SHAKESPEARE, COURT

Shakespeare, Court Dramatist centres around the contention that the courts of both Elizabeth I and James I loomed much larger in Shakespeare's creative life than is usually appreciated. Richard Dutton argues that many, perhaps most, of Shakespeare's plays have survived in versions adapted for court presentation, where length was no object (and indeed encouraged) and rhetorical virtuosity was appreciated. The first half of the study examines the court's patronage of the theatre during Shakespeare's lifetime and the crucial role of its Masters of the Revels, who supervised all performances there (as well as censoring plays for public performance). Dutton examines the emergence of the Lord Chamberlain's Men and the King's Men, to whom Shakespeare was attached as their 'ordinary poet', and reviews what is known about the revision of plays in the early modern period. The second half of the study focuses in detail on six of Shakespeare's plays which exist in shorter, less polished texts as well as longer, more familiar ones: *Henry VI Part II* and *III*, *Romeo and Juliet*, *Henry V*, *Hamlet*, and *The Merry Wives of Windsor*. Dutton argues that they are not cut down from those familiar versions, but poorly reported originals which Shakespeare revised for court performance into what we know best today. More localized revisions in such plays as *Titus Andronicus*, *Richard II*, and *Henry IV Part II* can also best be explained in this context. The court, Richard Dutton argues, is what made Shakespeare Shakespeare.

RICHARD DUTTON was educated at King's College, Cambridge and the University of Nottingham. He taught for many years at Lancaster University before becoming Humanities Distinguished Professor of English at The Ohio State University in 2003, and retiring in 2016. Richard Dutton is now Professor of English at Queen's University, Belfast. He has published numerous monographs, scholarly editions, and edited collections relating to the early modern period, mostly focusing on the censorship of the drama, the authors Shakespeare and Ben Jonson, and theatre history. His most recent book is *Shakespeare's Theater: A History* (Blackwell).

Shakespeare, Court Dramatist

RICHARD DUTTON

UNIVERSITY PRESS

Great Clarendon Street, Oxford, OX2 6DP,
United Kingdom

Oxford University Press is a department of the University of Oxford.
It furthers the University's objective of excellence in research, scholarship,
and education by publishing worldwide. Oxford is a registered trade mark of
Oxford University Press in the UK and in certain other countries

© Richard Dutton 2016

The moral rights of the author have been asserted

First published 2016
First published in paperback 2018

All rights reserved. No part of this publication may be reproduced, stored in
a retrieval system, or transmitted, in any form or by any means, without the
prior permission in writing of Oxford University Press, or as expressly permitted
by law, by licence or under terms agreed with the appropriate reprographics
rights organization. Enquiries concerning reproduction outside the scope of the
above should be sent to the Rights Department, Oxford University Press, at the
address above

You must not circulate this work in any other form
and you must impose this same condition on any acquirer

Published in the United States of America by Oxford University Press
198 Madison Avenue, New York, NY 10016, United States of America

British Library Cataloguing in Publication Data
Data available

Library of Congress Cataloging in Publication Data
Data available

ISBN 978–0–19–877774–8 (Hbk.)
ISBN 978–0–19–882225–7 (Pbk.)

Links to third party websites are provided by Oxford in good faith and
for information only. Oxford disclaims any responsibility for the materials
contained in any third party website referenced in this work.

This one, belatedly, is for Claire

Preface and Acknowledgements

The plays of Shakespeare are among the most widely read, performed, and revered texts in the world. But relatively few of those who encounter them realize just how problematic many of those texts actually are, how much editorial effort goes into producing the quietly authoritative (and silently modernized) versions that most of us use. About half of all the plays have survived in multiple early forms, often quite radically different from each other. Does Hamlet encounter Fortinbras, leading his army to Poland (4.4 in some modern editions) and speak the soliloquy 'How all occasions do inform against me' as a result? Or not? Is the Dauphin, heir to the French throne, at the battle of Agincourt in *Henry V*, or not? Does Edgar speak the closing lines of *King Lear*, or is it the Duke of Albany?

The mixed witness of the early versions of these plays poses these questions, and myriad others—large and small—besides. A Professor of Mechanics once looked into the origins of the now proverbial expression, 'an engineer hoist with his own petard', which derives from *Hamlet*.[1] He was shocked to discover that it does not appear in the First Folio text of the play (1623), the version edited after Shakespeare's death by John Heminge and Henry Condell, Shakespeare's old colleagues—and the version which many people assume is the most authoritative. Indeed, this Professor of Mechanics was forced to the realization that 'Hamlet is, or was, not one clear item but an indefinite thing which is in parts of uncertain authenticity' (Johnson 1987: 597). He had stumbled upon the buried world of Shakespearean editorial scholarship. It is the job of editors in reputable editions to consider the issues of 'uncertain authenticity' on our behalf and produce a readable text. They justify their decisions in textual essays and annotations of various sorts, but most readers (certainly most of my students) pay little attention to such matters. They accept 'Shakespeare's' text on its own, apparently unproblematic terms.

This is, to say the least, regrettable. For all the attention paid to Shakespeare's works, we actually know very little about the processes by which he composed them or the practical, day-to-day constraints within which he had to write. As I shall be arguing, the multiple states of so many of the texts actually offer us significant insights into such matters. That is because, in my view, many of the differences are of Shakespeare's own making, the results of revising his own works. That claim would have seemed unexceptionable to Alexander Pope and other editors of Shakespeare in the eighteenth century. Since then, however, it has often ranked as heresy in influential editorial circles, where it was long an article of faith that he did not change his texts once he had completed them: credit any changes to his fellow actors or to the printers, but not to the man himself.

---

[1] The original reads 'For 'tis the sport to have the engineer / Hoist with his own petard' (in Act 3, Scene 4 of modern editions, where it appears). It only appears in the Second Quarto of *Hamlet* (1604/5)—not in the First Quarto (1603) or the First Folio (1623).

Scholars these days are less certain about this. The idea of Shakespeare as a regular, detailed reviser of his own work drew new life in the 1980s and 1990s, but has dampened down since; it has certainly not generated a great deal of enthusiasm with his editors or, I regret to say, theatre historians (see pp. 148–67). This must in part be because there has been no obvious rationale for why, as a busy and practical man of the theatre who was clearly under some compulsion to produce new plays at regular intervals, he should spend valuable time revising old ones. The argument of this book is that the relationship of Shakespeare's acting company to the royal courts of Elizabeth I and James I offers such a rationale, one consonant with the documented practices of the era.

This argument emerged from the confluence of two hitherto discrete streams of my own scholarship. On the one hand, I have some experience of editing early modern plays—not, as it happens, those of Shakespeare but of his contemporaries, Ben Jonson, Thomas Middleton, and Thomas Drue. On the other hand, I have now spent twenty-five years studying the Masters of the Revels, the royal officials who regulated theatrical activity in the London region throughout Shakespeare's time and the decades that followed. These men licensed and censored plays for public performance, and that has been the focus of most of my study. But this was actually a secondary consequence of their original and still primary function of providing suitable entertainment at court. It was in this role, we may suppose, that Edmund Tilney and Sir George Buc (the two Masters of the Revels during Shakespeare's career) developed with the playwright their most important—and perhaps creative—relationships. This book brings together both that editorial insight and a knowledge of theatre history to cast new light, I hope, on the multiple texts of the man whose plays were staged at court far more frequently during his lifetime than those of any other dramatist.

* * *

These separate streams of my scholarship flowed together accidentally over several assignments and the book then presented itself to me as a fait accompli. In the course of all this I acquired a range of debts. I was firstly asked by Paulina Kewes to write on Shakespeare's English history plays for the *Huntington Library Quarterly*, and I wrote on the dating of the two early texts of *Henry V*. The editorial tradition has it that the quarto (published in 1600) is a trimmed-down and corrupted version of the pre-existing 1623 folio text (Dutton 2005). I became convinced that the folio text *followed* the quarto, was a revised expansion of it, rather than vice versa.

Shortly thereafter I was invited to give a paper at a conference in Toronto on 'Shakespeare and the Queen's Men' (October 2006), organized by Helen Ostovitch, Holger Syme, and others. This gave me an opportunity to look in detail at the old Queen's Men's play, *The Famous Victories of Henry V*, which has long been recognized as a source of sorts for Shakespeare's *Henry V* play, but not a very significant one, because the 1623 version is so much richer, more varied, and sophisticated. But when we compare the 1600 version of *Henry V* with the second half of *The Famous Victories*, we can see that the latter is an extremely strong narrative source for the

Shakespeare quarto text, not just an occasional point of departure (Dutton 2009c; see also Marino 2011: 125). These two papers lie behind Chapter 5a in this book.

In December 2006 I was invited to take part in a BBC Radio 4 programme to mark the 400th anniversary of the first known performance of *King Lear*, on St Stephen's Day (26 December) 1606, at the court in Whitehall, before King James I; the producer was Beaty Rubens. My particular remit was to address the role of the Master of the Revels, Edmund Tilney, in putting on such a production at court. This was a welcome opportunity to think further about his role of ensuring high-quality dramatic entertainment for the courts of Elizabeth I and her successor. I gave particular thought to the claim on the title page of the 1608 quarto text of *King Lear*: 'As it was played before the King's Majesty at Whitehall upon St Stephen's Night'. This parallels similar claims on other texts from the period. I concluded, and said on the programme, that this very probably meant that this text was not *King Lear* as it was regularly played at the Globe, the King's Men's usual theatre. Evidence, in particular, from the so-called *Diary* of the theatrical financier, Philip Henslowe, suggested that revision of plays—sometimes quite extensive revision of plays—was a regular feature of preparing them for performance at court. It was about now, perhaps as I was flying back from London, that the idea of this book sprang, fully formed, out of my head.

At the Shakespeare Association of America meeting the following year, Lukas Erne and Patrick Cheney organized a seminar on Shakespearean Authorship, which they invited me to join. My paper for the seminar offered a very rough draft of that fully formed idea, bringing together my work on *Henry V* and my thinking about *King Lear* (Dutton 2009b). Patrick Cheney was later kind enough to invite me to take part in two other discussions of Shakespeare as an author: a Shakespeare Authorship Forum at Penn State University, at which Jeffrey Knapp and I were the invited speakers, and an Authorship Forum in the journal, *Shakespeare Studies*, to which I was one of twelve invited contributors (Dutton 2008). Both of these prompted me to carry my thinking further, as did a subsequent invitation from Roslyn L. Knutson and Zabelle Stodola to give a talk in the Cooper Honors Program in the English department at the University of Arkansas, Little Rock. Different versions of that talk were subsequently given at Lincoln College, Oxford (at the invitation of Paulina Kewes and Susan Brigden) and at the Shakespeare Institute in Stratford-upon-Avon, courtesy of Kate McLuskie. I have since given papers on *The Merry Wives of Windsor* as it relates to the argument of the book at the Massachusetts Center for Interdisciplinary Renaissance Studies, at the invitation of Arthur Kinney, and on *Hamlet* and court performance at the English department of the University of Nevada, Las Vegas, at the invitation of Richard Harp (Dutton 2011; 2014). In October 2013 I gave a paper on the broad scope of the book at the Ohio Valley Shakespeare Conference in Cleveland.

I had the great good fortune to be awarded a fellowship by the National Endowment for the Humanities to work on this project for the academic year 2008–9 and want to record here my heartfelt gratitude for the free time this gave me. My chair at the time, the irrespressible Valerie Lee, was instrumental in securing this award and in freeing me of teaching duties and of my responsibilities as Vice Chair in the Department of English. My fellow Renaissance scholars in the Columbus English department—John King, Luke Wilson, Chris Highley, Alan Farmer, and Jennifer Higginbotham—have been supportive throughout; I am particularly grateful to Alan for allowing me early access to the invaluable *Database of Early English Playbooks* which he and Zach Lesser have created. Anyone interested in the subject of this book who has not seen it should do so (<http://deep.sas.upenn.edu/>). I am also grateful for particular insights and assistance from Lee Emrich, Peter Greenfield, William B. Long, Randall Martin, Tom Rutter, Dan Seward, David MacInnis, and Paul Werstine, which are recorded at appropriate junctures in the notes. Also for the comments of the two anonymous readers for Oxford University Press, which helped me back into the work after long interruptions by administrative duties.

I have had great support throughout my work from the staff of the Thompson Library at Ohio State, especially Anne Field, and from those in the Rare Books and Manuscripts Library, notably Geoff Smith, Rebecca Jewett, and Eric Johnson. And I have had invaluable help from various graduate students who have worked for me as research assistants while the project has evolved: Rachel Clark, Marisa Cull, Amanda Gerber, Erin Kelly, Erin McCarthy, and Elizabeth Steinway, who is largely responsible for the index.

My warmest thanks to everyone named here, and profound apologies for any kindnesses I may have overlooked.

Columbus, Ohio
July 2015

Contents

Introduction	1

I. PLAYING AND THE COURT

1. Shakespeare, Patronage, and the Court	13
2. Court Revels and Their Masters	38
3. Line Lengths, Playing Times, and Ben Jonson	67
4. The Revision of Early Modern Play Texts	97
a. The Revision of Plays in Shakespeare's Day	99
b. Thinking About the Revision of Shakespeare's Texts in Modern Times	138

II. SHAKESPEARE'S MULTIPLE TEXTS

5. More Sophisticated Histories	173
a. The Famous Victories of Shakespeare's *Henry V*	173
b. *2* and *3 Henry VI*—A True Contention	200
6. Augmentations	211
a. *Romeo and Juliet*	211
b. *Hamlet* and Succession	226
c. A Jacobean *Merry Wives*?	245
7. Last Thoughts	259
a. Single Sequence Additions	259
b. Jacobean Shakespeare	267
Conclusions	286
Bibliography	291
Index of Offices and Organizations, Events and Editions, Things and Theories	309
Index of Plays and Other Dramatic Texts	313
Index of Persons	317

Introduction

> And now what rests but that we spend the time
> With stately triumphs, mirthful comic shows,
> Such as befits the pleasure of the court?
> Sound drums and trumpets! Farewell sour annoy!
> (*3 Henry VI*, 5.7.42–5)[1]

THE ISSUE

The argument of this book is simply stated: it is that Shakespeare's plays were frequently and specifically revised for presentation at the courts of Elizabeth I and James I. And that the texts which have come down to us often bear the marks of those revisions. One of those marks, I argue, is the sheer length of many of Shakespeare's plays, which far exceed the norms of the public stage in his day but would have found a ready audience in the royal palaces.

It is in that sense that I nominate Shakespeare a court dramatist, because many of his plays as we know them (including all the great tragedies, except *Macbeth*) have come down to us in versions which were most likely prepared for court presentation rather than for acting at the Theatre, Curtain, Globe, or Blackfriars playhouses, which his companies used at various times. Of course, his plays were also performed there—apparently to great applause. But very probably not in the form in which many of them have survived.

Others have, of course, commented on Shakespeare's affinity with the court. It used to be commonplace, for example, to lament in Whiggish fashion James I's taking of all the major playing companies under royal patronage; this was seen as an act of Stuart absolutism, identifying the theatre with the court to the detriment of its art (Wickham 1959–81: 2:1, 92, 105; Danby 1965; Cohen 1985: 265). More recently the issue has been approached less censoriously by, for example, David M. Bergeron in *Shakespeare's Romances and the Royal Family*, Alvin Kernan in *Shakespeare, the King's Playwright: Theatre in the Stuart Court, 1603–1613*, and Paul Yachnin in his notion of 'populuxe theatre', first advanced in *The Culture of Playgoing in Shakespeare's England* (with Anthony Dawson). None of these, however, has commented on the way in which writing for the court affected not only the subject matter of Shakespeare's plays but also the precise state of the texts he

---

[1] Quoted from Bevington 2008. On the choice of editions cited in this book, see pp. 9–10.

left behind. Nor is it yet widely appreciated that the Elizabethan Shakespeare was just as much a court dramatist as the Jacobean one.

THE DEBATE

Why this should not have been observed before is something of a mystery to me, though there has long been strong ideological pressure to think of Shakespeare primarily as a popular dramatist. Alfred Harbage set the tone in his *Shakespeare's Audience*: 'I believe that Shakespeare's audience was a large and receptive assemblage of men and women of all ages and all classes... Unlike some other audiences existing in and near his time, Shakespeare's audience was literally popular, ascending through each gradation from potboy to prince' (1941: 158–9). But the failure to recognize the role of the court in shaping Shakespeare's texts must also be partly a consequence of the forms of contention that have surrounded the debate over those texts, which essentially began a century ago with A. W. Pollard's *Shakespeare's Folios and Quartos: A Study in the Bibliography of Shakespeare's Plays 1594–1685* (1909) and which focused heavily on the means and motives of their publication as the key to the differences between them.

A further key issue has been the question of revision. On the one hand there has been a general consensus (which happens to be wrong) that early modern plays were frequently revised for commercial purposes; the famous revisions of Kyd's *The Spanish Tragedy* and Marlowe's *Dr Faustus*, neither performed by their authors, have helped to lock this in people's minds. But there has been a separate, localized debate about the revision of Shakespeare's plays and how it might explain the multiple versions that have survived. The plays of no other dramatist have survived in so many varied states, which is a matter of note in itself, though often overlooked by those who immerse themselves in Shakespeare to the exclusion of what was going on around him. He was different and distinctive in this, as in so much else; only Ben Jonson offers anything like a parallel example. But the variations in his plays were, as I shall show, very different.

It may be helpful if I spell out the sheer scale of the issue. Let us start with the First Folio of *Comedies, Histories and Tragedies of Mr William Shakespeare*, overseen by Shakespeare's long-time colleagues, John Heminge and Henry Condell, and published in 1623. The folio was a prestigious and expensive volume, and the texts of the plays that it contained have the undoubted virtue of the authentication provided by fellow members of his acting company, the King's Men. Unfortunately, this does not necessarily mean that it provides the best texts of those plays, depending on how we define 'best'. The First Folio contained thirty-six plays, all but two of the works that subsequent scholarship has determined that Shakespeare wrote, at least in good part. The exceptions are *Pericles*, first published in quarto in 1609 and *The Two Noble Kinsmen*, not printed in quarto until 1634.[2] Of the plays in the

---

[2] It is usually thought that *Pericles* and *The Two Noble Kinsmen* were not included in the First Folio because in each case a co-author wrote a significant part of the text: George Wilkins and John Fletcher

First Folio, eighteen—exactly half—had never been printed before. These were, in putative order of composition:[3]

> *The Two Gentlemen of Verona, The Taming of the Shrew, 1 Henry VI, The Comedy of Errors, King John, Julius Caesar, As You Like It, Twelfth Night, Measure for Measure, All's Well that Ends Well, Timon of Athens, Macbeth, Antony and Cleopatra, Coriolanus, The Winter's Tale, Cymbeline, The Tempest,* and *Henry VIII* (performed as *All Is True*).[4]

The First Folio provides the only versions of any consequence of these plays.

But earlier, alternative versions of the other eighteen plays also survive. Each of these plays was first printed on its own, normally in a small, relatively cheap quarto format, about the size of a modest modern paperback.[5] And in some cases there were multiple early quartos. This is the full list, with dates of all pre-1623 printings:

> *2 Henry VI* (originally *The First Part of the Contention of the Two Famous Houses of York and Lancaster*, 1594, 1600, 1619), *3 Henry VI* (originally *The True Tragedy of Richard Duke of York, and the death of good King Henry VI*, 1595, 1600, 1619), *Richard III* (1597, 1598, 1603, 1605, 1612, 1622), *Titus Andronicus* (1594, 1600, 1611), *Love's Labour's Lost* (1598),[6] *A Midsummer Night's Dream* (1600, 1619), *Romeo and Juliet* (1597, 1599, 1609, 1622), *Much Ado About Nothing* (1600), *Richard II* (1597, 1598 twice, 1608, 1615), *The Merchant of Venice* (1600, 1619), *1 Henry IV* (1598, 1599, 1604, 1608, 1613),[7] *Merry Wives of Windsor* (1602, 1619), *2 Henry IV* (1600), *Henry V* (1600, 1602, 1619), *Hamlet* (1603, 1604/5, 1611), *Troilus and Cressida* (1609), *Othello* (1622), and *King Lear* (1608, 1619).[8] *Pericles* (1609, 1619) was also printed

---

respectively. The case for George Wilkins as co-author of *Pericles*, responsible for the first two acts, is now widely accepted: see Gossett 2004, 54–76; Vickers 2002; Jackson 2003. *The Two Noble Kinsmen* was published as by Fletcher and Shakespeare, and no one has seriously doubted the attribution. Shakespeare is also widely thought to have had a lesser hand in at least two other extant plays, *Sir Thomas More* (which survives in manuscript) and *Edward III* (quarto, 1596). Jonathan Bate and Eric Rasmussen have recently expanded the number of plays in which Shakespeare's hand is now suspected to include *Locrine*; *The London Prodigal*; *A Yorkshire Tragedy*; *Thomas Lord Cromwell*, *Arden of Feversham*; *The Spanish Tragedy* (1602 version); *Mucedorus* (1610 version); and *Double Falsehood*, supposedly derived from the lost *Cardenio* (Bate and Rasmussen 2013). But the jury is still out on many of these claims, and they are not relevant to the issue of the publication of Shakespeare's more securely canonical texts.

[3] I have followed the order proposed by *The Oxford Shakespeare*, general editors Stanley Wells and Gary Taylor (1986), and justified in 'The Canon and Chronology of Shakespeare's Plays' in the accompanying *Textual Companion* (1987: 69–144). As will be apparent later, I disagree with their dating of *Merry Wives*, but this is not the place to argue that issue.

[4] In the cases of *The Taming of the Shrew* and *King John* I have to impose my own editorial judgement. There are earlier plays to which Shakespeare's are undoubtedly related: *The Taming of a Shrew* (quarto, 1594) and *The Troublesome Reign of King John* (quarto, 1591). Are these *versions* of what Shakespeare originally wrote, or are they source-works from which he developed his own plays? My judgement here is that *A Shrew* and *Troublesome Reign* are sources, not versions. But there is no general consensus on this, and see Marino 2011, esp. 48–74.

[5] *The True Tragedy* (early *3 Henry VI*) was printed in the even smaller octavo format.

[6] See Chapter 4, n. 52.

[7] In the case of *1 Henry IV*, eight pages have survived of what was apparently an earlier version than the first complete extant quarto text of 1598. I have not counted it in the run of reprints. This is a useful reminder that some editions may have disappeared without trace. Only one copy of the 1594 quarto of *Titus Andronicus*, for example, has survived.

[8] All texts printed in 1619 formed part of a series of reprints commissioned by the stationers, Thomas Pavier and William Jaggard, apparently aimed at producing a collected edition of those works

twice, though it did not appear in the Folio. In addition, although both *2 Henry IV* and *Troilus and Cressida* were only printed once in quarto, in each case they were altered during the print run, producing distinctively different copies.

It will be apparent that there are many early versions of some of Shakespeare's plays and it has been the ongoing job of editors and bibliographers to try to determine either what Shakespeare actually wrote or what his actors staged. They are not helped in this by the fact that Shakespeare himself had no visible hand in the publication of any of his plays. His two narrative poems, *Venus and Adonis* (1593) and *The Rape of Lucrece* (1594), both bear Shakespeare's signed dedications to the Earl of Southampton, and some such touch is usually the mark of a play in this era which was printed with the blessing of its author. None of Shakespeare's plays carries such a mark. For none of the quartos do we know how copy reached the printer, however ingenious or plausible our guesses may be. Even with the First Folio, though we know the texts had the blessing of the actors, we do not know how or where they acquired them in those precise forms.

In many cases the differences between early versions of the same play are relatively slight and inconsequential. Every text in the early modern era had to be set by hand and compositors were quite liberal (by modern standards) in such matters as spelling and punctuation, and always liable to make mistakes because of eye-skips, poor handwriting in the copy, an inability to distinguish between verse and prose, or for any number of other reasons. So even when a printer set out with no higher aim than to reprint an earlier version, it never turned out exactly the same. In such cases there was often an attempt to correct egregious errors (or what were perceived to be errors), but these were often compounded by further errors of their own creation. And to complicate matters even further, we always have to take into account the fact that printers changed their texts during the printing process itself, so that hardly any two copies of an early modern text (even as prestigious a text as the First Folio) are absolutely identical.[9] The early textual history of *Richard III*, in particular, is an education in such matters.

These are very properly the concerns of editors of the plays, who want to determine the most authentic texts possible. But those relatively minor differences are not relevant to this study. I am concerned with the fact that some of these early texts are substantially different from each other. Some versions of *Titus Andronicus*, *Richard II*, and *2 Henry IV*, for example, contain a whole scene which does not appear in earlier versions of that play. *The First Part of the Contention* and *The True*

---

of Shakespeare already in print, the so-called False Folio. (They also included some plays not by Shakespeare, though credited to him, like *1 Sir John Oldcastle*.) On 3 May 1619 the Lord Chamberlain successfully interceded with the Stationers' Company on behalf of the King's Men to get this stopped. Possibly to get around these restrictions, the 1619 texts of both *Henry V* and *Lear* are dated 1608 on their title pages; those of *A Midsummer Night's Dream* and *The Merchant of Venice* are dated 1600 (Johnson 1992; Marino 2011: 108–26). I have only included the dates of reprintings prior to the publication of the 1623 First Folio. They continued to the Restoration and beyond, but those are not relevant to the present study.

[9] The classic work on variations within the First Folio was done by Charlton Hinman in his *The First Folio of Shakespeare, Based on Folios in the Folger Shakespeare Collection*, 1996 (1968).

Tragedy are so different from (and so much shorter than) what the First Folio tidily dubs *2* and *3 Henry VI* that they used to be thought Shakespeare's sources rather than versions of his own work. The 1600 quarto of *Henry V* does not have the familiar choruses, or the 'Once more unto the breach' speech, or the Dauphin at the Battle of Agincourt, besides much else—unlike, in each case, the 1623 folio version; it is, moreover, at 1,623 lines, barely half the length of the folio's 3,166.[10] *Hamlet* is the most notorious and problematic example. The 1603 first quarto of the play (2,154 lines) is some three-fifths the length of the other two surviving versions, its verse is palpably poorer, and it contains a scene between the Queen and Horatio which does not appear anywhere else. The 1604/5 quarto of the play contains 3,668 lines and is better by virtually any aesthetic criterion—though it takes well over four buttock-numbing hours to perform in full.[11] The folio text (3,537 lines) agrees with Q1604/5 in most important respects, but it contains the famous passage on the strident child actors, the 'little eyases', which appears nowhere else, and does not contain that passage in which Hamlet sees Fortinbras's army and speaks his 'How all occasions do inform against me' soliloquy, which is unique to Q1604/5.

How and why such differences may have arisen is the central question which this book explores. Ever since the time of Pollard a vocabulary has grown up to account for them. We have been told tales of 'bad' quartos, of 'foul papers', of 'memorial reconstructions' by more-or-less disaffected actors, of piracy by unscrupulous publishers, of performances transcribed by shorthand, of texts shortened for touring productions when plague drove the actors out into the country. More recently we have been told that they were shortened even for London performances, Shakespeare regularly writing plays that were too long to perform (Gurr 1999; Erne 2003: 225). And more recently still we have been told that the shorter versions were *expanded*, as much by the actors as by Shakespeare (Menzer 2008; Marino 2011).

The problem is that we have no hard evidence to substantiate any of these scenarios, though they are often advanced as given fact. The argument, for example, that plays would have been cut to reduce the number of actors required rarely squares with the practical reality of doubling smaller roles. G. I. Duthie was once thought conclusively to have established that no known early form of shorthand was capable of handling even the shorter versions of *2* and *3 Henry VI*, *Merry Wives*, *Romeo and Juliet*, *Henry V*, or *Hamlet* (1949). But Tiffany Stern has recently shown that he could well have been wrong (2013).

---

[10] Line-counting of these plays, especially such as will give reasonable comparisons between different versions, is quite tricky. How do you deal with prose, the number of lines of which (unlike verse) varies with the width of the page? Do you include stage directions or not? In the end precise figures—say, to closer than a hundred lines—are not going to be critical to my argument. I have normally used the figures compiled by Alfred Hart (1932: 21; 1934: 148), supplemented with those of Lukas Erne (2003: 141, 194).

[11] I designate it Q1604/5 because half of the surviving copies are dated 1604, the other half 1605, but they are otherwise the same text.

The fact is that we simply do not know why such different versions of these plays exist and got into print. That statement will be so heretical in some quarters that I shall repeat it, because it is an essential bottom line in everything that follows. The fact is that we simply do not know why such different versions of these plays exist and got into print. My argument that revision of the plays for court performance may explain some of the most problematic examples is, like all the others, a hypothetical one since we have no smoking-gun evidence. It has this distinction, however: it is based on a known theatrical practice, for which we have irrefutable evidence in Philip Henslowe's *Diary* and in Thomas Heywood's *Apology for Actors* (*c.* 1607/8, printed 1612), where he speaks of 'the office of the Revels, where our court plays have been in late days yearly *rehearsed, perfected*, and *corrected* before they come to the public view of the prince and the nobility' (E1v; my emphasis). When we combine that evidence with the fact that Shakespeare's plays were overwhelmingly the most popular ones at court during his working lifetime (as I demonstrate later), the circumstantial case becomes very compelling.

This book is therefore in conversation with the theory and practice of editing Shakespeare's plays. This is not the place for a comprehensive review of the issue, such as can readily be found elsewhere (see, for example, Maguire 1996; Maguire and Berger 1998; Murphy 2003, 2007; Egan 2010). And I shall deal with the elements that most impact my own argument in due course. But let me offer a brief overview, so that we can take our bearings. For much of the twentieth century our assumptions about Shakespeare's texts were largely shaped by the so-called New Bibliographers, most notably R. B. McKerrow and W. W. Greg, who influenced at least two generations of editors of Shakespeare's plays; the Arden 2 Shakespeare edition and the first edition of *The Riverside Shakespeare* are their most lasting legacies. And, as James Marino puts it, 'the New Bibliography continues to shape the ways that editing and textual scholarship are done...damaged and undermined as it has been by more recent scholars, [it] still remains the privileged starting place for discussions of dating Shakespeare's plays' (2011: 13). To this extent it will be necessary to understand something of what the New Bibliographers were looking for in Shakespeare's texts, as well as why more recent editors and thinkers have been looking for other things. For the most part their Holy Grail was the authentic words of Shakespeare, unsullied by their use in the theatre or by their abuse at the hands of publishers and printers. In the pursuit of this it became virtually axiomatic, especially with Greg, the most influential of them, that Shakespeare did not himself revise his texts once he had passed them to his acting colleagues (Greg 1954: 41, 60–1, 78, 89).

The *Oxford Shakespeare* of 1986, edited by Stanley Wells and Gary Taylor, marked a radical change of direction in editorial thinking. Wells and Taylor took as their aim not to recover the 'Shakespeare' behind his 'maimed' texts, but to reconstruct the plays *as they were first performed*. Their Shakespeare was not a transcendent poet but a theatrical professional. A surprising amount of Shakespearean scholarship prior to this (including that of the most influential New Bibliographers) had paid lip service to him as a 'man of the theatre', but actually did its best to separate the author of his poetry from its contamination with the practical business of playing. William B. Long put it well when he said that 'the investigation of the texts of Shakespeare and others has stagnated badly. Existing evidence has been ignored regularly; knowledge of working theatre avoided studiously' (1997: 53).[12]

My own 'court dramatist' emerges from the new generation of editorial and authorial scholarship which followed Wells and Taylor's lead and heeded the strictures of such as Long. I would particularly single out Andrew Gurr, Roslyn Lander Knutson, William Ingram, John Astington, W. R. Streitberger, Patrick Cheney, Scott McMillin, and Sally-Beth MacLean as scholars with whom I have been in long conversation, and Lukas Erne, Paul Menzer, James Marino, and Tiffany Stern with whom I have engaged more recently. My Shakespeare wrote to order and within the busy, demanding schedule of professional theatre. This book aligns me squarely with an argument summarized (and challenged) by Lukas Erne: '[Shakespeare's] play texts may be longer than those of his contemporaries, and several of his plays may survive in variant forms of very different lengths, but even his longest texts reflect an exclusive theatrical teleology' (2013: 10). Perhaps '*primary* theatrical teleology' would more precisely characterize my position; I do not say that Shakespeare was indifferent to print, only that it was always at most a secondary consideration among busy professional demands. It is almost certain that he had a contract when he became part of the Lord Chamberlain's Men in 1594, and this would have differed from the contracts of other shareholder actors in the company, in that it specified the writing of plays as part of his duties, and would have stipulated a schedule by which they should be written—probably two a year, which seems to have been his normal rate for most of the late 1590s (see Van Es 2013: 41–5, 99–112). It may well also have made stipulations about their possible publication. I discuss these matters further on pp. 269ff.

By the same token, Shakespeare's contract may well have included stipulations about 'patching' or revising plays—his own and other people's—as the occasion arose. It is very clear that this was expected of one of his successor playwrights for the King's Men, Philip Massinger (Bentley 1971: 235). Tiffany Stern suggests: 'When there was a resident or regular company dramatist, of course, he was likely to be a main prologue- and epilogue-writer: writing stage orations may have been an aspect of his job as company wordsmith' (2009a: 111). And this need not have been limited to his own plays. Stern cites Sonia Massai as claiming that 'there is every reason to think that Shakespeare as a company man was reviser/epilogue-writer of [*Locrine*]', an old play 'Newly set forth, ouerseen and corrected, By *W. S.*' in 1595.[13] It remains a matter of debate, however, how extensive such 'patching' might be (see Bate and Rasmussen 2013).

---

[12] Although recent editorial fashion has moved to a degree to take more account of performance in its emphases, it has not altogether absolved itself of Long's charge. 'Shakespeare' now often denotes a general collaborative theatrical effort, which need not account for the particular evolution of individual texts.

[13] Quoting from an unpublished paper, 'Shakespeare, Text and Paratext', given at the International Shakespeare Conference in Stratford-upon-Avon, 2008. I am also grateful to Sonia Massai for sharing the paper with me.

As we shall see in detail later, there were certainly occasions when plays were revised—for whatever reason—but less often than is popularly supposed. Sometimes this was done by the author, as Dekker revised his own *Phaeton*, now lost. But there were occasions when the author was not available: Kyd and Marlowe were both dead when, respectively, their *Spanish Tragedy* and *Dr Faustus* were revised. The Lord Admiral's Men, who did not at the time employ an 'ordinary poet', advanced money to Ben Jonson on two occasions (25 September 1601 and 22 June 1602) for 'additions for Hieronymo' (i.e. *The Spanish Tragedy*). Similarly, they paid William Bird and Samuel Rowley to write new scenes for *Dr Faustus* (Foakes 2002: 206, 182, 203). It is the main contention of this book that the Lord Chamberlain's Men regularly employed Shakespeare to 'patch' his own plays (and perhaps on occasion those of other writers) for the particular demands of the court. My method will, somewhat unusually, mix theatre history and editorial theory. There are many ways of explaining the extraordinarily rich and (one of his own favourite words) strange—wondrous, admirable—subject which is Shakespeare. And what I will say will by no means preclude, or render redundant, many of the others. But I think I have something new and distinctive to add to this debate, and I shall be advancing that as clearly as possible—and in terms which I hope general readers will understand, not just experts—not getting bogged down in too many ifs, buts, and possible alternative explanations. I have no doubt that others will be along to supply them for me.

I proceed according to the following plan. The book will fall into two halves: 'Playing and the Court' and 'Shakespeare's Multiple Texts'. Hingeing the two halves together will be a separate chapter on the revision of early modern plays. The three chapters of 'Playing and the Court' look firstly at the patronage practices governing Elizabethan theatre and how they both tied the most successful companies to the court and permitted an élite few to reap the commercial rewards of regular London playing. Secondly they examine the Revels culture of the Elizabethan court, the role within it of the Masters of the Revels, and most particularly the role of the one with whom Shakespeare most closely worked, Edmund Tilney (in office 1579–1610). I latterly focus on 1597/8 as a critical year in my narrative. Thirdly I look at the length of texts and differences in playing times between the public theatres and the court; I also look at the special case of Jonson and his distinctive texts.

The hinge chapter on 'The Revision of Early Modern Play Texts' examines vexed questions surrounding the revision of early modern play texts, and particularly those of Shakespeare; I review the practices spelled out in Philip Henslowe's *Diary*, look at various non-Shakespearean texts we know to have been revised, and review what title pages tell us. I also address how the modern editing of Shakespeare has responded to this information.

'Shakespeare's Multiple Texts' firstly looks in detail at *Henry V*, which is (I argue) unique among Shakespeare's plays in that we can trace its development from an immediate dramatic source in *The Famous Victories of Henry V*, through a preliminary version of Shakespeare's own in the 1600 quarto of *Henry V*, to the final version in the 1623 folio. No other play offers us such a clear trace of Shakespeare's working methods. A subsequent section of that chapter looks at the revision of *2* and *3 Henry VI*, suggesting that the revision of *Henry V* might be tied to the sequence of the history plays as it was to appear in the First Folio. In Chapter 6 I examine *Romeo and Juliet*, *The Merry Wives of Windsor*, and *Hamlet* in the light of what the earlier chapters establish. A final chapter looks at three plays that were revised on a lesser scale, briefly considers the very different textual evidence from the Jacobean period, and offers some concluding remarks.

Before proceeding I need to explain some of my practices. In the hope that the book will be read not solely by specialists, I have decided to modernize my quotations. It may be entertaining to engage with, say, Philip Henslowe's colourful spelling, deducing that 'adicyones in docter fostes' means 'additions in Doctor Faustus'. But this is also a major barrier and distraction even sometimes for the initiated. So whenever I cite from a text in original spelling (such as E. K. Chambers' *The Elizabethan Stage* or R. A. Foakes's edition of *Henslowe's Diary*), I have silently modernized it.

This is of particular consequence in respect of quotations from Shakespeare himself. Because the issues I discuss here are deeply implicated in the processes which produce the editions that most of us read, it is problematic for me to quote from those editions. But the original texts are, of course, in old spelling, and copies are often not readily accessible to most readers. Happily that is less true than it was only ten years ago, because those texts are now very effectively reproduced online. A convenient and highly reputable site is *Internet Shakespeare Editions*, based at the University of Victoria in British Columbia, under the General Textual Editor, Eric Rasmussen, and Coordinating Editor, Michael Best (<http://internetshakespeare.uvic.ca/Library/facsimile/>).

Nevertheless, the originals have neither line numbering nor, in most instances, page numbering as we are used to it, which makes it difficult to trace particular passages. So I have settled on the following compromise. I shall normally identify passages from the 'good' texts of the plays (the fuller quartos or folio versions with which we are most familiar) by reference to David Bevington's *The Complete Works of William Shakespeare* (6th edition, 2008). This is a relatively conservative edition, which limits its speculation about the relationship between the different versions. Where I refer to what used to be known as the 'bad' quartos, I use the following (modernized) editions: *The First Quarto of King Henry V*, edited by Andrew Gurr (2000); *The First Quarto of Romeo and Juliet*, edited by Lukas Erne (2007); and *The First Quarto of Hamlet*, edited by Kathleen O. Irace (1999). These are all in *The Early Quartos* subset of the *New Cambridge Shakespeare*. Unfortunately, as yet, neither they nor anyone else have equivalent editions of *The First Part of the Contention*, or of *The True Tragedy* (the early texts of *2* and *3 Henry VI*), or of *The Merry Wives of Windsor*. I am therefore obliged to settle on the photographic reproductions of the (old spelling) original texts that are reproduced as appendices in the Arden 3 editions of, respectively, *2 Henry VI*, ed. Ronald Knowles (1999), *3 Henry VI*, ed. John D. Cox and Eric Rasmussen (2001), and *Merry Wives*, ed. Giorgio Melchiori (2000). This is a clumsy expedient, but at least these editions are reasonably accessible. In all cases I continue silently to modernize where necessary.

In addition, for those who prefer to consult the original texts, I shall cite them, normally by page signature (in the quartos and the one octavo) and by the Through-Line-Numbering (TLN) of folio texts in Charlton Hinman's facsimile of the First Folio (1996).[14] Note that the TLN includes stage directions as well as the spoken lines.

Dating: England in Shakespeare's lifetime still formally used the old Julian calendar, and the year for some official purposes began on 25 March. However, in other contexts 1 January was recognized as New Year's Day. So any date in January, February, or most of March might be regarded as belonging either to the old year (Old or Annunciation-Style) or to the new (New Style). Queen Elizabeth, for example, died on 24 March, the last day of 1602 Old Style, though of course we would always say 1603. I shall normally give the date New Style, whatever my source text says. Occasionally it is impossible to tell whether the date is Old Style or New, in which case I shall flag the ambiguity.

Money: The pound (£) in Shakespeare's England contained 20 shillings (s) and each shilling contained 12 pennies (d from the Latin *denarius*), which subdivided into halfpennies and quarter ones, called farthings. It will give you some idea of values to tell you that standing room admission to the Globe cost 1d and the best seats 6d. Unbound copies of the Shakespeare First Folio cost 15s, those bound in calf-skin £1 (Blayney 1991: 25–32). Hired workers, such as clothworkers or butchers, might earn £5 or £6 a year, not much more than 2s per week. (Think of the 'rude mechanicals' in *A Midsummer Night's Dream*, dreaming of 'sixpence a day' for life as reward from Theseus.) The schoolmaster in Stratford-upon-Avon was paid £20 a year, plus board.

---

[14] Before modern page numbering, *signatures* (letters and numbers at the foot of a page) helped printers to determine page order. In a quarto the paper would be folded twice to produce four double-sided pages; the first collection of pages would normally be marked—on front sides only, known as the *recto*—A (implicitly A1), A2, A3, A4, the second collection B, B2, and so on. The reverse side of each page is called the *verso*, so it is referred to in the form A1^v, though such forms never appear in the originals. So, for example, you would find the 'To be or not to be' speech in the first (1603) quarto of *Hamlet* on D4^v and in the second (1604/5) quarto on G2. In the first example D4 is not actually marked—a common occurrence. But you can infer it by tracking back to D3^v. Through-Line-Numbering (TLN), devised by Charlton Hinman for his facsimile of the Shakespeare First Folio, relates a passage to its place in the whole sequence of the play, not scene by scene.

PART I
PLAYING AND THE COURT

1
Shakespeare, Patronage, and the Court

The court made possible early modern theatre in the forms that it actually took. And the court made possible the career that William Shakespeare actually had. Without the court it is certain that the kinds of theatre which flourished in the reigns of Elizabeth I and James I, and the plays written for them, would have been very different. By this I do not mean to perpetuate the old Whiggish tales of an enlightened, drama-loving court defending theatre against the killjoy puritans. The precise circumstances in which the court defended the players were more limited and self-interested than that. And they defined in numerous respects the kinds of theatre that were allowed to flourish.

I shall start by countering the usual objection to making the court so central—the fact that Shakespeare and his fellows made the great majority of their money from playing in the public theatres. I shall then look at the court's interest in playing, focusing on the career of the official who oversaw theatricals at the court itself, Edmund Tilney, from 1579 Master of the Revels. And I shall show how the mutual interests of the court and of a select body of actors—including Shakespeare—met and merged in the years 1594 to 1603. In order to provide a succinct account of this history I have deferred until Chapter 2 writing in detail about Tilney himself, the evolution of his role, and the influence of senior court officials such as the Lord Chamberlains. Some readers, however, may prefer to read that first.

MONEY

The actors received £10 for a performance at court, which was technically a fee of £6 13s 4d (two-thirds of that), rounded up by the free gift of Elizabeth or James. In Elizabeth's reign Shakespeare's company might expect to play at court three or four times a year, and even though this doubled and trebled under James, these rewards would never have constituted a major proportion of their income, as Bernard Beckerman argues (here speaking for most twentieth-century theatre historians):

> From Elizabeth, and later from James, the Chamberlain-King's Men received £873 between 1599 and 1609, of which amount £70 was for relief of the company during plague time, and £30 for reimbursement for expenses incurred during unusually lengthy travel to and from the Court. Thus the annual average for playing was £77.6s., with the court payments in the later years substantially greater than in the early ones. Grants from Elizabeth never totaled more than 5 per cent of the income the company

earned at the Globe. Under James the percentage rose to a high of about fifteen by 1609. The increase in Court support, evident in these figures, ultimately led the Globe company to appeal increasingly to an aristocratic audience. But throughout the decade we are considering [1599–1609], the actors depend on the pence of a large, heterogeneous public more than upon the bounty of their prince.   (Beckerman 1962: 22–3, using figures from Chambers 1923: 4.166–75)

Beckerman concedes that 'The players certainly tendered courtesy and respect to the Court, which after all was their main defense against puritanical suppression' (23), but the economics of the situation required them to cater first and foremost to 'a large, heterogeneous public'. This, I suggest, is the logic of the twentieth century, not of the sixteenth and seventeenth centuries.

Firstly, and most crucially, the Lord Chamberlain's Men were only able to make the very substantial sums we presume that they did at the Globe *because* the court protected them and gave them very significant privileges. It was not only puritans who wanted to 'suppress' the theatre. The City of London authorities had genuine public order and health concerns, in an era before modern policing, about auditoria that held upwards of two thousand people at a time. The company only existed at all, and certainly only flourished in their metropolitan situation, because they were expressly servants of the court, providing entertainment when needed for the Queen and her guests. This was their *raison d'être*, as her Privy Council never tired of reminding successive Lord Mayors of London.

But there were also other cultural pressures at work which made money—though, of course, very important—somewhat less than the complete bottom line. In broad terms the business of playing in Shakespeare's time passed from being part of a gift-exchange economy to being part of a proto-capitalist one, as I explain further in this chapter and the next. But aspects of the old order persisted (in ways that Beckerman does not recognize) even as the shareholding arrangements of the leading companies and changes in the ownership of the theatres they used flagged the future. Two major social developments accelerated these changes. One was the growing mobility of the population. Sometimes they were displaced by the enclosure of common land, more often simply drawn towards greater opportunities in the towns. This produced significant numbers of vagabonds or masterless men who seriously alarmed the authorities, and at times itinerant actors were counted among them. The second major change was the growth of London to a population of around 200,000 by the end of the sixteenth century, making it one of the biggest cities in Europe. This also made it a major target for the acting companies, and from 1576 onwards (when Shakespeare was twelve) there were purpose-built auditoria in the suburbs to accommodate them, as well as up to four converted inns within the city itself. By 1590, around the time Shakespeare moved to London, some of the companies were looking to perform in the city year-round. This created significant friction between the city authorities and the court.

At the beginning of Elizabeth's reign (1558) most troupes of actors were household servants of peers and members of the gentry, who sometimes made money for themselves by touring locally or further afield, showing their patrons' liveries and demonstrating their magnificence.[1] In all of their journeys from great house to great house, and town to town, they would have worn their patron's livery. At a time when the status of the greatest was measured by the numbers of their liveried servants, it was doubtless part of the motivation of those aristocrats who chose to patronize players that theirs should represent them around the country (at no regular cost to themselves), most especially in areas where their interests were particularly strong. And regular itineraries were established accordingly.

As such activity grew the actors were increasingly likely to be identified as masterless men. In 1572 Parliament passed an Act for the Punishment of Vagabonds, which expressly limited the right to patronize actors to members of the aristocracy, the elite group of about eighty families which effectively controlled the country; this removed the right of members of the gentry, a rather wider social grouping, to such patronage.[2] The legislation prompted the Earl of Leicester's Men, the leading troupe of the era, to petition their patron:

> To the right honourable Earl of Leicester, their good lord and master:
> May it please your honour to understand that forasmuch as there is a certain proclamation out for the reviving of a statute as touching retainers, as your lordship knoweth better than we can inform you thereof, we therefore, your humble servants and daily orators your players, for avoiding all inconvenience that may grow by reason of the said statute, are bold to trouble your lordship with this our suit, humbly desiring your honour that (as you have been always our good lord and master) you will now vouchsafe to retain us at this present as your household servants and daily waiters, not that we mean to crave any further stipend or benefit at your lordship's hands but our liveries as we have had, and also to certify that we are your household servants when we shall have occasion to travel amongst our friends as we do usually once a year, and as other noblemen's players do and have done in time past, whereby we may enjoy our faculty in your lordship's name as we have done heretofore. (Wickham et al. 2000: 205)

Here we see the reciprocity of the gift-exchange economy: by virtue of his status, Leicester is able to extend patronage to the actors, which costs him nothing except their livery; they are thereby enabled to make a living, in the course of which they advertise Leicester's magnificence. The pattern expanded in other directions too when they were called upon to perform at court. Leicester's status as an earl was a gift from the Queen, and a performance by players he patronized was a gift in return: these were gifts that kept on giving, reflecting honour on the giver and the recipient. And these reciprocities extended to the actors' dealings with those they visited on their travels. These would not be selected at random but chosen from their lord's neighbours, friends, allies, and relations: the performances were gifts, binding them more closely together. Of course, money was involved, though much sustenance was in kind—food and shelter. But it was boosted with a gratuity from their hosts, rather than a strictly commercial fee.

---

[1] On household theatricals, see Westfall 1990; Somerset 2009. On the Earl of Leicester and the Earls of Derby as prominent patrons, see MacLean 2002 and 2003.
[2] There was an exception to allow Justices of the Peace to license local troupes to travel within their own county.

When they visited towns the actors would similarly put on 'free' performances for the mayor or bailiff and the local worthies, often at the Town Hall or Guildhall, for which in turn they would receive a gratuity graduated to the status of their patron (Greenfield 2009). For example, when Leicester's Men visited Coventry in August 1587 they received 30 shillings (one and a half pounds) from the Mayor. Lord Admiral Howard's Men in the same period rated 20 shillings, while Lord Chandos's Men only rated 6s 8d. But when the Queen's Men had visited in 1585/6 they had received an impressive 40 shillings (£2). All such rewards would be regarded, in effect, as gift-exchanges with the actors' patrons. Thereafter the players would be given permission to put on a strictly regulated number of more frankly commercial performances in and around the town; their payments thus accrued from a mixed range of sources. Even when a town had reasons for preferring that no performances should take place, it was normal that the actors would receive a reward, as when Leicester's Men visited Norwich in 1584/5 and were turned away with 40 shillings, or again when they visited in Oxford in 1587/8 and were dismissed with 20 shillings 'so that they would depart with their plays (or pastimes) without greater trouble to the University'.[3]

As we shall see, the principle of gift exchange was always particularly visible at court, where, in the early years of Elizabeth's reign, performances were often staged by choir schools (before they became commercial operations) and the Inns of Court. But even in the late 1590s, when the troupes of only two patrons performed at court—the Lord Chamberlain and the Lord Admiral—both of these men were cousins of the Queen. Royal theatricals were in spirit a family present-giving. The actors privileged to be at the heart of it knew very well by what authority they were allowed to make real profits in the public theatres. And the relatively modest fees they received for performing at court were, in a sense, free gifts—since that performance, always at night, would probably have been in addition to their regular offering in the public theatre earlier in the day. Such duplication was not often available to them, though they did occasionally perform at private houses in the city. Beckerman's claim—that the increasing proportion of income which the King's Men derived from the court 'ultimately led' to their appealing 'increasingly to an aristocratic audience'—is simply back-to-front. Pleasing the aristocratic, and especially the courtly, audience was always their first concern. Everything else was, by definition, secondary.

* * *

In theory, the Act for the Punishment of Vagabonds reinforced the old gift-exchange culture in the business of playing by more clearly defining and narrowing the ranks of those entitled to participate. But in the longer view it was a mark of changing values. When the status of a company even as prestigious as that of the Earl of Leicester could not be taken for granted, the situation called for a clearer definition of their relationship (and that of other leading companies) to the central

---

[3] All of the payments and comments quoted here are from the REED (Records of Early English Drama) *Patrons and Performances* website, accessed via <http://link.library.utoronto.ca/reed/>.

authority of the court. The court's solution to this, a straw in the wind of what was to follow, was in May 1574 to issue Leicester's Men's with a royal patent, reinforcing Leicester's authority with the Queen's own. It addressed civic officials throughout the land:

> Know ye that we of our especial grace, certain knowledge, and mere motion have licensed and authorised, and by these presents do license and authorise, our loving subjects...servants to our trusty and well beloved cousin and counsellor the Earl of Leicester, to use, exercise, and occupy the art and faculty of playing comedies, tragedies, interludes, stage plays, and such other like...as well for the recreation of our loving subjects, as for our solace and pleasure when we shall think good to see them...as well within our City of London and liberties of the same, as also within the liberties and freedoms of any our cities, towns, boroughs, etc....throughout our realm of England. Provided that the said comedies, tragedies, interludes, and stage plays be by the Master of our Revels for the time being before seen and allowed, and that the same be not published or shown in the time of common prayer, or in the time of great and common plague in our said City of London. (Wickham *et al.* 2000: 206)

It is a document of many subtexts, which was to serve as a model for the patents of other major companies in the future. The first is the barely veiled assertion that royal authority takes precedence over all other, including that of the City of London, which was particularly concerned to control playing—though not necessarily to eradicate it. It makes a direct correlation between the actors' licence to play in public and their function to provide 'our solace and pleasure when we shall think good to see them', a formula which would be developed repeatedly over the next quarter of a century. And it directly answers the most common complaints raised by the City authorities: there should be no playing in time of plague, no playing at the time of church services, and (this was critical) no playing without the specific 'allowance' of their scripts by the court's own Master of the Revels (Wickham *et al.* 2000: 53–61). This latter was an attempt to pre-empt the City authorities from imposing their own system of licensing on the premier companies, which would inevitably cut across the authority of the court.

London and its Playhouses

An Act of London's Common Council in December 1574 can be read as a response to Leicester's Men's patent and is commonly cited as evidence of the London authorities' intransigent puritanical resistance to playing. In fact the situation was more complex than that, as we see in the authorities' treatment of the playhouses already under their jurisdiction—at least four inns, which were the sites of some of the earliest London theatre. As David Kathman puts it, the Act specified, at great length, that before any innkeeper or tavern keeper could have a play or interlude performed on his premises, he must have the playscript and playing place approved by the relevant authorities, post a bond with the Chamberlain of London, and pay a fee earmarked for the City hospitals (citing Chambers 1923: 4.273–6). Although this Act has often been seen as an attempt to suppress playing within the City, the Common Council went out of its way not to suppress such playing entirely, but merely to regulate it more strictly. While the Act undoubtedly did have something to do with the rise of the suburban playhouses shortly afterward, the greater cost of land within the City must also have been a significant factor. The new regulations did not prevent the Bull, the Bell Savage, the Cross Keys, and the Bell from hosting plays regularly for the next twenty years or more.[4] All four were well-established businesses that continued as inns throughout their lives as playhouses (2009: 156). Kathman cites William Ingram's argument in *The Business of Playing* that the Act was mainly intended to fund the impoverished City hospitals, but that it had the unintended consequence of driving many of the actors outside the jurisdiction of the City authorities altogether (Ingram 1992: 119–49).

In 1576 James Burbage, a former joiner and one of Leicester's players who had written the 1572 letter, went into partnership with his brother-in-law, John Brayne, and they built the Theatre, the first successful, purpose-built theatre in England for more than a thousand years.[5] This was in Shoreditch, some 500 yards north-east of the City walls, and under the jurisdiction of the Justices of the Peace of Middlesex (as the Bankside theatres like the Globe were to be under that of the Surrey Justices), not of the City authorities.

At this time no one seems to have contemplated that a company would occupy a playhouse like the Theatre on a permanent or exclusive basis. Touring was the established norm and, for a prestigious company, presumably a satisfactory way of conducting business. A company may well also have calculated that it could not fill an auditorium capable of holding perhaps 3,000 people year-round from a London population of probably not more than 150,000 at this time. Even if they could, they would have to find a way of securing many more playscripts; on tour they only needed a small repertoire, which they could permutate as they moved from place to place. It would not be until the late 1580s that they found a solution to this particular problem.

Nevertheless, it seems logical to assume that Burbage anticipated that his own company, Leicester's Men, would take advantage of the Theatre whenever their schedule brought them to London. It was capable of holding many more spectators than any of the city inns, and so was potentially a much more lucrative venue. Moreover, the authority of the company's royal patent would be respected there by the local justices, and would not come into conflict with the kinds of control being proposed by the City authorities. In *The Place of the Stage*, Steven Mullaney argued in cultural materialist mode that the location of the post-1576 playhouses made them marginal to respectable society and ambivalent in their relationship to authority (1995). All the great outdoor theatres did indeed follow the Theatre into the suburbs of the city, often (notably those on the Bankside) alongside brothels and madhouses; and the post-1599 boy actors' theatres were all in liberties,

---

[4] On possible playing in inns beyond 1596, see Menzer 2006.

[5] In 1567 Brayne had converted an inn, the Red Lion in Whitechapel, into a theatre, but it did not flourish (Wickham *et al.* 2000: 290–4). 'Successful' may overstate the point about the Theatre. Brayne and Burbage fell out and went to law over its costs, and there were numerous other setbacks. But it did remain in business until the late 1590s and might well have continued so if the owner of the land on which it stood had not refused to renew the lease (Wickham *et al.* 2000: 330–87). It certainly inspired others to emulate it.

formerly religious communities, like the Blackfriars and the Whitefriars which, even within the city walls, were exempt from the authority of the City fathers.[6]

But these locations actually represented something other than marginality. They represented a conscious and deliberate choosing of sides, an alignment of theatre companies with the authority of the court against that of the City. We need not read this teleologically down to Parliament's closing of the theatres in 1642, but it was a straw in that wind. Newington Butts was constructed south of the Bankside at almost the same time as the Theatre, and there too, like Burbage, the key entrepreneur was an actor with one of the troupes associated with the court: Jerome Savage, who led a new company under the patronage of the Earl of Warwick, first recorded at court in February 1575 (Wickham *et al.* 2000: 320–9; Ingram 1992: 150–81). The company played at Newington Butts until 1580 when it was dissolved, but revived without Savage as the Earl of Oxford's Men—another company received at court—who quite possibly continued to perform there. As we shall see, from the time of relatively settled London playing—say, the building of the Rose on the Bankside in 1587—there was an ever-closer identification between the companies playing at the supposedly marginal theatres and the court. This included, until they temporarily went out of business in the early 1590s, the boy companies, whose origins in chartered choir schools formally linked them with the court.

CHANGES AT COURT

Around the time that the first theatres were constructed in London there was a crisis over entertainment at court. The Revels Office, which oversaw such matters, had been poorly managed under its last Master, Sir Thomas Benger: costs were out of control and the quality could be erratic (see pp. 41–6). Benger was eventually replaced by Edmund Tilney, who was associated with the Office by February 1578 and appointed its Master by patent in July 1579. He was a kinsman of the powerful Howard family and his particular patron was Lord Howard of Effingham, later celebrated as the Lord Admiral who defeated the Spanish Armada, a first cousin of the Queen on the Boleyn side and a critical supporter of the players throughout the last quarter of the sixteenth century (Gurr 2002). Howard deputized for the Earl of Sussex, another mutual cousin, when he was ill in 1574–5, and succeeded him as Lord Chamberlain when he died in 1583. These were influential aristocrats who not only supervised matters at court but, through their positions on the Privy Council, effectively ran the country.

The Lord Chamberlain was ultimately responsible for the efficient running of most aspects of the royal household indoors; court theatricals were one small part of his remit, though at this date he had no managerial control over the Revels Office. It was obviously convenient, therefore, to have a Master of that office who

---

[6] The other 'public' theatres (outdoor auditoria) were, with locations and dates: Newington Butts, Southwark, south of the river, *c.* 1576; the Curtain, close by the Theatre in Shoreditch, 1577; the Rose, the Swan, and the Globe, all on the Bankside, 1587, 1597, and 1599 respectively; the Fortune, northwest of the City limits, 1600; the Hope, Bankside, 1614.

would be attentive to his concerns. It can hardly be accidental in all this that Howard first started patronizing his own company of players in 1576, when Sussex returned to his duties. It seems likely that he already anticipated one day succeeding Sussex as Lord Chamberlain and thought this an appropriate advertisement of his status for that role. His company performed at court twice in the 1576/7 season and again in 1578.[7]

Howard's support must have been highly significant in Tilney's early years, but it is apparent that Tilney also had pronounced managerial skills. In the first accounts that he submitted as Master (1579/80), he included a claim 'for his attendance at the Court 12 weeks after Ash Wednesday to sue out the warrant and for horse hire and riding charges divers times to Nonesuch [Palace] to satisfy her Majesty, my Lord Treasurer and my Lord Chamberlain in matters concerning the office' (Feuillerat 1908: 326). The Master normally claimed fees only for attendance at court during the Revels season. That ran in full from 1 November to Ash Wednesday. But Tilney only claimed for days when he would actually be in attendance to oversee performances—normally the twelve days of Christmas, plus Candlemas and Shrovetide. For the rest of the year his duties largely consisted of supervising the process of airing, cleaning, and repairing the vast stock of valuable costumes, cloths, and other properties held by the Office, then situated in his capacious quarters in the former Priory of St John in Clerkenwell. But on this occasion his Spring was devoted to sorting out the management of the Office with the most senior persons in the royal household. We may infer that he convinced them of his business plan from a letter sent that August by the Privy Council to the Master of the Tents and Toils and to the Lieutenant of the Tower of London, instructing them to 'take a view and peruse the stuff which remaineth [in the Revels Office] in what estate it is in', make an inventory of 'such stuff as shall seem serviceable... and deliver the same by Indenture to Edmund Tilney now Master of the said Office' (Feuillerat 1908: 330). This reads like a drawing of a line under the past, allowing Tilney to make a fresh start in the position.

The Privy Council wrote to the Lord Mayor of London on 24 December 1578, just before the first shows of the season were to be staged at court. Their minutes record:

> A letter to the Lord Mayor, &c., requiring him to suffer the Children of her Majesty's Chapel, the servants of the Lord Chamberlain, the Earl of Warwick, the Earl of Leicester, the Earl of Essex and the Children of Paul's, and no companies else, to exercise playing within the City, whom their Lordships have only allowed thereunto by reason that the companies aforenamed are appointed to play this time of Christmas before her Majesty.   (Gurr 1996: 55)

This spells out for the first time that there was an élite and privileged group of companies whose public performances in London that winter could very literally be regarded as rehearsals for appearances at court, and indeed all but Essex's Men

---

[7] For a rare sidelight on Howard's interest in theatre, and on the theatrical entrepreneurs Burbage and Brayne, see Mateer 2006.

did appear that season.[8] All of the adult companies who did perform were patronized by powerful aristocrats who held major offices at court. These were the companies Tilney was expected to work with. Those of Lord Chamberlain Sussex and the two Dudley Earls of Leicester and Warwick—men always high in the Queen's favour—all had solid track records at court, as did the boys of the Chapel Royal and St Paul's. Moreover, whereas the companies of many aristocrats would naturally gravitate towards their masters' country seats for the Revels season, these leading figures of the royal household would inevitably be waiting on the Queen at court.[9] In coming to serve the Queen, their companies would also be serving their lords. They all had experience of working with Tilney's predecessors and he could build on that in the years ahead.

In effect this directive extended to all of these companies the prerogatives individually extended to Leicester's Men in their royal patent. It is interesting to speculate on precisely why the Privy Council regarded this as necessary, since they all had possible bases outside the City's jurisdiction. Leicester's Men would have use of the Theatre and Warwick's of Newington Butts, while Sussex's Men could have taken over the Curtain. The Master of the Chapel Boys, Richard Farrant, had constructed a theatre for them in the Blackfriars liberty.[10] And the playhouse used by Paul's boys was within the Cathedral precinct and so also outside the jurisdiction of the Lord Mayor. A likely implication is that the adult companies wanted to use the city inns for their winter playing, which they always preferred, probably because audiences found them more convenient as the nights drew in. This is something we find the Lord Chamberlain's Men angling for at least as late as 1594 (see p. 70). But whatever lay behind the sending of this 1578 letter, it clearly drew a line between the court and the City: certain companies were to be regarded as having the specific authority of the court behind them.

The situation identified here—an élite group of court-identified companies—was to be at the heart of Tilney's working life from here on. Membership of the group would change over time as patrons died and specific circumstances intervened, some of which we shall note. But the group was never larger than the six listed here, and in the periods 1590–99 and again after 1613 (when there were once more no boy companies) it was often down to four. From 1594 to 1599—a critical fact in Shakespeare's career—it was down to two. Tilney's authority would, on paper, extend to cover playing companies throughout the country. But in fact his business was very largely focused on this small but exclusive group. They in turn would be the most successful troupes of their era and the vast majority of the plays which were published were written for, and performed by, them. When we

---

[8] The third Earl of Essex was still only thirteen, two years after his father's death. The company had appeared at court on the Shrove Tuesday of the 1577/8 season, designated as Lady Essex's Men, a last-minute replacement for Leicester's Men. But the Earl's mother had that year incurred the Queen's wrath by marrying the Earl of Leicester. The company never appeared at court again.
[9] Besides Lord Chamberlain Sussex, Leicester was Master of the Horse and Warwick Master of the Ordnance.
[10] This was different from the second Blackfriars theatre, built by James Burbage in 1596 and used by Shakespeare's company after 1608.

speak of 'Elizabethan drama' we in fact overwhelmingly mean the plays of these few companies.

This was at least in part because Tilney made them central to his business plan for the Revels Office. As W. R. Streitberger puts it, 'The main reason for Tyllney's success... was his reliance on the play rather than the masque as the mainstay of his entertainment schedule... during Tyllney's first season as Master, 1579–80, he furnished nine plays at an average cost of roughly £25 each. Reliance on the play rather than the masque further reduced the costs of costumes, for gradually over the course of Tyllney's early Mastership companies seem to have been expected to supply their own' (1986a: xviii–xix). That is, the unit costs were one-third of what they had been in, for example, the 1573–4 season and the total annual charges were radically reduced (Feuillerat 1908: 332). Leicester's Men supplied 'furniture' for plays they performed at court as early as 1573 and 1578 (Graves 1913: 84). But this became the normal expectation in years ahead, as companies settled into London quarters. In today's language, the costs of costumes and properties—together normally with their upkeep and transport to court and back—were outsourced. And this was a particular bargain, because the companies continued only to receive the traditional £10 fee, even though so many more of the costs fell to them. As I have argued, however, significant other benefits flowed from this to the companies.

In 1581 Tilney's patent was reinforced with a two-part special commission. The first part gave him warrant to purchase whatever he needed for the creation of costumes and properties 'at reasonable prices' and similarly to hire transport to move them to wherever they were needed. He was also given the powers to imprison anyone who should 'obstinately disobey or refuse' to carry out orders under this commission, and also to protect from arrest anyone working for him on urgent business. The second part of the commission gave him authority

> to warn, command and appoint in all places within this our Realm of England, as well within franchises and liberties as without, all and every player or players with their play-makers either belonging to any nobleman or otherwise bearing the name or names of using the faculty of play-makers or players of Comedies, Tragedies, Interludes, or what other shows soever from time to time and at all times to appear before him with all such plays, Tragedies, Comedies or shows as they shall have in readiness, or mean to set forth, and them to present and recite before our said Servant or his sufficient deputy whom we ordain, appoint and authorise by these presents of all such shows, plays, players and playmakers, together with their playing places, to order and reform, authorise and put down, as shall be thought meet or unmeet unto himself or his said deputy in that behalf. (Wickham *et al.* 2000: 70–1)[11]

He was also given powers to enforce this authority.

It is the second half of this commission to which I and others have paid most attention, because it was the basis of Tilney's role as licenser and censor of the

---

[11] The document is mislabelled in Wickham *et al.* 2000. It is not 'Elizabeth I's Patent appointing Edmund Tilney' (which was dated 24 July 1579 and is reproduced in Feuillerat 1908: 55) but a special commission.

professional theatre in the London region and beyond. It is the role in which he is most familiar to students of English Renaissance drama and in which he was amusingly travestied in *Shakespeare in Love* (see, e.g., Wickham, 1959–81: 2.1:94; Clare 1990: 11–12; Dutton 1991: 47ff). But I want here to consider it in relation to his primary role, that as provider of theatrical entertainment at court (Streitberger 1978). One reason for the Revels Office disarray before Tilney is that the court was notoriously bad, or at the very least slow, about paying its bills. Benger in fact died chronically in debt, largely as a result of having to carry the charges of the office personally for long periods, while Tilney's successor, Sir George Buc, was to go mad in office, almost certainly because of the pressure of debts (Streitberger 2004; Eccles 1933b). Given these circumstances, workmen were often reluctant to be employed, while merchants were only prepared to sell goods at inflated prices to cover their losses. The provisions of the first part of the special commission addressed both of these issues.

The provisions of the second part—although they did indeed institute Tilney's role as licenser of the public theatres—were primarily aimed at reinforcing his ability to provide entertainment of a suitable quality and cost at court. He might concentrate his attention on the companies patronized by leading courtiers, but he had *carte-blanche* powers to summon any company to court and in effect compel them to perform. And he used those powers decisively in 1583 to create an élite troupe of players patronized by the Queen herself. Tilney received a summons to court (10 March) from the secretary of the Privy Council, Sir Francis Walsingham, and was instructed 'to choose out a company of players for her majesty'. In his 1615 edition of John Stow's *Annals*, Edmund Howes describes the process, noting how

> twelve of the best [were] chosen [from the service of divers great lords], and... they were sworn the Queen's servants and were allowed wages and liveries as grooms of the chamber... Among these twelve players were two rare men, viz. Thomas [i.e. Robert] Wilson, for a quick, delicate, refined, extemporal wit, and Richard Tarlton, for a wondrous plentiful pleasant extemporal wit, he was the wonder of his time.   (Wickham *et al.* 2000: 208)

Scholars have varied in their explanations of what exactly was going on here. Andrew Gurr, for example, suggests that the formation of the Queen's Men arose from more or less open personal and factional competition within the Privy Council spilling over into the choice of companies to perform at court; he also argues that the key figure behind the scenes is likely to have been Tilney's patron, Howard of Effingham, who was shortly to succeed the ailing Sussex as Lord Chamberlain. Scott McMillin and Sally-Beth MacLean have suggested rather that the new troupe was the particular brainchild of the Leicester–Walsingham grouping within the Privy Council, proponents of an aggressive foreign policy against Spain, who wanted their brand of Protestant nationalism transmitted around the country by this company—still very much a touring operation, only returning to London at required times—which would carry all the prestige of the Queen's own livery. W. R. Streitberger argues that it was a much less charged product of normal

Privy Council attention to the Queen's needs, with Lord Chamberlain Sussex—who had only taken on oversight of the Revels Office in the wake of Benger's extravagance—taking an appropriate leading role (Gurr 1996: 197–201; McMillin and MacLean 1999: 18–36; Streitberger 2007).

From the perspective of this study, the micro-politics of the creation of the Queen's Men is less important than the consequences for court performance. In the first place, it eviscerated the previous leading companies. Sussex's Men, which had been growing in prestige, lost at least two leading players including the incomparable clown, Tarlton. Leicester's Men lost at least three, including the notable William Knell; Oxford's at least one. And the Queen's Men took on the fine actor-playwright, Robert Wilson (Tilney's powers extended over 'play-makers' as well as players). They were instantly the outstanding company of their time, and also larger in personnel than anything that had gone before: Stow suggests that there were twelve original sharers (core members of the company, with a financial stake in it), though soon their plays required as many as fifteen players. All of this was promptly reflected in their court privileges. In the 1583/4 and 1584/5 seasons they were the only adult players called to perform. This exclusive position eased somewhat from 1585/6, when Howard's company (he was now Lord Admiral, after two years as Lord Chamberlain) began to reappear in the schedules, and Leicester's Men appeared one last time before their patron's death in 1588. The Queen's Men still dominated in 1590/1, with five performances out of a total seven. But in 1591/2 they were all but eclipsed by Strange's Men, a company patronized by the son of the Earl of Derby, and their last court appearance was on Twelfth Night 1594.

The Queen's Men, we may conclude, suited the court's purposes—and Tilney's requirements—perfectly, if only for a time. The only question that remains is why they made no apparent effort to sustain their unique pre-eminence. Robert Wilson was allowed to join those of Leicester's Men who accompanied their patron on his ill-fated military expedition to the Netherlands in 1585; William Knell died in a duel with a fellow actor in 1587; Tarlton died in 1588. They still had well-known actors, including the Dutton brothers, John and Laurence. But it was no longer the all-star operation it had been, and others like Strange's Men were able to give them serious competition even at court. Possibly over time Tilney appreciated the risks of putting all the eggs in a single basket. Whatever the case, the key lesson about the creation of the Queen's Men is that the court was prepared peremptorily to intervene in the 'free market' of the theatrical business to ensure that it got what it wanted out of it. Everything else was secondary.

Another feature of Tilney's special commission was that it in effect addressed the question of his own remuneration. Over the next two decades various schemes were tried to cap Revels expenses, and these touched on the Master's own fees. It had been traditional to base them on expenses per day (and per night) for actual attendance on business and this had usually generated an income of about £30 for the Master. Some time before 1593 this system was changed so that all the officers of the Revels between them received fixed fees totalling £40, of which Tilney only received £21, a significant loss. The system reverted to something more like the old one under James I, and Tilney's attendance fees alone in 1603/4 totalled £62 8s—an issue to which I shall return (Streitberger 1978: 23–4).

But as sole licenser of theatres and of the plays performed in them, Tilney also had a distinct income, which was almost certainly more reliable than that from the court, except when plague interrupted business. It was a classic instance of the way in which Elizabeth and James rewarded their courtiers without having to pay them a proper wage: a monopoly in which court authority was translated into cash value. Tilney got fees for licensing each play for public performance (Buc would also get fees for licensing them for print); and he got fees for allowing each theatre to operate. We can see tabulations of such payments in Philip Henslowe's *Diary*, the single most revealing document we possess in relation to the business operations of Elizabethan theatre. Henslowe built the Rose playhouse, and the *Diary* (although sometimes difficult to follow) records many of the payments he made in its running between 1592 and 1603; he also records much of the business activity of the acting companies who were his tenants, most notably (from 1594) the Lord Admiral's Men, for whom he was landlord, banker, and eventually a manager of sorts.

Some of the apparent anomalies in the *Diary* have been explained as attempts to keep a precise record of what was due to the Master of the Revels. As its editor, R. A. Foakes, observes, 'These payments seem to have constituted fees paid to the Master for permission to stage plays in the theatre... Clearly, over the years from 1592 to 1597 the system of paying the Master was modified; what began as a weekly payment had become by the summer of 1597 a monthly payment' (2002: xxxii–xxxiii). The weekly payments were 5s, paid in four-weekly sums of 20s by January 1597 (75); by October 1599 Tilney was receiving £3 a month, a very substantial increase, which I discuss further later in this chapter (2002: 162–3). He received 7s for licensing individual plays, as in 'p[ai]d unto the Mr of the Revels' man for licensing of a Book called Damon & Pythias the 16 of May 1600 sum of...7s.' (134).

These payments all refer to the Lord Admiral's Men, firstly at the Rose and latterly at the Fortune. But there would have been a parallel income from the Theatre and the Chamberlain's Men, and eventually from other playhouse operations. Since occupation of the London playhouses increasingly went hand-in-hand with invitations to perform at court, Tilney would normally have been dealing with a self-contained group of privileged performers. Their payments to him were a tax on their livelihood, but they must always have been conscious that without Tilney they might well not have a livelihood at all, certainly not one as privileged as they had. It was a reciprocally advantageous arrangement in which, as T. H. Howard-Hill put it (referring to Buc), 'his relationship with the players although ultimately authoritarian was more collegial than adversarial' (1988: 43).

Tilney's special commission thus defined the terms and conditions of playing in London for actors during Shakespeare's working lifetime. It entrenched the relationship between professional theatre (in its most prominent companies) and the court, in a way that effectively sidelined the City of London authorities. Those authorities were well aware of this and continued to try to bring pressure to bear wherever they could. In 1589 they seem to have convinced the Privy Council that Tilney was not doing an adequate job of censoring the plays 'in that the players do take upon them to handle in their plays certain matters of divinity and of state unfit to be suffered'. The proposed solution was a licensing commission, composed of Tilney, 'a sufficient person learned and of judgement' to be appointed by the Lord Mayor, and 'some fit person well learned in divinity [to] be appointed by' the Archbishop of Canterbury (Wickham *et al.* 2000: 94–5). There is no evidence that this commission ever in fact operated, but if it did it had certainly broken down by February 1592 when the Lord Mayor wrote to John Whitgift, the Archbishop of Canterbury, with a proposal (discreetly expressed) to buy Tilney out. Anticipating at least one part of the reply, the Lord Mayor had his own solution for providing plays for the court:

> And because we understand that the Queen's Majesty is and must be served at certain times by this sort of people, for which purpose she hath granted her Letters Patent to Mr Tilney, Master of her Revels, by virtue whereof he being authorised to reform, exercise or suppress all manner of players, plays and playing houses whatsoever, did first license the said playing houses within this City for her Majesty's said service, which before that time lay open to all the Statutes for the punishing of these and such like disorders. We are most humbly and earnestly to beseech your Grace to call unto you the said Master of Her Majesty's Revels, with whom also we have conferred of late to that purpose, and to treat with him, if by any means it may be devised, that her Majesty may be served with these recreations as hath been accustomed (which in our opinions may easily be done by the private exercise of Her Majesty's own players in convenient place), and the City freed from these continual disorders which thereby do grow and increase among us... (Wickham *et al.* 2000: 96)

Subsequent correspondence made clear that the delicately phrased 'if by any means it may be devised' actually meant a 'consideration to be made to Mr Tilney' (97), recompensing him for the loss of his income under the proposed arrangements. The proposal went nowhere, almost certainly because the Livery Companies who would have had to foot the bill jibbed at paying off Tilney (98). So no one took up the Lord Mayor's suggestion that the Queen could be served simply by having her own players rehearse in private and entirely at her own charge. The mutually supportive blending of court patronage culture and of nascent capitalist enterprise, which is implicit in Tilney's special commission, survived and flourished down to the 1642 closing of the theatres.

By the time of this attempt to buy Tilney out the Queen's Men were almost a spent force at court. As we noted, they lost several of their irreplaceable leading lights early on. But other forces may also have been at play. A distinctive feature of this company is that they maintained a very substantial touring schedule; by 1587 if not earlier they were in the habit of splitting into two groups, covering different routes and so fully exploiting the gift-exchange culture of royal patronage (McMillin and MacLean 1999: 37–83). We know that they did perform in London, because Howard as Lord Chamberlain secured City permission for them to play at specified inns, and they may at other times have played at the Theatre or the Curtain, though there is no record of it (Gurr 1996: 201–2). It seems, in particular, that they came together there before performances at court, which might involve the whole company.[12] After 1594, however, they became exclusively a touring unit and there is no record of them in London; they certainly did not perform at court again. But they were the last major company for whom touring predominated over resident playing in London, and Tilney doubtless recognized the sea-change that was taking place as they slipped out of his schedules.

However, 1589 is a critical date in the theatre history of the era because at precisely that point—with Shakespeare poised to enter the picture—the records fail us in multiple ways. Much of the record of court entertainment that I have been able to put together here and in Chapter 2 derives from the accounts which successive Masters of the Revels submitted to various offices, and which Albert Feuillerat meticulously reconstructed from a variety of manuscripts. From this point on, until James's reign, those accounts have not survived, probably lost in one of the various fires that ravaged Whitehall in the period. In earlier years we often have the titles and dates of plays performed at court, sometimes with details of the Master's involvement; but rarely (except for those of John Lyly) have the texts survived. During Shakespeare's career, as we shall see, we generally know the dates when companies performed at court—but we rarely know which plays they put on.

In this sense we are in the odd situation of generally knowing more in some respects about court theatricals in the first three decades of Elizabeth's reign than we do about them in the last. Tilney's own few surviving accounts are actually less detailed, and certainly less colourful, than those of his predecessors and we have to go back as far as 1585 to find any play titles recorded even there. But the loss of them from 1590 to 1602 is a serious blow. So too is the loss of Tilney's office-book in which he presumably kept a record of his dealings with the acting companies, including his licensing of their plays for performance and his choices for court presentation. That too has disappeared completely, as has that of Tilney's successor, Sir George Buc. Not until the time of Sir Henry Herbert, in office 1623–42, has such information survived (Bawcutt 1996).

What we are left with are records of payments for performances which identify the relevant company, but which give us no indication even of the titles of what they played or of Tilney's interactions with them. The record is similarly blank on how the Lord Chamberlain's Men came into being in 1594 and what the Privy Council were thinking in 1597 when they ordered all the playhouses to be torn down (but, thankfully, relented: Wickham *et al.* 2000: 100–1). On the positive side, we have the immense blessing of Philip Henslowe's *Diary*—which I explore further in Chapter 2—though that (except very briefly) deals with rival companies, not with Shakespeare's own. As in so many things to do with Shakespeare, we see as in glass darkly.

My main concern about Tilney's rather anonymous accounts, compounded by this significant gap in their middle, is that they give the impression that his relationship with the actors became a simple, utilitarian, and commercial one: he saw

---

[12] McMillin and MacLean argue for relatively meagre returns of a touring company even as privileged as the Queen's Men (1999: 61). But see also Greenfield 2009: 294–5.

their plays and ordered the best ones to come to court. That is, that he broke with the premises of his predecessors, who saw the winter Revels season as entertainment by the court, for the court, and substantially shaped by their own imaginative input. This is commonly the picture painted by histories of the drama of the period. As I hope to show, it is wrong.

WILLIAM SHAKESPEARE AND THE ELIZABETHAN COURT

Our very first tangible record of Shakespeare as an actor/dramatist places him at the court. On 15 March 1595, together with William Kemp and Richard Burbage, he received payment on behalf of all the shareholders of the Lord Chamberlain's Men for performances at court on 26 and 28 December 1594.[13] Of course, we know well enough that Shakespeare had been active in the theatre before this. Thomas Nashe's salute to what we know as *1 Henry VI* and Robert Greene's sour deathbed denunciation of the 'upstart crow' are evidence enough (Schoenbaum 1987: 160, 149–53). But no one has been able to locate him with a specific company or theatre earlier than this. Terence G. Schoone-Jongen, the latest person to try, concludes: 'Ultimately, it seems Shakespeare's pre-1594 company affiliations present the biographer with a jigsaw puzzle. Yet because the puzzle is missing key pieces, it cannot be fully assembled. Or, more to the point, it can be assembled in a number of different, plausible-yet-incomplete ways' (Schoone-Jongen 2008: 199).

We may, however, safely assume that Shakespeare was part of this new company—Henry Carey, Lord Hunsdon, now the Lord Chamberlain, had not retained a company of players since 1589/90—when it made a brief appearance in Philip Henslowe's *Diary*. He records that 'my Lord Admiral's men and my Lord Chamberlain's men' played at Newington Butts from 3 to 13 June 1594 (Foakes 2002: 21). We do not know if this means that they played together as a joint company, or perhaps on alternate days. But thereafter they played separately, and Henslowe records the activities of the Admiral's Men in minute detail—but nothing more of the Chamberlain's Men.

The March 1595 record, however, already tells us a lot. The Chamberlain's Men had been accorded the honour of leading off the Revels season at court, a slot previously reserved almost exclusively for the Queen's Men. They performed on 26 December, St Stephen's Day, every year for the rest of Elizabeth's reign. It suggests that Shakespeare was already a senior member of this company and trusted by his fellows, that he should have been given the responsibility of receiving payment. Kemp was the leading comic actor of the company; Thomas Nashe dubbed him 'vicegerent general to the ghost of Dick Tarlton' in *An Almond for a Parrot* (1590). Burbage would quickly emerge as the leading serious actor of the company, but perhaps was accorded seniority here as the son of James Burbage, owner of the

---

[13] 28 December is almost certainly a mistake for 27 December. The Lord Admiral's Men also received payment for playing on the 28th, and that night the Lord Chamberlain's Men played a famously disastrous performance of *The Comedy of Errors* at Gray's Inn (Chambers 1923: 2.194).

Theatre where the company was then regularly playing. Shakespeare had no great reputation as an actor, so it was most likely in his established capacity as 'playmaker' that he was accorded this honour.

The plague years of 1592 to 1594 had decimated the population of London and played havoc with the acting world. Of the leading companies discussed earlier, Warwick's never flourished beyond 1580, while Leicester's had dissolved when their patron died in 1588. The fate of those that succeed them is amply indicated by the title page of the 1594 quarto of *Titus Andronicus*, which declares it to have been performed by 'the Earl of Derby, Earl of Pembroke, and Earl of Sussex their servants'—either as a combined group or successively.[14] None of these companies was still functioning at the highest level when the plague relented in 1594, though their remnants can be traced in the provincial records. I have already described the declining status of the Queen's Men. The boy companies were all out of business before the plague struck. There was a void to be filled in the theatrical world, and the new Chamberlain's and a reformed Admiral's Men filled it.

In the absence of firm evidence, scholars are divided over whether this was a commercially driven development or one engineered (as the formation of the Queen's Men had been) by the court. Roslyn Lander Knutson argues for 'cooperative commercial strategies that accommodated change and promoted growth' (Knutson 2001: 47; see also Knutson 2010). In her view, one company developed around the Burbages and their need to keep the Theatre in business, and James Burbage had been wearing Lord Hunsdon's livery for at least twelve years; the other developed around the most famous actor of the day, Edward Alleyn, who had been with the Lord Admiral's Men since around 1587 and whose father-in-law, Henslowe, owned and managed the Rose. Andrew Gurr, on the other hand, sees at least court collusion in all of this, under the guiding hands of Lord Admiral Howard and his father-in-law, Hunsdon:

> Whether Carey and Howard knowingly contrived their drastic bending of the *status quo ante* we cannot be sure, but the delicate precision with which the new set-up was established does suggest that they were both working to appease the anger of the city fathers against the players, and had seen how in the face of that the Lord Chamberlain might continue enacting his office's most sensitive duty, providing the queen with her Christmas shows. The crucial novelty in the idea was to allocate each company to a suburban playhouse and with it ban the players from using any of the inns inside the city. The two companies set up to run as a duopoly of playing in London were given similarly strong repertoires of plays, Shakespeare to the one and Marlowe to the other. (Gurr 2004a: 2)

Holger Syme, however, has challenged Gurr's much-reiterated account of 1594 as a watershed turning point in theatre history, overseen by members of the Privy

---

[14] Ferdinando Stanley, Lord Strange, was Earl of Derby from September 1593 to April 1594, when he died, and this refers to the company better known as Strange's Men; Henry Herbert, second Earl of Pembroke, was patron of a company that enters the records on several occasions in the 1590s but never quite established itself in the first rank; the Earl of Sussex referred to was either Henry Radcliffe, fourth earl and brother of the former Lord Chamberlain, or Robert his son, who succeeded him in December 1593.

Council. He questions the notion of a 'duopoly' and the teleological Shakespeare-centred narrative (2012: 214).

Yet it was certainly the case that the Admiral's and the Chamberlain's Men were the only playing companies with access to the court for the next five years and the only ones with more-or-less permanent London bases—respectively the Rose and the Theatre (and, after its lease ran out, the Curtain). And in 1598 the Privy Council formally announced this arrangement to be court policy. It was as perfect a marriage of commercial and courtly requirements as can be imagined, and I would only add that no one was better placed than Edmund Tilney to engineer it. He would be motivated simultaneously by the responsibility he had of supplying high-quality theatre to the court and the wish to maintain his own income.

I shall pick up the narrative of Shakespeare's work for the court in Chapter 2. For now I want simply to emphasize how perfectly his emergence into the public record coincides with an alliance between the court and the top ranks of the theatrical profession which had been in the making for the past twenty years. The two companies were the first of their kind to sustain London playing more-or-less year-round for so long;[15] their patrons were closely allied by marriage, and both were cousins of the Queen. Edmund Tilney, who oversaw them both in what they performed in public and what they offered at court, had been in office for sixteen years, and knew more about the London theatre than any man alive.

THE 1597/8 WATERSHED

The last piece of theatre history we need to consider here is the sequence of sometimes perplexing events in 1597 and 1598 which ultimately confirmed the special status of the Lord Chamberlain's Men and the Lord Admiral's Men in relation to the court. The conundrums begin on 28 July 1597, when the Privy Council—apparently *reversing* its policies of the past twenty years—wrote to the magistrates in Middlesex and Surrey, ordering that 'those playhouses that are erected and built only for such purposes shall be plucked down' both in Shoreditch, where the Theatre and Curtain were, and in Southwark, where the Rose and Swan stood (Wickham *et al.* 2000: 100–1; see also Dutton 1991: 102–16; Dutton 2000: 16–40). They also imposed a suspension of all playing. That was the very day that the Privy Council received what seems, on the face of it, to be yet another routine complaint from the London authorities (here the Court of Common Council), listing their usual objections to the theatres—immorality, crime, absenteeism, spread of plague—and petitioning 'for the present stay, and final suppressing, of the said stage plays' (Wickham *et al.* 2000: 99). Nothing suggests why the Privy Council should have reacted to this in the unprecedented manner that they did.

---

[15] See Lawrence Manley and Sally-Beth MacLean (2014) on Strange's Men, probably the first company to attempt a London-based strategy; they were thwarted by the plague and by the death of their patron. Normally speaking, closure of the theatres because of plague was the only reason the Chamberlain's and Admiral's Men left London and toured, though the Admiral's Men did occasionally take to the road for no defined reason, possibly at the behest of their patron.

But there is also no indication that anyone acted on the order to pluck the playhouses down.

Suspicion has focused on what was happening at this time around the newest of the theatres, the Swan. It had been occupied by the Earl of Pembroke's Men, who at this date clearly constituted rivals to the Admiral's Men, playing along the Southwark Bankside in the Rose. As early as that February, two of the sharers in the Admiral's Men had defected to join Pembroke's; in July another leading figure, Martin Slater, joined them (Gurr 1996: 239). However, by 6 August Henslowe records that he had bound Richard Jones back into service with the Admiral's Men and had further advanced him 2d to secure the services of one of the original Pembroke's Men, Robert Shaa or Shaw (Foakes 2002: 239–40). Moreover, on 10 August another of Pembroke's Men, William Bird or Bourne, bound himself to the Admiral's Men, and by 5 October Thomas Downton had bound himself to return to the fold (240).

It seems highly likely that this flow of key players from Pembroke's Men back to the Admiral's was linked with the Council's action against a play of theirs, *The Isle of Dogs*, co-written by Thomas Nashe and Ben Jonson; Jonson also performed in it. And it may well have been this, rather than the petition from the Court of Common Council, which prompted the Privy Council's actions against the playhouses (Wickham *et al.* 2000: 101). By 15 August they certainly had Jonson and other players in custody for their parts in this play 'containing very seditious and slanderous matter' (102). Moreover, they were employing the notorious inquisitor and licensed torturer, Richard Topcliffe, in pursuit of those responsible—the only time in the entire era that they demonstrated such naked aggression in their response to theatrical infractions.

One clear outcome of all this—which a cynical observer might conclude had been intended all along—was that Pembroke's Men were driven out of business and the Swan was largely unused for several years (Ingram 1978: 167–86, 313–14). On 19 February Privy Council letters went out simultaneously to the Middlesex and Surrey magistrates and to Edmund Tilney:

> Whereas licence hath been granted unto two companies of stage players retained unto us, the Lord Admiral and Lord Chamberlain, to use and practice stage plays, whereby they might be better enabled and prepared to show such plays before Her Majesty as they shall be required at times meet and accustomed, to which end they have been chiefly licensed and tolerated as aforesaid; and whereas there is also a third company who of late (as we are informed) have by way of intrusion used likewise to play, having neither prepared any play for Her Majesty nor are bound to you, the Master of the Revels, for performing such orders as have been enjoined to be observed by the other two companies before mentioned. We have therefore thought good to require you upon receipt hereof to take order that the aforesaid third company may be suppressed, and none suffered hereafter to play but those two formerly named belonging to us, the Lord Admiral and Lord Chamberlain, unless you shall receive other direction from us. (Wickham *et al.* 2000: 104)

No earlier document is as explicit about the interrelationship of these two 'licensed' and 'tolerated' companies, the Master of the Revels, and the provision of plays for the Queen. But this is unequivocal. Whatever understandings may have surrounded the emergence of these companies in 1594, these were now publicly stated policies of the Privy Council as far as the authorities in and around London were concerned.[16]

It is surely not coincidence that these developments broadly overlap with changes a) in the nature of what Henslowe recorded in his *Diary*; b) in the nature of his relationship with the Admiral's Men; and c) in the relationship of both the actors and their landlord with the Master of the Revels. Henslowe changed the nature of his entries in the *Diary* more than once. They detail theatrical business going back to 1591 and earlier entries are particularly valuable in what they tell us about the ever-changing repertoire and the receipts for individual performances. But that kind of information ceases late in 1597 and Henslowe starts listing, among other things, payments and loans to writers for particular plays (Foakes 2002: 72).

The explanation seems to be that, even as the *Isle of Dogs* business was unwinding, Henslowe ceased simply to be merely the Admiral's Men's landlord at the Rose (recording performances to keep track of what he was owed from the profits, and what was owed to Tilney), and became their banker, making the payments he details on their behalf. There must be a good possibility that this was linked with the publicly recognized status of the company's relationship to the court that all the parties must have known was about to emerge. The company was, very simply, a more secure business prospect. This supposition is reinforced by what seems to happen in their relations with Tilney. R. A. Foakes, the distinguished editor of the *Diary*, has this to say about the evolving pattern of entries in it, which he links with the need to keep records of what was due to Tilney:

> The daily entries come to an end in November 1597, about the time when Henslowe seems to have become not merely landlord but banker to the company; the payments to the Master of the Revels continued, and in October 1598, Henslowe made a single payment covering the previous three months... It may be that as the basis of payment changed, it became no longer important for Henslowe to keep a list of daily performances, if one reason for doing so initially was to provide evidence for the Master or his man of actual performances, and a check for himself of what he should be paying; a close relationship between performance and payments may have decayed until the payments became a customary formality. (xxxiii, citing Greg 1904–8: 2. 127, 133; Chambers 1923: 1. 361–2)

This makes a lot of sense *especially* if we see here a kind of three-way bonding—not just Henslowe becoming banker, and effectively business manager, of the Admiral's

---

[16] The relief for both companies must have been palpable, but all the more so for Shakespeare's company, whose patronage situation became precarious in 1596. The first Lord Hunsdon died that year and was replaced as Lord Chamberlain by Lord Cobham, a man who did not patronize players. Lord Hunsdon's son took over their patronage, but at that time he held no court office. Fortunately for the company, however, Lord Cobham died early in 1597 and was replaced as Lord Chamberlain by the younger Lord Hunsdon. The Howard–Carey family alliance in the Privy Council which had stood these two companies in such good stead looked firmer than ever, and must have played its part in the 1598 outcomes.

Men, but both becoming close enough to Tilney that his payments—and those from the Admiral's Men—became 'a customary formality' rather than something requiring painstaking daily accounts. They were all parties who could expect to benefit from the court's newly settled relationship with its privileged acting companies—and Tilney most certainly benefited, in that his fees for licensing the theatres effectively trebled (see p. 25). We may assume a parallel closening between Tilney and the Chamberlain's Men, though no record of it has survived.

The 1597/8 settlements put a very public seal, and a financial premium, on the symbiotic relationship between the Master and the privileged playing companies. As we shall see in Chapter 4, it was also at this time that Henslowe started recording payments to Henry Chettle and Thomas Dekker for revisions of plays 'for the court' and other payments for the acquisition of new items for their production; and that plays by the two privileged companies appeared, advertising themselves variously as revised and/or performed at court. While it is entirely possible that such revising of plays had been going on for some time, unrecorded, the timing offers grounds for supposing that these were fresh practices, linked to the companies' newly formalized status at court. The investments of the Chamberlain's and Admiral's Men in working up enhanced versions of some of their plays for the benefit of the court were very likely implicit thanks—gift offerings—for the privileged positions in which they were now publicly installed.

These understandings between the court and their favoured players may subsequently have given the senior sharers in the Chamberlain's Men the confidence to invest in the Globe and Henslowe to invest in the Fortune. The court's policies were further narrowed and refined by orders of 22 June 1600, which reconfirmed the special status of the Chamberlain's and Admiral's Men but now specifically tied their playing to the Globe (built in 1599 from the timbers of the Theatre) and, when it would be ready, the Fortune (1601), and barred them from playing in the city inns. It further restricted the playing of each company to 'twice a week and no oftener', not on Sundays, in Lent, or during time of plague (Wickham *et al.* 2000: 107). It was implicit in these orders that all other playhouses—the Curtain, Rose, and Swan—should be either put to other uses or 'plucked down'.

How many of these stipulations were enforced it is not easy to say. It seems unlikely, for example, that the actors confined themselves long to only playing twice a week. And by the time of Buc, if not before, the companies could buy licences to allow performances even in Lent.[17] Certainly none of the theatres was demolished. Moreover, these orders are oddly blinkered; they ignore the fact that the Privy Council had already relaxed its restraints on London playing, admitting the Earl of Derby's Men, who must have been licensed by Tilney to play regularly at the newly adapted Boar's Head in the suburb of Whitechapel (Wickham *et al.* 2000: 105–6). Serious patronage carried weight, even in the face of established policy, and Derby's Men were even able to gain an entrée at court. The company did not last in London but were replaced—both at court and at the Boar's Head—by

---

[17] Holy Week was excepted, as were Sundays and sermon-days, then fixed as Wednesdays and Fridays (Adams 1917: 47–8).

Worcester's Men in 1601/2. Worcester had the advantage over Derby and Pembroke of being a Privy Councillor; he was also backed by the Earl of Oxford, some of whose players merged with his own. They, along with the Chamberlain's and Admiral's Men, would be taken into royal patronage in the coming new reign.

The orders of June 1600 also said nothing about the two boy companies, the Children of the Chapel and Paul's Boys, which reopened around then under licensing arrangements different from those of the adult players, though still subject to Tilney's authority. It may well be supposed that they came back into being—now very clearly commercial enterprises, and shortly to lose privileges which derived from their choir school origins—precisely because the Privy Council's constraints created a demand in the market (Wickham *et al.* 2000: 509–11). The June 1600 orders may well have been a show of force for the benefit of the City authorities and not intended to square precisely with the realities on the ground, which the Privy Council understood well enough.

The stage was set for the next logical step, in 1603/4, when all the leading companies were taken into direct royal patronage: the Chamberlain's Men became the King's Men, the Admiral's became Prince Henry's Men, Worcester's became the Queen's (i.e. Queen Anna's) Men, and the Children of the Chapel became the Children of the Queen's Revels. This was not new thinking, but a logical outcome from what had developed over the last thirty years, which made all the more sense given the increased number of royal households.

As I spelled out at the beginning of this chapter, the court's patronage was the key that unlocked the players' regular access to the City's paying customers. I shall unpack aspects of this in subsequent chapters. In Chapter 2, I examine these developments in relation to the court tradition of midwinter Revels. In Chapter 3, I examine the linked issues of the length of plays and their playing times, concluding with a section on Ben Jonson, whose published plays defy all the norms. In Chapter 4, I look at all this in the wider context of plays being revised during the period, about which there are many myths. But firstly I want to give some impression of the quantitative impact of Shakespeare's own plays on the court Revels during his working lifetime.

Shakespeare at Court

From 1594 to the end of Elizabeth's reign in 1603 the Chamberlain's Men performed at court thirty-three times, against twenty-one times by the Admiral's Men. As I have indicated, towards the end of the reign this duopoly at court was breached several times: three times by the revived Derby's Men, once by Worcester's Men (combined with Oxford's), and once by the Earl of Hertford's; the revived Children of the Chapel played five times and Paul's Boys twice.[18] But these breaches did not

---

[18] These figures include the anomalous Twelfth Night in 1601, when the Chamberlain's, Admiral's, and Derby's Men, with the Children of the Chapel, are all recorded as having appeared. They could hardly all have performed full plays. On the term 'duopoly' (Dutton 1991: 111): it was never my intention to suggest that the Chamberlain's and Admiral's Men were the only companies that performed in London. But for the best part of five years they were the only ones privileged to perform at

seriously undermine the special status of the court duopoly, and the Chamberlain's Men in particular performed at court as often as all the other troupes put together.

Unfortunately, as I have indicated, we know really very little about what they performed. The only plays we definitely know they played in this time are Shakespeare's *Love's Labour's Lost* (published 1598) and *Merry Wives of Windsor* (1602), both proclaiming on title pages that they had been performed before the Queen. But we are not sure of the occasions when this happened.[19] For the Admiral's Men we similarly know specifically of two court plays, both as it happens by Dekker, *Old Fortunatus* (1600), 'As it was played before the Queen's Majesty this Christmas' and *The Shoemakers' Holiday* (1600), 'As it was acted before the Queen's most excellent Majesty on New Year's day at night last'—the latter date of 1 January 1600 being the only one on which we can confidently attach a particular play to a specific performance at court in the last decade of Elizabeth's reign.[20]

How many plays by Shakespeare were brought to court among the other thirty-one Chamberlain's Men performances? We must suspect that there were many. It would be natural to showcase their resident star playwright. But the best evidence we have is from the Jacobean years of Shakespeare's career when the records, albeit very patchy, are fuller.[21] In the period 1603/4–1612/13—Shakespeare's years with the King's Men—we can reliably identify sixty-two plays, including repetitions: twenty-two are by Shakespeare, more than a third, against forty-one by all others combined.[22] These are *A Midsummer Night's Dream* (New Year 1604); *Othello, Merry Wives, Measure for Measure, Comedy of Errors, Henry V, Love's Labour's Lost,*

court, and what happened to Pembroke's Men over the *Isle of Dogs* affair seems effectively to have meant that no other company was able to set up a permanent London base in that time.

[19] Re *Love's Labour's Lost*, see pp. 109, 129 and n. 52. There is a good chance that they also played Jonson's *Every Man Out of His Humour* there (see pp. 89, 91).

[20] The only other plays published after 1590 and before 1603 which declare court affiliations are the last of Lyly's plays, *Midas* (pub. 1592) and *The Woman in the Moon* (1597), Greene's *Orlando Furioso* (pub. 1599), and the anonymous children's play, *The Contention between Liberality and Prodigality* (1602), all from an earlier era. It is highly unlikely that any of these was performed at court after 1594, unless they were somehow adopted by the Chamberlain's or Admiral's Men.

[21] As I shall argue in the final chapter, there are good reasons for treating the Elizabethan and Jacobean phases of Shakespeare's career separately in respect of his plays at court. But in this context there is nowhere else to turn for evidence. Our chief evidence about playing at court comes from various versions of two sets of accounts: the Chamber Accounts, which are extant throughout Shakespeare's working lifetime, but normally only record payments to the companies and sometimes the dates on which they played, though in 1612/13 they anomalously list titles; and the Revels Accounts, which give the titles of plays and sometimes their authors, but they are only extant for 1604/5 and 1611/12.

The authenticity of these Revels Accounts has been challenged several times since they were first published in 1842 by Peter Cunningham. But they have been subjected by experts to several palaeographic, microscopic, and chemical tests and each time declared to be genuine. E. K. Chambers reviewed the arguments and concluded 'I do not think that, in view of the palaeographical investigation, it is any longer possible to reject the genuineness of the 1604–5 list, and although that of 1611–12 has not been so minutely tested, it is pretty obviously of a piece with the "book" of which it forms a part, and had it stood alone, probably no suspicion would have fallen upon it' (1923: 4.136–41, 139). W. R. Streitberger, the editor of the Jacobean and Caroline Revels Accounts, also reviewed the controversy, including A. E. Stamp's apparently definitive analysis of 1930: 'He concluded that the accounts were authentic, and there the controversy came to an end' (1986a: xxx–xxxi).

[22] Figures are from Astington 1999: Appendix, 'Performances at Court', 221–67.

Merchant of Venice (twice), all in 1604/5; *King Lear* (1606); *The Tempest*, *The Winter's Tale* (1611/12); *1* and *2*(?) *Henry IV*, *Julius Caesar*, *Much Ado* (twice), *Othello*, *The Winter's Tale*, *The Tempest*, *Cardenio* (twice), all in 1612/13.[23] In the same period the King's Men are known to have performed the following plays by other authors at court: anon. *The Fair Maid of Bristow* (1603/4); Ben Jonson, *Every Man Out of His Humour* and *Every Man In His Humour*, anon. *The Spanish Maze* (1604/5); Barnabe Barnes, *The Devil's Charter* (1607); anon. *Mucedorus* (1610 or 1611); Beaumont and Fletcher, *A King and No King*, Richard Nicholls (?), *The Twins' Tragedy*, Thomas Heywood, *The Silver Age* and *The Rape of Lucrece*, Cyril Tourneur, *The Nobleman* (1611/12); Jonson, *The Alchemist*, Beaumont and Fletcher, *Philaster* (twice), *The Maid's Tragedy*, *A King and No King*, and *The Captain*, Tourneur, *The Nobleman*, Nicholls (?), *The Twins' Tragedy*, John Ford (?), *A Bad Beginning Makes a Good Ending*, anon. *The Merry Devil of Edmonton* and *Knot of Fools* (1612/13).

That is also a total of twenty-two. The inclusion of the two Heywood plays somewhat inflates the figure, since they must surely have been in essence performances by Queen Anna's Men (the company to which Heywood belonged), augmented by personnel from the King's Men.[24] But we can broadly say that these figures suggest that the King's Men gave one play by Shakespeare for one play by anyone else—and that they might have been significantly more biased towards Shakespeare if the period had not overlapped at the end with the first great enthusiasm for Beaumont and Fletcher, whose plays were to outnumber his by the 1630s. If these figures have any representative force whatever, fourteen or fifteen of the thirty-one unidentified plays by the Chamberlain's Men at Elizabeth's court would have been Shakespeare's. Within the relevant Jacobean period the King's Men appeared a total of 125 times, leaving (after twenty-two by Shakespeare and twenty-two by their other dramatists) eighty-one appearances in which the plays performed are not accounted for. Looking at the period as a whole, it seems highly likely that virtually everything Shakespeare ever wrote was performed at court at least once and some plays several times.[25]

The question, then, is not whether Shakespeare's plays were performed at court, but what form they took there. It is the contention of this book that they were, on occasion, revised from the form in which they were performed in the public theatres

---

[23] Humphrey Mosely entered the lost *Cardenio* in the Stationers' Register (9 Sept. 1653) as 'by Mr Fletcher & Shakespeare'. There is no further proof of authorship. But given its apparent popularity at court, performed twice in the 1612/13 season, this is not an unreasonable ascription. *The Two Noble Kinsmen*, also by Fletcher and Shakespeare, was not printed until 1634; that play, incidentally, was almost certainly played at court in 1613/14, since Jonson made fun of it in *Bartholomew Fair*, which led off the Revels season the following year.

[24] John Heminge of the King's Men is, nevertheless, recorded as having received the unusual payment of £26 13s 4d for the two performances (Chambers 1923: 4.178).

[25] These figures are approximate in a variety of ways. They include, as noted, instances such as January 1612, when the King's Men twice joined forces with Queen Anna's Men to perform two plays by Heywood. They also include the lost *Cardenio*, which Shakespeare is believed to have co-written with John Fletcher. They assume that 'The Hotspur' means *1 Henry IV* (this has been disputed), and that 'Sir John Falstaffe' means *2 Henry IV*. The figures for 1612/13 are swollen by the festivities for the marriage of Princess Elizabeth to the Elector Palatine.

for those performances at court. And that the multiple texts of some of the plays reflect something of those revisions. That will be the subject of subsequent chapters. On the whole, attempts to show that Shakespeare wrote or adapted his plays for the court have tended to focus on particularly suitable subject-matter, such as the 'show of eight Kings, and Banquo last, with a glass in his hand' in *Macbeth* (4.1.111.1–2; TLN 1657–8), which would have been most effective with King James present, Banquo's heir (James was also known to be interested in witchcraft). And Prospero's entertainment for Ferdinand and Miranda in *The Tempest*, which is actually a wedding masque and so highly appropriate for the festivities surrounding Princess Elizabeth and the Elector Palatine's marriage in 1612/13, but less so for the betrothal event it celebrates within the fiction. Ironically, these are two of the shortest plays in the Shakespeare canon and it will be part of my argument that plays revised for court are longer than normal; I suspect that the texts of both of these plays as we have them reflect performance at the Blackfriars theatre rather than court (see p. 281).

Such conjectures have been made with no reference to the general likelihood of special revisions, or to any regular mechanism that would have brought them into being. In fact it is very clear that there was such a mechanism associated with court performances, as I shall show. It is not my primary intention, however, to look for topical or specifically courtly references in the plays. Length—a playing time beyond what was normal on the public stages—is one of the best markers we have of plays quite probably adapted for the court. The Revels, we must remember, were expressly instituted to fill the cold, dark hours of midwinter and were not inhibited by the time constraints of everyday public playing. Another marker is small but telling changes to a familiar text, such as the revisions to the very popular *Mucedorus*, which entertained the court on Shrove Sunday of 1610 or 1611. These will be the concerns of most of the rest of this book. But first I look further into the Revels Office and its Masters, the figures behind the scenes who supervised these revisions.

2
Court Revels and Their Masters

Revels [from the Fr. Reveiller, to awake from sleep] are with us, sports of Dancing, Masking, Comedies, and such like, used formerly in the Kings House, the Inns of Court, or in the Houses of other great personages; And are so called, because they are most used by night, when otherwise men commonly sleep: There is also an Officer, called, The Master of the Revels, who has the ordering and command of these pastimes.

Thomas Blount, *Glossographia* (1656)

Theatricals of various sorts had been a mainstay of court life since time immemorial, a relief from the long, dark nights of an English midwinter. John Donne talks of St Lucy's Day (13 December in the old calendar), 'who scarce seven hours herself unmasks', and that is no exaggeration in those northern climes.[1] Shakespeare and his contemporaries also lived through a mini ice-age, when the Thames more than once froze over. For those with the time and money nighttime theatricals were an ideal distraction from the bleak world outside. So the court institutionalized playing into a Revels season, which ran at its longest from Hallowmas (All Saints' Day, 1 November) until Shrove Tuesday, a date in February or just possibly March, determined by the fall of Easter. Court theatricals might be called for on special occasions at other times in the year, when matters of state required entertainment. But normally they fell into the Revels season.

When it actually started in any particular year depended upon the movements and wishes of the monarch. Elizabeth's Revels seasons never commenced before St Stephen's Day, the day after Christmas, usually at one of the four principal palaces then in use (Windsor, Whitehall, Hampton Court, and her favourite, Greenwich). James's Revels seasons usually started earlier than that and sometimes (increasingly often as the reign wore on) as early as 1 November itself. After the first year of his reign, when the London plague kept him at the safe distance of Hampton Court, it was almost always at Whitehall. The court, however, was not a particular place but the body of persons who surrounded the monarch at all times, the most important of whom were aristocrats and gentry: they were not only the main audience of these theatricals (together perhaps with visiting dignitaries, such as foreign ambassadors) but also in earlier years often the principal performers.

In the practice which Elizabeth's court inherited, theatrical entertainment usually focused on the traditional twelve days of Christmas and again around

---

[1] 'A Nocturnal upon St Lucy's Day, Being the Shortest Day', line 2.

Shrovetide. So, for example, in 1551/2 and 1552/3 Edward VI and his Privy Council gave over the twelve days of Christmas to a Lord of Misrule, a role performed in both years by the courtier, Member of Parliament, and poet, George Ferrers (Woudhuysen 2004). That first year, when everything cost a staggering £500, he purported to have arrived from the moon; the next year, from '*vastum vacuum*'. In the second year he had a large retinue, including a herald-trumpeter, an orator, and 'an interpreter or truchman', who made an embassy to King Edward on Christmas Day; an admiral to greet Ferrers when he arrived at court the next day by barge, a master of the horse, four pages, 'six counsellors at the least', a divine, a philosopher, an astronomer, a poet, a physician, an apothecary, a master of requests, two gentlemen ushers, 'besides jugglers, tumblers, fools, friars and such other' (Feuillerat 1914: 89ff). Clearly there was much impromptu business as Ferrers's Misrule Court parodied the real thing, but on 1 January there was a scheduled jousting on hobby-horses, and on 4 January the 'Lord' and his retinue paid a ceremonial visit to the City of London. Everything culminated on Twelfth Night with a Triumph or Play of Cupid, Venus, and Mars, apparently penned by Ferrers's 'master of the horse', Sir George Howard, and probably some masquing. Separate events at Shrovetide did not, however, go forward because the king was ill.

I have described this at some length in order to emphasize a key feature of mid-century revels, which is that they were by the court, for the court. No professionals were employed to entertain them. This was the king and his immediate circle letting their collective hair down. And there was a whole court office—the Revels Office, then located in Blackfriars—to supply such costumes, scenery, properties, etc. as were required; it was supervised by the Master of the Revels, then Sir Thomas Cawarden, with a clerk-controller, yeoman, and clerk. King Edward did in fact patronize a company of players, and on occasion (such as Christmas Day 1551) they would appear at court. But this was the exception, and far from the rule. The same holds true under Queen Mary. In the Revels season of 1554/5, for example, there was a masque of 'Arclules' [Hercules] with mariners for their torchbearers on St Andrew's Day (30 November); there were masques of Venetian senators, with galley-slaves for their torchbearers, and of 'Venuses' with Cupids and torchbearers over Christmas; then at Shrovetide there were masques of Turkish magistrates, with 'Turks archers' for their torchbearers and of 'Goddesses, huntresses' with 'Turkey women' for their torchbearers (Feuillerat 1914: xiv). These masques were usually elaborate masked dancing, rather than the more familiar quasi-theatrical events staged under James and Charles.

In the absence of a Lord of Misrule, the Master of the Revels assumed the responsibility of being what we might call the director and creative consultant for the Revels season: it fell to him to devise the masques and other entertainments, as well as to ensure the quality of the performances put on by the actors and (in particular) any choristers invited in. In those masques of 'Arclules', of Venetian senators, and Turkish magistrates, all the principal figures would have been courtiers and their attendants, dressed in gorgeous or exotic costumes by teams of tailors arranged by the Revels Office, and rehearsed in their non-speaking parts by

Cawarden—who, as a knight, was one of them.² The omnipresent torchbearers are a reminder that these events took place indoors in the dead of winter, and mainly at night, and it was a key responsibility of the Revels Office throughout the period to provide an appropriate blaze of light to dispel the gloom. Much of this came from candles held up by copper wiring that was strung from wall to wall in whichever room was designated for the event; the whole room was lit, not just a 'stage' area since, even when under James masques were increasingly focused in carefully structured locations, the theatricals were never more important than those being entertained. These events were, once again, of the court, for the court. The royal family and the great grandees of the court were always the real focus of attention.

In this particular season Cawarden also received explicit directions from Queen Mary to do whatever was necessary to help Nicholas Udall, who 'hath at sundry seasons convenient heretofore showed, and mindeth hereafter to show, his diligence in setting forth of dialogues and interludes before us for our regal disport and recreation' (Feuillerat 1914: 159). Udall was the author of *Ralph Roister-Doister*, the seminal early English comedy, and very probably also of the political allegory, *Respublica*, presented at court in 1553 (Steggle 2004). His role here was very likely connected with his recent appointment as master at Westminster School. The performance of plays was favoured in the curriculum of Tudor grammar and choir schools, to enhance the boys' rhetorical skills and singing.³ In the first half of Elizabeth's reign such performances by schoolboys were her favourite entertainments. As W. R. Streitberger observes, up to 1572 only eleven plays by adult professional companies were performed at court, a record 'vastly overshadowed by the at least thirty-five performances by boy companies' (2004).

This is not exactly the court entertaining itself, though the Chapels Royal at both Windsor and Whitehall were certainly part of the Queen's household, while the schools at Westminster and St Paul's were also closely associated with it. Nor, however, is it appropriate to think of this as commercial theatre, bought in by the court. That was certainly the situation with the revived boy companies after 1599/1600, when entrepreneurs exploited the phenomenon. And it was going in that direction in the 1580s, when John Lyly wrote plays for both the Children of the Chapel and the Children of Paul's, which were played with equal success at court and to the public. But in the mid-century it is more appropriate to think of these court appearances as gifts-in-kind from the masters or choirmasters of the schools, all of whom were appointed directly by the monarch or by those close to her, reciprocal gestures of obligation and reward.⁴ In this sense they were on a par with the gift-entertainments presented at court by the Gentlemen of Gray's Inn in March 1565 and by Sir Percival Hart's sons in February of the same year. There

---

² Tilney, the Master of the Revels with whom we will mainly be concerned, was never actually knighted, though he was entitled to be marshalled with the knights on ceremonial occasions—he shared their status (Streitberger 1980).

³ On the history and practices of the pre-1590 children's companies, see Hillebrand 1964; Shapiro 1977; Gair 1982. For an account of a particular court presentation by the boys of Westminster School, see Shapiro 2006.

⁴ On the reciprocities of patronage under Elizabeth, see MacCaffrey 1961; Scott 2006.

were no direct payments for such occasions, though expenses might be covered and the Revels Office expended large sums in costuming and staging them. This was also the case on the rare occasions when Elizabeth left the court itself to receive such gifts, as famously in 1561/2 when she attended the Inner Temple Christmas festivities, presided over by Robert Dudley, where she saw *Gorboduc* and two masques, *The Prince of Pallaphilos* and *Beauty and Desire*.

By the time of Elizabeth, the masters of the schools (Sebastian Westcott at St Paul's, William Hunnis at the Whitehall Chapel Royal, Richard Farrant at Windsor, John Taylor at Westminster, and latterly Richard Muncaster at Merchant Taylors' School) certainly did receive a standard £6 13s 4d per performance, raised after 1575 by an *ex gratia* fee to £10. But this was almost certainly seen as appropriate recompense for the effort of writing and mounting these plays specifically for the court. Although performances by these boy companies greatly outweighed those of adult companies at court in Elizabeth's early years, that changed over time. Early in the 1560s there were three performances by the company of the most favoured of all Elizabeth's courtiers, Robert Dudley, later Earl of Leicester, and in 1564/5 two by that of his brother, the Earl of Warwick. Lord Rich's Men performed twice in 1567/8 and again once a year in the following two Revels seasons. Sir Robert Lane's Men performed twice in 1571/2. But from then on performances by adult players—notably the players of the Earls of Leicester and Warwick, and Lord Admiral Clinton—mount steadily in number to rival those of the boys.

CRISIS IN THE REVELS OFFICE

Cawarden died in 1559 and was replaced as Master of the Revels by Sir Thomas Benger. Under Benger, however, the organization and, in particular, expenses of the Revels Office got completely out of hand. He was one of the small group of those who stayed loyal to Elizabeth while she was detained at Hatfield under Mary, and suffered for it (Streitberger 2004: 670–2). His appointment as Master was doubtless a reward for this, and there is no doubt that he had the primary qualification of understanding Elizabeth's taste: the concentration on boy companies was his policy. It is also clear that Benger understood that he was meant to bring down costs, as in the rather self-satisfied estimates that he returned in his first year: 'Memorandum that the charges for making of masques came never to so little a sum [£227 11s 2d] as they do this year for the same did ever amount as well in the Queen's Highness's time that now is, as at all other times heretofore, to the sum of [£400] always when it was least' (Feuillerat 1908: 54). Unfortunately, he could not keep it up, and for the next decade as W. R. Streitberger has shown, he made 'an annual average expenditure of about £570' (2004: 673). The Clerk Controller who served under him, Richard Leys, refused to sign the Revels Accounts from 1559 to 1567, 'perceiving that in his conscience her Majesty hath been and is overcharged in that behalf' (ibid).

The outlay was largely on costumes and materials, which were all inevitably of the most costly kind, especially for masques. But beyond that it is clear that Benger took his role as revels-master very seriously and was prepared to go to exceptional lengths to stage all events—plays as well as masques—with style and detail, amounting to something strangely like verisimilitude. In the accounts for 1571/2, for example, we find payments to John Carow, who was a property-maker in the Revels Office for many years:

> for sundry parcels of stuff by him bought and provided for the use of this office & for the plays, masks & shows set forth thereof by the said Master's commandment, videlicet. spars, rafters, boards, punchyns [pointed instruments?], nails, vices, hooks, hinges, horsetails, hobby horses, pitchers, paper, branches of silk & other garniture for pageants, feathers, ffagbroches [not identified], tow, trenchers, gloves black, scepters, wheat sheaves, bodies of men in timber, dishes for devil's eyes, devices for hell, & hell mouth, staves for banners &c., bows, bills, dags, targets, swords, fawchins [broadswords], firework, bosses for bits, spears, pate, glue, packthread, whipcord, holly, ivy & other green boughs, bays & strewing herbs & such like implements by him employed at the court & in the office to acceptable purposes with carriages & rewards by him paid in all... [£14 2s 2d]   (Feuillerat 1908: 140)

And this was all for one season, building up a properties department which would have been the envy of any modern film studio. When Carow died in 1574 the accounts listed similar items for which his widow should be paid, but also including 'monsters, mountains, forests, beasts, serpents' (241). Another regular, but at times particularly lavish expense, was on the building of 'houses' or booths, a very common feature of court staging though not of the public playhouses. They were used for entrances and exits, and holding properties and costumes, in buildings which did not conveniently accommodate such business. In the 1571/2 season we find William Lyzard paid the equivalent of a respectable year's salary just for the paints used for these: 'for gold, silver and sundry other colours by him spent in painting the houses that served for the plays, & players at the court... [£13 15s 1d]' (141).

And in that same season we also find certain exceptional outlays for the play of *Narcissus* performed by the Children of the Chapel on Twelfth Night:[5]

> John Tryce for money to him due for leashes, & doghooks, with staves, & other necessaries: by him provided for the hunters that made the cry after the fox (let loose in the court) with their hounds, horns, and hallowing, in the play of Narcissus, which cry was made, of purpose even as the words then in utterance, & the part then played, did require... [20s 8d]   (141)

> John Izard for money to him due for his device in counterfeiting thunder & lightning in the play of Narcissus being requested thereunto by the said Master of this office... [22s]   (142)

I detect a defensiveness on the part of the clerk writing all of this up. Both entries in fact are quite explicit that Benger personally required these outlays, and the former goes out of its way to justify the use of a live fox, loosed at court, and all the

---

[5] As I shall argue, particularly extravagant productions were associated with key dates on the festive calendar, including Twelfth Night.

paraphernalia of hunters, live dogs, and staves to keep them in order, as necessary to the dramatic impact of the scene. Nothing seems to have been too much for Benger to enhance a play and make it fit, as he saw it, for the court. Around 1571/2, towards the end of his time as Master, when performances by adult players began to be a more significant element in the court equation, we can begin to see how his attention to plays by professional actors figures more explicitly in the account returns than it had. A general statement covering the whole period from Christmas to Shrovetide outlines the duties in the office of:

> Devising, providing, preparing, new-making, translating, repairing, fitting, garnishing, setting forth, attending, well ordering, taking in again, safe-bestowing, and safe-keeping, of all the apparel & implements of the said office...with the properties, houses, and necessaries incident thereunto chiefly [*interlined*] for the appareling, disguising, fitting, furnishing & setting forth of sundry [*interlined*] men, women & children in the [6] plays & [6] masques mentioned more at large in the end of this book. (Feuillerat 1908: 132)

The same formula comprehends both plays and masques, though we may suppose that Benger did more 'devising' of masques and boy company plays than he did of plays for the adult actors. But they were still a factor. Later in the same accounts he focuses specifically on the six plays, two by an adult company, Sir Robert Lane's Men (*Lady Barbara*, 27 December, and *Cloridon and Radiamanta*, Shrove Sunday), and four by boy companies:

> All which [6] plays being chosen out of many and found to be the best that then were to be had. The same also being perused, & necessarily corrected & amended (by all the aforesaid officers). Then, they being so orderly addressed: were likewise thoroughly appareled, & furnished with sundry kinds, and suits, of apparel, & furniture, fitted and garnished necessarily: and answerable to the matter, person, and part to be played: having also apt houses: made of canvas, framed, fashioned & painted accordingly: as might best serve their several purposes. Together with sundry properties incident: fashioned, painted, garnished, and bestowed as the parties themselves required & needed. (Feuillerat 1908: 145)

This was, of course, before companies had built up significant reserves of costumes and properties, so much of the Office's business is given over to supplying those. But note that the business starts with a sifting process, identifying 'the best that then were to be had'—a process at that date involving all four of the Revels officers, not just the Master—and 'The same also being perused, & necessarily corrected & amended'. They would be 'perused' *in performance*, not just on paper.

We can see why, as W. R. Streitberger puts it:

> To imagine revels at Elizabeth I's court from 1559 to 1572 requires setting aside the usual generalizations made about performances in the later public theatres, where plays were staged without scenery and with few properties...Rather, we are invited to imagine startling, visually oriented productions, using three-dimensional scenery, spectacular effects, verisimilar performances, and a wide variety of subject-matter in elaborate and expensive masques performed principally by amateurs, and in lavishly produced plays performed principally by boys. (2004: 681)

We can also see why it cost so much. It may have been magnificent, but it is perhaps not surprising that when Benger died in 1572, he was not replaced as Master. The office was firstly put in commission under the joint oversight of the Master of the Great Wardrobe and the Master of the Tents, two related household departments, while Lord Burghley as Lord Treasurer instigated a review of the whole operation. The point of the exercise was to control the costs. From 1573 the Lord Chamberlain, the Earl of Sussex, took responsibility for the office, and the Clerk of the Revels, Thomas Blagrave, was appointed as acting Master on a yearly basis.

This did not, however, solve the problem: 'In 1573-4... Blagrave furnished six plays and three masques, at an average cost of roughly £75 each', totalling a princely £672 14s 2d for the season, among the highest Revels bills of the entire reign (Streitberger 1986a: xviii; Feuillerat 1908: 193–221). Equally unfortunately, the quality of the entertainment he provided was distinctly questionable. Under the subsection of accounts for Candlemas (12 January–5 February) we find a list of charges for:

> the new-making, translating, fitting, furnishing, garnishing, setting foorth and taking in again of sundry kinds of apparel, properties and necessaries incident for one play ['*Timoclia at the sege of Thebes.* by Alexander' interlined] shown at Hampton Court before her Majesty by Mr Mulcaster's Children, and one masque ['of Ladies with lights being 6 virtues' interlined] likewise prepared & brought thither in readiness but not shown for the tediousness of the play that night.   (Feuillerat 1908: 206)

In all £63 4s 6d were spent on a show by Mulcaster's Merchant Taylors' boys, which everyone found tedious, and on a masque that was never performed because of it. Blagrave had apparently done his best to salvage the play, visiting the school to help rehearsals. But to no avail.

The accounts show that Blagrave was assiduous, but in the end he was not up to doing what was required. In 1574/5 his claims included: '26 November. Horse-hire and charges by the way at Windsor staying there [2] days in November, [4] days for perusing & reforming of Farrant's play etc. [42s 6d]' (all quotations in this sequence are from Feuillerat 1908: 238). On 5 December he went to Hampton Court to 'confer with my [acting] Lord Chamberlain the Lord Howard' and consult with 'Mr Knevett [Gentleman of the Privy Chamber and keeper of stores at both Westminster and Windsor] upon certain devices & peruse Farrant's play there again [3] days, the charges whereof with horsemeat at Kingston is [26s 8d]'. On 14 December, 'The expenses and charges where my Lord Chamberlain's players did show the history of Phedrastus & Phigon and Lucia together amount-eth unto [9s 4d]'. This was evidently at the Master's lodgings in the Palace of St John's, Clerkenwell, which became Edmund Tilney's base until he was required to move in 1607. Shakespeare must have known it well, since that is where all court plays by the professional actors were rehearsed. Blagrave carefully claims for the coals bought to keep the place warm enough for this purpose. From details like these we can often tell how long a company would have to reform a play and rehearse it. It is not clear when precisely the Chamberlain's Men (i.e. Sussex's) performed but it could not have been before 28 December (allowing for other known performances), giving them perhaps two weeks to put things into final shape. Farrant's boys from Windsor performed on Twelfth Night, so they had something like a month and a half to get it right after Blagrave's four-day initial visit: this was evidently a problematic production, in which he invested a lot of effort. After the dismal showing of *Timoclia at the Siege of Thebes* the previous season, he was taking no chances.

Blagrave also claimed, under 18 December, for 'The expences and charges where my Lord of Leicester's men showed their matter of Panaceia. [10s]' as well as, under 20 December, for 'The charges and expences where my Lord Clinton's players rehearsed a matter called Pretestus [13s]' and, under the following day, for 'The charges and expenses where they showed [2] other plays with [3s] for torches & [4d] for an hourglass. [13s 4d]'. Leicester's Men performed (presumably *Panecia*) on New Year's Day, so they certainly had two weeks in which to whip things into shape. Lord Admiral Clinton's Men performed on 27 December and again on 2 January, so they had barely a week to be sure the first show (possibly *Pretestus*) was fit, with only a further five days to work on whatever was shown then, maybe one play, maybe two. Clinton's Men at this point were led by Laurence Dutton, one of the star actors of the period, so Blagrave perhaps calculated that they were the most reliable. But Leicester's and Sussex's Men were given more than enough time, by the standards of the day, to acquire extra properties and costumes, most of which at this time the Revels Office itself would supply.

The following accounts are more explicit about items for the boy companies, specifying them by the names of their masters ('Farrant', 'Sebastian', 'Hunnis'), but there is an item for 'carriage of [4] loads of timber for the Rock (which Mr Ross made for my Lord of Leicester's men's play) & for other frames and players' houses' and probably much more routine stuff besides (244). There was also doubtless time, if Blagrave saw the need for it, to 'study a speech of some dozen or sixteen lines which I would set down and insert in't' (*Hamlet*, 2.2.541–2)—and indeed, considerably more, from what we know of their rehearsal schedules (Stern 2000).

Blagrave was also responsible for *The Peddler's Masque* that Revels season (besides several other boy company plays, of which he records little except expenses for properties), and though we know very little about that production, it doubtless required far more of his personal attention than any one of his plays, since it is likely that he would have been involved from its imaginative inception and would have been expected to be a driving force in realizing its full potential. It must inevitably have been, like all Revels seasons, a frenetic time, planning to have some nine productions court ready in a six- or seven-week period. It is not surprising therefore, that he needed help, and claimed for payment to someone 'for his pains in perusing and reforming of plays sundry times as need required for her Majesty's liking paid by Dodmer [his servant] by the special appointment of the said Mr Blagrave [40s]'. Unfortunately he did not name this assistant.

Possibly the schedule for preparing all of these shows to a standard fit for the court was just too tight, or possibly Blagrave did not have the theatrical skills to make the necessary judgements. Whatever was the case, new solutions were needed.

TILNEY

When Edmund Tilney was formally installed in 1579 as the new Master he had an explicit charge to rein in costs. His strategy for doing this, as I have already observed, was based on what we should now call outsourcing. Most entertainment was to be bought in from the professional acting companies—specifically the most successful of them, patronized by the leading courtiers, plus the most accomplished boy companies, which were rapidly becoming commercial operations. Although stages still needed to be erected for them, and lit, the actors supplied their own costumes and properties, and the only other real cost was the standard £10 honorarium per show. Since for the rest of the reign there were rarely more than ten shows in a season, and more commonly six or seven, the savings were obviously significant. What did this mean for the role of the Master of the Revels? Did it, in effect, reduce him to the level of a booking agent, simply reviewing the talent available and hiring it in accordingly? Or did he retain any of the functions of what I have categorized as 'director and creative consultant for the Revels season'?

Although Tilney was to prove a good business manager, he was expected to have a wider range of skills. These were outlined, ironically, by Blagrave, his unsuccessful competitor for the post. In 'Orders to be Observed in the Better Management of the Office', Blagrave opined that 'The Master of the office... ought to be a man of good engine [ingenuity, artfulness], inventive wit and experience, as well for variety of strange devices delectable as to weigh what most aptly and fitly furnisheth the time, place, presence and state'. Blagrave further recommended that 'he also be of such learning wit and experience as able of himself to make and devise such shows and devices as may best fit and furnish the time, place, and state with least burden' (Feuillerat 1908: Table 1, 17; see also 432–3, 441–4). It was not to be the way of the future that the Master of the Revels would 'devise' shows. Yet it was still part of the expectation when Tilney was appointed and suggests that it was assumed that he could, as the need arose, negotiate with actors and their play-makers on knowledgeable terms.

There is evidence that Tilney and his successors did exactly that. They did not simply hire in from the actors' repertoire, as it were 'off the shelf', but intervened to make their shows as appropriate as possible for the court. Thomas Heywood's testimony in *An Apology for Actors* that 'our court plays have been in late days yearly rehearsed, perfected, and corrected before they come to the public view of the Prince and the nobility' gives us some indication that shows were not simply transported from the playhouses to court (1612, E1v). They were, at the very least, polished. But this gives us no idea of what lengths Tilney and the others may have gone to in order to 'perfect' and 'correct' them. Tilney's successor, Sir George Buc, wrote a treatise on the art of revels, certainly suggesting that he saw it as more than a managerial or mechanical process. But it is lost, like so much documentation of theatre in the period.

The best surviving evidence of how Tilney approached his Revels season responsibilities lies in the accounts he submitted, though as I have said those from 1588 to 1603—including the whole court careers of the Chamberlain's and Admiral's

Men—are lost. Tilney's first accounts, those for 1578/9, say little about 'perusing' and 'reforming' plays, perhaps because they cover a period before he was confirmed in office. His comments on the Christmas plays do, however, show a business mind at work, recording the level of demands that they made on the Office. So the first play, by Warwick's Men, was 'furnished in this office with sundry things as was requisite for the same'; that for the Children of the Chapel was similarly furnished 'with very many things aptly fitted for the same'; that for Sussex's Men 'with sundry things'; that for the Children of Paul's with 'some things in this office'; and the two plays by Leicester's Men 'with some things in this office' and 'many things for them' respectively (Feuillerat 1908: 286).[6] Evidently at this date the Revels Office still had to supply some properties and perhaps costumes. At the same time it is also clear that Tilney's mind was very much on '[2] masques shown before her Majesty, the [French] ambassador being there on Sunday night the [11]th of January' (289), which would still have required more personal attention from him than the plays did.

The following year (1579/80) points us more clearly in the direction where Tilney's management would lead, with a total of nine plays (only two by boys) and no masques. Each of the plays is listed, with a more detailed account of what it required than that furnished the year before. The last, for example, was 'The history of Serpedon shown at Whitehall on Shrove Tuesday at night enacted by the lord Chamberlain's servants wholly furnished in this office whereon was employed for head attires for women and scarves [11] ells of sarsenet, a great city, a wood a castle and [6] pair of gloves' (321).[7] Head 'attires' for women (or boys playing women)—elaborate hair arrangements—were a constant and expensive charge; when Shakespeare lodged with the Mountjoys in Cripplegate in 1604, his landlady, Mary Mountjoy, made such items and supplied them to ladies at the court (see Nicholl 2008). And it was a matter of court etiquette that all the leading players should receive a pair of gloves, which they were expected to wear during the performance. The 'great city' was presumably a backdrop of some description, whereas it is less clear whether the woods and the castle were pictorial or actual properties.

But the accounts pointedly commence 'from the first day of November 1579... The beginning was making choice of sundry plays, comedies and inventions at divers and sundry times aforesaid until the [19th] day of December then next following at which times the works began as well for furnishing & setting forth of sundry of the said plays, comedies and inventions' (320). The whole period from 1 November to the performance of *Sarpendon* on 16 February would constitute 108 days, but Tilney only claimed attendance allowances for himself and the three other Revels officers, on the traditional basis, for 39 days and 21 nights, bringing himself £12 and the others £6 each. This depended on a strict reckoning

---

[6] There are similar discriminations for the Candlemas and Shrovetide plays, where Warwick's and Sussex's Men were fitted out with 'sundry garments and properties' and 'sundry things', whereas the Children of the Chapel had 'very many rich garments and properties aptly fitted for the same'. The boy companies were clearly not the cheapest option.
[7] This was the company patronized by the Earl of Sussex, not Shakespeare's company.

of the precise Christmas, Candlemas, and Shrovetide periods when they were actually present at court, starting at 19 December but with breaks after Twelfth Night.

But he had laid a marker that his work had actually started earlier than this, and other charges indicate the business that went on, as it were, unseen: 'Charges of the players, the carriage and recarriage of their stuff for examining and rehearsing of divers plays and choice making of [10] of them to be shown before her Majesty... To one Porter and [3] other attendants at several times after the rate of [12]d apiece a day for their attendance and service at the rehearsals and choice making of the said [10] plays'—£10 for each of these (one play was apparently dropped along the way). The emphasis shifts from the office *providing* the actors' costumes and properties to paying for their transportation. Tilney was not directly paid for 'examining and rehearsing' the plays, but he made sure not to be out of pocket for doing it, especially in the matter of having no fewer than four attendants with him (as distinct from his fellow officers of the Revels), which thereafter becomes a regular charge.

The last surviving Elizabethan accounts left by Tilney for a single year are those for 1587/8.[8] His preamble states that the claims 'did arise... by means of attending, making choice, perusing, reforming & altering of such plays, comedies, masques and inventions as were prepared set forth & presented before her Majesty'. That year the Office presented 'seven plays besides feats of activity & other shows', spread between the Queen's Men, the Children of Paul's (possibly showing Lyly's *Galathea* and *Endimion*), and the Gentlemen of Gray's Inn (*The Misfortunes of Arthur*, a tragedy of sorts). This was not a particularly heavy year in terms of the number of items staged, but Tilney's attendance claims expanded considerably: I examine this in the next section.

It is useful to bear in mind that, although the repertory of shows was increasingly slanted towards commercial drama—the Children of Paul's at this date as much as the adult groups—there were still occasional 'gift' performances, such as that from one of the Inns of Court. There were also usually arrangements for events that were not simply plays, such as tumbling (acrobatics; John Symons and his company were paid several times in the late 1580s) or dancing, usually on one of the last nights before New Year. Sometimes the regular acting companies contributed to these, other times not. In 1588/9, for example, the Lord Admiral's Men were paid for two plays and for 'sundry feats of activity, tumbling and matachins' (Feuillerat 1908: 388). 'Feats of activity' were gymnastics; 'matachins' were sword dances related to morris dancing. They still only received the regular £10 per play.

Within all this—and it runs from Benger through Tilney to Buc in the Jacobean period, despite other changes—certain days in the Revels calendar were much more likely to involve *unusually rich or prolonged* festivities than others. The first day of the season—normally St Stephen's Day (26 December) under Elizabeth, though often earlier under James—was one of these. So too was Twelfth Night

---

[8] There is another version of the 1587/8 accounts which runs them together with those for 1588/9 (Feuillerat 1908: 387–95), but it is more difficult on those to make the distinctions between the Master and the other officers which are critical to my analysis.

(6 January), and either or both of Shrove Sunday and Shrove Tuesday, whenever they fell. New Year's Day and Candlemas (2 February) were also often specially marked (Kernan 1995: 17). The nature of the records is such that this is only intermittently apparent, but over the period as a whole the cumulative evidence is conclusive. The records for 1573/4 are particularly detailed and show how the court's own masquing might extend those nights. The season opened not only with Leicester's Men performing *Predor and Lucia*, but also with a masque of lance-knights;[9] New Year's Day not only had the Children of Westminster playing *Truth, Faithfulness, and Mercy* but also a masque of Foresters and Wild Men; Twelfth Night had the Children of Windsor Chapel performing *Quintus Fabius*, followed by a masque of Sages; Candlemas was the occasion of the disastrous *Timoclia at the Siege of Thebes*, when a masque of Virtues was prepared but not shown; and the season ended lavishly on Shrove Tuesday (23 February that year) with Merchant Taylors' boys performing *Perseus and Andromeda*, followed by twin masques of Warriors and Ladies.

The 1574/5 season opened on 26 December with Leicester's Men, but we also learn that Blagrave paid 'for gloves for my Lord of Leicester's boys [that] played at the court' (Feuillerat 1908: 239). Leicester never patronized a separate boy company, so this sounds very much like the importation of specially gifted boy performers (see Mateer 2006). Twelfth Night that season was marked by an unusual joint performance (*Mutius Scaevola*) by the Children of the Chapel and the boys of the Chapel of Windsor, while Shrove Tuesday saw both *Titus and Gisippus* by Paul's Boys and a masque of children. The 1578/9 season was doubtless inflated by various foreign presences, but it went out in style on Shrove Tuesday with Sussex's Men performing *Murderous Michael*, followed by a 'device' of the Earls of Oxford and Surrey (and other nobles); a morris masque was also prepared but not danced. On Twelfth Night 1581 *Pompey* by Paul's Boys was followed by a challenge at tilt.

On Twelfth Night 1585 the Queen's Men played something called *Five Plays in One*, while on Shrove Sunday they had *Three Plays in One* prepared but it was not shown; on Shrove Tuesday they performed both an 'antic' play and a comedy.[10] On Twelfth Night 1586 Howard's and Hunsdon's Men both performed, though we do not know if this was separately or together. Similarly on Twelfth Night 1591 Howard's Men (now known as the Lord Admiral's) appeared with Strange's in a play and activities, and on Shrove Sunday 1596 (we are now in Shakespeare's own era) they appeared with the Chamberlain's Men. On Twelfth Night 1598 the Chamberlain's Men were followed by a gift-masque of Passions, presented by the Middle Temple lawyers. On Twelfth Night 1601 the Chamberlain's, Admiral's, and Derby's Men somehow all appeared, as did the Children of the Chapel, who offered a 'show' of some description, while on Shrove Sunday 1602 the Chamberlain's Men and the Children of the Chapel both performed.

---

[9] Lance-knights were mercenary foot-soldiers, armed with lances or pikes.
[10] 'Antic' entertainments involved elements of the grotesque or incongruous.

These patterns of extended or elaborate performances continued in James's reign. Twelfth Night was sometimes the night for a masque (1604, 1605, 1612), which in that era would normally be the outstanding event of the season but that could be varied with barriers (martial exercises in the lists; 1606, 1610), or by the King's Men performing two plays in 1608; in 1607 there was both a King's Men's play and Campion's masque for the wedding of Lord Hay. (Jacobean masques, we may recall, were much more theatrically elaborate than their Elizabethan predecessors—lavishly staged, costumed, and choreographed—and commonly occupied a whole evening, well into the early hours.) New Year's Day 1604 also warranted two plays from the King's Men. At Candlemas 1605 there were rumours that Queen Anna's brother, the Duke of Holstein, would present a masque, but the only recorded performance is of the King's Men in Jonson's *Every Man In His Humour* (Chambers 1923: 3.377–8).

It is striking, lastly, that when plays were published as having been performed at court and a date is specified (as it usually is), that date is invariably one of the key festive dates, suggesting some affinity between the text and its courtly performance. Among Lyly's plays, for example, we are told that *Sappho and Phao* was performed on Shrove Tuesday (c. 1583), *Campaspe* on Twelfth Night (1583), *Endymion* on Candlemas (1588), *Galathea* on New Year's Day (c. 1585), and *Midas* on Twelfth Night (1589). A few others on this far from complete list are Dekker's *The Shoemakers' Holiday* (New Year, 1599), Shakespeare's *King Lear* (St Stephen's Day, 1606), Barnabe Barnes's *The Devil's Charter* (Candlemas, 1607), Middleton's *A Trick to Catch the Old One* (New Year, 1609), *Mucedorus* (Shrove Sunday, 1610 or 1611), and Jonson's *Bartholomew Fair* (All Saints, 1 November 1614). We must assume that these plays received closer attention from the Masters of the Revels than most. In the case of the 1610/11 performance of *Mucedorus*, the title page of the subsequent edition tells us that it was 'Amplified with new additions' (see p. 113). I do not mean to suggest that all of these plays were revised, expanded, or even specially written for these specific performances, though some of them certainly were. But the evidence suggests that they did make a particular mark at court, which printers evidently thought of as a selling point.

Patchy as some of this evidence is—and there are certainly sporadic instances of extended theatricals that do not relate to these specific dates—there is an unmistakable pattern of intensified, and prolonged, activity associated with those key festive milestones. Unfortunately, from 1594/5 onwards the level of detail in the records diminishes markedly. As I have said, we do know that the Chamberlain's Men opened the season every year from 1594 to 1603 (while from 1597 to 1602 the Admiral's Men almost invariably followed them the next evening, St John's Night). What is missing, however, is the level of evidence of what may have been done specially or differently on the key festive days. Nevertheless, the records over Elizabeth's reign overall are sufficiently detailed to show ongoing attention to these key dates, which must surely have required the particular involvement of Tilney and his fellows in ways that went beyond merely hiring in shows 'off the shelf'.

TILNEY'S GROWING BUSINESS

If anything, the repertory for 1587/8 (the last year of Tilney's surviving Elizabethan accounts) represented slightly less business than that in 1579/80, his first. Yet Tilney's personal claims for attendance expanded out of all recognition. The attendance times for the other officers remained much as they had been—38 days for the Yeoman, 28 each for the Clerk and the Clerk Controller, plus 14 nights for each of them. Yet Tilney claimed for himself 116 days and 14 nights, not simply for attendance but for 'choice-making & reforming of plays and comedies' (Feuillerat 1908: 379). He was now claiming for *all* the work he was putting in. At 4s per day this amounted to £26. He also claimed for his four attendants throughout the same period, which at 1s per day for each came to exactly the same total. Tilney is not specific about when these dates fell, except that they were 'during Christmas & Shrovetide'. But it looks as though he was claiming for virtually the whole of the festive season (1 November to Shrove Tuesday) rather than just those dates crowded round actual performances.

And this is confirmed when the extant record of his accounts recommences under King James. His first claim for wages and entertainments runs:

> Edmund Tilney...for his own attendance and four men [i.e. attendants, not officers] from the last of October 1603 until Ash Wednesday following, as well for rehearsals and making choice of plays and comedies and reforming them as for his other attendance for devices to be showed before the King and Queen's Ma[jesties] by the space of 113 days and 17 nights together with three days' attendance at the Triumph and other three at the receiving of the Constable of Spain, amounting in all to 136 days. (Streitberger 1986a: 5)[11]

He calculated the total at £57 8s, of which exactly half would be his own wage—just about the same as in 1589, allowing for the extra ceremonial duties this year (relating to the presence of the Constable of Spain, in England for the Treaty of London).[12]

This pattern remains good until his very last accounts, those for 1609/10, which he drew up himself but which had to be submitted by his cousin and executor, Thomas Tilney, since Edmund was buried 6 October 1610, to be succeeded by Buc. He claimed for his own attendance, and that of four servants, 'from the first of November 1609 until the [21st] of Febr. 1609 [i.e. 1610] next following being Ash Wednesday (both days included) as well for rehearsals and making choice of plays & comedies and reforming them as for other attendances for masques and

---

[11] Skipping to 1603 glosses over major changes to the finances of the Revels Office in the 1590s, including a fixed sum of money to cover the wages of the officers, described in detail in Chambers 1923: 1.90–4. These changes clearly reflect the reduction of work, as responsibility for masques and other extraordinary events was transferred elsewhere. But at the start of James I's reign there was a reversion to paying the officers on a per diem basis, so in that regard there is a real continuity between the 1589 and 1603 figures.

[12] Tilney actually tacked on a further twenty days for 'the airing of the robes, garments and other stuff', creating a total figure of £62 8s. That claim was made separately in earlier accounts, so I have excluded it in order to retain focus on my chief concern, his 'rehearsals and making choice of plays and comedies and reforming them'.

devices', a total of 112 days and 12 nights (Streitberger 1986a: 39).[13] This last phrasing confirms one important distinction between Tilney's Elizabethan and Jacobean accounts. At some point in the 1590s, and certainly before 1597, the Revels Office was relieved of virtually all responsibility for masques at court (Chambers 1923: 1.208). Although they had thinned in number as the reign wore on, such masques as *were* staged had become progressively more elaborate and expensive until it was decided that their budgets needed to pass into the control of senior members of the royal household, normally the Lord Chamberlain or the Master of the Horse. The Revels still provided some services, such as lighting, but the Master himself was no longer engaged in the creation and staging of what, of course, were to become even more elaborate and expensive affairs under James. But he was expected to attend.

To sum up: between the end of Benger's time, through Blagrave's temporary position, and throughout Tilney's long tenure, the accounts show a process in which the Master of the Revels is progressively less involved with shows that are genuinely of the court and by the court (even those which might be regarded as marginally of the court, such as the choir schools and the Inns of Court). Conversely, he became more responsible for drama provided by professional companies.[14] Yet over that period, Tilney's quantification of the time spent actually on the job expanded quite dramatically, from a relatively narrow window around the dates of specific performances from St Stephen's Day to Twelfth Night and again at Candlemas and Shrovetide, to encompass virtually the whole of the Revels season. This might be more understandable if there had been a steady growth in the number of plays given each season, but that was not the case. The number given in 1587/8, when he was already making these expanded claims, was seven and that was about average for the remainder of Elizabeth's reign.

The first year of James's reign, when there were fifteen nights with plays, on two of which (1 January and 20 February) two plays were performed, plus three masques and a tilt, must have been a tremendous shock to a settled system. But the extra work did not all fall on Tilney. His office was only responsible for plays specifically commissioned and paid for by the King; the major increase came about because the other royal households—initially Queen Anna's and Prince Henry's, and later Prince Charles's—also commissioned performances. The households naturally favoured the companies patronized by their head, but never exclusively. In the extended season of 1611/12, for example, we find the following distribution: the King sponsored six plays by the King's Men, two by Prince Henry's Men, two by the Queen's Men, one by Lady Elizabeth's Men, and possibly one (a dubious reading) by the Children of the Queen's Chapel. Prince Henry on his own

---

[13] This is the most tangible proof we have that Tilney remained in office up to his death. For years it was assumed that Sir George Buc deputized for him, either from 1603 or from some later date. This seems to have arisen from confusion about the status of Buc's patent to be Master of the Revels *in reversion*, compounded by the fact that in 1606 he received the authority to license plays *for printing* (but not for performance).

[14] The boy companies went out of business in the early 1590s, but were revived again in 1599/1600 and promptly returned to the court calendar. By then they were unequivocally commercial enterprises.

sponsored two by his own players and one by the King's Men. In conjunction with his sister, Elizabeth, and/or his brother, Charles, Henry sponsored no fewer than twelve performances by the King's Men, two by the Queen's Men, and two by Lady Elizabeth's Men. The Queen and Prince Henry jointly sponsored performance of two of Heywood's *Ages* plays, with the combined forces of the King's and Queen's Men. Prince Charles and Princess Elizabeth jointly sponsored four performances by the Prince's own players (generally then known as the Duke of York's Men) and one by the King's Men. Princess Elizabeth on her own sponsored one performance by the King's Men and one by Prince Henry's Men. Notice that *everyone* wanted a piece of the King's Men. There must have been some central coordination to ensure an agreeable distribution of plays and companies across the season.

My key point remains that even by the 1580s Tilney had found what was obviously a plausible case for personally claiming a full season's attendance fees (plus those of four attendants), even though he had less and less to do with time-consuming masques. And this at a time when Lord Burghley and his successors were making strenuous efforts to keep down court costs. (The other Revels officers received no increase in attendance fees.) The nub of this was, as repeatedly stated, 'examining and rehearsing of divers plays and choice making...of them to be shown before her Majesty', 'for rehearsals and making choice of plays and comedies and reforming them'. The change of reigns did not essentially affect this, despite the massive increase in the consumption of court drama.

But what exactly did it entail? We simply do not know. It is entirely counter-intuitive that Tilney should be able to claim greatly increased attendance allowances in a period both when the Revels Office was losing all its main responsibilities for in-house entertainments, such as masques, and when the favoured companies in the suburban amphitheatres were building up a significant stock of their own costumes and properties, which meant that they would need to draw much less on Revels Office time and funds.[15] As far as I know E. K. Chambers is the only person to have reflected on Tilney's expanded attendance claims: he speculates that Tilney 'possibly exercised a more detailed supervision of his Office than either Benger or Cawarden had attempted...Probably he liked to be at Court, whether there was much to do or not' (1923: 1.93–4). This will hardly do. How would he be exercising 'a more detailed supervision' of an office with dramatically less to do? And is it likely that he would have been allowed to claim for being at court 'whether there was much to do or not' and moreover to double the cost of this by also charging for four attendants? Right up to his death in 1597 Lord Burghley was trying by all means possible to reduce the costs of the Office, so that such gratuitous claims would hardly have passed his notice.

I suggest that Tilney was able to make these claims because he was able to substantiate the argument that 'perfecting', 'correcting', or 'reforming' the plays that would be shown at court really did constitute a full-time job throughout the Revels season. This would have to have been the case even when virtually all the

---

[15] See, for example, those inventoried by Henslowe for the Admiral's Men on 10 March 1598 (Foakes 2002: 317–23).

shows for which he was responsible were presented by the most talented professionals available.

Whether as a result of commercial competition or by direct court action, the adult companies called to court after 1583 were, as we have seen, the best of the best, and any who managed to squeeze into the privileged circle (as Strange's Men did in the early 1590s, and Derby's and Worcester's Men did after 1599) must have reached an impressive standard to do so, in addition to having particularly influential patrons. And the boy companies who reappeared after 1599 would have been no less professional and could draw on some of the best dramatists around, including Marston, Jonson, and Chapman.

What then did this leave Tilney to do? John Astington paints a rather bleak picture of the Revels Office 'as a rather marginal department of the household' by this date, stripped of most of its responsibilities for masques and other ad-hoc entertainments (1999: 24). Nor did it play any significant role in constructing the playing spaces the actors would use at court, though these were elaborately furnished. 'Stages there did not suddenly lapse into a Swan-like plainness with the scaling down of the Revels operations, we may take it. One or more of the other royal Offices—the Works and the Wardrobe principally—would have been charged with ensuring that what the Queen and the court looked at was fittingly decorated, and matched the splendour of the rest of the theatre, and of the audience' (107–8). The court could not be outfaced in such matters. But, as Astington's account suggests, staging no longer engaged Tilney; it fell to other offices.

What remained for Tilney—but not for the other officers of the Revels Office—was 'apting' plays for the court. That is, ensuring material that was fit to be performed *on* these stages. The role of the Masters of the Revels had always been to supply entertainment which was *suitable* for the court. The fact that by the end of Elizabeth's reign he had significant outside professional resources on which to draw did not necessarily mean that what they had to offer would readily meet the tastes and expectations of the Queen and her courtiers. It seems highly likely that, with his wealth of theatrical experience, Tilney's time was invested in reviewing the scripts of plays themselves, rehearsing them in his Clerkenwell quarters, possibly calling for changes, additions, embellishments—the kind of work we shall find Thomas Dekker and Henry Chettle engaged in for the Admiral's Men when we look at Henslowe's *Diary* in Chapter 3. This is the single most controversial claim that I shall make in this book and it will require some justification, because it is on the strength of this that my arguments about the effects of court performance on the texts of Shakespeare's plays depend.

QUALIFICATIONS OF THE MASTERS OF THE REVELS

For now, I want to say something about Tilney and his successors as likely supervisors of/collaborators in the revision of plays for the court. There is no smoking-gun proof that Tilney was at all intimately involved in the transformations of these plays. But the fact that his approval was an absolute prerequisite for performance there puts it almost beyond doubt. By the time Shakespeare appears in the records in 1595, Tilney had been in office sixteen years, had read every playbook written for the major companies before licensing it, and had outlasted early masters of the stage like William Knell and Richard Tarlton and the whole generation of 'University Wits' (Marlowe, Kyd, and Greene were all dead, Peele was dying, Lodge and Nashe had retired from the stage or would do so shortly). He had seen their successors grow up and knew more about the London theatrical scene than any man alive. His successors certainly had a private box in each of the theatres and it is likely that he did too (Bawcutt 1996: 214). He could thus catch a performance whenever he felt inclined—or, equally, he had the power to require the companies to come and perform whatever he chose before him. At the same time, knowing the court's taste intimately, no one was better qualified to recognize a tried and tested product, one with court potential, or one that might be transformed into something even more impressive.

He no longer had the extensive material resources within the Revels Office that his predecessors had enjoyed, and which to a degree had still been there in the first half of his tenure as Master. But he had the ready ear of acting companies who were growing increasingly wealthy and becoming well resourced as a result of the privilege and patronage that flowed directly from his office. (Henslowe's records, as we shall see, make it plain that the Admiral's Men sometimes acquired costumes and properties expressly for court use in the first instance.) And he knew that there were ways to enhance a dramatic performance other than simply with spectacle.

Tilney's role as censor of plays makes it very easy for us to pigeonhole him as a faceless bureaucrat, even an antagonist of plays and players. But the nature of his double role, both within and without the court, ensured that this could hardly have been the case. If he was to fulfil his role as the supplier of high-quality entertainment for the court, he had to collaborate with the players—and their playwrights—at least as much as he kept a tight rein on them. The evidence of the claims for attendance fees (which we have already observed) strongly shows that, in developing these skills, Tilney broke with the earlier practice of collaborating with the other officers of the Revels Office in 'perusing' and 'reforming' plays for court performance. His way of running things involved him personally in a much more hands-on operation over the whole Revels season, with four attendants to carry through his instructions, while the roles of the other officers seem to have remained much as they had been in the past, dealing with other kinds of office business.

Weight of patronage was always as likely to carry the day in an appointment of this nature as straight ability; Tilney's associations with Lord Howard of Effingham must have been critical there. The same would be true in the race for the reversion of the office after him. John Lyly, in the 1580s associated with the Earl of Oxford, believed he had a promise of it, and surely no one could have been better qualified in any of the practical considerations of stagecraft. He later complained that the Queen herself had told him that he 'should aim with all his courses at the Revels (I dare not say with a promise, but with a hopeful item of the reversion)' (Hunter 1962:

77, 356 n. 63). But all of this came to nothing and the reversion eventually went—not until the next reign, 23 June 1603—to Sir George Buc (or Buck), a rather distant cousin of Tilney's but, more to the point, another client of Howard, by then Earl of Nottingham. It may also have weighed in Buc's favour that he had done diplomatic service for Sir Robert Cecil, son of Lord Burghley and the man who engineered James I's peaceful succession; Cecil was an influential voice in all court appointments in the first hectic months of the reign.

There is no direct evidence of Tilney's dramatic skills. His *Flower of Friendship* (1568), a Castiglione-type debate on the duties of marriage, dedicated to the Queen, was sufficiently to the taste of the time that it went through at least five editions in his lifetime and offers sound evidence of literary competence (Tilney 1992). The massive 'Topographical descriptions, regiments, and policies' of eight key European countries, which he left unpublished at his death, is a strong testament to his knowledge of international history, customs, diplomacy, and genealogy, and attests to his patience, his attention to detail, and his powers of research. He compiled it from the 1590s on, intending to present it (handsomely decorated with the coats of arms of many of Europe's leading families) to Elizabeth in a bid, backed by Howard, for promotion to a new post as Master of Ceremonies. This would have left the way open for Buc earlier. But Elizabeth died before he could present it; he worked on a new version for James but never completed it (Streitberger 1986b).

Buc's literary and scholarly achievements were no less impressive. He was primarily a historian and mixed in later years in the circle of Sir Robert Cotton, a serious scholar who allowed his friends, including Ben Jonson, to use his extensive library (Sharpe 1979). His first published work was *Daphnis Polystephanos: an Eclog Treating of Crownes, and of Garlandes*, a poem honouring James I's coronation and celebrating the king's ancestors. The original *Dictionary of National Biography* laughably described this as a work of horticulture, but it is actually a deeply learned piece of genealogy expressed with some grace (Eccles 1933b). Other published work included Buc's account of the 1596 Cadiz expedition under Lord Admiral Howard, which first appeared anonymously in John Stow's *Annals* (1601); and his 'Third University of England', which was printed as an appendix to the 1615 continuation of the *Annals*, and surveyed the subjects—the arts, sciences, and professions (law, divinity, medicine)—which could effectively be studied in London, with histories of the foundations that professed them, even though the city boasted no university.

Buc's most important works, however, were not published at all in his lifetime and some have not survived in any form. For historians the most important of these is a revisionist *History of King Richard the Third*, which offers a much more sympathetic account of this maligned king than the one we know from Sir Thomas More and Shakespeare (Buck 1982). Of more immediate import in his own day was probably *The Baron*, a massive historical review of English titles and offices, but sadly only some notes towards it have survived. Saddest of all, from the point of view of this study, is that we know he wrote an 'art of revels', but none of that survives. The very fact that he wrote it, however, indicates that he saw his court post as something that involved far more than simply importing the best commercial fare available.

Buc probably licensed the very last of Shakespeare's plays: *The Tempest, All Is True* (*Henry VIII*), and the lost *Cardenio*. He certainly oversaw all court productions of his plays after August 1610, when he succeeded Tilney; these included a significant proportion of those we happen to know about during Shakespeare's own lifetime, including all of those around the time of the wedding of Princess Elizabeth and the Elector Palatine. Although I shall be considering Shakespeare's Jacobean writing in a separate chapter, there is no reason to suppose that Buc's relationship with Shakespeare would have been significantly different from that he had with Tilney. So I discuss him here to flesh out our sense of what Shakespeare's experience of working with the Revels Office is likely to have been like throughout his career.

We can capture brief glimpses of Buc's engagement with theatre and revels in some of his surviving writings. In the 'Third University', for example, he claims that his duties as Master of the Revels required expertise in grammar, rhetoric, logic, philosophy, history, music, mathematics, and other arts (sig. Oooo 3*v*). He was not, of course, thinking here exclusively—or even primarily—of plays. His responsibilities also extended at times to such entertainments as tilts, running the ring, dances, bear- and lion-baitings, fencing, feats of activity (gymnastics) on ropes, an annual accession-day triumph, and, in some peripheral ways, masques: variety was a key consideration in keeping the court entertained. But Buc's list of required expertise clearly harks back to the definitions of what was looked for in a Master after Benger died, a creative polymath who knew how to give the court what it wanted. That resulted in the appointment of Tilney, and he projects himself as in the same mould.

At the same time he expresses an elevated opinion of what the theatre of his day had achieved: 'Here be also in this city poets excelling in all kinds of poesy... That first and most ancient kind of poesy, the dramatic is so lively expressed and represented upon the public stages & theaters of this city, as Rome in the age of her pomp & glory never saw it better performed (I mean in respect of action, and art, and not the cost and sumptuousness, for therein the Romans exceeded all nations of the world). Of this art have written largely Petrus Victorius, Petrus Crinitus, Caelius Rodiginus, Carlo Gatto, Ludovico Dulce, Georgius Fabritius, Julius Caesar Scaliger, and who hath written so much and so well (and being an author in all good poet's hands) as it were in vain for me to say anything of the art, besides that I have written thereof, a particular treatise' (Buc, 'Third University', Chapter 38 'Of Poets and Musicians', p. 984). Buc assembles a scholarly bibliography of Renaissance writers who had addressed aspects of drama, culminating with the polymathic J. C. Scaliger. Buc was placing himself and his knowledge of the subject in impressive company. Like Heywood in *An Apology for Actors*, and indeed several foreign visitors to London, he connects ancient Roman theatre with that of his own life and time—something the players encouraged in the ways they decorated their playhouses.

But Buc's interest in theatre was not just theoretical or academic. He was an avid collector of playbooks, particularly but not exclusively of those from the pre-1594 era, several of which contain comments by him. These have been studied by Alan Nelson (1998). He has identified sixteen plays that are certainly inscribed by Buc, often with a slightly enigmatic 'E' on the title page, and a further four that may be. Among the more interesting annotations is that in a 1595 copy of *Locrine*: 'Charles Tilney wrot[e a] tragedy of this matter [which] he named *Estrild* [which] I think is this. It was [lost] by his death, & now s[ome] fellow hath published [it]. I made dumb shows for it, which I yet have. G. B.'[16] (Re *Locrine* and Shakespeare, see p. 7.) Charles Tilney was one of those executed in 1586 for his part in the Babington plot to assassinate Elizabeth and free Mary, Queen of Scots, so if he did write the play (he has no other known affiliation with the theatre) it must have been earlier than that. Tilney was a cousin of Edmund and was somewhat more distantly related to Buc, which makes this both intriguing and plausible. Buc himself would have been twenty-six in 1586, so he could have devised the dumb-shows, though the play as printed was probably revised by a later hand.

The possibility that Buc was on the fringes of the play-writing world as a young man may help explain why he had an interest in identifying the authors of anonymously printed plays. He variously identified authors or expanded title-page initials on copies of George Peele's *The Arraignment of Paris* (1584), *Edward I* (1599), and *Sir Clyomon and Clamydes* (1599), Robert Greene's *Alphonsus, King of Aragon* (1599), and Henry Chettle's *Patient Grissell* (1603, co-written with Thomas Dekker). The most intriguing of all these inscriptions is that in his copy of *George a Greene, the Pinner of Wakefield* (1599), which contains two depositions about the authorship of that play: 'Written by ...... a minister, who ac[ted] the pinners part in it himself. Teste W. Shakespea[re]'; 'Ed. Juby saith that this play was made by Ro. Gree[ne]' (Nelson 1998). On the witness of William Shakespeare: this is the only moment in the entire period when we can tangibly put Shakespeare face-to-face with a Master of the Revels, though we cannot say for sure when it happened or whether Buc held the post by then.

A quarter of Buc's playbooks that have come to light were printed in 1598/9 (and there were a similar number in 1603), the years when his name is first associated with reversion to the office and when he actually achieved it. Possibly he started to prepare himself for his eventual role around the turn of the century by buying these texts and enquiring into them. Shakespeare was by then very clearly the longest-surviving dramatist, the only one still active whose career went back before the 1592/4 plague, and so the one best placed to know who might have written this old play. Buc sought him out to ask. Edward Juby was one of the actor-sharers with the post-1594 Admiral's Men, and it is likely that his career also dated back some time before then. Shakespeare's answer on the face of it seems rather quirky, but we are wrong to assume that all plays of the era were written by 'professional' dramatists. The Chamberlain's/King's Men employed some distinctly odd 'amateurs' in addition to their august 'ordinary poet', including Barnabe Barnes, who wrote *The Devil's Charter*, and George Wilkins, who probably co-wrote *Pericles* with Shakespeare (Nicholl 2008: 221–5; Gossett 2004: 38–81; see p. 275).

[16] The relevant copy is in the Bibliotheca Bodmeriana, Cologny-Genève.

Some of Buc's other annotations reflect his genuine engagement with the material. In *The Tragedy of Tancred and Gismund* (1592), an Inner Temple gift-piece to the Queen by Robert Wilmot and others, he has marked one passage 'The Scene Salerno in Sicil'. In Greene's *The Scottish History of James the Fourth* (1598), he has altered the title to 'The SCOTTISH Historie *or rather fiction of English & Scotish matters comicall*', which is exactly right—the play has precious little to do with the actual Scots king who died at Flodden.

Shakespeare would have found Tilney much more knowledgeable than himself about the ways of London theatre when he first encountered him, in the late 1580s or early 1590s. In his first encounters with Buc he would have found someone very earnest about the job he was going to do, interested in the history of London theatre of which Shakespeare himself was such a part, and keenly aware of the intellectual traditions. These were both men with whom he should have been able to work. He did not live to work with Sir Henry Herbert.[17] But Herbert too was a cultured man of letters, as we might expect of the brother of the poets Lord Herbert of Cherbury and George Herbert. He actually went one step further than his predecessors in writing a full-length play, *The Emperor Otho*, which survives in manuscript but has never been given anything like its due.[18] It shows him to be a perfectly competent dramatist. One intriguing feature is that Herbert kept a very careful tally of the line count throughout. On the final sheet, remembering to add in a revised scene of 50 lines, he calculates it at 2,117 lines. That would be a very comfortable playing length at the Blackfriars theatre, and I am at a loss to explain why he would have been so particular about the length unless he had expectations of its being performed, professionally or otherwise.[19] But the very existence of the play underlines my key point. The Masters of the Revels were not faceless bureaucrats. They were every bit as much theatrical professionals as the dramatists whose works they licensed, men with whom they could and did do business.

OUR USUAL MANAGER OF MIRTH

It so happens that Shakespeare offers us a comic portrait of a Master of the Revels, Theseus' 'usual manager of mirth' in *A Midsummer Night's Dream*. By a further good fortune he contrives to do so in a context that provides a convenient and apt

---

[17] Formally speaking Sir John Astley succeeded Buc in 1622, the son of some of Elizabeth's intimates in the old Hatfield days, like Benger. But he effectively sold the post to Herbert the following year. Technically Astley retained the title, and Herbert was his deputy, but Herbert exercised full powers—a situation which apparently led to an early misunderstanding with Lady Elizabeth's Men over *The Martyred Soldier* (see pp. 159–60). Ben Jonson received a reversion to the Mastership and would have succeeded Astley, but he died before him (see pp. 90, 160). See Dutton 1991: 218–48.

[18] It is in the National Library of Wales at Aberystwyth, NLW 5302B.

[19] I am grateful to William B. Long and Paul Werstine, who have much wider experience of the surviving early modern playbooks than I do, for confirming in private conversation that they know of no other script from the period where the lines are counted in this way. The second reader of this book for Oxford University Press kindly informs me that an anonymous seventeenth-century translation of *Medea* in the Bodleian Library is marked with line numbers (MS Eng poet e 34) but I have no idea of its derivation.

example of revision to one of his texts—though in this instance there are few of the signs which I shall suggest are normally indicative of change for court performance. There is certainly scope, however, for speculation. It is the presentation of this character which most strikingly changes between the only two authoritative versions of the play. *A Midsummer Night's Dream* was first printed (Q1) in 1600; there is a wide consensus that this was set from a manuscript copy, perhaps in Shakespeare's own hand, which is why it has usually been adopted as the copy-text by modern editors. The 1623 folio text (F) follows Q1 in most respects, except that it seems to contain additions from a theatrical copy, marking divisions into acts and giving numerous other stage directions.[20] That apart, the most significant differences between them relate to what is Scene 8 in Q1 (G2^v–G4^r) and 5.1 in F (TLN 1,791–883).[21]

The differences lie not in the dialogue, which is identical in both versions, but in who speaks it. In both versions Theseus sends for 'our usual manager of mirth' to know 'What revels are in hand?' (5.1.35–6; TLN 1,830–1).[22] In Q1 the character who performs this role is Philostrate. To Theseus' request for entertainment, he hands him 'a brief, how many sports are ripe' (42, G3^r). The Duke reads the brief aloud, commenting on each in turn until he comes to *Pyramus and Thisbe*, the description of which perplexes him. Philostrate explains that it is a completely inept amateur offering, devised by players who are Athenian labourers, who have concocted the play 'against your nuptial'. Theseus resolves to hear it. His Master of the Revels tries to insist that 'it is nothing, nothing in the world' (5.1.78; GR3^v), but Theseus is adamant, declaring that nothing can be amiss 'When simpleness and duty tender it' (5.1.84).

In F the 'usual manager of mirth' turns out to be Egeus, Hermia's father. He speaks exactly the same lines as Philostrate, and Theseus' part remains the same except that Lysander reads the titles from the brief for him; Theseus merely supplies the comments. Though editorial policy throughout the twentieth century was overwhelmingly in favour of the Q1 version, the editors of the *Oxford Shakespeare* broke with that tradition, saying: 'we have found no reason to doubt that the bulk of the Folio directions represent the play as originally and authoritatively staged. Those directions which clearly envisage a different staging from that implied by Q

---

[20] There was a second quarto (Q2) in 1619, part of what is sometimes known as the False Folio (see p. 3 n. 8). F was actually set from this, rather than from Q1. But Q2 substantially follows Q1, except for making some corrections and introducing even more errors. It does not record any substantive changes.

[21] Since the textual differences here are between two equally 'good' texts, I shall give the Bevington citation for all quotations, as well as the Q1 signature and the folio TLN. The editors of the *Oxford Shakespeare* suspect that Shakespeare had tinkered with this passage even before Q1 was printed, since there is significant mis-lineation of it there. They assume that passages were added in the margin which the compositor found difficult to follow, and they offer a conjectural version of how the passage originally looked (see Wells and Taylor 1987: 279; and Wells and Taylor 1986: 333). This does not affect my discussion of the changes between Q1 and F as the play was printed and almost certainly performed.

[22] Although it is unlikely during Shakespeare's career that the monarch ever had a choice of entertainments on the night, there are numerous reports of a prepared play or show being put off. On 3 February 1605, for example, the King's Men had a play ready but it was 'not shown'.

seem to us dramatic improvements for which Shakespeare was probably responsible' (Wells and Taylor 1987: 280). So in their text—and others based upon it since—this passage appears in its folio form.

Which version came first? It is tempting to assume that a version printed in 1600 was written before one printed in 1623, but it is not necessarily the case (and in the editing of Shakespeare, as we shall see, it is commonly argued that the earliest printed versions were *not* written first). In this case, however, there is a good chance that it is so. In both versions Philostrate appears right at the beginning of the play, where he receives the order to 'Stir up the Athenian youth to merriments. / Awake the pert and nimble spirit of mirth' (1.1.12–13; A2r; TLN 16–17); he leaves without speaking. So it *looks* as though Shakespeare had him in mind from the beginning, but switched Egeus into most of his role at some later point. This does not quite explain why Philostrate survives in this tiny, wordless role in F, but Egeus cannot handle that early business because he is about to bring Hermia before Theseus to insist that she marry Demetrius. So presumably Shakespeare (or whoever made the changes) let it stand, a tiny detail that would not be noticed in performance.

Why then and when was Q1 changed to F? The introduction of act divisions in F is usually ascribed to changes in staging practices required when the King's Men began to perform at the indoor Blackfriars playhouse after 1608. In particular, the use of candles for overhead lighting required occasional breaks to attend to them. So at the end of Act 3 a stage direction in F tells us that Hermia and Helena 'sleep all the act' (TLN 1,507)—that is, throughout an intermission—whereas at the Theatre or the Globe the action would have been continuous. So the revision *from* Q1 *to* F looks to be later than 1608. And it may be quite a bit later. F also introduces a stage direction 'Tawyer with a trumpet before them' immediately before 'Pyramus and Thisbe' begins (TLN 1,924); there is no other record of the trumpeter, William Tawyer, before 1624. Of course it was by no means necessary that all the revisions reflected in F should have happened at the same time. We must conclude simply that the revision(s) occurred between 1608 and 1623.

Does any of this help to explain the switch of Master of the Revels roles from Philostrate to Egeus? It is hard to see how it would. The change would not, for example, reduce the number of actors. Permutating apparent options, Philostrate could always be one of Theseus' 'train' of attendant lords. But what of differences to the play at what we may call an artistic level? Do they help to explain the changes? In Q1 Egeus is last seen in what we know as Act 4, overruled by Theseus and unreconciled to the fact that Hermia is going to marry Lysander—an unresolved element in the comedy, like Shylock or Malvolio. His role in F as Master of the Revels to Theseus puts everything in a new light: he is onstage throughout 5.1 and can be assumed (although he says nothing) to become a party to the court's festive spirit, as represented in the to-and-fro of Theseus and Lysander's exchanges. He at least has the opportunity to reconcile with Hermia, though nothing is scripted (see Hodgdon 1986).

What is lost in the change is the unrelenting spotlight that briefly falls in this scene on the 'usual manager of mirth', who is embarrassed to be in any way responsible for the execrable fare on offer that night. It is, in effect, a role of comic humiliation, deepening throughout his attempt to dissuade the Duke from *Pyramus and Thisbe* and climaxing with an announcement through clenched teeth: 'So please your Grace, the Prologue is addressed' (5.1.106; G4r). That is, for example, how the comedian, John Sessions, played the role in Michael Hoffman's 1999 movie. In the folio version, much of that comedy evaporates, because Egeus' involvement in the play's romantic entanglements is more critical than his personal embarrassment (and the Theseus–Lysander double-act deflects some of the attention from him).

In the 1590s any Master of the Revels depicted onstage could hardly avoid being equated with Edmund Tilney, the man who licensed all plays for public performance as well as choosing those for court performance. It says something about Shakespeare's working relationship with Tilney that he felt comfortable creating the comic role in this way, offering a humorous version of his company's overseer even as he offers a travesty of himself and the Chamberlain's Men in Quince and the 'rude mechicals'. As 400 years of performance have shown, this is comedy that can work *anywhere*. But Q would always have been distinctively effective when acted at court, with Tilney himself in attendance. Unfortunately, we have no record of its being so acted—but that, as I have shown, tells us nothing (see p. 237 n. 24).

Yet of all plays this is one where scholars have repeatedly proposed that it might have been written—or at least adapted—for an actual wedding attended by the 'fair vestal throned by the west', Queen Elizabeth (2.1.158; C1r; TLN 535). To mention only two of the weddings which have been suggested, that of the sixth Earl of Derby with Lady Elizabeth Vere on 25 January 1595 coincides with a Chamberlain's Men's slot in the court calendar (while celebrations continued at Burghley House from 30 January to 1 February, with the Queen attending, another possible venue). Another possibility falls on 19 February 1596, when Elizabeth Carey, granddaughter of Lord Chamberlain Hunsdon, married Thomas, son of Henry Lord Berkeley, at her father's house in the Blackfriars. But final proof has proved elusive.

In truth, such speculation is hardly necessary. The odds are very strong that Elizabeth would have seen *A Midsummer Night's Dream* (Q) at court in the regular way, even though we have no records to prove it. It was popular enough that by 1607 Edward Sharpham's *The Fleire* was able to mock Thisbe stabbing herself with the handle of her knife and expect audiences to recognize the allusion. And if it did not appear at court beforehand, it did so (presumably still the Q version) on 1 January 1604, when '*Robin Goodfellow*' was presented before King James—with Tilney, as he was required to be, in attendance. The King's Men performed Quince's 'rude mechanicals' for the embarrassment of Philostrate and the (presumed) delight of Tilney and his royal master. That level of in-joking, a regular feature of Revels performances, as we shall see, is diminished in the folio version. Both versions, however, carried Theseus' proclamation 'A fortnight hold we this solemnity, / In nightly Revels and new jollity' (5.1.364–5; H3v; TLN 2,151–2), which would have had an extra frisson for a courtly audience, where such extended revelry was a reality few others could indulge.

But, as W. W. Greg first suggested, the sequence with the fairies that follows might have had even more of a frisson for that audience (1955: 242). It comes despite Theseus having resolved on 'No epilogue', since 'The iron tongue of midnight hath told twelve', settling for a bergomask danced by two of the comedians instead (5.1.351, 358; H3v; TLN 2,138, 2,146). As we shall see, *Merry Wives* contains a similar reference to 'one o'clock'—hours when normally no one would be acting at all, except at court (see p. 254). In the masque-like sequence with which *A Midsummer Night's Dream* actually concludes, Oberon promises the ministrations of his fairies 'Now until the break of day' (5.1.396; H4; TLN 2,185). This of course is all within the metatheatrics of the play. But if it were performed at court, in the dead of night, it would have the added resonance of sending the audience home in those witching hours which the fairies traditionally inhabit. Is it possible that the fairy masque was added for a court performance some time before 1600? That can only be the purest conjecture, though the fact that the whole sequence is structurally *unnecessary* gives it a little weight.

We can only guess at why Shakespeare or his fellows chose to dispense with the jokes at Philostrate's expense in the F version. Possibly his ritual humiliation had become so associated with Tilney that it did not seem fit to continue it once he died in 1610. Or Buc may not have been so inclined to identify with the comedy. Or indeed the change may have been made for entirely artistic reasons. The switch to Egeus, with his wider engagement in the action, and the introduction of Lysander as a third party in these exchanges, offers a completely different comic dynamic to this sequence, one perhaps felt to be more appropriate to the resolution of the play.

All we can finally say is that *A Midsummer Night's Dream* was, as Q's 1600 title-page tells us, 'sundry times publicly acted by the Right Honourable, the Lord Chamberlain his servants'; acted at least once at court, in 1604; and printed in a version with quite circumscribed revisions in 1623. It is a play which is quite substantially *about* the way in which public drama might become court drama and—in its worries about what might scare the ladies—about the nature of the 'allowance' that might make it possible. In the end, however, the changes we can trace do not seem to relate to those issues. Rather, the 'publicly acted' Q text seems to have been ready-fitted for court performance by nature of its subject-matter, in the event that 'our play is preferred' (4.2.36–7; G2ᵛ; TLN 1,783). It is also, strikingly, a perfect example of a play revised entirely within the confines of its 'allowed book', its dialogue preserved though redistributed. Elsewhere the changes in plays I examine—suggestive, as I argue, of revision specifically for the court—will be very different both in nature and in scale. But *A Midsummer Night's Dream* offers two important object-lessons: as early as 1595 Shakespeare, the 'ordinary poet' of one of the privileged London companies, was self-conscious that he was expected to produce entertainment for the court; and when the play was, for whatever reason, revised, it was done with strict adherence to the 'allowed book'.

THE INFLUENCE OF MASTERS OF THE REVELS ON COURT PLAYS

Given how little has survived of the records of Tilney and of Buc, it is not surprising that we have virtually no trace of their specific impact on the playwrights in respect of the plays they wrote or revised for performance at court. Even in the case of Sir Henry Herbert, much of whose office-book has survived, it tells us much less about his court duties than it does about licensing the public theatres. Yet *some* indication of their influence can be found. The court revels season of 1606/7 is interesting in this regard. We only know two of the plays presented then. One was *King Lear*, which opened the season on the day after Christmas: *As it was played before the King's Majesty at Whitehall upon S. Stephen's Night in Christmas Holidays*. Leah Marcus has adroitly explored the 'local readings' of the text of *Lear* and of the event of its court performance (Marcus 1988: 148–59). Prince Henry was also Duke of Cornwall, Prince Charles was Duke of Albany (and both of them may well have been at the performance), so that the division of ancient Britain between Cornwall and Albany in the play could hardly but have spoken to James's ambition formally to unite England and Scotland in a single Parliament. And, as Andrew Gurr puts it: 'It is difficult not to assume from this that the Master of the Revels could only have approved *King Lear* for a performance at court because he thought the play supported the king's position over the…uniting of the kingdoms' (Gurr 1996: 33). Indeed Tilney, as an expert genealogist, would not have missed the point, and he must at the least have sanctioned the use of the Princes' titles (which Shakespeare varies from those in his sources) in the royal presence(s).

But in the broader context that I am adumbrating, Tilney would not have been a passive gatekeeper in such matters. There is every likelihood that he collaborated with Shakespeare and the company to produce this explicitly court version of the play. What unfortunately we cannot know is how this compared with whatever version of *King Lear* the patrons of the Globe saw. This is a text (like *Bartholomew Fair*) which transgresses our usual assumptions about the length of performances in public theatres and it must be likely that the Globe version was significantly shorter. But whether it came *before* the court version and was expanded, or *after* it and was carved from it, we have no way of knowing (see p. 87).

The other known text from the 1606/7 season is far less familiar: *The Devil's Charter* by Barnabe Barnes, which was printed *As it was played before the King's Majesty, upon Candlemas night last*. Several issues arise here. In the opening line of the play proper (after an induction of diabolical magic), King Charles of France greets 'Renowned Lodowick our warlike cousin'. Lodowick Sforza was an actual historical figure, but at Whitehall in early 1607 the line must surely have evoked King James's own cousin, Lodowick Stuart, Duke of Lennox, the most prominent of the Scots to follow James to England; shortly thereafter, if there was any doubt, King Charles receives news from someone called 'Daubigny', which must in turn have evoked Lennox's younger brother, Esmé Stuart, Seigneur D'Aubigny, then living in London and patronizing, among others, Ben Jonson (Barnes 1980: lines 81, 147). Leaving aside possible wider political agendas, Shakespeare's play pays a tribute of sorts to the king's sons, Barnes's to his cousins—gracious touches for the court performances, which must have been negotiated with Tilney, if not actually required by him.

It is surely not accidental either that the two plays have other features in common. Both are about dealing with devils: in *Lear*, Edgar as Poor Tom famously draws on Samuel Harsnett's *Declaration of Egregious Popish Impostures* (1603) for his language of diabolic possession; *The Devil's Charter* is about a pact with the devil, who drags the Borgia Pope, Alexander VI, to hell before his expected time. The play is a rabidly anti-papist cross between *Dr. Faustus* and *The Revenger's Tragedy*, calculated to speak to anti-Catholic feeling in the wake of the Gunpowder Plot. But, as everyone knew, demonology was a subject on which James had written, and in which he continued to take a lively interest. It could hardly have been pure chance that two plays on that subject were chosen for the same Revels season.[23] Was this a result of the players anticipating the court taste? Or might Tilney have prompted them, and if so at what point in the writing/revision process? An intriguing dimension in all of this is the figure of Barnabe Barnes. He was a colourful character, once tried in Star Chamber for a poisoning, and clearly looking for advancement at court; in 1606 he dedicated his *Four Books of Offices* to the king, a substantial work on the four cardinal virtues for the benefit of princes. No other play by Barnes has survived, and this may have been his only work for the stage (Eccles 1933a). Would it have been Barnes himself, or Shakespeare, or even conceivably Tilney who proposed that he write a play so closely attuned to courtly preoccupations and linked thematically with the lead play of the season?

There is also evidence elsewhere of the court revels season being structured or thematized beyond what could reasonably have been expected if the Masters of the Revels had simply trawled whatever happened to be in the repertoire of the current 'allowed' companies. The 1604/5 season, for example, opened with *Othello*—and the Twelfth Night masque was *The Masque of Blackness*, in which Queen Anna and her ladies all wore black make-up, as Richard Burbage would have done as the Moor. In 1633 Shakespeare's *The Taming of the Shrew* and Fletcher's continuation, *The Woman's Prize* were acted before the King and Queen at St. James's Palace on 26 and 28 November respectively. In that case we can say categorically that the pairing was not planned more than a month beforehand, since it was only on 19 October that Sir Henry Herbert heard about the revival of Fletcher's play and peremptorily ordered the King's Men not to play it until it had been revised to his satisfaction (Dutton 2000: 41–61; see p. 153). Herbert carefully noted that *The Taming of the Shrew* was 'liked' (presumably by the King), while *The Woman's Prize* was 'very well liked' (Bawcutt 1996: 185).

Another intriguing pairing is Thomas Heywood's two-part *Fair Maid of the West*; both parts were published together in 1631, with identical phrasing on their title pages: 'As it was lately acted before the King and Queen, with approved liking. By the Queen's Majesty's Comedians'. All the evidence suggests that the first part had been revived after some thirty years, since it strongly evokes dramatic styles from the end of Queen Elizabeth's reign; the second part, very different in tone and style, may well, however, be Caroline. As G. E. Bentley puts it: 'The fact that both title pages boast of a court performance suggests that they were acted together, a

---

[23] *Volpone* (pub. 1607) and *The Merry Devil of Edmonton* (pub. 1608) were also both in the King's Men's repertoire at this time, and both deal in different ways with demonology. But we have no record of either at court at this time.

suggestion apparently confirmed by the fact that there is no epilogue for Part I and no prologue for Part II, but only a prologue addressed to the court before Part I and an epilogue obviously to the court to Part II' (Bentley 1984: 273).

Was it Heywood's own idea to write the continuation, some thirty years later? Herbert must at least have consented to the court performances. Is it possible that he was involved earlier, encouraging if not actually instigating this theatrical double-header? He doubtless recognized that there was something of an Elizabethan revival going on—the following year saw both the second Shakespeare folio and a collection of Lyly plays, besides the revival of numerous other Elizabethan plays and writings—and this resuscitation of Heywood in print, after a long dormant period, seems to have been a calculated intervention in it.[24] Herbert clearly played his part to the extent of bringing the plays to court. This may also be true of other revivals. Chapman's late rewriting of *Bussy D'Ambois* may well be related to its pairing with the sequel, *The Revenge of Bussy D'Ambois* (Tricomi 1971–2; 1973; see p. 132).

In such ways that we can only hazily trace, the Masters of the Revels were early impresarios, not just finding talent for the court where they could, but promoting it, stage-managing it, adding grace-notes to it, and 'apting' it for royal courts with increasingly insatiable appetites for theatre.

---

[24] No play by Heywood was published between *The Four Prentices of London* in 1615 and the *Fair Maid of the West* duo in 1631. Indeed it is not easy to trace much of Heywood's theatrical career at all between those dates, though Martin Wiggins' multi-volumed *British Drama 1533–1642: A Catalogue* promises a fuller picture (Oxford: Oxford University Press, 2011–).

3
Line Lengths, Playing Times, and Ben Jonson

THE LENGTH OF ELIZABETHAN PLAY PERFORMANCES

The normal performance length of Elizabethan plays bears directly on the question of why it might have been necessary—in some instances—to revise (and, I argue, implicitly expand) play texts for performance at court. All of the 'bad' quartos have line lengths, and so presumably playing times, comfortably within the average of texts known to have been performed in public theatres; the 'good' counterparts of three of them—*Romeo and Juliet*, *Henry V*, and *Hamlet*—are all very significantly longer.

How long it normally took for plays to be performed at the public playhouses is an issue on which a good deal of ingenuity and ink has been spilled, precisely because it has a bearing on our understanding of the reasons for the different versions of Shakespeare's plays; I review it below (see Hart 1934: 77–153 and 1942: 18–20; Klein 1967; Orgel 1988; Gurr 1999; Erne 2003: 131–73; Hirrel 2010; Urkowitz 2012). But the secondary question of whether this differed from the regular playing time at court—another venue where the plays were commonly performed—is one which hardly anyone asks. A battery of imponderables makes it impossible to answer these questions as categorically as some have tried to do, but there is a good deal of evidence to suggest that—at times—there were differences.

When W. L. Halstead looked at *Old Fortunatus* to try to determine what could be seen of the changes for the court that we can track in Henslowe's *Diary*, he observed that 'after altering, the play was nearly 3000 lines long, and this was too long for performance in the London theatres' (Halstead 1939: 352 note; see pp. 106–8). J. R. Mulryne, who edited *The Spanish Tragedy*, came to a similar conclusion about the 1602 revision of that play. At some 2,737 lines, the 1592 text was already on the long side; the 1602 additions push it over 3,000 and he felt this made it unplayably long: 'It is most unlikely in fact that the 1602 text, including the "Additions", was ever performed in its existing state. It is, for one thing, exceptionally long. It is more likely that the additional passages were intended to replace parts of Kyd's text which were felt by 1602 to be either old fashioned or weak' (Kyd 1989: xxxiii–iv).[1]

---

[1] Of course, one place the 1602 text *might* have been performed, as this book argues, was at court. It seems inconceivable that one of the most popular plays of the era was not performed there, in whatever version, but no evidence has survived to show that it was.

In this both Halstead and Mulryne were following criteria developed by Alfred Hart in the 1930s, in which he attempted to reconcile the varying line length of extant plays with supposed playing times. Hart knew that there is substantial unanimity among Shakespeare's contemporaries to the effect that performances in the theatres took two hours. The prologue of *Romeo and Juliet* famously speaks of 'the two hours' traffic of our stage' (line 12), and this is echoed by that of *The Two Noble Kinsmen* ('Two hours' travail', 29) and William Davenant's *The Unfortunate Lovers* ('in two hours', 20). *Henry VIII*, we are told, lasts 'two short hours' (Prologue 13). Dekker admittedly breaks the pattern once when he refers to 'three hours of mirth' in the epilogue (line 5) to *If It Be Not Good, the Devil is In It*, and there are other exceptions, as we shall see. But Hart tries to show that these are out of line when he concludes that 'Shakespeare, Jonson, Fletcher, Beaumont, Percy, Middleton, Barry, Tailor, Beeston and Dekker [elsewhere] all speak of "two hours" as the time spent in the representation of the play' (Hart 1934: 104). And Andrew Gurr speaks for most twentieth-century commentators in concurring that 'Two hours was the standard time for a performance' (Gurr 1999: 68). When we reflect, however, that the same prologue which introduced the 1597 quarto of *Romeo and Juliet* as 'two hours' traffic of our stage' (2,215 lines) also introduced the 1599 one (2,989 lines), two hours hardly constitutes the hard-and-fast measure of a performance it at first seems.

In reviewing literature on the subject since Hart, we see a clear trend towards opening up the apparent two-hour limit. David Klein was the first to challenge Hart, in a brief but pungent note. He introduces a range of instances not considered by Hart and concludes: 'on the basis of the evidence, it seems clear that the theory of a two-hour *allotment* is untenable' (1967: 438; my emphasis). That is, he regards the two hours as a conventional figure of speech, but one which did not actually constrain (or imply the external constraint of) playing lengths. Steven Orgel ignored this and stuck with Hart's norms, arguing that 'with very few exceptions, every printed Shakespeare text is far too long for the two to two-and-a-half hours that is universally accepted as the performing time of plays in the period' (1988: 7). In many respects Andrew Gurr followed suit in his 1999 essay, remaining convinced of two-hour playing norms.[2] Lukas Erne in *Shakespeare as Literary Dramatist* tried to negotiate a liberal accommodation with Hart, arguing that: 'There is no reason why the length of performances should not have varied between less than two and, say, two-and-a-half hours, excluding the final jig, inter-act music, and other additional entertainment...the performance time of an Elizabethan play usually was *in the proximity of* two hours, though there seems to have been considerable variety' (2003: 143, 147; my emphasis). That is, there were pressures (of whatever kind) to keep the performances of plays close to two hours in length, with additional materials such as jigs in the public theatres and inter-act music in the private ones taking unspecified extra time, which might have pushed total playing time out to, say, three hours.

---

[2] In other contexts, Gurr has seemed more liberal. In *Playgoing in Shakespeare's London*, for example, he suggested that 'The likely duration of most performances...was likely to have been close to three hours' (2004b: 39)—but this did include extra-textual elements, and implicitly he still stood by the two-hour *play*. That seems broadly his position elsewhere.

Michael J. Hirrel, however, has tried to open up the possibilities considerably further than that, arguing that 'The time available for theatrical events could, and regularly did, approach four hours' (2010: 181). But I am not convinced by the evidence he adduces. For example, he includes records of practices prior to settled London playing in the 1590s—a period from which precious few commercial playtexts survive, and none of them are likely to take anything like four hours to perform (161–2). It must be questionable whether these records reflect practice after 1594, the period to which most other commentators on the subject implicitly direct their attention, when settled London playing required different accommodations with the City authorities than the sometimes ad-hoc arrangements that had prevailed before. The evidence suggests that, pre-1594, performances in the City inns commonly did not start until after evensong—that is, somewhere between 3.30 and 4 p.m.—though it is less clear whether that also applied to the suburban amphitheatres, over which those authorities had no control (Chambers 1923: 4.223, 225, 298–302). How late these shows went on is also far from clear, despite Hirrel's attempts to pin it 'after 7.30 and even as late as 8:00 p.m.'—the latter time relating to a single incident when a group of apprentices tried to excuse their disorderly presence as related to attending a play (162). It is notable, however, that the correspondence in this period contains both complaints from the actors in Middlesex (at the Theatre or the Curtain) that 'the dark do carry *inconvenience*' (Chambers: 301), and worries from the Lord Mayor (13 April 1582) that restraining the start of plays till after evensong 'would drive the action of their plays into very *inconvenient* time of night' (ibid; my emphases). These are, I suggest, pressing factors which require further attention than Hirrel allows, when he describes 'the City facetiously' suggesting that 'no playing be in the dark' (162).

As we have observed, the relationship between the court and London playing was significantly different after the 1592/4 plague (see pp. 29–30). As part of this, the Privy Council and the City authorities seem to have faced up to the realities of permanent playing in London, rather than occasional playing dictated by touring schedules. The new Lord Chamberlain's Men and a revamped Lord Admiral's Men were the only companies who would perform at court for the next five years, and it was understood that each was more or less permanently resident at one of the suburban amphitheatres, the Theatre in Shoreditch and the Rose on the Bankside respectively. Other companies might continue to use the Curtain when their touring brought them to London, and over time new playhouses would be built, the Swan and the Boar's Head, where troupes would try to compete with the two privileged companies. But the latters' established ties to the court gave them considerable advantages, and these would be publicly asserted by the Privy Council from February 1598 onwards.

One part of the settlement with these privileged companies was evidently an agreement over performance times. This may or may not have been reached in conjunction with the City of London authorities, who still had jurisdiction over the City inns, where the companies still preferred to perform during the winter—though that option seems finally to have been closed to them from around 1596 or perhaps a little later (Kathman 2009: 160; Menzer 2006). The first we hear of this settlement, in fact, is in a letter of Lord Chamberlain Hunsdon to Sir Richard Martin, the Lord Mayor, on 8 October 1594, asking permission for his company to perform at the Cross Keys that winter:

> Where my now company of players have been accustomed for the better exercise of their quality, and for the service of her Majesty if need so require, to play this winter time within the City at the Cross Keys in Gracious Street. These are to require & pray your lordship (the time being such as, thanks be to God, there is now no danger of the sickness) to permit and suffer them so to do. The which I pray you the rather to do for that they have undertaken to me that, where heretofore they began not their plays till towards four o'clock, they will now begin at two, and have done between four and five, and will not use any drums or trumpets at all for the calling of people together, and shall be contributories to the poor of the parish where they play, according to their abilities. (Wickham *et al.* 2000: 304)

The old soldier manages briskly, if not indeed brusquely (signing off 'And so not doubting of your willingness to yield hereunto, upon these reasonable conditions'), to encapsulate many old arguments for the benefit of the Lord Mayor. The actors play to rehearse for the Queen; his new troupe are privileged in that regard; there is now no plague; it is winter; they will not make loud noises; and they will pay a reasonable sum for the upkeep of the local poor.

The biggest change, however, is that 'where heretofore they began not their plays till towards four o'clock, they will now begin at two, and have done between four and five'. It is rarely observed that this reversed two decades of attempts to keep the players out of competition with churches conducting evensong between two o'clock and four, and must have been unpopular in many quarters (not least the Church itself: see later in this chapter about Paul's Boys). Leicester's Men's 1574 patent, for example, had included the stipulation that plays 'be not published or shown in the time of common prayer' (see Wickham *et al.* 2000: 55, 58, 77–8). To sweeten this deal, Hunsdon explicitly undertakes that the players will 'have done between four and five'. This is the most explicit statement anywhere of start and end times for playing in the same document, setting a limit of between two and three hours.

If we ask why such a schedule should be acceptable both to the players and to the City authorities (who are being asked/told to forgo the respect they normally accord church services), the answer most probably lies with the issue which both sides raised in the 1580s: the players insisted that 'the dark do carry inconvenience' when they performed out at Shoreditch, and the Lord Mayor worried that restraining the start of plays till after evensong 'would drive the action of their plays into very inconvenient time of night'. This new arrangement would avoid inconveniences to both. It is a solution for a modern metropolis, in which settled playing was to be a fact of life.

There are reasons to suppose that these understandings also applied to the suburban amphitheatres. The Swiss visitor, Thomas Platter, records a 2 p.m. start as normal for a play in 1599. He describes his own visit to an early performance of *Julius Caesar* at the Globe: 'After dinner on the 21st of September, at about two o'clock, I went with my companions over the water'. Then, after describing another 'after dinner' play visit (most likely at the Curtain), he reflects that 'thus every day at two o'clock in the afternoon in the city of London two and sometimes three comedies are performed' (Chambers 1923: 4.365). Unfortunately Platter does not give an end-time to these performances, so that I cannot categorically deny that these performances extended late into the evening, but the logic behind these conditions—as in Hunsdon's letter—was evidently to avoid that.

And the balance of likelihood is against it, especially in winter. The first consideration was always likely to be lighting. In a country as far north as England the light fails fatally early in the winter months, and this is critical in open-air auditoria with little or no artificial lighting.[3] Webster's famous complaint about the first performance of *The White Devil* at the Red Bull theatre—'it was acted in so dull a time of winter, presented in so open and black a theatre, that it wanted...a full and understanding auditory'—underscores the problems of performing in such conditions ('To the Reader', in Webster 1995, 1: 140–1). 'The assumption that a complete entertainment at the theater lasted between two and three hours means that some representations finished in twilight. Even if plays began promptly at 2 p.m., a three-hour duration would push the end of the play past sunset for four months a year, from the second week in October until the third week in February. When plays began at three o'clock [see later in this chapter], the end of a three-hour play would continue past sunset for half the year, from the middle of September until the middle of March' (Graves 1999: 83). As Graves himself observes, the eye can certainly adapt to follow action in twilight, and we do know that at least one outdoor theatre had some very rudimentary lighting.[4] But the splendid clothing in which the actors invested so much of their capital would have been wasted in these conditions.

Being able to see the show, however, may not have been the prime consideration. Hunsdon's brusque note to Lord Mayor Martin suggests other practicalities. For the Lord Mayor, audiences at playhouses were primarily a public order issue; having several hundred emerge from one of the inns into the unlit streets after sunset would never have been an attractive prospect. But larger invasions of the City after dark from the suburban amphitheatres, each capable of holding 2–3,000 people, would have been even less acceptable. Moreover, respectable citizens very likely had their own reservations about being out after dark and would have welcomed being home by supper time (see later in this chapter). If a performance within the City walls was expected to end between 4 and 5 p.m., what of the suburbs?

---

[3] Many of my American acquaintances fail to appreciate that England is at the same latitude as Labrador and is only protected from sub-Arctic weather by the Gulf Stream and other effects of the Atlantic Ocean.

[4] The Boar's Head paid out for 'rushes and cresset lights in winter, which some weeks came to ten or twelve shillings' (Berry 1986: 116). This fell far short of the candelabra used in the indoor theatres. Hirrel cites this evidence of indoor lighting at the Boar's Head in support of the view that performances were regularly longer than the supposed 'two hours' traffic', but such lighting would not have made a significant difference. He also mentions an engraving of a well-lit performance in the 1650s, which he believes to have been at an outdoor theatre, the Red Bull; I follow R. B. Graves, whom he cites, in believing this to be a picture of an indoor theatre (2010: 168–9). As I suggest, absence of lighting on the audience's way home was more critical than lighting within the public theatres.

A citizen attending the Theatre or the Curtain in Shoreditch had to negotiate the open spaces of Finsbury Fields and Moorfields before they even entered the City walls. And one attending the Rose or the Globe had either to hire a boat across the Thames or take a longer walk around, across London Bridge. In the dead of winter—and we recall that the early seventeenth century was a mini ice-age, in which the Thames froze over more than once—this would not have been an attractive proposition long after sunset. This was the 'inconvenience' these arrangements were facing up to. Again, the pressure for performances to be over by 5 p.m.— from both audiences and City authorities alike—seems quite probable.

After 1594, 2 p.m. was not a universal start-time, though Platter certainly suggests that it was a norm. A later start is recorded in the contract of the actor, Robert Dawes, with the management of the new Hope theatre in 1614, where he is required 'every day whereon any play is or ought to be played [to] be ready apparelled and—to begin the play at the hour of three of the clock in the afternoon' (Bentley 1984: 49). There are likely explanations for this, at the later date; it may well have been a practical concession to the established dominance of the neighbouring King's Men at the Globe. It would not be good for either company to have hundreds of customers converging on the Bankside at the same time, especially given the demand for water-taxis across the Thames—nor, by the same token, for them all to be leaving and expecting transport back at the same time. The City authorities, likewise, would presumably also have been pleased to have their influx of returning citizens staggered. Dawes signed his contract on 7 April, about a month before the Globe's normal summer season began.[5] The contract may implicitly have reflected summer conditions. Between October and April the Hope would have had no competition on the Bankside, since the King's Men were performing across the Thames at the Blackfriars during those months, and in those circumstances a 2 p.m. start may have been both possible and desirable.

The last piece of evidence about performance times is certainly anomalous, but helps to confirm some of the parameters I have been suggesting. The amateur dramatist, William Percy, wrote plays with Paul's Boys in mind and the surviving manuscript contains a general note to their Master, saying that if they 'but overreach in length (the children not to begin before four after prayers and the gates of Paul's shutting at six) the time of supper, that then...you do let pass some of the songs and make the consort the shorter, for I suppose these plays to be somewhat too long for that place' (Kincaid 1999: 1: 69). The boys' theatre, being in the precinct of St Paul's, was subject to the cathedral's regulations when it reopened in 1599, which meant that they could not start playing until evensong finished at 4 p.m. So they were still bound by the rule which had affected everyone in the 1570s and 1580s, but which by now everyone else had abandoned. Moreover, they had to stop—and the audience be gone—before 6 p.m., when cathedral premises were closed. This would indeed have required plays to run well *less* than two hours. It may well explain why plays for Paul's Boys were on the short side, and the whole

---

[5] The King's Men's normal summer schedule was delayed this year because the Globe was having to be rebuilt, following the 1613 fire: it was ready to reopen by 30 June (Chambers 1923: 2.218).

situation may explain why they were never as robust as their rivals and went out of business by 1606. Percy's reminder that the whole Paul's precinct, like much of respectable London, closed at 6 p.m. (which he regarded as 'the time for supper'), offers a useful perspective on the timings we have been tracking elsewhere. For much of the year, the pressure to complete performances while there was still adequate light, and to get audiences safely returned to their City homes and supper while there was at least twilight to guide them, must have united players, audiences, and the City authorities in thinking that 5 p.m. was an appropriate time for most performances to end.

Let us now return to Hirrel's arguments for longer playing times than this. When he addresses the post-1594 era he suggests that 'London gallants, many informants tell us, often spent their whole afternoons between midday dinner and evening suppers at the theaters' (165). His principal evidence on this is a John Davies epigram from the late 1590s, where 'Fuscus' regularly 'goes to Giles's, where he doth eat till one / Then sees a play till six, and sups at seven' (Davies 1876: 2: 37–8).[6] But this is satirical fiction, not documentary reporting. It fits Davies's depiction of the hedonistic Fuscus that theatre schedules should stretch to indulge his whims in an endless cycle which is only broken when he 'falls into a whore-house' instead of a playhouse. There is no precision here about the time a performance ends, or how long it takes Fuscus to get to wherever he sups (and Percy, at least, thought that supper-time was 6 p.m.). The whole *experience* of attending the play—perhaps arriving early to get the best seats and lingering late to socialize—is emblematic of the burgeoning early modern entertainment industry, catering particularly for those who did not have to work. The specifics of play times are only incidental. This is an issue whenever we try to read fiction as documentary.

But there is a similar imprecision built into the 1619 petition of Blackfriars residents, complaining about the coaches which crowd the precinct's streets during the winter playing season there. They are described as a nuisance 'almost every day in the winter time (not forbearing the time of Lent) from one or two of the clock till six at night' (Hirrel 2010: 165). Some patrons would certainly have arrived at 1 p.m. to catch the pre-show concert offered by the Blackfriars' resident consort of musicians. But I cannot agree with Hirrel's suggestion that 'this suggests that performances lasted from two until sometime approaching six' (ibid). The key question is how long it took the coaches which assembled between 1 and 2 p.m. to get out of the narrow medieval alleys and courtyards surrounding the Blackfriars, which were not designed for such traffic. Jacobean coaches were large and cumbersome status symbols, and their use had expanded dramatically since the second Blackfriars theatre opened in 1600. That use would expand even further (and the issue be compounded by the introduction of sedan chairs) into the Caroline period.[7] The point of the 1619 petition is in part how long it took to clear the jam once the performance

---

[6] I have rendered 'Gyls' as 'Giles's', presumably a reference to St. Giles-without-Cripplegate, adjacent to the Shoreditch playhouses.

[7] Hirrel introduces some Caroline evidence, by when the issue was even more aggravated (165).

ended, and that was more likely an hour than a few minutes. This probably speaks to a playing time from 2 until 5, rather than 6 p.m.

Hirrel is also one of several commentators who invokes the 'performance schedule' built into *The Tempest* as evidence of actual practice:

> The play's characters identify times that correspond to the passage of actual time in the theatre. Soon after the play begins, Prospero asks Ariel, 'What is the time of day?' He answers his own question, 'At least two glasses' (after two) and continues, 'The time twixt six and now / Must by us both be spent most preciously' (1.2.239–42). Near the play's conclusion, Prospero asks Ariel, 'How's the day?' Ariel answers, 'On the sixth hour, at which time, my lord, / You said our work should cease' (5.1.3–5). That is, between five and six, but approaching six o'clock, when their work was to cease. (166)

Hirrel is determined to make this span four hours ('approaching six o'clock') but 'On the sixth hour' probably means 'approaching the sixth hour', not late within it, as two further comments make clear. The boatswain announces that 'our ship, / Which but three glasses since we gave out split, / Is tight and yare' (5.1.222–4). Three glasses are three *hour*-glasses. Similarly, Alonso wonders at Ferdinand's attachment to Miranda: 'Your eld'st acquaintance cannot be three hour' (186). While Prospero initially envisions a four-hour span, the reality is a three-hour one—only one of the 'strange' disjunctions (rather than correspondences) between art and reality in this play. What is really curious about this is that *The Tempest*, of all plays, takes nothing like even three hours to perform. Indeed, ironically, it is one of 'the very few exceptions' in the entire Shakespeare canon that Steven Orgel believes could realistically be performed within the conventional 'two hours' traffic of the stage' (1988: 7).[8] An explanation probably lies in the play having been written for the Blackfriars, where there would have been inter-act music: the total show thus perhaps extended for three hours.

There is an instructive parallel here with Jonson's *The Alchemist*, to which Shakespeare's play is commonly thought a riposte or companion piece. It too is most likely to have been written for performance at the Blackfriars, its action located in Lovewit's house in that precinct and carefully tied to a specific date: 1 November 1610. The timing of its action is even more precisely spelled out than that of *The Tempest*, starting with Dapper's tardy appearance, late in the morning (1.2.6); he is sent off to reappear 'against one o'clock' (164), which he does. As Peter Holland and William Sherman observe, the play then 'unfolds in continuous time for the first two acts' (Jonson 2012b: 545). Within this, the play 'construct[s] a series of deadlines and appointments for its characters' and hurries them forward with 'effectively an hour's time-gap between Acts 2 and 3' (565). When Lovewit unexpectedly returns, 'it is still "yet not deep i'the afternoon"' (5.2.30). The Prologue's "two short hours" (1) for the performance come remarkably close to the play's fictional time-span' (ibid).[9]

---

[8] The other two are *The Comedy of Errors* and, with reservations, *Macbeth* (7).

[9] All quotations from Jonson are from *The Cambridge Edition of the Works of Ben Jonson* (Jonson 2012a). Individual works within the edition have separate volume citations.

The play thus encourages us to think that the action unfolds (with a one-hour gap) in 'real time'. The farcical pace accelerates in the second half, yet all within the most scrupulous unity of time. But as with *The Tempest*, there is an illusion at work in the play. *The Alchemist*, at 3,058 lines, is half as long again as *The Tempest*. Far from playing in 'two short hours', even those who believe the first actors of these plays delivered their lines faster than their modern counterparts (see later in this chapter), would accept that *The Alchemist* would take over two-and-a-half hours to perform, and that is without consideration of inter-act breaks. *The Alchemist* is thus a perfect mirror-image of *The Tempest*: even ignoring breaks, the action (sticking rigidly to the classical unities) takes longer to perform than the text tells us it does, whereas that of *The Tempest* (driven by the 'strange' conventions of early modern romance) takes *less* time to perform than the text tells us it does. It is not impossible that the playwrights were having fun at each other's expense, working through their very different intuitions about how drama works.

To return, however, to Michael J. Hirrel's argument: neither of these plays argues for a four-hour playing time. Paradoxes apart, *The Tempest* might, with longer breaks, reach its three hours. *The Alchemist*, with more expeditious breaks, could probably be played in the same time. Adding this to my earlier reservations about the evidence he adduces, I cannot follow Steven Urkowitz in accepting that Hirrel establishes that public performances 'fill[ed] out a roughly four hour span of time' (2012: 240). I see nothing to convince me that anything beyond three hours was normal.

So far, however, I have—as it were—only been telling one side of a story. None of the scholars we have discussed is interested in determining performance lengths purely as an end in itself. Each of them is at least as interested (and often more so) in the implication of performance length for the nature and length of the play scripts that were performed. Alfred Hart was convinced that no play longer than between 2,300 and 2,400 lines could be completed in two hours. Since he was convinced that the two-hour figure applied literally, it followed that all plays longer than that must have been cut for normal performance—in the cases of Shakespeare and Jonson, the playwrights who most commonly exceeded even 2,800 lines, quite drastically cut. Similarly, Steven Orgel, on a quest to determine what we mean by 'authentic' Shakespeare, felt the need to confront certain implications of Hart's analysis. For him it meant that 'Shakespeare habitually began with more than he needed, that the scripts offered the company a range of possibilities, and that the process of production was a collaborative one of selection as well as of realization and interpretation' (1988: 7).

Andrew Gurr approached a similar assessment of the factual situation from a different perspective, one based on an important dimension of theatre history (1999). As we have seen, the Master of the Revels had a special commission that required all plays to be censored and licensed by him before they could be performed in public (Dutton 1991: 47ff). One copy of the play, known as the 'allowed book', bore his licence and seal; this was important verification of his authority, could be used in any dispute with other authorities about performing that play, conferred a performance copyright of sorts, and so was extremely valuable to the acting company which possessed it. Gurr's contention is that the 'allowed book' would be a 'maximal' version of the play, containing perhaps considerably more than could ever be performed; and that 'minimal' performance versions could be derived from it, as long as they did not introduce material that had not been authorized.

The maximal 'allowed copy' would by definition be quite close to what the author originally wrote, though its value to the company would normally preclude its use for publication; that would more likely be based on the author's own papers, or other copies derived from them; 'minimal' texts would reflect the author's work as it had been reworked and negotiated with his acting colleagues: 'The "allowed" book and its comprehensive text... was maximal. The conditions that determined the performed text always pushed it in the direction of the minimal... The absence of the six famous choruses from the 1600 quarto of *Henry V*, a text much nearer the play as performed than the author's first manuscript on which the Folio text is based, probably indicates that the original players never actually did ask their audiences to piece out their imperfections with their thoughts' (70). Gurr does not ask how or why the players might have been constrained to a two-hour playing time; that does not seem to have been imposed or enforced by the Master of the Revels. But the existence of texts like the 1600 *Henry V* (1,623 lines)—or the 1597 *Romeo and Juliet* (2,215) and 1603 *Hamlet* (2,154)—confirms for him that such constraints did exist. It used commonly to be asserted (on no actual authority) that such texts were prepared for touring purposes, not for regular London playing. But Gurr will have none of that.

Lukas Erne's analysis is much more wide-ranging, in the sense of reviewing more plays and specific texts in greater depth, and reassessing the evidence on which Hart, in particular, based his case. His conclusions, however, are remarkably similar in key respects to those of Gurr: there are maximal and minimal texts. The maximal texts are not necessarily to be associated with the 'allowed books' (he does not rule this out, but is not really interested in the issue). They represent for him, rather, versions written with a view to readership and publication. The minimal texts, as with Gurr, represent what the acting company made of these overlong reading versions for performance purposes.

As Erne puts it: 'I will argue that Shakespeare, "privileged playwright" that he was, could afford to write plays for the stage and the page' (2003: 19–20). 'From the very beginning... Shakespeare's plays... were designed to be not only staged performances but also printed texts... The problem of the length of many of Shakespeare's plays becomes soluble, I argue, once we accept that the play as it has come down to us may be more than a reflection of what would have been spoken on stage' (135). In the first half of his book Erne does in fact make an excellent job of dispelling the old myth that the Chamberlain's Men consistently fought against the publication of Shakespeare's plays, showing that virtually all of those over which they held rights were in fact printed.[10] But that is not the same thing as

---

[10] As I shall argue later, I am less convinced about Erne's account of what was going on in the Jacobean phase of Shakespeare's career.

proving that they were '*designed* to be not only staged performances but also printed texts' (my emphasis). Nor does it prove (and this goes for Hart and Gurr too) that they were necessarily over-length *in the first instance*. None of those I have cited considers the possibility that the minimal texts might actually have been purpose-written to begin with, to fit the time available, and only expanded when a specific demand arose for them to be. That, in a nutshell, is my own argument.

Erne is particularly sensitive to the issues of playing speeds and the practical realities of 'two hours' traffic'. Hart had concluded: 'It can be proved that the average length of plays with sound texts written for representation on the public stage during the years 1590–1616 did not much exceed 2,500 lines, and that, apart from Shakespeare and Jonson, five dramatists only out of about fifty wrote even one play of [3,000 lines]' (1932: 24).[11] This statistic led him to suppose that the two-hour figure was a strict one ('if they wrote "two hours" we have no option but to think that they meant exactly what they said') and that frequent instances of lines being marked for deletion in the mere nineteen manuscript playbooks which have survived indicates a certain ruthlessness of practice: 'all plays exceeding 2300 to 2400 lines in length would be liable to abridgement and usually would be abridged' (1934: 104; 1942: 122).[12]

Even to allow this number of lines, Hart had to suppose that Elizabethan actors spoke more rapidly than their modern counterparts. As Steven Urkowitz recapitulates: 'Hart estimates a rate of delivery of verse drama at about 1200 lines an hour (a speed achieved today by troupes unencumbered by modern production values of scenery, variable lighting, and intermissions but which includes time for stage combat and songs as called for in the scripts)' (2012: 241). Urkowitz is thinking of such troupes as that at the American Shakespeare Center, performing normally at the Blackfriars Theater in Staunton, Virginia.[13] This may be compared with the Royal Shakespeare Company's average delivery of 900 lines per hour (the figure used by Gregory Doran in his Director's Talk about the production of *Hamlet* at the Courtyard theatre, 5 August 2008). It squares readily with instances Erne uses, an RSC *Lear* that lasted three-and-a-half hours, despite a 400-line cut; and a 1997 *Cymbeline* that ran almost three hours despite cuts of 1,000 lines (2003: 137).

By Hart's standards, only seven of Shakespeare's plays in their folio versions would have escaped some abridgement: *The Tempest*, *The Two Gentlemen of Verona*, *The Comedy of Errors*, *A Midsummer Night's Dream*, *Timon of Athens*, and *Macbeth*, plus *Pericles*. *Merry Wives*, *Measure for Measure*, *Much Ado*, *Love's Labour's Lost*, *The Merchant of Venice*, *As You Like It*, *The Taming of the Shrew*, *A Winter's Tale*, *King John*, *Richard II*, *1 Henry IV*, *1* and *3 Henry VI*, *Henry VIII*, and *Titus Andronicus* would all have had to lose between 150 and 500 lines to squeeze under the 2,400

---

[11] Virtually all of Jonson's surviving plays are more than 3,000 lines long and self-evidently a 'special case'. I consider this at pp. 87ff.

[12] On the surviving manuscript playbooks, which do not in fact bear out Hart's view of ruthless uniformity as to length, see Long 1999 and Erne 2003: 158–65. Passages are in some instances marked for deletion, but never on anything like the scale that would be necessary to reduce, say, Q2 *Romeo and Juliet* or *Hamlet* to their Q1 lengths.

[13] Erne also takes note of this company, in its earlier incarnation as the Shenandoah Shakespeare Express (2003: 137 and n).

lines. *2 Henry IV*, *Henry V*, *2 Henry VI*, *Richard III*, *Troilus and Cressida*, *Coriolanus*, *Hamlet*, *Othello*, *Antony and Cleopatra*, and *Cymbeline*, and the quarto version of *King Lear*, which are all over 3,000 lines, would have had to lose much more. The 1604/5 *Hamlet*, at 3,668 lines, would need to lose more than a third of its length. At Royal Shakespeare Company levels, the cuts would need to be a quarter deeper still.

Given that Hart had already allowed for faster delivery of the text, Erne saw no further margins in that direction. He did, however, see reasons to relax the two-hour performance limit to which Hart had held fast. He argued that 'the performance time of an Elizabethan play usually was in the proximity of two hours, though there seems to have been considerable variety. The "two houres and a halfe, and somewhat more" of Jonson's *Bartholomew Fair*... is likely to indicate close to the maximal length a performance could have that was not drawn out by inter-act music or dances... Hart believed that plays would have a more or less uniform length of between 2,300 and 2,400 lines, but we are likely to be closer to the truth if we assume that the lengths varied from less than 2,000 to about 2,800 lines' (2003: 147). Crucially, from the point of view of Erne's wider thesis, this still left fourteen Shakespeare texts, more than a third of them, that exceeded the 2,800 threshold. These constitute for Erne the primary evidence that Shakespeare wrote as much for readers as for what his fellow actors could mine from his raw material for their performances.

The pay-off for Michael J. Hirrel of performance times lasting up to four hours, even if some of that time might be given over to incidental entertainments like jigs or inter-act music, is that *all* of Shakespeare's plays could be performed without cuts, and even virtually all of Jonson's. He hypothesizes that, with a start-time at 2 p.m. and a finish around 5.45 p.m., there could be up to 'three hours and a quarter' for the play proper: 'A play performed in that time at the speed calculated by Hart would comprise about 3,900 lines. None of Shakespeare's plays is that long' (2010: 181). Steven Urkowitz happily steps into the breach which he believes Hirrel has opened up, brushing aside Hart, Orgel, Erne, and Gurr for 'glumly imagin[ing] that Shakespeare was part of a team that regularly debased and reduced the artistic value of the plays they staged in order to fit them within strict but never-articulated demands for brevity and simplicity' (2012: 257). On the contrary 'I believe that Shakespeare and his company participated in bold, risk-taking and expansive theatrical ventures... they wrote, revised and played more and more daring, more and more demanding, and, yes, more and more lengthy scripts that may perhaps have been copied and printed for private reading but primarily were played at full length (or approximately full length) for public, private, and courtly performances in London and on tour for crowds of attentive listeners and observers' (ibid).

The evidence, sadly, is all too elastic. Known starting times vary in the course of the period, or for localized reasons; ending times and so the supposed length of play performances (with or without other, incidental entertainments) are never verifiable. And this is before we even question the use of line lengths as the measure of a performance. Even if we agree on a common accounting—whether stage directions are included, for example—there are serious questions about comparability.

Comedies, especially if we are talking about Shakespeare, average lower line lengths than histories and tragedies. But might that not be because they include a higher proportion of (often unscripted) songs, dances, masques, and other diversions that would actually have used up a good deal of stage time? Conversely, we have to acknowledge that Jonson's comedies are among the longest texts of the entire era, so there is no general principle we can apply here.

Speed of performance is another notoriously imprecise measure. I have myself seen the former Shenandoah Shakespeare Express and its successor company at the American Shakespeare Center, who often perform at the speeds envisioned by Hart and Erne, and always enjoyed their shows—brisk, lucid, engaging. But whether they actually reflect conditions on the Elizabethan stage—and particularly the outdoor stages, communicating with audiences of up to 3,000—is another matter. Projecting in an amphitheatre like the Globe would surely slow things down, compared with an intimate indoor space like the Blackfriars at Staunton. Moreover, we know that the acting companies invested in fabulously expensive costumes for some of their shows. Consider *All Is True/Henry VIII* on the day that the Globe burned down, 'with many extraordinary circumstances of pomp and majesty, even to the matting of the stage; the Knights of the Order with their Georges and garters, the guards with their embroidered coats, and the like: sufficient in truth within a while to make greatness very familiar, if not ridiculous'.[14] It was a theatre of display, and often of ceremony, which would hardly have registered at 1,200 lines an hour. Moreover, how would the special talents of an Edward Alleyn or Richard Burbage (or Will Kemp or Robert Armin) have imprinted themselves on an audience at such a pace which, to modern appearances, is one of a workmanlike ensemble rather than a company looking to highlight its stars. There are reasons why the Royal Shakespeare Company proceeds at about 900 lines per hour, which are fundamentally to do with resonance and effect.

All our measures are imperfect and, as we have seen, capable of being combined in order to endorse a wide variety of conclusions. Bearing all that in mind, let me now try to insert myself into this debate. As I have already indicated, I do not find Hirrel's arguments for four-hour performance times—and so Urkowitz's visions of untrammelled experimentation—plausible. I do think it likely that constraints existed, but not as draconian as those envisaged by Hart, Orgel, Gurr, or even possibly Erne; nor do I think that those constraints necessarily operated in the ways they imagine.

I thus stick my colours to the mast in arguing that, after 1594, the usual time for performances was normally between 2 p.m. and at the outside 5 p.m. There is no evidence of regulation on this, but it would seem to have fulfilled the interests of all concerned and to square with all the, admittedly imperfect, evidence. This span might reasonably be designated as either two hours or three hours, with Hunsdon's business-like promise that his men would 'have done between four and five' splitting the difference between the two, as we may suppose was often what happened. This is, as it happens, in line with the overwhelming majority of commentary from

---

[14] Sir Henry Wotton to Sir Edmund Bacon; *ES* 2: 419.

the period, especially from the dramatists when they address the two or three hours' traffic of the stage that they have generated. Three hours would, however, have to incorporate ancillary entertainment such as jigs in the public playhouses or inter-act music in the private ones. So it is unlikely that a play, on its own, could run much longer than two hours and twenty minutes, which (at a playing speed of 1,200 lines per hour, however problematic that may be) would allow up to 2,800 lines, the very figure that Erne reaches as his own cut-off point. It is always worth bearing in mind that when the King's Men converted *The Malcontent* to perform at the Globe, the play contained 2,531 lines, a figure we might regard as normative (see p. 118).

This still leaves many plays, not least by Shakespeare, which could not conceivably be performed in that time. Does this mean that we must suppose—along with Hart, Orgel, Gurr, and Erne (not to mention the New Bibliographers)—that *somebody* cut down the texts of *Hamlet*, *Henry V*, *King Lear*, and the others for regular performance purposes? Hart, convinced that this is what necessarily must have happened, allowed himself flights of fancy about how Shakespeare would have reacted to it all:

> He had almost invariably filled from the copious overflowings of that mind more leaves of manuscript than were necessary for a two-hour play. He did not measure out his lines as a draper does yards of calico for a customer, and never troubled, probably did not know how, to exercise that economy of effort which experience taught Heywood, Dekker, Fletcher, Webster and even voluminous Jonson. He was, methinks, without the vanity of smaller men, and smiled philosophically while some friend butchered his verse to make a groundling's holiday. If his was the job of cutting down outside plays, he would play the Roman father to his own... he wrote as an artist what his partners turned into a play. (1944: 178–9)

We may smile ('methinks') at a certain faux-poetic tone here, but this in essence has become a standard account of how some of the shorter, quarto versions of certain plays came into being. We have already seen Andrew Gurr arguing the same point, less poetically, in respect of *Henry V*, and he reiterates it in his edition of the quarto text: 'the quarto text of *Henry V* offers the best evidence we have of what routinely happened to the scripts that the Shakespeare company bought from their resident playwright... the quarto [is] the prime case in point to test the view that the plays were radically altered between their first drafting and their first appearance on stage' (2000: ix). And this is in essence Lukas Erne's view (2003: 189–203).[15] What once was decried as a piratical mangling of Shakespeare's texts has become a normal and acceptable piece of theatrical business (Pollard 1909).

Yet none of these are *necessary* assumptions. One of the benefits of the more settled arrangements from 1594 onwards, at least for the Lord Chamberlain's and Lord Admiral's Men, is that they knew exactly how long a normal playing time would be and they could expect their playwrights (and not least their 'ordinary poet', if they had one) to produce plays that could be performed within those

---

[15] Steven Urkowitz is, of course, appalled at the idea (2012). But if Hirrel's arguments for four-hour performances are, as I suggest, unsustainable, he needs other grounds for rejecting the idea.

limits. Indeed, when we look at the pattern of Shakespeare's 'overlong' plays, it is one not driven so much by genre, as is commonly held, but by date. 'Overlong' plays are (with exceptions I shall address) a luxury of the second half of his career. Although we know nothing about how Shakespeare's early plays were able, apparently, to follow him to the Lord Chamberlain's Men, or how their texts may have changed over time, a review of everything written up to 1596 shows that it was almost all (on the textual evidence that survives) under 2,800 lines and so playable within the parameters we have been discussing:

> *The Two Gentlemen of Verona* (2,193 lines); *The Comedy of Errors* (1,753); *Love's Labour's Lost* (2,651, even after it had been 'augmented', according to the 1598 quarto); *A Midsummer Night's Dream* (2,102); *The Taming of the Shrew* (2,552); *King John* (2,570); *Richard II* (without the deposition scene, 2,589; with, 2,755); *1 Henry VI* (2,676); *The First Part of the Contention of the Two Famous Houses of York and Lancaster* (1,973); *The True Tragedy of Richard, Duke of York* (2,124); *Titus Andronicus* (2,437, without 3.2 which first appears in the First Folio; 2,522 with); *Romeo and Juliet* (1,597 Q1, 2,215).

When I include *The First Part of the Contention* and *The True Tragedy*, rather than *2* and *3 Henry VI*, and the first quarto of *Romeo and Juliet*, rather than the more familiar 1599 second quarto, I am simply recording the texts which we know existed by 1596/7. Had the later versions never been published, we should all assume that these were the plays as Shakespeare wrote them—possibly with collaborators, in the cases of *The First Part of the Contention* and *The True Tragedy*. And that is the assumption I am making here: we have no idea when *2* and *3 Henry VI* came into being in their First Folio form; we have no evidence that the second quarto version of *Romeo and Juliet* existed before 1599. My real point is that the publication record, imperfect as it is, shows us an early Shakespeare working within the performance parameters we have been discussing.[16]

The glaring exception to this rule is *Richard III*, which was published in 1597 in a quarto of 3,389 lines (the First Folio version has 3,570). I have no hesitation in supposing that this is a text revised from a lost shorter original, almost certainly for performance at court; on the evidence of eight editions before the Civil War, it was one of the most popular of all Shakespeare's plays, and was performed on Queen Henrietta Maria's birthday in the Revels season of 1633 (Bawcutt 1996: 184; see p. 137). At exactly the same time, other big texts begin to appear: *1 Henry IV* (c. 1596/7; 2,968 lines), *2 Henry IV* (c. 1597/8; between 2,898 and 3,140 lines in its two quarto versions), the second quarto of *Romeo and Juliet* (1599; 2,989 lines). It is important to remember, however, that indisputably *new* plays continued to be written at lengths which posed no problem to the normal playing times we have discussed: *The Merchant of Venice* (2,554), *Much Ado About Nothing* (2,535), *Julius Caesar* (2,450), *As You Like It* (2,608), and—as I would argue—the earliest and shortest versions of *Merry Wives*, *Henry V*, and *Hamlet*.

---

[16] I discuss in Chapter 4 James Marino's radical argument that some of these early works were not by Shakespeare at all, but only later assigned to him by the Chamberlain's Men as the company asserted its performance privileges (see p. 163).

COURT TIME

As I shall show in Chapter 4, the period when the bigger texts begin to appear (1597–1600) exactly coincides with the sequences in Henslowe's *Diary* which detail Admiral's Men's plays being revised 'for the court'. As I shall demonstrate, this is the one documented context in which plays were regularly 'corrected' and 'perfected', in a way that sometimes demonstrably left them longer than they had been—rather than 'butchered' (as Hart graphically has it), to a point where they were, beyond any reasonable doubt in the mathematics, capable of having been played on the public stages. This was when they were 'perused' by the Master of the Revels for possible adoption at court, with Edmund Tilney putting in over 100 days' attendance at court to get everything right. Since Shakespeare's company performed there far more often than any other during the span of his working lifetime, and since they put on his plays far more often than those of anyone else, *it must follow* that those plays were revised (and by revised we probably mean augmented) in this way more often than others in any repertory.

Why this would have been necessary is simple. If the circumstances of public playing tended to constrict the length of performances to not very much more than two hours, the demands of court were regularly for entertainment of three hours—and sometimes significantly more (Chambers 1930: 1:214–15).

The whole idea of 'revelling'—of enjoying oneself in warmth and candlelight while ordinary mortals took to their beds—was an extravagance for the privileged few and the longer it went on the better. (See the epigraph to Chapter 2.) Performances at court, at least in the Shakespearean period, invariably started after supper, the main evening meal, normally around 9 p.m. (already very late by most people's standards), and commonly lasted till 1 a.m., but sometimes later. This is not to say that *every* play at court dragged into the early hours of the following morning. But some of them certainly did, often padded out with other entertainments and invariably with food; the obligatory 'banquet' was not, however, the modern multi-course meal, but a light repast of rich and sophisticated food and drink—an inter-act diversion. Sometimes the late entertainment was to impress special guests, sometimes to mark those special days in the festive season we have talked about—the opening day of the season, St Stephen's Day, New Year's Day, Twelfth Night, Candlemas, Shrovetide. Sometimes (especially with James and Charles) it was a particular interest in the play that led to prolonged performances, though this is better documented in respect of university drama than it is of professional plays. In an era when domestic clocks were still a rarity, correspondents are often unobligingly vague about precise times, but the following instances (usually from diplomats, who strove to convey the grandeur of court affairs) will give a sense of how fully the night might be spent in revelry.

Early in Elizabeth's reign the Spanish Ambassador, Don Diego Guzman de Silva, was particularly assiduous in reporting court entertainments to his king, Philip II. In July 1564 the Queen was entertained by Sir Richard Sackville: ' "after supper…the Queen came out to the hall, which was lit with many torches where the comedy was represented. I should not have understood much of it, if the

Queen had not interpreted, as she told me she would do. They generally deal with a marriage in the comedies... The comedy ended, and then there was a mask of certain gentlemen who entered dressed in black and white, which the Queen told me were her colours, and after dancing a while one of them approached and handed the Queen a sonnet in English, praising her." A banquet followed, ending at 2 a.m.' (Chambers 1923: 1.161, quoting Hume 1892–99: 1.367, 385). De Silva also witnessed a revel after a foot-tourney or 'barriers' on Shrove Tuesday (6 March) 1565: 'a comedy in English of which I understood just as much as the Queen told me. The plot was founded on the question of marriage, discussed between Juno and Diana, Juno advocating marriage and Diana chastity. Jupiter gave a verdict in favour of matrimony, after many things had passed on both sides in defence of the respective arguments. The Queen turned to me and said, "This is all against me." After the comedy there was a masquerade of satyrs or wild gods, who danced with the ladies, and when this was finished there entered ten parties of 12 gentlemen each, the same who fought in the foot tourney, and these, all armed as they were, danced with the ladies; a very novel ball' (Chambers 1923: 1.161, quoting Hume 1892–99: 1.404). This whole event was hosted by the Earl of Leicester, and the specially written play was performed by the gentlemen of Gray's Inn. We have no precise timing, but it was evidently a very full evening.

Thomas Birch expressly informs us that the very last court performance of the Queen's Men (6 January 1594) was part of entertainment that lasted until 1 a.m.: 'Mr [Anthony] Standen was at the play and dancing at twelfth-night, which lasted till one after midnight...' (Chambers 1923: 4.108, n. 14, quoting Birch 1754: 1: 146). Likewise, the French ambassador, Antoine de La Broderie, describes an entertainment of Queen Anna by the Earl of Arundel on 25 May 1607 which included a play of *Aeneas and Dido* and went on until 'two hours after midnight' (Chambers 1923: 4.122, n. 2, quoting de La Broderie 1750: 2. 247, 264). We know that a play by Prince Henry's Men on 7 January 1610 did not start until 10 p.m., following a supper hosted by the Prince, but unfortunately we do not know when it ended (Chambers 1923: 4.124, n. 2).

The most detailed account we have of a Shakespearean performance at court relates to events at Whitehall in May 1619 to mark the departure of the French Ambassador, La Trémoille, which were hosted by the King's cousin, the Duke of Lennox. The King's Men performed *Pericles* for the event:

> The Marquise Trenell on Thursday last took leave of the King: that night was feasted at White Hall, by the Duke of Lennox in the Queen's great chamber... In the King's great Chamber they went to see the play of Pericles, Prince of Tyre, which lasted till 2 o'clock. After two acts, the players ceased till the French all refreshed them with sweetmeats brought on chiney voiders, & wine & ale in bottles, after the players began anew.[17]

---

[17] Sir Gerrard Herbert, writing to Sir Dudley Carleton, quoted in Chambers 1930: 2.346. I am grateful to John Astington for drawing this account to my attention. Voiders were baskets or trays for serving or removing food; 'chiney' presumably means these were of (expensive) china, perhaps platters.

Limited as it is, this is the most precisely timed and detailed description of a court play (as distinct from masque) that we have. Assuming they had supper at the usual time, the performance began before 10 p.m. and certainly finished at 2 a.m. It was interrupted for what seems to have been a relatively modest banquet after the second act, but we have no way of knowing how much time that took.[18] Of course, the fact that plays at court took breaks for refreshments (like modern intermissions), not to mention that they had seating for the majority of those present, must have made the performance of ultra-long plays like *Hamlet* or *Bartholomew Fair* far more acceptable from an audience's point of view.[19]

Other forms of entertainment also absorbed the court into the early hours. E. K. Chambers characterizes court masques as spanning 'a considerable number of hours', most particularly because of the dancing involved (1923: 1.195). 'The mask, beginning after supper, was prolonged far into the night. That at Sir Philip Herbert's wedding lasted three hours; *Tethys' Festival* was not over until hard upon sunrise' (1.206). Sir Ralph Winwood described its ending: 'By that time these had done, it was high time to go to bed, for it was within half an hour of the sun's, not setting, but rising. Howbeit, a farther time was to be spent in viewing and scrambling at one of the most magnificent banquets that I have seen' (1725: 3: 179). *Tethys' Festival* was unusual in that it was given during the summer (5 June 1610), as part of the festivities for the creation of Prince Henry as Prince of Wales. So dawn would have been as early as 4.45 a.m. Even so, it was a long night, which broke up with the usual unseemly rush for the banquet at the end.

And clearly such long nights could take their toll, as happened when three masques were planned on successive nights for the wedding celebrations of Princess Elizabeth and the Elector Palatine in 1613. On the third night, when the gentlemen of Gray's Inn and the Inner Temple, under the direction of Francis Bacon, were to perform Beaumont's *Marriage of Thames and Rhine*, the king put his foot down. '[B]ut the worst of it was that the King was so wearied and sleepy with sitting up almost two whole nights before, that he had no edge to it. Whereupon, Sir Francis Bacon adventured to entreat of his Majesty that by this difference he would not, as it were, bury them quick; and I hear the King should answer, that then they must bury him quick, for he could last no longer, but withal gave them very good words, and appointed them to come again on Saturday' (Chamberlain 1939: 1.426).

That may have been extreme, but we know that leading courtiers tried to reproduce such revelry in their own houses. In January 1598 Sir Robert Sidney's correspondent, Rowland Whyte, reported that 'My Lord Compton, my Lord Cobham, Sir Walter Ralegh, my Lord Southampton, do severally feast Mr Secretary [Sir Robert Cecil] before he departs [on a diplomatic mission to France], and have plays and

---

[18] This was the occasion when the Earl of Pembroke, the Lord Chamberlain, excused his absence from the play so soon after the death of Richard Burbage: 'which I being tender-hearted could not endure to see so soon after the loss of my old acquaintance Burbage' (cited in Chambers 1923: 2.308). Nothing better demonstrates how close the actors, and most notably the King's Men who performed there most often, must have come to the grandees of the court.
[19] On seating at court, see Astington 1999: 84, 117, 172–3.

banquets'; the following month the rival political camp at Essex House did likewise: 'Sir Gelly Meyrick made at Essex House yesternight a very great supper. There were at it, my Ladies Leicester, Northumberland, Bedford, Essex, Rich; and my Lords of Essex, Rutland, Montjoy, and others. They had 2 plays, which kept them up till 1 a clock after midnight' (Collins 1746: 2.86, 90).

The most striking evidence we have of extremely long performances, however, relates to academic theatricals at which royalty were present. In each case we must assume that the Master of the Revels vetted the material before it was presented, though Oxford and Cambridge scholars might be presumed to understand what was acceptable. So when Elizabeth visited Cambridge in August 1564 she sat through a three-hour performance of Plautus' *Aulularia* in the chapel of King's College, Cambridge. This was in the original Latin, which made it wearisome to courtiers who were not used to spoken Latin, but Elizabeth herself sat through it with no sign of fatigue (Chambers 1923: 1.127). On subsequent nights she saw *Dido*, a Latin tragedy, and *Ezechias*, an English comedy by Nicholas Udall. All of these shows started at 9 p.m. But on the fourth night she drew the line at hearing a Latin translation of Sophocles' *Ajax Flagellifer*. As with James and the masques for Princess Elizabeth's wedding, there were limits to how many nights of entertainment were actually bearable (Boas 1914: 93–7; Nelson 1989: 230–6).

But James could also register intense enthusiasm when presented with something he really enjoyed. One can only imagine that George Buc anticipated something of this when he sanctioned a performance of George Ruggles' Latin comedy, *Ignoramus*, on a visit to Cambridge in March 1615. Plays were staged over four nights in the hall of Trinity College, which was so arranged that '2000 persons were conveniently placed' (Chamberlain 1939: 1.587). 'The second night was a comedy of Clare Hall with the help of two or three good actors from other houses, wherein David Drummond in a hobby horse, and Brakin, the recorder of the town under the name of Ignoramus, a common lawyer, bare great parts: the thing was full of mirth and variety, with many excellent actors...but more than half marred with extreme length.'

The extant play would take some five hours to perform—and certainly did so when it was performed a second time. John Chamberlain, the assiduous purveyor of news, may have felt that it was 'half marred with extreme length' but it is apparent that James did not. Alvin Kernan offers an explanation for why not:

> Ignoramus was intended as a caricature of the Cambridge town recorder, but the audience immediately identified the stage character as Sir Edward Coke...as Lord Chief Justice of the King's Bench, he was engaged in a bitter struggle with his monarch. James roared with laughter, clapped frequently, and called out 'Plaudite' as Ignoramus-Coke, spouting pig Latin and legalese, strutted the stage, attacked bishops and laymen, and courted a young girl with bawdy macaronic verses: '*Et dabo* fee simple, *si monstras* love's pretty dimple.'

James could not stop laughing, and he tried to have the play brought to London. When that proved impossible, he returned to the university two months later...to see *Ignoramus* again. The play was put on for him a second time, according to James Tabor, registrar of the university: 'About 8 of the clock the play began and ended about one: his majesty was much delighted with the play, and laughed exceedingly; and oftentimes with his hands and by words applauded it'.[20]

It seems unlikely that the Cambridge authorities would have risked the wrath of a weary James—who did not hesitate to let performers know when he was unhappy—if they did not have some prior assurance that the king might sit out five hours of a play. His visit to Oxford in August 1605 could not have offered them a good precedent, since at a performance of a Latin *Ajax Flagellifer* in Christ Church Hall, 'The King was very weary before he came thither, but much more wearied by it, and spoke many words of dislike'.[21] The next night was no better: 'That night, after supper, about nine, began their Comedy call *Vertumnus*, very well and learnedly penned by Dr Gwynn...yet the King was so over-wearied at St. Mary's, that after a while he distasted it, and fell asleep; when he awaked, he would have been gone, saying, "I marvel what they think me to be," with such other like speeches showing his dislike thereof, yet he did tarry till they ended it, which was after one of the clock' (Nichols 1828: 1.550, 552). The Cambridge people had perhaps done their homework in the intervening years to ensure that they did not make the same mistakes. Part of that must surely have involved finding out what worked at court, where the Master of the Revels' first responsibility was to minimize such outbursts.

The most astounding incidence of academic theatre offered to a monarch falls outside of our period, but is worth mentioning as an example of the extremes *theoretically* possible. Charles I and Queen Henrietta Maria visited Cambridge in March 1632. The University staged for them a performance of Dr Peter Hausted's *The Rival Friends*, a seven-hour-long play filled with anti-Puritan and anti-sectarian satire, which was presumably expected to chime with the King's known Laudian views. The University authorities banned tobacco and warned the students in advance to refrain from 'any rude or immodest exclamations...nor any humming, hawking, whistling, hissing, or laughing...or any stamping or knocking, nor any such uncivil or unscholarlike or boyish behavior', or even applauding until the end, unless their betters did so first (Gurr 2004b: 54). For all their precautions, the performance was a disaster, a near riot in the presence of the King and Queen. The vice-chancellor, Henry Butts, felt the shame so personally that he committed suicide on Easter Sunday. Perhaps the authorities had been advised that Charles would be prepared to sit through seven hours of anti-Puritan satire, suitably interspersed with breaks and refreshments. But they should have known better than to subject their students to seven hours of anything, king or no king.

There is no evidence that any court play (as distinct from masque) ever lasted five hours, much less seven. But these academic plays give us some idea of the relaxed and expansive conditions under which theatre might be enjoyed in privileged contexts, outside the usual constraints of professional playing. And they help

---

[20] Kernan 1995: 191–2. His account of the identification of Ignoramus with Sir Edward Coke owes something to Bowen 1956. The Tabor quotation is from Mullinger 1873: II 544.
[21] It is not recorded if this was the same play that Elizabeth declined to see on her visit to Cambridge. But it presumably derived from the same source, Sophocles.

to explain how it might be that, on some occasions, the court might look for something richer and fuller to consume a winter's night than the customers of the Globe and the Fortune could expect. Sometimes they got two plays on one night, or three plays in one, or a show of acrobats or jugglers in addition to a play. Sometimes what they got—as we shall see—was something akin to Dekker's revised and expanded *Old Fortunatus* (with new properties or costumes) rather than the one the people of London had grown used to.

I stress again that I do not suppose for a minute that this happened to every play performed at court. But I think we may take some measure of it from the plays which we know were chosen to *open* Revels seasons—a detail which, like so many others, we have only very sketchily. Within Shakespeare's working lifetime, the earliest extant play which we know opened a season is *Othello* (1 November 1604); then *King Lear* (26 December 1606); and finally *Bartholomew Fair* (1 November 1614)—all three among the longest plays of the era, at respectively 3,222 (folio), 3,092 (quarto), and 4,344 (prose) lines.[22] In the 1630s we also know of *Richard III* (16 November 1633), 3,389 (quarto) or 3,570 (folio) lines; and *Catiline* (9 November 1634), 3,405 lines.[23]

JONSON

Bartholomew Fair is the longest of all plays in the era written by a professional playwright, and it repays particularly close attention. The discrepancies between the *Induction*'s account of the play's playing time and the actualities of the surviving printed text can only be accounted for by supposing that there were at least two distinct versions of the play. Lukas Erne observes: 'the "Articles of Agreement"... promise a playing time of "two houres and a halfe, and somewhat more"... Even by Jonsonian standards, *Bartholomew Fair*, at 4344 prose lines is very long... Performed at... the average speed of the Royal Shakespeare Company, the unabridged play would take more than five hours to perform. At the higher speed at which Elizabethan players may well have delivered their lines, a performance of the full text would have taken close to four hours. Jonson's precise indication thus suggests that when *Bartholomew Fair* was acted, performances were some seventy to eighty minutes shorter than they would have been if the play had been performed in its entirety' (Erne 2003: 143–4, citing Hart 1934: 103, and Klein 1967).

---

[22] *The Tempest* is the earliest-named of plays in the 1611/12 season, being staged on 1 November, All Saints. It is certainly *not* an overlong play as we have it (at 2,015 lines) and must have been chosen to show off the company's new repertory from the Blackfriars. But the King's Men anomalously performed an unnamed play on 31 October, so *The Tempest* did not lead off the season.

[23] The Shakespeare plays all reflect the argument of this book about plays being expanded (if not originally written) for festive holidays at court; I discuss the special case of Jonson shortly. The exceptions to this rule of thumb about seasons kicking off with long plays are a number which commenced with plays by Fletcher, all written for indoor theatres, usually the Blackfriars. The versions which have survived all reflect the smaller length of plays written for such venues: *The Maid in the Mill* (1 November 1623); *Rule a Wife and Have a Wife* (2 November 1624); *The Coxcomb* (17 November 1636); and *The Mad Lover* (5 November 1630), which are all in the range of 2,150 to 2,500 lines. Clearly a different aesthetic applied.

But Erne, who is concerned to argue that the longer texts of Jonson and Shakespeare were written with a *reading* audience in mind, ignores the unique production circumstances of *Bartholomew Fair*. We know of only two Jacobean performances: on 31 October 1614 at the Hope theatre, for which the *Induction* was expressly written; and the following day at court, for which a separate prologue was provided, directly addressed to King James.

The *Induction* is, of course, teasing in its ultra-precision about the timing of the performance, but this is all part of the mock-legalese of the supposed 'contract' between the author and the audience. It is most unlikely that anyone at the Hope had a timepiece with which to measure his veracity. But any audience would have noticed the difference between 'two hours and a half, and somewhat more' (which is, I have argued, about the *normal* length of commercial plays in the period) and a performance of four to five hours (*Induction* 59–60; Jonson 2012c). I infer, therefore, that there were in fact two versions of the play, one which approximately measured up to the promises of the *Induction*, the other the printed version that has survived. And I presume that the printed version is that which was presented at court, with its prologue to the king, on All Hallows Night, the usual start of the Jacobean Revels season. It would, of course, have made extraordinary demands on the actors, with more opportunities for confusion.

Yet the schedule of revisions which, in the next chapter, we shall observe Dekker making to *Phaeton* and *Old Fortunatus* for the court, must have placed similar burdens upon the actors in terms of last-minute learning of new lines, cues, business, running sequence, etc. for plays with which they were already familiar. Given the phenomenal number of roles these actors had to carry in their head at any one time in order to handle an ever-changing repertory, the challenge of a play in two versions may not have seemed so great. Moreover, this court performance of *Bartholomew Fair* was a unique opportunity for Jonson's protégé, Nathan Field, and his company, Lady Elizabeth's Men.[24] They were displacing the King's Men from the opening slot of the Revels season, and they were doing so in a vehicle specially written for them by a man who was all but formally Poet Laureate. It was worth the effort.

Jonson, then, apparently produced both versions of *Bartholomew Fair* at the same time, anticipating a special court performance from the outset: this could only have come about at the instigation, or at least the prior approval, of Sir George Buc, as Master of the Revels. The true dress rehearsal for the court performance would not have been the event at the Hope (which doubled as a bear-baiting arena) but the run-through at Buc's Revels Office quarters, which were by then located in the Blackfriars district. It would have been under his watchful eye that the parallels between Justice Overdo and King James remained on the right side of respectful jocularity. Overdo's pose as a Ciceronian magistrate, lurking in dark corners to expose enormities, and his denunciation of tobacco in particular—'who can tell if, before the gathering and making up thereof, the alligator hath not pissed

---

[24] 'Nat Field was his scholar, and he had read to him the satires of Horace, and some epigrams of Martial' (*Informations* lines 121–2, Jonson 2012j).

thereon?' (2.6.21–2)—steer sufficiently close to James's public pronouncements on the nature of his own kingship and to his *A Counterblast to Tobacco* (1604) that the point could hardly be missed (McPherson 1976). This goes well beyond the gestures towards Albany and Cornwall in *King Lear* and to Lennox and Aubigny in *The Devil's Charter* (see p. 64). But Jonson by this point had almost a decade's experience of entertaining the king in his masques and he knew exactly how to play to his tastes.

The issue of the length of Jonson's plays is one that we cannot ignore. The figures are so remarkably out of line with those of any other dramatist in the era that when Alfred Hart did the first serious studies of line lengths he consistently left them out of his averages, on the grounds that he could not be comparing like with like. One set of his computations, relating to the period 1594–1616, demonstrates the scale of the discrepancy: 'Thirty-three known authors contributed 179 plays in all. Jonson wrote eleven of these, averaging 3580 lines a play, Shakespeare thirty-two, averaging 2744 lines. The remaining thirty-one dramatists provided 136 plays that average 2430 lines' (1934: 88).

But no one is ever really surprised that Jonson wrote plays at such length, because it is widely taken for granted that he was writing for readers at least as much as for audiences, and probably more so. Lukas Erne is typical in this:

> We have no problems understanding why Jonson's plays are inconveniently long from the point of view of the stage. Considering himself an author rather than a provider for the stage, he held the players in low esteem and, at times, explicitly wrote for a readership rather than for a theatre audience. The title-page of *Every Man Out of His Humour* (Q1, 1600) famously points out that the text contains 'more than hath been Publicly Spoken or Acted'. (2003: 140)

But what does this phrase actually mean? It is often coupled with the declaration on the title page of Webster's *Duchess of Malfi* (1623) that it contains 'The perfect and exact copy, with diverse things printed, that the length of the play would not bear in the presentment'. But that is not actually what Jonson's text declares. What he denies is that the *whole* of his text has been performed *in public*. As Randall Martin puts it: 'The phrase implies that the staged version of the play at the Globe Theatre in 1599 was shorter and different from the one printed here' (Jonson 2012i: 1.250, n. 7). Jonson could simply be drawing attention to the extensive para textual material in the edition. But he might equally be implying a situation identical to that of *Bartholomew Fair*, in which there was a text for the public theatres and another one (this one) for the most exclusive of theatres, *for the court*. He could, in effect, be making the same claim as that which appears in some copies of the 1609 *Troilus and Cressida* (see p. 285). Of course Jonson had his eye on readers. But before that he had his eye on court patronage.

Jonson's career was focused on the court far more exclusively than Shakespeare's. After the early associations with the Lord Admiral's Men reflected in Henslowe's *Diary*, he distanced himself as far as a working dramatist could from the acting companies. He placed his plays with several different companies but always (after the Henslowe years) with an apparent eye on the likelihood of court performance.

In *Satiromastix* (pub. 1602) Dekker aimed a strangely prescient blow at the Jonson who had recently written *Cynthia's Revels* and *Poetaster* for the Children of the Chapel Royal at the Blackfriars. He accuses 'Horace' (a thinly veiled Jonson) of aiming to 'beget...the reversion of the Master of the King's Revels' (4.1.189–90: cited from Dekker 1953–61b, Dutton 1993). In fact Jonson did indeed acquire such a reversion twenty years later, in 1621; he would have become Master of the Revels if he had outlived two men who held prior rights, Buc (already in office) and Sir John Astley (see Chapter 2, note 17). The striking thing is that Dekker should have known so early where Jonson's ambitions lay, some years before the Jacobean court masques—at a time when he was still labouring as a common playwright for the Chamberlain's and Admiral's Men, as well as the Blackfriars boys, in order to make a living.[25]

With uniquely focused ambition, Jonson pursued the route that had almost secured the reversion for John Lyly, providing superior entertainment which was clearly slanted towards court tastes (see p. 55). Where for a time Lyly also acquired strong patronage from the Earl of Oxford, Jonson was to attach himself in mid-career to the Earl of Pembroke (see p. 94 and n. 32). The court masques which Jonson wrote almost yearly from *The Masque of Blackness* (1605) were the most conspicuous contributions to this bid for royal patronage. But I suggest that the plays—the ones he *chose* to publish, with conspicuous flaunting of his own authorship, learning, and ability—also played their part. We *know* that by the time he published his *Works* in 1616 at least *Every Man In His Humour*, *Every Man Out of His Humour* (twice), *Cynthia's Revels* (probably), *The Alchemist*, and *Bartholomew Fair* had been performed at court. There are also good circumstantial reasons for supposing that *Sejanus* and *Volpone* had early court performances.[26] Before the closing of the theatres in 1642 *Volpone* (at least three times), *Epicene* (at least twice), *Catiline*, *The Staple of News*, and *A Tale of a Tub* had certainly joined them.

Dekker observed Jonson's aspiration in the three plays that are the focus of his mockery in *Satiromastix*, the 'comical satires' (Jonson's own term), *Every Man Out of His Humour*, *Cynthia's Revels*, and *Poetaster*. Each of these is to varying degrees about courts, courtiers, and their hangers on, offering mordantly amusing reflections on the vanity, hypocrisy, and hollowness to be found there. In each, however, Jonson has a figure of right-reason, ultimately a poet-counsellor of the monarch, who is able to see through the folly and vice and rectify it: Asper/Maciliente, Criticus, and Horace. Naturally Dekker saw these as grandiose wish-fulfilment

---

[25] 'Playwright' was apparently Jonson's own derisive coinage, on the model of cartwright or wheelwright, for dramatists who wrote as a form of manual labour. He always referred to himself as a 'poet'.

[26] Jonson's claim in the folio text that *Sejanus* was performed by the King's Men in 1603 is difficult to square with our understanding that the public theatres were closed by plague for a year after Elizabeth's death—unless that performance was at court. See also p. 187 on the possibility that choruses running throughout a play were marks of work intended for court. *Volpone* deals with demonic possession, making it a natural companion-piece to *King Lear* and *The Devil's Charter* in the Revels season of 1606/7, the first year it would have been available. There must also be a very good chance that *Epicene* was one of the five plays offered by the newly formed Children of the Whitefriars in the 1609/10 season, unless Lady Arbella Stuart's protests succeeded in having it suppressed. According to the Venetian ambassador the play was 'suppressed' and the king's cousin was looking to the forthcoming Parliament to punish those involved (Jonson 2008: 72–3).

self-projections on Jonson's part, and in *Satiromastix* mocks Horace/Jonson for it. He suggests that Jonson's satire had not gone down well at the court itself 'because thy sputtering chaps yelp that arrogance and impudence and ignorance are the essential parts of a courtier' (5.3188–90). Horace/Jonson is made to swear that 'when your plays are mis-liked at court, you shall not cry mew like a pussy-cat, and say you write out of the courtier's element' (324–6). This and other gibes must have borne some resemblance to the truth to have had any chance of being funny.

We learn from the 1616 folio text of *Every Man Out* that the play was performed at court, before Queen Elizabeth.[27] Its satire is only partly aimed at the court, mainly in the figure of the courtier Fastidious Brisk. But the ending—at least the *planned* ending—makes its courtly ambition clear enough. In a postscript to the 1600 quarto text, Jonson explains that he originally intended a boy actor to appear, costumed as Queen Elizabeth—the sight of which stripped Macilente of his envy. This had been blocked by unnamed persons who objected to the impersonation. Instead Macilente is scripted simply to lose his motivating envy when he runs out of creatures to be jealous of. But in the folio text we discover that he provided yet another ending 'Which in the presentation before Queen Elizabeth was thus varied by Macilente', such that sight of the *actual* Queen cured him (Jonson 2012i: 426). That twist must have given Jonson particular satisfaction, even if we accept Dekker's testimony that the play was not well received at court.

There is also a good chance that Dekker particularly had *The Fountain of Self-Love, or Cynthia's Revels* in mind when he claimed that 'your plays are mis-liked at court', though there is no specific record of its performance there (Jonson 2012d: 431). It was Jonson's first for the Blackfriars boys, and *Satiromastix* was joint-commissioned by the Chamberlain's Men and the other boys group, the Children of Paul's, in response to his work for them. Cynthia is a very thinly disguised Elizabeth, in the mode of Lyly's mythologized court drama (though the satirical tone of the play is very different), and the whole work reads like a riposte to those who objected to the original ending of *Every Man Out*. It was certainly designed with the court in mind. As David Riggs puts it, 'Jonson did not merely, or even primarily, write the play for the Blackfriars clientele; he was also offering the Queen his services as a maker of court entertainments' (1989: 70).

In the spirit of that aspiration, *Cynthia's Revels* contains what E. K. Chambers describes as a 'full-blown Court mask' (Chambers 1923: 3.364). This was Jonson setting out his wares, and it must have been especially galling (though it should not have been surprising) if the court, the supposed 'Special Fountain of Manners', had

---

[27] *Every Man Out of His Humour* was the first play that Jonson had published, a measure of its significance to him. There is no other testimony of its performance before Elizabeth, though there was certainly one before King James on 8 January 1605—when again the text must have been changed in some untraceable way, since a representation of the late Queen would certainly not have been appropriate. But any version of the play that vindicated Jonson's 'comical satire' with an image or actuality of royalty would have suited his purpose. There is no evidence that *Poetaster* was ever performed at court, but that is not to say that it was not; the Children of the Chapel performed three unknown plays early in 1602. Set in Augustan Rome, *Poetaster* is Jonson's most elaborate exploration of poetic virtue and courtly politics.

really responded more like the 'Fountain of Self-Love' which he had satirically accused it of being. The play is also textually interesting. Here we have a close approximation to the situation we have with Shakespeare, where a play might appear first in shorter version and later in a longer, possibly more authoritative version. In this case, however, it is clear that Jonson was personally responsible for both the shorter 1601 quarto and the longer 1616 folio texts, and neither could be described in any sense as 'bad'.

The differences lie not in the quality of the imprint but in what Jonson chose to include. Chambers summarizes: '*Criticus* is renamed *Crites*, and the latter half of the play is given in longer form, parts of iv.i and iv.iii, and the whole of v.i–iv appearing in F1 alone' (3.363). These involve the addition of a new subplot and hundreds of minor changes, adding around 1,000 new lines to the 2,640 of the quarto. Chambers follows the explanation traditionally applied to Shakespeare's multi-text plays: 'I think the explanation is to be found in a shortening of the original text for representation, rather than subsequent additions' (ibid). He assumes that an overlong original was trimmed for performance purposes. The play's latest editors, Eric Rasmussen and Matthew Steggle, disagree, concurring with Ralph W. Berringer's arguments in the context of the 'War of the Theatres' (1943): 'This edition agrees with Berringer in supposing that the F1-only sections should be treated as later additions, a basis for this view being the inconsistencies that they introduce into a previously more coherent text' (Jonson 2012e: 3).

The quarto text is expressly printed '*As it hath been sundry times privately acted in the Blackfriars by the Children of Her Majesty's Chapel*'. It was at the extreme limits of performance possible there—on the arguments I adduced earlier in this chapter—if there was (as we must suppose) accompanying music. There is every possibility that the folio text—which is specifically dedicated to the court—is a version that was *augmented* for performance before the Queen. If so, it would have been when the Blackfriars boys were at court on 22 February 1601. It would have required a major additional investment of time and effort on Jonson's part, and that of the company, but given the stakes—the court patronage he was seeking and that which the company was seeking to recover—that would have been worth it; it seems a more credible motivation than expanding the text for purely literary reasons in the 1616 *Works*.

As with *Bartholomew Fair*, *Cynthia's Revels* very possibly shows us a Jonson who was prepared to produce two versions of a play simultaneously, or at least in very short order, one lasting the space of 'two hours and a half and somewhat more' and another lasting considerably longer in the only plausible venue—at court. The title page of *Every Man Out*, as we have seen, hints at the same possibility. In the cases of both *Cynthia's Revels* and *Bartholomew Fair*, at least, we must suppose the early and active involvement of the Master of the Revels. The former would only have been worthwhile if Jonson and the Children of the Chapel (the Blackfriars boys) had Tilney's prior assurance that the play would in fact be presented at court. The latter must also have had Buc's blessing from an early date. In both these instances it may well have been a factor that the companies would have had a particular interest in making their mark at court—the Children of the Chapel looking to regain their old popularity with Elizabeth, the Lady Elizabeth's Men trying to assert itself in an unusually crowded market, dominated by the King's Men, but also containing the Queen's, Palsgrave's, and Prince Charles's Men.[28]

This is a different model of (re)writing for the court than I shall be concentrating on in the next chapter, where the likes of Dekker and Chettle reworked plays—by themselves or others—that were months or even a few years old, and which (I argue) Shakespeare followed, at least in the cases of *Romeo and Juliet*, *Henry V*, *Merry Wives*, *2* and *3 Henry VI*, and *Hamlet*. But the model I propose for Jonson would make sense firstly in the context of the Blackfriars boys, who did not at that time have a back-catalogue of plays, and secondly in the context of Jonson's unique ambitions. It may also have set a model for Shakespeare's later career (see pp. 279ff).

As the need for quality drama at court expanded in the Jacobean period, especially in relation to the key festive dates, a model in which plays by the most successful dramatists could be nurtured from an early date for the court would have been advantageous all round. *Othello* and *King Lear* might well fit that mould. In Jonson's case *Epicene*, set in the West End near Whitehall, seems to have been commissioned by the newly constituted Children of the Whitefriars (another troupe of which Nathan Field was a leader) as a major draw for their new theatre; similarly, *The Alchemist*, set explicitly in the Blackfriars, seems to have been an early commission by the King's Men after they were able to use the Blackfriars theatre. Both were surely conceived of also as fare for the court, and recognized as such by Tilney and then Buc.[29]

Jonson certainly achieved his goal of becoming the court's resident showmaker. And, when he came to celebrate the fact in his 1616 *Works*, the magnificent sequence of nine plays that he chose to reproduce there stand alongside other items specifically commissioned by and for royalty. It has long been understood that the folio volume is not a *collected* works, but a highly *selective* sampling (Kay 1995: 70–1). Jonson wrote plays for the Admiral's Men at the same time as he was writing the *Every Man* plays for the Chamberlain's Men, but none of them ever saw print. These included *Robert II of Scotland* (*The Scots Tragedy*), *Hot Anger Soon Cold*, *Page of Plymouth*, and *Richard Crookback*, besides such piecework as adding new scenes to *The Spanish Tragedy* (Foakes 2002: 100, 123, 124, 203). The usual assumption has been that Jonson regarded these as hack-work, much of it co-written, and not worthy of commemoration in print.[30] Conversely, the plays performed by the Chamberlain's Men and the boy companies, all single-authored pieces (once he had replaced the parts of *Sejanus* originally written by 'a second

---

[28] In this the Lady Elizabeth's Men failed. They merged temporarily with Prince Charles's Men, and their leading player, Nathan Field, defected to the King's Men.

[29] Re *Epicene*, see note 26. *The Alchemist* was certainly given at court in 1612/13, but might well have appeared earlier.

[30] Other known collaborative texts include *The Isle of Dogs*, co-written with Thomas Nashe for Pembroke's Men, which has not survived; *Sejanus*, for which Jonson rewrote a collaborator's parts before he published it in quarto (1605); and *Eastward Ho!*, co-written with Chapman and Marston for the Blackfriars boys, and published in 1605 without Jonson's apparent involvement.

pen'), were thought to represent his real literary skill. Jonson's publication of select plays in quarto, and then again in his *Works* of 1616, was thus a careful process of literary self-fashioning. I am arguing that it may have been even more selective than has been appreciated.

In his selection of occasional pieces to be printed (either around the time of their commission or later in the *Works*)—everything from masques and shows to brief entertainments—Jonson deliberately excluded items which did not have predominantly royal associations. He particularly ignored items that had civic or guild links. For example, he never printed the Lord Mayor's Show for 1604, for which he was commissioned by the Haberdashers' Company.[31] Nor did he ever print the opulent entertainment at the Merchant Taylors' Company in 1607 or the 'Entertainment at Britain's Burse', written for the opening of the Earl of Salisbury's New Exchange in 1609. On the other hand, he did print all his court masques to date, as well as such items as his contribution to James's formal entry into London in 1604 and several slight pieces for the entertainment of the royal family. It is highly likely that his choice of plays for print was dictated by similar considerations. Certainly the dedications which he attached to them in the 1616 volume collectively bind them to the court: two were dedicated to members of the royal family (*Sejanus*, Lord D'Aubigny; *Epicene*, Sir Francis Stewart), one to the court itself (*Cynthia's Revels*), and one to its Lord Chamberlain (*Catiline*, the Earl of Pembroke).[32] Three of the plays, *Sejanus*, *Volpone*, and *The Alchemist*, contain 'arguments' which, as Tiffany Stern has shown, were not merely literary affectations, but kinds of authorial self-presentations of the work, which might be distributed by the author at first performances—or at court (2009a: 63–80).

How much of this is a retrospective invention it would be difficult to say. As I have indicated, it is not at all clear how many of the earlier plays (of those he chose to preserve) actually appeared at court, at least when they were new. No titlepage ever claims that they did. *Every Man In His Humour* is a prime example. It stands at the very head of the *Works*, the first work we meet. But there is no evidence that it went to court when it was new in 1598; if it did it was a completely different play from the one that appears in the *Works*. Compared with its 1601 quarto, the setting of the folio text has moved from Italy to London and the names of characters have been anglicized. The quality of the play has been improved at every level—language, psychology, dramatic pacing; a somewhat naïve emphasis on poetry as a humanistic redemptive force has been toned down, and the ending

---

[31] This despite his own membership of the Tylers and Bricklayers' Company (lasting till at least 1611), which gave him certain privileges as a citizen of London, but of which he was never publicly proud. See Kay 1995: 15 and n. 9; on the Lord Mayor's Show, see Kay: 65. For 'The Entertainment at Britain's Burse', see Jonson 2012f.

[32] As Martin Butler has pointed out, the volume celebrates not only Jonson's general association with the court, but specifically with the Pembroke/Herbert/Sidney faction which was in the ascendancy at the time of its publication. This helps explain the dedication of *The Alchemist* to Lady Mary Wroth (née Sidney), the Earl of Pembroke's cousin: see Butler 1993. On the little-known Francis Stewart, see Butler 1995.

has been completely rewritten (Dutton 1974).[33] We do not know when the rewriting took place, but there are two major schools of thought.

One is that it was revised for the only *known* court performance, on 2 February (Candlemas) 1605. This was the Revels season of Jonson's first great triumph as a masque-writer, *The Masque of Blackness*, performed on Twelfth Night. The King's Men, as by now they were, underscored his success by reviving both of the *Every Man* plays (*Every Man Out* was given on 8 January): in terms of the written record, this is where Jonson's rise to be Poet Laureate and lay claim to be Master of the Revels began. E. K. Chambers held that the court performance 'would be the natural time for a revision, and in fact seems to me on the whole the most likely date' (1923: 3.360). The other argument, represented by some who have studied the print history of the *Works*, holds that the play was revised specifically for its prominent position in that volume, where its Prologue (itself a new item) stands as a preface to the whole volume (see Riddell 1997; Gants 1999). When William Stansby started printing the *Works* he left space for it and completed other items first, suggesting that he was waiting for Jonson to supply the copy.

It is, of course, always possible that the revision took place in more than one stage. David Bevington, the latest scholar to edit both versions, is relatively agnostic about the cause and timing of the revision, finding none of the evidence conclusive. But he finally tilts towards revision for the known court performance: 'On balance, there appears to be no compelling reason to place all of the folio revisions as late as 1610–12, even if some revising work does indeed seem to have continued into the printing process... At all events, the invitation to present the play at court in 1605 might well have provided an apt incentive for Jonson to rework his earlier play, even if internal evidence cannot conclusively support this date' (Jonson 2012h: 621).

So whether or not *Every Man In* was originally part of Jonson's design to become a writer of court entertainments, it certainly became one in the select version of his career that was represented in the *Works*. The 1616 dedication of the play to William Camden is strategically brilliant in terms of defining the span of Jonson's career. Camden had been his headmaster at Westminster School, acknowledged in the *Epigrams* for 'All that I am in arts, all that I know'. But the play is specifically dedicated to 'Mr Camden, Clarentiaux'. By 1616 Camden was Clarenceux King of Arms, a senior figure in the College of Heralds and so also of the royal household. Like Jonson, though by a different route, he has come to court.

In short, though we cannot be certain that all of Jonson's published plays were actually performed at court—or even what the texts of those that were looked like at the time—it is unquestionably the case that in the 1616 *Works* Jonson associates the plays that appear there with his status as a court writer. And that cannot be separated from their extreme length. The cases of *Cynthia's Revels* and *Bartholomew*

---

[33] Somewhat remarkably, given the extent of the revision, the one thing that did not change was the length of the text (apart from the addition of a Prologue). In J. K. Lever's parallel text edition of the play (Jonson 1971), which treats the extensive prose in both versions identically—often the most difficult item to allow for in comparing lengths of texts—the quarto is 2,901 lines and the folio 2,902: both very long, but neither more so than the other.

Fair (written 1614, but omitted from the *Works*, probably for lack of space) strongly suggest that Jonson was prepared to produce both theatrical *and* courtly versions, and that it was the latter which predominantly got into print. Long before the folio *Works* became a reality, Jonson can be seen to have been working towards it. As the masque-writing career took off—each event commemorated in increasingly elaborate, annotated texts (at least until *The Masque of Queens* in 1609)—the production of play-texts worthy to stand alongside those royal commissions took on a self-assured air. The quarto and folio versions of, notably, *Volpone*, *The Alchemist*, and *Catiline* are virtually identical, but for typographical details.[34] And very, very long.

Lukas Erne calls his chapter on the playing time of plays 'Why Size Matters'. In his view anything longer than could realistically be performed on the public stage (which he sets at 2,800 lines) was primarily aimed at readers. My point is that size also has other connotations: notably status, the freedom to perform where time is no object, and the presence of an élite, discriminating audience, typified by D'Aubigny and Pembroke. Of course, in choosing to put his plays into print—and so publicly associating them with the 'Jonson' name he chose in order to distinguish himself from all the other Johnsons and Johnstones—he was cultivating a readership. But I suggest that this was a secondary consequence of firstly cultivating the court *as a dramatist*. For Jonson size matters because it confirmed his standing in the most competitive patronage race there was, that for court favour.

---

[34] No extant quarto of *Epicene* appeared until 1620; it too is virtually identical to the folio version.

4

The Revision of Early Modern Play Texts

When Alexander Pope edited Shakespeare's plays in 1725, and observed the differences between the quarto text of *Merry Wives* and its folio equivalent, he saw absolutely nothing problematic.

> The play was written in the Author's best and ripest years, after Henry the Fourth, by the command of Queen Elizabeth. There is a tradition that it was composed at a fortnight's warning. But that must be meant only of the first imperfect sketch of this Comedy, which is yet extant in an old Quarto edition, printed in 1619. This which we here have was altered and improved by the author almost in every speech.[1]

Pope, who was to revise his own masterwork, *The Dunciad*, saw no problem with a Shakespeare who 'altered and improved' the quarto to produce the folio version of this play. And John Roberts, who wrote *An Answer to Mr Pope's Preface to Shakespear*, was happy to concur that Shakespeare 'frequently revised and altered his plays'. Samuel Johnson in his own edition of the *Plays* agreed with Pope about *Merry Wives*, referring to the quarto version as 'the first sketch of this play, which, as Mr. Pope observes is much inferior to the latter performance'. And George Steevens expanded the observation to embrace several of the quarto-version plays which also exist in more substantial folio versions, including *King John*, *Henry V*, *Henry VI*, *Merry Wives*, and *Romeo and Juliet*. In the quarto versions, he felt, 'we may discern as much as will be found in the hasty outlines of the pencil', which may be contrasted with their folio versions, where we may observe the 'fair prospect of that perfection to which he brought every performance he took pains to retouch'.[2]

I do not intend to trace the entire editorial history of *Merry Wives* or any other play. That would seriously distract us from the purpose of this book. Suffice it now to look at two recent editions of *Merry Wives* and their editors' views of the relationship between the quarto and folio texts. In his New Cambridge edition, David

---

[1] Pope 1725: I.viii.223. On the circumstances of the play's composition, see pp. 246ff. Pope had only seen the 1619 third quarto of *Merry Wives*, not the 1602 original, but there is no substantive difference between their texts. I must acknowledge my debt here and in what follows on *Merry Wives* in the eighteenth century to Roberts 1976: 144ff. Anyone interested in the waywardness of taste in the editing of Shakespeare would be well advised to read this essay.

[2] Roberts 1729: 28; Johnson 1765: II. 557n; Steevens 1766: 7. Dr Johnson emphatically endorsed the authority of the First Folio; Steevens was unusual in seeing virtue in the quartos, even in some that were later to be dubbed 'bad' quartos, and his edition of twenty quarto texts was ahead of its time. The 1603 quarto of *Hamlet* was not rediscovered until 1823: see Lesser 2015. On *King John*, see Introduction, note 5.

Crane argues that the First Folio text is 'very close to Shakespeare's foul papers, the earliest state of the play', and by definition the quarto is inferior and derivative from it (Crane 1997: 1).[3] Giorgio Melchiori in his Arden 3 edition more complicatedly argues that the quarto is a 'memorial reconstruction of an authorial acting version of the play' (Melchiori 2000: 109). What matters here is that Crane locates the folio text of *Merry Wives* as close to the hand of Shakespeare himself as it is possible to imagine, and he does so in such a way as to suggest that the quarto text is subsequent and a falling-off (in ways for which Shakespeare is not held to be personally responsible). Melchiori also argues that the folio version came first. But he is a little kinder to the quarto, which he at least thinks reflects an 'authorial' acting version of the play, one designed by Shakespeare himself—albeit one corrupted and refracted on its way to us by 'memorial reconstruction', another staple of twentieth-century editorial theory. I discuss in more detail the terms 'foul papers' and 'memorial reconstruction' at pp. 143ff.

My immediate point here is that everyone—eighteenth century, twentieth century—is united in believing that the folio version of *Merry Wives* is superior. But whereas Pope and his era assumed this was because Shakespeare revised the earlier quarto text, modern editors—as far as I can see, all of them—assume that the folio text (or something like it) came first, and that the quarto text is a poorly transmitted version of something derived from it. That became until quite recently the almost universal view of the relationship between all of the 'superior' versions of Shakespeare's texts and the 'bad' alternatives, including the ones I shall mainly be concerned with: *2 and 3 Henry VI, Romeo and Juliet, Henry V, Merry Wives*, and *Hamlet*. And it remains a key paradigm in Shakespearean editorial theory to be confronted.

---

[3] Although David Crane's 2010 'updated edition' revises some features of his textual analysis, he remains committed to the basics: 'the F text of *The Merry Wives of Windsor* is very close to Shakespeare's foul papers, the earliest state of the play... there is good reason for dating the first performance of this play to St George's Day (23 April) 1597' (2010: 1) and 'there is good evidence... that Q is the product of a corrupt memorial report of *The Merry Wives of Windsor* for a printer to produce a pirated or "bad" quarto of the play for illicit profits' (167).

a. The Revision of Plays in Shakespeare's Day

Somewhat ironically, when we look at plays of the era *other than by Shakespeare*, a different paradigm has prevailed (see Ioppolo 1991: 12ff). Where two versions exist it is generally assumed that one of them (invariably published later and usually somewhat longer) is the result of deliberate revision at the behest of the playing company that owned it. The assumption was that revisions were most *normally* made because plays had been out of the repertory for some time and would need to be spruced up to attract an audience on revival. As G. E. Bentley put it: 'the refurbishing of old plays in the repertory seems to have been the universal practice in the London theatres from 1590 to 1642' (1971: 263). And it is still widely taken for granted, as we see with Katharine Eisaman Maus in the general introduction to the Norton Anthology of *English Renaissance Drama*, where she speaks of it being 'routine to compose new scenes for revivals' (Bevington 2002: xxi).

The instances of *Dr Faustus* and *The Spanish Tragedy* are often cited in support of this view, in part because of their familiarity, but also because we have some chapter-and-verse facts in Henslowe's *Diary*. William Bird [aka Bourne] and Samuel Rowley were paid £4 for 'additions in Doctor Faustus' on 22 November 1602 (Foakes 2002: 206), and Ben Jonson was paid a similar amount for 'additions in Hieronimo' (as Henslowe refers to *The Spanish Tragedy*), spread over 1601/2 (see p. 101). These are very substantial sums of money, given that Henslowe often only paid £6 for whole new plays. Apparently corresponding to these payments, a version of *Dr Faustus* was published in 1616 which is significantly longer (and remodelled in other ways) than the first quarto of 1604 (Marlowe 1993: 62–77). The first surviving version of *The Spanish Tragedy* dates from 1592 and was reprinted twice; in 1602 a new version was printed with five additional passages, one reprinted many times thereafter (Kyd 1986: xxi–xxvi).[4] In both cases occasional doubts have been raised as to whether these revisions do actually correspond to Henslowe's recorded payments, but that is not material to my argument.[5] What we do know from this is that the Lord Admiral's Men were prepared on occasion to pay quite substantial sums for *additions* to old plays, some of which eventually reached print.

---

[4] The 1592 imprint mentions an even earlier edition, but no copy of that is extant. Jonson in the Praeludium to *Cynthia's Revels* (printed 1601) jokingly affirmed ' "that the old *Hieronimo*", as it was first acted, "was the only, best, and judiciously penned play of Europe" ' (Jonson 2012d: Praeludium, lines 166–7, p. 451). This suggests that one revision was already extant—if not necessarily in print—before 1601.

[5] There has been a heavy industry in recent years trying to credit Shakespeare with the 1602 *Spanish Tragedy* additions: see Vickers 2012; Bate and Rasmussen 2013; Bruster 2013.

We must balance this, however, against Roslyn Landor Knutson's detailed wider study of Henslowe's *Diary*—the one document of the era where we have evidence of a company's business practices over time. For the uninitiated I should firstly stress that Henslowe was only the financier in these transactions. Members of the Lord Admiral's Men made the business decision to pay for the additions. The money for Bird and Rowley was 'Lent unto the company', while Jonson's payment was 'Lent...at the appointment of E Alleyn'. Suspicion of Henslowe himself as a moneylender and pawnbroker (not to mention his erratic spelling) has often needlessly coloured what his records reveal. Knutson's study of payments for revising plays found that they were distinctly *exceptions* and not the rule: 'the repertory companies in the 1590s did not see the payment for revisions to accompany a revival as a commercially necessary or profitable venture' (1985: 11). She acknowledges the revisions of *The Spanish Tragedy* and *Dr Faustus* but shows how unusual they were, suggesting that they relate to 'a period of unusual business activity' (14). She concludes: 'From the evidence in the diary, the Admiral's men and Worcester's men (and by association, all adult companies) operated their businesses as economically as possible. If they invested in substantial revisions, they did so because of pressing circumstances in their commercial world. The normative and preferred practice in the Elizabethan playhouse is seen in the revivals of such plays as *The Jew of Malta* and *The Wise Man of West Chester*, which could be returned to the stage every few years at essentially no cost' (15).

In the course of this argument Knutson does note some specific occasions 'for which the Admiral's men commissioned alterations, mendings, and additions. Of the sixteen plays in these entries, most were altered either during their maiden run or for a presentation at Court', observing that the cost of such revisions was typically negligible. 'In several cases, however, the company paid sums seemingly out of proportion with the return they could have expected for a single performance at Court... Possibly the players transferred the dramas to the public stage in order to recover expenses' (12). It is these *out of proportion* cases with which I am concerned; most of them were demonstrably related to court performances (and others may have been too). They defy the economic laws of business which, as she so ably shows, pertained in relation to most of the companies' commercial affairs. While it is likely that they did indeed try to recover costs by subsequently using some of these revisions on the public stages, we may wonder why they did not simply use the money to invest, as they usually did, in their most lucrative products—new plays. It is part of the argument of this book that the answer to this is tied up with the companies' intimate dependence upon, and patronage relationship with, the court.

Here is a complete list of Henslowe's payments for 'additions', 'mending', and 'altering' (the only terms he uses) in the years where such items are listed, 1598–1603:

18 November 1598, to Henry Chettle 'upon the mending of the First Part of *Robin Hood*' (10s) and 25 November 'for mending of *Robin Hood* for the court' (10s)

31 [sic] November 1599, to Thomas Dekker 'for the altering of the book of *The Whole History of Fortunatus*' (20s) and 12 December 'for the end of *Fortunatus* for the court' (40s)

14 December 1600, to Dekker 'for his pains in *Phaeton*... for the court' (10s), and 22 December, 'for altering of *Phaeton* for the court' (30s)

28 June 1601, to Chettle 'for the altering of the book of *Cardinal Wolsey*' (20s) and 4 July 'for the book of *Cardinal Wolsey* in full payment' (40s)[6]

25 September 1601, to Ben Jonson for 'additions in *Hieronimo*' (40s) (plus a subsequent payment on 22 June 1602: see note 32 in this chapter)

16 January 1601/2, to Dekker 'toward the altering of *Tasso*' [*Tasso's Melancholy*] (20s) and 3 November 1602, 'for mending of the play of *Tasso*' (40s)

21 January 1601/2, to Chettle for 'mending the book of *The Proud Woman*' (10s)

17 August 1602, to Dekker 'for new additions in *Oldcastle*' (40s) and 7 September 1602 'for his additions in *Oldcastle*' (10s)

20 September 1602, to Thomas Heywood 'for the new additions of *Cutting Dick*' (20s)

22 November 1602, to William Bird and Samuel Rowley, 'for their additions in *Dr Faustus*' (£4)

24 February 1602/3, to '4 poets', 'for their additions for the 2nd Part of *The Black Dog*' (20s)

Besides these items, Henslowe lists the following payments for prologues and epilogues:

12 January 1601/2, to Dekker 'for a prologue and epilogue for the play of *Pontius Pilate*' (10s)

29 December 1602, to Chettle 'for a prologue and epilogue for the court' [play unnamed] (5s)[7]

14 December 1602, to Thomas Middleton 'for a prologue and a epilogue for the play of [*Friar*] *Bacon* for the court' (5s)[8]

---

[6] There were at least two plays about Cardinal Wolsey, and Henslowe laid out considerable sums of money to pay for properties for one or both of them: see p. 155.

[7] The 5 shilling payment may be an underestimate, in that on the same day (29 December) he was paid another 5 shillings, via the same member of the Lord Admiral's Men, Thomas Downton, this time specifically for part-payment in respect of *The Tragedy of Hoffman*. The two payments together could represent extra, court-related work on the same play. Prologues and epilogues were often treated as ephemera and only staged for special occasions, most notably for performances at court. Note, for example, the epilogue to *2 Henry IV*, in which the speaker kneels to pray for the Queen, something he may have done in her presence: see Hattaway 2009: 162–3.

[8] On prologues and epilogues appended to plays, see Stern 2009a: 81–119. Specifically for the court, see 83, 100, 109, 110, 118, 153, 253. Juliet Dusinberre identified a poem ('As the dial hand tells o'er') as an epilogue to *As You Like It*, specifically associated with performance at court at Shrovetide 1599, but this has by no means been universally accepted (Dusinberre 2003; Hattaway 2009; Hackett 2012).

There is much about these entries that is debatable. There were at least two plays about each of Robin Hood, Fortunatus, Cardinal Wolsey, and Sir John Oldcastle, and it is not always certain which Henslowe is referring to in a particular entry. Why was Chettle apparently 'altering' *Cardinal Wolsey* before he had received payment for completing it? Why are the payments for 'altering' and 'mending' *Tasso*, or those of Jonson for *Hiernomio*, so far apart—were these separate commissions? And so on. But some things are clear, despite the doubts. Firstly, these are a very small proportion of all entries relating to payments for plays. There are typically only one or two a year, except for 1601/2, which was much busier in this regard. Most payments total between 20 shillings and 40 shillings (say, one-sixth and one-third of a typical payment for a new play). The payments to Bird and Rowley for *Dr Faustus* are way off the scale.

The *only* reason ever given for additions, mendings, alterings, or commissioning prologues and epilogues is that they are 'for the court'. And most payments are made in the months from November to February, matching the court Revels schedule. It is an open question whether there were other reasons when Henslowe chooses not to be specific. Of the plays mentioned, five are extant and four (*Robin Hood* [*The Downfall of Robert, Earl of Huntington*], *Old Fortunatus*, *The Spanish Tragedy*, and *Dr Faustus*) show, or may show, signs of revision in those texts. They will be discussed later. *The First Part of Sir John Oldcastle* was published in 1600, before Dekker's 'additions'.

Although Knutson's ground-breaking work is acknowledged, for example, by the editors of the *Oxford Shakespeare*, it has had little impact on the editing of Shakespeare plays since its publication (Wells and Taylor 1987: 15). Grace Ioppolo, in championing Shakespeare as a regular reviser, dismisses Knutson's conclusions as 'invalidated by a great deal of external and internal evidence in this period' (1991: 95). She does not, however, consider how much of that evidence conforms to the specific, limited circumstances within which Knutson finds revision taking place, notably when it is 'for the court' (see pp. 103–24). The loose assumptions voiced by Bentley are still commonly in circulation. This is unfortunate, since what Henslowe's *Diary* specifically tells us about the revision of plays for the Lord Admiral's Men is very likely to shed light on what was going on in the rival camp. Let us focus firstly on the three earliest entries, which all involve revisions for the court. Henry Chettle was apparently paid a total of 20 shillings for 'mending of the first part of *Robin Hood*' in November 1598, expressly 'for the court' (Foakes 2002: 101, 102).[9] This identifies it as what was published as *The Downfall of Robert, Earl of Huntington* (rather than its sequel, *The Death of Robert, Earl of Huntington*), for which Anthony Munday was originally paid as recently as February of that year. Both are Robin Hood plays. I examine below the possibility that the published text of *The Downfall* reflects that 'mending' and was performed at court.

---

[9] The detail that this was 'for the court' is interlined, perhaps an afterthought but one worth preserving.

A parallel sequence of entries occurs in respect of the play *Phaeton*, for which Henslowe originally paid Thomas Dekker in January 1597, and also lent money for 'a suit' and 'a white satin doublet'. In December 1600, he paid Dekker a total of 40 shillings 'for altering of *Phaeton* for the court', while on 2 January 1601 William Bird was advanced 20 shillings 'for divers things about about [sic] the play of *Phaeton* for the court' (137–8). *Phaeton* has not survived at all. But both of these sets of entries show us that money was changing hands to adapt plays—and plays quite fresh to the repertoire—'for the court'. The latter instance also shows that the Lord Admiral's Men were prepared to invest in new properties ('divers things') associated with the play, specifically for a court performance. It seems likely that a play about Phaeton driving the sun chariot ideally called for special properties or effects.[10]

Munday's *The Downfall of Robert, Earl of Huntington* was planned from an early date (if not perhaps the beginning) as the first part of a two-part play.[11] He was paid £5 for each part and Edmund Tilney was paid for both their licences on 28 March 1598. Chettle's 'mending' of the first part 'for the court' only nine months later presumably brought something new to the mix.[12] The surviving text does show *The Downfall* as the plausible recipient of such a revision, though in some respects it is so erratic (about the characters' names and the nature of the ending, for example) that it is difficult to be sure; the text as we have it is unplayable, showing clear changes of mind by either Munday or Chettle which are never fully resolved. The feature most suggestive of a revision for the court is a distinctive framing structure in which the play proper is being rehearsed for performance before Henry VIII, giving the whole play specifically courtly dimensions. Among the cast are a courtier, Sir John Eltham (who plays Little John in the show), the poet John Skelton (who plays Friar Tuck), and a Clown (who plays Much, the Miller's son in clown mode). The first scene—141 lines—involves a discussion of the play and what it will contain, and includes dumb shows which (to a narration by Eltham) spell out the key features of the eventual plot; it ends with what will be the most distinctive feature of the framing, Skelton/Tuck's repeated use of what

---

[10] In his inventories of the Lord Admiral's Men's properties, drawn up on 10 March 1598, Henslowe lists several items specifically associated with *Phaeton*, some of which are difficult to make sense of: '8 lances, 1 pair of stayers [stairs?]', '1 hecfor [heifer?] for the play of Faeton, the limes [limbs?] dead', 'Faeton's limes, & Faeton charete [chariot]', and '1 Faytone sewte' (319, 322). R. A. Foakes also suggests that 'j crown with a sone [sun]' would have been for *Phaeton* (321n). The point is that the company had already invested considerably in the play before Bird was given money to spend another pound on it at the time of these revisions for the court.

[11] Munday and his printers consistently make the title Earl of Huntington. The name of the town, and of the various earldoms associated with it, is more regularly rendered as Huntingdon. Hence John C. Meagher modernizes/corrects the title of his edition to *The Downfall of Robert Earl of Huntingdon 1601* (1965), while retaining Huntington within the text.

[12] Strictly speaking the second November entry of payment to Chettle is problematic for two reasons. Firstly, it is interlined with another entry, in earnest of a comedy by Chettle called *'Tis No Deceit to Deceive the Deceiver*, but only a single payment of 10 shillings is mentioned. Secondly, it is not certain if this entry refers to the First or Second Part of the play. Nevertheless, given the entry of the week before, and the absence of any evidence that Part Two was ever revised, it is not unreasonable to see this 10 shillings as the final reckoning for revising Part One.

Eltham characterizes as 'ribble rabble rhymes Skeltonical', very short rhyming lines in the real Skelton's familiar mode (Munday 1965: line 2,235, using Through-Line-Numbering). We find them again at lines 846–89, where Eltham has to stop Skelton/Tuck when he shows signs of running on indefinitely:

> Stop, master Skelton: whither will you run?
> *Fri(ar Tuck)*: God's pity, Sir John Eltham, little John,
>   I had forgotten myself; but to our play. (890–2)

And we find them latterly at 2,242–7, immediately after Eltham has asked him to desist: Skelton/Tuck is incorrigible. We also find them at lines 1,587–607 and 2,146–53, though these do not explicitly refer us to the framing structure. That structure is completed by discussions between Skelton and Eltham about the outcome of the play, at 2,208–47 and in the closing sequence, 2,783–840.

In *Work and Play on the Shakespearean Stage* Tom Rutter argues that these sequences were part of the play as Munday originally wrote it, and not Chettle's later interpolations:

> there are aesthetic grounds for assuming the Induction was a feature of the play as Munday conceived it for the public stage... These moments, fostering the conceit that we are watching a rehearsal of the Robin Hood play rather than the real thing do not detach easily from *The Downfall of Robert, Earl of Huntingdon* as a whole, suggesting that they were in the play from the start.   (2008: 53)[13]

On the contrary, these moments can be detached very easily, as the sequence I quote (890–2) readily shows. There is no doubt that Tuck's Skeltonics add a comic brio to the play and the meta-theatrical nature of the framing structure is entertaining in itself: the play is better off for them. But that is not the same thing as saying that they must have been there from the beginning. In fact the dumb shows at the opening could have been there all along, without the 'rehearsal' conceit and there is no real need for the later discussions of what the play will show—except that they are linked to the make-believe that the play is being made good enough to entertain Henry VIII. This would add a further level of meta-theatricality if these lines were actually inserted into a revised text for a real performance before his daughter.

It must always have been part of the rationale of the two Robin Hood plays that the Nottingham connections of the character would help to celebrate the elevation of the company's patron to the status of Earl of Nottingham, which happened in 1596. (The early quartos of *The Downfall* and *The Death* both accord the Lord Admiral his earldom.) So a line assuring us that the villainous Warman will 'not be earl of Nottingham' (947–8) need not be an addition for the court, though it would doubtless go down well there. Chettle's revisions were completed by 25 November 1598. The Lord Admiral's/Nottingham's Men performed at court that season on 27 December, 6 January, and 18 February, so they would have had at least a month to adapt to the new version.

---

[13] I am grateful to Tom Rutter for the suggestion that I revisit *The Downfall of Robert, Earl of Huntingdon*.

The strongest arguments against *The Downfall* as we have it being the version revised for court relate to the clearly unfinished nature of the text. John C. Meagher in his edition of the play points to four 'incomplete and unfinished' features (Munday 1965: vi–vii): several names change after line 781—Lord Lacy becomes Lord Fitzwater; his daughter Marian becomes Matilda (only later to be redubbed Maid Marian); Leicester becomes Salisbury, making way for a very different Leicester; the sequence beginning at line 1,024 does not properly relate to what goes before it; between lines 1,554 and 1,628 there are two entrances of the Friar and Jinny, one clearly redundant; the discussion of the play at 2,208–47 promises that it will end with Robin's tragedy (i.e. death), whereas that at the end (2,783–840) explains that it will be deferred to the sequel, *The Death*.

Several of these anomalies must relate to a belated decision (probably but not necessarily by Munday) to follow the Robin Hood material in Michael Drayton's *Matilda, the fair and chaste daughter of Lord R. Fitzwater* (1594; expanded edition 1596). This explains the change of names after 781 and very probably the decision to make a two-part play: the sequel is very substantially based on Drayton's story. And for Meagher these awkwardnesses in the text argue against its being the version as revised by Chettle: 'Such an unsettled and unfinished text clearly makes it improbable that Chettle's additions, composed some nine months after the settled and finished version of the play had been presented to the Admiral's Men, are in any way represented here' (Munday 1965: vii).

But these arguments can readily be turned on their heads. Would Chettle have worked on a fair copy of the 'settled and finished version of the play' that Munday had delivered? It would be sensible thrift to allow him to work out his 'mending' on Munday's working papers, with all their gaps and inconsistencies—the resolutions to which Chettle would know well enough from stage performances. If his 'mending' was indeed the imposition of the rehearsal framing structure, the only inconsistency within what would be *new* material is Skelton's promise of Robin's 'tale tragical' and death in the sequence 2,208–47, when the sequel already existed. Possibly he flirted with the idea of merging elements of both parts of the play for the court revision, before conceding that the revamped Part One was quite long enough in itself. Indeed the conclusion of the play dwells on the length:

> *Sir John*: Then Skelton here I see you will conclude.
> *Skelton*: And reason good: have we not held too long?
> *Sir John*: No in good sadness, I dare gage my life
>   His Highness will accept it very kindly. (2,783–6)

Eltham then recounts all the elements of the story that still remain to be told, concluding:

> Skelton, there are many other things,
> That ask long time to tell them lineally:
> But ten times longer will the action be. (2,805–7)

Skelton, confessing 'i'faith I know not what to do', resolves upon the sequel, begging Eltham to 'crave the king / To see two parts'.

Unless Chettle's labours were in vain, it seems likely that Elizabeth saw Part One (as I would argue, in a version not too far removed from this published text, though with inconsistencies smoothed over). We have no evidence that she ever saw Part Two, though it is entirely possible that both parts were performed in the Revels season of 1598/9: such thematic groupings were a feature of the Master of the Revels's choices (see p. 65). In Meagher's edition *The Downfall* is some 2,840 lines long, significantly longer than the average Rose/Globe play, though just beyond what in Chapter 3 I reckoned acceptable length for regular public playing. Length alone is not conclusive evidence of a court version of a play, but for reasons we have discussed, it is often a marker, especially when it can be associated with other distinctive features, such as revision or details that would resonate at court. And the final length of *The Downfall of Robert, Earl of Huntingdon* is almost identical to that which Dekker was to give to *Old Fortunatus*. The various elements I have characterized as the framing structure comprise some 315 lines of the play—without them the play would be 2,535 lines long, a distinctly more average length.[14] But at least as important as the added length is the super-added fiction of a performance in the making for Henry VIII, a gracious gesture to his daughter. That could well have been worth the 20 shillings that Henslowe paid Chettle on behalf of the company, and is not untypical of the kinds of 'mending' which we see in numerous other instances—relatively modest embellishments, unfamiliar flourishes, that make the court version a bit special. (See, for example, the discussions of *Mucedorus* and *Titus Andronicus*: pp. 113, 259.)

It is, however, a significantly smaller payment than Dekker received for revisions to *Old Fortunatus*, which were evidently on a much more substantial scale. Since this is the one play of all those that Henslowe mentions that indisputably survives in its revised form, it warrants close attention. The problematic question arising from Henslowe's entries on it, yet again, is whether we are dealing with one play or two. Some entries doubtless relate to the play designated 'the i p [First Part?] of fortunatus' which Henslowe recorded as performed several times in 1595 and 1596 (Foakes 2002: 34, 35, 36, 37). But a sequel (*The Whole History of Fortunatus*) is also involved, as well as substantial rewriting—either of the original or of the sequel.

The full picture is more complicated than my abstract of revision entries in the *Diary* suggests. On 9 November 1599 Dekker was advanced 40 shillings 'in earnest of a book called the whole history of Fortunatus' (126); on 24 November

---

[14] I acknowledge that it is problematic including stage directions in assessing the length of a play, as the Malone Society Reprints do in their Through Line Numbering, which is what I am going by here. And Charlton Hinman's Through Line Numbering of his facsimile of the Shakespeare First Folio does the same. But it is equally problematic *not* including the stage directions, since they are often the only pointer we have to action which would have added significantly to the length of a performance. The stage directions in the opening scene of *The Downfall*, including the dumb shows (which I have suggested may or may not have been part of Munday's original conception), amount to some 35 of the 315 lines.

he was advanced a further £3. On 30 November he received 20 shillings 'in full payment of his book of fortunatus' (127). That is, over the month he received a total of £6, commonly the fee for a new work. But the very next day (31 November, in Henslowe's sometimes erratic reckoning) he was paid a further 20 shillings 'for the altering of the book of the whole history of fortunatus', and shortly thereafter Henslowe records: 'paid unto m^r Dekker the 12 of December 1599 for the end of fortunatus for the court...the sum of...40s' (128). So in December Dekker received a total of £3, half as much again, apparently to revise either the original or a play which he had just written. That the revision was to *The Whole History of Fortunatus*, which carries the story beyond the death of Fortunatus himself, is attested by June Schlueter's demonstration that a German play of *Fortunatus*, published in 1620, was based on *The Whole History* before its revision (2013).[15]

From the level of payment, Chettle's two stints of work on 'Robin hood' equated to at least twice the effort of supplying a prologue and an epilogue. But Dekker's payments for both *Phaeton* and *Fortunatus* were of a different order again. He received a total of £2 (beside the £1 that went to Bird) for work on *Phaeton* expressly for the court; and even if we discount the £6 that he first received in November 1599 for *The Whole History of Fortunatus* (on the grounds that it must have been for a new play), it is inescapable that he still received a further £3 to revise it again for the court. Such payments amount to a third or a half of what was commonly paid for a new play, and so represented a significant investment on the part of the Lord Admiral's Men. And we may add to this that, in an undated entry in the *Diary* (between entries for 3 and 12 December 1599), Thomas Downton, an actor with the company, acknowledged receiving the princely sum of £10 'for to buy things for Fortunatus' (128). A 'tree of golden apples' recorded in Henslowe's 1598 inventory may well have been for the original play. But no expense was to be spared in making an impression with this revised version.

In the case of Fortunatus we indisputably have the finished product of these revisions, *The pleasant comedy of old Fortunatus As it was played before the Queen's Majesty this Christmas* (printed 1600). Brian Walsh describes it as 'a wild and fantastic mess of a play'—but Dekker and the company (and almost as certainly the Master of the Revels) invested a good deal of time, effort, and money to produce that 'fantastic mess', evidently expecting that it would make its mark at court (Walsh 2009: 6). And Schlueter's analysis of the 1620 German *Fortunatus* makes it possible to see with unusual specificity, in *Old Fortunatus*, what Dekker's revisions amounted to: 'Scholars have long agreed that the playwright's embellishments included the Prologue and Epilogue, which are explicit in their identification with the court and their praise of Gloriana; the allegory of Vice and Virtue; and, taking their cue from *Henslowe's Diary*, the ending. With the 1620 play representing *The Whole History*, we can not only confirm these assumptions, but also employ a more considered perspective on Dekker's "altrenges"' (124; Hoy 1980: 1.73). She argues that 'Dekker's revisionary efforts are heavily invested in the supernatural subplot'

---

[15] I am grateful to David McInnis for introducing me to June Schlueter's work on *Old Fortunatus* and for more general conversations on the play.

(ibid), and its 'otherworldly characters—especially the condemned Spirits and Virtue and Vice', who (she points out) 'participate in the grand spectacle that turns an unhappy tale into *A Pleasant Comedy*' (121; Hunt 1911: 34). That would appear to be the sequence for which Dekker was paid last, 'for the end of fortunatus for the court'. All of this squares with Tiffany Stern's argument that prologues and epilogues on their own were usually ephemera, often written for a single performance, at the court or in the playhouse (Stern 2009a: 81–119, esp. 110, 118). Dekker's assignment here was on a substantially greater scale.

This computation adds at least 491 lines to an existing text of 2,331—more than a fifth.[16] As we noted (p. 67), this length led W. L. Halstead—who first suggested that the Vice–Virtue subplot was a result of the late alterations—to conclude that 'Performance on the public stage...seems...doubtful, since, after altering, the play was nearly 3,000 lines long, and this was too long for performance in the London theatres'.[17] He was working on Alfred Hart's computations, which were certainly over-strict. But it is incontrovertible that what Dekker did to *Old Fortunatus* took it from an average playhouse length to beyond even the average length of a *Shakespeare* play (2,751 lines, in Hart's computation). He was doubtless paid not simply in relation to the quota of lines, but also the aptness with which he could integrate the old material with the new and make it appropriate for a royal audience, at which he succeeded with some aplomb. He included, for example, an aerial ascent for Fortunatus, which it is unlikely the Admiral's Men could have staged at the Rose (see p. 281, note 29). The Vice–Virtue material includes a very elaborate dumb-show introduction to the third scene, with Vice ('with a gilded face and horns on her head') and Virtue ('a coxcomb on her head, and all white before') both dressed—as are their attendants—in symbolically decorated costumes, coming before Fortune to plant their trees: Vice's 'a fair tree of gold with apples on it', Virtue's 'a tree with green and withered leaves mingled together, and little fruit on it'. This presumably gives us some indication of what Downton spent the £10 on. The Admiral's Men had twelve days between Dekker's final payment (12 December) and the likely first performance of the revised play, on 27 December at court.[18]

All three of these instances in Henslowe—*Robin Hood*, *Phaeton*, and *Old Fortunatus*—square entirely with what we know of the schedule followed by Edmund Tilney when (as Heywood tells us) he 'rehearsed, perfected, and corrected' plays for court performance; there is no doubt that he would have had to approve each of them, and every reason to suppose that he would have been

---

[16] Schlueter notes other lesser details which are neither in the source material nor the 1620 German play, such as 'the cameo role for Insultado the Spanish dancer', which may have been new (127).

[17] Halstead 1939: 352. My figures are based on the edition of *Old Fortunatus* in Bowers 1953–61a: 1.105–206. My count of the original length excludes a prologue that presumably antedated that for the court (24 lines), so the net additional length might be 467 lines.

[18] Their only other performance that season, on New Year's Day 1600, was *The Shoemakers' Holiday*. That is the only court date to which we can confidently attach a specific play in the last decade of Elizabeth's reign. It seems to have been presented without alterations, as was doubtless *usually* the case.

involved in discussions about what would be suitable. They are important models to bear in mind when considering Shakespeare's revised texts at this point in his career, starting with *Romeo and Juliet* and *Henry V*.

It is intriguing that when we look to the repertory of the Chamberlain's Men (for whom, of course, we have no such accounts) in the 1598 time frame, we find newly printed *A pleasant conceited comedy called Love's Labour's Lost As it was presented before her Highness this last Christmas. Newly corrected and augmented by W. Shakespere*. This is the earliest instance of any Shakespeare play that we *know* being performed at court (though it is highly unlikely that others were not performed before this). And it is the earliest of any play by a dramatist writing for an adult playing company to make the fact of performance at court a selling point on the title page.[19] Given the Old Style/New Style uncertainties about dating in the era, however, the title page is ambiguous about when it occurred. As John Astington says, 'the court performance may have been in the season 1597–98 or that of 1598–99' (2009: 307). The former would make it a year earlier than *Robin Hood*; the latter would put it in the same Revels season. But either puts the two plays in sufficiently close proximity to make us suspect that it may be part of the same phenomenon: *Love's Labour's Lost* is not only printed as *Newly corrected and augmented by W. Shakespere* but also *As it was presented before her Highness this last Christmas*, as if the two facts are linked.

Before I go on to consider the implications of *Newly corrected and augmented*, let us first note what this title page does *not* tell us. If we look at the earliest texts of Shakespeare's plays, their title pages tend to be formulaic in the information they convey about the text and/or its performance, though this evolves over time. To begin with they identify the acting company by patron. *Titus Andronicus* (1594) declares itself to be 'as it was played by the Right Honourable the Earl of Derby, Earl of Pembroke and Earl of Sussex their servants'.[20] *The True Tragedy* appears 'as it was sundry times acted by the Right Honourable the Earl of Pembroke his servants'. Thereafter *Richard III* (1597) is 'As it hath been lately acted by the Right Honourable the Lord Chamberlain his servants', while *The Merchant of Venice* and *Henry V* (1600) both have similar formulae ('As it hath been divers times acted', 'As it hath been sundry times played', etc.).

But the first ('bad') quarto of *Romeo and Juliet* (1597) appeared 'As it hath been often (with great applause) played *publicly*, by the Right Honourable the Lord of Hunsdon his servants' (my emphasis).[21] Thereafter *Richard II* (1597) appeared as 'publicly acted', while *A Midsummer Night's Dream* (1600), *2 Henry IV* (1600), and

---

[19] There are, of course, a number of earlier extant plays written for the children's companies which were performed at court, and the fact is advertised on their title pages. These include notably several plays by Lyly, such as *Campaspe, Sapho and Phao, Gallathea, Endimion, Midas*, and *The Woman in the Moon*.

[20] There has been much debate about whether these companies combined to perform during the plague years of 1593/4, or whether each took it on successively. The second quarto (1600) adds 'and the Lord Chamberlain' to the list of patrons, which in that context surely means that the play was passed from the last company which owned it to Shakespeare's new company.

[21] This publication was in the brief period in 1596/7, between the death of the first Lord Hunsdon and the appointment of his son as Lord Chamberlain.

Much Ado About Nothing (1600) all appeared as 'sundry times publicly acted'. In the period 1597–1602, when an unusually large number of Shakespeare's plays (ten) first got into print, half of them made a point of stressing that their texts were as *'publicly* acted'.[22] *Love's Labour's Lost,* with its *As it was presented before her Highness this last Christmas,* is clearly sending a different message: this is not the play as it was staged 'publicly' but in private, at court—the same distinction as made in the 1600 quarto of *Cynthia's Revels* (see p. 89). This is even more emphatically the case with *King Lear* (1608): *As it was played before the King's Majesty at Whitehall upon S. Stephen's Night in Christmas Holidays* is a very precise statement of where and when *this* text was performed, strongly suggesting that other (public) performances would have been different. That suggestion is reinforced with the further information that it was acted '*By His Majesty's servants playing usually at the Globe on the Bankside'*—as if to underline that this was not the version of the play that they would 'usually' play at the Globe.[23]

Having established this contextual frame, I return to the claim that *Love's Labour's Lost* had been *Newly corrected and augmented* before its court performance and subsequent publication. Other texts were clearly being revised in this same time frame. The second ('good') quarto of *Romeo and Juliet* appeared in 1599, advertised as '*Newly corrected, augmented, and amended'*. The quarto of *Henry V* appeared in 1600, with the folio version being written shortly before or (as I argue) after. *2 Henry IV* was also printed in 1600; the first state of the quarto lacks what in modern editions is 3.1, where King Henry meditates on the passage of time, but it appears in the second state (see p. 263). The second quarto of *1 Henry IV* (1599) appears as '*Newly corrected'*, while the third quarto of *Richard III* (1602) advertises itself as '*Newly augmented,* By *William Shakespeare'*; in both cases they are much the same as versions published earlier—an issue I discuss later in this chapter. The early states of *Hamlet* and *The Merry Wives of Windsor* seem to have come into being around 1600/1, and both were revised (as I shall argue) by 1604. At which point what we might characterize as a period of intense textual ferment in Shakespeare's career dies down.[24] Or,

---

[22] Omitting reprints, eight title pages by other authors make similar claims up to 1594, then none till 1597. In the same 1597–1602 time frame, eight non-Shakespearean plays were published as 'publicly acted': *The Blind Beggar of Alexandria, James IV of Scotland, A Humorous Day's Mirth, 1* and *2 Edward IV, Every Man Out of His Humour, Every Man In His Humour,* and *Satiromastix.* 'Privately acted'—meaning performed by one of the boy troupes—does not occur before Jonson's *Cynthia's Revels* in 1601, a year or so after the reopening of their playhouses, which had been out of use for a decade. 'Publicly acted' does not originally seem, therefore, to have been used in contradistinction to playing in the indoor theatres, though it clearly has that sense in *Satiromastix* (1602), which was performed both by the Chamberlain's Men and by the Children of Paul's.

[23] The evidence from other plays is more equivocal. Although Q2 *Romeo and Juliet* appeared '*Newly corrected, augmented, and amended'*, it is also advertised as 'As it hath been sundry times publicly acted by the Right Honourable Lord Chamberlain his servants'. The 1602 quarto of *The Merry Wives of Windsor* is 'As it hath been divers times acted by the Right Honourable my Lord Chamberlain's servants. Both before her Majesty and elsewhere', suggesting that the same text suited multiple venues. Q2 *Hamlet* says nothing about performance at all.

[24] Quite a few of Shakespeare's other plays first see print during this 'window', though their texts do not necessarily show signs of revision: *Richard II* (1597), *1 Henry IV* (1598), *Much Ado About Nothing*

more precisely, the evidence just dries up. And as it happens, the evidence from Henslowe dries up too. The regular entries in the *Diary* cease in the early months of 1603.

It is pure chance that the windows in which we can see a pattern of the Admiral's Men revising plays for the court, and Shakespeare revising some of his plays (almost certainly for the same reason), coincide and mirror each other. But it is distinctly likely that the shared practice of *Newly correct[ing] and augment[ing]* plays for performance at court specifically arose at this time as a reciprocal gesture of thanks, an obeisance to their most important patrons, the court, for the privileged position it publicly accorded them in this period. And this allows us to see Shakespeare's writing practice at this time in a wholly new light.

* * *

John Kerrigan's essay, 'Revision, Adaptation, and the Fool in *King Lear*', remains one of the most insightful studies we have of the ways in which early modern dramatists revised plays, their own and other people's. It was included in Gary Taylor and Michael Warren's *The Division of the Kingdoms* (1983), the volume which first convinced most scholars that *The Tragedy of King Lear* in the First Folio is a purposeful revision of the quarto *History of King Lear*, probably by Shakespeare himself.[25] This directly challenged the old orthodoxy, which held that both texts derived from the same Shakespearean original.[26] While Kerrigan's essay is essentially a study of the role of the Fool in the two versions of the play, it starts with a ground-clearing review of what we can learn about the revision of early modern play texts from some of the most clear-cut instances. The opening paragraph is worth quoting at length:

> When Hamlet adapts *The Murder of Gonzago* for performance at court, he does not subject it to a rigorous line-by-line revision. Instead, he inserts into the old play 'a speech of some dosen lines or sixteen lines', specially composed for the occasion. He substantially interpolates; he does not tinker. Now while the Prince is in some ways an atypical dramatic adapter...he does seem to work in a representative way. The available evidence strongly suggests that when, in the early seventeenth century, one man of the theatre overhauled another's play, he cut, inserted and substituted sizeable pieces of text without altering the details of his precursor's dialogue. Revising authors, by contrast, though they sometimes worked just with large textual fractions, tended to tinker, introducing small additions, small cuts and indifferent single-word substitutions. A survey of rewritten plays reveals two kinds of textual variation then, one rarely authorial in origin, the other characteristically so. (196)

(1600), *A Midsummer Night's Dream* (1600). See, however, Chapter 2, p. 59 about *A Midsummer Night's Dream* and Chapter 7 on *Richard II*.

[25] There is an early earnest of the collaborative volume in Warren 1978.
[26] It followed from this that the old editorial tradition of conflating the two texts was misguided. Hence the decision in the 1986 *Oxford Shakespeare* to publish *both* the *History* and the *Tragedy*, a practice widely followed since.

In this analysis—which Kerrigan substantiates with compelling ease—those who revise plays usually emerge as either interpolators or tinkerers. Interpolators *may* be the original authors, but tinkerers almost *always* are. Jonson is the author who most consistently and unmistakably 'reveal[s] the presence of a fidgeting authorial reviser' (209) or tinkerer, in all the plays first published in quarto and then republished in his 1616 *Works*. The tinkering is on a grand scale in early works like *Every Man In His Humour* and *Cynthia's Revels*, but is unmistakably there—in minute details—even in plays as late as *The Alchemist* (1610) and *Catiline* (1611). Another clear instance is Chapman's revision of *Bussy D'Ambois*, from the version printed in 1607 to that printed in 1641, which seems truthfully to declare on its title page that the tragedy was '*much corrected and amended by the Author before his death*'. By contrast, changes to notably revised texts such as the 1602 *Spanish Tragedy*, the 1610 anonymous *Mucedorus*, and the 1619 *A Fair Quarrel* by Middleton and Rowley (all discussed later in this chapter) emerge as works of interpolation, with no significant adjustments to the text except brief cuts and the insertion of discrete sequences of new material (insertions significantly outweighing excisions). In the case of *A Fair Quarrel*, even though there is no evidence of tinkering, it seems indisputable that the new material was by its author(s).

The big pay-off for Kerrigan is that this establishes the folio *King Lear* as the work of 'a fidgeting authorial reviser' of the 1608 quarto of the play. He concisely suggests that similar relationships exist between Q1604/5 and the folio *Hamlet* and the quarto and folio *Othello* (212–13), in all of which I concur. His analysis works most clearly and convincingly when there are two 'good' (and, as it happens, strikingly long) versions of a play; he has nothing to say about the relationship between traditionally conceived 'bad' and 'good' versions (say, of *Hamlet*), where the changes represent considerably more than either limited interpolation or fidgeting.[27] But the model of his analysis of *King Lear* gives us grounds to think of a Shakespeare who would revise a *whole* text, rather than simply make discrete interpolations and isolated changes. The position which Shakespeare enjoyed as the 'ordinary poet' of the most successful acting company of his time clearly gave him the opportunity to write an unusually high proportion of his plays on his own—'without a coadjutor, / Novice, journeyman, or tutor', as Jonson puts it (Prologue to *Volpone*, Jonson 2012k: 17–18). He may well have exercised the same proprietorial independence when there was a need to revise those plays.

Kerrigan's comments on non-Shakespearean revision, however, invite us to consider other ways in which they may throw light on the revision of Shakespeare's own. Here I review some of the most notable instances.

---

[27] It is hardly accidental that Menzer and Marino both fall back on 'continuous copy'—the idea that a play might go through regular changes at the hands of the actors—in respect of *Hamlet*, the most intractable editorial conundrum of them all. Menzer's *The Hamlets* is entirely dedicated to it; Marino's *Owning William Shakespeare* has a key, driving chapter on it (2011: 75–106).

MUCEDORUS

If frequency of reprinting is any guide, *Mucedorus*, which might loosely be described as an Arcadian romance, was one of the mainstays of Shakespeare's company and one of the most popular plays of the whole era. First printed in 1598, it went through no fewer than seventeen imprints before 1668. Of these, the second and third are of particular interest: 'The new edition of *Mucedorus*, which came out in 1606, contains revisions in the epilogue that alter the monarch addressed from a queen to a king, thus implying a performance before King James, perhaps in 1605–06' (Knutson 1991: 110, citing Thornberry 1977). But the third quarto of 1610 was even more different from its predecessors, as the title page tells us: 'Amplified with new additions, as it was / acted before the King's Majesty at / Whitehall on Shrove- / Sunday night. / By his Highness's Servants usually / playing at the Globe.' It thus fits perfectly the pattern of more modest revisions 'for the court' recorded by Henslowe. The company has taken a play out of its regular repertoire, which was already familiar to many in the court audience, and spiced it up with new additions—six discrete passages. Which of course make it somewhat longer (approximately 215 lines are added, though about 30 of the original are dropped), but not greatly so. They might represent a quarter of an hour's playing time.

The revisions, however, quite adroitly redirect the play's emphases in ways that give it a distinct Jacobean flavour. For example, Mucedorus's identity as son and heir to the King of Valencia—not revealed in the original till the end of the play—is now announced in the opening scene, allowing for subsequent scenes in which the King actually appears, firstly lamenting the apparent death of his son, latterly taking part in the final festivities. The dramatic pattern is more that of Fletcherian tragicomedy, while parallels with *The Winter's Tale* (lost royal children) are quite pronounced. The role of Mouse, the clown (probably played by Robert Armin, Kemp's successor), is enhanced to include giving him a bottle [bundle] of hay to carry and different stage business with the bear that pursues him. The bear was always part of *Mucedorus*, but the changes draw new attention to it, and again inevitably point towards *The Winter's Tale*.

The reshaped epilogue expressly recognizes the Jacobean court and the King. In doing so, the characters distance themselves from the kind of pointed political satire which had been the stock-in-trade of the Blackfriars boys and had latterly lost them their licence in 1608—a circumstance which made it possible for the King's Men to take over their theatre. Envy threatens Comedy that he will 'fly me to a puisant magistrate' and 'rehearse those galls [bitter quarrels] / With some additions, so lately vented in your theater'. She expects this to lead to 'your great danger, or at least restraint'. But Comedy laughs off her 'folly'. 'This is a trap for boys, not men, nor such...Whose staid discretion rules their purposes. I and my faction do eschew those vices' (Jupin 1987: Addition 5, lines 32–42, after line 14 of the original Epilogue). Stressing their own 'staid discretion' over the 'galls' vented by their predecessors in the Blackfriars, they then kneel before the 'Glorious and wise Arch-Caesar on this earth' (52)

(Pyle 1969: 182, n. 1).[28] It adds a diverting twist to the most escapist of entertainment, especially for those who were expecting the old ending. We are expressly told that this was played on one of the peak court Revels holidays, Shrove Sunday, though Old Style/New Style differences mean it could have been in 1610 or 1611.

A FAIR QUARREL

A Fair Quarrel is a tragicomedy by William Rowley and Thomas Middleton, written for Prince Charles's Men, of whom Rowley was the leader and principal comedian. The play was first published in 1617, proclaiming itself to be 'As it was acted before the King and divers times publicly by the Prince his Highness's Servants'. But this was quickly followed by a second issue (not a reprint, but the original printing with additional material and an altered title page), which contained a new scene as an appendix, something which the revised title page was at pains to advertise: 'With new Additions of Mr Chough's and Tristram's Roaring, and the Bawd's Song. Never before Printed. As it was acted before the King, by the Prince his Highness's Servaunts'. Suzanne Gossett, the play's most recent editor, suggests that 'The play was probably composed in 1615–1616, in which years the invasion of private property to search for saltpetre (1.1.240–4), roaring boys, and duels were all much in the public eye' (2007c: 399). She adds that 'The additional scene, expanding on interest in the roaring boys and probably on the theatrical success of Chough and Trimtram, was most likely added early in 1617. This would allow time after the performance for it to be printed and inserted in the remaining copies of the first issue, and for the second issue still to be dated 1617' (2007c: 400).[29]

Given Roslyn Knutson's view that it was unusual for the acting companies to go to the trouble and expense of adding new material to a play already in the repertory (see p. 100), we may wonder why Prince Charles's Men asked Rowley, who is almost certainly the sole author here, to add this 242 lines to the original 2,272, and when (Hart 1934: 138). There is, in fact, a compelling circumstantial case for thinking that this might well have been specifically during the Revels season of 1616–17, when the company appeared at court an unprecedented (and unrepeated) thirteen times, which must really have stretched their repertoire. For once they even outfaced the King's Men, who only appeared eleven times. This higher representation must have been connected with the creation of Prince Charles as Prince of Wales in 1616. Rowley underlines his company's affiliation in print by dedicating the play to 'Robert Grey Esquire, one of the grooms of his Highness's Bedchamber'.

They were basking in the reflected glory of their patron's enhanced status and must have called upon all their resources to do him credit. Predictably, this involved something we encounter repeatedly in revisions for court, the addition of a scene

---

[28] On the issue of whether Shakespeare could have revised the play, see p. 277.
[29] A second quarto of the play appeared in 1622, with the new scene in its proper place as 4.4.

which is not strictly necessary, though it would enhance the theatrical experience. Gossett says of the scene (4.4.) and its place in the structure:

> The additional scene is tightly integrated into the play. It forms a counterpart to 4.1, in which Chough learns at the roaring school the lessons he practises in 4.4.; it fills out the tripartite plot structure; it elaborates both the character of Chough and the theme of women's questionable virtue; it slyly satirizes the military pomp of Captain Ager and the Colonel through Captain Albo. Given Priss's meta-theatrical reference to the 'new play', the additional material seems to be an afterthought capitalizing on the popularity of the original roaring scene. (2007b: 633)

It doubtless helped Rowley to write such a well-integrated scene that it involved the character he himself almost certainly played, Chough; he was a regular exponent of fat-fool roles like Lollio in *The Changeling* and the Fat Bishop in *A Game at Chess*. Chough is characterized in the *Oxford Middleton* as 'a simple Cornish gentleman of great estate' (Middleton and Rowley 2007c: 1,212).[30] London audiences were, of course, fond of making fun of their country cousins, but at court this one would have had an extra resonance, because Charles was Duke of Cornwall before he was Prince of Wales.[31] Anyone physically less like the diminutive prince than the rotund Rowley would be difficult to imagine, but that would be part of the joke.

The claim in the revised title page that the play was 'Never before Printed' rather stretches the truth: only the new scene had not been printed. But while the boast of performance before the King may simply reiterate that of the first impression, in context it actually makes a new claim: that the play *as it had never been printed before* had been acted 'before the King' and *not* 'divers times publicly', as the original version had been. The evidence is only inferential, but it is of a piece with what we find elsewhere in plays 'augmented' for court performance.

A scene of 242 lines would barely add twenty minutes to the playing time. But this was artfully designed to enhance Rowley's own key role, which doubtless generated much of the comedy in the play, 'capitalizing on the popularity of the original roaring scene'. It was an added gesture, an encore of sorts, something unanticipated in a play which (if we can trust the title pages) had already appeared at court in its original form. This must often have been the level of novelty—modest but memorable—which was looked for in texts revised for court.

THE SPANISH TRAGEDY

With these instances in mind we can revisit the two most famously revised texts, *The Spanish Tragedy* and *Dr Faustus*. *The Spanish Tragedy* more resembles *Mucedorus*, in being a well-established play (Henslowe's *Diary* records twenty-nine performances at the Rose between 1592 and 1597, while extant unrevised editions date

---

[30] The Persons of the Play, p. 1,212. Chough has a servant, Trimtram, which is obviously a play on Tristan/Tristram, the great mythical Cornish hero. And both have heavy stage-Cornish accents.
[31] Duke of Cornwall is the default senior title of the eldest son of a monarch, prior to his formal elevation as Prince of Wales. Charles inherited it when Prince Henry died.

from 1592, 1594, and 1599), to which five new passages were added in 1602, comprising some 320 lines. These do not, however, significantly impinge upon the original plot. Most are quite brief, except for the famous Painter scene (inserted between what modern editions of the 1592 text make 3.12 and 3.13), which takes up fully half of the new lines. It offers the actor playing Hieronimo a striking opportunity to expand what he can show of grief and madness.

There is nothing in the text to suggest why the additions were made. As we have seen, Roslyn Knutson ascribes them to 'a period of unusual business activity', though without speculating what made it so (p. 116). One obvious possibility is that it was connected to the Admiral's Men's move from the Rose to the Fortune, effected late in 1600. The company doubtless had to lure customers from the Bankside to St. Giles, and new touches to the old favourite might have been part of the strategy. Or, if we knew precisely the process of Edward Alleyn's retirement from the stage, we might be able to associate it with that (Cerasano 1998). Could the changes have been crafted to enhance his return to the role of Hieronimo after some time away? Or to give his replacement in the role more scope to make it his own? Only recently it has been argued by Douglas Bruster, Jonathan Bate, and others that the play had been acquired by the Chamberlain's Men and the additions were by Shakespeare to give Burbage something distinctive in the role—which I doubt, but it is not impossible (Vickers 2012; Bate and Rasmussen 2013; Bruster 2013).[32] But it is difficult to avoid the conclusion that the additions had *something* to do with enhancing the star role—something that I shall argue later may well have been a factor in revisions of *Titus*, *Richard II*, *2 Henry IV*, and *Henry V*, not to mention *Hamlet*. As we have already noted, one consequence of the additions was to make the play 'exceptionally long', leading some to doubt if it could have been performed on the public stage (see p. 67). That the changes were for court performance thus cannot be ruled out.

DR FAUSTUS

The differences between the two early texts of *Dr Faustus* follow none of these patterns, and the greater length of the 1616 version (commonly known as the B text, as opposed to the A text of 1604) can hardly be explained, for instance, as an attempt to enhance the star role. The clowning is what is actually expanded most, but that hardly begins to describe the real differences. The B text introduces nine new passages, one as short as five lines, up to the largest, which is 214 lines, adding

---

[32] It is not critical to my argument whether Shakespeare revised *The Spanish Tragedy* or not. I doubt it mainly on the licensing grounds. Although it first appears in Henslowe's *Diary* in the repertory of Strange's Men, it is securely with the Admiral's Men from 1597 and they did pay Ben Jonson quite a bit for 'additions to *Hieronimo*' in 1601/2 (see p. 101), which is hardly the action of a company contemplating selling on their interest in it. Tilney would not have let it change hands without their formal agreement: I trust that more than I do any stylometric tests, computerized or otherwise. The famous 'Elegy on Burbage' does associate 'old Hieronimo' with Shakespeare's colleague, but it is not the most reliable of texts (Chambers 1923: 2.309).

a very substantial 676 lines to the A text, while losing some 40 in the process (Marlowe 1993: 63; Kerrigan 1983: 196–8). The A text, however, was very short to begin with, some 1,540 lines, so the B text remains on the short side by the standards of the day for a play from the public theatres, especially a tragedy. Beyond this the B text introduces 'thousands of verbal changes' (Marlowe 1993: 62).

Modern scholarship is now virtually unanimous in believing that the A text is closest (however imperfectly) to what Marlowe wrote and that the B text came later, probably significantly later.[33] But this was not always so. W. W. Greg, for example, in his parallel-texts edition of the play, characteristically approached them as he did the disputed Shakespeare texts, regarding the A text as a 'bad' quarto compiled by memorial reconstruction, its deficiencies the result of cuts for touring or faulty memory (Marlowe 1950). Perhaps betraying his anti-theatrical instincts, he thus did not accept that the B text incorporates the 'additions in Doctor Faustus' for which Henslowe paid Bird and Rowley, which most scholars now regard as a very reasonable assumption. John Kerrigan certainly accepts it but fights hard—it is in many ways the play which most challenges his theories—to establish that, while the new passages (or most of them) derive from Bird and Rowley, the 'verbal changes' cannot be ascribed to them (197–8). They are, rather, corruptions acquired during various transmissions of the text over the years. In terms of purposeful revision, then, this is a case of interpolation, not of 'tinkering' or 'fidgeting'.

Bevington and Rasmussen are not altogether convinced (Marlowe 1993). They suspect more phases of revision than the one we happen to know about, adding up to 'a thorough if intermittent reworking of concept and language' (77)—interpolation *plus* tinkering, which Kerrigan would normally regard as a sign of the author at work. But Marlowe was dead by 1593 and—assuming the priority of the A text—these revisions could hardly be by him, nor do we know why they were made. That includes the Bird/Rowley work in 1602; the fact that it was paid for late in November, with the Revels season looming, may point to an explanation, though Henslowe does not mark the fact.[34] We could speculate that the B text was somehow related to versions of the play performed in Germany in the early seventeenth century—but speculation is all it would be (Herz 1903: 66). In this instance I fall back on the mantra I invoked in respect of Shakespeare's plays: *We simply do not know how or why such different versions of these plays exist and got into print.* But this is the only play outside the Shakespeare canon about which I feel such doubt.

---

[33] The case was most fully made by Eric Rasmussen (1993) and carried over into the two parallel-text editions of *Dr Faustus* which Rasmussen has co-edited with David Bevington (Marlowe 1993 and 1995). Their lead has been followed by Mark Thornton Burnett (Marlowe 1999) and David Scott Kastan (Marlowe 2005) in their own parallel-text editions. The only dissonant note of any substance has been Michael Keefer, in his revised edition of the play (Marlowe 2007).

[34] As with *The Spanish Tragedy*, it is inconceivable that a play so popular—reprinted at least ten times between 1604 and 1631 (1604 text in 1609 and 1611; 1616 text in 1619, 1620, 1624, 1628, and 1631)—was not performed at court on some occasion. We just have no record of it.

THE MALCONTENT

In the case of *The Malcontent* there are very few doubts at all about the nature of the revisions to the play and the reasons for them. The play was written by John Marston for the Children of the Chapel, and twice printed in 1604 as it would have been played by them at James Burbage's indoor Blackfriars theatre. Somehow, however, the King's Men acquired the play, and later in the year the same printer and publisher (Valentine Sims, William Aspley) published a distinctively different version, proclaiming on the title page that it was 'Augmented by Marston. With the additions played by the Kings Majesty's servants. Written by John Webster.'[35] Scholars generally agree this means that Marston wrote most of the 'additions' to his own boy-company play to facilitate its performance by the King's Men, including a role for an Armin-type fool, which was not a feature of boy-company plays; and Webster wrote the induction (in which some members of the King's Men appear as 'themselves'), plus a few lesser 'additions'. The original text of 1,908 lines was expanded to 2,531 lines, as Richard Burbage (playing 'himself' in the Induction) explains, 'to entertain a little more time, and to abridge the not-received custom of music in our theatre' (83–4). The consort of musicians at the Blackfriars played before and during performances, and inter-act divisions were observed to allow for the trimming of candles—practices the King's Men would inherit with that theatre after 1608, but not at the Globe. Marston and Webster knew exactly how much extra stage-time was expected at the Globe, something like 2,500 lines being the norm there, whereas something closer to 2,000 lines was adequate for the indoor theatres. This is perhaps the best indicator we have of what was normal at the two kinds of theatre and how conscious theatrical professionals were of this. Such movement of plays between different companies and theatres was unusual during Shakespeare's lifetime and it is unclear whether this was an amicable arrangement or the King's Men had some score to settle with the 'little eyases' at the Blackfriars.[36]

PHILASTER

Beaumont and Fletcher's *Philaster, Or Love Lies A-Bleeding* is one of the relatively rare plays in the period whose texts seem to mirror quite closely the situation we

---

[35] As I have argued, *The Spanish Tragedy* would not have changed hands without Tilney's permission (see note 32).

[36] How precisely the King's Men were able to perform the play remains obscure. The Induction suggests that they were paying back the newly named Children of the Queen's Revels for the theft of one of their own plays. It is also not impossible that there was an amicable agreement between the two companies. But it seems most likely that Samuel Daniel's acquisition of the licensing responsibilities for the children's company—depriving Tilney of his monopoly and fudging the protocols—played its part in allowing the 'theft' to happen. When all the leading companies were taken into royal patronage, Queen Anna appointed Daniel as the licenser of her Children of the Revels, breaking the Elizabethan pattern of having a single licenser for all plays. He seems to have been singularly ill-suited to the post and there is some evidence that he sold it within a year or so. But who then licensed the Revels boys until Sir George Buc took on a reformed company of them in 1610, alongside his other licensing duties, is not known.

find with so many of Shakespeare's—a 'bad' version published first and a 'good' one later. As is always the case with Shakespeare, we find that the situation is not simply that the first-published version is a poorly communicated version of the later one. There are substantive differences between the two versions. At some point purposeful changes were introduced to the basic plotting and characterization of the play, changes which cannot simply be explained away by poor transmission of the first-printed version. In the case of *Philaster* these occur very noticeably at the beginning and end of the text.

Philaster seems to have been written *c.* 1609/10 for the King's Men, one of the first plays—if not the very first—by Beaumont and Fletcher for them. Its popularity was immediate, certainly at court. It was apparently played there twice in the 1612/13 Revels season and was one of the plays considered for court performance between 1615 and 1622.[37] It was certainly played there again on 21 February 1637 (Bawcutt 1996: 201). It also came to be one of the most reprinted plays of the era, though not till a decade after it was first performed, with quartos published in 1620, 1622, 1628, 1634, 1639 (two issues), 1652, and two more, probably early in the Restoration (when it was also back onstage). It was then included in the Second Beaumont and Fletcher Folio of 1679.

Our concern is only with the first two of these, Q1 and Q2, the only versions with independent authority, all subsequent imprints deriving from Q2. Q1 was published as 'PHILASTER. Or Love Lies a-Bleeding. Acted at the Globe by his Majesty's Servants... 1620'. Q2 repeats this information, but adds that it had also 'been diverse times acted, at... the Black-Friars' and that this was 'The second impression, corrected, and amended... 1622'. The publisher expanded the claim that this copy was 'corrected, and amended' with a note 'To the Reader' which wittily plays on the subtitle: 'Philaster and Arethusa his love have lain so long a-bleeding, by reason of some dangerous and gaping holes which they received in the first impression... Although they were hurt neither by me nor the printer, yet I... have adventured to bind up their wounds... so maimed and deformed as they at the first were... assuredly they will now find double favour, being reformed and set forth suitable to their birth and breeding' (Beaumont and Fletcher 2003: 3).

The claim is borne out to the extent, as Andrew Gurr puts it, that 'Q1 undoubtedly does present a text inferior in almost all respects to that of Q2. The two texts differ in numerous words and phrases throughout. Q1 is shorter by some 200 lines; in particular the first and last few hundred lines are widely divergent from Q2, evidently written by a different hand from those of the authors, with only resemblances of plot in the first section and occasional verbal echoes in the last' (lxxv). Q1 is a 'bad' quarto—Gurr describes it as 'a botched text throughout' (lxxvi)—to Q2's 'good' quarto, the latter based possibly on an authorial text. That

---

[37] Chambers 1923: 4.127. The consideration was noted on one of four scraps of paper listing plays found within the manuscript of Buc's *History of Richard III*. They were first published by Marcham, Frank (1925); E. K. Chambers first suggested that they represented plays considered to be performed at court and has been misrepresented as suggesting that they date narrowly from 1619 or 1620. As Gary Taylor shows, the range of possibilities is wider than that (2007: 331–4).

view is held by Leo Kirschbaum and most editors of the play (1945: 707). While we may no longer wish to talk in terms of piracy about a text like Q1, it certainly has all the hallmarks of having been transcribed by oral/aural means with, for example, little attention to line endings or the difference between prose and verse (see pp. 141, 148). Q2 looks more like a version based on a decent manuscript, and one that shows no signs of having been tidied up for the stage.

The debate over the play's textual history has been bedevilled by the assumption that the versions which lie behind Q1 and Q2 must *both* have existed *c.* 1610, so that all references within the text must relate to that time frame.[38] Whether the term is used or not, the 'foul papers' hypothesis holds sway: a 'good' version (Q2) looks to be based on a generally respectable manuscript, so it is deemed originary and authoritative. Oral/aural transmission can explain how so much of the language of the Q1 text is poorer and clumsier than that we encounter in Q2.[39] But it is much more difficult to explain how the author of Q1 arbitrarily decides to marry off Galatea to Clerimont and Bellario to Trasiline as a way of rounding off the action, while in Q2 Galatea is not involved in the ending at all and Bellario/Euphrasia is accepted by Princess Arethusa as an unmarried companion.[40] This somehow reflects a change of mind, authorial or otherwise. The question is how and when this change came about.

At least one significant difference between Q1 and Q2 can best be explained if the change was made closer to 1622 than to 1610. This is the treatment of Pharamond (Pharamont in Q1), the Spanish prince promised to Princess Arethusa. In both versions he is introduced with appropriate dignity, feted by the King, and apparently accepted—however reluctantly—by Arethusa. Only when Philaster confronts him ('you foreign man' [1.1.174]) does Pharamond's true villainous nature, entirely predictable in early Jacobean Protestant England, begin to emerge. He has an affair with his female counterpart, Megra; slanders Arethusa (with the consequence that Philaster is condemned to death); and is held hostage by the people to save Philaster, mock-threatening to castrate and dismember him. This underscores the point that he is a *comic* villain, whose schemes are doomed to fail in a tragicomic structure which flags from the beginning an inevitably happy ending, though the means of finding that happiness are unpredictable. The danger not the death is the classic motive force of Fletcherian tragicomedy.

But here the two versions diverge. In Q1 Philaster saves Pharamont, who thanks him with a scant two lines (Beaumont and Fletcher 2003: Appendix A, Q1 5.4.77–8). Thereafter he is made to experience the utmost discomfort as his schemes are revealed and his failure made apparent. When the King hands the

---

[38] See Savage 1949. He assumes that the cross-dressed Bellario must allude to Lady Arbella Stuart's awkward situation at court (see p. 90), and that the unaccountable decision in Q1 to marry her off to Cleremont (and Galatea to Thrasiline) was a change forced on the authors to minimize the parallels (ibid).

[39] See Beaumont and Fletcher 2003: lxxvi–lxxvii for examples of Q1's 'misreadings'; Appendix B addresses questions of lineation in both versions: 132–6.

[40] My spelling of the names reflects the different usages in Q1 and Q2.

crown of Sicily to Philaster and claims him as his son, Pharamont sputters: 'How Sir, yer son, what am I then, your Daughter you gave to me' (Appendix A, Q1 5.5.115). When Leon (Q2's Dion) reveals that Philaster and Arethusa are already married, Pharamont protests: 'How married? I hope your highness will not use me so, I came not to be disgraced, and return alone' (Appendix A, Q1 5.5.124–5). Finally, as the King banishes Megra from the court but orders her confined until he decides on her fate, Pharamont tries to leave with what little dignity he has left: 'Here's such an age of transformation, that I do not know how to trust myself; I'll get me gone too: Sir, the disparagement you have done must be called in question. I have power to right myself, and will' (Appendix A, Q1 5.5.167–70). Like Malvolio's threat in *Twelfth Night* to 'be revenged on the whole pack of you' (5.1.378), it is the bluster of a man humiliated beyond bearing, perhaps uncomfortable in its comedy.

Q2 is very different. Pharamond thanks Philaster for saving him from the citizens with something approaching grace ('Sir, there is some humanity in you, / You have a noble soul', 5.4.99–100) and then makes genuine comedy out of his relief to be spared from 'these wild dogs' (111). Philaster assures the people that 'there is no danger in him' (119). When the King hails Philaster as 'My son' (5.5.8), Pharamond says nothing. Philaster then grants him 'full leave / to make an honourable voyage home' (20–1), suggesting (perhaps jokingly) that he might take Megra with him. Pharamond still remains silent. But then Megra tries to stir up mischief by implying that Arethusa has had improper relations with Bellario. Q2 examines the consequences of this slander in far more detail than Q1: the revelation that 'Bellario' is actually Euphrasia solves nothing, because then there is a suggestion of impropriety between her and Philaster. Threats of death and torture, and Philaster's offer twice to commit suicide, now form the emotional centre of the play's ending, replacing the marriages of Galatea and Bellario.

As the passion subsides, with Arethusa's decision not to be jealous of 'Bellario', the spotlight returns to Megra and Pharamond. Philaster argues that they should not 'Wrong...the freedom of our souls so much / To think to take revenge of that base woman; / Her malice cannot hurt us. Set her free' (5.5.206–8). The King agrees, though he banishes her from the court. And he treats Pharamond—who has remained silent and somewhat overshadowed in this scene—with diplomatic courtesy:

> You, Pharamond,
> Shall have free passage, and a conduct home
> Worthy so great a Prince. When you come there
> Remember 'twas your faults lost you her [i.e. Arethusa]
> And not my purposed will.
> *Pharamond*:   I do confess,
>   Renownèd sir.   (5.5.211–16)

So Philaster is able to demonstrate royal magnanimity, which the King endorses, while Pharamond is allowed to show some humanity, even remorse, and to retire with dignity.

These endings are significantly different. We have no objective way of knowing how they came about, but it is implausible that both were created *c*. 1610. The likeliest explanation for the different treatment of Pharamond is surely a change in diplomatic relations with Spain. King James was always more pro-Spanish than his English subjects and had negotiated peace with Spain in 1604. At the time the play was first written the idea of a Spanish match for one of his children (such as that Pharamond sought) was not an immediate possibility, and there was no reason to object to a comic villain acting out a fantasy such as we find in Q1.[41] By the end of 1619, however, James was actively looking into a Spanish match for Prince Charles, who since the death of Prince Henry in 1612 had been heir to the throne. Any time after 1619 it is unlikely that James (or Sir George Buc) would have welcomed a gratuitously offensive depiction of a Spanish royal seeking a dynastic marriage.[42] In Q2 of *Philaster* Pharamond remains a comic villain, but the ending is far less brutal, allowing him a degree of dignity.

I conclude that the new elements of Q2 were probably produced for a court performance of the play at some time between 1619 and 1622. I cannot prove this, but it fits all the known circumstances. The fact that Q1 was published in 1620 suggests that the King's Men already had it in revival about that time, since publication often accompanied or followed shortly after a revival (Knutson 1991: 12–13, 81). In this scenario Beaumont (whom scholars credit with most of the Q1 text) could not have been the reviser; he retired from the stage in 1613 and died in 1616. But Fletcher continued to work as the 'ordinary poet' for the King's Men until his death in 1625 and might well have been employed in such a 'diplomatic' revision. There is, however, not enough evidence upon which to base a stylistic judgement, and it is not material to my argument who in fact made the changes. (See Beaumont and Fletcher 2003: xxiv–xxv.)

My point is to establish that there is a very similar pattern here to that which pertains with the Shakespeare 'bad' and 'good' texts. Q1 was very probably based on *Philaster* as Beaumont and Fletcher originally wrote it, but seriously corrupted (probably) by oral/aural transmission of the text. The most plausible explanation for Q2 is that the play was revised for court performance, under pressure from the new diplomatic situation; this gave rise both to a better-quality manuscript and to significantly altered elements of plot and characterization. The 'foul papers' editorial tradition (which has invariably favoured Q2) has led us to think of those altered elements as not only aesthetic improvements—which I think most people

---

[41] James certainly harboured ambitions of marrying his heir apparent, Prince Henry, to the Spanish Infanta, though Henry himself resisted the idea and nothing concrete was in prospect. In 1610 the Infanta was secretly engaged to the Dauphin of France, finally putting an end to the possibility.

[42] In 1623 Charles and the Duke of Buckingham went to Madrid, hoping to secure marriage with the (new) Spanish Infanta, but the bid failed. They joined the anti-Spanish voices in the country and James was reluctantly pushed towards war with Spain. This is probably what gave Sir Henry Herbert the confidence to license Middleton's strongly anti-Spanish *A Game at Chess* in 1624. In 1631 Herbert declined to license Massinger's *Believe as Ye List* 'because it did contain dangerous matter, as the deposing of Sebastian king of Portugal, by Philip the Second, and there being a peace sworn twixt the kings of England and Spain' (Bawcutt 1996: 52). The Masters of the Revels had constantly to be alert to such diplomatic nuances.

would concede—but also part of the authors' original conception. But it is not so heretical to allow that second thoughts might result in improvement.

The important truth to take away from this is that Q1 is *not* a corrupt version of Q2. The scenario I have outlined to explain the differences between them is, and only can be, conjectural; but it highlights real differences which it is implausible to suggest might come about in some clumsy process of redaction—or, indeed, in 'continuous copy', progressive changes made by the actors (see pp. 151, 163). Whichever in fact came first, and whatever circumstances required it, *substantive*, *consistent*, and *intentional* changes were made to the plotting and characterization. This, I suggest, is what we will also repeatedly find in the parallel cases of *Romeo and Juliet*, *Merry Wives of Windsor*, *Hamlet*, *Henry V*, and *2* and *3 Henry VI*.

THE MAID'S TRAGEDY

The textual history of *The Maid's Tragedy* is quite parallel to that of *Philaster*. It was written by 1611 and first published in 1619 (Q1), though in this case in a perfectly respectable text. A second edition appeared in 1622 (Q2), containing some 80 lines which are not in Q1, in seven discrete passages. There are also more than 400 minor localized variants, maybe half of which can be ascribed to compositorial practice. But in perhaps 200 places we must suspect authorial intervention—in Kerrigan's terms, it has been quite 'tinkered' or 'fidgeted' with (see p. 112). It looks as though an author—rather than a printer—has gone through it systematically, changing things at will, though there is nothing like the decisive change in plotting that we find in *Philaster*.[43]

There are, however, certain elements in the changes which would be particularly consistent with freshening it up for a new performance at court. Within the 80 lines there are no fewer than three songs not in the original.[44] The additions within the masque in 1.2. (lines 256–71) include 'To bed, to bed, come Hymen lead the bride', and within those at 2.1.79–97 Aspatia sings 'Lay a garland on my hearse of the dismal yew' and Dula sings 'I could never have the power'. Songs, of course, are not unique to courtly drama, but three additional ones might well constitute the kind of small embellishments, unexpected extras, calculated to please an audience that probably knew the play quite well. They would doubtless also consume more time than a

---

[43] Modern scholarship suggests that Beaumont wrote the majority of *The Maid's Tragedy*, with Fletcher only adding a few scenes. But Beaumont had retired from the stage by 1613. If it was he that 'fidgeted', he must have done so early, as indeed Robert K. Turner concluded he had done (Turner 1957). But that analysis was yet another one in thrall to 'foul papers' editorial theory and avoids the practical questions of a) why the Q2 text was not printed in the first place, in 1619; and b) why the publisher of Q2 would have gone to the trouble and expense of setting another old manuscript in place of the perfectly adequate one used for Q1. The likeliest explanation has to be that the Q2 text was not available in 1619, but seemed—for whatever reason—a saleable commodity in 1622. If so, Fletcher, as the King's Men's 'ordinary poet', once more probably did the 'fidgeting' for his dead partner.

[44] On the portability of songs in plays, see Stern 2009a: 120–73; on their addition to existing texts, sometimes for court performances, see 147–53.

simple line-count would suggest. In another fresh passage within the masque (1.2.148–57), Cynthia, the moon-goddess, addresses her sister goddess, Night:

> Yet whil'st our reign lasts, let us stretch our power
> To give our servants one contented hour,
> With such unwonted solemn grace and state
> As may forever after force them hate
> Our brother's glorious beams.   (148–52)

This is one of several instances where court plays draw attention to night-time and revelling, consuming the dark hours as pleasurably as possible. (In the folio *Merry Wives of Windsor* we shall see a reference to it being one o'clock in the morning: see p. 254.) Of course a night-time masque at court was always part of the fiction of the play, but this new passage would take on a meta-theatrical resonance in the actuality of a late-night court performance.

I conclude, therefore, that—like *Philaster*—*The Maid's Tragedy* was probably revised to be performed at court at some time between 1615 and 1622, and most likely after 1619 (see p. 122). The second quartos of both plays were published by Francis Constable, and in the same year. That of *Philaster* is modestly described on the title page as 'corrected, and amended', though in fact the text is quite extensively changed from that of Q1. That of *The Maid's Tragedy* is much more dramatically advertised as 'Newly perused, augmented, and enlarged' on the strength of 80 new lines. Both do, however, seem essentially to tell the truth. It is time to consider what title pages actually tell us.

* * *

TITLE PAGES: 'AUGMENTED', 'ENLARGED', 'AMENDED', 'WITH ADDITIONS', 'CORRECTED'

Not all plays that were revised signify as much on their title pages. Of the plays we have already considered, it will be apparent that any or all of *'augmented'*, *'enlarged'*, *'amended'*, *'with additions'*, and *'corrected'*—the only terms which signal any changes to a text in the Shakespearean era—might have appeared on the title page of Dekker's *Old Fortunatus*. But none of them did. Moreover, not even all plays that had earlier been published in different versions register the change. When the revised text of *Dr Faustus* appeared in 1616 it boasted a splendid new wood-cut but said nothing about the revision. It was not until 1619 that a printing modestly announced 'With new additions'. This was all at the publisher's whim.

We must also recognize that information is not necessarily true because it appears on a title page. When the printer of the 1602 *Merry Wives of Windsor* (a train-wreck of a text in so many ways) tells us that it is 'Intermixed with sundry variable and pleasing humours, of Sir *Hugh* the Welch Knight', rather than priest, it does not instil in us any confidence that anyone involved in the product has either seen or read the play. All we can really say for sure is that someone thought that whatever appeared (or did not appear) on the title page of a play improved its chances of selling. On the other hand, as we shall see, where we can check against the facts, very few claims about changes to a text are completely dishonest—or, at least, beyond reasonable explanation. Many of the doubts voiced about their claims in the past were, in fact, tied to 'foul papers' editorial theory, which virtually required that the 'better' version of a text (where there was more than one) must have been the author's original work. Where title pages contradicted this it was convenient to dismiss them as salesmanship, or to construe them tortuously. They do repay attention. It says something, for instance, that three out of five of the terms specifically claim an *expansion* of the text, not simply a revision, much less a contraction. For reasons I advance throughout this book, I believe that plays which either were longer than average or were expanded (however modestly) were particularly likely to be associated with court performances.

The significance of all five of the terms signalling change has been much disputed, especially in the Shakespearean instances. I want to put this into context by considering all of their uses, which turn out, perhaps surprisingly, to be quite limited (and to tend to recur repetitively in a small circle of texts), though Shakespearean examples are disproportionately high.[45] As I have said, these are the only title page terms used to describe changes to performed play texts during Shakespeare's working lifetime. (I have stretched this from 1590 to the publication of the First Folio. For the sake of completeness, I do follow them down to the 1642 watershed, but you will note their rarity after 1623.) 'Revised', for example, is not seen before 1630, when it is first used in the third quarto of *The Maid's Tragedy*; no one uses 'restored' at all.[46]

By the same token I have not found any references to the revision of plays in paratextual material within this time frame. There are instances from the 1630s, such as Heywood's Prologue for the eighth reprint of the first part of *If You Know Not Me, You Know Nobody*, where he claims to have reclaimed the true text from early corruptions (though in truth his changes are minimal).[47] But such changes seem to relate to the 'Elizabethan revival' of the Caroline period, trying to project these texts as classics; they are quite separate from the kinds of earlier revision with which I am concerned.

Most of the extant plays which we know to have been performed at court in the period I have defined are discussed somewhere within this book. The very few exceptions are *The Contention Between Liberality and Prodigality* (pub. 1602); *The Fair Maid of Bristow* (pub. 1605); Middleton's *The Phoenix* (pub. 1607); and Nathan Field's *A Woman Is a Weathercock* (pub. 1612).[48] I have not discussed them because their texts show no signs of having been revised and their lengths are not remarkable.

[45] I want once more to acknowledge the *DEEP Database of Early English Playbooks* created by Alan Farmer and Zachary Lesser, without which an exercise of this nature would be infinitely more time-consuming.
[46] 'Revised' also appears in Heywood's 1632 *Four Prentices of London* and his 1638 *Rape of Lucrece*, and may well be the author's own choice.
[47] Heywood similarly revised the fourth imprint of part 2 of *If You Know Not Me, You Know Nobody* in 1633, but there is no reference to it on the title page or in any paratext.
[48] Several other court plays were also published in the period, such as some by Lyly, but they derive from the 1580s or very early 1590s; Robert Greene's old Queen's Men's play, *Orlando Furioso*, also appeared in print (1594) but was somewhat earlier.

Table 4.1 Title page uses of 'augmented', 'enlarged', 'amended', 'with additions', 'corrected'

Augmented			
	Love's Labour's Lost*	Q1 1598	'Newly corrected and augmented By W. Shakespere'
	Romeo and Juliet*	Q2 1599	'Newly corrected, augmented, and amended'
	Richard III	Q3 1602	'Newly augmented, By William Shakespeare'
	The Malcontent* (Marston)	Q3 1604	'Augmented by Marston. With the additions played by the Kings Maiesties servants. Written by Ihon Webster.'
	The Devil's Charter* (Barnes)	Q1 1607	'As it was plaide before the Kings Maiestie, vpon Candlemasse night last: by his Maiesties Seruants. But more exactly reveewed, corrected, and augmented since by the author, for the more pleasure and profit of the reader.'
	The Maid's Tragedy* (Beaumont & Fletcher)	Q2 1622	'Newly perused, augmented, and inlarged'
Enlarged			
	The Spanish Tragedy* (Kyd)	Q4 1602	'Newly corrected, amended, and enlarged with new additions of the Painters part, and others.'
	Hamlet	Q2 1604/5	'Newly imprinted and enlarged to almost as much againe as it was, according to the true and perfect Coppie.'
	'The Whole Contention betweene the two Famous Houses, LANCASTER and YORKE.*	1619. Second imprint of The First Part of the Contention and The True Tragedy	'Diuided into two Parts: And newly corrected and enlarged. Written by William Shakespeare, Gent.'
	The Maid's Tragedy* (Beaumont & Fletcher)	Q2 1622	'Newly perused, augmented, and inlarged.'
Amended			
	The Spanish Tragedy (Kyd).*	Q1 1592	'Newly corrected and amended of such grosse faults as passed in the first impression.'
	Soliman and Perseda* (anon)	Q2 1599	'Newly corrected and amended.'
	Romeo and Juliet*	Q2 1599	'Newly corrected, augmented, and amended'
	The Spanish Tragedy* (Kyd)	Q4 1602	'Newly corrected, amended, and enlarged with new additions of the Painters part, and others.'

	Philaster (Beaumont & Fletcher)*	Q2 1622	'The second Impression, corrected, and amended.'
	Bussy D'Ambois (Chapman)*	Q2 1641	'Being much corrected and amended by the Author before his death.'
With Additions			
	*The Spanish Tragedy** (Kyd)	Q4 1602	'Newly corrected, amended, and enlarged with new additions of the Painters part, and others.'
	The Malcontent (Marston)	Q3 1604	'Augmented by Marston. With the additions played by the Kings Maiesties servants. Written by Ihon Webster.'
	Richard II (Shakespeare)	Q4 1608	'With new additions of the Parliament Sceane, and the deposing of King Richard.' (Not in all copies.)
	Mucedorus (Anonymous)	Q2 1610	'Amplified with new additions.'
	A Faire Quarrell (Rowley & Middleton)	Q1b 1617	'With new Additions of Mr. Chaughs and Trimtrams Roaring, and the Bauds Song. Neuer before Printed.'
	Doctor Faustus (Marlowe)	Q4 1619	'With new Additions.' (The additions first appeared in Q3 1616, but that edition did not advertise them.)
Corrected			
	The Spanish Tragedy (Kyd)*	Q1 1592	'Newly corrected and amended of such grosse faults as passed in the first impression.'
	Locrine (Charles Tilney? Peele?)	Q1 1595	'Newly set foorth, ouerseene and corrected, By W. S.'
	*Love's Labour's Lost**	Q1 1598	'Newly corrected and augmented By W. Shakespere.'
	*Soliman and Perseda** (anon)	Q2 1599	'Newly corrected and amended.'
	*Romeo and Juliet**	Q2 1599	'Newly corrected, augmented, and amended.'
	1 Henry IV	Q2[49] 1599	'Newly corrected by W. Shake-speare.'
	*The Spanish Tragedy** (Kyd)	Q4 1602	'Newly corrected, amended, and enlarged with new additions of the Painters part, and others.'
	Parasitaster, or The Fawne (Marston)	Q2 1606	'And now corrected of many faults, which by reason of the Authors absence, were let slip in the first edition.'

(*continued*)

---

[49] Q2 *1 Henry IV*. There were evidently two editions of *1 Henry IV* in 1598, but only a fragment of one of these—usually known as Q0—remains; that *could* have been the version by which Q2's 'Newly corrected' measures itself. The other, generally known as Q1, survives in three more or less complete copies, and that is the version which the 1599 text (Q2) is based upon. See Kastan 2002: 106–11.

Table 4.1 Continued

The Devil's Charter* (Barnes)	Q1 1607	'As it was plaide before the Kings Maiestie, vpon Candlemasse night last: by his Maiesties Seruants. But more exactly reuewed, corrected, and augmented since by the author, for the more pleasure and profit of the reader.'
Jack Drum's Entertainment (Marston)	Q2 1616	'Newly corrected.'
The Whole Contention betweene the two Famous Houses, LANCASTER and YORKE.*	Q2s 1619	'Diuided into two Parts: And newly corrected and enlarged. Written by William Shakespeare, Gent.'
Philaster (Beaumont & Fletcher)*	Q2 1622	'The second Impression, corrected, and amended.'
The Faithful Shepherdess (Beaumont & Fletcher)	Q2 1629	'Newly corrected.'
Merry Wives of Windsor	Q3 1630	'Newly corrected.'
Love's Mistress (Heywood)	Q2 1638	'corrected by the Author, THOMAS HEYWOOD'
Bussy D'Ambois* (Chapman)	Q2 1641	'Being much corrected and amended by the Author before his death.'

(* indicates that a text appears under more than one head)[50]

The instances I cite are *all* the *first* usages of my key terms—'augmented', 'enlarged', 'amended', 'with additions', 'corrected'—as they were applied to plays performed on public stages down to 1642. It should be understood that once these statements appear on an edition, they will probably also appear on subsequent imprints of the same play, though I shall not tabulate or discuss those here. This means that plays like *The Spanish Tragedy*, *Romeo and Juliet*, *Mucedorus*, *Philaster*, and *1 Henry IV*, which were often reprinted, kept this vocabulary alive. But it seems more significant that later publishers either had less call to use it or were reluctant to adopt it.

Augmented

'Augmented' seems to have been coined specifically for the works of Shakespeare, since the first three usages all apply to his texts: *Love's Labour's Lost* (1598), *Romeo and Juliet* (1599), and *Richard III* (1602).[51] We can ascribe its first uses to Cuthbert

---

[50] I have not followed my usual practice of modernizing these title-page entries since they are all accessible as they stand and give authentic flavour. I have not included 'perused' or 'reviewed' in the list of key terms, because they indicate a possible disposition to change but not actual change itself. All their usages are actually coupled with one or more of my five key terms.

[51] Lukas Erne comments on 'corrected', 'augmented', or 'enlarged' in Shakespeare's plays as 'important for the *literary* status of playbooks generally' (2013: 98, my emphasis). There is doubtless some truth in this. But my argument is that they firstly flag a change in the text for different *playing* conditions.

Burby, the publisher of the first two, and this was then imitated by Thomas Creede, who printed the third. In the case of *Love's Labour's Lost* the claim seems to be in respect of an earlier, shorter text. Editors *invariably* assume that the reference is to a lost *printed* text, but nothing requires this to be the case.[52] The text as printed shows considerable muddle (especially in such matters as speech prefixes) which could either betoken Shakespeare's working methods—careless about details that could be tidied up later, quick to insert second thoughts without thoroughly cancelling first ones—or could reflect a substantial revision, the details of which were incomplete in the printer's copy. G. R. Hibbard's *Oxford Shakespeare* edition (1990), for example, argues for the former; the 1923 New Cambridge edition, by Sir Arthur Quiller-Couch and John Dover Wilson, enthusiastically champions the latter. Signs of possible revision include the introduction of *three* French Lords in 2.1, two of whom quietly disappear before the end of 4.1, confusion over the naming of the French ladies, and utter confusion over the names of Holofernes and Nathaniel from about a third of the way through 4.2. The text is certainly 'augmented' to the extent that we have two separate passages where both first thoughts and expanded second thoughts are included. As Hibbard puts it: 'At 4.3.293, twenty-three lines of a first draft have been expanded into a revised version of forty-eight lines; and at 5.2.819 the thirty-five lines of dialogue between Biron and Rosaline that follow are clearly meant to replace a mere six lines of dialogue between them that began originally as 5.2.805' (76). Grace Ioppolo discusses some of these 'second thoughts' in detail, speaking of 'particular, specific and deliberately crafted revisions in the texts of *Love's Labour's Lost* [that] show Shakespeare reshaping and redefining the role of Berowne' and how 'in revising Berowne, [he] revised his hero, his play, and his own artistic role, function, and method' (1991: 102, 98). Such revision, as I shall argue, is typical of Shakespeare's reworkings for the court. At 2,651 lines, although unexceptional by the standard of Shakespeare's own histories and tragedies, the play is the longest of the 1590s romantic comedies. So there is at least a case for 'augmented', which is specifically linked with advertising that the text is *As it was presented before her Highness this last Christmas*.

In the case of Q2 *Romeo and Juliet's* 'augmented' we encounter a classic instance of the 'bad' quarto issue (see pp. 139–40). Brian Gibbons, in the full flight of Greg's 'foul papers' certainties, follows Pollard in dubbing the 1597 Q1 of the play 'a Bad Quarto, piratical and dependent on an especially unreliable means of transmission of the text'. He consequently states categorically that the wording on the Q2 title page 'means that it is a replacement of the first edition, not a revision of an earlier version of the play' (1980: 1). This makes adequate sense of the 'corrected' and 'amended' in that wording, but implicitly reduces 'augmented' to mean something like restoring the wordage that got lost by the 'unreliable means

---

[52] Arthur Freeman and Paul Grinke identified a reference to a '1597' edition of *Love's Labour's Lost* in an inventory of the books of Edward Conway, second Viscount Conway (2002: 18). But, as Lukas Erne has shown, the inventory is not error-free and without further corroboration this remains speculative (Erne 2013: 207–8; Murphy 2003: 461).

of transmission' behind Q1. And this is hardly an adequate explanation of the differences between the two texts (see pp. 211–13). It is certainly not unreasonable to suppose that Q2 is what it implicitly claims to be, a revised and expanded version of what first appeared as Q1. No external evidence connects this with court performance, but at 2,989 lines, it is long for the public stage (pp. 77–80).

No one has set much stock by the claim of Q3 *Richard III* to be '*Newly augmented, By William Shakespeare*'. Neither Anthony Hammond (1982) nor Janis Lull (1999), for example, notices it at all. Ioppolo presumably has it in mind when she talks of 'later reprints of Quartos which contain no major variants [but which]... misleadingly announce that they have been "augmented"' (1991: 6). John Jowett observes: 'The claim on the title-page... is misleading, for there is no new dialogue, but the text does introduce some new stage directions' (2000: 116). These in no meaningful sense 'augment' the text of either Q1 or Q2 (which are very similar to each other) so that it is tempting to think that Creede simply borrowed the term as a sales ploy. All of the surviving texts of *Richard III* are much of a length, and all are exceptionally long. Q1 (1597) has 3,389 lines; Q2 and all subsequent quartos (each reset from its predecessors, without apparent recourse to manuscripts) have two extra lines of dialogue. The folio text clearly did refer to another manuscript and has 3,570 lines, some never printed before, though it also omits a passage from the quartos. So it is apparent that there were at least two broadly Shakespearean versions of the play, neither of which, however, was probably playable on the public stage because of its extreme length. However, whenever a play has only survived in versions of extreme length, it is quite likely that a shorter one also existed for use in the Theatre or the Globe, which never found its way into print (see p. 110). So there is a possibility—no more than that—that Q3's '*Newly augmented*' is not just publisher's hype but belatedly acknowledges an expansion of the original text—dating from *c.* 1592–3—some time before 1597. (See later in this chapter on the 'With Additions' in Q1619 of *Dr Faustus* and 'Newly corrected' in Q3 *1 Henry IV*.)

These Shakespeare texts apart, only three other texts used 'augmented', and each use is distinct and intelligible. We have already observed that the 'augmented' in *The Malcontent* (Q3 1604) is fully justified. The next 'augmented' text was Barnabe Barnes's, *The Devil's Charter* (1607). This is a very long play, at 3,026 spoken lines and 274 lines of stage directions, and the fact of its performance on one of the key dates in the Revels season makes it very tempting to enlist it in the argument for a link between marked length and court performances.[53] But Barnes makes it clear that he added to it *after* the performance, so this leaves room for doubt. It joins Webster's *The Duchess of Malfi* (1623) as one of only two texts which explicitly tell us that they contain more material than was ever performed (as distinct from 'publicly' performed: see p. 89). Webster is the only one, however, who categorically tells us that he composed, apparently from the outset, a play that was too long to stage: 'with diverse things printed, that the length of the play would not bear in the

---

[53] In R. B. McKerrow's edition (Barnes 1904) the through-line numbering gives a count of 3,330. If the play as printed were performed it would certainly be on a par with Q2 *Hamlet*.

presentment' (see p. 89). The whole thesis of Lukas Erne's *Shakespeare as Literary Dramatist* is that many Shakespeare plays also fit that category, though none was published saying as much. The last play published as 'augmented' was *The Maid's Tragedy* (Q2, 1622), which we have considered, and its claim is at least modestly justified.

Enlarged

'Enlarged' first entered the booksellers' vocabulary for plays in 1602, when it was applied to the fourth quarto of *The Spanish Tragedy*. Again, this is indisputably a true claim, in that the text contains some 320 lines not in any of the earlier quartos, including a whole new scene with the painter (see p. 116). The claim of Q2 *Hamlet* (1604–5) to be 'enlarged' is also certainly true by comparison with the 1603 first quarto. A debate exists (to which we shall return in due course) as to whether this means that its 'true and perfect copy' existed before 1603, or whether it only came into being with the enlargement. I would merely point out here that all the 'augmented' and 'enlarged' texts we have looked at so far mean exactly that: they were first published (and presumably written) smaller and then made larger.

The next instance of plays being advertised as 'enlarged' is in some ways the most problematic. It is the 1619 reissue of *The First Part of the Contention* and *The True Tragedy* (i.e. the early versions of *2* and *3 Henry VI*) as 'The Whole Contention between the two Famous Houses, LANCASTER and YORK.' This formed part of the so-called 'False Folio' published by William Jaggard and printed (for the most part) by Thomas Pavier. The most pronounced new feature of this text is the linking of the two plays as a continuous item, though that hardly counts as enlargement. There is, however, an unusual level of attention to the text of *The Contention* in an edition often regarded as a piece of unscrupulous sales practice, where 'enlarged' might deceive buyers who perhaps knew that longer versions of these plays did exist.[54] There are six short passages which alter what appears in Q1594, the most notable of which is a correction of York's false recitation of the seven sons of Edward III.[55] In *The Contention* he forgets the second-born William of Hatfield and promotes Edmund of Langley, Duke of York (actually fifth born), to that position; he also incorrectly names an Earl of March as the fifth son. This would likewise be corrected in *2 Henry VI* (2.2.10–17), in similar but not identical language. The six items between them add fewer than ten new lines to the text, such that the claim to enlargement is highly dubious.[56]

---

[54] More intriguing than the 'enlarged' is the claim that the *Whole Contention* is 'Divided into two Parts', since we assume that it started life as two separate plays. Was there a tradition of playing the two works together? The *Contention* at 1,973 lines and the *True Tragedy* at 2,124 lines would together amount to over 4,000 lines. Court would seem to be the only plausible venue for such a production.

[55] The passage appears on C4r in both Q1 *The Contention* and *The Whole Contention*.

[56] The other five new passages (listed in Hattaway's edition of *2 Henry VI* [1991: 235–6]) find counterparts in F, but never in identical language. It would seem, as William Montgomery put it, that 'Q3 somehow had access to a supplementary report not available to those responsible for Q1' (Wells

The *'augmented, and inlarged'* claim for *The Maid's Tragedy* seems just to be tautology.

Amended

The earliest play advertised as 'amended' was the first extant edition of *The Spanish Tragedy* (1592). The claim refers to a lost 'first impression' and to creating a more accurate imprint of the play, rather than to any changes in Kyd's underlying script. Presumably the term still carries that sense in the 1602 fourth quarto, which, however, *also* claims to be 'enlarged'—a distinct term and, as we have said, justified. The next text to claim to be 'amended' was the second version of the old Queen's Men's play, *Soliman and Perseda* (1599), which announces itself as '*Newly corrected and amended*'. In fact this line only appears in some copies of this imprint and may be stamped in by hand (Greg 1939–59: 109 (i), 109 (ii)). There are no substantive departures from the Q1 text of 1592, so it is certain nothing had been amended '*Newly*'. This late advertisement was perhaps prompted by another instance of 'amended' that year, in Q2 *Romeo and Juliet* (discussed earlier)—one printer borrowing another's sales ploy. There again, the claim *seems* to relate to the accuracy of the text, not to changes in the original play. 'Amended' does not appear again until 1622 and the second quarto of *Philaster*. This 'amended' in fact flags significantly more than producing a more accurate text. As we have seen, this is a purposely revised text of the play (with much 'fidgeting').

The last use of 'amended' on a title page also proves to flag more than a tidying up of the text. This was the 1641 second quarto of *Bussy D'Ambois*. As Kerrigan's analysis showed, the claim that this was 'amended' by Chapman before his death may well tell the truth. One court performance of the play is recorded on 7 April 1634, only a month before Chapman died—which accords very closely with the claim of the Q2 title page (Bawcutt 1996: 188). There are some 228 variants between this and the original 1607/8 version, 'including thirty long alterations and additions and five excisions; their extent and tone show a concern only an author could feel' (Logan and Smith 1977: 150–1). In Kerrigan's terms, there are clear signs of fidgeting but also significant interpolations. He connects this with Albert H. Tricomi's demonstration that the revisions were probably made to make the play more congruent with its sequel, *The Revenge of Bussy D'Ambois* (1971–2; 1973). The most likely reason for doing that would be if the plays were to be produced in tandem and one of the likeliest contexts in which that might happen would be during a court Revels season (see pp. 65–6). In as much as the relatively small number of uses of 'amended' over the period is at all representative, it seems that the earlier uses make claims (whether truthfully or not) of improving the quality of the printing and/or its relationship to an underlying manuscript, whereas later usages (1622 and after) refer to changes in the underlying text itself.

---

and Taylor 1987: 180)—conceivably even the manuscript that ultimately lay behind Q1. It is difficult to understand why they made such limited use of whatever access they had.

With Additions

This category is easily dealt with because in each case the claim is categorically true. We have already effectively dealt with *The Spanish Tragedy*, *The Malcontent*, *Mucedorus*, and *A Fair Quarrel* under different heads. This leaves only *Dr Faustus*, perhaps the most famous set of 'additions' in the field, and the only Shakespearean instance, the 1608 *Richard II*.[57] In respect of *Dr Faustus*, it is perhaps surprising how long it took for those additions to appear in print (by comparison, say, with equally popular works like *The Spanish Tragedy* and *Mucedorus*)—that is, if the printed additions really are those mentioned in Henslowe's *Diary*, which there is no way of knowing. But even more surprising is that the 1616 imprint, where they first appeared, draws no attention to them. Not until 1619 do we get a seemingly casual '*With new Additions*'. This demonstrates that the title-page claim of a changed text *could* be legitimate, even if the referent was not the antecedent version in print. The '*new Additions*' in the 1619 *Faustus* dated back at least to 1616 and possibly to 1602—but they certainly existed. This could well be significant in relation to the Q3 *Richard III* (1602) (see under 'Augmented' earlier in this chapter), and the Q2 *1 Henry IV* (1599) and the Q3 *Merry Wives of Windsor* (1630) (see under 'Corrected' below).

I shall consider the 1608 *Richard II* ('*With new additions of the Parliament Sceane, and the deposing of King Richard*') in Chapter 7a (pp. 261–3). The claim of '*additions*' is irrefutable; the question is whether '*new*' means newly written or just newly printed.

Corrected

'Corrected', as will be apparent, often appears in conjunction with one or more of these other terms; indeed, nothing is 'amended' that is not also 'corrected', which suggests a degree of redundancy in these usages. 'Corrected' first appears—yet again—in the 1592 *Spanish Tragedy* (and again in the undoubtedly revised 1602 version), then in the 1598 *Love's Labour's Lost*, 1599 *Soliman and Perseda*, 1599 *Romeo and Juliet*, *The Devil's Charter* (1608), the 1619 *Whole Contention*, 1622 *Philaster*, and 1641 *Bussy D'Ambois*. To those instances we can add the sole edition of *Locrine* (1595), the second exant quarto of *1 Henry IV* (1599), the second quarto of Marston's *Parasitaster, or The Fawn* (1606), the second quarto of Marston's *Jack Drum's Entertainment*, the second quarto of *The Faithful Shepherdess* (1629), and the third quarto of *Merry Wives* (1630).

It is unlikely that a consistent sense is being used in all of these instances. Quite a few seem to want to imply the sense explicit in *Parasitaster*, *The Devil's Charter*, and *Bussy D'Ambois*—that the author himself had brought the text into line with his own intentions: '*now corrected of many faults, which by reason of the Authors absence, were let slip in the first edition*', and so on. Those who knew that Kyd wrote *The Spanish Tragedy* and that Shakespeare wrote *Romeo and Juliet* might infer that sense

---

[57] For the possibility that Shakespeare also wrote the 'additions' to the 1602 *Spanish Tragedy*, see p. 116 and n. 32.

from their 1592 and 1599 texts respectively, though the authors are not named and there is no evidence that they were involved with either publication. Kyd, who died in 1594, was certainly *not* the one who 'corrected' the 1602 version, any more than Marston, who abandoned the stage by 1608 at the latest, 'corrected' the 1616 *Jack Drum's Entertainment*. In most cases it seems likely that the 'correcting' is to be understood to mark the printer's doing a more accurate and professional job than was done in an earlier imprint—which is expressly what the 1592 *Spanish Tragedy* claims to be doing. Of course, whether the claim is true or not is another matter.

The situation becomes characteristically muddy when we look at the Shakespeare examples of 'corrected'; these, we note, are again the most numerous. *Love's Labour's Lost* is problematic in part because the title page is (apparently) explicit that Shakespeare 'corrected' and 'augmented' the play, but not that he wrote it in the first place. Moreover, while many assume that the 'corrected' refers to some previous (and lost) printed edition of that play, nothing actually says so. It may simply refer to an earlier manuscript/acting version. So too with *Romeo and Juliet* (1599): '*Newly corrected, augmented, and amended*' may suggest considerable, and purposeful, change from the earlier, first quarto, and it is certainly true that there are significant differences between those texts. But it could equally refer to another, lost acting version. Moreover, it is far from certain that only one individual was responsible for all three distinctly signalled versions of change and, if so, that the individual was Shakespeare. And, as we have already noted under 'augmented', we cannot be sure in 'bad' quarto territory whether Q2 represents an *earlier* version of the text, of which Q1 is a corruption, or whether it represents a *later* version, a purposeful improvement upon Q1. My purpose here is simply to examine what the wording of the title pages does (and does not) tell us—and 'corrected' tells us precious little, except that someone thought it would help to sell copies.

We have already discussed the *Whole Contention* under 'Enlarged', the claim for which is dubious (p. 131). Yet the attention paid to the text of *The Contention* might well be said to go beyond what we would normally expect of a simple reprint. And that might warrant the description 'corrected', though it is difficult to understand why the changes are so limited in scope, given the access the printers apparently had to previously unpublished information. It is not impossible that the correction of the listing of the seven sons of Edward III (a relatively familiar piece of genealogy) was noted at some point when *2 Henry VI* was performed; but it is difficult to see how this could have been the case for the other five changed passages. We have no evidence that Shakespeare or his fellow actors were involved, but it is difficult to see how it happened otherwise. To that degree it is reasonable to agree that this edition was 'corrected', in the sense of brought more into line with what would appear (as *2 Henry VI*) in the First Folio.

The 1630 *Merry Wives* is different again, since it differs from Q1 (1602) and Q2 (1619) in being a reprint of the 1623 folio text.[58] In that sense there is truth *of a*

---

[58] Practice varied after 1623 as to whether fresh quartos reprinted earlier quartos or the folio text. *Love's Labour's Lost* is another that follows its folio text. But *Richard III*, *1 Henry IV*, and *Hamlet* follow earlier quarto versions (in the case of *Hamlet* Q2 1604/5). *Othello* (1630) conflates its folio and quarto versions.

kind in its claim that it is 'newly corrected'. By the same token, there may be truth *of a kind* in the claim of 1599 *1 Henry IV* to be '*Newly corrected by W. Shake-speare*'. The text is no more than a reprint of the first-surviving 1598 version of the play, which has led editors to discount the title-page claims (see p. 127). As David Scott Kastan puts it, 'the assertion is a marketing ploy rather than a bibliographical fact...what differences exist are not the result of the author's corrections or revisions but of the normal procedures of a printing house' (2002: 111). There is, however, the same possibility as we noted exists with Q3 *Richard III*'s '*Newly augmented*', that the title page is belatedly comparing the text with a version of *1 Henry IV* that antedates any of the versions that found their way into print (no more belatedly, for example, than the 1619 *Dr Faustus*'s 'With new additions'). Here again, all surviving copies of the play, quarto and folio, are long (only a few dozen lines short of 3,000, and many of those in wordy prose), making it unlikely that they were performed entire on the public stage.

This is, however, the first version of the play to identify *1 Henry IV* with Shakespeare and the 'corrected' claim may have been invented partly with the purpose of impressing that on potential customers. From this date onwards Shakespeare's name is invoked often enough, even on items that he had nothing to do with (such as the 1619 reprint of *Sir John Oldcastle*), as to suggest that it sold copies. The tantalizing '*Newly set foorth, ouerseene and corrected, By W. S.*' which appeared on the 1595 *Locrine* makes it tempting to suppose that the publisher felt that aficionados would be interested in his association (real or imagined) with that old text, even at such an early date (see p. 7; Erne 2013: 56ff). Such considerations make it even more difficult to know how much trust to place in the claims made on title pages.

CONCLUSIONS

Given all the repetition, imprecision, and possibility of outright lying associated with the use of these five terms, it might be reasonable to conclude that we can learn nothing from them. Yet limited consistencies do emerge which tell us something about, in particular, the marketing of Shakespeare's texts, especially in the decade from 1598 to 1608. And some of these point us in the direction of changes made to texts for court purposes.

Of the five terms with which we began, 'corrected' is the one which has most readily been discounted—by editors—in respect of Shakespeare's texts, because it seems to be the most casually applied. Often it appears to refer to no more than regular print-house practices; more often than is the case with the other terms, it has been suspected of being simply a marketing ploy; where it might refer to meaningful intervention by an author, the text tends to spell that out with other terms. The Shakespeare texts where 'corrected' has seemed most likely to flag his personal involvement in changes to a text as printed are *Love's Labour's Lost*, where we do not have an original with which to compare it, and the 1599 *Romeo and Juliet*, where it is virtually redundant because that is also described as '*augmented, and amended*'. Yet, *pace* the editorial tradition on these matters, we cannot entirely discount the possibility that 'corrected' on Q2 *1 Henry IV* and Q3 *Merry Wives* actually might have flagged to early readers that the text is not as it was originally composed and performed. 'Amended', as I have already suggested, seems to have been virtually synonymous with 'corrected' during Shakespeare's lifetime, and so gets us little further. 'With additions' is normally straightforward but only affects one (particularly slippery) Shakespeare text, *Richard II*.

The two really loaded terms, it transpires, are the other pair of apparent synonyms, 'augmented' and 'enlarged'. As I have suggested, 'augmented' seems to have been *invented* for Shakespeare's texts—1598 *Love's Labour's Lost*, 1599 *Romeo and Juliet*, 1602 *Richard III*. Two other usages—*The Malcontent* and *The Devil's Charter*—both proclaim their attachment to the King's Men (a unique departure for Marston, a unique event for Barnes) and may be inviting comparison with Shakespeare's authorial persona. If we leave aside the probable salesmanship of 'enlarged' in relation to *The Whole Contention*, by itself 'augmented' only applies to two texts—the 1602 *Spanish Tragedy* (which, given the play's enormous popularity, must have been a well-known exemplum) and the 1604/5 *Hamlet*. Then, belatedly, the 1622 *Maid's Tragedy* appeared as *both* 'augmented and inlarged'. With that single exception, every instance of 'augmented' and 'enlarged' falls between 1598 and 1608—four to Shakespeare, and one each to the revisers of Kyd, to Marston and Webster, and to Barnes. Half of all instances of 'with additions' also fall between those dates. A preponderance of all these uses falls between 1598 and 1604.

This closely overlaps with the main period (1598–1603) when Henslowe's *Diary* tells us incontrovertibly that plays are being altered, mended, and added to, and plays by Shakespeare and Dekker are specifically advertised as having been performed at court; I suggest that the two phenomena were linked in publishers' and readers' minds. This is expressly the case with *Love's Labour's Lost*, advertised as both 'augmented' and performed before the Queen. We have seen that the same joint claim could have been made of *Old Fortunatus*, though the publisher or printer chose only to flag the court connection. It would also have been true of *Phaeton* and *Tasso's Melancholy*, had anyone published them at all. Other cases—notably *Romeo and Juliet* and *Hamlet*—have strong claims, which I shall pursue elsewhere. For a limited time publishers were keen to associate plays by Shakespeare with being 'augmented' or 'enlarged': it was a distinctive selling-point, unique to him until the third edition of *The Malcontent*. This almost certainly explains the claim—bogus or not—of Q3 *Richard III* to be '*Newly augmented, By William Shakespeare*'. As Grace Ioppolo puts it: 'There is enough evidence within these texts to indicate that printers used the terms "augmented", "amended", and "enlarged" to advertize the recent *authorial alterations* of existing passages and *additions* of new ones' (1991: 88, my emphases).

Of the five plays explicitly designated as 'augmented' or 'enlarged', *Love's Labour's Lost*, *1 Henry IV*, and *Richard III* were incontrovertibly performed at court (even if the surviving evidence only puts the latter two there many years after these editions appeared).⁵⁹ And it seems most unlikely that *Romeo and Juliet* and *Hamlet*—two of Shakespeare's most reprinted, imitated, and talked-about texts—were not also presented there. The fact that we have no explicit evidence of this is a measure of just how limited our knowledge actually is. If we look at the whole range of our key terms, leaving aside only 'corrected' as too imprecise, a significant number of them are applied to plays which we *know* to have been worked on for court performances (*Love's Labour's Lost*, *The Devil's Charter*, *Mucedorus*) or have reason, as I have shown, to think that may have been the case (all the other Shakespeare texts, plus *A Fair Quarrel*, *The Maid's Tragedy*, *Philaster*, and *Bussy D'Ambois*). The instances of *The Spanish Tragedy* and *Dr Faustus* may simply relate to the return of Alleyn to the stage (or his absence from it), though a court pay-off may also have been anticipated. Only the instance of *The Malcontent*, unique in so many other ways, seems entirely unrelated.

One final thought about all the non-Shakespearean texts which have survived in more than one version, with an edition that claims to be 'augmented', 'enlarged', 'amended', or 'with additions'. In every case the version that makes the claim is longer, is published *after* versions that do not make the claim, and there are strong grounds for supposing that the changes were made *after* (often quite a long time after) the play's original staging—*The Spanish Tragedy*, *Dr Faustus*, *Mucedorus*, *Bussy D'Ambois*, *A Fair Quarrel*, *The Maid's Tragedy*, and *Philaster* also all point in that commonsensical direction. Only the discredited 'foul papers' theory of composition (discussed later), which resists the idea of authorial revision after first performance, would lead anyone to suppose otherwise. In this I concur with a more recent theorist, James Marino, even if I differ on how revisions were made (see pp. 163ff). By the same token, no one—not Henslowe, nor any publisher (saving only John Webster's publisher on the title page of *The Duchess of Malfi*)—ever speaks of a play being *cut* from its original length, for touring purposes or any other. Some play texts do represent themselves as containing more than was 'publicly presented', but that could as readily mean that they were augmented—presumably for court performance—as that they were cut. Jonson, always the exception, may have developed a habit of creating shorter versions for public performance and longer ones for court virtually simultaneously. But if plays changed at all, they almost invariably—like all those we have reviewed in Henslowe's *Diary*—started smaller and got bigger.

I shall be applying that same logic to the multiple-text Shakespeare plays, whether or not their publishers chose to comment on their title pages. Firstly, however, we need to review something of the way people in the modern world have thought about those multiple texts and applied that thinking to the editing of Shakespeare's plays—remember those editors of *Merry Wives*, early in this chapter, talking confidently of 'foul papers' and 'memorial reconstruction'? We need to be clear about our terms here.

---

⁵⁹ Herbert records performances of 'The First Part of Sir John Falstaff' on New Year's Day 1625 and of *Richard III* on Queen Henrietta Maria's birthday, 16 November 1633. These were evidently old court favourites (Bawcutt 1996: 159, 184).

b. Thinking About the Revision of Shakespeare's Texts in Modern Times

For much of the twentieth century there was a deep-rooted predisposition in the editorial and bibliographical tradition against the idea of Shakespeare revising his own texts at all. If they were changed after he completed them, it was widely supposed to have been done by scriveners working in the playhouse, by his fellow actors, by people copying them surreptitiously with shorthand, or by printers—by anybody but Shakespeare. And by definition such changes represented a corruption of the Shakespearean original. This pattern of response can be laid directly at the door of the most influential of the so-called New Bibliographers of the early twentieth century, W. W. Greg. Greg's two most visible and lasting contributions to the Shakespearean editorial debate were the idea of 'foul papers' as markers of the most authentic Shakespearean manuscripts behind the surviving early texts, and a quasi-scientific demonstration of how 'memorial [re]construction' was supposed to have played its part in creating some of the less satisfactory texts. We need to backtrack a little to understand why these should have acquired the authoritative force they did in Shakespearean editing.

'STOLNE, AND SURREPTITIOUS COPIES'

A fundamental issue in Shakespearean textual scholarship is the relationship between the First Folio of 1623 and all the precedent quartos. The debate starts with the First Folio itself where, in their address 'To the great Variety of Readers', John Heminge and Henry Condell made this claim for the volume they had edited, first regretting that Shakespeare did not live to do it himself:

> But since it hath been ordained otherwise, and he by death departed from that right, we pray you do not envy his friends, the office of their care and pain, to have collected & published them; and so to have published them, as where (before) you were abused with diverse stolen, and surreptitious copies, maimed, and deformed by the frauds and stealths of injurious impostors, that exposed them: even those, are now offered to your view, cured, and perfect of their limbs; and all the rest, absolute in their numbers, as he conceived them.   (sig. A3)

This gave rise to the assumption which it was surely designed to promote: that all the pre-existing Shakespeare quartos were 'stolen and surreptitious copies' and that only the First Folio, prepared by colleagues to whom Shakespeare had bequeathed memorial rings in his will, had any textual authority at all. Until the twentieth century scholars did not realize that Heminge and Condell, who oversaw the creation of the volume though it is less clear how personally involved they were, had themselves often based their texts on the quartos they affected to despise.

'Bad' quartos

The overriding authority of the First Folio was thus virtually an article of faith from the time of Dr Johnson and the great Shakespeare scholar, Edmond Malone (1741–1812), to the early twentieth century, when it was partly challenged by A. W. Pollard in his landmark *Shakespeare Folios and Quartos* (1909). Pollard insisted for the first time that there was a line to be drawn between good and bad quartos, and this is how he drew it:

> if we take the quartos which have 'bad' texts, differing widely and for the worse from the First Folio, we shall find that they also agree in one point, that is in either not being entered prior to first publication in the Stationers' Register at all, or in having an entry of an unusual nature, entitling us to suspect something wrong. These plays are (i) Danter's edition of *Romeo and Juliet* [first quarto, 1597], and Busby and Millington's *Henry V* [first quarto, 1600], of both of which there are no entries prior to publication; (ii) the first quarto of *Hamlet* [1603] and also *Pericles* [1609], both of which were published without having been licensed to the firms publishing them; (iii) *The Merry Wives of Windsor* [1602], transferred to another publisher on the day of entry...we are surely justified in arguing...that there is some causal relation at work which connects a good text with regular entry prior to publication in the Stationers' Register. (65)[60]

Pollard's list of 'bad' quartos might well have been at least two longer, if he had not shared the then-common belief that *The First Part of the Contention* and *The True Tragedy* were source-texts for, respectively, Shakespeare's *2 Henry VI* and *3 Henry VI*, rather than versions of his own work.[61] The quality of their texts, by comparison with the Folio versions, is very similar to the five plays he singles out; they do not, however, square with his theory about a relationship between poor quality and improper entry in the Stationers' Register. *The First Part of the Contention* was entered for Thomas Millington on 12 March 1594 in perfectly proper fashion and printed that year. There is, admittedly, no entry for *The True Tragedy*, which Millington also published [1595], but as Randall Martin points out, 'the publication in any event may have been covered by the entry for *The First Part of the Contention*' (Martin 2001: 103).

At all events, editorial practice after Pollard's book appeared was for many years almost universally to treat the five texts he nominated (and eventually the other two) as 'bad' quartos, worthy of no authority. As late as 1982, Harold Jenkins could confidently assert of the 1603 quarto of *Hamlet* that it 'is now recognized to belong to a category of quartos which it is one of the achievements of twentieth-century textual scholarship to have distinguished. It is, in the sense in which

---

[60] Of these five texts, *Pericles* is not relevant to this study, since it only survives in one early version.
[61] See Introduction, note 4 about *The Troublesome Reign of King John* (1591) and *The Taming of a Shrew* (1594).

the word is now used, a "bad" quarto' (1982: 19). But the central plank in Pollard's case for piracy in this restricted group of texts had been to associate them with supposed impropriety in their licensing: 'It is believed that the prevalence of piracy has been somewhat exaggerated, but it is part of our case that it existed' (79).

Publication practices

Not until 1960 was this undermined in part by C. J. Sisson (1960) and then discredited by a series of revisionist essays by Peter Blayney, culminating with 'The Publication of Playbooks' (1987, 1989, 1997). In this Blayney painstakingly elucidated the terminology surrounding the publication of play texts, relating to the practices of the Stationers' Company, which held a virtual monopoly of printing in early modern England. This had been widely misunderstood by generations of literary historians. The key issue was the granting of the Company's licence. This established ownership of copy, which is to say the exclusive right to print a particular text—and so to block attempts by others to publish anything that might prevent the owner from making a return on his investment in a work:

> The owner of a copy had not only the exclusive right to reprint the text, but also the right to a fair chance to recover his costs. He could therefore seek the Company's protection if any book—not necessarily a reprint or plagiarism of his own copy—threatened his ability to dispose of unsold copies of an existing edition... When Millington and Busby tried to license Shakespeare's *Henry V* in 1600, therefore, the wardens would not have cared about either the authorship or the 'Badness' of the text—but they would have required the consent of Thomas Creede, who had published (and printed) *The Famous Victories of Henry the Fifth* in 1598. Creede presumably did consent, on condition that he be hired (and therefore paid) to print the rival play. (1997: 399)

An entry in the Stationers' Register was not required of someone who already had the Company's licence:

> Certainly before 1622... a stationer was not required to spend money on an entry in the register. An entry was an insurance policy: paid for, it provided the best possible protection, but the price had to be weighed against the risk... License was mandatory, and the Company punished evasion whenever it was detected. But entrance was voluntary, and its absence is never sufficient reason for suspecting anything furtive, dishonest, or illegal. (1997: 404)

With that, Pollard's attempt to connect his five 'bad' quartos with publishing impropriety was dead in the water.

SHORTHAND COPYING

The 'bad' quarto label has lingered, however, because it implies an aesthetic judgement as much as a moral one. The texts which Pollard had identified (and the two

Henry VI ones) are markedly shorter than the corresponding versions in the First Folio, with whole scenes missing; the verse is generally less rich and sometimes not distinguished from prose; they contain clumsy disjunctions. It seemed clear that they could not have been supplied to their publishers by either the author or his acting company. In summing up his case that, of the nineteen Shakespeare quartos, 'five are by universal consent thoroughly bad', Pollard added 'three of these being demonstrably derived from shorthand copies taken down at the theatre or from quotations from memory' (1909: 79). Furtive shorthand was then a commonplace explanation for how such poor texts might have come into being. Thomas Heywood claims in the preface to *The Rape of Lucrece* (1608) that 'some of my plays have...accidentally come into the printers' hands...copied only by the ear' (A2ʳ). And in a prologue he wrote for a revival of *If You Know Not Me, You Know Nobody*, he complained about earlier printings: 'some by stenography drew / The plot: put it in print: (scarce one word true)' (1637: 249). Yet G. I. Duthie so convincingly argued the case against the practicability of shorthand for these purposes in *Elizabethan Shorthand and the First Quarto of 'King Lear'* that Laurie Maguire could claim: 'The connection between suspect texts and shorthand reports has not been a component of studies of suspect texts for many years, having been cogently disproved by G. I. Duthie in 1949' (1996: 18). Nevertheless, Tiffany Stern recently offered a compelling case for the 1603 quarto of *Hamlet* being derived from shorthand (2013). In the study of Shakespeare's texts, few speculations are ever definitively laid to rest.

MEMORIAL RECONSTRUCTION (1)

Pollard also offers 'quotations from memory' as an explanation of the source of the 'bad' quartos and—variously known as memorial 'construction' or 'reconstruction'—it became the most common explanation of how they came about. The thought that actors might have been involved in putting together some of the less satisfactory Shakespeare texts had been around from the middle of the nineteenth century (Mommsen 1857: 182). But W. W. Greg was the first to demonstrate in detail how this might have affected a text, in the introduction to his facsimile of the 'bad' quarto of *The Merry Wives of Windsor, 1602*, which was cited reverentially by his followers long after Greg himself had had second thoughts about some of his assumptions (Greg 1910).

He approached the text as one characterized by 'gross corruption, constant mutilation, meaningless inversion and clumsy transposition...The playhouse thief reveals himself in every scene, corrupting, mutilating, rewriting' (xxvi–xxvii). From the start, 'memorial reconstruction' is associated with illicit activity. Greg went looking for a thief and found him: 'that mine Host had a main finger in the work I feel convinced' (xli), a detection worthy of Sherlock Holmes. That actor 'as the result of a week or two's labour with a not very ready pen, [drafted] a rough reconstruction of the play, in which naturally enough, his own part...was the only one rendered throughout with tolerable accuracy' (xliii). In fact that is simply not true.

The Host's own role is less convincingly rendered in later parts of the play, whereas scenes where he is not present are quite competently delivered.

By 1928 Greg was prepared to admit that it was 'very likely mistaken' (1928: 202). But this was overshadowed by Peter Alexander's *Shakespeare's Henry VI and Richard III*, which sought to establish the fact of memorial reconstruction with even more systematic rigour, even in texts which had not originally figured in 'bad' quarto debates (1929). And Greg himself later seemed to think that the widespread acceptance of memorial reconstruction as an explanation for flaws in a wide range of texts substantiated its *bona fides*. Indeed almost anywhere one looks in the mid-century years, it is paraded as a given fact in editions of plays with 'bad' or suspect quartos. See, for example, Walter 1954: xxxiv–xxxv; Green 1965: 148; Gibbons 1980: 2; Jenkins 1982: 19–20.

MEMORIAL RECONSTRUCTION (2), WITH THE 'ABRIDGED RURAL PROMPT-BOOK THEORY'

The emphasis on the illicitness of 'bad' quartos was partly countered early on by the possibility that some 'memorial construction' might have arisen from relatively normal theatrical practice. A. W. Pollard and John Dover Wilson published a series of articles, 'The "Stolne and Surreptitious" Shakespearian Texts' (1918/19). These argued that 'bad' quartos might have derived from the practice of actors who, while touring the provinces in smaller numbers and lacking their regular script, might have pooled their memories to produce an ad hoc prompt copy of the play. In this 'abridged rural prompt-book theory', as W. L. Lawrence sardonically dubbed it, such texts might have come legitimately into existence: only their sale to unscrupulous publishers constituted piracy (1919). Abridgement for provincial touring is nowhere attested in the records of early modern theatre, and it is particularly difficult to square with the limited touring of Shakespeare's Lord Chamberlain's Men. But it quickly became a very close ally of 'memorial reconstruction'. All of the editions cited at the end of the last section speak of it in the same breath. Incidentally, all attempts to prove that cutting in the process of 'memorial reconstruction' would reduce the number of actors needed to go on tour have failed.

The first really cogent objections to 'memorial construction', especially as it was coupled with the provincial touring hypothesis, were delivered in Paul Werstine's landmark essay, 'Narratives About Printed Shakespeare Texts: "Foul Papers" and "Bad" Quartos' (1990).[62] Laurie E. Maguire then subjected the whole body of 'memorial construction' theory to unprecedented scrutiny, concluding that the body of texts which might conceivably have come into existence in this fashion was much smaller than had been assumed (1996). Werstine followed up with further

---

[62] Other valuable works, not otherwise cited here, that have played their part in the decline in the fortunes of 'bad' quarto as a category for play texts include McLeod 1982; Ioppolo 1991; Bradley 1992; Irace 1994; Spong 1996.

hammer blows in, notably, 'Touring and the Construction of Textual Criticism' (1998) and 'A Century of "Bad" Shakespeare Quartos' (1999). The latter shows with great clarity how all attempts to tie memorial constructions to identifiable perpetrators have been deeply flawed. Janette Dillon meanwhile challenged the whole idea that 'bad' quartos were performance texts of any description (1994), leading Werstine to observe: 'As Dillon contends, it may be acceptance of the memorial-construction hypothesis that has produced the assumption that the "bad" quartos are self-evidently performance text' (1999: 329). Two hypotheses which had propped each other up for the best part of a century tumbled like the monuments of ousted dictators.

FOUL PAPERS

Greg's other great legacy to the editing of Shakespeare—in many ways the exact antithesis of the 'memorial construction'—was the promotion to prominence of the idea of an author's 'foul papers'. Contrary to the immediate connotations of 'foul', these papers, if they could be found, would be the Holy Grail of an editor's search, since they comprehend 'a copy representing the play more or less as the author intended it to stand, but not in itself clear or tidy enough to serve as a promptbook'.[63]

The issue is critical because editors began to enquire about the kind of copy that lay immediately behind the 'good' texts, whether in quarto or in folio. Two principal categories suggested themselves—the playhouse 'book', which would have carried the 'allowance' of the Master of the Revels, together perhaps with necessary business inserted by the company bookkeeper, such as stage directions; and the dramatist's own copy, as delivered to the company. But what was the relationship between these two? Was the dramatist's copy converted into the 'book'? Was there indeed only one version of the dramatist's copy—his working papers? Or might a dramatist produce a 'fair copy' of his finished work, in his own hand or in that of a professional scrivener?[64] What was at stake here was nothing less than the word of Shakespeare himself. In the absence of manuscripts and of any evidence that he oversaw the printing of his plays, the text that Shakespeare wrote is mediated by at least the work of the printer and of the compositors who set it in print. But how many other layers might also intervene, even in a 'good' text?

As Paul Werstine has shown, it was in 1927 that Greg first took a particular interest in the term 'foul papers', which he identified as a very specific form of manuscript— the closest possible to the finished thoughts of the originating author (2009, 2012: 12–59). He found it in a manuscript copy of John Fletcher's play, *Bonduca*, which had been transcribed after the author's death (1625) by the bookkeeper of the King's

---

[63] The quotation is from an essay by Greg, 'The Final Revision of *Bonduca*', written in 1927 but never published in full. It is now in the Huntington Library. Quoted from Werstine 2009: 33. I am grateful to Professor Werstine for letting me have a copy of this prior to publication.

[64] On the work of one such scrivener, Ralph Crane, see pp. 162–3, 256–8.

Men, Edward Knight. Knight inserted a note which seemed to establish that Fletcher's 'foul papers' and 'the book where by it was first acted from' were distinct entities (Fletcher 1951: 30). Greg knew that a fuller version of *Bonduca*, containing scenes missing from the manuscript, had been published in the 1647 first folio of the plays of Beaumont and Fletcher. He concluded from lacunae and other deficiencies in the manuscript that Fletcher's 'foul papers' were indeed 'foul'—sloppy and incomplete—and that the 'book' (on which the folio text was apparently based) was evidently in much better shape and must have been made from a copy prepared by Fletcher himself, the only person capable of perfecting his own working draft. So it was possible to see, side-by-side, authoritative copies both of the 'foul papers' of a King's Men's play and also of its 'book'.[65] All of this offered a model for thinking about how two such versions of Shakespeare's plays might have compared with one another, and how either might have made it from the playhouse to the printers. And Greg found what he thought was substantiating evidence in the papers of the theatre owner, Philip Henslowe (1907: 78).

In the 1930s another of the New Bibliographers, R. B. McKerrow, published two essays which had a direct bearing on all of this (1931, 1935; see also Bald 1942: 165). In one he argued that even 'good' play texts (for example, of the 1604/5 *Hamlet*) are sometimes worse printed—contain a higher level of mistakes—than other kinds of texts produced by the same printers (1931). This led him to suppose that the copy for these play texts was probably an author's draft, with all its putative false starts, corrections, interlinings, and so on, posing multiple problems for the printers and their compositors. In the other paper he particularly focused on the erratic or skimpy identification of characters as a further way of identifying such authorial manuscripts (Greg's 'foul papers') behind the printed texts (1935). As he observed, 'A prompter of a repertory theatre could hardly be expected to remember that Bertram was the same person as Rossillion, or Armado the same as Braggart' (464). In such inconsistent details, or in the naming of the actor rather than his role, we identify the almost unvarnished creative hand of Shakespeare at work.

Although McKerrow preferred the term 'draft' ('the author's rough draft much corrected and never put in order for the press': 275), these arguments confirmed to Greg the special significance of 'foul papers' in the pantheon of dramatic manuscripts, and he advanced the case for them with increasing confidence between his two major general statements on Shakespeare's texts, *The Editorial Problem in Shakespeare* (first ed. 1942) and *The Shakespeare First Folio* (1955).[66] He admits that such an investigation involves entering 'a misty mid region of Weir, a land of shadowy shapes and melting outlines, where not even the most patient inquiry and

---

[65] As Paul Werstine shows, Greg in fact got the status of the manuscript, and its relationship to the folio version, wrong in some important ways (2009). In particular, he underestimated how significant it might have been that Knight was producing an elegant copy for a client rather than striving for a meticulously accurate transcript. But that does not affect the subsequent history of 'foul papers' in Greg's thinking.

[66] *The Editorial Problem* was first delivered as the Clark Lectures at Cambridge in 1939, printed in 1942, and reissued in slightly different editions in both 1951 and 1954. I quote from the third edition but the arguments I follow all date back to the original lectures.

the most penetrating analysis can hope to arrive at any but tentative and proximate conclusions' (1955: 105). Yet 'foul papers' are always a privileged thread running through the possibilities he reviews. And Fredson Bowers, the great textual theorist of the mid-century, endorsed their existence and significance, claiming that 'the author's last complete draft in a shape satisfactory to him for transfer to fair copy' was 'known at the time and subsequently as his "foul papers"' (1955: 107–8, 13).[67]

Underlying all this was Greg's resolute resistance to the idea that Shakespeare might have revised his texts once he had delivered them to his fellow actors. The issue recurs with surprising frequency and urgency in his key text, *The Editorial Problem in Shakespeare* (2nd revision 1954). When he considers what the so-called 'bad' quartos may represent, he is anxious that they should not count as evidence of Shakespeare's revision of his texts:

> I believe that the theory that regards 'bad' quartos as essentially reports of the full Shakespearian texts is the true one. Whether they are reports of the texts exactly as we have them is of course a more difficult question. It is possible that after the reports were made the plays may have undergone revision. This view is still held by many, and it is not possible to disprove it. At the same time, except in a few instances of minor importance, there seems to me *little specific evidence of alteration or addition, while for any general practice of literary textual revision there is none at all*. We shall be wise not to postulate revision except on evidence of a cogent nature.   (60–1; my emphasis)

This patrician wariness becomes a little tetchy when faced with theories of revision to account for the differences between the first quarto of *Richard III* and the folio version: 'I have commented before on the absence of any external evidence that could predispose us to admit the likelihood in Shakespeare's plays of such stylistic revision as is here contemplated' (78). And Greg rises to a height of disdain when faced with Madeleine Doran's *The Text of 'King Lear'*: 'we have no evidence whatever that such persistent and wholesale revision was anything but exceptional in Elizabethan dramaturgy, and further it appears particularly unlikely in the work of so fluent a writer as Shakespeare' (89). Doran's 1931 work in many ways anticipated Gary Taylor and Michael Warren's *The Division of the Kingdoms* (see p. 111).

Once the 'foul papers' had been surrendered, Shakespeare's role was supposed to be at an end. Scriveners might then mis-transcribe it; actors might reduce, adapt, or garble it; compositors might mis-set it: it was the work of modern editors to search out the untarnished original. And that is what Shakespeare editors did throughout the mid years of the twentieth century. In some ways it lives on in the work of those like Lukas Erne and Andrew Gurr, who believe that Shakespeare habitually wrote unactably long plays for readers, which his colleagues would then mine for acting versions.[68]

* * *

---

[67] Bowers did argue that a fair copy, possibly authorial, might sometimes have intervened between the foul papers and the prompt copy. But he did not repudiate foul papers and their significance as such.
[68] Greg indeed anticipated Erne in some respects: 'I do not myself believe that Shakespeare, at any rate in his maturity, wrote only for the stage—he must have known and recognised the value of the

Over the next thirty years, however, different aspects of the 'foul papers' hypothesis were fairly comprehensively discredited. E. A. J. Honigmann challenged Greg's over-narrow and specific use of the term (1965: 17). Peter Blayney convincingly challenged McKerrow's claims about the unusually poor printing of even the best playbooks (1982). And in ' "A Bed / for Woodstock": a Warning for the Unwary', William B. Long undermined the ease with which Greg and others had claimed to be able to distinguish between 'foul papers' and 'prompt-copies' by showing from direct manuscript observation that the latter often did not in fact have the characteristics which they claimed for them (1985).

Then in his 'Narratives About Printed Shakespeare Texts', Paul Werstine systematically traced the inconsistencies in Greg's construction of 'foul papers' as such a distinctive and authoritative form of manuscript (1990); the great edifices of 'memorial construction' and 'foul papers' crumbled together. Werstine has since produced related works, each putting further nails in the coffin of the Pollard/Greg/McKerrow New Bibliographical agenda of Shakespearean editing (1998, 1999, 2009, 2012; see also Stern 2009a: 20–1). Over the twentieth century 'good' and 'bad' quartos, piracy, shorthand transcription, memorial reconstruction, abridgement for touring purposes, and foul papers and prompt copies all flourished as explanations for the radical differences we find between Shakespearean texts—and all of them have been quite categorically found wanting, at least in the terms in which they were first advanced. Of course there were 'foul papers' and playhouse 'books', and there may well have been 'memorial reconstructions'—but they did not relate to the printed Shakespeare texts in the manner that their proponents suggested. Nevertheless, many of these notions continue to find currency; myths are remarkably resilient in Shakespeare studies.

But just as the New Bibliographical paradigms were in reality on their last legs, the rules changed.

THE OXFORD SHAKESPEARE

William Shakespeare: The Complete Works, of which the general editors were Stanley Wells and Gary Taylor (1986), with assistance from John Jowett and William Montgomery, was the most radical edition of Shakespeare of the twentieth century and has since become the most influential.[69] It was implicit throughout much of their agenda that what mattered above all to the New Bibliographers were the words of Shakespeare himself, as he wrote them. In as much as any of them were literary critics, they were Arnoldians, convinced of Shakespeare's transcendent genius and dedicated above all to reconstructing precisely what he wrote, through

---

enduring element of his creation—but he wrote primarily for the stage and was content that its accidents should mould the fashion of his art' (1954: 157).

[69] The *Complete Works* (1986) needs to be distinguished from the single-volume *Oxford Shakespeare* edition. The volumes in the series do not necessarily subscribe to the principles espoused in the *Complete Works*.

the fog of subsequent interpositions. The Wells and Taylor *Oxford Shakespeare* broke decisively with all that. Their focus was not on the transcendent poet but on the man who wrote play scripts. As they put it in their General Introduction:

> it is in performance that the plays lived and had their being. Performance is the end to which they were created, and in this edition we have devoted our efforts to recovering and presenting texts of Shakespeare's plays as they were acted in the London playhouses which stood at the centre of his professional life. (1986: xxxix)

The accompanying *Textual Companion* makes explicit what that means for their choice of copy texts: 'Where matters of verbal and theatrical substance are involved, we have [therefore] chosen, in our tradition, to prefer—where there is a choice— the text closer to the prompt book of Shakespeare's company' (1987: 15). Although they still often use the language of foul papers, these are no longer the Holy Grail that they seek.

My own book is in part heir to the thinking about Shakespeare's texts which the *Oxford Shakespeare* ushered in. Shakespeare wrote for performance. Where I principally differ is in believing that court performance 'stood at the centre of [Shakespeare's] professional life' to a degree which Wells and Taylor (and virtually everyone else) have not appreciated. And that it impacted significantly on the texts that have survived, especially the 'good' quartos. Wells and Taylor led the rehabilitation of the 'bad' quartos. They assume that, whatever the origins of these texts and however 'corrupt' they may be deemed, they are records of a sort of authentic performances and so have an authority in an edition like theirs. These 'reported texts' or 'post-performance texts', as they habitually and non-judgementally call them, 'are not without value in helping us to judge how Shakespeare's plays were originally performed' (1986: xxxii–xxxiii).

For example, in their introduction to *Henry V*, they explain that while they use the folio version as their copy text, their 'edition draws on the 1600 quarto in the attempt to represent the play as acted by Shakespeare's company. The principal difference is the reversion to historical authenticity in the substitution at Agincourt of the Duke of Bourbon for the Dauphin' (1986: 567). I would argue, however, that the First Folio text of *Henry V* is as much a performance text as the 1600 quarto, one produced at a different moment and in another context—that of a presentation at court (see pp. 173–99). Any conflation of Shakespearean texts is highly questionable. Each version represents—however inadequately—a particular moment in the play's evolution, and we need extraordinary grounds for supposing that conflations of them will get us any closer either to what Shakespeare wrote or to what audiences saw onstage.

MEMORIAL RECONSTRUCTION (3), ONE MORE TIME

This new orthodoxy has breathed fresh life into the 'memorial reconstruction' hypothesis.

One appealing feature of that hypothesis is that *parts* of it do seem to square with *some* of the characteristics of the 'bad' texts. That is, some of the kinds of clumsiness found in texts may well derive from a speaker or speakers dictating to a scribe, rather than a scribe working from a written or typeset script; as Wells and Taylor put it, 'such texts derive from a process of aural transmission' (1987: 27).[70] And once again we find the contention that 'memorial texts represent—however imperfectly—the performance script of a play' (28). Through them—'however imperfectly'—we see the plays, not necessarily as they were staged in some remote market town, but perhaps at the Theatre or the Globe.

Scott McMillin also revisited memorial construction, looking to make non-piratical sense of the practice in relation to texts left by the Queen's Men.[71] He concentrated in particular on two texts that had been compared to Shakespearean 'bad' quartos and identified a common feature in them: 'Both *Famous Victories of Henry V* and *True Tragedy of Richard III* are printed with long stretches of mislineation—verse printed as prose, or (the more interesting case) prose printed as verse' (1999: 113). It was not generally in the interests of printers to render prose as verse because it consumed more paper.

> We propose that our two mislined Queen's Men's texts were prepared by dictation in the playhouse, with actors reciting their parts after they had memorized them, and with a scribe recording those recitations in order to have a temporary copy... Our hypothesis is that these two texts... faithfully record the order of the speeches but carry an extra element of error introduced by transcription from dictation... Books created in this way would have been imperfect. They would have suffered from aural mistakes, but they would have served their purpose in performance. (114, 119)

McMillin specifically related this to the practice of the Queen's Men splitting into two groups for touring, which might plausibly create a need for ad hoc copies. It is less obvious in the case of other companies, which did not divide. But the idea of companies creating temporary acting versions of plays has caught the imagination of some editors of Shakespeare. This, after all, might accord with Heywood's complaints about his work 'copied only by the ear' or even by 'stenography'. McMillin sees nothing in the practice as being piratical, only that it produced clumsy and inadequate texts for readers. In such ways 'memorial reconstruction' remains very much on the editorial agenda (if far from fully explained), though stripped of its original 'stolen and surreptitious' associations.

THE TURN OF THE CENTURY

Taylor and Warren's *The Division of the Kingdoms* inspired some to find Shakespeare's revision of his own plays in texts other than *King Lear*. Grace Ioppolo's *Revising Shakespeare* is a notable case in point, tracing in Shakespeare's plays a repeated habit

---

[70] The General Introduction to the *Textual Companion* is signed by Gary Taylor alone.
[71] *The Queen's Men and their Plays* (1999) was co-authored by Scott McMillin and Sally-Beth MacLean, but the section on 'the nature of the texts' (Chapter 5) was primarily McMillin's work.

of revision, often within the original process of composition itself, but preserved by printers who failed to appreciate that one version should have been excised. She sees her work as a contribution to an 'irreversible and irrevocable movement towards Shakespearian revision', reaching such conclusions as that the 'Quarto and Folio texts of *Hamlet, Troilus and Cressida,* and *Othello*...offer substantiating canonical evidence of consciously planned and deliberately made authorial revision' (1991: 16, 159). Another passionate supporter of the argument that Shakespeare regularly revised his own work is John Jones, whose *Shakespeare at Work* appeared in 1995. He too sees *The Division of the Kingdoms* as crossing a line over which there can be no going back: 'For the conflationists, for the lost archetype men, the game was up' (160). The 'conflationists' were those who believed that both texts of *Lear* derived from a single original manuscript and might therefore profitably be conflated in order to recover Shakespeare's intentions (see note 24 in this chapter). Jones's own book enthusiastically expands the argument to include, in particular, *Hamlet* and *Othello*, reaching conclusions such as this: 'You have only to place the two versions of *The Tragedy of Othello, The Moor of Venice* side by side for much of what has just been said to appear perfectly obvious. Why, then, has it not long been well known, why is it not even now a commonplace and an interesting subject for discussion, that Shakespeare revised this play?' (247).

Some of this spirit carried over into the burst of revived Shakespearean editing that came in the 1990s and 2000s, with notable contributions (for example) from Eric Rasmussen, one of the most active recent editors of the plays (see Cox and Rasmussen 2001; Bate and Rasmussen 2007, 2013). But the specific surge of enthusiasm for Shakespeare as a purposeful reviser of his own works has not carried all before it, as Ioppolo and Jones expected. From the beginning there were sceptics, even in respect of *King Lear* (see Thomas 1984; Vickers 2006). Nor has it been much extended to the texts with which I am primarily concerned, those which carry with them so-called 'bad' quartos. John Jones himself is adamant 'that *Hamlet, Othello* and *King Lear* are the only cases of work begun and declared finished that was thought about again, and thought about as a whole' (50).[72] There has been more conviction that Shakespeare might have been a reviser of texts where two 'good' versions have survived than otherwise. Moreover, there is no consensus among the various works considered here—or even very much interest—about why Shakespeare, a busy professional, should have revised as much as he apparently did, beyond some artistic or aesthetic impulse. Grace Ioppolo, for example, acknowledges 'the many stages during which revisions may have been made by the author' (45), but does not look for particular causes, seeing revision as a general condition of the theatrical marketplace.

Perhaps more importantly the changed priorities announced by the *Oxford Shakespeare* have often relegated Shakespeare's own hand in the creative process—at best—to the status of first among equals rather than that of the transcendent

---

[72] When Jones talks of *Hamlet* he means the Q2 and F texts. Q1 is simply cordoned off as inauthentic: 'The preferred hypothesis here is that *Hamlet* was pirated for rival production, and later made its way to the print shop' (37n).

'author'. Meanwhile the conviction that the once-reviled 'bad' quartos probably reflected (however poorly) something of the original staging gave them a credibility which Pollard and his era could never have imagined in their worst nightmares, ushering in a radical redefinition of the hierarchy of Shakespearean texts.

It opened the way, for example, for the *Shakespearean Originals* series edited by Graham Holderness and Bryan Loughrey, which sought in a cultural materialist spirit to promote the 'bad' quartos as examples of genuinely popular—and inherently radical—theatre.[73] Similarly, the current *New Cambridge Shakespeare* publishes a series of 'First Quartos', to parallel the volumes in their regular series. Their very existence is a measure of the revolution that has occurred. They are now regularly claimed as authentic evidence of what the actors routinely did to Shakespeare's overlong originals when adapting them for the stage (see Gurr 2000, cited p. 80). This has become a new orthodoxy, though it has not gone unchallenged (see Dillon 1994; Werstine 1999). And I am furthering that challenge.

These series are also symptomatic of the wider Shakespearean publishing bonanza I mentioned that reached its height around the turn of the century, which breathed new life into old series like the *Arden*, *Oxford*, and *New Cambridge Shakespeares* and generated new series, like the *Folger Shakespeare Editions*. The result has been something of an editorial free-for-all. The break with the past is most starkly apparent in the Arden 3 *Hamlet*. Where for Arden 2 Harold Jenkins had scorned the first quarto and conflated the second quarto with the folio text as he saw fit (see pp. 226–9), Ann Thompson and Neil Taylor would reconstruct the play's editorial Gordian knot, publishing all three versions of the play on equal terms, rather than trying to find a definitive text among them (Thompson and Taylor 2006). As Jill Levenson observed in her *Oxford Shakespeare* edition of *Romeo and Juliet*, all the old editorial certainties have collapsed:

> Under fresh scrutiny... their narratives are breaking down, and with them the binaries that have defined the study of early modern play-texts: author versus stage, good quartos versus bad quartos, memorial reconstruction versus foul papers, prompt books versus foul papers, touring versions versus London versions. As the century turns, the vocabulary and grammar for historicizing such texts are undergoing significant adjustment. Without the narratives, dualism, authority, and other constructions, early drama-texts look different, unstable and shifting. When there are multiple versions of the same play, the relationship between them establishes a field of energy for the viewer's imagination and perhaps an analogue for the play's origins in changing theatrical or other socio-economic factors. (2000: 105–6)

This is very liberating from a literary critical perspective, but runs the risk of losing touch with certain realities on the ground that have not in fact disappeared: Henslowe does give us quite a clear picture of how plays were revised, at least for a time; and Herbert assures us that there was a fairly robust licensing system, with which the actors cooperated most of the time, because in the long run it was in their interest to do so. Such realities seem to me to have been overlooked, or perhaps

---

[73] The *Shakespearean Originals* series was published by Harvester Wheatsheaf (Hemel Hempstead, 1992ff).

circumvented, in this editorial free-for-all, one important result of which has been the resurrection of the notion of the 'continuous copy' in Shakespeare's texts.

CONTINUOUS COPY AND ITS ATTRACTIONS

As we noted earlier, Pollard and Dover Wilson introduced the idea that Shakespeare's texts might have been revised for touring performances (Pollard and Wilson 1918–19; see p. 142). But those same articles also constituted a wider challenge to Greg on the question of Shakespearean revision by proposing what E. K. Chambers later dubbed the theory of 'continuous copy', arguing that the plays were repeatedly subject to revision for playing purposes. 'According to [this] an author's original draft, after receiving the licence of the Master of the Revels, became the official prompt-book, was annotated by the book-keeper, was cut or expanded according to the demands of circumstances, and during a long theatrical career was freely revised or rewritten, sometimes in the margin, sometimes by means of inserted or substituted slips or leaves' (Greg 1955: 102).

Dover Wilson continued to propound and popularize this notion in the volumes of the *New Cambridge Shakespeare* which he edited, though it never gained much support from the scholarly community or especially from other editors. It was anathema to Greg, since it would make the business of retrieving Shakespeare's own text, even in 'good' copies, virtually impossible; he was clearly relieved that E. K. Chambers set his considerable authority against it (1930: 1.151–2; 1933).[74] Greg once characterized Dover Wilson's inventive theories as 'the careerings of a not too captive balloon in a high wind' (quoted in Hyman 1955: 184). It is easy to see why he would find them disturbing. These may seem to be old and settled arguments but—as Greg's own influence has declined and the effects of the *Oxford Shakespeare* have worked their way through—they have re-emerged recently, explicitly in such influential works as Paul Menzer's *The 'Hamlets': Cues, Qs and Remembered Texts* (2008) and implicitly in Tiffany Stern's *Documents of Performance in Early Modern England* (2009a) and James Marino's *Owning William Shakespeare: The King's Men and Their Intellectual Property* (2011). These are important contributions to current debates about the revision of (in particular) Shakespeare's plays; and I need to explain why, for all their other virtues, they do not offer convincing explanations of how plays might have changed and expanded within the playhouses.

Pollard and Wilson first formulated their theory around the manuscript of *The Book of Sir Thomas More*, which they took to be more representative than it actually is. *More* contains a first version of the play in the hand of Anthony Munday, which is marked by significant interventions from Edmund Tilney in his role as censor; these most notably require drastic changes in its depiction of the notorious 1517

---

[74] Chambers himself was more concerned with ways in which this theory was applied to argue for the 'disintegration' of the Shakespearean canon (seeing texts like *The Taming of the Shrew*, *King John*, and *2* and *3 Henry VI* as early, collaborative works which Shakespeare rewrote over time) than about revision as such.

Ill May Day riots. But the manuscript also contains a number of passages in other hands (including, supposedly, Shakespeare's own) which were apparently contributions towards revising the play. It is not altogether clear that all the revisions were aimed at responding to Tilney's objections; but Tilney had neither affixed his licence to the text, nor marked any of the revisions. So it is simply wrong to conclude that revisions like this could be made unsupervised to a text which had *already* been licensed. Whether the revision was ever completed, whether Tilney ever licensed it, or whether it was ever performed are all unknown. But it is certainly the case that the revised version would have had to be licensed before any performance would have been tolerated. Had it already been licensed, we know that Sir Henry Herbert—Master of the Revels in the 1620s and 30s—would have charged a half-fee (by then 10 shillings) for allowing a new scene in a play (Bawcutt 1996: 39).

The most critical issue here—as it is in the books by Menzer, Stern, and Marino—is the relationship between the 'allowed book', which carried the Master of the Revels' authority for performance, and the play as it was actually performed. If we accept Gurr's argument that the 'allowed book' *was* the maximal text, this is unproblematic; the Master's licence might indeed be valid for any (minimal) version of the play which was derived from it, *assuming that it contained no additions or alterations*. But Menzer, Stern, and Marino all approach their texts from the opposite direction, and assume that the licensing arrangements might give scope for actors and authors together to revise texts without being restricted to the 'allowed book' or the oversight of the Master of the Revels.

Since both Menzer and Stern quote my own work in support of this argument, I want to make my position quite clear. Menzer quotes me as saying that the Master's 'ambiguous relationship with the actors...must always have been perceived as collaboration as much as of regulation' (2008: 73), and Stern quotes me as saying that 'the censorship of English Renaissance drama was neither as totalitarian nor draconian as it is often held to be' (2009a: 232).[75] In both of these instances what I had in mind was that, where we have evidence of the Masters at work on texts—as with Tilney on *Sir Thomas More*, Buc on *Sir John van Olden Barnavelt*, or Herbert on *Believe as Ye List*—their aim was consistently to try to render them workable rather than to ban them outright. And this despite the fact that all three plays clearly dealt with subjects which the authorities of the day would regard as 'dangerous matter'. In the case of Massinger's *Believe as Ye List*, Herbert licensed what was quite transparently a new version of a text to which he had refused a licence earlier, on the grounds that it was critical of Anglo-Spanish relations at a time when there was diplomatic accord between the two countries. By transposing the action from modern Spain and Portugal to Asia Minor in classical times, Massinger had removed the overt offence to Spain, even though audiences were free to draw whatever analogies they wished (Dutton 2000: 6–7).

Herbert clearly understood Massinger's views and intentions, but did not see it as his responsibility to interrogate them, so long as offence to persons of conse-

---

[75] The quotations are from Dutton 1991: 135 and ix.

quence (including friendly foreign powers) was avoided. It is in this sense that I talk of the Masters' 'collaboration' with the actors, their regimes 'neither as totalitarian nor draconian as [they are] often held to be'. I never intended to imply that this meant laxness, much less ignoring or turning a blind eye to revisions of an 'allowed book'.

The licence on that book was the tangible presence of their authority in every performance staged, and recognition of that authority was the prime precondition of the Masters' 'collegiality' with the players. When, in fevered moments, the King's Men staged *The Spanish Viceroy* without a licence in 1624, and William Beeston's boy players staged an unlicensed play relating to 'the K[ing's] journey in to the North' in May 1640, Herbert promptly called them to account (Bawcutt 1996: 183, 208). This rare aberration by the King's Men occurred as the country prepared for a long-awaited war with Spain and they had doubtless hoped to duck under Herbert's radar, but failed. Herbert required them to sign an explicit letter of submission to his authority and kept it against further 'disorders', only placing it in his office book at the time of troubles over a revival of *The Tamer Tamed* in 1633 (of which more later). Eviscerating the most successful company of the era would seriously have challenged his ability to stage the Revels season satisfactorily at court. But we should not doubt his readiness to do so if they transgressed again. Beeston, for his part, spent months in prison and William Davenant took over his company for a time. But in most circumstances the two parties, actors and licensers, knew they needed each other, and collaborated accordingly.

And the evidence suggests that this normally extended to respecting the integrity of 'the allowed book'. Passages might be omitted, though there is nothing in Henslowe's *Diary* to show that anyone was paid to make such revisions. It is possible that the 'allowed book' acquired some details of stage business, as we see in the manuscript of *The Second Maiden's Tragedy*, though these fall short of what we would expect of a prompt book today (see p. 277). It is even conceivable that passages might be recast in the manner of 5.1 in the folio text of *A Midsummer Night's Dream* which, as we have seen, retains the language of the quarto, but redistributes it among the characters. But nothing in the evidence convinces me that this extended to unsupervised additions or alterations of the dialogue in the 'book'.

Arguing that 'throughout this study, "revision" implies a wide range of collaborative textual acts, particularly those of the players', Paul Menzer addresses this question head-on, suggesting that the actors in effect ignored or circumvented the Masters' authority (2008: 32, 72–80). He wants to establish, specifically, that the actors reduced their plays to 'parts' (from which they might rehearse, and which in turn they might adapt during those rehearsals) and also invested in expensive properties for those plays *before* they had a licence: 'we might even assume that the Master's imprimatur was a foregone conclusion' (74). Unfortunately, he misconstrues the circumstances of the instance in Sir Henry Herbert's office book on which he bases his case, the King's Men's attempt to stage Fletcher's *The Tamer Tamed* (also known as *The Woman's Prize*) in October 1633:

> Most pertinent to this book's argument, companies evidently presumed upon the Master's approval, for they would apparently transcribe parts before the book was licensed. In his note to Knight [the King's Men's bookkeeper] quoted above, Herbert tells the bookholder to tell the players to 'purge their parts, as I have the book'... Herbert assumes that the King's Men have already broken the play into parts, and that Mr. Knight will have to transfer the Master's alterations from the licensed book to each impacted part. Herbert's awareness of this manuscript's state argues either intimacy with the case of this particular play or a working familiarity with theatrical practice. It is uncertain whether the instance is anomaly or exemplary, but the Master of the Revels presumes that the book he is reviewing has already generated the players' parts. He testily concludes that 'the players ought not to study their parts till I have allowed of the book'. (74, citing Bawcutt: 182–3)

The instance is most definitely *anomaly*. What Menzer does not take into account is that *The Tamer Tamed* was not a new play. Most scholars think Fletcher wrote it around 1611, more than twenty years earlier. So of course the play had already been broken into parts; it had been available in the repertory all that time. It was a *revival* of the play which had thrown Herbert into panic mode, for reasons which may not be all that difficult to guess at: *The Tamer Tamed* was Fletcher's sequel to *The Taming of the Shrew*; it contains a domineering female called Maria and also, in its original form, a good deal of anti-Catholic material. When King Charles was married to an ostentatiously Catholic queen, Henrietta-Maria, whose influence at court was a matter of deep suspicion and resentment, it was potentially explosive to stage (Dutton 2000: 48–61).

Herbert evidently made up new policy to address this. His predecessors' licences had been good indefinitely, and the players were under no obligation to inform the current Master when they revived a play. But Herbert somehow heard about *this* planned revival on the morning of Friday 18 October and sent peremptory orders that it should not be staged 'this afternoon, or any more till you have leave from me: and this at your peril' (Bawcutt: 182). 'On Saturday morning following the book was brought me, and at my Lord Holland's request I returned it to the players the Monday morning after, purged of oaths, profaneness, and ribaldry' (ibid).[76]

From this Herbert resolved that:

> it concerns the Master of the Revels to be careful of their old revived plays, as of their new, since they may contain offensive matter, which ought not to be allowed in any time.
>
> The Master ought to have copies of their new plays left with him, that he may be able to show what he hath allowed or disallowed.
>
> All old plays ought to be brought to the Master of the Revels, and have his allowance to them for which he should have his fee, since they may be full of offensive things against church and state, the rather that in former time the poets took greater liberty than is allowed them by me. (182–3)

---

[76] The players' use of the Earl of Holland as an intermediary was shrewd, since he was known to be close to Henrietta Maria.

It was in that context that he then wrote 'The players ought not to study their parts until I have allowed of the book': in the case of an old, revived play, he was going to relicense it, and the players should not dig out their parts until he had done so. Any amendments should be made to those parts as well as to the 'allowed book', via Edward Knight, the bookkeeper. It was all resolved very professionally. Herbert recorded that his rulings 'raised some discourse in the players, though no disobedience', but all the companies eventually acceded to his demand that old, revived plays be relicensed, and that he be paid for it. This was shrewd of Herbert on two counts.[77] The resolution not only reasserted Herbert's authority but extended it further, in the process enhancing his income. The companies were commissioning fewer and fewer new plays, since they had a great stock of old ones to draw upon; to be paid for relicensing those old plays—and checking them for 'dangerous' content—was restitution of a sort. Herbert carefully recorded the restitution of collegial relations with the King's Men: 'Lowin and Swanston were sorry for their ill manners, and craved my pardon, which I gave them in presence of Mr. Taylor and Mr. Benfield' (Bawcutt: 183). The leading sharers in the company thus restored their working relations with the man they knew they ultimately had to answer to.

The case of Herbert and *The Tamer Tamed* does not, therefore, tell us that the actors prepared the parts for a *new* play before the Master of the Revels had signed and licensed the 'allowed book'. I need also to enter a *caveat* about the evidence that Menzer derives from Henslowe's *Diary* about the possibility that the players would begin to put a play into production before it had been licensed. In this he builds on Scott McMillin's claim that 'Philip Henslowe's records make it clear that plays often went into rehearsal while the authors were still completing the texts or making final revisions' (McMillin 1987: 37–8, cited p. 75). But this is based on a misunderstanding of the pattern of Henslowe's payments for licensing. Menzer is quite correct in showing that, in the cases of both *The Third Part of Thomas Strowde* and a play of *Cardinal Wolsey*, Henslowe disbursed various sums in payment to their authors and then to other persons to create or procure costumes and properties for those plays *before Tilney was paid for licensing them*.[78] In the case of *3 Thomas Strowde*, payments started being paid to John Day and William Haughton on 21 May 1601 and concluded ('in full payment') on 30 July; on 27 August money was lent to Dover the tailor to buy 'divers things' for the production, and on 1 and 3 September for him to 'make' certain items for it, including a 'suit for a fire drake'. Then finally 'Lent unto the company the 3 of September 1601 to pay unto the Mr. of the Revels for licensing both 3 part of *Thom Strowde* & the remainder of *Cardinal Wolsey*: 10s' (181).

---

[77] Archbishop Laud's Arminian reforms to the Church of England were highly controversial; Herbert's insistence on purging 'oaths, profaneness, and ribaldry' seems in part to have been code for making sure that nothing offensive to Laud and his Court of High Commission should get through. Herbert had himself fallen foul of Laud and the High Commission over the licensing of Jonson's *The Magnetic Lady*, which is the subject of an entry in the office book for 24 October 1633 (Bawcutt: 184). This records Herbert's and Jonson's exoneration, while the 'whole fault' was laid 'upon the players'. This must further have coloured the dealings over *The Tamer Tamed* days earlier.

[78] There were at least two *Cardinal Wolsey* plays, *The Rise* and *The Life*. Quite which 'the Remainder of Cardinal Wolsey' mentioned here related to is unclear.

So it may seem that preparations for staging *3 Thomas Strowde* were afoot *before* it was licensed, and so too with *Cardinal Wolsey*: 'Again: playbook, costumes, license' (79). Payment for the licence for 'the remainder of *Cardinal Wolsey*' was made at the same time as that for *3 Thomas Strowde* which, however, is a clue that the system was not quite as Menzer assumes. As R. A. Foakes notes in his edition of the *Diary*: 'Clearly, over the years from 1592 to 1597 the system of paying the Master was modified; what began as a weekly payment had become by the summer of 1597 a monthly payment' (xxxiii). This refers specifically to payments for which Henslowe was personally responsible as landlord of the theatre, fees simply to put on performances—not the fees for which the *company* was responsible, for the licensing of individual plays. But those fees too, at least after 1597, were paid to the Master in arrears, *not at the time a licence was issued*.

Henslowe sometimes mentions the titles of plays for which he is advancing money to pay for licences, as when he records 'for the licensing of 2 book [sic]...called *The Two Parts of Robart Hood*' (88; see also 106, 121). But more commonly he is much less specific, recording 'for licensing of two books', 'licensing of 3 books', 'licensing of two plays' (86, 94, 105). Such vague accounting suggests that Tilney did not pocket the money on the day that he issued the licence (which would have made him look far too much like a tradesman), but that there was a settling-up some time after the event, which would cover however many licences had been issued in the intervening period. All of this was of a piece with the new status accorded to the Admiral's and Chamberlain's Men in 1597/8 (see p. 30).

Post-1597 the payment of such fees settled onto a monthly basis, like those that Henslowe himself paid for using the theatre. The *Diary* contains an acquittance (receipt) from Tilney's agent, William Playstowe, dated 8 July 1602, in respect of Henslowe's fees for that June (195). But more interesting is the next acquittance from Playstowe in the sequence, from early August 1602; it is not in the *Diary*, but Foakes prints it as a cognate item: 'Received of Mr. Henslowe the 4th of August 1602 for one month's pay: due unto my master, Edmund Tilney, upon the 30th day of July last past the sum of £3' (296). And to this Playstowe appends a list of 'books owing for / 5', which he itemizes as *Baxter's Tragedy*, *Tobias Comedy*, *Jephthah Judge of Israel* & *The Cardinal*, and *Love Parts Friendship*. All of these plays have evidently been licensed, but as yet the fees for them have not been paid. Playstowe was gently reminding the company, via Henslowe.

If we apply the same principle to a similar but missing acquittance from a year earlier, dated early in September 1601, relating to *3 Thomas Strowde* and 'the remainder of *Cardinal Wolsey*', it will be apparent that those plays might have been licensed at any time in August 1601. But they were *not* licensed on the date of the acquittance itself. In the case of *3 Thomas Strowde* Henslowe paid out nothing to put the play into production until 27 August, and in respect of *Cardinal Wolsey* he similarly paid out nothing towards the production before 7 August. In both cases it is entirely likely that the plays had been licensed before anyone paid out money to mount the production.

This entry in the *Diary* does, however, raise an interesting further possibility. Henslowe's 3 September payment is for *3 Thomas Strowde* and 'the *remainder* of

Cardinal Wolsey' (my emphasis) and the fee, anomalously, was 10 shillings. Tilney's regular fee for a licence at this date was 7 shillings. The inference has to be that this represented a full fee for *3 Thomas Strowde* and a partial fee for 'the remainder of *Cardinal Wolsey*', presumably somewhat less than half of the play. A further inference would be that Henslowe had paid the other 4 shillings for *Cardinal Wolsey* the month before. This opens up the distinct possibility that Tilney was prepared to licence plays *in sections*, rather than wait for the completed item. This would be particularly useful for the players, since they could start the process of transcribing and learning their parts, and acquiring properties, earlier than would otherwise be possible—but still safely within the licensing system. The settlement of debts was evidently conducted on a gentlemanly timetable, in arrears, such that a single payment might normally cover all the partial licensings of a single play or even multiple plays.

This would also square with another piece of evidence sometimes adduced to suggest that parts were written up and learned before the book had been allowed (Stern 2009a: 236). In June 1613 Robert Daborne wrote to Philip Henslowe to explain the 'extraordinary pains' he is taking to finish the play *Machiavelli and the Devil*. He confirms that he has finally written the ending of the play, and moreover he has also altered 'one other scene in the third act which they *now have in parts*' (Greg 1907: 73). It is entirely plausible that Daborn might have revised a scene in the light of company concerns, or simply to make it consistent with later scenes as they were written—and *then* had it licensed and reduced to parts. There is nothing necessarily illicit here.

All of this squares moreover with the one account we have of Tilney actually issuing a licence, which on the face of it is odd. Early in 1603 Paul's Boys performed *The Old Joiner of Aldgate*, a play which later proved to reflect on several local persons and so became the subject of extensive litigation (Sisson 1936: 12–79; Gair 1982: 147–51). One thing we learn is that it was the author, George Chapman, who brought the play to Tilney and readily acquired a licence from him (Dutton 1991: 181; Sisson: 69–70).[79] This makes no sense unless Chapman was certain that the finished play was acceptable to the management of Paul's Boys, and that would be much more likely if he had been delivering the play in sections to the company as he went along—and getting them licensed by Tilney in turn once they were satisfied. It makes no sense that Tilney would have the time to read and amend the full text of a play while Chapman waited somewhere in his quarters in Clerkenwell.

It also squares with something most apparent in Henslowe's *Diary*—that the great majority of the plays the Admiral's Men commissioned were delivered, and paid for, in sections. Taking examples at random, we see that Henry Chettle was paid £1 'in earnest' of *The Stepmother's Tragedy* on 23 August 1599, and a further £1 two days later 'for his book called *The Stepmother's Tragedy*' (Foakes: 123). This

---

[79] No one in the litigation suggests that Tilney was at fault in issuing the licence or that he knew anything about the brewing scandal, though it is difficult to believe that he knew nothing about it. Chapman had been personally hired by one of those 'personated' in the play to write it, at above his usual fee.

was evidently not the complete book, but Chettle must have produced enough to justify a further payment. Then on 14 October Henslowe released £4 'to pay H. Chettle in full payment of a book called *The Stepmother's Tragedy*' (125). Henry Porter was presumably already well advanced with the second part of *The Two Angry Women of Abingdon* when he received £5 on 22 December 1598; he was given a further £2 on 12 February 1599 'in full payment'. These practices are usually cited as evidence that the playwrights who worked for Henslowe's companies lived hand-to-mouth, as some of them evidently did, and could not afford to wait for a final payment when everything was concluded. But they may also record an important company practice: receiving *and licensing* plays in sections, as they were completed, so as to ease them into the densely packed schedule for launching new plays.

In short, neither Sir Henry Herbert's office book nor Henslowe's *Diary* offers us grounds for supposing that the players divided their plays into parts, or began rehearsing them, before they were licensed (or partly licensed). The whole logic of the 'allowed book' had to be that the play as performed—and so the actors' parts—had to derive from it, and not deviate from it in any but trivial ways which were inevitable with transcription. Conversely, any changes in the play as performed needed to be reflected in the 'allowed book', and a fee would be due for relicensing. This was why, at the outset of his tenure as Master, Herbert was so scrupulous about his handling of two 'old' plays. On 19 August 1623 he made two entries in his office book: 'For the Prince's servants at the Red Bull—an old <play called the> *Peaceable King or the Lord Mendall,* former<ly allowed of by Sir> George Buc & likewise by me & because <it was free from addition> or reformation I took no fee'; 'For the King's players. An old play called *Winter's Tale*, formerly allowed of by Sir George Buc, and likewise by me on Mr. Heminge his word that there was nothing profane added or reformed, though the allowed book was missing; and therefore I returned it without a fee' (142). Quite why *The Peaceable King* needed attention at all is unclear; this was a decade before the revival of *The Tamer Tamed* which led to the paid relicensing of revived old plays. Probably its allowed book had also gone missing; in the case of *The Winter's Tale* we might guess that the same had happened during the creation of the Shakespeare First Folio.[80]

The key point, however, is that Herbert determined in both cases—even if only by taking the word of the company's representatives (a genuine mark of collegiality, implying trust between the two parties)—that they were 'free from addition or reformation' or 'there was nothing profane added or reformed'. It would be utterly pointless to confirm that the 'allowed book' was unchanged if the performance text was actually different. On the other hand, if there *were* changes, Herbert had a scale of fees determined by their extent: 'For allowing of a new act in an old play, this 13 May 1629: 10s' (168); 'For allowing of an old play, new written or fur-

---

[80] We do not know what version of *The Winter's Tale* replaced the old 'allowed book'. There has been much conjecture that it might have been the relevant sheets of the First Folio. Other examples of old plays being treated in the same way include *Match Me in London* for Lady Elizabeth's Men (143), and *More Dissemblers Besides Women* and *The Honest Man's Fortune*, both for the King's Men (146, 160).

bished by Mr Beeston, the 12th of January 1631: £1'—the standard fee; (15 May 1636) 'received of old Cartwright for allowing the <Fortune> company to add scenes to an old play, and give it out for a new one—£1' (199).

None of this is, to my mind, critical to Menzer's central analysis of the three early states of *Hamlet* and the relationship between them, focusing in particular on the actors' cues and how these are affected by changes in the text. I find this brilliantly illuminating, especially in defining the very different status of Q1 (1603) from both Q2 (1604/5) and the First Folio (1623). But he does desperately *want* many of the changes to have been made by the actors in rehearsal and performance rather than by a single author: 'Rather than ascribing F1's modifications to Shakespeare, however, I argue that the Folio *Hamlet* represents an "aggregation", an anthology of changes that were made over time and that do not necessarily involve the playwright, thus rehabilitating the long rejected concept of "continuous copy" in the playhouse' (20). As with the works of Marino and Stern, this is a legacy of the *Oxford Shakespeare*'s refocusing of thinking about plays as products of the playhouse. But there are limits to what we may agree was possible. Unfortunately, neither the licensing records of Sir Henry Herbert nor Philip Henslowe's *Diary* offers him the support he thought they did in 'rehabilitating... "continuous copy"'. And a revision or revisions by an individual who thoroughly understood playhouse practice (including the need to preserve cues wherever possible) is more in line with what those documents reveal than any other explanation. The logical person to do it was the company's 'ordinary poet' and there are no grounds for supposing that he attempted to circumvent licensing as he did it. As with several examples I have discussed—*Mucedorus*, *A Fair Quarrel*, *Philaster*, *A Maid's Tragedy*, and *Bussy D'Ambois*—revision for court performance is the likeliest context in which revisions would be made, safely under the direction of the Master of the Revels.

Tiffany Stern's *Documents of Performance in Early Modern England* (2009a) offers us an important reconsideration of the extensive 'patchwork' of documents needed to put a play into production. Her final chapter, 'The approved "book" and performance' (232–52), engages with some of the issues we have just observed in Menzer. Like Menzer, she wants to argue for a version of 'continuous copy', suggesting that the players were freer to adapt and rewrite their plays than I believe was the case. She firstly explores the issue of the degree of trust that had to run through relations between players and the Master of the Revels, if the system was to work at all; clearly he did not have the resources to supervise the state of their 'books' and parts on a regular basis and normally had to take it on trust that they were abiding by his licensing authority. There are, of course, a number of instances when that trust was broken so that, Stern maintains, 'uncensored material was in fact frequently spoken onstage' (232). But the devil is usually in the detail of these cases, and it is certainly so in the case of the first example she adduces, Henry Shirley's *The Martyred Soldier*, which Henry Herbert called in and 'reformed' only a month into his term of office, in August 1623. He then re-examined the 'book' he had allowed and found that his 'reformations... were not observed, for to every cross they added a stet [leave as is] of their own' (Bawcutt: 143).

This *sounds* like outright contempt for Herbert's authority, but there is more to it than meets the eye. Rather like *The Tamer Tamed* (discussed earlier), *The Martyred Soldier* was not a new play. Herbert in fact calls it 'an old play...formerly allowed by Sir John Ashley [or Astley]' (ibid). Astley was the man who had sold the post of Master of the Revels to Herbert after he had only served in office for sixteen months, so the play could not have been older than that (see Chapter 2, note 17). We have to wonder why it was that Herbert saw fit to re-examine such a play so assiduously at precisely the same time as he was allowing older plays like *The Winter's Tale* and *Match Me In London* to pass merely on the word of the players and without exacting a fee.[81] It is likely that he had heard bad things about *The Martyred Soldier* and found in fact that the text Astley had allowed did not meet his own standards. So it was 'reallowed with reformations'. We must then assume that the Lady Elizabeth's Men were furious to find that a play which was properly licensed and paid for, and which they been playing for a year or more, had been altered in this way. Formally speaking, Astley was still Master of the Revels and Herbert his deputy, even though in practice this was never observed. But only a month into the new regime the actors may have felt that they could make something of it, possibly appealing to Astley. In repeatedly marking the text with 'stet' where Herbert had set his crosses, they were insisting that Astley's 'allowed book' was still valid, whatever Herbert thought. So it is not strictly true that 'uncensored material was...spoken on stage' in this instance. They were simply continuing to follow Astley's censorship, rather than Herbert's (see Egan 2011: sections 16–17).

Of course this was an affront to Herbert's authority, but it was not an outright disregard for his office. It amounted to a trial of strength with the new Master, a struggle of wills which the company clearly lost in the end. Herbert confiscated the book, having charged his £1 fee for licensing it. Five days later Herbert transferred the book to the Palsgrave's Men, who were desperate for new plays following the loss of their old ones when the Fortune burned down. He doubtless insisted that *his* reformations were to be followed, and charged them a further £1.

Other instances that Stern considers prove equally problematic. Nashe and Jonson's *Isle of Dogs* (1597) was indeed accused of 'containing very seditious and slanderous matter', but it is far from certain that Tilney would have licensed work for an 'incoming' company like Pembroke's Men, who were not part of the privileged circle (234).[82] Moreover, the circumstances surrounding the play and its performance were far from normal: see my earlier discussion of the play and its consequences (p. 31). Instances involving the Blackfriars boys after 1604 are similarly almost impossible to untangle since they had a separate licenser in Samuel Daniel (see pp. 118 n. 36, 240 n. 26). If he was replaced after the humiliation of his own *Philotas* we do not know by whom, but scandal after scandal suggests that the job was not done with the rigour that normally characterized the Masters of the

---

[81] *Meet Me in London* was freely relicensed by Herbert for Lady Elizabeth's Men only two days (21/23 August) before he drew the line with their *The Martyred Soldier* (Bawcutt 1996: 143).

[82] As late as 1624, Henry Herbert was still circumspect about licensing plays for touring players who 'were none of the *four* companies', that is, not officially sanctioned to perform in London (Bawcutt 1996: 145).

Revels. The fact that *Eastward Ho!* was performed by the boys without a licence at all exposed Jonson and Chapman to the possibility of judicial mutilation, the punishment for seditious slander from which the operations of the Masters of the Revels normally protected players and their writers (Jonson 2012a: 5, 373). That must normally have been a serious consideration with the players, weighing against temptations to circumvent the Masters and their fees.

Stern links the unlicensed *Eastward Ho!* with circumstances in 1633 which we have already considered (pp. 153ff); like Menzer she seems not to recognize that *The Tamer Tamed* was an old play, and one for which it was quite natural that 'parts' already existed (234). What was unusual was that Herbert wanted to review and very probably change them. She also mentions the actors' contrition over staging *The Spanish Viceroy* without a licence, as if this was an issue at the same time (but see above, p. 153). It was only as similar questions about his authority gathered around the revival of *The Tamer Tamed* that Herbert placed the signed submission from nine years before in his office book 'for a remembrance against their disorders' (Bawcutt: 183).

We could go on considering instances, but once we exclude anything that went on at the Blackfriars between 1604 and 1608, moments of intense nationalistic fervour, such as 1624, and fraught issues around Archbishop Laud and Henrietta Maria in the early 1630s, what we find is that instances when the companies defied the Masters of the Revels, or tried to circumvent their authority, were few and far between. Indeed, they normally fell over themselves to keep him happy. They presented Herbert's wife with gloves 'that cost...at least twenty shillings' (Bawcutt: 181); they presented him a copy of Sidney's *Arcadia* for allowing a play whose 'book' was lost (160); when Richard Brome's *The Honour of Young Ladies* proved a particular success they made him a gift of £2; they gave him Christmas and New Year's gifts (148, 149, 159, 214); and they allowed him two benefit performances a year, of plays of his own choice (this was later converted to two cash payments of £10: 166, 167, 168, 172, 173, 174, 176, 179, 184). And all this was on top of his regular fees for licensing playhouses and plays. They did everything they could, in short, to keep him happy.

This—and Herbert's prompt reprisals when he felt his authority was challenged—convince me that the players normally respected the Master of the Revels and the licensing regime which he represented. It was an essential ingredient of their own continued success, and for that reason they would have hesitated to produce 'parts' which strayed in anything but incidentals from the 'allowed books'. The ultimate test case *seems* to be an exception to that rule, but again is not as straightforward as it looks. 'That approved page and subsequent staging were not the same is illustrated by the story of Jonson's *The Magnetic Lady*', which was referred over Herbert's head to Archbishop Laud and the Court of High Commission (233). It is most likely that something was spoken onstage that referred to Laud's Arminian reforms (Butler 1992). The players claimed they performed nothing but what was in the 'allowed book', written by Jonson and licensed by Herbert, and initially the court agreed with them. But at a second hearing '[the High Commission court] did me right in my care to purge the [actors'] plays of all offence. My Lord's Grace of Canterbury...laid the whole fault of their play called *The Magnetic Lady* upon the players' (Bawcutt: 184).

This is more puzzling than Stern allows. The 'allowed book' must have been available, so that the court could readily see what Herbert had licensed. If the offensive words were not there, the fault logically lay with the players. But in their first ruling the court seems to have found that the material *was* there, vindicating the players. In their second ruling they either changed their minds (but why?) or it was somehow demonstrated that the objectionable material had not been present when the book was licensed. If the latter, it must have been very professionally integrated with the original to escape initial detection; it could hardly simply have been interleaved or pasted in. So what caused the court to change its mind? What belatedly attached the objectionable material to the players rather than to Jonson? Conceivably someone in the know confessed. But the most plausible scenario is that the players—who could hardly have imagined that the matter would be carried so far—were made to see that the benefits of winning this case were distinctly outweighed by the likely consequences of losing Herbert, and opted for the devil they knew, even if they had not in fact been guilty. There is a distinct possibility that Jonson did write the offensive material and that Herbert somehow missed its resonances. If not, the King's Men went to extraordinary lengths to disguise the material they added to the licensed book. Straying from the 'allowed book', straying from the umbrella of protection afforded by the Master of the Revels licence, was always a risk and one only worth taking in extreme circumstances.

Stern then goes on to consider the implications of what she supposes to have been loose oversight in the licensing regime for the actors' parts. Like Menzer and Marino, she is inclined to think that parts were transcribed before the 'book' was licensed. She raises the case of Daborne's *Machiavelli and the Devil*, discussed earlier, and continues to misunderstand the implications of *The Tamer Tamed* being an old play in 1633 (236–7).[83] She introduces the case of the surviving manuscript of *Sir John van Olden Barnavelt*, by Fletcher and Massinger, and what it might tell us about when actors' parts were copied. The manuscript is puzzling because it is a fair copy in the handwriting of Ralph Crane, copyist for the King's Men in the late 1610s and 20s, and it has been censored by Sir George Buc in quite close detail, very probably because it touches on delicate diplomatic issues. But it does not bear Buc's licence. Presumably a new version, incorporating his amendments, was going to be required; in this instance, unlike *Sir Thomas More*, we do know that the play was licensed and staged (Dutton 1991: 207). T. H. Howard-Hill tentatively considered that Crane's copy represents that 'from which actors' parts were made but not the prompter's copy', opening the possibility that those parts were created early in the process of making copies, and prior to licensing (Stern: 237). He did so, however, on the understanding that virtually all the markings on the text—in a mixture of ink and pencil—derived from Buc and no playhouse intervention. But F. J. Stephenson, who has found more markings on the manuscript than Howard-Hill

---

[83] See above, pp. 157, 153.

did, ascribes some of them to a 'book-keeper' (Stephenson 2006: 522). So the manuscript was probably prepared at a later stage of the play's copying than Howard-Hill assumed and there is nothing to associate it with the creation of 'parts' either pre- or post-licensing.

Stern points out that the whole process of transcription (even after licensing) would inevitably have led to minor variations and small creative adjustments—she points to the two manuscript copies of *A Game at Chess* in Middleton's own handwriting, which contain multiple differences (241), and it is certainly the case that even an extremely meticulous copyist like Ralph Crane *edited* at a verbal level rather than attempting to create a diplomatic copy of the original (Middleton 1999: xl–xli). But that is far removed from the kind of laissez-faire freedom to create actors' parts pre-licensing, or adapt them post-licensing, that she, Menzer, and Marino all want to believe in. Yes, it was a system based on trust, and yes that trust was sometimes broken. But on the whole it worked as it was meant to work; everyone conformed to the umbrella of official licence, because it was normally in everyone's self-interest that they should do so.

Menzer's supposition that 'the manuscripts could remain "obstinately in process" and continue to accrete handwritten additions and revisions' (29) parallels James Marino's argument in *Owning William Shakespeare*. Inspired in part by Steven Urkowitz's *Shakespeare's Revision of 'King Lear'* (1987), Marino is determined to make the actors major agents in the process of changing 'Shakespeare's' texts: 'Isolating and eliminating the contributions to Shakespeare's plays by other agents in the playhouse is neither empirically feasible nor genuinely worthwhile... When the company changed the texts of the plays, they were not adapting them. They were continuing the process of creating them... Revision, for the players, was the essence of theatrical possession' (11–12, 12, 33). This is 'continuous copy' in all but name.

These convictions underlie much broader claims about the revision of plays to which Shakespeare's name became attached and their place in building the King's Men's intellectual property. So, for example, Marino claims that 'the King's Men had maintained theatrical control of the plays that predated their company through revision, producing new and superior texts to *King John*, *Taming of a Shrew*, *Hamlet* and the *Henry VI* plays, among others' (125). And he sees this largely as the actors' own work. Speaking specifically of *Hamlet*, he claims 'changes could easily have been made incrementally, and many might have been made on the working texts in the playhouse rather than on fresh sheets at the poet's desk', envisaging 'continual incremental revisions' (79). 'What we know of early modern stage practice does not suggest that the playing companies limited their methods of revision to a choice between minor adjustments on one hand and global rewriting on the other, or that they limited the occasions of revision to special events or altered venues' (84).

There is a good deal of Marino's argument with which I wholeheartedly agree and which indeed endorses the thesis of this book. For one thing, he fights much the same battle with the New Bibliographers as I do, noting in particular that 'From the viewpoint of the so-called New Bibliographers, the idea that a longer, later-published text was a revision of a shorter, earlier and often inferior text seemed at odds with common sense' (13: see pp. 138ff above). From his perspective (and mine) it is perverse that the 'canonical text is presumed to precede any texts printed before it' or that 'arguments that variant editions of the play were created in the same order in which they are published are typically met with demands for positive evidence, reversing the usual burden of proof' (15). In the case of many of 'Shakespeare's' plays—including early works like *King John*, the shorter *Henry VI* plays, the *ur-Hamlet*, and *King Leir* which may not originally have been written solely by him (if at all)—we do see a compelling case for 'arguments that variant editions of the play were created in the same order in which they are published'.[84] The later versions were added to, augmented. And that in this process the King's Men's intellectual property was enhanced and consolidated.

Where I differ with Marino is in his assumptions about how these changes took place—especially the privileged role he gives to the actors in this—and more widely about 'what we know of early modern stage practice' in this regard. I would firstly ask where the actors were supposed to have found the time. Tiffany Stern's *Rehearsal from Shakespeare to Sheridan* (2000) and subsequent works have graphically demonstrated how little free time actors actually had, staging six different plays a week in the afternoons, and learning and rehearsing a new play every three weeks or so. These are the conditions reflected in Henslowe's *Diary* in the mid to late 1590s. As Andrew Gurr observes, 'Pre-rehearsal preparations might run for no more than two or three weeks, which would include the reading and formal acceptance of a text, casting the roles and annotating the playbook and getting it licensed by the Master of the Revels, transcribing all the "parts", getting costumes and special properties ready, and running through the play itself in rehearsal' (1996: 101–2).[85] But the real emphasis was on actors learning their individual 'parts', which they would only loosely know in relation to the wider plot.

Rehearsals as we know them were something of a luxury: 'At least one collective rehearsal was desirable, but it was also, if necessary, disposable, in ways that conning a part at home was not. Hence professional theatre contracts of the time suggest that not attending rehearsal was a finable offence' (Stern 2009b: 509). Collective rehearsal was an unpaid chore, which it might be tempting to skip. And sometimes it might simply be impossible to schedule. As Neil Carson asks, in his analysis of short times between the delivery of texts and their performance, in Henslowe's *Diary*: 'But what are we to make of cases such as *1 Civil Wars* (f.50v), *Fortunatus* (f.66), or *Jephtha* (ff. 105v–106v), when the prompt-books were prepared and presumably rehearsals begun in nine, six, and three days respectively?' (1988: 74). Collective rehearsals, when they did happen, seem to have focused on stage business rather than on the text and seem not normally to have been called for with a revived play, as distinct from a new one. Under all this

---

[84] Terri Bourus has, however, recently urged the case for the *ur-Hamlet* being what we know as the 1603 Q1 text, and by Shakespeare (2014).

[85] Readings seem to have been deliberately informal, even celebratory. Henslowe records payments to the Admiral's Men 'for to spend at the reading of that book [*Henry I*] at the Sun in New Fishstreet' and 'Laid out for the company when they read the play of Jephtha for wine at the tavern' (Foakes 2002: 88, 201).

remorseless pressure, and lack of collective engagement before performance, where would the actors find the time, or indeed the inclination, to consider making a collective revision to their texts?

There is certainly nothing in Henslowe's *Diary* that speaks to *actors* revising texts, though we have seen that several of the company's playwrights were paid on occasion for doing so. Marino rather ducks the implications of this when he claims that 'Henslowe's *Diary* indicates just how routine paying for additions was' (53). But he did not pay actors to do it, nor did he do it *routinely*. See on pp. 100–1 the sum total of revisions Henslowe lists, including prologues and epilogues; there is some ambiguity, given multiple plays with similar names, but Roslyn Knutson calculated the total as sixteen items (1985: 15); this against 280 plays mentioned in the *Diary* as a whole (Carson 1988: 82–4). As Knutson concludes, revisions were *not* routine: 'The normative and preferred practice in the Elizabethan playhouse is seen in the revivals of such plays as *The Jew of Malta* and *The Wise Man of West Chester*, which could be returned to the stage every few years at essentially no cost' (11, 15; see p. 100).

Underlying all these other reservations lie doubts about the ways in which Marino effectively glosses over the powers of the Masters of the Revels in respect both of revisions and of the licensing of plays for performance. In respect of revisions, the issues are exactly as they were with Menzer and Stern, so I need not rehearse them here (see pp. 153, 159). In respect of licensing practices, although he acknowledges that the Master's licence gave exclusive authority for a single company to stage a play, at least in the London region, he constantly looks for possible breaches of that principle. So, for example, he notes 'repeated examples of Henslowe, Alleyn, or both supplying the same play to multiple companies while retaining control themselves of the playbook and the performance rights' or where confusions of Falstaff/Oldcastle titles seem to offer the possibility that one company might have transgressed another's licence (26, 122–3). The control exercised by Henslowe and Alleyn by the late 1590s amounted to a new form of theatrical management, one in which ownership of the licensed London theatres gave them considerable leverage over the companies which used them. They took over, in effect, some of the autonomous authority previously enjoyed by those companies, especially when the companies fell into debt to them.[86] In that context it is not surprising that they should abrogate the performance rights of some plays to themselves and lease them out to successive companies using their playhouses. It would not infringe the exclusivity of the licence, which ensured that multiple companies should not be staging the same play in competition with each other. In respect of Falstaff/Oldcastle, it is entirely possible that all the supposed cross-licensing boiled down to nothing more than the notoriously strong memory of Shakespeare having changed the name he originally gave to his most popular character. As I observe in my chapter on *The Merry Wives of*

---

[86] This would become even clearer in 1614 when Henslowe became co-owner of the Hope playhouse and signed up actors to play there under contract to himself and his partner, Jacob Meade, rather than to a patronized company.

Windsor, it is notable that as late as 1709 Nicholas Rowe knew that Shakespeare had been forced to drop Oldcastle for Falstaff and knew the family which had required it. 'Oldcastle' quite possibly tells us nothing about the licensing of these plays.

Under normal circumstances, however, the Master of the Revels' authority underwrote the *performing* rights of the company which licensed a play with him; Marino gives a good deal of attention to the *publishing* rights attached to a play, which were entirely another matter. A Stationers' Company licence might protect the rights to a number of texts relating to the same subject (Blayney 1997, cited on p. 140). But no such understanding applied to performing rights, which were specific and exclusive. A key thrust of Marino's argument is that the Chamberlain's Men somehow acquired the texts for various pre-1594 plays, including early versions of *King John*, *2* and *3 Henry VI*, *Hamlet*, and *The Taming of the Shrew*, and multiple plays formerly belonging to the Queen's Men, including *The Famous Victories of Henry V* and *King Leir* (see p. 26). And that they essentially established their own performing rights to these plays by revising (and expanding) them, eventually wrapping them in the authority of Shakespeare's growing reputation, whether or not he had written the originals or he had personally been responsible for the changes the company made.

At the very least this could not have been done without Edmund Tilney's acquiescence. As we have seen, Andrew Gurr has argued repeatedly that it was more than that, part of a wider act of policy imposed by Tilney's superiors in the Privy Council: 'each company was given a set of already famous plays. One secured [the Admiral's Men] Marlowe's, the other [the Chamberlain's Men] Shakespeare's' (2004a: xiii). As we have also seen, this has been widely challenged itself, in particular by Roslyn Knutson and Holger Syme (see p. 29). Any explanation, however, has to account for how the playing licences *changed hands*. They were too valuable simply to surrender or allow to lapse. The Queen's Men ceased to be one of the court companies in 1594 and became exclusively a touring company; if at that point they knew that they would no longer be exercising their London performing rights to their old plays, they might well have sold them to the Chamberlain's Men. Similarly, companies like Strange's, Pembroke's, and Sussex's Men, which had broken up or refocused during the 1592–4 plague, might also have been prepared to cash in their performing licences to a company which could use them. And the Chamberlain's Men may then have sought to make the most of them, perhaps even presenting them as new plays (with higher prices for first performances) by revising them almost out of recognition. I do not think, however, that we have any grounds for assuming that this process took place *outside* of the licensing system, by what amounts to a process of piracy, or that the mere fact of revision (even revision by the actors themselves) somehow conferred on the Chamberlain's Men a greater right to perform plays if they did not in fact possess such licences.

Marino is careful not to ascribe all the changes to plays to incremental alterations made by the actors, recognizing that some changes would seem to have required more centralized planning. 'Some changes, like the changes in *Hamlet's* plot sequence, are more drastic and require a number of consequent changes, while other adjustments are more local and convenient to make. The Chamberlain's Men could have made all the changes between the texts of *Hamlet* at one time, if they chose, but there is no special reason to insist that they did so' (93). On the contrary, there is every reason to suppose that they did so. Incremental change by the actors (other, perhaps, than *reductions* in the text) are an unproved supposition, which runs as I have argued against the logic of the licensing system and for which there is no evidence either in Henslowe's records or in other documents of the era. The actors were quite busy enough as it was rehearsing and performing; and the Chamberlain's Men, in particular, had a resident 'ordinary poet' who was better placed than anyone to change their texts, 'drastically' or otherwise, and it made sense for him to do it 'at one time' rather than piecemeal. As I argue throughout the book, the most compelling evidence for when and why such changes might be called for is linked with revisions 'for the court'.

RECAPITULATION: REVISION OLD AND NEW

As I conclude the multi-faceted theatre- and textual-history side of this book and move on to look at specific Shakespearean texts, I would like to point out how many pieces of evidence point in the same direction. The interests of the court and of the leading theatrical companies steadily converged in the last quarter of the sixteenth century, when settled London playing became a realistic possibility. In 1598 those interests were publicly acknowledged as identical, as the Chamberlain's Men and the Admiral's Men were given privileged positions in London playing as well as at court. The fact that other companies later joined the privileged circle did not undermine the principle here, given the striking increase in demand for theatre at court under King James, with the new reality of multiple royal households (see pp. 52–3).

The court Revels season, over the protracted midwinter festivals, was a long-established institution, though its nature changed over time; this was especially so with growing dependence on plays brought to court by the leading theatrical companies over the last twenty years of Elizabeth's reign. It is a mistake, however, to assume that all of those performances simply replicated the plays as they were staged in the public theatres. Henslowe's *Diary* contains compelling evidence (between 1598 and 1603) that certain plays of the Lord Admiral's Men were chosen for 'additions', 'alterings', or 'mendings', sometimes at quite substantial cost; and the only explanation ever given for this is that they were 'for the court'.

Dekker's revision of *Old Fortunatus* is the clearest-cut example we have of a play receiving such 'additions' and ending up at a length that some theatre historians have argued would not have been acceptable in the public theatres. However, the one place we know where there was no constraint of playing times was the court, where performances are known to have gone on (with intermissions) until 1 or 2 o'clock in the morning. We also know that the Master of the

Revels, who was responsible for overseeing the Revels season at court, significantly *increased* his claims for attendance fees in the period when the court became more dependent on commercial drama, even though he lost responsibility for in-house entertainments like masques. The only logical explanation is that he was taking very seriously the understanding (expressed by Thomas Heywood) that plays should be 'perfected...before they come to the public view of the Prince and the Nobility'. That is, he was actively engaged in the revision processes of the Admiral's Men described in Henslowe's *Diary*—and equally engaged in those of the rival Chamberlain's Men, centring on their 'ordinary poet', William Shakespeare.

While all this was going on—in a window from 1598 to 1604, fortuitously almost exactly overlapping that in Henslowe's *Diary*—some publishers took to describing their play texts as 'augmented', 'enlarged', or 'amended'. These were preponderantly plays of Shakespeare, which for the first time are linked with him by name. One of these, *Love's Labour's Lost*, also links such augmentation with performance at court; *Old Fortunatus* could have done the same, but in fact neither Dekker's name nor the fact of augmentation is mentioned on the title page.[87]

Virtually all of this has been ignored in the changing fashions that have held sway over the editing of Shakespeare's texts for the last century. When the New Bibliographers were at their most influential, the early revisions of Shakespeare's plays were invariably deemed to have been conducted by people other than Shakespeare—actors, stenographers, printers—and from originating 'foul papers' to some more corrupt form. As my analysis of the 'bad' quartos will show, that ignores evidence which points to those texts being imaginatively reconceived and expanded rather than cut. Conversely, as the influence of Greg has diminished, a new enthusiasm has emerged for a much more fluid pattern of revision within the playhouses ('continuous copy'), though here again Shakespeare himself is largely sidelined. But this fluidity can only be imagined if it was possible to ignore or circumvent the licensing machinery of the day, which I dispute was normally the case.

I find no compelling evidence in Menzer, Stern, or Marino that the actors' parts were written out *prior* to licensing, or that plays were in a process of 'continuous copy'—by the actors or others—*after* licensing. Both are at odds with the logic of the licensing of an 'allowed book', which was central to the authority of the Master of the Revels. And while we can identify a small number of examples, in unusual or pressurized circumstances, when that authority was challenged, it was overwhelmingly respected by the players for the simple reason that it was in their long-term interests to do so. Revision was normally conducted in the orderly manner apparent from Henslowe's *Diary*, and licensed (for a fee) by the Master of the Revels—except when it was done for court performance, directly under the Master's personal control. Revisions that Shakespeare made in this context were overseen and implicitly licensed by Edmund Tilney or latterly Sir George Buc. It is to such revisions that we now turn.

---

[87] Dekker's name appears, unusually, at the very foot of the play's last page (L3v).

PART II

SHAKESPEARE'S MULTIPLE TEXTS

PREAMBLE

The first half of this book has sketched out a context in which it made compelling sense for Shakespeare personally to be the reviser of his own plays (and possibly plays originally co-authored with others, which he made his own) during his years with the Chamberlain's Men. This explains why there were multiple versions of so many of them. The company were mandated to entertain the court and it was his role as the company's 'ordinary poet' to take the lead in doing this as impressively as possible. There was a clear incentive, not present within the public theatres, to write expansively and with increased rhetorical range.

My argument about each of the once-called 'bad' quartos—*The First Part of the Contention*, *The True Tragedy*, *Romeo and Juliet* (Q1, 1597), *Henry V* (Q1, 1600), *Merry Wives of Windsor* (Q1, 1602), and *Hamlet* (Q1, 1603)—is essentially the same, though there are several variations on the one theme. Each is an early version of a play which was later adapted—and in each case significantly expanded—into the versions with which we are much more familiar. Each is, in its own way, a poorly reported version of that early play; it does not derive closely from an authorial manuscript but in my view was probably transmitted (at least in part) by actors who performed in it, though in the case of *Hamlet* shorthand may have played its part (Stern 2013). And that transmission was probably (again, at least in part) oral/aural, a form of 'memorial reconstruction' akin to that described by Scott McMillin (see p. 148), such as to give rise to a lot of the roughness—words misheard, speech prefixes confused, repetition, narrative sequences disrupted, verse rendered as prose and vice versa (though it sometimes gave rise to much more detailed stage directions than are found in later texts). The 'good' versions, by contrast, all derive directly from authorial manuscripts or written versions based closely upon them.

This makes it impossible to compare the early and late texts on a like-to-like basis, as we perhaps can with, say, *Othello* and *King Lear*. If Shakespeare did revise these plays, he did so starting with the original manuscripts—not with their poorly transmitted print versions. So we can never be sure what exactly he was working from. Moreover, it is always possible that there was more than one stage of adaptation between the versions that have survived, missing links that we simply cannot take into account. What I think we *can* trace when we compare the texts are developments in plotting, characterization, and conceptual range (as well, of course, as verbal richness) that we would expect of a dramatist of Shakespeare's calibre when he reimagined an earlier play.

Those who would argue that the later versions were written first rarely face up to the difficulty inherent in *un-imagining* such features. It is easy enough, of course, to imagine a redactor—conceivably Shakespeare himself—trimming the luxuriant language of *Romeo and Juliet* if a shorter version was needed. It is much more difficult to imagine that person (much less some actors' collective) reducing the caring and latterly deeply contrite figure of Friar Laurence we see at the end of Q2 to the much less focused figure we see in Q1. By the same token, it defies plausibility that anyone could or would have deconstructed the orchestrated functions which Shakespeare built into Will Kemp's roles as the company clown in Q2. In both these instances (and others throughout these plays) what we have is not a *reduction* from one to the other, a process that would surely have left traces of the earlier achievement; we have creativity operating at different levels. And in the difference between the two we can see something—however obscured by the impenetrability of some of the evidence—of Shakespeare's dramatic imagination at work, an opportunity which prevailing attitudes to the 'bad' quartos (more recent as well as older) have denied us. That is why this matters.

I shall, therefore, largely be tracing developments in plotting, characterization, and language which seem to me inherently typical of augmentation rather than of its reverse. In addressing *Henry V* first it is my intention, as it were, to make the one example stand for them all in challenging a range of the traditional assumptions about these plays, so that I do not have to keep traversing the same territory with each of them. There is, however, one argument about the relationships between the two sets of texts that I would like to address here collectively, hoping to clear some ground. Lukas Erne seeks to undermine the very thesis I have just outlined by demonstrating that the versions of some passages in Q1 *Romeo and Juliet* can only render adequate sense by reference to Q2, supposedly proving that the latter is the earlier text:

> the derivative nature of most of the 'bad' quartos is strongly suggested by passages whose sense only becomes entirely clear after a comparison with the 'good' text...Q1 reads:
>
>> JULIET A blister on that tongue! He was not born to shame.
>> Upon his face shame is ashamed to sit.
>> But wherefore, villain didst thou kill my cousin?
>> That villain cousin would have killed my husband.
>> All this is comfort.   (11.41–5)

It is not entirely clear what 'All this' refers to. The second quarto adds a passage between lines 44 and 45 with which Juliet's concluding words make better sense:

>> Back, foolish tears, back to your native spring,
>> Your tributary drops belong to woe,

> Which you mistaking offer up to joy.
> My husband lives that Tybalt would have slain,
> And Tybalt's dead that would have slain my husband.
> All this I comfort... (3.2.102–7)   (Erne 2007: 9–10)

Of course Q2 makes better sense. But none of this—or any of the many other examples that can be adduced—proves that Q2 was written before Q1.[1] All it really proves is the inadequacy of the Q1 text, whether as a result of poor 'memorial reconstruction' or however else we account for its various inadequacies. Yes, the passage that is better reported in Q2 *Romeo and Juliet* was very probably in the originary text. But that could just as readily have been a lost manuscript somewhere behind Q1 as Q2 itself. The reporter simply failed to reproduce it adequately. It does not follow that all the other dramatic and linguistic sophistications of Q2 were already in existence. Indeed the very fact that the earlier texts fail to register even traces of so many of those sophistications is more telling than that they should omit passages of the type Erne details. We will see similar instances in the next section, on *Henry V*.

Let me just add that I have not attempted to engage with every modern edition of the plays I am concerned with (though I have done my best to consult them all). As I have explained before, I am here advancing a new explanation for the state of these texts, one which seems to me to have been strangely overlooked in the history of Shakespeare editing. I am not concerned, therefore, to explore other possible explanations for their own sake. I engage with those I have found which best help me to advance my own case, while also illustrating some of the limitations of other explanations still widely in circulation.

---

[1] Erne cites Chambers 1930: 1.341 and Hart 1942: 184–90 'for further passages which do not make perfect sense in Q1 because of Q2 cuts'. He acknowledges 'It is true that some of these examples have little weight' but insists 'the cumulative case remains strong' (Note 33: 9).

5

More Sophisticated Histories
a. The Famous Victories of Shakespeare's *Henry V*

Henry V is the most revealing Shakespeare text in relation to the thesis of this book. That is so because we possess a short, earlier version of the play (the 1600 quarto, henceforth Q1; 1,623 lines in length) and a long, later one (the much more familiar 1623 folio version, F; 3,166 lines); but we uniquely also have close source texts, alongside which we can trace something of Shakespeare's creative practice in building his own play not once but twice. There is nothing in that last sentence which I am not going to have to argue from the ground up. But my hope is that this can reduce the time I shall need to spend on these issues in the discussion of the other plays in this category. Q1 *Henry V* is not the earliest of them, but sequence is not important here.

Firstly, then, let me lay out something of the differences between the two Shakespearean texts of this same play, and in what senses Q1 may be said to be inferior. I am assuming that readers will be better acquainted with something resembling F, the longer version, which is instantly recognizable from its choruses.[1] Q1 will be less familiar and can most easily be described in terms of what it does *not* have, compared with F—though such language perhaps predisposes us towards a view of their relationship which I do not share. These, therefore, are all of what I hesitantly describe as the 'omissions' in Q1 greater than about ten lines in length, referenced against Bevington's edition of the F text: all the Choruses, including Prologue and Epilogue; 1.1. entire (the scheming bishops); 2.2.102–39 (Henry's sententious reflections on the traitors; TLN 732–79); 2.4.1–14 (the French King's worried reaction to English invasion; TLN 888–901); 3.1. entire (Harfleur: 'Once more unto the breach'; TLN 1,082–117); 3.2.27–46 (the Boy's reflections on Pistol, Nim, and Bardolph; TLN 1,145–63) and 64–139 (the roles of Jamy and Macmorris; TLN 1,183–258); 3.3.11–41 (Henry's threats to the Governor of Harfleur; TLN 1,269–300); 3.5.27–60 (French king and nobles anticipating Agincourt; TLN 1,406–40); 3.7.7–18, 21–39, 50–9, 69–79, 125–57 (overconfident French nobles; TLN 1,632–43; 1,646–65; 1,676–86; 1,695–705; 1,753–87); 4.1.1–35 (Henry bidding goodnight to his brothers and Erpingham before the battle; TLN 1,845–92) and 118–33 (part of Henry's conversation with Bates, Court, and Williams; TLN 1,967–81); 228–86 ('Upon the king...'; 'ceremony';

---

[1] I say 'something resembling F' deliberately, since some notable modern editions (e.g. *The Oxford Shakespeare*, *The Norton Shakespeare*), while based on F, incorporate features from Q. This is an issue to which I shall return.

TLN 2,079–140); 4.2. entire (The French nobles taking to the field of battle); 4.3.19–29 (beginning of the 'Crispin Crispian' day speech; TLN 2,262–73); 4.4.2–11, 14–24, 51–66, 68–79 (i.e. most of the scene involving Pistol, the Boy, and M. le Fer; TLN 2,387–95; 2,397–405; 2,431–44; 2,446–56); 4.8.82–91 (numbers of the French dead; TLN 2,801–10); 5.1.46–54, 68–78 (Pistol, Fluellen, Gower, and leeks; TLN 2,944–51; 2,965–74); 5.2.98–282, 273–328, 345–58 (most of the last scene, including Burgundy's lament for the state of France, much of Henry's wooing of Katherine, and the peace negotiations; TLN 3,086–268; 3,271–319; 3,335–49).[2] The issue is whether F was written first, and these passages later excised—either by Shakespeare or by others; or whether Q1 was written first and these passages added, in a complete rewrite.

My contention is that Q1 was not only published first, but also *written* first; and that F was a later expansion. I am by no means the first to suggest this. Back in 1881 Brinsley Nicholson argued the case, as did Hardin Craig in 1927, and there may be others. But the twentieth-century editorial tradition of Shakespeare's *Henry V*, heavily driven by Greg's 'foul papers' theory, unanimously supported the assumption that F came first, drowning out contrary voices.[3] I believe that we can substantiate the primacy of Q1 by reference to Shakespeare's acknowledged sources, Holinshed's *Chronicles* and the old, anonymous Queen's Men's play, *The Famous Victories of Henry V*, first published in 1598. In this analysis I shall focus on three 'amendments' or 'augmentations' which seem to me to signal developments from Q1 to F, rather than vice versa: the likely creation of Q1 itself; changes in the play's adherence to historical evidence; and changes in the play's rhetorical strategies.

This contention turns two pieces of 'established' wisdom about Shakespeare's play on their head. Firstly, if Q1 really was written first, it can no longer be dismissed as an inadequate—and ignorable—redaction of the much larger folio text, the role it enjoys almost universally in the editorial tradition: in Andrew Gurr's words, 'a cheap paste copy of the Shakespearean diamond' (2000: ix). It is a (version of a) play that was almost certainly written and performed in its own right in 1599—and it deserves more attention in its own right than it has generally received. We have testimony, possibly from Sir George Buc himself, that Q1 *Henry V* is 'much ye same with that in Shakespeare'. Even before he became Master of the Revels, Buc was better placed than most to know if another, radically different version of the play had been performed.[4]

My contention secondly challenges established wisdom about the extent of Shakespeare's indebtedness to *The Famous Victories* in writing *Henry V*. It has long been widely recognized that the entire *Henriad—1 Henry IV, 2 Henry IV,* and

---

[2] A full list of the material not in Q—there are many smaller omissions—can be found in Taylor 1982: Appendix F, 312–15. Note, however, that this does not always map directly on to Bevington 2008, because of differences in lineation, especially in prose scenes.

[3] To mention only some of the most prominent editions that advance the F-came-first case: Walter 1954; Humphreys 1980; Taylor 1982; Wells and Taylor 1986; Gurr 1992; Craik 1995; Greenblatt 1997; Gurr 2000.

[4] The comment is in a copy of Q1. Alan Nelson judges that it *may* be by Buc, though he is not certain: see pp. 57–9. The quarto comes from the period just before and after 1600 when Buc bought numerous play texts but, if it *is* his comment, there is no way of knowing when he wrote it.

Henry V—owes something to this play, if not perhaps to precisely the version that made its way into print in 1598.⁵ The version we have offers a somewhat chaotic account of the folk-tale history of Henry, misled in his youth by an Oldcastle-like Vice, who miraculously converts on the death of his father to become the great warrior who defeats the French at Agincourt: in broad-brush terms, the story Shakespeare also tells. But the early parts of the play are at best only sketchily related to Shakespeare's *Henry IV* plays, and the later parts (dealing with the warrior Henry) only intermittently bear any resemblance to the familiar folio version of *Henry V*. They bear a *striking* resemblance, however, to the much-overlooked Q1.

THE FAMOUS VICTORIES OF HENRY V AND Q1

The Famous Victories consists of twenty scenes: Sc. 1 to the first part of Sc. 9 correspond loosely with parts of the *Henry IV* plays; but the remainder of Sc. 9 to Sc. 20 (more than half the play) correspond closely with Q1 *Henry V*. Q1 picks up the material at exactly the same point in Sc. 9, with the Archbishop of Canterbury ('Bishop' in Q1) summoned to give his views of Henry's claim to France, and expounding at some length on Salic Law; Henry and his counsellors discuss the Scottish threat; the Dauphin/Dolphin's gift of tennis balls is received and defied; John Cobbler, his wife, and Derick provide comedy in scenes which will readily transpose to those of Pistol, Nym, and the others; the siege of Harfleur is mentioned but not shown (neither gives Henry a piece of rousing oratory); the Dauphin is prevented by his father from taking part in the battle of Agincourt; the French troops regard the English as easy prey; Henry tells the French herald that he refuses to be ransomed, whatever the outcome, and leads his troops with a stirring patriotic/religious battle-cry: 'cry "Saint George!" and "God and Saint George help us"!' (*Famous Victories*, 14.52–3);⁶ 'The Battle' itself is hardly scripted; Henry and his nobles review their astonishingly light casualties, the Duke of York being the most notable; Derick has an encounter with a French prisoner; Henry debates with the French King the precise terms of the peace treaty, demanding the crown immediately but, as negotiations overrun, wooing and winning Princess Katherine; there is a last comic scene of John Cobbler and Derick, involving many captured French shoes; Henry finally agrees to accept the French crown when the present king dies, as long as the French nobility swear allegiance to him (which they do), and the play ends—as Q1 does—with Henry proclaiming that he will wed Katherine very soon.

There are few *verbal* links between *The Famous Victories* and Q1, but enough to suggest Shakespeare's acquaintance with the earlier play, either in performance or in

---

⁵ See, for example, Humphreys 1960: xxxii–iv. Several commentators have suggested that *The Famous Victories* represents what may be a collapsing of two original Queen's Men's plays into one, and that more of their material may have been available to Shakespeare, lying behind *1* and *2 Henry IV*. The *Henry V* material, however, seems relatively intact.

⁶ References to *The Famous Victories of Henry V* are to the text in Corbin and Sedge 1991; those to Q1 are to Gurr 2000.

the 1598 text: the interchange between Henry and the French Ambassador over whether the latter should feel free to speak his mind (*Famous Victories*, 9.107–10; Q1, 1.160–8); the description of the Dolphin's present as a 'tun' of tennis balls/treasure (*Famous Victories*, 9.105; Q1, 1.176); the Herald's request after Agincourt for leave to bury the dead (*Famous Victories*, 15.22–4; Q1, 16.47–50). The scene of Derick with his French prisoner is strongly reminiscent of Pistol with M. le Fer, while Henry's wooing of Katherine is similar in both texts: both sequences strongly suggest some acquaintance (Smith 1998). None of these suggests close attention by Shakespeare to the *verbal* play of *The Famous Victories*, which he evidently reinvented in his own idiom, just as he went to Holinshed's *Chronicles* to flesh out the historical (as distinct from legendary) features of Henry's life; but some details and situations seem to have stuck with him.[7] They only did so, however, as far as Q1: none of the material in F that does not pre-exist in Q1 derives from *The Famous Victories* at all.

Shakespeare has reinvented the verse and prose of *The Famous Victories* in Q1 at every level. He has entirely re-imagined the comic scenes in the persons of Pistol, Nym, and their associates, carried over from the *Henry IV* plays, replacing those written for the great clown, Richard Tarlton, who originally played 'Derick'. Shakespeare has also imagined Henry's army as a much fuller cross-section of English (and Welsh) male society. In *The Famous Victories*, Henry only ever speaks to his aristocratic commanders who—contrary to the chronicles—include a prominent Earl of Oxford; in Q1 Henry speaks to, or about, Shakespeare's own historically questionable selection of aristocrats, but also to the captains, Gower and Llewellyn, and three ordinary soldiers (the Bates, Court, and Williams of F), besides Pistol of his old tavern companions.[8] And Shakespeare has added an early scene for Katherine, plus an entirely distinct sequence of some substance (deriving from Holinshed), the traitor scene. He has also found space in which to kill off Falstaff.

So Shakespeare has produced a distinctively different play, but within the structural confines of its predecessor. It seems irrefutable that *The Famous Victories* has provided Shakespeare with the essential *shape* of Q1. They start and end in exactly the same place. Neither version gives us a scene at Harfleur; in neither version is the Dauphin at Agincourt (in this they follow the chronicles, as F does not); in both versions the triumph at Agincourt is rounded off with a mirroring triumph in the wooing of Katherine, which is undercut neither by Burgundy's lament over war-torn France nor by a reminder of how short-lived Henry's achievements were to prove, as it is in F.

---

[7] Cf Roger Warren's characterization of the relationship between the two versions of 2 *Henry VI*, where he speaks of 'several occasions where F and Q represent different versions of the material', emphasizing the difference between content and expression (see p. 201).

[8] *The Famous Victories* and Shakespeare (somewhat differently in Q1 and F) both took considerable licence over the choice of aristocrats present at Agincourt. See Pitcher 1961: 183–95. Q1 focuses on the royal family—Exeter (Henry's uncle), Clarence and Gloucester (brothers), York (cousin), plus the Earl of Warwick. F reduces Clarence to a cypher but replaces him with his brother, Bedford; it also supplements Warwick with the Earls of Westmorland, Salisbury, and Shrewsbury (Talbot), seemingly concentrating on warriors already made famous in *1 Henry VI*. I return to this later.

But the editorial tradition of *Henry V* assumes, either implicitly or explicitly, that *The Famous Victories* had relatively little influence on the play (i.e. F), which of course—being twice the length, with much more detail—it only patchily resembles.[9] Conversely, it could only be the merest chance that a process which converted F to Q1 would do so in such a way as to emphasize so many resemblances (and so few differences) between Q1 and *The Famous Victories*. It is highly improbable. My argument is that Shakespeare, ever the focused professional, firstly produced a robustly playable text, Q1, a workmanlike revamping of the old Queen's Men's play. In *1599: A Year in the Life of William Shakespeare* (2005), James Shapiro has argued that the year of the opening of The Globe was an unusually busy one for Shakespeare, with the writing of as many as four new plays, against his usual yearly tally of two: 'In the course of 1599 Shakespeare completed *Henry the Fifth*, wrote *Julius Caesar* and *As You Like It* in quick succession, and then drafted *Hamlet*' (Preface: xi–xii). He was certainly exceptionally busy. And *As You Like It* is an interesting text to lay alongside Q1 *Henry V*, since it too is remarkably faithful to its primary source text, Thomas Lodge's prose romance, *Rosalynde*. Shakespeare reduced it to dramatic form with hardly any deviations/additions: it is an exemplary instance of efficient generic translation. By the same token, his first use of Plutarch as a source, in *Julius Caesar*, involved a highly focused economy: 'the white heat of Shakespeare's drama, even from the Lupercalia, comes from four folio pages, 786–9, of *Caesar* in North's 1595 Plutarch' (Daniell 1998: 87).

This was probably not always Shakespeare's way of working, but circumstances perhaps demanded it. *The Famous Victories* gave him the dramatic form for a play about Henry V: what he produced from it was a play with closer attention to the real history (Holinshed) and verbal energy of an entirely different order. I suggest that he only produced the much fuller and the multiply-layered F, the third longest text he ever wrote—even more dependent on Holinshed, but also in places disregarding that history, as we shall see—later, when time permitted and circumstances called for it.[10] It is, of course, my argument throughout this book that a court

---

[9] See, for example, Taylor 1982: 27–8; Craik 1995: 7–9; Gurr 1992: 226–30.

[10] I think it likely that F belongs to 1602, after the decisive (Agincourt-like) Battle of Kinsale (Dutton 2005). That is not a *necessary* condition for the purposes of this book. But the chorus to Act 5 of F, with its optimistic aspirations for the return of 'the General of our gracious Empress', could hardly have been staged anywhere between September 1599 (Essex's ignominious return from Ireland) and the end of 1601 (Mountjoy's victory at Kinsale).

James Bednarz argues that the Choruses were in public performance as early as 1599 (2006). He points to a passage in Jonson's *Every Man Out of His Humour* which appears to mock the calls to *Henry V*'s audience to exercise their imaginations: 'let your imagination be swifter than an oar …' (Grex, 4.5.141–45, in Jonson 2012i). It is a plausible allusion, but not a necessary one. Dekker's *Old Fortunatus* also contains Choruses which exhort the audience to use their imaginations to make allowance for an inadequate theatre and specifically to transport the characters overseas: 'And for this small circumference must stand / For the imagined surface of much land / Of many kingdoms, and since many a mile / Should here be measured out, our muse intreats / Your thoughts to help poor art' (Prologue, 15–19); 'The world to the circumference of heaven / Is as a small point in geometry, / Whose greatness is so little that a less / Cannot be made. Into that narrow room / Your quick imaginations we must charm / To turn that world, and (turned) again to part it / Into large kingdoms, and within one moment / To carry Fortunatus on the wings / Of active thought, many a thousand miles. / Suppose then, since you last beheld him here, that you have sailed with him upon the seas…' (Chorus to Act 2, 1–11). *Old Fortunatus* was very probably played at court on 27 December 1597; the Prologue and Choruses were presumably retained when it was transferred to the public stage, as it

performance was always the likeliest occasion for a rewrite on such a scale. That may at this time have been a recurrent working method for Shakespeare.[11]

THE DEFICIENCIES OF Q1 AS A TEXT

Q1 *Henry V* was one of Arthur Pollard's original 'bad' quartos, commonly thought to have derived from unauthorized—indeed piratical—reconstructions from memory by small numbers of actors. Q1 fit the category in part because it lacked whole scenes and sections that appeared in F, but also because the language is sometimes clumsy, versification is erratic, and several passages are inconsistent or patently incomplete. In my analysis, of course, the absence of substantial material from F is irrelevant: the Choruses and other major items were added later. The other inadequacies of Q1, however, resemble those deriving from some sort of oral/aural transmission, probably non-piratical 'memorial construction', which I have discussed elsewhere (pp. 147–8).

The belief persists that it was first mined from a longer, more finished Shakespearean original. In Andrew Gurr's terms it was a minimal text derived from a maximal one (see p. 76). Starting from that premise he offers the most thorough analysis of the quarto's deficiencies in his edition of Q1 (2000: 9–28). Gurr argues that it ultimately derives from F (which, of course, I dispute) but via 'a copy which had been radically revised by the company for performance at the Globe. It was put together for performance in London and elsewhere in late 1599 or early 1600 by several members of the company. It was undoubtedly an authoritative players' text. At least two, possibly more, of the company's players who had speaking parts shared the work. Most of the manuscript was recorded by dictation, chiefly from the rough playscript, helped in places by the players' memories of their parts' (9). But inevitably the process introduced errors and confusion:

> The surviving text in Q1 is some way from being a perfect representation of what was actually said and done on stage in 1599. It has confusions that come from the revision of the original copy to make an acting version as well as mistakes made in the process of transcription, not only by the copyists but by the Q1 compositor. Each error might come from any one of the steps of the process. (13)

Again, I resist the F-to-Q1 suggestion implicit in the phrasing about 'revision of the original copy to make an acting version'. But the scope for confusion, between the actors who dictated it to a scribe and the printer's compositor (the man who set it in type), was indeed considerable.

---

would soon have been to recoup the investment, though the special Prologue and Epilogue 'at court' would have been dropped. In any case, the play was entered in the Stationers' Register on 20 February 1600, more than a month before *Every Man Out of His Humour* (8 April). Jonson may well have been poking fun at Dekker's Choruses, which certainly existed before his own play was in print, rather than those of *Henry V*, which may well not have done.

[11] See p. 201 on Randall Martin's analysis of the relationship between the texts of *The True Tragedy* and *3 Henry VI*.

Gurr gives many examples of errors in Q1 that might result from mishearings during dictation. For example:

> 1.32, where Q conflates Sala and Elbe. Salic Law was given its name from the river called Sala or Salia. Here Sala is mistranscribed by infection from the other river's name. Simpler cases are 1.45 Q's 'the function' from F's 'defunction'; 1.46 'Godly' for F's 'Idly', and in the same initial section Q's 'fate' for F's 'state' at 1.119. The same process generated 2.33 'talke' for 'take', 2.73 'tashan' for 'tertian'... Other examples include 5.40 'demonstrated' for F's 'demonstrative', 5.62 Q's 'hear' for F's 'him', 5.81 Q's 'musters' for F 'masters', 9.29 'Packs' for F's 'pax', 9.34 'approach' for F's 'reproach', 9.79 'abraided' for 'vpbrayded', and 11.102 'chanceries' for F's 'chantries'. (16)

Other mistakes suggest that at times transcription was made directly from a written text, though one that was sometimes difficult to read. This need not have been the author's manuscript; it could, for example, have been some of the players' parts (Palfrey and Stern 2007). Gurr cites Q1's 'rackte at 5.38' for F's 'rakt' (raked) and 11.61 Q1's 'gift' for F's 'guilt'—both more likely misreadings rather than mishearings (17). But mishearings of a kind that fail to register, for instance, differences between prose and verse are much more common. In all of this it is evident that a more perfect manuscript lay somewhere behind Q1 than the printer managed to represent. But it need not have been F or have derived from F. If you lay F alongside Q1 it is certainly not *unreasonable* to conclude that the latter was a poor attempt to reconstruct the former, any more than it is unreasonable to assume that the sun revolves around the earth. But there are other explanations.

While Q1 is clearly inferior in the parts of the text it shares with F, it gives no indication that those substantial parts of F which it did *not* represent existed at all in 1599/1600—for example, the Choruses; 1.1 (the scheming bishops); 3.1 (Harfleur and 'Once more unto the breach'); the roles of Jamy and Macmorris in 3.3; 4.2 (the French nobles taking the field of battle); and large swathes of Act 5. Perhaps even more telling than whole sections that are simply missing are the instances of Henry's own oratory that are absent from Q1 but do not announce their absence by any clumsiness in the text—notably 2.2.102–39 (Henry's sententious reflections on the traitors; TLN 732–79); 4.1.228–86 ('Upon the king...'; 'ceremony'; TLN 2,079–140); and the beginning of the 'Crispin Crispian' day speech at 4.3.19–29 (TLN 2,262–73). Each of these is readily detachable, what John Kerrigan might characterize as an *interpolation* (see p. 112), and just as likely to be an *addition* to a later F as an excision from what existed in 1599.

THE LONG AND THE SHORT OF *HENRY V*

As the 'bad' quarto orthodoxy of the New Bibliographers waned, this new orthodoxy—that the shorter texts represent stage-worthy adaptations of Shakespeare's overlong creativity—has waxed in its place, especially in respect of *Henry V*. It perfectly accords with Lucas Erne's argument in *Shakespeare as Literary Dramatist*:

> There are good reasons to believe, then, that the first quartos of *Romeo and Juliet*, *Henry V*, and *Hamlet* reflect, or at least dimly reflect, what Shakespeare and his fellows

performed in London and elsewhere... the 'long' extant texts of these and other Shakespeare plays do not appear to have been meant for performance before undergoing abridgement and adaptation for the stage.   (2003: 219)

On the contrary, he maintains, they were meant to be read.

So we are expected to believe that, in the course of one of the busiest years of his life, Shakespeare originally wrote a play twice as long as was needed for performance (F)—for the benefit of unknown manuscript readers; that one or more persons (by most accounts not Shakespeare himself) then abridged and adapted this for the stage; and that finally this stage version became somewhat muddled—possibly because of an aural transmission of versions of the text at some point in the process—before it emerged as Q1. In this account Shakespeare apparently paid little attention to *The Famous Victories*, but the whole process of adaptation somehow produced a Q1 with remarkable similarities to the earlier play.

How improbable this all is will become even more apparent when we consider in some detail exactly what would have had to be cut from F to produce Q1. And—this seems to me the most critical issue—what needed not merely to be cut from F but deliberately *changed*, in a way that does not sit readily with a process merely of adaptation to the stage. However we read this process—Q1 to F or F to Q1, and however many stages now invisible to us it may have involved—it constituted a *reinterpretation* of the subject-matter. Put simply, the Henry of Q1 is not the Henry of F, nor are his noble companions.

Gary Taylor gives this nuanced account of what would have been cut from F (amounting to half the text) to create Q1, noting that the quarto:

> omits, from the play as we know it, the opening scene (with its revelation of mixed ecclesiastical motives for supporting Henry's claim to France), lines 115–35 of 1.2 (which culminate in the Archbishop's offer of church financing for the war), all reference in 2.1. to Henry's personal responsibility for Falstaff's condition, Cambridge's hint of motives other than simple bribery for the conspiracy against Henry (2.2.154–9), the bloodthirsty MacMorris and most of Henry's savage ultimatum in 3.3, all of Burgundy's description of the devastation Henry has wreaked on France (5.2.38–62).[12] Whoever was responsible for them, the effect of the differences between this text and the one printed in all modern editions is to remove almost every difficulty in the way of an unambiguously patriotic interpretation of Henry and his war.   (1982: 12)[13]

That is to say, yet again, to make it remarkably like *The Famous Victories*, which is nothing if not unequivocally patriotic in its depiction of Henry.

Yet the material in F but not in Q1 does not *only* problematize 'an unambiguously patriotic interpretation of Henry and his war'. The single most prominent feature of F does precisely the opposite. The Chorus throughout F is an unashamed apologist for 'the mirror of all Christian kings' (TLN 469; 2.0.6); famously evoking an endearing 'little touch of Harry in the night' (TLN 1,836; 4.0.47); then telling of him returning from France 'free from vainness and self-glorious

---

[12] Cambridge's motives for his treachery are discussed later.
[13] NB: The line references in the quotation are to Taylor's own 1982 edition, not to Bevington 2008.

pride' (TLN 2,870; 5.0.20); lamenting 'This star of England' (TLN 3,373; Epilogue 6). If the point of 'cutting' F was to produce an 'unambiguously patriotic interpretation of Henry', why on earth did they cut the Choruses? By the same token, why did they 'cut' the stirring 'Once more unto the breach, dear friends, once more' speech at the siege of Harfleur, today enshrined as one of the most quotable pieces of jingoism in the language? And why did they 'cut', as the fuller list of omissions from Q1 demonstrates, almost all of the material showing the French aristocrats as complacent and boastful opponents—surely grist to the mill for any 'patriotic' telling of this tale? Is it not easier and more logical (Occam's Razor) to assume a process in which Q1 always resembled *The Famous Victories*, and that the major differences in F were a product of later and complex rethinking, blending the negative account of Henry outlined by Taylor with the positive ones of the Chorus?

The fact is that the unique elements in F pull in two directions at once, the Choruses embellishing the folk-tale version of Henry's life to the level of myth, while other parts of the play not in Q1 problematize that myth in a variety of ways, emphasizing the realpolitik, cold-bloodedness, and ruthless determination by which Henry achieves what he does: his apparent politicking with the bishops; discussion of his treatment of Falstaff; the failure of 'Once more unto the breach' to achieve its military object, resulting in his 'savage ultimatum' to the Governor of Harfleur; the hanging of Bardolph; the devastation caused to France by his campaign. F is not only much longer than Q1, it is also a much more sophisticated play, and it would have required equal sophistication—not merely stage know-how—to strip it down to the much less multi-vocal text of the quarto. I discuss this further later, in relation to F's overall rhetorical strategy.

Another feature notably absent from either Q1 or *The Famous Victories* is any *trace* of a reference to Ireland. In F, the Dauphin derides the Constable for riding 'like a kern of Ireland' (F, 3.7.53) and warns of 'fall[ing] into foul bogs' (57; TLN 1,679, 1,684), while Pistol cockily sings 'calemie custure me', a corruption of the Irish refrain 'cailin og a' stor' (4.4.4; TLN 2,389). Three Irish elements in F have generated much more comment in modern times: one is the whole role of Macmorris in the second half of 3.2 ('What ish my nation? Who talks of my nation?' 3.2.122–3; TLN 1,240). Another is the play's most famous textual crux: at 5.2.12 Queen Isabella greets Henry as 'brother Ireland' (TLN 2,999). This is universally amended in modern editions to 'brother England', either as a compositor's misreading of 'Ingland' or because it is, as Gary Taylor puts it, 'Shakespeare's own "Freudian slip"—a slip natural enough in 1599, a hundred lines after Shakespeare's reference to the Essex expedition in 5.0' (1982: 18).[14] Why should it be a slip at all? Henry shortly assures Princess Katherine that 'England is thine, Ireland is thine, France is thine' (5.2.240–1; TLN 3,226–7). It might be unusual to address Henry by his second title, but it is not improper or disrespectful: in the context of negotiations towards the Treaty of Troyes, it is a gracious way of acknowledging that Henry was on the point of adding a *third* crown to the *two* he already possessed.

[14] See also the notes to the line in Wilson 1947 and Walter 1954.

Most vexed of all is that supposed 'reference to the Essex expedition in 5.0', which evokes

> the General of our gracious Empress
> As in good time he may, from Ireland coming,
> Bringing rebellion broachèd on his sword.
> (5.0.30–2; TLN 2,880–2)

In the universal editorial consensus that something like F existed in 1599, these lines are invariably glossed as a reference to the Earl of Essex's expedition to Ireland in the spring and summer of that year. But if this and the other Choruses are *later* additions, this must be a reference to the man who did indeed 'Bring rebellion broached on his sword', Charles Blount, Lord Mountjoy, the victor of Kinsale—the 1601 battle which saved England from what Essex had left looking like inevitable defeat.[15] It is, of course, just possible that all of these Irish references just happened to get trimmed in a process that redacted F to Q1 or that press censorship removed them from Q1 in 1600, when Essex's failure was all too apparent (though the odds of any censor recognizing 'calemie custure me' as Irish seem pretty thin). But it is at least equally plausible that they were never there in 1599. They were certainly not in *The Famous Victories*.

Although, as I have tried to show, it is more realistic to assume that Shakespeare started with a small, serviceable version of *Henry V* and only later developed the much more sophisticated version with which we are more familiar, I recognize that the issue of adding/cutting can be argued both ways in most instances. There is more we can say, however, about Shakespeare's use of his other main source—Holinshed's *Chronicles*—which may cast more specific light on the issue.

HOLINSHED

Shakespeare's debt to Holinshed is indisputable.[16] Besides many smaller borrowings, F contains four sustained passages where he virtually paraphrases the *Chronicles* into verse: 1.1.1–21 (the bill to strip the church of many of its holdings; TLN 39–57); 1.2.35–101 and 130–5 (Canterbury's exposition of Salic Law; TLN 182–248, 277–82); 2.2.165–77 (part of Henry's accusations of the traitors; TLN 795–807); and 4.8.74–104 (details of the French and English dead after Agincourt; TLN 2,791–823). Q1, of course, does not contain the material from 1.1. It also lacks the second passage from 1.2 and ten lines (80–9) from 4.8 (so, on my analysis, Shakespeare would have returned to Holinshed to expand Q1 into F); but the debt to Holinshed is still clear, not least in the traitors' scene, which is Q1's most notable addition to the narrative in *The Famous Victories*. That play contains rudi-

---

[15] See p. 188. If F was broadly the version of the play performed at court in 1605, these lines (with 'Empress' presumably amended to 'Emperor') must surely *there* have been received as a compliment to Mountjoy, by then elevated to the earldom of Devonshire for his success (Dutton 2005).

[16] It is also apparent that he consulted, as often before, Edward Hall's *The Union of the Two Noble and Illustre Families of Lancaster and York* (1548), though this appears in details rather than in sustained narrative passages.

mentary versions of 1.2 and 4.8 but Shakespeare has completely reinvented them in Holinshed's detail and idiom.

None of this is conclusive in respect of the order of Q1 and F. But the situation changes when we turn our attention to the personnel in the two versions of *Henry V*. Firstly, there is the question of the presence or otherwise of Henry's brothers—Thomas, Duke of Clarence, John, Duke of Bedford, and Humphrey, Duke of Gloucester—in the two versions. Q1 is not absolutely punctilious about following Holinshed's authority in this, but it is markedly more so than F, particularly in the disposition of Bedford. To take the brothers one at a time: the stage directions in Q1 explicitly place Clarence onstage four times: in the first scene, in scene 9 (the condemnation of Bardolph), in 12 ('Crispin Crispian'), and again in 17 (the dispute between Llewellen and the second soldier); he only actually speaks (2 lines) in scene 12. (He may also implicitly be onstage in other scenes that specify only 'Lords' or 'nobles'—3, 6, 15, 16, 19.) In fact Clarence returned to England after Harfleur (scene 6), though Holinshed wrongly places him at Agincourt, and Shakespeare may simply have been following his source in making him present for much of the action.

Gloucester is explicitly onstage in scenes 3, 9, and 12, speaking briefly in all of them; he too may also implicitly be in scenes of 'Lords' or 'nobles'. He was in fact wounded at Agincourt, though neither Q1 nor F mentions this, but both put him at the battle. Neither he nor Clarence is scripted to be in 19, the closing scene which depicts the final treaty negotiations, presumably because they were not historically present. Bedford does not appear in the play at all, which is appropriate because he was not in France during any of the activity shown in it; Henry named him Lieutenant of England for much of the period.[17] The only quasi-exception to this is in Henry's Crispin Crispian's Day, where Bedford is invoked as one of the names that will emerge as 'household words' (12.34) from the Battle of Agincourt: 'Harry the King, / Bedford and Exeter, Clarence and Gloster / Warwick and York' (31–3).[18] Editors sometimes invoke this as evidence that Q1 derives from F, since Bedford is quite prominent in F and this may seem to be an overlooked instance in a text from which Bedford has been excised. But the passage forcefully compresses the solidarity of the royal family (Exeter was an uncle, York—the chief English casualty in the battle—a cousin) at the head of the national enterprise, and this may have counted for more than historical accuracy at this critical moment.

In F, by contrast, Clarence all but disappears. A stage direction places him in 1.2 and he is addressed in 5.2, but he says nothing. Gloucester appears frequently (1.2, 3.1, 3.6, 4.1, 4.3, 4.7, 4.8, and 5.2) and might also appear in 3.3 and 4.6, among the king's 'train'; he speaks briefly in about half his appearances. Bedford is unequivocally (and unhistorically) a character, who speaks briefly in two appearances, in 2.2 (the traitors' scene) and 4.3 (Crispin Crispian), and stage directions place

---

[17] He did in fact figure in a naval victory over the French and in relieving Harfleur from a siege after it fell to the English. But Shakespeare chooses to show none of this.
[18] Warwick was not related to the king, but was a close ally since they fought together in the Welsh Marches. He was involved in the French campaign and had a strong military record; like Bedford, however, he was not at Agincourt, nor does Holinshed place him there.

him in 1.2 and 5.2.[19] The latter instance is rather odd, since Henry specifically addresses Gloucester and Clarence, but ignores Bedford altogether: 'Go, uncle Exeter / And brother Clarence, and you, brother Gloucester' (5.2.83–4; TLN 3,071–2). Compared with Q1, it looks as if someone has tried to overwrite Clarence with the person of Bedford but not made a perfect job of it. That suspicion is reinforced by the reference to the royal family in the Crispin Crispian's day speech, which in F becomes: 'Harry the king, Bedford and Exeter, / Warwick and Talbot, Salisbury and Gloucester' (4.3.53–4; TLN 2,296–7). Clarence has disappeared, supplanted by the non-royals, Talbot and Salisbury.

Those (mainly editors) who have looked for an explanation of these matters have usually assumed, of course, that F came first and that the virtual excision of Bedford from Q1 was a matter of trimming the parts to produce a version of the play that could be performed with a smaller cast, perhaps on tour.[20] But in effect the ghostly role of Clarence in F grows in Q1 to replace Bedford, so there is no net loss. If we start from Q1, however, what we have is something that follows the historical record reasonably closely—or, more precisely, follows Holinshed, who for Shakespeare and his contemporaries virtually *was* the historical record. According to Holinshed, Clarence and Gloucester both accompanied Henry to France and fought at Agincourt (though in fact Clarence was not at the battle); Bedford did not. None of the brothers is scripted to appear in the closing scene at Troyes— uncle Exeter is Henry's key counsellor there—which is historically accurate.[21] Within the framework of a commercial drama Q1 does a creditable job of replacing the utterly unhistorical collection of aristocrats celebrated in *The Famous Victories* with something closer to what Holinshed recorded.

F, however, gives us something quite different. Clarence and Gloucester both appear at Troyes, and Bedford appears at both Agincourt and Troyes, all contrary to Holinshed. Moreover, of the non-royal aristocrats celebrated in the Crispin Crispian's day—Warwick, Talbot, Salisbury—only Salisbury had actually been at Agincourt, or been credited by Holinshed with being there. The effect of all this is very noticeably to increase the prominence in F of those who also appear in the *Henry VI* plays—Warwick, Salisbury, and Talbot (later Earl of Shrewsbury) all appear in *1 Henry VI*, where Talbot is the hero of the English forces in France. Clarence died before King Henry did, so it fell to Bedford, as Regent of France in *1 Henry VI*, and Gloucester (Duke Humphrey) as Protector of England in *1* and *2 Henry VI*, to try (unsuccessfully) to protect Henry's legacy for his infant son, Henry VI—'Which oft our stage hath shown', as the final Chorus reminds us.

F *Henry V* is thus conscious, in ways that Q1 is not, of its place as the last piece in the Lancastrian/Yorkist historical arc that runs from *Richard II* to *Richard III*.

---

[19] Those who remember Kenneth Branagh's movie of *Henry V* may recall how powerful a presence Bedford made, in the person of the burly, bearded Brian Blessed, despite having almost nothing to say.

[20] Such suppositions are often made by people who have no experience of staging. There are distinct limits on how much doubling of roles can be done, given the requirements for characters to appear in specific scenes and for actors to change costumes. Shorter plays actually make this more difficult.

[21] Holinshed also places Exeter at Agincourt and gives him command of the rearguard; Shakespeare follows this in both Q and F, though it was not actually true.

The (unhistorical) introduction of Westmoreland at Agincourt points us backwards to *1* and *2 Henry IV*, where (as a cousin by marriage) he supported the king, alongside Bedford who, as Prince John of Lancaster, was already a familiar figure on the stage. Clarence and Gloucester joined them in *2 Henry IV*. And, as the closing Chorus intimates, Bedford, Gloucester, Warwick, Salisbury, and Talbot carry us forward to the unhappy next phase of the history in *1 Henry VI*.[22] Whatever else was involved in the translation of Q1 to F, or vice versa, it is difficult not to conclude that the role of the play in that whole theatrical sequence was to the fore of the mind when F was compiled, while more parochial issues—an uncomplicated, patriotic play; reasonable historical accuracy—dominated the workmanlike creation of Q1. F comfortably takes its place in the long sequence of *Henry*-titled plays with which the First Folio neatly packages this era of English history. Perhaps more importantly, it maintains continuities between the *Henry IV* and *Henry VI* plays (at the price of some historical accuracy) which would be helpful any time these plays were performed in sequence. That was less a factor in the creation of Q1.

Grace Ioppolo has argued that 'evidence in Folio *Richard III* and Folio *2 Henry IV* strongly suggest that at some point after the four *Henry VI* plays and the four *Henry IV* plays were completed, Shakespeare reworked portions of the later plays by which characters recall events already presented in the early plays, in order to provide a sense of dramatic and theatrical unity and continuity among all four of the plays in each sequence, perhaps in anticipation of performing the four plays together in repertory' (1991: 130). I am suggesting that the revisions to the roles of Henry's brothers between Q1 and F *Henry V* point to attempts to create better 'dramatic and theatrical...continuity' not merely within each sequence but between the two tetralogies, moving them in the direction of the seamless sequence of eight plays in which they appear in the First Folio.

Before we consider the wider implication of all this for the sequence of writing the two *Henry V* plays, we should also observe the single most striking change in the narrative between the two texts. Holinshed, *The Famous Victories*, and Q1 are at one in agreeing that the Dolphin/Dauphin—heir to the French throne—did *not* take part in the Battle of Agincourt. In scene 8 of Q1, the French King insists 'Son Dauphin, you shall stay in Rouen with me' (21), and despite the Dauphin's protests that is what happens. The Constable, who died in the battle, and the Dukes of Bourbon and Orleans (captured for ransom) led the French troops. But F is radically different; the Dauphin evidently ignores his father's command and does appear in two scenes on the eve of the battle (3.7 and 4.2), in the former mainly speaking lines that in Q1 (scene 10) had been assigned to Bourbon, boasting about his horse. In this one respect Shakespeare *radically* changed Holinshed's history.

The only reasonable explanation for this change is that Shakespeare wanted to stage a confrontation between Henry and someone of his own royal standing, to underline the magnitude of his victory—though in fact no such *direct* confrontation

---

[22] I am happy to acknowledge that I owe much of the thinking about the roles of Gloucester and Bedford to my former student, Lee Emrich.

is scripted in F and Henry's greatest personal achievement in the battle is apparently the capture of Bourbon (4.7.52.02; TLN 2,578). As part of the terms at Troyes, Henry is named 'Notre très cher fils' and '*Haeres Franciae*' by King Charles VI, our very dear son and heir of France on Charles's death (5.2.338/41; TLN 3,330/2). Spectators of the play would have every reason to suppose that the Dauphin they have seen in the losing battle (Louis) is being disinherited in the peace negotiations. In fact he died in the same year as the battle (1415) and was succeeded by his brother, John, who died in 1417. The disinherited Dauphin in the 1420 treaty was actually Charles, the one we see in *1 Henry VI*, who eventually became Charles VII with Joan of Arc's assistance and overturned that part of Henry V's legacy. But that is a level of historical detail that F is quite prepared to gloss over.

If we link together Shakespeare's playing fast-and-loose in F with the English aristocrats involved in Henry's campaigns and his readiness to place the Dauphin at Agincourt, it seems reasonable to assume that he is striving for a bitter-sweet effect that the final Chorus underlines—to show Henry as absolute and unequivocal victor in the French wars, 'This star of England' (6), while keeping firmly in our mind the fate of his infant son, Henry VI, 'Whose state so many had the managing / That they lost France and made his England bleed' (11–12; TLN 3,373, 3,378–9).

The question here is whether it seems more reasonable to suppose that Shakespeare first drafted *Henry V* with these sophisticated ironies about the outcome of Henry's ambitions, overlaid with close attention to the pivotal role of the play in the two sequences of Lancastrian and Yorkist history. And then that he or someone else went back to Holinshed and cut out the unhistorical elements (and the ironies) to reinvent the play in the tone and shape of *The Famous Victories*. Or is it more realistic to assume that he first drafted an uncomplicated but perfectly playable Q1, using the structure provided by *The Famous Victories* and for the most part following Holinshed in the history? And only later developed a much more nuanced portrait of Henry, one that more forcefully locates it (rewriting history if needs be) in the longer pattern of English medieval history; a portrait in which the adulation of the Chorus is repeatedly in tension with what we see of his actions and their consequences? I suggest that the latter is a much more credible scenario.

THE COURT

If we accept that F did in fact follow Q1, is there anything about the text which makes it likely that court performance lay behind the revision? As we have noted, sheer length (in the case of histories and tragedies) is a likely indicator, though not an infallible one. As the third longest of all Shakespeare's surviving texts, F *Henry V* must qualify very highly by this criterion: it is an epic that would unfold much more comfortably for a seated audience indoors through the dark hours of a winter night, with breaks to trim the candles and to enjoy a light banquet, than exposed to the elements and the more challenging amenities of the Globe or the Curtain.

Moreover, this is a text which has clearly been adapted for a five-act performance (while Q1 is equally clearly a text of 19 scenes, designed to be played continuously).

Many of the plays in the 1623 folio carry the trappings of five act divisions, but in some cases it is perfunctory and may be no more than a nod to the tradition of presenting classical drama in such a format (see p. 260). But in the case of *Henry V* each act break is (or is *meant* to be) reinforced with a Chorus, asking us to 'Piece out our imperfections with your thoughts' (Prologue, 23; TLN 24). These are a taxing five acts for an audience.

The Choruses themselves may or may not speak to a courtly origin. Distinctive prologues and epilogues were a feature of most of the play texts marketed as having been performed at court—though not, for some reason, Shakespeare's own three (*Love's Labour's Lost*, *Merry Wives*, and *King Lear*). Such items, as Tiffany Stern has argued, were always somewhat disposable, and their appearance in print must always have been something of a matter of chance (Stern 2009a: 81–119, esp. 110, 118). Lyly's *Campaspe*, *Endimion*, *Gallathea*, and *Sappho and Phao* all have such court-specific items, as do plays more contemporary with *Henry V*, such as Dekker's *The Shoemakers' Holiday* and *Old Fortunatus*. But all of these specifically address the Queen herself. *Henry V*, by contrast, consistently addresses its audience as 'gentles all' (Prologue 8; TLN 9)—deferential enough for the court, but also (in the spirit of Henry's battlefield 'band of brothers') for the public theatre. The extent to which the Chorus keeps drawing the audience into the imaginary workings of the play might explain why it would be impolitic to address the Queen directly. But it is difficult to generalize. A Chorus that reappears throughout the play is unusual in the era; only *Pericles*, of all Shakespeare's other plays, has one.[23] Interestingly, *Old Fortunatus* has one, in addition to its explicitly courtly Prologue and Epilogue; it has striking parallels with *Henry V* in apologizing for the inadequacy of the theatre and asking audiences to draw on their imaginations. This may well have been part of the play that Elizabeth saw, but there are also grounds for believing that it was used in public performances (see note 10).[24] So this does not allow us to say for certain that such running Choruses were a distinctive mark of courtly performance, though it is not unlikely.

The possibility that the Chorus may be inviting us to piece out the imperfections of a *court* performance challenges one of our most fondly settled notions about Henry V: that when Shakespeare acknowledges the inadequacies of the 'cockpit' or 'wooden O' to stage this great saga he is referring to the Globe or Curtain, a public theatre.[25] If the *Prologue* had existed in 1599 the references to the 'cockpit' and the 'wooden O' might have been particularly appropriate as an

---

[23] Jonson has more than most, with a chorus of musicians in *Sejanus* and classical-style choruses in *Catiline*. *Every Man Out of His Humour* has what he calls a Grex of two characters who comment on the action at various points, not just between the acts. *The Magnetic Lady* has an Induction and what Jonson calls Intermeans, in which two characters, rather than commenting upon the action, have it explained to them.

[24] In addition to the Prologue and Epilogue 'at court', *Old Fortunatus* has a Prologue and Choruses to Acts 2 and 4, but not 3 and 5.

[25] Whether it ever could have been the Globe is itself a moot point. The playhouse was not ready for use until the autumn of 1599. The performance of *Julius Caesar* seen there by Thomas Platter on 21 September seems to have been one of its earliest shows. Essex returned to London from Ireland in panic and disgrace on 28 September, so the Chorus to Act 5 which imagines 'the General to our gracious Empress' could hardly have been performed after that. If the 'wooden O' really was an outdoor

apology for the old and undistinguished Curtain, where Q1 was very likely staged (see note 25). But these terms in fact could be used to describe virtually any of the playing-spaces used in Elizabethan and Jacobean England, which tended to be built internally to quasi-circular designs. Dekker in *Old Fortunatus* tells how 'this small circumference must stand / For the imagined surface of much land' (Prologue, 15–16), and he too may well have had a court theatre in mind. In the reign of James I an actual cockpit at Whitehall Palace was used on occasion for the performance of plays (Chambers 1923: 1.212). Since the reference to the 'General of our gracious Empress' does constrain us to the reign of Elizabeth, a plausible courtly candidate would be the wooden banqueting house built at Whitehall in 1581 and in use until it was replaced in 1607. Warren D. Smith long ago made the case for this, in tandem with the suggestion (which I also support) that the 'General' is not Essex but his incomparably more effective successor, Lord Mountjoy (1954). His argument has been completely ignored in the juggernaut of editorial conviction that F came first and existed in 1599—and, at least until relatively recently, that it was the version performed in the public theatres. *Any* theatre is in various ways inadequate to handle the epic material of *Henry V* (even the version in Q1), so the provenance of the Prologue and Choruses remains uncertain.

One possible indicator that the Choruses were written for a specific event, such as a court presentation, is the fact that, when Heminge and Condell assembled the *Henry V* text for the 1623 folio, they encountered serious difficulties.[26] The Chorus that in all modern editions introduces Act 2 ('Now all the youth of England are on fire': TLN 463) is in its familiar position—it follows what we think of as 1.2 (Henry's rebuff of the Dauphin's insulting tennis balls) and precedes 2.1 (Bardolph, Nym, Pistol, and Mistress Quickly lamenting the decline of Falstaff). But the text in no way recognizes this as an act-break: all of these items, Chorus included, are presented as part of Act 1. And Act 2 ('Actus Secundus') is not marked to begin until what we know as the Chorus to Act 3 ('Thus with imagined wings our swift Scene flies': TLN 1,045), by which time Henry's French campaign is well advanced. Act Three ('Actus Tertius') is marked to begin with 'Now entertain conjecture of a time' (TLN 1,790), what we think of as the Chorus to Act 4. Act 4 is marked (without a Chorus) in the middle of the Battle of Agincourt, immediately after Henry orders 'Then every soldier kill his prisoners' in what modern editions make 4.6 (TLN 2,524) and before 4.7, where Fluellen seeks to compare Henry with 'Alexander the Pig'. The sequence then rights itself, and the Chorus to 'Actus Quintus' ('Vouchsafe to those that have not read the story': TLN 2,851) appears in

---

theatre, it was likely to have been the Curtain, the house which the Lord Chamberlain's Men used between the tearing down of the Theatre and its reconstruction as the Globe.

[26] The precise contribution of Heminge and Condell to the preparation of the First Folio is unknown. As the oldest surviving members of the King's Men, they signed the dedication of the volume to the brother Earls of Pembroke and Montgomery and the address 'To the Great Variety of Readers'. But neither acted in the unlicensed *Spanish Viceroy* the following year and both were apparently semi-retired, though they may have retained managerial roles (as they certainly retained shares in both the company's playhouses). So how active they were in editing the Folio is a moot point. But surely whoever did the work could have called on them to make sense of the older manuscripts.

its familiar place. The superstructure of Choruses and act-divisions is an utter mess (all tidily sorted out, of course, in modern editions).

Moreover, the unlabelled Chorus to Act 2 contains its own conundrum. Having clearly stated that 'the scene / Is now transported, gentles, to Southampton' (2.0.34–5; TLN 506–7), it contradicts itself in a closing couplet: 'But till the King come forth and not till then / Unto Southampton do we shift our scene' (41–2; TLN 503–4). Since the lines immediately before (39–40) are themselves a rhyming couplet, presumably originally intended to close the Chorus, this looks like a rather desperate attempt to excuse the inclusion of 2.1, which actually transports us to Pistol, Nym, and others of Falstaff's circle in an unspecified location, presumably London. Only in the subsequent traitors' scene do we actually move to Southampton. Possibly 2.1 was an afterthought, and this was an expedient to include it without seriously reworking the Chorus.[27]

However we attempt to explain all this, it seems indisputable that at least one of the Choruses was involved in some last-minute revision, while in 1623 some of the Choruses were not in their proper places among the papers that went to the printers; that in itself may not have been unusual, but if the printers referred the issue back to Heminge and Condell, they did not know how to resolve any of it (cf. Stern 2009a: 106–9). This strongly suggests that the Choruses were disposable or adaptable items and only used on limited occasions; and that the last time they had been used was so far back by 1623 that Heminge and Condell, or their assistants, could not remember how to reconstruct the proper placement. It is entirely possible that they had been composed for one or more performances at Elizabeth's court and not used thereafter.[28]

THE COURT AND 'AMPLIFICATIO'

As we have noted, in *Shakespeare as Literary Dramatist* Lukas Erne is among those who account for the differences between the quarto and folio texts of *Henry V* in terms of *cuts* from the longer version rather than (as I have argued) *additions* to the shorter one. The nub of his case is that Shakespeare at times consciously wrote material which was more suitable for readers than for theatrical performance, expecting that it would subsequently be cut in performing texts, which Erne assumes that the shorter versions (however clumsily) represent:

> I have argued... that some passages present in the long, literary texts are omitted or abridged in the short, theatrical texts because they are chiefly of value for readers and not for spectators... It may seem surprising that Shakespeare wrote purple patches into his dramatic texts in the knowledge that they might well be omitted on stage. Such a passage may seem less surprising, however, once we realize that these passages would have been particularly appreciated by readers. (2003: 225, 227)

---

[27] This clumsiness has given rise to speculation that Shakespeare's decision to kill off Falstaff—contrary to the promise at the end of *2 Henry IV* to bring him back—was a late one, requiring last-minute solutions as to how to handle Pistol and the others. But this can only be conjecture.

[28] There is no record of the play being performed after its court appearance in January 1605. For that performance the Chorus to Act 5 at the very least must have been changed, since no reference to a 'General of our gracious empress' was any longer appropriate.

I think these are odd assumptions to make about a professional dramatist and player, under contract to a company of fellow players. But more importantly I think they derive from narrow and unwarranted assumptions about what is 'theatrical', especially in an era when rhetorical skill and decorum were among the most cherished accomplishments of those who watched these plays at court, being essential tools in the business of government.

To start with a small but telling example, he compares passages from the folio and quarto versions of *Henry V* (4.7.54–68; TLN 2,580–97: corresponding to Sc. 16; F1r). A chastened Montjoy, herald of the French, comes once more to speak to Henry after the Battle of Agincourt is fought. And Erne focuses on the fact that, amid some other apparent trimming, two particular lines are omitted in Q1:

> Exe[ter]: Here comes the herald of the French, my liege.
> Glou[cester]: His eyes are humbler than they used to be. (4.7.65–6)

He suggests:

> If we understand the Folio text and the script behind Q1 as designed for two different media, what seems significant about the two missing lines is that they can be *acted* and therefore do not need to be *spoken*. In performance the words would unnecessarily reiterate what the actor conveys through body language. For readers to be aware of Mountjoy's appearance—contrasting sharply with his proud demeanor prior to the battle—they need to be told so either in dramatic dialogue or in a stage direction... the two lines present in the readerly but absent from the theatrical text are thus crucial for what Harry Berger calls 'imaginary audition.' They allow a reader to imagine a point of stage business that could otherwise only be conveyed by performance. (222)

This analysis of what *needs* to be spoken applies much more readily to proscenium-arch staging—in which actors for the most part face an audience broadly focused on a single perspective—than it does to the kind of staging used by the Chamberlain's Men. The latter placed the audience on at least three sides, whether in the public theatre or at court. At the Globe the actors not only had groundlings standing around the thrust stage with, beyond them, three tiers of seated spectators; they also had the gentlemen's rooms on either side of the stage; and the lords' room (the most expensive and prestigious of all) located in an upper tier of the *frons scenae*—in what *we* would call the back of the stage. So they must truly have played in the round—in the process ensuring that at least half of the audience could not see at any one time the particulars of what was going on.

At court, much of the seated audience would be on three sides of the stage, but the monarch and most favoured guests in a position of honour (analogous to the lords' room in the playhouse)—a position in which *they*, rather than the theatricals, could best be seen and to which inevitably much key action would have been addressed.[29] Moreover the flickering overhead candlelight of a night-time performance

---

[29] At Oxford and Cambridge stages were constructed with 'scaffold seating for college dignitaries and noble visitors above the stage, at the upper end of the hall; and scaffold seating and floor space for students and for visitors from the town below the stage, toward the lower end of the hall' (Nelson 1999: 59–60). So the lower orders observed their superiors (including members of royalty when they visited)

could only have given most of the audience an indifferent view of the actors' faces. In either arrangement half of the audience certainly could not see the expression on an actor's face which, without the benefits of modern lighting, was never going to be all that visible to begin with.

'Imaginary audition' was always a function of Elizabethan *theatre*, as much as of the printed page. That is the whole import of the Choruses in F *Henry V*, which expressly address the *theatrical* situation, and repeatedly exhort us to 'Piece out our imperfections' (those of the actors and stage, not of the text or author) and to 'entertain conjecture' of scenes which the play as often as not then shows in action, like the traitors or 'A little touch of Harry in the night' (TLN 24, 1,790, 1,836). The quarto is no more 'theatrical' here than the folio, unless by theatrical we always mean something brisker, less detailed, less nuanced, more given over to action than to words (which is true in general of the short quartos of Shakespeare's plays). The folio text of *Henry V* is, in virtually all respects, simply *fuller* than the quarto, *expanding* the theatrical and rhetorical experience in as many ways as possible.

This is also true of passages which are not linked to action at all. Among numerous other examples, Erne quotes from Burgundy's long speech about the desolation of France in Act 5 of the folio *Henry V*:

> Her vine, the merry cheerer of the heart,
> Unprunèd dies; her hedges even-pleached,
> Like prisoners wildly overgrown with hair,
> Put forth disordered twigs; her fallow leas,
> The darnel, hemlock, and rank fumitory
> Doth root upon, while that the coulter rusts,
> That should deracinate such savagery.
> The even mead, that erst brought sweetly forth
> The freckled cowslip, burnet, and green clover,
> Wanting the scythe, all uncorrected, rank,
> Conceives by idleness, and nothing teems
> But hateful docks, rough thistles, kecksies, burrs,
> Losing both beauty and utility.   (5.2.42–53; TLN 3,028–40)

'And so on. It is hardly surprising that Q1 omits all but four of the forty-five lines of this speech. Whatever the reason for which Shakespeare wrote this speech, it seems hardly to have been for recital on stage' (226). Surveying other such passages, he concludes:

> These passages share certain characteristics. They are not necessary for the understanding of the plot. Most of them are not particularly stage-worthy. They are good reading material, appealing to a fairly educated readership. In short they are 'stuff to please the wiser sort,' as Harvey put it.   (226)

Erne does concede that 'The point to be made about the omission of poetic passages in the stage version is not that a theatre audience would have been unable to

---

through the action of the play. Though it is less fully documented elsewhere, it seems very likely that there were similar configurations at the Inns of Court, in great houses, guild halls, and the like.

appreciate them. People able to absorb long and complex sermons must have had aural faculties that allowed them to cope with intricate poetic language' (227). Yet he is convinced that in live theatre such people were only interested in understanding the plot and engaging with 'stageworthy' material (what I characterize as 'more given over to action than to words'), not in applying those 'aural faculties'.

The 'wiser sort' which Erne, quoting Gabriel Harvey, identifies as Shakespeare's potential readers, were nowhere if not at the court—the very institution which, as I argue, allowed Shakespeare's theatre to flourish specifically as it did.[30] There above all 'aural faculties' flourished. It is axiomatic in books of manners and of rhetoric, from Castiglione's *Book of the Courtier* (1528; 1561 in Sir Thomas Hoby's English translation) and Sir Thomas Elyot's *Book Named The Governor* (1531) to George Puttenham's *The Art of English Poesy* (1589) that the pursuit of eloquence is a hallmark of all courtiers, men and women, and that the court itself was a place where ornamented speech was especially to be expected in the presence of the monarch. Here is Puttenham's chief example of *inappropriate* oratory before a monarch; it relates to the confirmation ceremony for a Marian Speaker of the House of Commons:

> I remember in the first year of Queen Mary's reign a knight of Yorkshire was chosen Speaker of the Parliament, a good gentleman and wise, in the affairs of his shire, and not unlearned in the laws of the realm, but as well for some lack of his teeth, as for want of language nothing well spoken, which at that time and business was most behooveful for him to have been. This man, after he had made his oration to the Queen—which ye know is of course to be done at the first assembly of both houses—a bencher of the Temple, both well learned and very eloquent, returning from the Parliament house asked another gentleman his friend how he liked Mr. Speaker's oration. 'Marry,' quoth the other, 'methinks I heard not a better alehouse tale told this seven years.' This happened because the good old knight made no difference between an oration or public speech to be delivered to the ear of a prince's majesty and state of a realm, than he would have done of an ordinary tale to be told at his table in the country, wherein all men know the odds is very great. (Puttenham 2007: Bk 3, Ch. 2, 223)[31]

Puttenham is determined to establish that appropriately ornamented speech is not a self-indulgent frippery but an essential feature of civil society at its highest level. He immediately contrasts the unnamed Speaker with two of Elizabeth's leading ministers, noted for their eloquence in pursuit of their governmental and judicial functions:

> And though grave and wise counselors in their consultations do not use much superfluous eloquence, and also in their judicial hearings do much mislike all scholastical rhetorics, yet in such a case as it may be (and as this Parliament was) if the Lord Chancellor of England or Archbishop of Canterbury himself were to speak, he ought to do it cunningly and eloquently, which can not be without the use of figures, and

---

[30] For Harvey, see Jenkins 1982: 573–4.
[31] Whigham and Rebhorn, Puttenham's editors, note that no Marian Speaker seems to fit his description, though at least one Elizabethan one might (406–7). As ever, Puttenham was probably being discreet. I am most grateful to Dr Dan Seward for bringing this passage to my attention.

> nevertheless none impeachment or blemish to the gravity of their persons or of the cause. Wherein I report me to them that knew Sir Nicholas Bacon, Lord Keeper of the Great Seale, or the now Lord Treasurer of England, and have been conversant with their speeches made in the Parliament house & Star Chamber. From whose lips I have seen to proceed more grave and natural eloquence than from all the orators of Oxford or Cambridge... (223–4)[32]

This praise of the two eloquent leading counsellors, Lord Keeper Bacon and his brother-in-law, Lord Treasurer Burghley, is of a piece with what Frank Whigham and Wayne Rebhorn call 'the core fantasy' of Puttenham's book, one in which the poet, by the use of all his rhetorical skills, may rise to the service of the monarch (Puttenham 2007: 1; 5; 61–9). And his book is a guide to how it might be done. Conflating the poet/courtier with his art, Puttenham sums up its achievement in fashioning such a person by claiming that he has

> appareled him to our seeming in all his gorgeous habiliments, and pulling him first from the cart to the school, and from thence to the court, and preferred him to your Majesty's service, in that place of great honor and magnificence to give entertainment to princes, ladies of honor, gentlewomen, and gentlemen, and by his many modes of skill to serve the many humors of men thither haunting and resorting. (378)

Puttenham was barely veiling his own aspirations, which as it happens were largely unfulfilled. The true embodiment of the poet/rhetorician who rose from nowhere, via a humanistic education, to the service of the Queen and the entertainment of her courtiers, was William Shakespeare. And he did it by cultivating precisely those eloquent flourishes of language which Erne designates 'not necessary for the understanding of the plot...not particularly stage-worthy...good reading material, appealing to a fairly educated readership..."stuff to please the wiser sort".' Rather than being cut out for the purposes of the public stage, they were (I contend) *added* for the delectation of an audience which recognized in its own superior skill with words a justification for its own standing.

Such additions were typically, I suggest, examples of one of the most fundamental skills of the early modern rhetorician, that of *amplification*, which was the subject at the heart of one of the most spectacularly successful school textbooks of the sixteenth century, Erasmus's *De verborum ac rerum Copia* (1512), 'On the abundance of expressions and ideas'. Later, expanded editions were entitled *De duplici copia verborum ac rerum*, 'On the twofold abundance ...'. There were at least 150 editions of this work published before 1572, and T. W. Baldwin showed that, having apparently been first written at the request of John Colet for use at his new St Paul's School, it was adopted at Eton, Canterbury, Worcester, Bangor, and numerous other grammar schools (see Rix 1946; Erasmus 1963: esp. 1–7; Baldwin 1944: 2. 179–80). It is highly likely that Shakespeare knew it from his own grammar school.

---

[32] Lord Treasurer Burghley achieved that post in 1572 and held it for the rest of his days. He was certainly well schooled in humanist rhetoric. Polonius' advice to Laertes is sometimes thought to offer a parody of his style.

As Marion Trousdale explains, Erasmus's 'true subject is eloquence. His exercises are structured to develop both kinds of verbal richness described by [Rudolph] Agricola: a small matter about which many words are said...or a matter itself enlarged by finding within it a heap of things. If properly done, such amplitude was to the age its own aesthetic justification. Something equated with both wisdom and pleasure could hardly be otherwise, and it is important to realize the extent to which copiousness was admired for its own sake' (Trousdale 1982: 43; see more generally 43–52). In Chapter 33 of Book 1 Erasmus notoriously found 148 inventively different ways of expressing a Latin sentence which translates as 'Your letter has delighted me very much'.

If we put Erasmus and Puttenham together here and review the changes to *Henry V*, it will be apparent that in both versions of the play Shakespeare was very conscious of the appropriateness of eloquence, of fertile and inventive language in courtly contexts. His Archbishop of Canterbury is never at a loss for dignified words, whether expounding the import of Salic Law or using the analogy of the beehive to justify the hierarchical structure of society. These are, to a degree, in both versions. But only the folio text precedes these two speeches with an opening scene of clerical intrigue which puts them in an ironic perspective. Is the Archbishop saying what he does because he believes it, or because it is what he knows Henry wants to hear (and hear in public) and so will help protect the Church? That first scene in effect goes to the heart of the *twofold abundance* of eloquence in exposing the difference between words and things upon which rhetorical theory depends.

The copiousness, the fluidity, the slipperiness of language derives precisely from the fact that it is not tied to actuality but is generated by human invention to fulfil specific social purposes. In being a rhetorical creature, the Archbishop is inevitably and inextricably also a political one. But only the folio text points us squarely at that conundrum. In Laurence Olivier's 1944 movie of *Henry V* the political manoeuvring of the clerics in F's first scene is muted, so that Canterbury's Salic Law speech emerges as rhetorical in a modern sense—empty, formulaic—and is reduced to a sequence of comic stage business for the benefit of the groundlings in audiences both old and new. In Kenneth Branagh's 1989 version the squarely politicized first scene put everything in perspective: the Salic Law speech was political rhetoric in deadly earnest, as Shakespeare's courtly audience would fully have understood. Everything hinges on the sound bite: 'May I with right and conscience make this claim?' (1.2.96; TLN 243).

In the case of Burgundy's speech, quoted earlier, we recall Erne's conclusion that 'Whatever the reason for which Shakespeare wrote this speech, it seems hardly to have been for recital on stage'. On the contrary, this is classic rhetorical fare for the *courtly* stage. In the quarto text Burgundy is no more than a cypher, a middle man who brings the English and French kings face-to-face and pleads with them for peace. He says nothing at all about why it should be so desirable. That is entirely added in the folio text, which is almost copybook *amplificatio*, exemplum piled upon detailed exemplum: it establishes the gravitas of a sovereign duke, one who is succeeding where the Holy Roman Emperor had failed before him (5.0.38–9; TLN 2,888–9). He is the equal in most respects of the kings he seeks to reconcile, in every sense avoiding the boorishness of Puttenham's Marian Speaker. It succeeds to the extent of changing the register of the play's rhetoric from Henry's repeated concerns with honour, warfare, and kingship—which all lie under the shadow of doubt cast by the questionable legitimacy of his personal causes.

Unlike Canterbury's Salic Law speech at the beginning of the play, Burgundy's speech at the end is unironic and unequivocal, a call to the warring parties to weigh the costs of what they have been doing. The whole tone of the final act changes with it, the emphasis shifting from war, to peace, to romance—while Henry's own rhetorical mode turns to that of the bluff, 'unartful' English lover, with which he woos French Katherine (and which we surely recognize as another artifice). In performing this role, Burgundy's speech inevitably calls into question Henry's whole policy of pursuing war with France. So it offers a rich alternative to—and should be appreciated alongside—the largest rhetorical addition to the folio text, the sequence of Choruses.

As I have suggested, these stand at a provocative angle to the action of the play. On the one hand, following the Prologue, they explore the distance between telling and showing, the constraints of the dramatic medium. But, on the other, in the process they seamlessly spin the myths of 'the mirror of Christian kings', the 'little touch of Harry in the night', as if the deficiencies of theatre itself somehow vouch for the *truth* of what is being represented: 'Minding true things by what their mockeries be' (4.0.53: TLN 1,842). The tensions here can be indicated by the sophistications introduced into the traitor scene as it appears in the quarto by the addition of the Chorus, 'Now all the youth of England are on fire'. The high-minded patriotism of that speech slips into another gear with the mention of 'A nest of hollow bosoms' who 'Have, for the gilt of France—O guilt indeed!— / Confirmed conspiracy with fearful France' (2.0.21, 26–7; TLN 483, 488–9). The memorable glibness of the pun is called into question when Henry confronts the traitors and accuses them specifically of doing it for money.

The Earl of Cambridge gnomically denies this: 'For me, the gold of France did not seduce, / Although I did admit it as a motive, / The sooner to effect what I intended' (2.2.154–6; TLN 784–6). What he in fact intended was to put his brother-in-law, Edmund Mortimer, 5th Earl of March, on the throne. Mortimer was the son of the man whom the childless Richard II had declared his heir and was felt by many to have a stronger claim to the throne than Henry IV (and thus Henry V), a claim which would eventually re-emerge as the Yorkist one in the Wars of the Roses. These lines are not in the quarto, where Cambridge is merely a paid traitor. Just briefly, therefore, the (folio) play threatens to open up something which all of Henry's claims to the French throne are meant to keep buried: that his claim to the *English* throne is far from perfect.[33] The stirring resolution to the traitor scene—'No King of England, if not King of France' (3.107; 2.2.190; TLN 822)—is exactly apposite. In the quarto it is pure, patriotic uplift. But in the folio, where the Chorus ignores the more complex realities that Cambridge hints at and rails so smugly against the guilt/gilt of France, it is sharply double-edged.

---

[33] The issue only surfaces unequivocally once, in both texts, on the eve of Agincourt, where Henry prays in private that God will not 'think on the fault / My father made in compassing the crown' (11.94–5; 4.1291–2; TLN 2,145–6).

For all the eloquence of the folio Chorus, Henry's situation is repeatedly undermined by the action. His increasingly strained conversation with Bates, Court, and Williams (which already exists in outline in the quarto, where the outcome is likewise a challenge to a duel) is hardly what we expect after the Chorus promises us a reassuring 'little touch of Harry in the night'. As a rhetorician, the Chorus's bluff is repeatedly called in such a way that he fails Puttenham's crucial test to 'worthily retain the credit of his place and profession of a very courtier, which is, in plain terms, cunningly to be able to dissemble' (Puttenham 2007: 379). It is, of course, Henry himself who most 'cunningly' passes the test, with 'dissembling' rhetoric carefully and opaquely modulated for all occasions: outrage against the Dauphin or the traitors, the spinner of beguiling fables for Williams, inspirational fervour (with the radical promise of 'brotherhood' for all) at Agincourt, the bluff and 'artless' English lover with Katherine. All of this rhetorical mastery is clearly scripted in Q1, as Henry acts out the role of the unimpeachable warrior king.

But in F it is both enhanced (not least by the support of the Choruses) and subject to greater scrutiny (as in Burgundy's paean to peace). In Q1 Henry is given six opportunities for sustained public oratory, attempting to impress or convince others: his response to the Dauphin's tennis balls ('We are glad the Dauphin is so pleasant with us', 1.180–215), his denunciation of the traitors ('The mercy which was quick in us but late', 3.57–82), two courteous responses to the French herald, Montjoy (9.96–120 and 12.62–93), his analogy of servants and sons in response to the second Soldier's talk of the king's 'heavy reckoning' (11.54–68), and the Saint Crispin's Day speech (12.12–48).

In F the denunciation of the traitors is more than doubled, to sixty-five lines long. And we get two quite distinctive additional soliloquies. The first is 'Once more unto the breach, dear friends, once more' (3.1.1ff; TLN 1,083ff)—blood-tingling rabble-rousing, before the military situation deteriorates into the desperation of Agincourt. Nothing could be more stirring—though we notice firstly that it has no effect on Pistol, Nym, and Bardolph, on whom Fluellen has to use violence to make them move; and then that it does not bring the siege of Harfleur to an end. That is only finally effected by his grim ultimatum to its Governor, which we have no reason to doubt that he will carry out. At the other extreme, in a bridge between the unresolved quarrel with Williams and prayers before the battle, we hear Henry in a very different mode, voicing something close to self-pity:

> Upon the King! Let us our lives, our souls,
> Our debts, our careful wives,
> Our children, and our sins, lay on the King!
> We must bear all.
>
> (4.3.228–31; TLN 2,079–82)

This is a note we have encountered before in the *Henriad*. *1 Henry IV* opens with the King clearly not enjoying the fruits of his usurpation:

> So shaken as we are, so wan with care,
> Find we a time for frighted peace to pant,

> And breathe short-winded accents of new broils
> To be commenced in strands afar remote.
>
> (1.1.1–4; TLN 5–8)

It becomes apparent that a particular burden of office is the wayward behaviour of Prince Hal:

> I know not whether God will have it so
> For some displeasing service I have done,
> That in his secret doom out of my blood
> He'll breed revengement and a scourge for me.
>
> (3.2.4–7; TLN 1,822–5)

In *2 Henry IV* a similar note of the King's world-weary self-pity appears in a late-added soliloquy of the quarto (see p. 263):

> How many thousands of my poorest subjects
> Are at this hour asleep! O sleep, O gentle sleep,
> Nature's soft nurse, how have I frighted thee.
>
> (3.14–6; TLN 1,425–7)

Kingship is a penance, not a pleasure; it is a weight of responsibilities to be carried that ordinary people know nothing of. This would be a particularly apposite *topos* at court, and in both *2 Henry IV* and *Henry V* Shakespeare seems to have contrived to give it a conspicuous airing in versions of the plays specifically re-engineered for that location. Such set-piece items must have been opportunities for the actors in Shakespeare's company to stretch their vocal chords and demonstrate the range of their emotive skills. We do not know which roles Richard Burbage played in the *Henriad*, but the opportunities provided for show-stopping soliloquies suggest that he probably played the title roles in each—graduating from Henry IV to the adult Henry V with the crown. A cardinal rule in embellishing plays for the court was doubtless to be sure to enrich Burbage's part, something Shakespeare was to do in spades with *Hamlet*.

In the case of the role of Henry V, the 'Upon the King' soliloquy seems a surprising departure from the performative rhetoric associated with Henry elsewhere in the play, each piece of it an appropriate contribution to his studied public role as king. As Derek Traversi long ago noted, in each public instance Henry contrives to evade personal responsibility for anything he does, from invading France, to condemning the traitors to death, to threatening the sack of Harfleur, to sending soldiers to their deaths, to fighting at Agincourt (Traversi 1957: 38, 40). Here at last, on the eve of desperate battle, we seem about to grasp the private man behind the evasive rhetoric. But in fact we do nothing of the sort. There is nothing here about his motives for war, his feelings about the traitors, any guilt he feels at the banishment of Falstaff or execution of Bardolph, any remorse for those he sends to their death in battle. Instead it is a performance of being the world-weary king, the mere mortal called upon to do what others can barely imagine. As such, Henry uses eloquence not to move his subjects and his enemies. He does it to evoke the audience's sympathy, in a final evasion of responsibility for his actions as king.

The play's last rhetorical gesture, the epilogue, brings together all the doubts that have accumulated around Henry's 'performance' with all the instabilities inherent in meta-theatrical frames of reference: 'In little room confining mighty men, / Mangling by starts the full course of their glory' (Epilogue 3–4; TLN 3,370–1). Henry was a 'star of England', but a short-lived one, and his infant son paid the biblical consequences: 'Whose state so many had the managing / That they lost France and made their England bleed: / Which oft our stage hath shown' (11–12; 3,378–9). The pluses and minuses of military greatness are called into question in ways that the quarto text never hints at, and finally wrapped in the remorseless circularity of the theatrical repertoire. The achievement of F's Henry is greater and more hard-won than that of Q1's, but its mixed motives, its price in blood, and its evanescence are more starkly under scrutiny.

Rhetorical embellishment is the stuff of courtly theatre, which is why it is the stuff of all Shakespeare's histories and tragedies. But it is also true of the comedies, where we can trace it. *Love's Labour's Lost* comes to us as 'corrected and augmented' though we do not know from what. But, as Grace Ioppolo has shown, we can trace in the 1598 quarto text some of his second thoughts (see p. 129). In discussing one such passage she says: 'what is undebatable and much more important is that the later and more poetically lush version, with its metaphor on the power a beloved's eyes transmits to the lover, intensifies the audience's view of Berowne as the play's eloquent and persuasive spokesperson for Platonic ideals of love' (1990: 96).[34] Indeed, Shakespeare is often the dramatist of lushness, of copiousness, especially where he wrote of courtly topics. Yes, it probably was aimed primarily at the 'wiser sort', but in the supremely *theatrical* context of the court.

As I have tried to demonstrate, once we recognize the foundations of Shakespeare's play in *The Famous Victories of Henry V* we can see a trajectory running through his two versions, in a way that is not possible for any other play in the canon. As we observe Q1 through the refractions of its poor transmission, we can see a workmanlike play that in many respects replicates its source in presenting an unambiguous account of a great English warrior king. But it does so with a much greater range of verbal and dramatic resources, drawing to an extent on a roster of characters already established in the *Henry IV* plays; and with a much closer attention to the historical record and personnel as determined, mainly, by Holinshed.

F, too, is not without its transmission problems; its five-act structure and attendant Choruses are in disarray, which suggests that the company had lost touch with their use. That apart, however, we see a much more ambitious play than Q1, one which draws on a whole range of rhetorical resources—some channelled through Henry himself, some through the Choruses, and some through other figures, like Burgundy, to produce a much more complex and nuanced picture of the king and his achievements. His victories are harder-won, but the values attached to them are scrutinized in uncomfortable depth. In the process Shakespeare has not been afraid to abandon some of the historical accuracy of Q1, most particularly in

---

[34] In Bevington the passage is at 4.3.324–7; see also the textual note to 4.3.291, on A-116. The original duplication is on F2v and F3r.

bringing the French Dauphin to Agincourt, but also in shuffling the pack of aristocrats who accompany Henry (his three brothers and uncle, plus Warwick, Salisbury, Westmoreland, and—at least in name—Talbot) in such a way as to locate this play as the centrepiece in that span of histories which runs from the deposition of Richard II to the defeat of Richard III (see pp. 184–5). There in particular we see what can only be a purposeful authorial intervention, reinventing the play's resonances. The idea that this complexity could be created and then deliberately, systematically erased (Irish references and all), in a process which produced a Q1 in the image of *The Famous Victories*, is simply less credible than that it was an achievement forged progressively, and with increasing poetic and rhetorical skills, in two major creative phases. And the most compelling reason to develop such sophistication would be to meet the tastes of an audience trained to appreciate it, in a venue where time was no object.

b. *2* and *3 Henry VI*—A True Contention

On 12 March 1594 'a book entitled the first part of the Contention of the two famous houses of York and Lancaster' was entered in the Stationers' Register (a common, but not universal practice before books were printed) in the name of the publisher, Thomas Millington. It appeared later that year in a quarto imprint. Its title page doubled duty as an advertisement of its contents: 'The First Part of the Contention betwixt the two famous Houses of York and Lancaster, with the death of the good Duke Humphrey: and the banishment and death of the Duke of Suffolk, and the tragical end of the proud Cardinal of Winchester, with the notable rebellion of Jack Cade: and the Duke of York's first claim unto the crown'. No mention is made of an author, which again was common at the time.[35] This is unfortunate, because the question of who wrote it has bedevilled discussion of the text ever since. Is it, in whole or in part, by Shakespeare? (See p. 139.) Or is it the work of lesser dramatists, such as George Peele or Robert Greene? Either way, it has *some* connection to the play which appears in the Shakespeare First Folio as *The second Part of Henry the Sixth, with the death of the Good Duke Humphrey* (see Marino 2011: 45–7).[36]

Before we consider what kind of connection that may be, it will be helpful to add the parallel case of the octavo volume published the following year by Millington, with this title page: 'The true tragedy of Richard Duke of York, and the death of good King Henry the Sixth, with the whole contention between the two Houses Lancaster and York, as it was sundry times acted by the Right Honourable the Earl of Pembroke his servants'. In exactly the same way, that play has *some* connection to what appears in the First Folio as *The third Part of Henry the Sixth, with the death of the Duke of York*. As far as I can determine, there is a universal scholarly consensus that the relationship between *The Contention* and *2 Henry VI* and that between *The True Tragedy* and *3 Henry VI* (as I shall henceforth call these texts) are at the very least parallel, and I shall treat them as such here. Evidence from the one will be treated as at least circumstantially relevant to the other, to avoid unproductive repetitions.

---

[35] There is no name attached either to the quarto of *Titus Andronicus*, also published that year. Shakespeare's name started appearing on title pages in 1598, on imprints of *Love's Labour's Lost*, *Richard III*, and *Richard II*.

[36] Note that there is no early text associated with what the First Folio calls *The first Part of Henry the Sixth*, which is concerned with the wars in France and not with the Wars of the Roses, as both the second and third parts are.

Why the relationship between the earlier printed versions and the folio texts is so problematic is usefully sketched out by Roger Warren in his *Oxford Shakespeare* edition of *2 Henry VI*:

> Q is roughly a third shorter than F, and differs from it in most of its readings, even though the basic material of each scene is the same. Only a handful of passages is identical in the two texts. Q's brevity is partly accounted for by the absence of short passages that involve figurative expressions or extended comparisons...the Folio also contains several longer passages which are absent from the Quarto [he lists nine of these]...Does the absence of these passages in Q suggest deliberate omission (perhaps cutting) in Q, or addition in F, or a mixture of the two? There are also several occasions where F and Q represent different versions of the *material* [of which he lists eleven]. (Warren 2002: 75–6)[37]

(Warren's characterization of the two versions as using the same *material* [his emphasis], but often different language and staging, is a useful distinction, to which I shall return. There are obvious parallels with Shakespeare's adaptation of *The Famous Victories of Henry V* for Q1 of his own Henry V play.) Randall Martin, editor of the *Oxford Shakespeare 3 Henry VI*, offers a parallel assessment of the relationship between the two versions of that play:

> In general, O [the 1595 octavo] is about a thousand lines, or one third, shorter than F. It omits a few minor roles...as well as verbal ornament, classical allusions, and metaphorical expressions. But there is no actual reduction in personnel...O's selection of historical events and its narrative sequence are also largely the same as F's. At particular moments, on the other hand, O's dialogue and scenic choreography are unique, and its substantial changes in characterization create different meanings and emotional effects. (Martin 2001: 104)

As early as the eighteenth century, there was a clear division of views on how these differences came about. Samuel Johnson held that they were garbled versions of the Shakespearean originals represented by the folio texts. Edmond Malone originally agreed with him, but included in his 1790 edition of Shakespeare a 'Dissertation on the Three Parts of *King Henry VI*'. In this he concluded that 'Shakespeare wrote *two* plays' about each of the later phases of King Henry's reign, 'a hasty sketch' and a 'more finished performance' (Malone 1790: 6.412). I argue here that he was right.

But Johnson's view gained powerful support early in the twentieth century from the 'foul papers'/'memorial reconstruction' lobby. Peter Alexander and Madeleine Doran in different ways advanced the view that the 'corruption' of *The Contention* and *The True Tragedy* derived from poor memorial reconstruction of Shakespeare's folio texts, probably by actors (Alexander 1924; Doran 1928; but see Urkowitz 1988). Michael Hattaway's analysis in his *New Cambridge* editions of the plays significantly squares with that line of thinking, though it accords more status

---

[37] Other editions to which I shall refer here, with their textual analyses, are Hattaway 1991: 215–20; Hattaway 1993: 201–7; Knowles 1999: 106–41; Cox and Rasmussen 2001: 148–76; and Martin 2001: 96–132.

to the early texts (in ways parallel to what we have seen with *Henry V*) as authentic insights into the early staging of the plays: 'F therefore stands revealed as the only authoritative text for the play as a whole, although there is no doubt that Q records details of staging of performances with which Shakespeare was probably associated' (1991: 217; see also Hattaway 1993: 204). In this respect he follows the lead of William Montgomery in the *Oxford Shakespeare*, which advanced the virtues of *The Contention* and *The True Tragedy* as performance texts (Wells and Taylor 1987: 175–8, 197–9). These represent the majority view of the relationships between these texts in the 1990s.

But the attacks launched around that time on the editorial assumptions on which they depend, notably the 'foul papers' assumption about authorial manuscripts, undermined the confidence of their successors. Paul Werstine's 'Narratives about printed Shakespeare texts' (1990) was particularly influential, as we see in Ronald Knowles's *2 Henry VI*, which conducts its textual analysis very much along the old assumptions, but abruptly recognizes that 'A recent and radical redirection of textual scholarship suggests that the theories and practices of the New Bibliography, and the editorial principles derived from them may be less scientifically based than was once supposed' and concludes that 'In the light of Werstine's scrutiny we have to acknowledge that there can be no certainty in discriminating among the possible various agents whose interventions may stand between authorial manuscripts and the printed texts of Q and F' (1999: 140–1).

John Cox and Eric Rasmussen, Arden 3 editors of *3 Henry VI*, pose the questions very clearly and reach frankly agnostic conclusions: 'The legendary difficulties associated with the texts of *The True Tragedy* and *3 Henry VI*...are due...to the overwhelming uncertainties about textual origins. Does the order of publication reflect the order of composition? That is, does O represent the original version of the play and F a subsequently enlarged version? Or was F the original and O a shortened version? Were the changes made intentionally by a revising playwright or accidentally by someone attempting to reconstruct the text from memory? Are the two texts versions of the same play...or are they, in fact, different plays written by different dramatists' (2001: 158). In the search for answers to these questions they interrogate two of the most deep-seated assumptions that have clung to these texts: that O is an unauthorized memorial reconstruction and that F is based on Shakespeare's own 'foul papers' (159–75). In both cases they unearth enough doubts to undermine these assumptions, but without entirely eradicating them. 'Our analysis of the Octavo text of *The True Tragedy* questions its origins in memorial reconstruction by touring actors and our analysis of the Folio text of *3 Henry VI* questions its "foul paper" status' (175). They opt not to champion any theory: 'We hope that the very inconclusiveness of our analysis will stimulate new ideas and fresh debate about these still enigmatic texts' (176).

This suggests that the evidence is so ambiguous that opting for one interpretation over another is pretty much a matter of inclination or fashion—or indifference. I want to suggest that is not the case. Of all recent editions of these plays, Randall Martin's *Oxford Shakespeare 3 Henry VI* (2001) most decisively breaks with the old assumptions, in effect reverting to Malone's position. While recognizing that 'at present there is less certainty about the historical relationship between O and F, and the integrity of O than there has been since earlier in the century just past' he argues 'that *True Tragedy* is a memorially reported early version of the play that Shakespeare *substantially revised* as *3 Henry VI*' (105, my emphasis).[38] Consequently, 'This edition is based on the First Folio text, which represents Shakespeare's expansion and revision of an earlier version of the play reported by O' (133).

This squares exactly with my own argument that the folio text reflects a revision with court performance in mind. Whatever the origins of *The True Tragedy*, *3 Henry VI* is a later version of the play. Martin stands by the standard argument that the copy behind it is a Shakespearean manuscript (characterized by indefinite, vague, or permissive stage directions, inconsistencies, and loose ends), but avoids the trap of claiming this as 'foul papers' which must have existed before O: 'F bears signs of being a draft which Shakespeare was in the later stages of composing *and/or revising*, rather than being in either a definitive or "final" state' (96, my emphasis). In a telling piece of scholarship Martin shows that a distinctive difference between O and F is that the former more commonly follows the version of events in Edward Hall's *Chronicle* (*The Union of the Noble and Illustre Families of Lancaster and York*, 1542) whereas F is more likely to follow Raphael Holinshed's *Chronicles England, Scotland, and Ireland* (second edition, 1587):

> While establishing the temporal priority of these differences often remains inferential, the nature of the differences between O and F in terms of factual details, diction, and interpretative commentary by Hall and Holinshed reasonably suggests a direction of change, as well as the presence of an informed agency at work in revising the play reported by O. (117)[39]

'Informed agency' is the key term here: the differences between the two versions cannot be ascribed to accidents of the transmission of a single originary text. At some point between them there has been deliberate revision, informed by a new study of the sources—parallel to F *Henry V*'s revision of the roles of the Dauphin, Clarence, Gloucester, and Bedford, and the greater reliance on Holinshed in certain scenes. Indeed, he suggests 'that Shakespeare's revision of *True Tragedy* was associated with an interpretive shift away from Hall towards Holinshed—a change that in wider terms accords with his evolving career as a playwright, and with the English history plays in particular' (119). Martin is careful to say that it is still difficult to *prove* whether F is a revision of O, or vice versa. But the fact that F is the fuller text, with richer verse and fuller characterization, makes it likely that it represents Shakespeare's later thoughts (see Martin 2001: 20, 95 on the roles of Henry VI and Queen Margaret). It would be unusual, to say the least, to strip out richer verse and characterization while at the same time changing the text in line with different sources.

---

[38] I am grateful to Professor Martin for pointing out to me at the 'Shakespeare and the Queen's Men' conference (October 2006) the similarity of my argument about Q1 and F *Henry V* and his own position on *3 Henry VI*.

[39] See further Martin 2002.

Martin's argument accords with my demonstration in Chapter 4 that the substantial revision of plays for court performance was, by inference from Henslowe's *Diary*, a regular feature of Shakespeare's working life, at least in the late 1590s and early 1600s. Sometimes, as with *Old Fortunatus*, this made the plays longer than we would normally expect for public staging, and that has certainly happened with *2 Henry VI* (3,069 lines) and *3 Henry VI* (2,904). If we revisit Roger Warren's account of the differences between *The Contention* and *2 Henry VI*, we can see something of how the expansion was effected—an 'absence of short passages that involve figurative expressions or extended comparisons' in the former, the two texts representing 'different versions of the *material*' (see p. 201).

This then involves both of the kinds of revision that John Kerrigan identifies as typical of such processes in early modern drama (see p. 112). The nine longer passages in F but not in Q are relatively self-contained 'interpolations', which he normally associates with a reviser working on a play that may not be his own. But the 'short passages' involving 'figurative expressions or extended comparisons' and the eleven instances 'where F and Q represent different versions of the *material*' in their different ways both represent examples of a 'tinkering' or 'fidgeting' author working on his own script. With the possible exception of *Dr Faustus*, however, Kerrigan did not consider revisions as extensive as I argue those of Shakespeare's so-called 'bad' quartos involve. Given the editorial orthodoxies prevailing when he wrote (1983), these would not usually have been considered authorial revisions. But I suggest that the examples we are considering here show us something of Shakespeare's creative method, let loose on a bare bones text like *The Contention*, whether he had a hand in its original writing or not. As with *Henry V*, he fidgeted on both large and small scales, making insertions large and small, and reinventing both dramatic structure and the local texture of the language at the same time.

There is a particularly marked example of this in perhaps the most famous passage in *2 Henry VI*, Young Clifford's discovery of his dead father. This sequence prompts Ronald Knowles, who in general resists the argument for Shakespeare's revision of his early text, to concede that there must have been *some* late revision of the play, even if not as much as I envision: 'All critics agree that the maturity of the verse in Young Clifford's speech at 5.2.31–49 indicates a revision of the manuscript later than Q' (1999: 140). Roger Warren similarly makes a small concession in that direction. Interestingly, he includes most of this passage in his list of 'longer passages which are absent from the Quarto' rather than (as I would do) one of the 'occasions where F and Q represent different versions of the *material*', which underscores how difficult it can be to separate out one creative process from another.

For this reason, Young Clifford's speech is worth examining in some detail. In *The Contention* he seeks his father on the battlefield:

> *Alarms, then enter Young Clifford alone.*
> Father of Cumberland,
> Where may I seek my aged father forth?
> Oh, dismal sight! See where he breathless lies,

> All smeared and weltered in his luke-warm blood.
> Ah, aged pillar of all Cumberland's true house,
> Sweet father, to thy murdered ghost I swear
> Immortal hate unto the house of York.
> Nor never shall I sleep secure one night
> Till I have furiously revenged thy death,
> And left not one of them to breathe on earth.
>   *He takes him up on his back.*
> And thus as old Anchises' son did bear
> His aged father on his manly back,
> And fought with him against the bloody Greeks,
> Even so will I. But stay, here's one of them,
> To whom my soul hath sworn immortal hate.
>   *Enter Richard, and then Clifford lays down his father,*
>   *fights with him, and Richard flies away again.*
> Out, crooked-back villain, get thee from my sight.
> But I will after thee and once again,
> When I have born my father to his tent,
> I'll try my fortune better with thee yet.
>   *Exit Young Clifford with his father.*   (H3r; 406)[40]

This is all perfectly functional verse, if limited in its emotional range. We get a verbalization of the facts of Old Clifford's dead body (which most in the audience would see well enough for themselves) rather than a subjective reaction to it. The vows of revenge against the house of York and its most hated member, Richard of Gloucester, are formulaic rather than heartfelt. It is what we would once have called poetry of the surface, though perfectly adequate within its dramatic function. Only the allusion to the well-known passage of the *Aeneid* in which Aeneas carries Anchises from the burning city of Troy gives the passage any wider resonance, but that is as much to call attention to the symbolism of the action—the son carrying the father—as it is to generate verbal intensity.

This is how the passage plays out in the folio (Bevington 2008):

> *Enter Young Clifford*
> Shame and confusion! All is on the rout.
> Fear frames disorder, and disorder wounds
> Where it should guard. O war, thou son of hell,
> Whom angry heavens do make their minister,
> Throw in the frozen bosoms of our part
> Hot coals of vengeance. Let no soldier fly.
> He that is truly dedicate to war
> Hath no self-love, nor he that loves himself
> Hath not essentially but by circumstance
> The name of valor. [*Seeing his dead father.*] Oh, let the vile world end
> And the premisèd flames of the last day

---

[40] In the absence of a modernized text of *The Contention*, my reference is to the original, as reproduced in Knowles 1999 as Appendix 1 (376–407). Page references are to that edition. The modernization is my own.

> Knit earth and heaven together!
> Now let the general trumpet blow his blast,
> Particularities and petty sounds
> To cease! Was't thou ordained, dear father,
> To lose thy youth in peace, and to achieve
> The silver livery of advisèd age,
> And in thy reverence and thy chair-days, thus
> To die in ruffian battle? Even at this sight
> My heart is turned to stone, and while 'tis mine,
> It shall be stony. York not our old men spares;
> No more will I their babes. Tears virginal
> Shall be to me even as the dew to fire,
> And beauty, that the tyrant oft reclaims,
> Shall to my flaming wrath be oil and flax.
> Henceforth I will not have to do with pity.
> Meet I an infant of the house of York,
> Into as many gobbets will I cut it
> As wild Medea young Absyrtus did.
> In cruelty will I seek out my fame.
> Come, thou new ruin of old Clifford's house:
> As did Aeneas old Anchises bear,
> So bear I thee upon my manly shoulders;
> But then Aeneas bare a living load,
> Nothing so heavy as these woes of mine. (5.2.30–65; TLN 3,253–87)

No wonder this has drawn the critical approval of which Knowles speaks. It has all the verbal, emotional, and psychological depth which the quarto text lacks; it will pass muster among Shakespeare's more mature works. Finding his dead father is not an isolated experience, but one located in the course of Young Clifford trying to rally troops in the midst of battle and to summon up the inhuman selflessness necessary there. This expands into images of the Day of Judgment and the end of time itself with the Last Trump as he catches sight of the body. We get no image of the corpse itself, but rather an exploration of Young Clifford's consciousness taking in one more harrowing reality of war amid so many others, reflecting on the painful ironies of a man dying thus in his old age, and allowing this to build into a cold-hearted dedication to revenge.[41]

This evokes the image of Medea chopping her brother into little pieces before we begin to rejoin the thread of the quarto narrative with the reference to Aeneas. But even here it is not the same, because Young Clifford now recognizes that the analogy is not exact. Aeneas was carrying his live father to safety, while he carries his dead father from the battlefield to his personal Day of Judgment. Shakespeare also seems to recognize that the token, inconclusive confrontation with Richard of

---

[41] It is typical of the differences between the two texts that the quarto stage directions are so full, whereas the folio's are so sparse—in the latter we have to intuit when Young Clifford first sees his father, and even his exit is not marked. The quarto at times seems to record an observed performance, and at other times gives directions for a staging. The folio has many of the characteristics of an authorial manuscript, with stage business only sketchily attended to.

Gloucester detracts both from the rhythms of mourning and from the sense of remorseless disaster which is befalling Henry VI's Lancastrian forces at the Battle of St Albans.[42] So he drops it and moves the fight between Richard and the Duke of Somerset, which in the quarto occurs earlier in the battle (H2r; 405), to pick up the action when the stage clears. The death of Somerset in that action is yet another hammer blow to the Lancastrians, contextualizing Clifford's treatment of the death of his father as one more event amid the shameful chaos of a war they are losing. Clifford's vows to take personal revenge on the House of York are the last sparks of Lancastrian energy in the play, engulfed by the Yorkists' total triumph—the only real promise that all is not yet over. This seems to be another instance of revision of the histories in the two tetralogies to fit them better into continuous sequences (see pp. 184–5).

It will be immediately apparent that the quarto version of this sequence is in no sense a misremembered or misreported account of what appears in the folio. They are two differently imagined renditions of the same event. And while no one can prove beyond a shadow of doubt that the folio version did not exist when the quarto version was created (which would mean that someone deliberately opted for workaday adequacy over inspired poetry), the odds are overwhelmingly against it. It may well be, as Peter Alexander famously argued, that some form of memorial reconstruction played its part in some deficiencies in the quarto; that does not mean that anything like the complete folio version lay behind it.[43] The quarto stylistically looks back to the stagecraft of the 1580s; the folio comes close in parts to the vibrant poetic drama of *Romeo and Juliet*. I do not pretend for a moment that the whole text of *2 Henry VI* matches the quality of Young Clifford's speech, but throughout we find infusions of metaphoric language, longer and richer speeches, and changes in the staging which are not merely casual.[44] Here in particular is a classic example of John Kerrigan's 'fidgeting' authorial reviser, one catching new fire as his more mature self re-engages with what Roger Warren calls 'the material'. The argument for the folio text being created by purposeful revision somewhat later than the quarto is overwhelming.

There is, then, suggestive evidence that both *2* and *3 Henry VI* are versions of earlier plays, revised by Shakespeare. What evidence is there that this had anything to do with court performances? Length is, of course, a prime consideration in the history plays and tragedies: at over 3,000 and 2,900 lines respectively (and both involving considerable onstage business in the battles) they are longer than most

---

[42] Richard was not in fact born at the time of the events depicted in *2 Henry VI*.

[43] The supposed clinching detail in Alexander's case is that the version of York's pedigree given in Q could only have been reported by someone who did not understand the facts of the case: 'The Quarto writer by making him declare his ancestor the Duke of York to be second son to Edward III renders further argument superfluous; he had now no need to claim the throne through a daughter of the third son as he proceeds to do' (1929: 62). Whoever compiled the quarto got other details wrong too, leaving out William of Hatfield, the actual second son, and wrongly including one of the Earls of March among Edward's sons. All this proves, however, is that the 'Quarto writer' for some reason mangled information that was probably correct in the text that lay behind his version. It does not prove that the whole of *2 Henry VI* as we know it existed at the time. The 1619 third quarto of the play (*The Whole Contention*) is the earliest edition of the play to correct Q1's errors (see p. 134).

[44] Warren, for example, examines a range of instances (2002: 90–7).

plays performed in the public theatres. But length alone is not the issue: it is the nature of the additional 1,000 lines which find their way into each of the folio texts. I showed in the case of *Henry V* we can uniquely observe Shakespeare transform a text which he did not write (*The Famous Victories of Henry V*) into a text that lies behind a 'bad' quarto version which he assuredly did (the 1600 quarto of *Henry V*), and later transform *that* into the folio text of *Henry V* (as I argue, to be performed at court). This is an important sequence, because it suggests the potential range and flexibility of Shakespeare as a reviser of plays. He starts with (to use Roger Warren's useful term) the relatively inert and unmetaphoric 'material' of *The Famous Victories*, and makes his own vigorous play of it, with much richer language and updated comic material, but the same basic shape. Later he goes beyond that, revisiting his sources, adding new material, making the language even more rhetorically rich and poetically compelling, and complicating his dramaturgy to produce the folio version with which we are most familiar.

In the case of *2* and *3 Henry VI* we see an analogous, but differently phased transformation. The earlier versions are more on a par with *The Famous Victories*, so that their translation into the folio versions requires a greater creative leap. But as we have observed, the results are metaphorically richer, usually metrically more regular, and (as we saw in the case of Young Clifford, but might equally have done with the role of Henry VI in *3 Henry VI*) much more imaginatively engaged with the characterization. They are also typically more allusive, widening the range of reference in the plays. In the case of *3 Henry VI* there are no fewer than twenty-nine classical quotations and references; *The True Tragedy* only has sixteen (Hart 1942: 151). Pronounced classical material sometimes marks a young dramatist showing off his humanist education, and there is something of this in *The True Tragedy*: the inevitable 'Et tu Brute' at E2r: 403; or Clifford invoking Phoebus/Phaeton (C3v: 389); or again Henry VI developing Richard of Gloucester's contemptuous reference to Prince Edward as Icarus (F1v–F2r: 407).[45]

But some of the instances unique to the folio version are far from commonplace. Young Rutland, for example, dies quoting Ovid: '*Di faciant laudis summa sit ista tua*': i.e. 'The gods grant that this may be the height of your glory' (1.3.48; TLN 452. *Heroides*, 2.66). As Cox and Ramussen observe: 'The line is spoken by Phyllis after Demophoön has abandoned her, and its bitter irony is therefore heightened in a play where so many people break their promises as soon as they make them' (2001: 211n). Rutland is, in fact, the first to suffer at the hands of Clifford, implacably pursuing revenge for the death of his father—the energy which directly links this play to *2 Henry VI*. As with Clifford recasting the Anchises reference (in the folio text of that play) while he carried off his father's body, new levels of thought are brought to bear. These are surely signs of Shakespeare writing for a more than usually educated audience, one which could be expected to rise to the challenge of sophisticated Latin references. A prime contender for such an audience, of course,

---

[45] In the absence of a modernized text of *The True Tragedy*, my references are to the original, as reproduced in Cox and Rasmussen 2001 as Appendix 1 (370–409). Page references are to that edition. The modernization is my own.

would be that at court. Elizabeth and James were both fluent in Latin, and many of their courtiers hardly less so.[46]

In all the cases we are considering, much of the evidence is at best ambiguous, and it is easy to understand why people might assume that the degraded language and clumsier stage-work of the shorter texts point to a falling off from their folio equivalents. But the instances I have focused on—the Young Clifford speech and Randall Martin's analysis of a greater reliance on Holinshed in *3 Henry VI*—both point to something which is difficult to account for other than by reference to purposeful, and probably authorial, revision. And that is something which could only realistically happen in a development from shorter texts to longer, not vice versa. No redactor for the stage is going to consult the relative credibility of Hall and Holinshed; nor is there any possibility that 'memorial reconstruction' could so utterly drain the poetic life of Young Clifford's folio speech at the same time as it rearranged the role of Richard of Gloucester in the closing sequence of *2 Henry VI* so as to reduce its dramatic impact. In both cases someone—almost certainly Shakespeare—was stamping his greater maturity on the folio text.

When, then, might these early texts have been revised and expanded?[47] Only Randall Martin, in his edition of *3 Henry VI*, offers such a dating, arguing that 'the revision of *True Tragedy* as the Folio-text *3 Henry VI*... took place between 1594 and 1596' (2001: 131). His main evidence derives from the folio text of the play, which names three of the actors who (presumably) were expected to play the minor roles to which they were assigned. The relevant stage directions are 'Enter Gabriel', for a messenger (1.2.47.1; TLN 361), and 'Sinklo, and Humphrey' for two gamekeepers (3.1.0.1; TLN 1,396–7). Given our limited knowledge of actors' names, these are probably Gabriel Spenser, John Sinklo or Sincler, and Humphrey Jeffes. Sinklo was a hired man (not a sharer) with the Chamberlain's Men, probably from their inception in 1594 and at least until 1604; he is similarly named in the Induction to (folio-only) *The Taming of the Shrew* and in the 1600 quarto of *2 Henry IV*. Spenser and Jeffes both seem also to have joined as hired men around 1594; both defected in 1597 to join the reinvigorated Pembroke's Men, later settling with the Admiral's Men. The possible window for this rewriting thus seems to me to be between 1594 and early 1597.

This makes it possible that the rewriting might have been connected with the anomalous 1596/7 Revels season, when the Chamberlain's Men were the only troupe at court, performing a then-unprecedented six plays. A revised sequence of

---

[46] In 1597 Elizabeth was unexpectedly subjected to a challenging oration in Latin by a Polish ambassador. Her response clearly impressed Sir Robert Cecil, who wrote to the Earl of Essex: 'To this I swear by the living God that her majesty made one of the best answers extempore in Latin that ever I heard, being much moved to be so challenged in public, especially so much against her expectation' (Elizabeth I 2000: 335). For James's response to George Ruggles's immensely long Latin play, *Ignoramus*, which the entire court sat through, see p. 85.

[47] The title page of *The True Tragedy* puts it in the repertory of Pembroke's Men, who flourished very briefly in London 1591–3, but then went broke. The only *recorded* performances of any of the *Henry VI* plays are those in Henslowe's *Diary*, between 1591 and January 1593, of 'Harry the vi' by Lord Strange's Men (Foakes 2002: 16–20). These are usually understood, on little real evidence, to refer to *1 Henry VI*.

Henry VI plays might have been a welcome novelty—and of a piece with other evidence we have seen that the tetralogies tracing the histories of the Houses of Lancaster and York were revised to make them run more smoothly as sequences. It is perhaps also noteworthy that both *The Contention* and *The True Tragedy* were reprinted in 1600, with no significant changes, except that the latter was now in quarto. This was also the date of the quartos of *2 Henry IV* and *Henry V*; and the quarto of *1 Henry IV* was reprinted again in 1599. *Richard II* and *Richard III* were both printed in 1597, and both reprinted within a year. Bearing in mind that the printing of playbooks often coincided with revivals, it is difficult to resist the conclusion that the plays of both tetralogies were mainstays of the Chamberlain's Men's repertoire in a four-year window, *c*. 1596–1600, very possibly in various sequences: 'as oft our stage hath shown', says the chorus at the end of F *Henry V* (see pp. 184–5).

6

Augmentations

a. *Romeo and Juliet*

Anyone looking for an object lesson in the changes that have overtaken Shakespearean editing over the past thirty years could hardly do better than to look at *Romeo and Juliet*. Back in 1980, Brian Gibbons's Arden 2 edition was state of the art. In confronting the reality of two significantly different early versions—a 1597 quarto (Q1) and a 1599 quarto (Q2)—Gibbons unhesitatingly followed W. W. Greg in regarding Q1 as a 'memorial reconstruction' of the text behind Q2, which was deemed to be Shakespeare's own 'foul papers', or just possibly a copy very close to them.[1]

> [I]t has come to be accepted that a number of Bad Quartos of Shakespeare's plays were reconstructed from memory by reporters who knew the play on the stage; *Romeo and Juliet* Q1 is such a text. It contains anticipations, recollections, transpositions, paraphrases, summaries, repetitions and omissions of words, phrases or lines correctly presented in Q2. Most of these features are evidence of the faulty memory of the reporters, though certain omissions, and a cut in the required number of players, may indicate that Q1, however abbreviated, derived from a version adapted for acting. (1980: 2)

By contrast, 'Q2 is nearly half as long again as Q1; it offers correct versions of corrupt or garbled passages in Q1; and its characteristics indicate that the copy was the author's foul papers from which the prompt book was derived' (3).

It should be said here that Q1 is nothing like as 'bad' as the earliest quartos of *Merry Wives* or *Hamlet*, or indeed as dysfunctional as Gibbons makes it sound. It is entirely coherent, follows the action in almost exactly the same sequence as Q2, and in many places runs closely parallel with it; indeed, some scholars think that parts of Q2, though mainly based on Shakespeare's own manuscript, were set by reference to Q1. The main difference is simply length (and accompanying verbal richness), with Q2 at 2,989 lines and Q1 2,215, every scene of the latter shorter than its Q2 counterpart. This is rarely because action is missing and mainly because some of its speeches lack passages (short and long) that only appear in Q2. Nevertheless, Q2 was inevitably adopted as the copy-text for Gibbons's edition, as it has been for virtually every scholarly edition of *Romeo and Juliet*, except

---

[1] There were two further quartos before the First Folio. But they, like the folio text, were all ultimately based on Q2, with some occasional reference to Q1 and to each other, and they carry no real authority.

those which single out Q1 as a curiosity (even if, these days, an honourable curiosity).[2]

We may contrast the Gibbons edition with that of Jill Levenson in the *Oxford Shakespeare* series (2000). She retains Q2 as her copy-text but demonstrates her respect for Q1 by printing it at the back of her edition, entire and (like the main text) modernized, on an almost equal footing. (Other modern editions commonly reproduce facsimiles of relevant 'bad' quartos, a step in the same direction and measure of their modern status.) Her introduction traces the remorseless decline in the confidence which scholars have placed in the New Bibliographers' editorial paradigms over the decades between Gibbons' edition and her own (see p. 150). The issue for her is how to respond to the growing indeterminacy this opens up. Where earlier editors attempted to close it down as far as possible, Levenson welcomes the freedom to explore it, discussing the history of the *Romeo and Juliet* text and her own editorial procedures under the banner of 'The Mobile Text' (103). This is welcome and liberating in many ways. But there are dangers in taking the idea of indeterminacy too literally, of imagining texts growing or proliferating uncontrollably—in effect imagining the 'continuous copy' of John Dover Wilson and some modern scholars (see pp. 142, 151). The licensing system was there precisely to prevent an unregulated proliferation of texts, any of which might be—*or might be made*—seditious, heretical, or abusive of those in power (pp. 152ff). Where we have multiple texts of the same play, therefore—and we believe that they were performed in texts pretty much resembling each of those configurations—we have to account for them within these specific constraints. And where possible we should *historicize* them as closely as possible, trying to recreate the contextual moment that separated one version of a text from another.

Lukas Erne's edition of *The First Quarto of Romeo and Juliet* (2007) sees Q1 and Q2 as distinct texts, the former a cut-down version of the latter for performance purposes. His analysis traverses much of the same material as Levenson's, exorcising the 'bad' quarto narratives, associations with piracy, memorial reconstruction (in its earlier incarnations), and adaptations for touring. But he finally follows the shape of Andrew Gurr's argument about the quarto of *Henry V* to identify Q1 as what is essentially the version of *Romeo and Juliet* for the public stage, adapted from an originating Q2: 'The first quarto of *Romeo and Juliet*... probably takes us as close as we can get to the play as it was performed by Shakespeare and his fellow players in London and elsewhere' (25). He accepts the idea that some of the differences between the texts can be explained by oral/aural distortions deriving from 'a process of memorisation' as it is more commonly understood today: that is a normal company activity, involving a significant number of players. But he also believes that some deliberate abridgement was involved, 'undertaken by a redactor or by Shakespeare himself' (24).[3]

---

[2] Such as Erne 2007 and Halio 2008.
[3] Cf. Grace Ioppolo, who speaks of Q1 *Romeo and Juliet* containing 'a number of cuts that may be due to abridgement for a smaller acting company, cuts probably made by Shakespeare himself' (1991: 89).

In the course of all this he confidently asserts that: 'The idea that Q1 constitutes a first draft which Shakespeare expanded to Q2 may safely be laid to rest' (24). I fear that I am here to exhume it, because it seems to me a more convincing explanation of the relationship between the two texts. Erne's main argument in support of his assertion is one I have already looked at in some detail, because it admirably encapsulates a common contention (see pp. 170ff): 'An obstacle to belief in this theory resides in the fact that the derivative nature of most of the "bad quartos" is strongly suggested by passages whose sense only becomes entirely clear after a comparison with the "good" text' (2007: 9ff).[4] As I countered earlier, such weaknesses are precisely the kind that will bedevil any text which relies to some extent (as Erne accepts this does) on memorization. He is arguing as if Q1 were a text directly derived from Q2, when (as he recognizes elsewhere) Q1 could only at best be an inadequate and indirect *version* of a text so derived, a reconstruction of it by some fallible parties. By the same token, his arguments about the abridgement of Q2 can all be turned on their head to suggest (as I shall) *augmentations* and purposeful *amendments* of an earlier Q1.

Tiffany Stern to a degree echoes Erne in reviving the old suggestion that Q2 *Romeo and Juliet* was an authorized text of the play, presumably released by the Chamberlain's Men, intended to efface the poor, unauthorized Q1: ' "corrected" plays were sometimes released, presumably by companies, in the wake of errant ones: *Romeo and Juliet* explains on its title page that it is "newly corrected, augmented, and amended" (1599), thus casting aspersions on the previous text' (2013: 10). But it may simply be drawing attention to a newly revised text. No 'explanation' of Q1 based on the argument that it was cut down from Q2, or even mangled by shorthand, can explain in the latter what I shall describe as deliberate revisions to the characterizations of Juliet and Friar Laurence, or to the clown's role played by Will Kemp. The 'newly corrected, augmented' here refers to something genuinely new and, I suggest, authorial.

All texts, including those based on Shakespeare's own manuscripts (or close copies of them), were tailored to quite specific playing conditions and to the licensing regime that contained them. Particular versions came together at given times to create the versions that have survived. In the case of a text like Q1, which seems not to be based closely on a manuscript and to involve some oral/aural transmission (of which any form of shorthand is only an alternative form), we can only really guess—in our current state of knowledge—how it might have come together. In the case of Q2, I think it can be shown that the manuscript behind it recorded an expansion and elaboration, not of Q1 itself, but of the play of which Q1 is only a somewhat inadequate record. That is, Q2 is exactly what it says it is on the title page. And the likeliest explanation for that is that it was done for a court performance.

Much of the evidence for this is, I again confess, ambiguous. When shorter scenes in Q1 are compared with longer versions in Q2, it is generally as easy to

---

[4] Erne is specifically responding to Bains 1995.

argue that the latter was cut as that the former was 'augmented'.[5] Yet that explanation becomes less plausible if we consider that a very significant number of the cuts or additions relate to the roles of two characters in particular, Juliet and Friar Laurence. The former is particularly suggestive, since it seems likely that the play was originally written between 1593 and 1596, while (on my argument) the expansion was presumably made between 1597 and 1599. The latter are precisely the dates when Shakespeare was writing some of his strongest and—in acting terms—most taxing female roles: Portia, Beatrice, and Rosalind. It is also the period in which *Love's Labour's Lost* was 'Newly corrected and augmented', with strong roles for the Princess and Rosaline. The explanation commonly advanced for this is that the Chamberlain's Men must at this time have had at least one exceptionally gifted boy actor who was capable of handling such long and sophisticated roles. Is it likely that, as he was creating those roles, Shakespeare was simultaneously slashing (or allowing his colleagues to slash) the part of his most striking female tragic protagonist to date? That can only, of course, be a rhetorical question. I shall, however, be looking at a parallel casting question, where the texts leave more concrete traces, and showing that the role(s) in *Romeo and Juliet* played by Will Kemp, the company's principal comedian, were also revised and expanded, in ways that point to a more general process.

Let us start with what most modern editions designate 2.4 or 2.5 (Sc. 8 in Erne), a scene of 77 lines in Q2 but barely half that (44) in Q1.[6] The great majority of the *added* lines (as I argue) go to Juliet, with some additional comedy from the Nurse. The scene opens identically, with Juliet longing for the Nurse's return to hear more of Romeo. But after three lines Q1 reads:

> O, she is lazy. Love's heralds should be thoughts
> And run more swift than hasty powder fired
> Doth hurry from the fearful cannon's mouth.   (8.4–6; E3v)[7]

Q2, however, has:

> Oh, she is lame! Love's heralds should be thoughts,
> Which ten times faster glides than the sun's beams,
> Driving back shadows over louring hills.   (2.5.4–6; E4v)

The speech then proceeds in Q2 for a further ten lines, reflecting on Cupid, the sun, the swifter/slower passing of time in youth and old age.[8] This whole longer passage rehearses the key recurrent themes of the mature play: the passing of time, youth, and death (whereas Q1's 'hasty powder' catches none of this). At the same time, 'lame' for 'lazy' is almost certainly not a misreading but sets up the comic

---

[5] See, for example, Halio 2008: 124–30.
[6] Levenson's Q2-based *Oxford Shakespeare*, for example, makes the scene 2.4; Gibbons's Arden 2 makes it 2.5, as does Bevington 2008. It depends on whether the exit of Benvolio and Mercutio around line 43 of 2.1 is treated as the end of a scene or not.
[7] References to Q1 are to Erne 2007, with the sig. reference to the 1597 text; references to Q2 are to Bevington 2008, with the sig. reference to the 1599 text.
[8] The last couplet of the ten lines are credited to '*M*', but there is no other suggestion of a second character present and it is almost certainly a mistake. Q4 and F give the lines correctly to Juliet.

business to come, centring on the Nurse's infirmity. Then, when the Nurse finally arrives, her 'man' Peter is with her. Peter, we know, was played by Will Kemp, and the audience would naturally have anticipated more of his comedy (see p. 28). It is not impossible that he extemporized at this point (he was famous for it), though nothing is scripted. But his mere presence adds to Juliet's frustration; she wants him out of the way so that she can speak of her love, and asks for him to be dismissed, which he is. (None of this is in Q1; more of it later.)

Both versions then develop a comic tension between the Nurse, who is too weary to speak (or, at least, to speak to the point), and Juliet, who is desperate for her news. But in Q1 this is only a sketch. In Q2 Juliet develops a strain of witty, anxious frustration, for which there is no equivalent in the other version:

> Oh, Lord, why lookest thou sad?
> Though news be sad, yet tell them merrily;
> If good, thou shamest the music of sweet news,
> By playing it to me with so sour a face. (2.5.21–4; F1r)
>
> How art thou out of breath, when thou hast breath
> To say to me that thou art out of breath?
> The excuse that thou dost make in this delay
> Is longer than the tale thou dost excuse.
> Is thy news good or bad? Answer to that;
> Say either, and I'll stay the circumstance.
> Let me be satisfied: is't good or bad? (2.5.31–7; F1r)

The Nurse's response to this is essentially the same as that in Q1—'you know not how to choose a man...He is not the flower of courtesy' (38–9, 43). And it is just as beside the point, but all the funnier because Juliet could hardly have been more explicit about precisely what she wants to hear. And her speech really ought to have given the Nurse the time to catch her breath. Instead, it gives her space to reflect on all her aches and pains together ('my head aches', 'ah my back, my back', 48, 50; F1r–F1v), rather than spaced out as in Q1, increasing Juliet's frustration to the breaking point of civility and leading to another attempt squarely to elicit the news:

> I'faith I am sorry that thou art not well.
> Sweet, sweet, sweet Nurse, tell me, what says my love? (53–4)

The remainder of the scene is essentially the same in both versions, with minor verbal adjustments (tinkering) such as any competent writer might make, given the opportunity to revisit his material. But the differences I have pointed out (developments, I would call them) show how unlikely it actually is that Q2 existed first and was somehow cut. They certainly rule out memorial (mis-)construction as a cause of difference, because it is not that Q1 garbles Q2, nor is it Q2-lite. Q2 has been re-imagined, deftly working within the framework of Q1, to give Juliet a fuller presence and her frustration at the Nurse's delays a more comic and credible rhythm. Q1 is certainly brisker, but it is not more dramatic. Q2 is psychologically more acute, both about Juliet and the Nurse, and the introduction of Peter/Kemp, only to have him immediately withdrawn, brilliantly mimics for the audience Juliet's frustration. *Something* of this would surely have survived in any redaction.

We may also glance here at the following brief scene, 2.5 or 2.6 in modern editions (Sc. 9 in Erne). The differences between the Q1 and Q2 versions of it are the most marked of any in the play, and Jay L. Halio singles it out for special comment (2008: 133–6). He believes that Q2 came first and he also generally believes that Shakespeare revised the text to produce Q1. But he cannot believe that Shakespeare is responsible for Q1's 2.5/6 (or several other parts of that text) and suggests that they may have been the corporate working of the acting company:

> The best example of what is very likely wholesale nonauthorial revision of Q1 *Romeo* is 2.6. Here Juliet meets Romeo at Friar Laurence's cell to be married, but the scene is entirely different from its counterpart in Q2, not only shorter by almost 50 percent, but completely rewritten. Although some vestiges of Shakespeare's original poetry appear (as in the day-sun image, recalling the imagery of 2.2), the verse is pedestrian and suggests that someone other than Shakespeare wrote it. In other respects, too, the scene differs from Q2's version. The action is swift: Juliet rushes in, speaks to and embraces Romeo, whereas in Q2 she more demurely addresses the Friar before turning to Romeo. Indeed, speed in Q1 replaces the more deliberate pace found in Q2. (134)

As with Lukas Erne's attempts to argue that Burgundy's major speech about war-torn France in the final act of *Henry V* is 'non-dramatic', speed here risks being confused with drama (see p. 191). But this whole scene is *about* speed, and it is apparent that the author of Q2 has something different to say about it from the author of Q1.

In Q1 Friar Laurence observes that 'Youth's love is quick, swifter than swiftest speed' and immediately the stage direction reads '*Enter* Juliet, *somewhat fast, and embraceth Romeo*' (9.9–9.10; E4r). As the lovers embrace and exchange endearments, it is the Friar who urges them to hurry: 'Come wantons, come, the stealing hours do pass', a theme which the lovers pick up. Romeo says 'Lead holy father, all delay seems long', and Juliet chimes in with 'Make haste, make haste, this lingering doth us wrong' (9.21, 25, 26; E4v). In Q2 a totally different perspective is announced by having the Friar speak the first, cautious lines:

> So smile the heavens upon this holy act
> That after hours with sorrow chide us not. (2.6.1–2; F1v)

As Romeo longs for 'one short minute...in her sight' (5; F2r), and defies 'love-devouring death' (7) so long as he and Juliet are married, the Friar injects an urgent note of caution for which there is absolutely no counterpart in Q1:

> These violent delights have violent ends,
> And in their triumph die like fire and powder...
> Therefore love moderately, long love doth so,
> Too swift arrives, as tardy as too slow. (9–10, 14–15)

These are the words that now ironically hang in the air as the direction reads '*Enter Juliet*'. This may not say explicitly that she enters '*somewhat fast*', but it is implicit in the dialogue. In Q1 Father Laurence celebrated her lightness of foot:

> So light of foot ne'er hurts the trodden flower
> Of love and joy, see, see the sovereign power. (9.11–12; E4r)

Here he extends the sense of wonder, but concludes it with an unexpected twist:

> Here comes the Lady. Oh so light a foot
> Will ne'er wear out the everlasting flint.
> A lover may bestride the gossamers
> That idles in the wanton summer air,
> And yet not fall, so light is vanity.   (2.6.16–20; F2r)

Juliet's lightness of foot has become the lightness of vanity. She does indeed greet her 'ghostly confessor', but she almost certainly does so from Romeo's arms, since the Friar's response—'Romeo shall thank thee, daughter, for us both' (22)—implies that Romeo will kiss her on both their behalves. The lovers then both try to find words to express the immensity of their joys, demonstrating the kind of elaborate wordplay which the title page of Q1 offers ('An Excellent Conceited Tragedy') but which the text of Q2 ('The Most Excellent and Lamentable Tragedy') much more fully delivers. Finally, and ironically, it is the Friar who now urges them to hurry ('Come, come with me, and we will make short work') but very specifically so that 'you shall not stay alone / Till holy Church incorporates two in one' (35–7). Speed is no longer a surrender to the lovers' desires, but a way to ensure that those desires are properly contained within the blessing of 'holy Church'.

Halio's 'deliberate pace' in this scene is actually a matter of the Friar trying to impose a seemly pace, one measured by a Christian perspective, on the self-absorbed impetuosity of the Q1 lovers (who have themselves become more 'conceitedly' proficient with words). It is in every sense—including the dramatic—a more sophisticated version. Of course I cannot prove that someone did not decide to ignore virtually all of it and substitute the altogether more one-dimensional version in Q1. But it seems to me suspicious that Halio is uncomfortable with the idea of that 'someone' being Shakespeare. In general he is prepared to accept that the adaptation from Q2 to Q1 (as he takes it) may have been by Shakespeare working in conjunction with his acting colleagues. But he seems to recognize that in 2.5/6 this amounts to something like a slur on the actors and casts around for alternatives, mentioning an old (and totally unwarranted) theory that the reviser here might have been Henry Chettle. All of these problems disappear if we accept that Q1 is an earlier, hastier, less reflective version of the play, which I for one have no problem crediting to a less practised Shakespeare; and that Q2 is a more studied revision, written by a more mature playwright for the wider canvas of a court performance.

To return specifically to Juliet, we can see this pattern again in even more pronounced form in what modern editions make 3.2 (Sc. 11 in Erne), where she enters once more urging time to fly, longing for the night: 'Gallop apace, you fiery-footed steeds' (11.1; F3r/3.2.1; G1r). In Q1 this speech is only four lines long; in Q2 it is thirty-one. The Q2 scene as a whole is 143 lines long, Q1 59.[9] The expansion, however, is very substantially that of Juliet's role. The Nurse gets only 12 more lines (20 to 32), whereas Juliet's part grows from 40 lines to 111. Even

---

[9] These figures vary slightly, depending on how you treat half-lines.

leaving aside the opening soliloquy, her role doubles. The twists and turns of her emotional state are followed with rhetorical embellishment. The soliloquy at the beginning opens into a hymn to night and blackness; her response to the news that Romeo has killed Tybalt expands into a study on the oxymoron:

> Beautiful tyrant, fiend angelical:
> Ravenous dove-feathered raven, wolvish-ravening lamb.   (3.2.75–6; G2v)

Her attempts to come to terms with the fact of Romeo 'banished', sketched in Q1, are elaborated and focused in a closing couplet:

> There is no end, no limit, measure, bound,
> In that word's death; no words that woe can sound.   (125–6; G3r)

And finally—an insight not reflected in Q1—she recognizes that she is likely to 'die maiden-widowèd' (135). At that point what I have characterized as rhetorical embellishment—a verbal simulacrum of her feelings—turns into a painful piece of self-realization, as the personal implications of the day's events sink home. The whole scene therefore describes a dramatic arc, from impatient expectation to a state of living death. It is a bravura piece, which surely only the most accomplished boy actor could handle.

When we turn to the case of Friar Laurence, it is clear that there has been a deliberate rewriting of the role, some of which we have already observed in 2.5/6, where his function has appreciably changed. The rewriting is also readily apparent in his long speech after Romeo's attempted suicide (3.3.108–58); twenty-five lines in Q1 double in Q2. Most of this is a prolonged passage (119–34) for which there is no equivalent in Q1. In it, the Friar attempts to make Romeo see his actions in a perspective beyond his own emotions:

> Why railest thou on thy birth, the heaven, and earth,
> Since birth, and heaven, and earth, all three do meet,
> In thee at once, which thou at once wouldst loose.   (119–21; H1r)

His theme is that everything transcendently human in Romeo is betrayed in the attempt at suicide: 'thou shamest thy shape, thy love, thy wit…/…Thy noble shape is but a form of wax…/…Thy dear love sworn but hollow perjury…/…Thy wit, that ornament to shape and love, / Mishapen in the conduct of them both' (3.3.122, 126, 128, 130–1; H1r–H1v). It is in effect a mini-sermon, and it is easy to see how it might be omitted if the play were being shortened. But this is also a further expansion of what we saw in 2.5/6, Friar Laurence taking seriously his role as a spiritual confessor, attempting to make Romeo and Juliet see the moral world beyond their mutual self-absorption. If it is much more plausible to think of the Q2 2.5/6 as a sophisticated development from Q1, it is logical that this passage in 3.3 should be an addition as well.

As a final piece of character evidence in the case, I point to the long speech which Friar Laurence gives at the end (5.3.223–269; M1r–M1v). Here length itself is hardly an issue: forty-one lines (Q1, 20:153–93) against forty-six (Q2). Yet the speech has been completely rewritten. Each version is entirely comprehensible in itself and there is little to choose in the quality of the verse. What has markedly changed is that in Q2 Friar Laurence is more accurate, more careful to distinguish between what he knows and what he can only guess at, and more heavily aware of just how guilty he must seem to others for what has happened. Both versions in fact conclude with him prepared to accept 'the rigor of severest law' 'if aught in this / Miscarried by my fault' (5.3.269, 266–7; M1v). But Q2 prefaces the whole speech with the Friar's recognition that circumstances point to his own guilt, so that what follows carries the twin functions of revealing what happened (at the risk of condemning himself) but also exonerating himself: 'And here I stand, both to impeach and purge / Myself condemnèd and myself excused' (226–7; M1r).

In Q2 he explains that Juliet pined for the banishment of Romeo, not for the death of Tybalt, as Paris had assumed (236; cf. 4.1.6, I2r). He tells of Juliet's 'wild looks' (240) as she desperately sought to avoid a second marriage. But he says nothing of Romeo, 'understanding by his man, / That Juliet was deceased' and so returning 'in post' (Q1 20.179–80; K3v), of which in fact he has no knowledge. He tells more simply how he found 'The noble Paris and the true Romeo dead' (259; M1v), and when Juliet awoke tried to coax her from the tomb 'And bear this work of heaven with patience' (261), a last flash of the would-be conscientious confessor, again not in Q1. He accurately reports how 'she, too desperate, would not go with me' and reasonably concludes 'But, as it seems, did violence on herself' (263–4). So he ends his account with the factually correct 'All this I know, and to the marriage / Her nurse is privy' (265–6). The Nurse's status as eyewitness is mentioned early in Q1; here it reinforces the Friar's own veracity. In sticking to the facts as he knew them, most particularly in reporting his own impressions of Juliet's state of mind, and in more fully owning up to his own possible guilt in all this, Friar Laurence in Q2 is a more convincing witness. It is surely inconceivable that anyone would go out of their way to lose all of that in a revision of Q1 that loses only five lines. And it is even less conceivable that any process of 'memorizing' Q2 would result in Q1.

The evidence from the characterization of Juliet and Friar Laurence consistently points to a richer and fuller realization of the roles in Q2 than in Q1, which is not simply a matter of having more lines to speak. There are advances in their motivations and self-awareness which would surely not have been lost so thoroughly and systematically in a stripping down of Q2 for the public theatre, much less its misremembering. They are much more credibly the result of a careful and deliberate expansion ('Newly corrected, augmented, and amended') of what lay behind the Q1 text.

Evidence of a rather different kind relates to the role(s) assigned in the play to Will Kemp. It is difficult to speak with absolute assurance on this because both Q1 and Q2 use a range of designations for what may be seen as a single 'character' or possibly a grouping of roles all subsumed within the function of the 'clown'. But these roles are all those of a serving-man in the Capulet household—in a play where serving-men figure very prominently. It is, after all, serving-men (in both versions) who precipitate the violence in the first scene: pairs of Capulets and Montagues face off, graphically demonstrating the ingrained and thoughtless antagonism between the two families. The key issue here is evidence of a rewrite in Kemp's role in the final scene of the play (5.3; Sc. 20), where in Q2 he is clearly scripted to appear, though he later unaccountably disappears. In Q1 he does not appear at all.

My analysis of Kemp's role in the play substantially accords with that of David Wiles in the most acute and insightful account we have of Kemp as a performer, though we differ on details (Wiles 1987: 84–92). Kemp first appeared, we agree, in the second scene as what Q1 dubs a serving-man (ostensibly the role he is performing), but what Q2 also describes on entry as 'the Clown'. This more fundamentally describes his role here, where his chief characteristic is to be illiterate—he has to ask Romeo to read the list of those he is to invite to the Capulets' feast—and designates the company's principal comedian, a role which in Kemp's hands was semi-autonomous. He was an attraction in himself that the audience came to see, not least for the jig he would often perform after the show proper (a satirical or farcical song and dance, often bawdy). In the roles that we know were written for Kemp—Dogberry in *Much Ado* is one, 'Peter' in this play another—he typically has problems with language, a rustic fellow who nevertheless often scores off his fellows and betters. So here, in both versions, he has 'dumb' fun teasing Romeo as to exactly where the guests to the feast should come—'Up', 'To our house', 'My master's'—before finally conceding: 'My master is the great rich Capulet' (2.67–74; 1.2.74–81). The joke, incidentally, suggests that Kemp must have been wearing his usual clown's 'motley', rather than his livery as a Capulet serving-man, which Romeo would immediately have recognized (Hotson 1952). This in itself indicates his half-in-role, half-not function in the performance.

Kemp then seems to have another brief entrance in the next scene, where the texts invert their designations: in Q1 'Enter Clown', while in Q2 'Enter Serving[man]' (3.70.1; 1.3.100.1). His function is merely to summon Juliet to dinner, but in three lines he pulls two jokes—'supper is ready, the Nurse cursed in the pantry, all things in extremity. Make haste, for I must be gone to wait'—a tart, passing gibe at the Nurse (with whom he is soon to be comically paired) and punning on the paradox that he 'must be gone to wait' [serve as a waiter]. Wiles assumes that Kemp then appeared as the lead serving-man in what modern texts designate either as a sequence within 1.4 or (like Bevington) as the start of a separate scene (1.5.1–15; C2v–C3r). The sequence does not occur at all in Q1 and this omission is worth considering in detail, because it tells us something not only about Kemp's more developed role in Q2 but more generally about that text's more imaginative staging.

It is one of the clearest instances of purposeful *theatrical* change between the two texts—not simply adding or subtracting lines ascribed to a character but altering the action. In Q1, Scene 4 (the famous 'Queen Mab' sequence, with Romeo, Benvolio, and Mercutio in masquers' disguise, on their way to the Capulets' ball) reaches line 92, with Romeo's 'On, lusty gentlemen'. The setting then unaccountably switches to the inside of the Capulets' house, with Old Capulet entering and greeting his guests, who include the Montague faction from the previous sequence: 'Welcome, gentlemen, welcome gentlemen!' A change of locale in normal Elizabethan staging conventions requires a new scene.

In Q2 Benvolio adds 'Strike, drum' to Romeo's 'On, lusty gentlemen' (1.4.114; C2v), and before Old Capulet appears a stage direction tells us 'They march about the stage and serving-men come forth with napkins'. These busy serving-men then set up for the ball, with cross-cutting orders, questions, and banter. As they leave, 'Enter all the guests and gentlewomen to the masquers', and Capulet begins to greet them. The serving-men are evidently introduced to gloss over the change of location, which would normally require a change of scene, and to ease the passage of Romeo, Benvolio, and Mercutio into the Capulets' boisterously disordered household—their 'march' intersects with the servants' bustle. It is a moment of simple domestic confusion, which would have no charge to it were it not for the presence of the Montagues in the house of their enemies. Wiles reckons that this is another Kemp scene; the lead serving-man—Kemp's presumptive role—is designated 'Ser.' in the speech prefixes, whereas the others are merely numbered 1, 2, and 3. If we accept this, we should note that it is the second occasion when Shakespeare contrives to have Kemp and Romeo onstage at the same time. There will be more, and we shall track them.

It is not until Erne's Scene 7 that Kemp enters in his most familiar guise in the play: 'Enter Nurse and her man' (both versions: 81.1, E2r; Q2, 2.4.99.1, E3r). In Q1 it is not until following 125.1 that Kemp speaks; the Nurse 'turns to Peter, her man' and berates him because 'thou like a knave must stand by and see every jack use me at his pleasure'—referring to the fun that Romeo, Benvolio, and Mercutio have been having at her expense (E3r). 'Peter' gives as good as he gets. As Wiles observes, 'there is no way in which the nurse, a servant herself, could technically be Peter's employer' (1987: 86). We are possibly to understand that he has been sent to chaperone her while she is out in the street (and subject to the banter of young Montagues), but they also seem to be playing a game of scornful mistress and her personal, far-from-overawed 'servant'. The scene is very similar in Q2, though he speaks a very grudging 'Anon' (2.4.103) to the Nurse as they enter and she demands her fan, which makes him a party of sorts to the ribbing she is to receive from the Montagues: 'Good Peter, to hide her face, for her fan's the fairer face', mocks Mercutio (2.4.105–6). This scene puts Kemp onstage with Romeo yet again in both versions, though the dialogue in Q2 draws more attention to it. We have already commented on the following scene, where 'Peter' enters briefly, trying Juliet's patience (in Q2 only: 2.5), but leaves without speaking; it is the last time we see him as the Nurse's 'man', though the designation 'Peter' intermittently remains with him in speech-headers.

It is possible that Kemp is the serving-man in Sc. 16 (4.2 in Q2) who bandies words with Capulet about inept cooks licking their fingers, since he later jokes with the musicians about the silver he was given to pay them (and the cooks) off with.[10] But in 4.4 (Q2) Kemp is expressly *not* one of the 'three or four' serving-men who bring in logs for the fire, since they are directed to 'Peter' (4.4.17; K1v) to find

[10] In Q1 there is a single serving-man; in Q2 'servingmen, two or three', but only one speaks.

drier ones. In Q1, the text's single serving-man is told even more revealingly that 'Will will tell you where thou shalt fetch them' (17.41–2), another indicator of the clown's quasi-autonomy and how closely Shakespeare identified the role with the actor.

In Scene 18 (4.5 in modern editions) Kemp was even more emphatically involved. Q2 reads 'Enter Will Kemp' (4.5.125.2), though his speech-headers read 'Peter'. (Q1's equivalent is 'Enter Serving-man'.) David Wiles calls this 'Peter's most important scene', in defiance of a long tradition of commentary which finds his joking with the musicians weak and/or in poor taste, given that Juliet is supposed to be dead (1987: 88). But his comic banter about silver and gold (playing on the fact that he is here to pay off the musicians for a performance that is no longer required) is actually appropriate here, because as yet there is every possibility that the play will end happily for the lovers. Friar Laurence's plan still has a chance of working.

It is in 5.3 that questions seriously arise about what Shakespeare was actually thinking—or perhaps rethinking—about Kemp's role. In Q1 the key stage direction is 'Enter Romeo and Balthasar, with a torch, a mattock, and a crow of iron' (20.14.1–2). Subsequently Romeo's companion is unequivocally 'Balt.' until Romeo enters the tomb alone; when Friar Laurence arrives and encounters him, he is 'Man', as he is ('Romeo's man') when he is discovered by the Watch. Only when the Prince demands that he accounts for himself is he expressly 'Balth' again. Q2 is intriguingly different. The stage direction is 'Enter Romeo and Peter', and the companion remains 'Pet.' until Romeo enters the tomb. Thereafter he is 'Man' and addressed as 'Romeo's man' exactly as in Q1, and finally 'Balth.' when he answers the Prince.

By Scene 18 (5.1 in Q2) Romeo has a 'man' or servant, called Balthasar. We also know that in Shakespeare's immediate source for the play—Arthur Brooke's *Tragicall Historye of Romeus and Juliet* (1567)—Romeo had a servant called Peter. So explanations for Romeo's curious accompaniment by Peter in Q2's 5.3 tend to focus on a lapse of memory by Shakespeare, passively following his source and forgetting both Balthasar and that he had already used 'Peter' for another character—one associated moreover with the Capulets, not the Montagues. The double lapse of memory seems, to say the least, unlikely. An alternative theory, that Kemp doubled as Peter and Balthasar, seems unlikely for a number of reasons that I pursue below.[11]

David Wiles has another suggestion, which begins with the supposition that Shakespeare wrote this scene first, with Kemp in mind, and then had second thoughts. Although I disagree with the premise about writing this scene first, there is much to recommend his analysis, which is grounded in this perception of the relationship between the clown role and Romeo:

> The intention behind 'Peter' seems plain. Romeo's rhetoric is frankly melodramatic, and the persona of Peter—i.e. the clown—obliges the audience to reject Romeo's own account of himself, temporarily, and to accept an alternative perspective...In Romeo there lay the possibility of transcending the melodramatic or burlesque norms of early Elizabethan tragedy. In Kemp, he had a clown whose presence would never allow

---

[11] See Levenson 2000, note to 5.3.21.2.

Romeo to dominate the stage, a clown whose presence would preclude even short-lived idealizing of Romeo's emotions. When he began the play at the beginning, therefore, Shakespeare relocated the clown as principal Capulet servant, retaining the English name of Peter. When he finally established the character of Romeo's servant in V.i., he gave this servant verse and an Italian name, to signal that this was a straight character, distanced from the immediate world of the London audience. (1987: 91–2)

Hence the comic potential of Peter/Kemp (rather than his own servant) accompanying Romeo to the tomb. Peter's entrance here in 5.3, laden with a torch, mattock, and crowbar, offers opportunities for bungling; his initial resolution to leave when they get to the tomb—'I will be gone, sir, and not trouble ye' (5.3.40; L2r)—could certainly be played for laughs.

Indeed, the logic of Peter/Kemp playing this role is a compelling one. To the objection that 'Peter' is a Capulet servant, not a Montague one, I say again that (unlike all the other servants) he is evidently not in livery, but in his clown's motley (p. 220). Like Feste in *Twelfth Night*, he has the clown's freedom to move from house to house, semi-independent of his assigned role. And, as in the scene with the musicians, it is important to bear in mind that the full tragic outcome is still nothing like a foregone conclusion, even though the Choruses (one in Q1, two in Q2) have warned us to expect it. Kemp's presence keeps the tragicomic possibility alive. Yes, Friar John has not delivered Friar Laurence's letter to Romeo, who has ominously purchased poison. But Friar Laurence could still get back to prevent the tragic sequence. It is only when Romeo encounters Paris within the tomb that the play tips irrevocably into tragedy.

Q1, where Romeo is accompanied by a Balthasar who is, as Wiles puts it, a verse-speaking, Italianate 'straight character', is already committed to a conventional tragic mode, sentimentally indulging what Wiles rightly identifies as the element of melodrama in Romeo's rhetoric—and indeed more generally in the tale of the star-crossed lovers. My suggestion is that Q2's version, with Kemp left quivering outside the tomb, is not a rejected first draft but actually the later version, a brilliantly original twist on romantic tragedy conventions, superimposed on the Q1 original—which, however, is still apparent in the final sequence, where the references to Romeo's 'Man' and the one speech-header for 'Balth' survive.

There can be little doubt that there was some confusion in the Q2 manuscript, and we can probably identify the point at which it occurs. At 20.53.2 (K1v) in Q1 the stage direction reads 'They fight' (meaning Romeo and Paris) and Paris's page (speech-header 'Boy') cries out 'O Lord, they fight. I will go call the watch'. At the equivalent point in Q2 (5.2.71; L2v) there is no stage direction, but the page's line is printed as if it *were* a stage direction (i.e. inset and in italics), without a speech-header. The confusion over the identity of Romeo's 'Man' in Q2 only begins at that point, presumably because the version in which he was unequivocally Kemp was not finished or sheets were mislaid.[12]

---

[12] Bevington and most modern editors leave the line with Paris's page, but one set of editors did not—those who compiled the First Folio text. They gave the line to 'Pet.'—that is to Kemp (TLN 2,924). This makes little sense, because all versions agree that it is the page/boy who rouses and brings

The possibility that Shakespeare intended to replace Balthasar with Kemp in 5.3 is given more credence when we recall that Romeo had encountered 'Peter' (then 'Clown' according to Q2) in 1.2 (Sc. 2) and read his list of banquet invitees for him; in the little bridging scene that gets Romeo, Mercutio, and Benvolio into the Capulet ball (between 1.4/5 in some editions: this in Q2 only); and again in 2.4 (Sc. 7) when Romeo, Mercutio, and Benvolio come across him with the Nurse. Wiles points out that the neoclassical tradition is for witty servants to be attached to the principal male character (as the Dromios are in *The Comedy of Errors*: 91). 'Peter' is obviously never Romeo's servant in this way (and Shakespeare does not need him to be while the playful mockery of Mercutio and Benvolio keeps Romeo's love-sickness in proportion). But Kemp's semi-detached clowning does shadow Romeo earlier in the play, and there is every reason why it should follow him to the mouth of Juliet's tomb, throwing into perspective the words and actions of the distracted lover.

Wiles's assumption that the lines ascribed to 'Peter' in 5.3 offer 'evidence of a preliminary version of the play' (90) accords with the traditional assumption that Q2 was close to Shakespeare's original manuscript or 'foul papers'. But they make much more sense as an inventive *revision* of the somewhat pedestrian Q1 at this point. As we shall see with the folio text of *The Merry Wives of Windsor*, the best explanation for what lay behind it is indeed an authorial manuscript (or something close to it), but one that incompletely or messily records an unfinished expansion/revision. And however we account for the differences between the two versions of *Romeo and Juliet*, they cannot be explained in terms of Q1 being a stage adaptation of a 'literary' Q2: the role of a clown, which can barely be contained by the words on a page, is a highly *theatrical* phenomenon. And Kemp's role is much fuller, stronger, and more inventive in Q2 than it is in Q1. It would have been a brave—and prosaically minded—man who cut it.

This accords with two other instances we have noted—both involving Kemp—where the stagecraft is markedly more sophisticated. The sequence in which Romeo, Mercutio, and Benvolio crash the Capulet ball wittily uses the domestic mayhem of the serving-men to occlude the transition from outside to inside. And Kemp's mute appearance in 2.4, just long enough to stretch out the rack of Juliet's

---

back the watch. But it does suggest that the compilers of the folio text, who presumably had some knowledge of the acting tradition, did associate 'Peter' with the scene. Moreover, they did *not* associate Balthasar with it. After the Romeo/Paris fight they follow both the earlier versions in designating Romeo's companion simply as 'Man'. But at the point where 'Romeo's man' gives his version of events to the Prince he has quite unaccountably become 'Boy' (TLN 3,146), rather than 'Balth', as in both the other versions. Balthasar is in fact a much more shadowy figure in both Q2 and F than he is in Q1—he is addressed by name once early in 5.1 (5.1.12, K4r; TLN 2,734) but is otherwise 'Man'. He is only otherwise 'Balth' in Q2 when he addresses the Prince. In F he is never Balthasar again. In respect of my argument that in Q2 it is *meant* to be 'Peter'/Kemp who accompanies Romeo to Juliet's tomb, it should be noted that Balthasar may only have come into being in 5.1 because Kemp was not available. The scene immediately before is 4.4 with the musicians and there would not have been time for him to morph into the role of Romeo's 'man'—which he has become by 5.3. The muddled states of Q2 and F may suggest that Shakespeare was looking for a way to dispense with Balthasar's role and give it to Kemp. It was not until Q4 of *Romeo and Juliet*, an undated edition later than the First Folio, that Balthasar was consistently established as Romeo's 'Man', as he clearly had been in Q1, though Q2 and F tell a different story.

frustration, is a telling example of the mature Shakespeare's grasp of the possibilities at his disposal with Kemp in the company. So too, I argue, is the reinvented 5.3. Q2 simply offers a more imaginatively staged version of the play than Q1. For Q1 to be a redaction of Q2 for public performance, we have to imagine that someone clinically cut a good deal of *theatrical* sophistication (much of it affecting Kemp) in addition to the hundreds of lines that it strips from all the main characters—lines that, in the case of Juliet, create a tragic heroine of credible substance for Romeo, and in that of Friar Laurence a very different pattern of motivation. No sign of those nuanced elaborations survives the transition.

Q1 is a perfectly playable, more than adequate telling of the story of *Romeo and Juliet*. But Q2 shows something with so much more ambition, both linguistic and theatrical. The ambition is even there in the size of the cast called for. As Romeo and the others make their way to the Capulets' ball (an indeterminate number of masquers in Q1, Sc. 4), the Q2 text calls for 'five or six other masquers' (1.4.0.1–2) and seems to expect them all to run into the four serving-men who are making ready (of whom there are no equivalents in Q1). In Sc. 17 of Q1 it is a single serving-man who enters with logs and coals (I1r); in Q2 it is 'three or four with spits and logs, and baskets' (4.4.13.1–2; K1v). In the 'foul papers' fantasy world such permissive cast numbers betray a Shakespeare who leaves the practical details to others. Here I suggest he is encouraging his fellow sharers in the company to put on as impressive a show for a court performance as the budget would allow.

The ambition is likewise there, for example, in the second Chorus, at the head of Act 2 (not in Q1), one of many examples of the play's self-conscious relationship to sonnets and their conventional intertwining of love and death. It is also there in Old Montague's expanded account of not knowing what afflicts Romeo (1.1.131–42, 146–55; A4v–B1r), which establishes a more substantial character for himself while stoking audience expectations about the entrance of the star actor—presumably Burbage. These can easily be dismissed as 'unnecessary' literary adornments, but I suggest that they are rather signs of *amplificatio* such as I discussed in relation to *Henry V* (see p. 193). They are markers, perhaps—like the truly imaginative expansion of Kemp's role throughout the play—of something 'Newly corrected, augmented, and amended' for the court.

b. *Hamlet* and Succession

Adam Gopnik: There are those who think that the late long First Folio *Hamlet* is a messy author's expansion of the short, stern early quarto, but they are a minority. (Gopnik 2007: 70)

Elizabeth Kolbert: Mapping [genetic differences between species of humans] is, in principle, pretty straightforward—no harder, say, than comparing rival editions of *Hamlet*. (Kolbert 2011: 72)

The challenge of understanding the relationship between the three surviving texts of *Hamlet* has become almost proverbial; and, like the Shakespeare authorship debate, it is a matter on which unwary amateurs often have a ready opinion. I do not pretend to have all the answers. But I do believe that the three versions contain traces within them that allow us to fix, within a few years, the moment that each of them came together approximately in the form that was printed. And I suggest, on the basis of the evidence advanced in this book, that the overwhelmingly most likely explanation for the most substantial differences—those between the earlier quarto (Q1, 1603), on the one hand, and the later quarto (Q2, 1604/5) and folio (F, 1623), on the other—is revision (*substantial* revision) for court performance.

I shall pursue my case in two stages, firstly looking at plot or structural differences between Q1 and the two later-published versions, and secondly looking at thematic traces within the differences. In the latter I shall yet again be following in the footsteps of Roslyn Knutson to locate some of those traces in the explanations given by each text for why the players of *The Murder of Gonzago* are touring. But I also want to shape my argument around another trace running through the three versions: the succession question.

Harold Jenkins' Arden 2 edition of *Hamlet* had been long awaited when it finally appeared in 1982. Jenkins was at the time general editor of the long-respected series which, more than any other, had championed the textual theory of W. W. Greg, R. B. McKerrow, and other New Bibliographers. And it was anticipated that he would bring the weight of its accumulated wisdom to bear on the most problematic of Shakespearean texts. He did not disappoint. He was categorical (with a conviction deeply fuelled by the 'foul papers' orthodoxy) that Q1, Q2, and F all derived ultimately from a single Shakespearean original, which suffered various forms of abuse as it was transmitted to posterity and which it was his responsibility, as far as possible, to reconstruct.

In respect of Q1, Jenkins could hardly have been more dismissive:

> Q1 is now recognized to belong to a category of quartos which it is one of the achievements of twentieth-century textual scholarship to have distinguished. It is, in the sense

in which the word is now used, a 'bad' quarto, one, that is to say, whose text, deriving from performance, lacks a direct manuscript link with what the author wrote... Objectors to 'memorial reconstruction' as the explanation of the bad quartos have sometimes complained that there is no contemporary 'testimony' to such a practice; but if you come upon a mutilated corpse you don't deny a murder because no one has reported one. (1982: 19–20)

Much of this is, of course, true. Such a text does 'lack a direct manuscript link with what the author wrote' and its deficiencies *may* largely derive from 'memorial reconstruction', though without the pejorative connotations which the analogy with murder here implies. What none of this proves, however—though it purports to, in the subsequent demonstration of the mangling of the text wrought by misremembering—is that Q2 or F, or something very like them, existed *before* Q1. All it proves is that a manuscript sharing *some* of the language of Q2 and F existed earlier—but whether it was (say) closer in length to Q1 or to Q2 there is no way of finally knowing.

Jenkins also blames larger apparent anomalies in Q1 to misremembering, including the transfer of 'whole stretches of dialogue from one part of the play to another' (31).[13] As he notes, 'the most remarkable of such transpositions brings forward the "nunnery" scene and with it the "To be or not to be" soliloquy... from the third act to the second' (ibid). But he is quick to stamp on any suggestion that this might be evidence of authorial revision: 'That the position of the nunnery scene in Q1 is erroneous has been perceived by the leading modern scholars, but their view that it represents a deliberate alteration and not just a lapse of memory I find wholly unacceptable. This prevalent belief is simply another legacy of former misconceptions about the status of Q1' (32). Those 'misconceptions', of course, centre on Q1 being written earlier than the other texts, and relate to 'continuous copy'-type explanations about the evolution of the text (see p. 151).

Jenkins' confidence finally falters in respect of 'other modifications in Q1 [which] are more problematical. A new scene between Horatio and the Queen is introduced, and two of the dramatis personae [Corambis/Polonius; Reynaldo/Montano] are given different names; and these things... can hardly be inadvertent' (33). He offers no satisfactory explanation for any of this, though he tries to ascribe the new scene to an extreme form of misremembering. 'The scene between Horatio and the Queen was presumably suggested by a recollection of the tête-à-tête between these two which F's contracted stage version gives us at the beginning of IV.v, but in matter it replaces IV.vi: instead of our seeing Horatio receiving Hamlet's letter, Q1 has Horatio telling the Queen he has received it. An account of Hamlet's changing the commissions is also incorporated here instead of being left for Hamlet to give in person at the beginning of V.ii' (ibid). As he sees it, a scene 'which thus amalgamates three episodes in one may well seem a well-contrived abridgement' (33), but he is loath to ascribe this to deliberate artistry,

---

[13] To anyone really interested in examining the relationship between the *Hamlet* texts, let me recommend *The Three-Text 'Hamlet'*, edited by Bernice W. Kliman and Paul Bertram (2003). It prints the three texts in parallel, with a separate column for Q1 transpositions.

explores what it may or may not owe to the reporter of the text's recollections of an *Ur-Hamlet* text and of *The Spanish Tragedy* (from which there are evident borrowings in the Queen's words), and concludes that what he takes to be changes from the Shakespearean original 'derive from the reporter's own attempt to sustain a coherent plot when memory faltered' (34).

But this will hardly do to account for what Jenkins recognizes as the more critical 'change': 'there is a divergence in the attitude of the Queen, who is shown in league with Hamlet against the King; and Q1 has anticipated this development by making her promise Hamlet, at the end of her scene in her closet (III.iv), to assist in his revenge' (33). However we cut this, there is a deliberate and sustained difference in the plotting, characterization, and scenic structure of Q1 from what we find in Q2 and F. This simply cannot be ascribed to faulty memory, though Jenkins effectively ducks behind the possibility that this too derives from muddled memory of a lost *Ur-Hamlet*.

Paul Menzer, in his meticulous, acting-focused examination of the relationship between the three versions of *Hamlet*, comes to a radically different kind of conclusion about Q1: 'I argue that the pattern of cues within Q1 (and their departures from those of Q2 and F) suggest that whoever the creator(s) was of the text, he was not intentionally trying to reproduce either Q2 or F or a "touring version" and that, furthermore, the manuscript was created solely for publication (or reading), as its cues render it virtually unactable...It recalls and rewrites the "Tragedy of Hamlet," performed at various times and in various places in the late sixteenth- and early seventeenth-century England' (2008: 24, 176; see also Lesser and Stallybrass 2008). Terri Bourus goes even further, arguing that Q1 *is* the so-called *ur-Hamlet*, which she believes was written *c.* 1588–89 (2014: 135–79).

Menzer's argument squares very readily with Tiffany Stern's recent re-exploration of the possible use of shorthand (and/or 'swift-writing') during performance in the creation of some play texts, asking whether 'it is worth exploring whether *Hamlet* Q1 might have its origins in a "noted" text' (2013: 11).[14] Her enquiry sheds extremely plausible new light on the verbal differences between that text and Q2 and F, and on such features as the stage directions—which are often observations rather than directions as such. It would also explain the unactable cues which Menzer finds. Her argument, however, becomes much less convincing when she confronts what we might call the structural differences between Q1 and the later-published texts: 'How, though, to explain the larger oddities of *Hamlet* Q1: the fact that the order of *Hamlet* Q1 is different from the order of Q2/F? That might, of course, reflect the version of the play that Q1 records. Yet significant reordering is a feature of noted sermons...Material of a similar kind tends to be pooled together' (15). From this she builds to explain actual additions to the play, compared with other versions: 'Larger additions in *Hamlet* Q1 simplify the play and are partly responsible for its sheer length. In the most major addition, Horatio relates to the Queen a letter he has received telling of Hamlet's escape from the ship taking him to England. The Queen then declares her disillusionment with the

---

[14] See, however, Terri Bourus's forceful challenge to Stern (2014: 69ff).

King and loyalty to Hamlet. This addition compresses 4.6 and 5.2, dispenses with some additional characters, and makes the Queen, who "was the character that lent itself most readily to... simplification with the least loss of subtlety", less complex and more sympathetic' (16; referring to Melchiori 1992: 202).

This comes remarkably close to the conclusions reached both by Jenkins (discussed earlier) and by Lukas Erne, though by different means. All three credit the changes to the supposed scribes of Q1, be it the actors involved in 'memorial reconstruction', those producing a 'minimal' text from Shakespeare's 'maximal' one, or the reporters taking the action down by shorthand: when memory fails, or they need to cover a lot of plot in a short scene, or they simply cannot keep up, they make up their own version to cover the gap. That is, they behave rather like dramatists... Erne ascribes the distinctively different plotting in Q1 to a deliberate, practical abridgement of a text close to Q2/F for the purposes of staging the play: 'This fusion of several sequences into one short scene considerably condenses the action where Q2 and F slows it down, thereby allowing for a swift, action-packed and exciting finale' (2003: 238). He sees a similar process in the characterization: 'In the play we know [the Queen] is a highly complex figure whose motives and allegiances are far from clear. In Q1, on the other hand, her allegiance to Horatio and Hamlet is unambiguous... It is a feature not just of Q1's Queen but of the short text as a whole that characterization is less multi-layered and complex than it is in the long texts' (239–40).

For either Stern's or Erne's scenarios to be true, we have to posit the existence of a note-taker (or note-takers) who make up plot when they cannot follow it or redactors of resolutely prosaic mind from among the actors, capable of draining imaginative vitality from a Shakespearean original—colleagues who will systematically shut down the ambiguity of the Queen's position, Hamlet's culpability in the deaths of Rosencrantz and Guildenstern, and lose the gathering suspense of Hamlet's stage-managed reappearance in Denmark as 'Hamlet the Dane' (Q2, M4v; 5.1.247).[15] What Stern describes when she talks about the insertion of the new scene in Q1, and the rearrangements of other scenes, sounds—as I have suggested—suspiciously like the work of a *dramatist*. And the same is true of Erne's putative actors. The fact is that anyone capable of devising the new scene in Q1 or draining Q2/F of such colour was perfectly capable of writing Q1 from scratch. However we understand the oddities of Q1, we have to understand that whoever devised it was familiar with elements of what we now recognize as Q2/F, though he (or they) did not do the best job of reporting them. But we should also understand that he saw a play that was different structurally in some respects, and less sophisticated in its characterizations. Is it not so much more plausible that such sophistications were the consequence of an imaginative re-engagement with a less complex original, a development from less to more such as we traced with *Henry V*?

---

[15] All quotations are from the relevant text in the Arden 3 edition of *Hamlet*, by Ann Thompson and Neil Taylor (2006), which offers modernized texts of all three versions. In this instance I have not thought it useful to cite details from the Bevington edition, which is based on Q2 but conflates material from F. I do, however, still include signature references to the quartos and Through-Line-Numbering to the folio.

And indeed that Q2 was, as advertised, *newly* 'enlarged to almost as much again as it was'?

THE 'MOMENTS' OF THE THREE TEXTS

The likelihood of such purposeful revision is further increased when we consider those trace elements in the three versions which can help us pin when each came together as it was printed.[16] These are to be found in moments when authorial intervention is overwhelmingly the most likely explanation for change: in the texts' discussions of the reasons why the players we see in the play have abandoned their city base to go on tour; and in their depiction of Fortinbras and the succession issue.

Let us start with Knutson's analysis, which to my mind is one of the most liberating documents ever written on the play. Concentrating on the passages in the different versions about the boy actors (only in Q1 and F—there is no equivalent in Q2), advanced to explain why the players are travelling, she concludes:

> the manuscript Shakespeare wrote in 1599–1600 was altered in a process of deletions and additions that produced Q1, Q2, and F (more or less directly, at different times, for different reasons)...the question is not *whether* Shakespeare's manuscript was revised but *when* and *in what ways*. I suggest the following textual history: a passage very like the 'humour of the children' passage existed in the *Hamlet* that was staged at the Globe in 1600; that passage was cut by 1604 and its place filled with the line about an inhibition, caused by an innovation; at a still later date (*circa* 1606), the 'little eyases' passage was added in the place formerly occupied by the 'humour of the children' passage in the *Hamlet* of 1600. (Knutson 2001: 112–13).[17]

It is important to recognize that Q1 does not simply reflect the text written *c.* 1600. Paul Menzer puts it well when he speaks of how 'it recalls and rewrites the "Tragedy of Hamlet," performed at various times and in various places in the late sixteenth- and early seventeenth-century England'. But within that it does preserve the earliest intimations we have of the play, including most particularly the reference to 'humour of the children'. The superficial resemblance between the references in Q1 and F to the boy actors had long fuelled the assumption that both passages derived from one mother-text. 'Gilderstone' in Q1 explains that the players are on the road because 'novelty carries it away. For the principal public audience that came to them are turned to private plays, and to the humour of children' (Q1, E3r; Sc. 7.271–3). 'Rosincrance', in a much longer passage in F, tells Hamlet that 'there

---

[16] An earlier advocate of the case for purposeful, possibly authorial revision as the reason for multiple versions of the play, to some extent responding to Jenkins' edition, was Philip Edwards in his New Cambridge edition, who argued that 'the variations in the text of *Hamlet* are not alternative versions of a single original text but representations of different stages in the play's development' (1984: 8).

[17] Bourus, who does not cite Knutson, has the following datings: Q1 1588–9; Q2 1603–4; F 1602 (2014: 135–79, 182–96, 191–207). I find Knutson's explanation of F's 'little eyases' passage, and consequent dating *c.* 1606–8, far more convincing.

is, sir, an eyrie of children, little eyases that cry out on the top of the question' (F, 2.2.337–9; TLN 1,386–91). There is a big difference between 'novelty' being the reason for drawing away audiences and 'cry[ing] out on the top of the question', making a scandalous noise like fledgling hawks. Knutson convincingly suggests that the former relates to the reopening of the indoor boy theatres—Paul's and the Children of the Queen's Chapel—in 1599/1600, after years of inactivity; while the latter refers to the notoriety of the Blackfriars boys around 1606–8, as they repeatedly staged political and satirical scandals—Daniel's *Philotas*, Chapman, Jonson, and Marston's *Eastward Ho!*, Day's *The Isle of Gulls*, Chapman's *Byron* plays, and others.[18]

The F passage more fully reads:

> *Rosincrance:* there is, sir, an eyrie of children, little eyases that cry out on the top of the question and are most tyrannically clapped for't. These are now the fashion, and so berattle the common stages (so they call them) that many wearing rapiers are afraid of goose-quills and dare scarce come thither.
>
> *Hamlet:* What, are they children? Who maintains 'em? How are they escotted? Will they pursue the quality no longer than they can sing?[19] Will they not say afterwards if they should grow themselves to common players—as it is most like if their means are no better—their writers do them wrong to make them exclaim against their own succession? (F, 2.2.337–49; TLN 1,386–98)

Shakespeare here joined Thomas Heywood, who in *An Apology for Actors* (written c. 1607/8) similarly decried this policy:

> now to speak of some abuse lately crept into the quality, as an inveighing against the state, the court, the law, the city, and their governments, with the particularizing of private men's humours (yet alive), noble-men and others. I know it distastes many; neither do I any way approve it, nor dare I by any means excuse it. The liberty which some arrogate to themselves, committing their bitterness and liberal invectives against all estates to the mouths of children, supposing their juniority to be a privilege for any railing, be it never so violent, I could advise all such to curb and limit this presumed liberty within the bands of discretion and government. (printed 1612, G3v)

Two senior figures from the public theatres thus rebuked the Blackfriars management for their provocative policies, which threatened all their livelihoods.[20]

---

[18] The Children of the Queen's Chapel had been reformed in 1604 as the Children of the Queen's Revels (i.e. Queen Anna's). By 1606 they had been stripped of the royal association, presumably because of the scandals. In 1608 their licence was withdrawn altogether. Their title changed so often in those times that it makes sense just to call them the Blackfriars boys, after their theatre. See Dutton 2002a.

[19] The acting profession was known as 'the quality'. Hamlet's concern is that this is a high-risk strategy for their long-term employment as actors, either because they will individually acquire bad reputations or (more likely) because the authorities will put the theatres out of business. Intriguingly this is one of only two passages in the play that use the word 'succession' (discussed later in this chapter), and this one only occurs in F.

[20] Compare this with the 1610 revisions to *Mucedorus*, which address the situation after the Blackfriars boys have been closed down and their theatre made available to the King's Men; see p. 113.

Significantly, all three of Knutson's proposed dates (Q1 1599–1600, Q2 by 1604, F around 1606) miss 1601, the year to which conflationists most commonly assign the original play from which they all supposedly derived (Jenkins 1982: 13). That assignment is largely because it was thought that the 'little eyases' passage referred not only to the revived boy actors but more specifically to the so-called 'War of the Theatres'—a lively exchange of satiric invective, mainly between authors writing for the two revived boy companies, though involving at least one intervention from the Chamberlain's Men (see Knutson 2001; Bednarz 2001; Hirschfeld 2004). The 'War' reached its height in 1601 with Jonson's *Poetaster* for the Children of the Chapel and Dekker's *Satiromastix*, a shared project of the Lord Chamberlain's Men and Paul's Boys (Jenkins 1982: 472–3; Loewenstein 1988). The particular passage that prompted this interpretation is Rosincrance's claim that 'There was for a while no money bid for argument unless the poet and the player went to cuffs on it' (F, 2.2.352–4; TLN 1,401–3). But in the context of Hamlet's concern for the boys' 'succession' this makes better sense as a reference to the later reckless scandal-mongering of the Blackfriars management than to the 'War of the Theatres', which was in essence little more than a publicity campaign generated by the competing acting companies and never anything like as serious. *Hamlet* was also assigned to 1601 because it was assumed that the passage in Q2 which replaces the passages about boy players in both other versions (about 'their inhibition' coming 'by means of the late innovation' [Q2, F2v; 2.2.295–6]), referred to the Earl of Essex's rebellion of February 1601 and so was written not long after it. In this assumption, too, I shall argue that the conflationists were wrong.

What I want to add to Knutson's analysis is a different mechanism to explain how and why the play was revised as it was, and especially how Q2 came into being at such gargantuan length. Q1 is only 2,154 lines long, notably short by comparison with most of Shakespeare's tragedies and histories. Q2 *Hamlet* accurately proclaims itself to be 'enlarged almost as much again as it was, according to the true and perfect copy'. At 3,668 lines it is the longest text in the Shakespeare canon, and David Bevington speaks the traditional wisdom when he says that 'the text of the second quarto is too long to be accommodated in the two hours' traffic of the stage' and assumes that it would have had to be cut to be performed at all (2008: Appendix 1, A-16). As readers will by now anticipate, my explanation for this dramatic 'enlargement' is that Q2 was prepared for performance in the one venue in early seventeenth-century England where length was little object: the court, and in this case specifically the court of James I.

Q1 AND SUCCESSION

The question of who was to succeed Elizabeth I—and how—hung over the drama of her reign from its first major work, *Gorboduc, or Ferrex and Porrex*, to *Hamlet*, one of its last. *Hamlet* is, of all plays, one most deeply informed by issues of regime change and succession anxieties. The play begins with a new king and replays obsessively the tale of how he came to the throne by murdering his brother; it depicts an attempt by Laertes, seeking to avenge his father, which could easily have ended with the overthrow of Claudius; but it ends instead with Claudius' death by other means and replacement by young Fortinbras of Norway, passing over the also dead Hamlet, 'Th'expectation and rose of the fair state' (Q2, G3r; 3.1.151). It is a sustained demonstration of how *not* to do it.

A good deal of this is inherent in the material that the Elizabethans inherited from Saxo Grammaticus and François de Belleforest, early tellers of the Hamlet story, and this doubtless helps to explain why they revisited it. But the figure of Fortinbras is new and distinctive in the only Elizabethan versions to have survived, those of Shakespeare's play. Fortinbras complicates succession issues radically by translating what had been an intra-family revenge plot into one of regime change. This new element makes him an ideal feature of the play to observe in relation to its evolution from 'bad' quarto through 'good' quarto to First Folio text.

Q1 *Hamlet* is, in Knutson's analysis, clearly an Elizabethan play, written around the time *Julius Caesar* contemplated the horrors of unregulated regime change and *As You Like It* conjured a pastoral comedy from the same concerns. It was entered in the Stationers' Register on 26 July 1602 and so certainly antedated the Queen's death. What relationship the text printed in 1603 had with any earlier Hamlet plays there is finally no way of knowing, despite Terri Bourus's robust claim that the *ur-Hamlet is* that text (2014). A play certainly existed by 1589, when Thomas Nashe's preface to Robert Greene's *Menaphon* satirically evoked 'English Seneca', who 'will afford you whole Hamlets, I should say handfuls of tragical speeches' (Nashe 1904–10: 3.315). This may have been the same *Hamlet* that Philip Henslowe records having a single performance at Newington Butts in June 1594, and again the one that Thomas Lodge saw which caused him to write in 1596 about the 'ghost which cried so miserably at the Theatre, like an oyster-wife, Hamlet, revenge' (Foakes 2002: 21; Lodge 1596: 56; Marino 2011: 75–8).

Knowing no more than these and other traces, however, we cannot know one thing which I have suggested is critical to Shakespeare's versions of *Hamlet*: who added the figure of Fortinbras? In the earliest tellings of the legend, to be found in Saxo Grammaticus' twelfth-century *Historiae Danicae*, there is no parallel to Fortinbras, because Amleth overcomes Feng (the ur-Claudius) and then is acclaimed king himself. And in this respect the French prose version that Shakespeare himself probably read, that by François de Belleforest in his *Histoires Tragique* (first published 1570), followed Saxo. The death of Hamlet in pursuing revenge for his father's murder, and with it the extinction of the Danish royal line, leaving a vacuum filled by Fortinbras, is first extant in Shakespeare's versions of the play.

I describe the addition of Fortinbras to the plot as 'critical' because it is the one narrative change which allows the succession issues in the play to map suggestively onto those of England as the reign of Elizabeth neared its end. The Tudor dynasty was bound to die with her. The search was not just for a new prince, but for a new line of princes. And there was every chance that this would not emerge from within the kingdom but would come—perhaps be imposed—from abroad. There was no shortage of claimants to the English throne which Elizabeth would leave vacant. At home the heirs of Edward Seymour, Earl of Hertford, carried the strongest claim through the Grey family. Lady Arbella Stuart's claim derived from Margaret Tudor, elder sister of Henry VIII, who married James IV of Scotland and later the Earl of Angus; the fact that she was an English resident landowner gave her precedence in some eyes. Overseas, Philip II—and subsequently Philip III—of Spain pressed the claim of their daughter/sister, the Spanish Infanta, which derived from John of Gaunt, Duke of Lancaster and father of Henry IV. But the most credible claim was always that of Elizabeth's 'cousin of Scotland', James VI, also descended from Margaret Tudor but by a senior and Scots royal line. In this world, a victorious, living Hamlet at the end of the play made no suggestive sense at all.

The ultimate role of Fortinbras in all three versions of Shakespeare's *Hamlet* is to pick up the pieces when Hamlet himself dies, to assume the throne of Denmark, and implicitly in the not-too-distant future—when the 'impotent and bed-rid' king, his uncle, dies (Q2, B4r; 1.2.29)—to assume also the throne of Norway, once held by his namesake father. It is little remarked that Denmark–Norway enjoyed a personal union of the crowns between 1536 and 1814, with a single king reigning over two politically distinct countries. There were other instances of this in Shakespeare's day: Philip II of Spain was also King of Portugal; Henri IV of France was also King of Navarre. But Denmark–Norway was the only instance in Northern Europe, and it spoke directly to the situation of James VI of Scotland, whose queen was from Denmark. When James finally did succeed to the English throne, he emulated his brother-in-law, Christian IV of Denmark–Norway, in bearing two crowns, those of a northern and a southern kingdom. Fortenbrasse (Q1) in the play of *Hamlet* foreshadows that outcome.

It is difficult to believe that contemporary audiences of Q1 did not see what we might call this wish-fulfilment element in the dramatic retelling of the old tale, though it is not heavily underscored. The path of Fortenbrasse's career, more familiar to us in the richer detail of Q2 and F, is sketched in: he plans to avenge his father's death at the hands of old Hamlet by attacking Denmark; following an embassy from the Danish king to old Norway he is ordered not to do this, and chooses instead to use his troops against the Poles; we briefly see him for the first time on Danish soil, seeking the pass he has negotiated through the country (Q1, G4v; Sc. 12.1–5); finally he appears at Elsinore after the deaths of the Queen, Leartes, the King, and Hamlet. And he stakes his claim almost as an afterthought:

> I have some rights of memory to this kingdom,
> Which now to claim my leisure doth invite me.
>
> (Q1, I4r; Sc. 17.126–7)

It is a functional solution, hardly a metaphysical one.

Q2 AND SUCCESSION: INHIBITION AND INNOVATION

The Q2 text, by contrast, invests the whole issue of succession with metaphysical circumstance, a good deal of it focused on Fortinbrasse (as he here appears). This can best be explained by the circumstances of its composition, which I further suggest were dictated by the expectation of presenting the vastly expanded play at the court of Fortinbrasse himself, James I. To pin this to the court of King James we need to consider its likely dating, which again is best deduced from the text's distinctly different explanation of why the players are travelling. In this version we hear nothing of 'novelty', 'the humour of children', or of 'little eyases'. We are, rather, confronted with a terse account which contains a famous crux.

Rosencraus explains that: 'I think their inhibition comes by the means of the late innovation' (Q2, F2v; 2.2.295–6). 'Inhibition' and 'innovation' have both been subjected to extreme scrutiny. The former seems to refer to a ban on playing, and there have been numerous attempts to identify this as a topical allusion to an actual ban in the real world (Knutson 2001: 115–18; Bourus 2014: 184–7). Many of the conflationists, convinced that the references to the boy actors in both Q1 and F pointed to the War of the Theatres in 1601, wanted to construe 'innovation' as an 'uprising' of some sort, that would most likely point to the Essex rebellion of February in that year. It seemed logical, therefore, to try to find an 'inhibition' in the same time frame, though in fact nothing we know of fits the bill. But if, as I argue, Q2 dates from a court revision of 1603/4, the strongest and most logical connotation of 'innovation' would be 'new regime'.

In fact this suggestion was first made as long ago as 1785 by John Monck Mason, who found such a usage in the Shirley play, *The Coronation*. The king, Demetrius, has been deposed in favour of someone masquerading as his elder brother, and two gentlemen discuss the outcome:

> Philocles: The new King has possession.
> Lisander: And is like
>   To keep't. We are alone: what dost think of
>   This innovation? Is't not a fine jig?[21]

As Mason suggested, this probably means 'the late change of government', for which of course in *Hamlet*—after 1603—the accession of James I would constitute a real-life equivalent (Mason 1785: 381). For many years, however, the primacy usually accorded F—where both the inhibition/innovation and the 'little eyases' passages appear, misleadingly seeming to point to 1601—made Mason's suggestion unthinkable.

Yet in the context of James's accession we have a perfect accompanying 'inhibition'. Looking to forestall any disturbances, the Privy Council closed the London theatres on 19 March 1603, in anticipation of Elizabeth's death. They may well not have reopened that year. Although Sir Robert Cecil—the kingmaker—proclaimed James king immediately after the old Queen died, there was anxiety as people waited to see if his accession was contested. Plague broke out in April and was certainly bad enough by 19 May also to have closed the theatres, since the King's Men's new patent contains a proviso about their licence to play only 'when the

---

[21] Shirley 1640: H3r. The 1640 quarto credits Fletcher as author and it was reprinted in the second Beaumont and Fletcher folio (1679), where Mason found it. Modern scholarship gives the play to Shirley.

infection of the plague shall decrease' (Gurr 2004a: 254). And it apparently did not do that until Easter 1604. Between the change of monarchs and the plague there were clearly overlapping 'inhibitions'.

So if the company played Q2 during the Revels season of 1603/4 it would have been immediately intelligible that the players in *Hamlet* were touring because of an 'inhibition' in the city that followed ('as a result of') an 'innovation'. The title page of Q1 tells us that the play is: 'As it hath been diverse times acted by his Highness's servants in the City of London: as also in the two Universities of Cambridge and Oxford, and else-where'. Given what we know of their touring, this must have been in the summer of either 1601 or 1603. There was no plague or other 'inhibition' to send them abroad in the earlier year (though the 'novelty' of competition from the boys might have been an issue), but in 1603 we have a record of them performing in Oxford (Gurr 2004a: 59). So there is a good chance that the King's Men, imitating their fictional counterparts, had toured *Hamlet* (a version of something imperfectly captured in Q1) in the summer when James came to England.

This wry piece of in-joking was probably all the more pointed in that the King's Men had to 'travel' further that winter than they normally did to perform for the court, which removed itself from London to avoid the worst of the plague—the 'inhibition' continued. Their first performance that Revels season was at the Earl of Pembroke's estate at Wilton, a journey so exceptional that John Heminge was paid £30 'for the pains and expenses of himself and the rest of the company in coming from Mortlake in the county of Surrey unto the court aforesaid and there p[re]senting before his Ma[jesty] one play' (Chambers 1923: 4.168). And all bar one of their other court performances that season were at Hampton Court, the furthest flung of the royal palaces regularly in use, some eleven miles upstream from London.[22]

Do any other circumstances give us reason to suppose that *Hamlet* was performed at court in 1603/4? Ordinarily we would have little chance of answering that, because so few of the records of the titles of plays performed there have survived. But, as we have seen, by the sheerest good luck we know what was performed there in the *following* Revels season, 1604/5 (see Chapter 1, pp. 35–6 and n. 21). That Christmastide the King's Men performed eleven times in all, and the plays were *Othello*, *Merry Wives*, *Measure for Measure*, *The Comedy of Errors*, *Love's Labour's Lost*, *Henry V*, *Every Man Out of His Humour*, *Every Man In His Humour*, *The Spanish Maze* (an anonymous, lost play), and *The Merchant of Venice* twice, repeated by the King's command. The sheer number of performances is staggering—almost twice as many as in the company's busiest Elizabethan season (1596/7), and three times a usual year. And they had performed nine times in 1603/4 (including Wilton). That is, over two seasons they performed twenty times—perhaps eighteen plays, allowing for repetitions.

The next remarkable fact, other than the sheer volume, is how many of the 1604/5 plays were by Shakespeare—eight, including the repetition. It is as if, faced with the need to impress the new royals, the King's Men pulled out the family

---

[22] The only exception was their last performance, at Whitehall—James's preferred residence—on Shrove Sunday.

silver, the repertory of their star 'ordinary poet'.²³ They would have had guidance on this from Tilney, who made the final decisions about what went on, but probably also from the one new sharing member of the company when they reformed as the King's Men. Laurence Fletcher had spent several years in Edinburgh entertaining the then James VI of Scotland (see p. 268). His knowledge of the King and Queen and their tastes must have been invaluable. At all events, if 1604/5 is any guide at all, it is a fair guess that a further five or six Shakespeare plays had been performed in 1603/4. If popularity or reputation is anything to go by, it is reasonable to suppose that these would have included *Richard III, 1 Henry IV, Romeo and Juliet, A Midsummer Night's Dream*—and *Hamlet*. Indeed, given that we know that *Othello* led off the 1604/5 season and *King Lear* led off 1606/7 it is very tempting to suppose that *Hamlet* was the first play James saw in his new kingdom.²⁴

Let us conjecture, then, that Edmund Tilney, drawing on his unrivalled knowledge of the drama of the day and contemplating the need to cater for a greatly expanded Revels season, suggested to the King's Men that *Hamlet* was a play ripe for revision and a prominent court performance. How might Shakespeare have set about it? As we have observed, John Kerrigan has described Shakespeare as a 'tinkering' reviser, what he also dubbed a 'fidgeting authorial reviser', rather than one who made mainly self-contained cuts and interpolations (see p. 112). That was largely on the evidence of the differences between the quarto and folio texts of *King Lear*. And a similar conclusion might be drawn from, say, the differences between the first quarto and folio texts of *Richard III*, which can best be accounted for by a thorough, 'tinkering' rewrite (see Hammond 1981: 2).

Both of those pairs of plays are much more similar to each other (in terms of both length and verbal quality) than Q1 and Q2 *Hamlet*. But the pattern seems to fit. Of course we cannot know at the level of language how exactly Shakespeare behaved in making the revision that produced Q2 *Hamlet*, since what he revised would have been the manuscript that ultimately lay behind Q1, not Q1 itself with all its deficiencies. But while, as we shall see, there are some entirely new passages, and a whole scene (that involving Gertrude and Horatio) is redistributed by different means, on the whole the revision takes the form of 'tinkering' on a grand scale, of a fundamental creative re-imagining of the text and its language. Shakespeare sat down to reinvent, not to patch and edit.

The theatres were closed for most of 1603. If Shakespeare did not tour with the company during this period, he would have had plenty of time—and incentive—to conduct a thorough, 'tinkering' revision of *Hamlet* before the first Revels season of the new reign. If I am right about this, Q2 (and indeed F) are both Jacobean

---

²³ They did something similar in 1612/13, the Revels season which included the wedding of Princess Elizabeth to the Elector Palatine, when we again have titles. The King's Men were called on to perform twenty plays and eight of them (nine, if we include *Cardenio*) were by Shakespeare.

²⁴ This is, of course, pure supposition. There is no record of *Hamlet* at court earlier than 1637 (Adams 1917: 76). There is some evidence for *A Midsummer Night's Dream*; Sir Dudley Carleton reported that 'On New Year's night we had a play of Robin Goodfellow' (Chambers 1923: 3.279). The only play that we *know* the King's Men performed in 1603/4 is the *Fair Maid of Bristow*, which was published in 1605 'As it was played at Hampton, before the King and Queen's most excellent Majesties'. This was the only Revels season under James held at Hampton Court.

texts, revised when the outcome of the succession was a fait accompli and it was possible to review events with some equanimity, whereas Q1 is an Elizabethan play, as fraught with anxieties about regime change as *Gorboduc* or *King Leir*. But it contains none of the particularities on the issue that we find in Q2 or F: nothing alluding to the Essex rebellion (which, on my dating, had not happened when the text from which it derives was written), nothing about Hamlet's sense of having been cheated of the throne, nothing about an 'inhibition' or an 'innovation', little about the workings of providence, little to underscore the parallels/contrasts between Hamlet and Fortenbrasse. These are all part of the Q2 revision.

When Shakespeare revised the play it is apparent, for example, that he approached it with classical precedents in mind. It is evident even in the naming of the characters. Q1 had set the precedent of mixing names of a Danish or Anglo-Saxon derivation (Hamlet himself, Gertred, Voltemar) with Roman ones (Horatio, Marcellus) and Greek (Leartes), and the oddly unexplained Corambis, which nevertheless *sounds* classical.[25] But Shakespeare tilts the balance further towards the classical in Q2 by renaming Corambis Polonius, which may relate to the play's interest in Poland but is unequivocally Latin in form. Much more significantly, however, he gives the king the name of Claudius—the Roman emperor who married his own niece, Agrippina, the mother of his eventual successor, Nero. In the text as we have it, this is never voiced; it only appears in the opening stage direction and speech prefix. But given the play's themes there is a good chance it was known or understood. King James, sternly tutored in his youth by the historian George Buchanan, would have known about Claudius as one whom Erasmus dubbed, in *The Education of a Christian Prince*, a type of the bad ruler. The incest theme and the uncle/stepfather role make the parallel instantly intelligible, as we might expect an educated courtly audience to appreciate, even if the name was not voiced. Other pointers also suggest that we should understand that Q2 Elsinore is reliving the internecine (and sexually excessive) power struggles of imperial Rome.

Something of this already lurked behind Q1. When Hamlet is summoned to see his mother, he resolves: 'O God, let ne'er / The heart of Nero enter this soft bosom. / Let me be cruel, not unnatural' (Q1, G1r; Sc. 9.233–5). The thought survives in both the later versions. Nero is infamous for the murder of his own mother, the very Agrippina who had incestuously married her own uncle, Claudius. Hamlet is trying to distance himself from the circle of unnatural sexuality and death with which Claudius and Gertrude have identified themselves. But the resonances of this are only fully realized in Q2 and F.

These resonances are further underscored by the first substantial interpolation in the Q2 text, for which there is no parallel in Q1 or even in F (Q2, B2r; 1.1.111–24). The passage includes Horatio's recitation of the portents said (in Plutarch and elsewhere) to have occurred before the assassination of Julius Caesar:

---

[25] There are also two with Italianate names, Francisco and Montano (who would unaccountably become Reynaldo in Q2). 'Cornelius' as he appears at TLN 213 could be classical, but it also had a modern Dutch usage. Horatio would be Horatius in true Latin, but was clearly marked out as 'more an antique Roman, / Than a Dane' (TLN 3,826–7) even in the earliest version. Laertes, the proper and Q2 form, was the father of Odysseus. It is an eclectic mix.

> In the most high and palmy state of Rome
> A little ere the mightiest Julius fell
> The graves stood tenantless and the sheeted dead
> Did squeak and gibber in the Roman streets;
> As stars with trains of fire and dews of blood,
> Disasters in the sun; and the moist star
> Upon whose influence Neptune's empire stands,
> Was sick almost to doomsday with eclipse.   (112–19)

It is commonly observed that Shakespeare had something of *Julius Caesar* in mind—written no more than a year earlier than Q1 *Hamlet*—when he has Corambis recall 'My lord, I did act Julius Caesar, I was killed in the Capitol' (Q1, F3r; Sc. 9.72–3). This foreshadows his own death. But Horatio's Q2 passage takes us far beyond Polonius' personal fate.

Disturbance in the macrocosm often mirrors disturbance in the microcosm in Shakespeare's plays at moments of regime change (e.g. *King Lear*, *Macbeth*). At such moments the affairs of men are closely in touch with otherworldly forces. Of course the Ghost flags something of this in all versions of *Hamlet*. But nothing in Q1 matches this broader Q2 reference to the definitive self-made ruler who was never quite a king, but might have been. The assassination of Julius Caesar prompted the archetypal historical example of a succession by civil war, as Rome pivoted between its republican past and imperial future. Horatio's words similarly look in two directions. He identifies the Ghost as 'prologue to the omen coming on' (Q2 B2v; 1.1.122). But it is actually the tale of a murderous regime change that has *already* secretly happened that the Ghost unfolds, prologue to his own poisoning. This will preoccupy the play at least until 'The Mousetrap', if not until Hamlet's confrontation with his mother. If the Ghost is indeed an omen of further regime change, it is a very early and indirect one. All these dimensions may be implicit or latent in Q1 but it is Q2 that realizes them.

As Q2 is the first text to discuss 'innovation', it is also the first to raise the question of how Claudius succeeded to the throne rather than (young) Hamlet. The answer is that Denmark historically had an elective monarchy, albeit one that tended to make its selection within the same royal family. A court whose Queen was sister of the King of Denmark might be expected to know this. It is never an issue in Q1. The closest we get to it is Hamlet's 'Why, I want preferment' (the universal complaint of early modern courtiers) in response to Rossencraft's attempt to elicit 'the cause and ground' of his discontent; to which Rossencraft replies 'I think not so my lord' (Q1, E2v; Sc. 7.250–1). Hamlet is, of course, toying with the old friends he no longer trusts, so it is difficult to know how serious he is.

This passage reappears in Q2 in much fuller, 'tinkered' form, and in a different place:

> Sir, I lack advancement.
> *Rosencraus*: How can that be when you have the voice of the
>   King himself for your succession in Denmark?   (Q2, H4r; 3.2.331–4)

This reiterates what Claudius had publicly said on his first appearance, repeatedly claiming Hamlet as his son: 'for let the world take note / You are the most immediate to our throne' (Q2, C1r; 1.2.108–9). The voice of the reigning monarch was obviously expected to weigh heavily in the choice of his successor.

In Q2 Hamlet does not, therefore, challenge Claudius' right to the throne until he knows that he only acquired it by murder. When he tells Rosencraus that he 'lack[s] advancement' he wraps his resentment in the language of any ambitious courtier. But when he unburdens himself to his mother in her bedroom he denounces Claudius as 'a vice of kings, / A cutpurse of the empire' who 'stole' the crown (Q2, I3v; 3.4.96–9); and he later complains to Horatio how Claudius 'Popped in between th'election and my hopes' (Q2, N1v; 5.2.64). None of this is in Q1, indicating how much more fully Q2 considers Hamlet's own ambitions, the rights and wrongs of succession, and the mechanisms that affect it, even in a constitution so alien to the English.

Another marked omission in Q1 *Hamlet* had been the lack of any reference to revolt or rebellion. In itself this does not prove that this version antedates the Essex rebellion, since any reference to that would surely have been censored in the months after the event.[26] But it is suggestive. Q1 shows Leartes returning alone, 'like a most desperate gamester' (Q1, H1v; Sc. 13.62). Q2 by contrast depicts Laertes returning from Paris 'in a riotous head' (Q2, L1r; 4.5.101) and expressly marks it as a 'rebellion [which] looks so giant-like' (121), in which Claudius' throne is at stake. He calls for his Swiss mercenary guard (97) and the messenger reports that 'the rabble' cry ' "Choose we: Laertes shall be king!" – / Caps, hands and tongue, applaud it to the clouds – / "Laertes shall be king! Laertes king!" ' (106–8). The messenger characterizes this as 'Antiquity forgot, custom not known' (104), an abandonment of the social practices by which kingship has been established and reverenced over the years. It is a reminder that, whatever divine right attends on kingship, its practical operation depends on a society's shared values, respected over time. When Q2 was performed (post-1603), this could hardly have been received without stirring memories of Essex, whose memory and earldom were rehabilitated under James. His young son became Prince Henry's companion. The Earl of Southampton, Essex's principal supporter during the rebellion, had been imprisoned for life but was freed on James's accession and restored in honour at court.

In short, Q1 *Hamlet* is not about rebellion at all; and it is only rather perfunctorily about succession—the extinction of the Danish royal family and the transfer of the throne to 'Fortenbrasse' are shown but hardly considered in depth. In this, the revenge play mirrors Shakespeare's comedies of *c.* 1598–1601 (notably *Much Ado About Nothing* and *As You Like It*), where the anxieties about succession are contained within conventional generic formulae. Q2 *Hamlet* is quite markedly and openly about both rebellion and succession, and the social practices of kingship; it

---

[26] *Some* references were censored significantly later. Daniel's *Philotas* was examined by the Privy Council in 1604 expressly because it was felt to shadow the Essex rebellion, and there is good reason to suppose that Chapman's *Byron* plays (1607–8) got into trouble partly because they 'glanced' at Essex. He remained a dangerous figure to discuss, despite his rehabilitation by James.

also picks up Q1's brief reference to the 'divinity' which 'doth wall a king' (Q1, H1v; Sc. 13.57), making it Claudius' last defence when his 'Swissers' fail and showing how it more generally (in Hamlet's own conviction) 'shapes our ends, / Rough-hew them how we will' (Q2, N1r; 5.2.10–11). There is no parallel to this conviction in Q1. So, luxuriating in its greater length, Q2 *Hamlet* contrives to be a reflection on the inscrutable processes by which a throne passes from king to king, about how it evades the threat of rebellion, and follows divine will in (eventually) effecting succession on a fitting heir. An evil king may rule for a time, even, ironically, taking *Gorboduc* to heart: he both marries and settles the succession, illegitimately wrapped for a time in the 'divinity' which walls a legitimate monarch (though it had not protected old Hamlet). The election may never in fact settle on young Hamlet, but in his death the state will be healed. A proper outcome should never ultimately be in doubt.

The most marked development in Q2 furthering this theme is the enhancement of the role of Fortenbrasse, and most particularly the expansion of what in modern texts is 4.4, where his army appears, crossing Denmark on its way to Poland. In Q1 this occupies a mere six lines (Q1, G4v; Sc. 12.1–5), and Hamlet is not involved. In Q2, Hamlet—en route to England with Rosencraus and Guyldensterne— observes the scene, questions a Norwegian captain about the campaign, and, incredulous that anyone could go to war for such a small cause, is prompted to another soliloquy: 'How all occasions do inform against me / And spur my dull revenge' (Q2, K3r&v; 4.4.31–4). So a man who veers between rashness and indecision to the point of perplexity observes and reflects upon a man who is resolutely steadfast, even where the object hardly warrants it.

The capriciousness of Hamlet's condition is underscored by the fact that the next passage of his life is dictated by the improbably romantic intervention of the pirates. Fortenbrasse, by contrast, determines his own fate. And steadfastness eventually wins the day. The dying Hamlet can only 'prophesy th'election lights / On Fortinbras: he has my dying voice' (Q2, O1v; 5.2.339–40; not in Q1). Fortinbrasse, of course, behaves as though he does not intend to wait for any election. Where in Q1 it is his 'leisure' which invites him to claim his 'rights of memory in this kingdom', in Q2 it is his 'vantage' (374). Fate has made him the right man in the right place; and he has an army to answer any doubters.

This was surely just what James I wanted to hear after his long wait in the wings. Q2 was a version 'augmented' for his first Revels season in his new kingdom, a meditation on the role he was born to play: he is Fortinbras, uniting the kingdoms of England and Scotland, as his dramatic counterpart does those of Norway and Denmark. He is also the consummate statesman who, like Claudius, fends off war with adroit diplomacy, another feature of the play much enhanced here. When his King's Men set out to entertain him, they came to Elsinore (or, very probably, Hampton Court or even Wilton), not driven out by the 'humour of children' or the 'little eyases', but to give proper thanks for their own good fortune in the wake of James's miraculously peaceful succession. In uniting the two crowns he had created a new empire of Great Britain, and this imperial theme of sovereign territories bound together under a single royal authority was to run throughout

Shakespeare's Jacobean plays (*King Lear*, *Antony and Cleopatra*, *The Winter's Tale*, and *The Tempest* being only the most obvious examples).

THE FOLIO 'HAMLET', AND AFTER

Q2 was, however, Fortenbrasse's textual high water-mark in the evolution of *Hamlet*. When Shakespeare revised it to produce the folio text, which I date at 1606/8 on the basis of the 'little eyases' passage, he did so, in Kerrigan's categorization, as if he were revising someone else's play: 'he cut, inserted and substituted sizeable pieces of text without altering the details of his precursor's dialogue'. So there is relatively little of the 'fidgeting' which characterizes the much more complex transformation of Q1 into Q2. And the whole exercise only results in a net loss of *c*. 130 lines (to 3,537), resulting in what is clearly still a version that could only be staged at court. But two major cuts and one major insertion stand out. The first cut is the eighteen lines involving Horatio's 'prologue to the omen coming on' (Q2 1.1.122); the second is the whole sixty lines of 4.4 in which Hamlet observes Fortinbras (as he finally becomes) in person; and the insertion is the 'little eyases' passage (F, 2.2.337–60; TLN 1,384–1,408) by which we have dated the revision.[27] The Q2 determination to parallel Fortinbras and Hamlet, and to contrast the role of providence in their fortunes, is relaxed. The succession question is now less topical, and the scandals of the Children of the Blackfriars who 'cry out on the top of the question' (F, 2.2.338; TLN 1,387) steal some of its thunder in the folio version.

There is evidence, moreover, that Fortinbras's role continued to diminish in public performances of the play over the next half century and more. Q2 was followed by three further quartos that substantially reprinted it, the last in 1637. But in 1676 Sir William Davenant's abridgement of *Hamlet* (often called *The Players' Hamlet*) was published. Based on the 1637 quarto, it nevertheless contained this note 'To the Reader' after the title page: 'This play being too long to be conveniently acted, such places as might be least prejudicial to the plot or sense, are left out upon the stage: but that we may no way wrong the incomparable author, are here inserted according to the original copy with this mark'. This represented the text as Davenant had worked on it for Thomas Betterton, who first played the lead in 1661, so it may be an entirely Restoration creation—and if so some of the shortening might have been required to allow for the afterpiece which commonly accompanied performances in that era. But Davenant was the most significant bridge between pre-Civil War theatre and Restoration practice, and it is not unlikely that the text represented something close to the play as it had been staged

---

[27] F rather clumsily offers *both* the old 'inhibition [which] comes by means of the late innovation' *and* the new popularity of the 'little eyases' ('tyrannically clapped') to explain why the players are travelling.

in the 1630s—if indeed not significantly earlier.[28] Q2 (and indeed F) were always 'too long to be conveniently acted'—except, as I have argued, at court.

When we analyse what Davenant left out as 'least prejudicial to the plot or sense' one of the first things that strikes us is that '[t]he omissions include nearly all references to Fortinbras before his final entrance (including Hamlet's "How all occasions do inform against me" soliloquy in 4.4.)' (Erne 2003: 167). Indeed his name and Polish expedition are not mentioned until the closing moments of the play. It is indeed as if the motivation which had prompted the addition of Fortinbras to the Saxo/Belleforest story had all but disappeared. The motivation to make him as prominent as he is in Q2 had certainly retreated. He is reduced to the minimal function, even less than in Q1, of filling a gap left by the annihilation of the Danish royal family. Nothing even suggests that the thrones of Denmark and of Norway will eventually merge in his person, since the Norwegian context is left so obscure.[29] By the Restoration, succession is not the key theme in *Hamlet* that it had been for the Elizabethans and, especially, the early Jacobeans. Other dimensions had begun to assert themselves. And this remained true for over a century: 'Eighteenth century versions by David Garrick and others often took out or severely reduced the Fortinbras plot' (Bevington 2008: 1096).

The Players' Hamlet raises a question which neither Lukas Erne nor (so far as I can see) anyone else has asked, and which has wider ramifications for the 'bad' quarto texts—and perhaps others. What is the relationship between the performed text reported there and Q1? Erne argues that 'the "bad" quartos are the best witness we have of what would actually have been performed on the London stages' (194). So why was it necessary for Davenant to adapt the text again? Q1—and the 'allowed book' that lay somewhere behind it—remained available after 1603. Why was it necessary for Davenant to reinvent the wheel? Why did he not simply go to the version that players were already supposed to have created for performance?[30] It is immediately apparent that he did not: the performance text of *The Players' Hamlet* bears no resemblance to Q1, not even a 'tidied up' Q1.

All of this gives weight to the growing conviction that Q1 *Hamlet* is not, certainly in any simplistic sense, a 'performance' text at all (Dillon 1994; Lesser and Stallybrass 2008; Menzer 2008: 24; Stern 2013). It might capture some features of the play in its earlier performances, such as stage directions which give us the Ghost under the stage or in his nightgown, or Ophelia with her hair down, playing a lute (D1ᵛ; G2ᵛ; G4ᵛ). In that sense Q1 represents earlier instantiations of the play, which were soon to be superseded; it may also contain elements of what later

---

[28] Mary Edmond spells out why Davenant's 'importance as a champion of continuity can hardly be overestimated' (1987: 141). It is probably not coincidental that 1637, the year of Q5, was also a year when we *know* that *Hamlet* was performed at court (24 January; see Adams 1917: 76). Revivals, reprints, and court performances seem commonly to have occurred together by the 1630s, and quite probably earlier.

[29] By this date, intriguingly, it is neither his 'leisure' (Q1) nor his 'vantage' (Q2, F), but his 'interest' which invites him to claim his 'rights of memory' in Denmark.

[30] Q1 was famously lost until 1823, the subject of Zachary Lesser's fascinating *'Hamlet' After Q1* (2015). But quite when it disappeared is unknown. It is entirely possible that copies were available to Davenant in the 1630s.

emerged as Q2 and of F, but that does not mean that either of these existed in their entirety by 1603. Once Q2 appeared, Q1 became defunct, for both reading and performance purposes.

By this logic, something akin to Davenant's version must have come into being parallel to Q2, in 1603/4, since neither Q2 nor F (being, as he puts it, 'too long to be conveniently acted') could realistically be used on the public stage. Whether the same is true of all Shakespeare's overlong plays for which there are no shorter companion texts (we are talking here primarily of Jacobean plays) must depend on whether his writing practices changed when the company became the King's Men (see section b of Chapter 7). If he continued to write first for the public stage and then revamped for the court, there would have been no need to produce equivalents of *The Players' Hamlet*. If, however, writing for the court became an enhanced priority—one that took precedence over other writing—there would indeed have been a need for such a version. But whether they would have been prepared by Shakespeare himself we have no way of knowing. Indeed, since none of them has survived (as either 'bad' or 'good' quartos), we are forced to conclude with Wittgenstein that 'What we cannot speak about we must pass over in silence'.

c. A Jacobean *Merry Wives*?

TEXTS

Of all Shakespeare's plays, *The Merry Wives of Windsor* is the one most bedevilled by a perfect storm of poor early texts and of beguiling (but unprovable) contexts. The 1602 quarto of the play (Q1) is perhaps the worst—clumsy, least intelligible— of those which A. W. Pollard originally dubbed as 'bad', while the 1623 folio text (F), despite being much fuller and very probably based on a copy by the highly competent scrivener, Ralph Crane, is also most unsatisfactory in a variety of ways. The differences between the two versions are concisely summarized by Giorgio Melchiori in his Arden 3 edition of the play: 'In the first place there are glaring omissions [in Q1]: 4.1 (the "Latin lesson"), 5.1, 5.2, 5.3, 5.4 and the Garter speech at [5.5.55–75] are totally missing. 3.4 and 3.5 are transposed, and there are further transpositions of passages within single scenes or from one scene to another. Finally all scenes are radically reduced in length, so that the Quarto version is less than 60 per cent of the length of that in the Folio...and the wording of the surviving speeches presents substantial variants' (2000: 32).[31] As readers might perhaps anticipate, I would argue for *additions* to F, rather than *omissions* from Q1.

But the relationship between the two versions is far from clear. Since the beginning of the twentieth century, however, the orthodoxy has been to assume that F most closely approximates to what Shakespeare originally wrote and that Q1 represents a serious corruption (or, at least, adaptation) of it. As we have seen, it was W. W. Greg's pioneering work on the play that established this (p. 141). In practice it has meant that modern editors have invariably used F as their copy-texts, though in fact it is one of the least satisfactory texts in the First Folio; so they have relied on Q1 in an effort to make it more intelligible. As Melchiori puts it: 'Editors of *The Merry Wives of Windsor* are given no alternative in the choice of their copy-text...[but] it appears that a number of inconsistencies in F can be at least in part explained by recourse to the earlier Q' (2000: 109). This has been particularly the case in respect of stage direction, the one feature of the text in which Q1 is demonstrably fuller. But such practices—coming close at times to a conflation of the

---

[31] See also Melchiori's more detailed analysis of the relationship between the scenes of the two versions: 324–5. References to Q1 are to the facsimile reproduced as an appendix in Melchiori 2000: 295–322, which divides the text into eighteen scenes. There is no modernized edition of Q1, nor indeed one that offers line numbering. I have silently modernized the text, and offer scene and signature references. References to the F text are to the version in Bevington 2008.

texts—are highly questionable. They rely far too heavily on a dubious and unproven relationship between them.³²

CONTEXTS

The mythology which surrounds *Merry Wives* to this day emerged remarkably fully formed at the beginning of the Shakespearean editorial tradition, in the Introduction to Nicholas Rowe's 1709 edition of the plays:

> [Elizabeth I] was so well pleased with that admirable character of Falstaff, in the two parts of *Henry the Fourth*, that she commanded him to continue it for one play more, and to show him in love. This is said to be the occasion of his writing *The Merry Wives of Windsor*. How well she was obeyed, the play itself is an admirable proof. Upon this occasion it may not be improper to observe that this part of Falstaff is said to have been written originally under the name of Oldcastle; some of that family being then remaining, the Queen was pleased to command him to alter it; upon which he made use of Falstaff. The present offence was indeed avoided; but I don't know whether the author may not have been somewhat to blame in his second choice, since it is certain that Sir John Falstaff, who was a Knight of the Garter, and a Lieutenant-General, was a name of distinguished merit in the wars in France in Henry the Fifth's and Henry the Sixth's Times. (3)

We now know that the first half of this may well be a fabrication. It can be traced back no earlier than the dedicatory epistle of John Dennis's 1702 adaptation of *Merry Wives*, *The Comical Gallant: or the Amours of Sir John Falstaff*, where he claims that 'this comedy was written at [the Queen's] command, and by her direction, and she was so eager to see it Acted, that she commanded it to be finished in fourteen days'. It was entirely in Dennis's self-interest to generate such gossip about a play which he was offering in the marketplace. But the measure of his success is that modern editors of the play can hardly bring themselves to ignore the story altogether. On the other hand, Rowe was substantially right about Oldcastle being the original name of Falstaff and about the intervention of the Cobham family (though unnamed by him) to get it changed. It is remarkable that the story had remained current for more than a century.

As we have already observed, when Alexander Pope edited the plays in 1725, blissfully unaware of W. W. Greg and 'foul papers', he linked the mythology surrounding Queen Elizabeth's supposed demands with the differences he observed between the two extant versions, but saw nothing problematic (see p. 97). The idea of a 'first imperfect sketch', hastily composed at the Queen's behest, that was revised and perfected at some later date struck him as the most natural thing. He

---

³² Melchiori's own edition, while based on F, draws far too extensively on Q1 to be helpful for the purposes of this book. Hence my preference in citations for Bevington 2008, which is more conservative.

was followed in this by all notable contemporary Shakespeareans and by most scholars for the following hundred years.

In the early twentieth century, scholars had little reason to doubt Pope's sense of where the play fell in the sequence of the plays Shakespeare wrote, even if they disagreed what version was written first. It seemed self-evidently to follow the two *Henry IV* plays, partly because Justice Shallow and Falstaff's boy (Robin) seem here to be familiar from *2 Henry IV*, where they had apparently first appeared. That might date it *c.* 1598/9. It also made sense that it would be written before Falstaff was killed off in *Henry V* (Q1 1600), the only other play in which Nym appears. Those factors inclined some to date it as late as 1599/1600, which is where E. K. Chambers tentatively dated it in *The Elizabethan Stage* (1923: 2.486).

But then contextual myths began to overtake editorial ones. In 1931 Leslie Hotson first suggested that the play was an occasional piece (in accord with the notion of its being written in fourteen days), designed to be performed at Westminster Palace on St George's Day (23 April) 1597 to celebrate the election of five new knights to the Order of the Garter (1931). The conclusive detail here was that the patron of Shakespeare's company, George Carey, Lord Hunsdon, was one of the new Garter Knights. Not only that, but on 14 April Hunsdon had become Lord Chamberlain and a Privy Councillor, thus achieving the positions which his father, the first Lord Hunsdon, had held before. The younger Hunsdon had in fact hoped to succeed his father on his death in July 1596, but William Brooke, tenth Lord Cobham, had been made Lord Chamberlain. The sudden death in turn of Cobham had reopened the way for Hunsdon to achieve his ambitions, in the process restoring the status quo for the actors he patronized, once more the Lord Chamberlain's Men.[33] There was an attractive argument to suggest that Shakespeare and his company might have written a play which openly alludes to the Order of the Garter, in order to celebrate their patron's success. Thirty years later William Green published *Shakespeare's Merry Wives of Windsor*, which very much more substantially spelled out this circumstantial case, further convincing all but a very few doubters (1962).

There were, however, a number of problems with the case. First among these was that it relied heavily on F, or something very like it, existing as early as 1597. Q1, though it does allude to Windsor and sets some of the action in the Garter Inn, has very little of the Garter material and, bluntly, if we did not also have F there would be little reason to associate the play with 1597. Happily for Hotson and Green, Greg's immensely influential 'foul papers' orthodoxy hardly allowed this question to arise: F, though not without its own mystifying features, seems manifestly closer to Shakespeare's pen, and so (the argument goes) closer to the originating document. Secondly, in the case against the 1597 dating, there is no record of *any* theatrical performance on the occasion of the Garter feast that year, nor on that of a subsequent Garter event in Windsor itself in May 1597, which might have been

---

[33] The company had been Lord Hunsdon's Men during Cobham's tenure of office.

equally apt. Thirdly, a date early in 1597 is impossible to square with the play having been written after the two *Henry IV* plays, much less after *Henry V*, which can hardly be earlier than 1599. Fourthly, it is difficult to understand why a *Merry Wives* performed early in 1597 would not have appeared in Francis Meres's list of Shakespeare's works in *Palladis Tamia* (1598). It was not, however, until 1994 that Barbara Freedman argued the case against a 1597 dating in compelling detail (1994).

The tensions between the Hotson/Green mythology and other forms of evidence are reflected in the *Oxford Shakespeare* and its *Textual Companion* (Wells and Taylor 1986; 1987). In their headnote to the play Stanley Wells and Gary Taylor edge close to endorsing the Hotson/Green position. 'Shakespeare's play was probably performed in association with this occasion, and may have been written especially for it' (1986: 483). They realized, however, that this dating created a very tight writing calendar for Shakespeare, who they imagined 'may have started to write [*2 Henry IV*] late in 1596, or in 1597, directly after *1 Henry IV*, but have laid it aside while he wrote *The Merry Wives of Windsor*' (509). In the *Textual Companion* they seem far less certain. They still maintain that the Hotson dating is 'plausible', but also consider it possible that *1 Henry IV* is as late as 1597, after the death of Lord Cobham. 'Queen Elizabeth's request for a play on Falstaff in love could have been made in anticipation of a later court performance that Whitehall season (on 26 February [1598])...*Merry Wives* could, on this interpretation, have recollected, rather than anticipated, the Garter ceremonies of 1597' (1987: 120).[34] This dedication to the mythology brings to mind the mordant line in John Ford's *The Man Who Shot Liberty Valance*: 'When the legend becomes fact, print the legend'.

Most editors nevertheless have continued to follow the Hotson/Green argument, with the notable exception of George Hibbard who, in his New Penguin edition, took seriously the absence of the record of performances at appropriate times in 1597. He hypothesized instead a much more modest entertainment than the full play at the Garter feast, perhaps provided at very short notice. 'Then later, when it was all long over, Shakespeare, with the economy so characteristic of him, salvaged the entertainment...and used it for the denouement of his new comedy' (1973). This hypothesis has the virtue of retaining all the contextual richness implicit in the Hotson/Green scenario, but without tying it to an unsustainable dating schedule. It squared the circle, which is perhaps why Giorgio Melchiori adopted and elaborated it in his Arden 3 edition of the play, where he concludes that 'neither version of the play that has reached us...can possibly be identified *in toto* with the presumptive 1597 entertainment—actually the Quarto omits the lines on the Garter ceremonies in the masque-like part of Act 5 that would have been most appropriate to the occasion' (2000: 30).

This gets close to identifying the elephant in the room about the 1597 hypothesis, but fails to do so. If we forget for a moment 'the lines on the Garter ceremonies in the masque-like part of Act 5 that would have been most appropriate to the

---

[34] There is an unaccountable reference later in the *Textual Companion* to 'the recorded court performance of 1597' (1987: 341). There is, of course, no 'recorded court performance' at that time.

occasion'—of which there are precisely 22, and only in F (5.1.54–75)—*Merry Wives* is an intensely *inappropriate* play to celebrate the election of someone to the Order of the Garter. It is not heroic, it is not festive; it is satiric and charivaric, and invests much of the energy of its climax in the ritual humiliation—virtually an exorcism—of its central character, Falstaff. Falstaff was actually a *degraded* Garter knight, the antithesis of what a new member of the Order should strive to be.

Shakespeare derived the new name for his Oldcastle character from the Sir John Falstaff whom the English hero, Talbot, strips of the Order of the Garter for cowardice in a memorable sequence in *1 Henry VI* (TLN 1,759–90; 4.1.9–47). This does scant justice to the historical Fastolfe, who had some reputation as a soldier. In some accounts his withdrawal at the battle of Patay only occurred when Talbot himself was in full retreat, and he was certainly later restored in honour, a circumstance which Shakespeare chose to overlook. When Shakespeare revived this character in the *Henry IV* plays he persisted in making him a quintessential cowardly knight. But nothing identifies him as a Knight of the Garter, either before or after his degrading—yet being a Garter knight was a distinction of supreme importance in the honour culture of Elizabethan England (James 1986).

Not until *Merry Wives* are we reminded of Falstaff's Garter associations, and in Q1 it is an incidental detail: he happens to be staying at the Garter Inn in Windsor. The Order of the Garter, founded in 1348, has always been associated with St George's Chapel in Windsor Castle, the oldest continually occupied royal residence. But this is, as Melchiori points out, an entirely inadequate basis for the Hotson/Green scenario, which depends upon the much greater elaboration of Garter material in F. That material is, as I shall argue, a distraction from the final scene's main business, which in F as in Q remains the humiliation of Falstaff.

It reads like one of several patched-in additions, as the play's editor, David Crane, observes. He notes, uniquely in F, 'matter of an upper-class and educated kind, such as the heraldic discussion with which the play begins, and William Page's Latin lesson at the beginning of Act 4' and 'a long speech by the Queen of Fairies about Windsor Castle and the Garter Chapel which in the specificity of its reference is even more easily detached from its surroundings than the heraldry or the Latin lesson' (1997: 1).[35] Anticipating in many respects my own argument, though tied to the 1597 and 'foul papers' orthodoxies, he 'suggests that the play [i.e. F] was angled towards an audience specifically of this [upper-class and educated] kind' (ibid). In my analysis these detachable items are late additions to the text, not part of the original plan.

* * *

I now return to the second half of Rowe's comments about the play, which address two distinct issues: that the Falstaff character was originally called Oldcastle, and that this gave rise to protests from the Cobham family whose title derived from the historical Oldcastle. This is certainly not fanciful mythology, as Gary Taylor has

---

[35] On Crane's view of the play's textual issues, in both the 1997 and updated 2010 versions of his edition, see Chapter 4, p. 98 and n. 3.

demonstrated in detail (1985; 1987). Whether Shakespeare intended deliberate offence to the Cobham family it is impossible to say, though the cumulative evidence is suggestive. Oldcastle was hardly an obscure figure. Once close to Henry V, he was latterly convicted of heresy for his Lollard (proto-Protestant) beliefs and gruesomely executed: hung in chains and burned. Allusions to this fate seem to cling to Shakespeare's Falstaff even though his association with Oldcastle was formally disowned in the epilogue to *2 Henry IV* ('for Oldcastle died a martyr, and this is not the man').[36]

Oldcastle was only a martyr as far as Protestants were concerned, the role he played in John Foxe's *Book of Martyrs*; in the Catholic tradition he remained a traitor to his kind and a heretic. He was thus a contentious figure in Shakespeare's day, and though the playwright could always point to Oldcastle's appearance in his source-text, *The Famous Victories of Henry V* (see p. 175), it was as predictable that the Cobhams would object to this travesty of him onstage as it was unlikely that Shakespeare would not anticipate their reaction. And even if *he* had not done so, it is inconceivable that Edmund Tilney, Master of the Revels and a notable genealogist, did not. Yet Tilney must have licensed the play for performance in its original form. At which point we slip back into all the problems associated with dating these plays.

1 Henry IV is usually located in 1596. If it was after July (as most editors have presumed) we might at least hazard a guess that the choice of Oldcastle was linked with Cobham's being preferred as Lord Chamberlain over the younger Hunsdon, though this would surely have been reckless: Cobham was in a position to ruin the company, if he chose. As we have seen, however, it is not impossible to stretch the dating of *1 Henry IV* later even than March 1597, by which time Lord Chamberlain Cobham was dead; in which case, the protest against Oldcastle would have been entered by his son, Henry Brooke, eleventh Lord Cobham. This is where my own contribution to squaring this enormously problematic circle begins.

One of the few certainties in this web of supposition is that by late February 1598—at least in courtly circles, and specifically among the associates of the Earl of Essex—the younger Cobham had become *identified* with Shakespeare's Falstaff. Essex wrote to Sir Robert Cecil, jestingly asking him to tell their friend Sir Alex Ratcliff that 'his sister is married to Sr. Jo. Falstaff'—rumour was linking Margaret Ratcliff with Brooke. The following July the Countess of Southampton wrote to her husband with the same joke (Hotson 1949: 148, 153–6). Whether this derived from one *Henry IV* play, or both of them, or also from *Merry Wives* there is no way of saying. But I suggest that the subsequent history of the Falstaff plays, and of *Merry Wives* in particular, was intimately tied up in this identification of Falstaff/Oldcastle with Brooke. And I suggest that the critical date in that history is not 1597 but 1599.

---

[36] This may have been a late addition. In the 1600 quarto text it comes at the very end, some lines after the speaker has knelt to pray for the Queen, which would normally conclude the play. In the folio the kneeling to pray is in its proper place.

In that year Henry, Lord Cobham was elected to the Order of the Garter. This was an instance of the delicate balancing of patronage and royal favour so typical of the court politics of the later 1590s. The ambitious younger Cobham had hoped to succeed *his* father as Lord Chamberlain in 1597, only to see it go (with the Garter) to the younger Hunsdon. Cobham *had*, however, succeeded his father in the equally prestigious post of Lord Warden of the Cinque Ports and was in turn raised to the Garter.[37] By April of 1599 he had been living under the shadow of the Oldcastle/Falstaff association in the *Henry IV* plays for at least two years, possibly longer. *1 Henry IV* was in print by 1598 and massively popular, going through three editions in two years (see p. 3 and n. 7). Its Oldcastle references are easy enough to ferret out if you look for them. *2 Henry IV*, probably first staged in 1598 (and printed in 1600), concluded with an epilogue, explicitly disavowing the link between Falstaff and Oldcastle but inevitably perpetuating that link in people's minds by doing so. It promised, moreover, to 'continue the story, with Sir John in it', speculating that 'for anything I know, Falstaff shall die of a sweat, unless already 'a be killed with your hard opinions' (Epilogue 25–30; TLN 3,345). This could not but keep court tongues wagging.

In the event Shakespeare did not bring Falstaff back in *Henry V*, except in the report of his death offstage. In Mistress Quickly's account he dies peacefully enough, 'babbling a green fields' in Theobald's famous amendment to the text.[38] He thus avoids the gruesome death which befell the historical Oldcastle for his Lollardry—but a fate indirectly echoed in the hanging of Bardolph, the only member of the Eastcheap crowd (other than Mistress Quickly) to have accompanied him in every play. The persistent Falstaff/Cobham associations may have made it impolitic to continue shadowing Oldcastle to the bitter end. But the elevation of the younger Cobham to the Garter once worn so ignominiously by his fictional alter-ego may (given the history between the Cobhams and the Chamberlain's Men) have prompted Shakespeare to a burlesque upon the character instead.

Q1 *Merry Wives* in 1599 or early 1600 would in this way have been a very timely resuscitation of the fat knight, counterpointing the account of his death in *Henry V*. It certainly stamps the associations of Cobham with the Falstaff role more explicitly than F does, since Master Ford uses the Cobham family name of 'Brooke' when he goes in disguise. The point is heavily underscored in the quarto text:

HOST: Hast thou no suit against my knight,
My guest, my cavaliero?
FORD: None I protest: but tell him my name
Is *Brooke*, only for a jest.
HOST: My hand, bully: thou shalt
Have egress and regress, and thy
Name shall be *Brooke*: (Scene 5; sig. C2r)

---

[37] The apparent rivalry between the Cobhams and Hunsdons was evidently related to the bitter factional rivalry between the Cecils and Essex in the late 1590s. See White 2002.
[38] The folio has 'a table of green fields' (TLN 839); the 1600 quarto, where the passage is on B4v, has him 'talk of flowers'.

'Brooke' is voiced a remorseless twenty-eight times in the brief quarto text, making it unmissable. It is yet another argument against the 1597 dating of *Merry Wives* that 'Brooke' should have found its way so prominently into print as late as 1602; if it had been closely contemporary with the original use of Oldcastle, it would surely have been revoked at the same time. The name would indeed be changed to 'Broome' in F. But if the change had actually happened in 1597 or thereabouts, we would expect it also to be respected in 1602. This is one of the clearest indicators that Q1 is in fact (as I am arguing) antecedent to F. The level of Garter detail which we find in Q1—light but legible—is also more appropriate for this 'humorous' satire of an unknightly buffoon than the elaborately decorous material which is foregrounded to celebrate the Order in F.[39] Q1 could hardly have been written to *celebrate* Hunsdon's elevation to the Garter—or anybody else's. But its robustly charivaric plot might well have been written to *mock* such an elevation, and Brooke/Cobham is overwhelmingly the likeliest candidate.

The degree to which the Cobham association with the Falstaff plays remained in the public mind is marked by how often *1 Henry IV* (one of the most popular of all Shakespeare's plays) was referred to as 'Oldcastle'.[40] Gary Taylor argued that this is evidence that the original, uncensored version of the play was performed on occasions, which is possible though by no means a necessary condition of my argument here: what really matters is that people heard Falstaff and thought Oldcastle. The earliest known instance of this relates to a performance of the play specially commissioned by Lord Chamberlain Hunsdon for the benefit of Flemish Ambassador Verreyken on 6 March 1600, and mentioned under the title of 'Sir John Old Castell' by Rowland White in one of his regular messages to Sir Robert Sidney (Kastan 2002: 54; see Marino 2011: 107ff). There were further instances at court on 6 January 1631 and 29 May 1638, by which time (as I shall suggest) the resonances of these associations with Brooke/Cobham were quite different.[41]

* * *

A defining turning point in the associations of Falstaff with Henry, Lord Cobham occurred with his implication in the 'Main Plot' in 1603. This aimed to depose James I, for religious reasons, and replace him with Lady Arbella Stuart. Cobham's younger brother, George, was implicated in the related 'Bye Plot', and executed. Cobham was also condemned to death but, like Sir Walter Ralegh, spared in a late act of clemency by the king. He spent most of the rest of his life in the Tower of

---

[39] Another circumstantial argument in favour of a 1599/1600 dating is the presence of the characters, Sir Hugh Evans and Fluellen in *Merry Wives* and *Henry V* respectively; it has been suggested that comic Welsh roles were a specialism of Robert Armin, who joined the company around this time, perhaps following the departure of Will Kemp. I am grateful to Peter Greenfield for this suggestion.

[40] Some of these instances *could* relate to *2 Henry IV*, though the print history suggests it was never as popular a play. But it does not really affect my argument which of the plays was meant.

[41] The performances are referred to respectively as 'Olde Castell' and 'ould Castel' and some scholars have assumed this means either *1* or *2 Sir John Oldcastle*. But both of these were written for the Admiral's Men, whereas these performances were by the King's Men. The balance of probabilities is that these were one or other of their own *Henry IV* plays. See McManaway 1969: 119–22; Marino 2011: 107–42.

London, dying in poverty in 1619.[42] In a striking instance of life imitating art, on 14 February 1604 Cobham was stripped of the Garter, like the prototype Falstaff character in *1 Henry VI* (the technical term is 'degraded'), and his insignia were removed from his stall in St George's Chapel, Windsor.

What resonances must there have been from this when, on 4 November 1604, *Merry Wives* was performed at court? The man who had for family reasons become synonymous with the role of Falstaff had, in a curious way, *become* the fictional degraded knight; and his absence from that performance at Whitehall, while his alter ego performed ludicrously onstage, must have been particularly marked. I suggest that *this* is very likely to have been the occasion for what we know as the folio version of the play, or something very like it. In the usual way of these things, the King's Men would have collaborated with Master of the Revels Tilney to decide the plays they would perform that festive season and make any necessary changes. It was his business to be aware of the implications of the Oldcastle/Cobham/Brooke/Falstaff traces: one of his primary responsibilities was to ensure that the actors did not show disrespect to persons of consequence. And it is likely that he thought long and hard before deciding that *Merry Wives* was suitable that season—or perhaps could be *made* suitable. Given the poor quality of both the texts it is difficult to be sure, but it looks as though a revision somewhere between the scale of that for *Mucedorus* and that for *Old Fortunatus* was required (see pp. 113–14, 106–8).

We have the assurance of the Q1 title page that a version of the play had already been played at court by 1602: 'A most pleasant and excellent conceited comedy of Sir John Falstaff and the merry wives of Windsor...As it hath been divers times acted by the Right Honorable my Lord Chamberlain's servants. Both before her Majesty, and elsewhere' (see p. 124). The fact of court performance does not figure very highly in the list of the items the publisher saw fit to advertise the play by. But there is no reason to doubt the court claim. The issue is: what version of the play did Elizabeth see? Greg, Hotson, Green, and virtually all editors have assumed it was something much closer to F than to Q1, but for all the reasons given I doubt that. Q1 as it stands is virtually unactable, but it cannot simply be dismissed as a poor 'memorial reconstruction' of F, to which it is only tangentially related. It is a very poor rendition of something else, now lost.

F makes most sense as a version of the play developed from that lost item; it was very probably constructed by Shakespeare, working under Tilney's direction, with the particular intention of court performance on 4 November 1604, during James I's first full Revels season at Whitehall (see pp. 35–6). As we have seen, the Audit Accounts have survived for that season, and they list the plays performed (see pp. 35–6 and n. 21). We do not know who was present that night, but it is highly likely that they included several for whom membership of the Order of the Garter was still a novelty. King James himself, now the Sovereign of the Order, had been a member since 1590, but appointed in his absence. In the first year of his reign he created no fewer than six new knights, a quarter of the total who could be members at any one time. Three of these were of the royal family: Prince Henry, Christian

---

[42] Ralegh was almost certainly innocent, though Cobham was probably not.

IV of Denmark (Queen Anna's brother, *in absentia*), and the Duke of Lennox, James's cousin. Another was one of James's Scottish counsellors, the Earl of Mar. The other two new knights were the leading contenders for the role of the 'fair youth' in Shakespeare's *Sonnets*, the 3rd Earl of Southampton (restored in honour after being imprisoned for his part in the Essex rebellion) and the 3rd Earl of Pembroke.

Older members included the cream of the Elizabethan aristocracy, the Earls of Nottingham, Shrewsbury, Cumberland, Derby, Devonshire, Worcester, Sussex, and Suffolk, and old Lord Treasurer Dorset, who as Thomas Sackville long since co-authored *Gorboduc*.[43] At the beginning of the first full court Revels season to be held at Whitehall, it is likely that a good many of these were in attendance, and hyper-conscious of Cobham's absence. If what they saw of *Merry Wives* approximated to F—and if they remembered a version approximating to Q1, played before Elizabeth—they would perhaps have appreciated that the play's satire of a degraded knight was now balanced by its decorous celebration of the revered and exclusive Order to which they all belonged, but which had lost one of its own. It also sported, probably for the first time, a comic Latin lesson which David Crane described as 'matter of an upper-class and educated kind'.

Several details in F are suggestive of a play adapted specifically for court performance, and some make better sense if they belong to a text later than Q1. The most daring gesture—one that Tilney surely had to approve—is Falstaff's first line in F: 'Now, Master Shallow, you'll complain of me to the King?' (1.1.103–4; TLN 105–6). There is no reference to a king—or a queen—within Q1, only the threat in the opening line of referring Falstaff to the (Privy) Council in its role as the Court of Star Chamber, which is retained in F. Within the historical fiction, the king is presumably Henry IV; but at Whitehall in 1604 the idea of someone complaining about 'Falstaff' to the king had completely different connotations. This was taking the bull by the horns, making the issue of Cobham's disgrace the open, if not quite spoken, subject of the play.

Another detail only in F—a far less loaded one—that would carry particular weight at court appears in the very passage most closely associated with the Order of the Garter. The 'Queen of Faery' directs her fairies: 'till 'tis one o'clock, / Our dance of custom, round about the oak / Of Herne the Hunter, let us not forget' (5.5.73–5; TLN 2,556–8). One o'clock in the morning, as we have observed, was commonly a time at which court performances concluded—part of the point of the court Revels season being precisely to while away the midwinter darkness with light, warmth, and entertainment that lesser mortals could not afford (see pp. 82–7). With no other apparent significance to fixing the time, this has the air of a self-reflexive gesture. There is no such line in Q1.

There are two topical jokes which appear in both texts of the play and which suggest that there were purposeful changes between Q1 and F (and in *that* direction). One relates to the change we have already noted, of Ford's disguise-name from Brooke to Broome. This makes utter nonsense of a Falstaff joke about flowing

---

[43] The second Lord Hunsdon, whom the mythology attaches to the play, had died in 1603.

alcohol: 'Such brooks are always welcome to me' (Q1; sig. H2r) becomes a meaningless 'such brooms are welcome to me, that o'erflows such liquour' (F, 2.2.143–4; TLN 911–12).[44] To anyone familiar with Cobham's association with the Falstaff character (virtually everyone at court, including his fellow Garter knights), the change from Brooke to Broome could have been no more than a fig leaf. But when the fig leaf renders a joke meaningless it draws attention to itself in a particularly pointed way.

The second joke constitutes a notable crux in Q1 about a 'Germain Duke come to de court' and 'three sorts of cousin garmombles' (Sc. 16; F4v).[45] These occur in the context of a plot by Sir Hugh Evans and Dr Caius (set up in what is 3.1 of the folio text) to be revenged on the Host of the Garter Inn for his deceit. They are widely supposed to refer to Count Frederick of Mömpelgard who had visited England in 1592 and left behind a bad reputation relating to a warrant (which may have been abused) for the free use of post horses.[46] The Count, who became Duke of Württemberg in 1593, lobbied hard for election to the Garter and succeeded in 1597 but failed to show up for the ceremonies and installation. The rather weak joking about 'cousins german' (i.e. first cousins) is an excuse to mix ideas of cozening ('Has cozened all de host of Brentford'; 'Is cozen all the host of Maidenhead & Readings', ibid) with a xenophobic slur against the Germans. The supposed cheating ascribed to Mömpelgard and his followers, here amounting to horse-stealing, not only pays back the Host's deceit but also mirrors Falstaff's unworthiness to be a Garter Knight.

The parallel passage in F is even more garbled, however, making an even weaker joke about 'cosen-germans' (it is now only one subplot in a whole sequence of cozenings) in a way that loses all specificity; 'garmombles' is never mentioned and the fact that the Host has made 'grand preparation for a duke de Jamany' is not mentioned until Dr Caius also avers that 'dere is no duke that the court is know to come' (F 4.5.74, 83, 84; TLN 2,288–305). Of course, in neither Q nor F was there any real horse-stealing by Germans; Bardolph is the one who makes off with the Host's horses, possibly with assistance. By 1604, however, the joke is less that Mömpelgard came and behaved badly (his unpronounceable earlier title has ceased to be a butt of the humour), but that the Duke never came at all, after his election, an act of discourtesy unworthy of a Garter knight. In fact King James had resolved the diplomatic awkwardness that arose from this in September of the previous year 'when the insignia were conferred upon him with pride, pomp, and circumstance...at Stuttgard' (Hart 1904: xlii–iii). Thus one blot on the honour of the Order had been removed, as those at the 1604 court performance would certainly remember and probably smile at.

---

[44] Bevington retains the 'Brookes' reading from Q1. On the Falstaff/Cobham joking in general, across all three Falstaff plays, see Scoufos 1979.
[45] Precise modernization is difficult because the words are *meant* to be garbled attempts at German.
[46] It is not impossible that Shakespeare has conflated the Count with a Frenchman, Monsieur de Chastes, who in 1596 did steal post horses in his haste to take to the French king news that he had been elected to the Garter. See Crofts 1937 and Freedman 1994: 206.

The biggest single difference between the texts of Q1 and F, however, lies in the masque of the Queen of Faery, from which the 'one o'clock' reference derives.[47] The guying of Falstaff at the hands of Mistress Quickly in Q1 gives way in F to something far more decorous and quasi-ceremonial, invoking a blessing on the Order of the Garter and its Chapel at Windsor. The text is confused and confusing on the matter. But the key change is flagged in Mistress Page's announcement that her daughter, Anne Page, is meant to play the role of the 'Queen' in F: 'My Nan shall be Queen of all the Fairies / Finely attirèd in a robe of white' (F 4.4.70–1; TLN 2,197–8); in Q1 the plan is only that she 'Shall like a little fairy be disguised' in 'a robe of white' (Sc. 16; F3v) and it is Mistress Quickly who enters 'like the Queen of Fairies' (Sc. 18; G2r). But as the scene is printed in F it is not at all clear if 'Nan' does indeed take the role of Queen; the typesetter gives the Queen's lines twice to 'Qu.' but also twice to 'Qui.' This of course leaves open the possibility that Mistress Quickly retained her role from Q1—a possibility which every editor I am familiar with has accepted.

It was entirely appropriate that Mistress Quickly should preside over the discomfiture of Falstaff in Q1, where it is the main focus of attention in the scene. But she is a very odd figure to announce the benediction over the Garter stalls in St George's Chapel (the most notable change/addition to the scene), the light solemnity of which is very much a counterpoint to what happens to Falstaff in F.[48] The confusion here must be connected to the problems over how precisely Nan's two unlucky suitors are misled by the colour-coding of the dresses, which are too complex to reproduce fully here. Neither Q nor F is internally coherent about this, but they are incoherent in different ways, suggesting some level of revision that Ralph Crane, the copyist of F, was unable to make sense of. Q contains a perfectly coherent stage direction of the action whereby each of the three suitors thinks he is stealing Nan away (though only Fenton is correct), but it does not square with the dialogue. The SD tells us that 'the Doctor comes one way and steals away a boy in red' but it is later Slender who complains that he failed to achieve Nan though 'I came to her in red as you bade me' (Sc. 18; G4r). In F Slender is set up to 'come to her in white' (5.2.5–6; TLN 2,436–7) but later complains that 'I went to her in green' (TLN 2,682).[49] F has no stage direction here. Modern editors, locked into the assumption that Q1 is a corrupted version of F, generally reproduce Q1's stage direction in some form, assuming that it applies to the action in their F copy-text. But if Nan does indeed play the Fairy Queen, the details of the action were very probably different—she was no longer just a fairy in the background, but the centre of attention perhaps until the song begins. No wonder Crane was confused. He recovered the song,

---

[47] Leah Marcus also makes the point that, while Q1 does mention Windsor, the action in general is given 'an urban setting strongly suggesting London or some provincial city' and does not have the 'numerous typographical references to the area [of Windsor], its palace, park, and surrounding villages' which are so prominent in F. These are distinctively *different* texts. See Marcus 1991: 173ff.

[48] Some editors try to get round this by suggesting that Shakespeare—since the copy-text is supposed to come from his hand—meant 'Qui' to indicate the actor who played Mistress Quickly, but who was no longer in that role, a pretty lame argument.

[49] Note that Bevington—like most editors—gives this as 'I went to her in white' (5.2193), attempting to sort out the confusion.

which is not printed in Q1, but failed to keep track of the revisions. The bottom line in all this remains, however, that Q1 is not a debased version of F. F is rather a revised version of Q1, albeit in incomplete and muddled form.

John H. Long argued many years ago that the Q1 masque is a better ending to the play than the one in F. Like David Crane (see p. 249), he sees it as a detachable item:

> Now, at the point where the little masque opens, the flow of dramatic action takes either of two courses; on one hand we have the light, genial, satirical, and rather vulgar masque of the Quarto, and, on the other hand, there is the ornate, courtly, somewhat stilted masque of the Folio. Both agree in only one respect; they both draw the action toward the same conclusion. In other respects, such as language and characterization, they are quite different. If we are interested in studying the masque as a genre, that is, a pseudo-dramatic production designed to flatter some person or to celebrate some important event, we find the Folio masque, with its prim address to Windsor Castle, its owner, and the Order of the Garter, an excellent miniature of the form. But if we are interested in the dramatic unity of the entire play (and most of us are), then the Quarto masque seems to be more appropriate.
>
> From the point of view of construction, atmosphere, language, characterization, and text, the Folio version is not well fitted into its context. The rollicking spirit of the farce comedy is considerably dampened by the dignity of the masque at a time when the comedy should reach a climax. The construction of the scene is loose—appropriately so for a masque, but not so for a dramatic scene as important to its context as this one. The florid language is assigned to Mistress Quickly and Sir Hugh, both of whom are unfitted for the lines they speak. Quickly is cast as the Queen of the Fairies and Evans as one of her assistants. (Long 1952: 40)

As I have suggested, the F text is more ambiguous about who plays the Queen of Fairies than Long allows, but he is right about Parson Evans, who also unaccountably loses his Welsh accent at this point in F, so it is less than obvious why Falstaff should exclaim 'Heavens defend me from that Welsh fairy' (F 5.5.81; TLN 2,563). He is also right that the Q1 masque is a better ending for the play—but only if you concede that comical satire at the expense of Falstaff is the driving force of the play, as it is in Q1. In F the intention at least seems to be that Shakespeare wanted to locate that satire in a wider, more ceremonial celebration of the Order of the Garter.

The F text, in short, shows all the signs of an incomplete revision, the elements of which (apparently) neither Ralph Crane as an expert scrivener, nor Heminge and Condell, the overseers of the folio, could by 1623 reconcile. It is quite parallel in this respect to Q2 *Romeo and Juliet* or indeed to the muddled Choruses in F *Henry V* (see pp. 222ff, 188–9). But if Anne Page *does* play the role of the Queen— at least in the decorous first half of the sequence—many of Long's objections are answered. She can bring a credible innocence and sincerity to the role of blessing the Chapel, before being whisked away to marry Fenton, her own preferred suitor, over those championed by her mother and father. A reasonable resolution of these conundrums, in fact, would be for Anne Page to perform as 'Queen' until the 'dance of custom' which she calls for at 5.5.74 (TLN 2,557): no dance is called for in Q1. The dance would offer the perfect opportunity for her and Fenton to slip away, while the other suitors go for the wrong colours; and at that point (Evans's 'But stay! I smell a man of middle earth': 5.5.80) for Mistress Quickly to take over as 'Queen of Fairies' and oversee Falstaff's ritual taunting, as in Q1.

I cannot, of course, prove that it was staged in that way, but I suggest that it would capture the spirit of what is scripted in F: satire, romance, and ceremonial blend (more or less) into one. The blessing of the Garter insignia puts the raucous comedy of Q1 into perspective, allowing a measured and appropriate act of retribution, rather than outright humiliation, against the disgraced knight. This version of the play not only guys a degraded Garter member, it also reaffirms the higher code of values invested in the Order itself, which live on in those members of the Order present at the performance at Whitehall that night. All of the iconography and associations of the Garter which William Green assembled in respect of a 1597 event, which almost certainly never happened, are entirely relevant to the 1604 event which certainly did. And they come together in the form of a mixed masque/anti-masque which, like the black-faced *Othello* staged at the beginning of the Revels season, nods to Queen Anna's much-anticipated Jones/Jonson masque in January (see p. 65).

By the same token, I cannot *prove* that Shakespeare rewrote *The Merry Wives of Windsor* for its only recorded court performance during his lifetime, any more than I can disprove that he wrote any version of it as early as 1597.[50] But if we can rid ourselves of the myths of 'foul papers', piratical 'memorial reconstructions', and a play written at short order for Queen Elizabeth; if we can resist the temptations of a 1597 (or even 1598) first dating, which may be seductive, but for which there is no evidence and which moreover goes against the most logical inferences we would otherwise make about the order of the Falstaff plays; if we acknowledge that Q1 is not just a poor report of the F version but has its own integrity (however limited), while F has a different integrity which identifies it as a piece for court performance: then I suggest that my argument makes the most compelling sense of the inadequate evidence we have.

The Hotson/Green thesis plausibly satisfied the myth about Elizabeth wanting to see Sir John in love, but it did nothing for the much more concrete historical reality of the Cobhams insisting that Oldcastle's name be changed. And nowhere have I seen an attempt to trace how the fortunes of Henry, Lord Cobham, elected to the Garter in 1599 and degraded from it in 1604, *must* have impacted the Shakespeare plays which were so closely associated with him and his family's name, not least *Merry Wives* with (in both versions, though differently) all its Garter associations.

---

[50] The text of the play printed in the 1623 folio was clearly stripped of profanity some time after the 1606 Act of Abuses and set from a copy prepared by the scrivener, Ralph Crane, who has not been associated with the King's Men earlier than 1618. Neither fact helps us to date the underlying copy. It perhaps says something, however, that Crane failed to make a very impressive job of bringing the text to tolerable order. Anyone who has seen his work on the manuscripts of *A Game at Chess*—so much neater and better organized than those of the author, Middleton—must conclude that what he was faced with was in some disarray (Dutton 1999). It would not be surprising if these were the papers in which Shakespeare had (not altogether transparently) translated the earlier version of the play into the later one.

7
Last Thoughts
a. Single Sequence Additions

In the Shakespeare corpus there are three texts which, over the course of their printing history, each acquired a single extra scene or long sequence which had not appeared in its earliest imprint. On the face of it, this gives grounds for suspecting that their history may have been similar to that of *A Fair Quarrel* (see p. 114), with the extra sequences being added for court performances—a slightly different enlivening twist from the spread revisions, say, to *Mucedorus* (1610) or *Philaster* (1622). But, to the best of my knowledge, this case had not been argued for any one of them. They are, in order of composition, *Titus Andronicus*, *Richard II*, and *2 Henry IV*.

TITUS ANDRONICUS

A quarto of *Titus* was published in 1594 (Q1); the reprints of 1600 and 1611 add little of consequence. But when the folio text appeared in 1623 (F) it contained a whole extra scene, that which appears in modern editions as 3.2 (TLN 1,451–539). It is often known as the fly scene, since the key action has Titus's brother, Marcus, killing a fly. This drives Titus into bizarre, insane reflections: 'How if that fly had a father and mother?' and so on (F 3.2.60; TLN 1,513). The scene was normally printed in twentieth-century editions, though little note was made of its anomalous origin. Jonathan Bate's Arden 3 edition (1995) was the first to make a real editorial point of this:

> A responsible modern edition of *Titus Andronicus* has to be based on Q1, which represents something unusually close to a play as Shakespeare wrote it and as it was first performed... at the same time there are good reasons for believing that the folio stage directions reflect early seventeenth century practice and that the fly-killing scene is authentic, so that a text should incorporate them. My text is, however, the first to draw attention to the different status of the fly-killing scene by printing it in a different typeface. (98)

Later Bate adds this comment: 'The first folio text includes one completely self-contained scene that had not previously been printed. It has all the marks of an addition to the action, like the celebrated added mad scenes in Kyd's *Spanish Tragedy*' (1995: 117).

There are several suggestive points here. The scene is indeed self-contained. It can be included or excluded in performance or print, without doing damage to the narrative coherence of the play. It is, in John Kerrigan's characterization, more typical of a non-authorial reviser, who 'inserted...sizeable pieces of text without altering the details of his precursor's dialogue', though *A Fair Quarrel* gives a very clear example of how an author might also revisit his text in this way (see pp. 114–15). The analogy with the added mad scenes in *The Spanish Tragedy* is also telling. Mad scenes were a stock-in-trade for the Elizabethans—Alan C. Dessen speaks of the 'plentiful *mad* scenes that start in the 1580s'—and for many this is sufficient to explain the addition of the 'fly' scene (Dessen 2009: 519). In his New Cambridge edition of the play, for example, Alan Hughes observes that 'Shakespeare seems to have added [3.2] sometime after 1594 to exploit a vogue for mad scenes' (2006: 48). Bate's comment that 'the folio stage directions reflect early seventeenth century practice', however, suggests that this may not have been a casual early addition but one associated with later staging. And this seems all the more likely when we examine that staging more closely, as Hughes does:

> The fact that 3.2 was printed for the first time in the Folio, as well as its relatively sophisticated verse, suggests that this is a later addition...The transition to 4.1 is awkward. Titus and Young Lucius exit with Lavinia to read in her closet, which implies that Marcus leaves by the other door. Next young Lucius runs on pursued by Lavinia; they meet Marcus and Titus, who evidently enter by the other door. Shakespeare avoids bringing actors on for another scene immediately after an exit. This re-entry requires a clumsy backstage regrouping, aggravated by the attendants, who would have to 'strike' the properties used in the 'banquet' [i.e. fly-killing scene] and rush into the tiring-house with their burdens just in time to collide with actors regrouping for their entrance in 4.1.
>   This is decidedly odd. The journeyman Shakespeare contrived smooth transitions between acts, but as an experienced craftsman adding a scene years later, he seems to have forgotten his skill. Perhaps playhouse custom had changed; where action had flowed continuously when *Titus Andronicus* was new, an interval was inserted between Acts 3 and 4, precisely where a modern audience would expect it. (2006: 173)

'Perhaps playhouse custom had changed...' There is no evidence that the practice of continuous staging ever changed at public amphitheatres like the Globe. They were, though, certainly different at the Blackfriars, where candles needed to be trimmed.

There is no evidence that Shakespeare's company ever staged old revenge tragedies like *Titus* at the Blackfriars, but it must be possible; *Othello*, for example, certainly transferred from the Globe to the Blackfriars (title pages of Q1 1622 and Q2 1630). But the one context in which they are very *likely* to have staged the play in this manner—by reputation one of their most successful properties—was the court. The even more lavish use of candles there, as we have discussed, required repeated interruptions to the action. It is commonly observed that the division of plays into acts in the First Folio was to fulfil a 1620s readerly expectation of plays printed in the same mode as the classical dramatists, notably Plautus and Terence. But that volume, for the most part, stopped short of Ben Jonson's practice, in his

1616 *Works*, of laying out his plays in strictly classical fashion, with a bunching of all the character names in a scene at its head. Whoever prepared the texts did insert (some) act and scene breaks, but they were far from consistent.[1] Whatever else act divisions may have denoted, they perfectly reflected their acting practice in staging the plays at court.

In the case of *Titus Andronicus*, an act break before 4.1 would readily resolve all the complications which Alan Hughes describes. There would be time for the 'banquet' to be cleared, and Titus, Young Lucius, Lavinia, and Marcus would have no problem regrouping for their re-entry. If the new scene was going to be staged at the Globe, however, further thought would have to be given to the problems Hughes identifies.

RICHARD II

Richard II was first published in a quarto (Q1) of 1597; it announced the play to be 'As it hath been publicly acted by the Right Honourable the Lord Chamberlain his servants'. What was in essence the same text, with only minor differences (one being the addition of Shakespeare's name to the title page), was reprinted twice in 1598. Then it was reprinted in 1608. The initial title page of Q4 looks very like those of the 1598 copies, except that the actors are now the King's Men. But then a second state of Q4 was issued in the same year and its title page flagged a revival and a significant difference: 'The tragedy of King Richard the Second with new additions of the Parliament Scene, and the deposing of King Richard. As it hath been lately acted by the King's Majesty's servants, at the Globe'.

It was as good as its word; indeed the earlier 1608 copies also had these additions, as the folio eventually would too (in a somewhat better copy). A single continuous passage—not, strictly, a 'scene'—is inserted at a point on H2r in the original 1597 text (4.1.155–321 in Bevington 2008). The Bishop of Carlisle denounces the plan to depose King Richard, and the Earl of Northumberland arrests him on charges of capital treason; he places Carlisle in the custody of the Abbot of Westminster, and immediately Bolingbroke announces that his coronation will take place the following Wednesday. Most of the assembled lords disperse, leaving only Carlisle, Aumerle, and Westminster, who laments 'A woeful pageant have we here beheld'. In the 1608 version, as soon as Carlisle is in custody, Northumberland continues with a parliamentary motion: 'May it please you Lords, to grant the common suit; / Fetch hither Richard, that in common view / He may surrender, so we shall proceed

---

[1] We do not know how 'hands on' Heminge and Condell were in preparing the First Folio. Ralph Crane, the one copyist we can identify from those who worked on its texts (including *The Tempest*, *The Two Gentlemen of Verona*, *Merry Wives*, and possibly also *Measure for Measure*, *The Winter's Tale*, and *Cymbeline*), was generally quite meticulous about marking act and scene breaks there and in those of his manuscripts which have survived, including those of *A Game at Chess*. We do not know, however, whether this was simply a personal preference or something required by his employers. For some reason he chose to use Jonson-style 'massed' headings for *Merry Wives*, but *only* that text. Some Folio texts, like *Romeo and Juliet* and *Antony and Cleopatra*, contain no directions for breaks after the opening scene.

without suspicion' (H1v). These proceedings continue for 166 lines: Richard II publicly surrenders his crown to Bolingbroke and abdicates with a sequence of rhetorical flourishes, culminating with a play on the order to 'convey him to the Tower': 'O good convey, conveyers are you all, / That rise thus nimbly by a true King's fall' (H3v). At which point Bolingbroke takes up again the old text with the announcement of his coronation the following week, and Carlisle, Aumerle, and Westminster are left once more to lament the woeful pageant.

The seamlessness of the insertion makes it difficult to be sure exactly what happened here. Westminster's 'woeful pageant' could either be Carlisle's peroration and arrest; or it could be Richard's rhetorically inflated abdication. The balance of scholarly opinion on this has generally weighed towards the latter, suspecting that the passage existed prior to 1597 but was censored (either prudentially by the actors or the printer, or directly by the authorities). Then for some reason the censorship was withdrawn in 1608 and the old passage was restored. When I confronted this issue in my *Mastering the Revels*, I was far from convinced that censorship was to blame (Dutton 1991: 124–7). The most perplexing feature of the censorship thesis is that the new (or restored) passage seems relatively innocuous: why censor the self-pitying abdication of a king, who in both versions has already sent word by York that he is prepared to stand down, when the scene of his murder is left untouched? 'Those who would see in all this evidence of a dangerous text finally being made available to the reading public have to weigh against it the equally strong possibility that Shakespeare and his colleagues felt it necessary to spice up the play with "new additions"... to make it worth reviving' (126).

Since then Cyndia Susan Clegg has published by far the most compelling explanation of why the passage might not have seemed so innocuous to the authorities in 1597 (1997). Her argument is that the Q4 scene is explicitly in Parliament, with the implication that Parliament has the authority to make and unmake kings. As Elizabeth's reign moved to its inevitable end, with no declared successor, such a doctrine would have been anathema to her. By 1608 James was on the throne and had three living children; the doctrine would doubtless have been equally objectionable to him, but the issue was no longer topically subversive. In support of this argument, Clegg notes that some of the stage directions have been tactfully changed. In 1597 the whole sequence we have been considering begins with 'Enter Bolingbroke with the Lords to Parliament' (G4r), which suggests a degree of ceremony that makes the whole context unmistakable. But of course we do not get the abdication/deposition. In 1608 we have a bare 'Enter Bolingbroke, Aumerle, and others' (G4v). It is left to Northumberland's words to make the point: the 'common suit' which he urges is a motion by the House of Commons that has been sent for consideration to the House of Lords. This is explicitly parliamentary business (as indeed the title page announced that it would be). And this leads directly to Richard's highly stylized resignation of his whole role and identity.

This explanation has made me lean over the past few years to the view that censorship might well have been at work here. But looking at the issue again in the wider context of texts revised for court performance, I find myself once more pulled in the other direction. It is clear in both versions that the power brokers in

Parliament, Bolingbroke and Northumberland, do in fact depose Richard. The scene at Flint Castle where Richard surrenders to the rebellious forces establishes that with its vivid imagery of the setting sun: 'Down, down I come, like glist'ring Phaeton' (Q1, G2r; 3.3.178). What the 1608 text gives us is not a new political reality but something of gloss on it, a metaphysical poem on the meaning of that reality for a Richard who peers into a looking glass, seeking a self which has been obliterated. It is a gift of a scene for Burbage, who presumably played the role. Yes, it is possible that dwelling on the issue at such length made a censor in the 1590s uncomfortable. But it is equally possible that these genuinely were 'new additions' for the Jacobean era, rhetorically copious in a way we have repeatedly found in texts reworked for the court—and on a subject which is repeatedly a subject in such augmentations, the nature of monarchy itself (see pp. 196–7, 263 below).

2 HENRY IV

The textual history of *2 Henry IV* is one of the most complex in Shakespeare's canon. The play appeared only in one quarto (Q, 1600), which has all the hallmarks of having been set from a manuscript in Shakespeare's own hand—the character name Silence, for example, is often spelled Scilens, in what appears to be Shakespeare's preferred spelling. But that quarto appeared in two distinct states (usually differentiated as QA and QB). And the First Folio text (F) is quite different in some respects from either version of Q, apparently relying in part on a manuscript other than the one on which Q was based. It contains, in particular, eight passages of some substance that do not appear in Q.[2] Some of these refer openly to Richard II or heavily involve the Archbishop of York as one of the leading rebels, and might well have been censored in relation to the dire political situation in Ireland in 1600 when the quarto was published: QA strikingly contains no reference at all to Richard II. Other passages, however, like Lady Percy's lament for the dead Hotspur, seem to have no such dangerous connotations.[3]

Amid all this, what critically distinguishes QB (and subsequently F) from QA is that it contains a whole scene not in the earlier imprint. That scene is 3.1 in Bevington 2008 and other modern editions. It is where Henry IV laments the miseries of kingship ('Uneasy lies the head that wears a crown': QB, E4r), and goes on to discuss the state of the rebellion with Warwick, wishing that it could be quashed so that he could pursue his dream of a crusade to the Holy Land. As with the abdication scene in Q4 *Richard II*, one can argue that it is aesthetically crucial: without it King Henry does not appear in the play that bears his name until what in modern texts is 4.3, where he is already on his deathbed. So it is commonly

---

[2] The passages which appear only in F are 1.1.166–79, TLN 225–38; 1.1.189–209, TLN 248–68; 1.3.21–4, TLN 522–5; 1.3.36–55, TLN 537–56; 1.3.85–108, TLN 588–611; 2.3.23–45, TLN 981–1,003; 4.1.55–79, TLN 1,923–47; and 4.1.103–39, TLN 1,969–2,005.

[3] Explanations for these differences are many and varied. See, for example, Humphreys 1966: lxviii–lxxiv; Jowett and Taylor 1987: 31–50; Jowett 1987: 351–3; Melchiori 1989: 189–202; Weis 1998: 78–99.

argued that the scene was always part of Shakespeare's plan for the play. A. W. Pollard pointed out that, at 108 lines, this was almost exactly double what Shakespeare seems commonly to have written on a folio side of paper, so that the entire scene might have occupied a single sheet, which could easily have been mislaid en route to the printer or by the printer himself (1920).

On the other hand, it is surely suspicious that the scene is so self-contained. Its omission from the text leaves out nothing critical to the narrative, which is true to the description on the quarto title pages: 'The Second part of Henry the fourth, continuing to his death, and coronation of Henry the fifth. With the humours of Sir John Falstaff, and swaggering Pistol' (Q; A1r). The king is only required to die; other than that the play is really about Falstaff, Pistol, and the Prince. And even if we grant the aesthetic case that Henry IV should appear earlier than he otherwise would, nothing would guarantee that Shakespeare should get it right in his first draft. There is every possibility that it is a second thought.

A factor often overlooked in attempts to unravel these textual mysteries is that we start with what is already a very long play. QA is 2,898 lines long, many of which are dense prose. QB, with this scene, expands to 3,012 lines. F expands again with the eight new (or restored) passages mentioned earlier, though it also loses some lines from Q; its total is 3,140 lines. By the criteria we have been following, it is doubtful if any version of the play was performed in its entirety on the public stage. But it is highly likely that they all were performed at court. The scene we know as 3.1 has all the hallmarks of a gracious embellishment for that venue. Like the parallel scenes in *Titus* and *Richard II*, it is self-contained and can be omitted without damaging the narrative. It provides Burbage (assuming he played the king) with two fine and resonant soliloquies: 'How many thousand of my poorest subjects... Uneasy lies the head that wears a crown' and 'O God, that one might read the book of fate...And the division of our amity' (E3v–E5r; 3.1.4–31; 45–79).[4]

And one of these complies with what is a virtual requisite of the *latest* versions of the Henriad plays, being a lament about the burdens of kingship. As early as *Richard II* Henry IV is not allowed to enjoy his usurpation: he is troubled from the start by his 'unthrifty son' (5.3.1). *1 Henry IV* actually starts with his 'So shaken as we are, so wan with care' (1.1.1). Even before the insertion of the new scene, QA of *2 Henry IV* had him regretting at length a reign which had been all about living with the consequences of seizing the throne illegally: 'God knows (my son) / By what by-paths, and indirect crooked ways, / I met this crown' (Q, I2r). But 3.1's earlier soliloquies raise this to a new pitch, and (as we noted: p. 197) that will be echoed again in one of the soliloquies added to the folio version of *Henry V*: 'Upon the King! Let us our lives, our souls, / Our Debts, our careful wives, / Our children, and our sins, lay on the King!' (F 4.1.228–82; TLN 2,079–134). There is a family likeness to these set pieces which perhaps suggests an author playing to a known audience's tastes.

All three of the *Henriad* plays are known to have been performed at court in Shakespeare's lifetime: *Henry V* in 1605 and both *1* and *2 Henry IV* (as 'The

---

[4] The signatures expand to E5 and (unmarked) E6 to accommodate the additions in QB.

Hotspur' and 'Sir John Falstaff') in 1612/13. This record is far too late to have affected QA and QB of *2 Henry IV*, but such was the popularity of Falstaff that there must be a very good chance that it was performed there unrecorded between 1598 and 1600. There is no record of either *Richard II* or *Titus Andronicus* at court. But, as I have shown, it is statistically likely that virtually all of Shakespeare's plays were performed there, in the Jacobean era (when the number of court performances was just so much greater) if not before. And that time frame would work for both these plays, whose extra scenes first appeared in 1608 and 1623 respectively.

And, like *2 Henry IV*, both of them stood a better-than-average chance of being called to court. The stubborn popularity of *Titus Andronicus* was notorious throughout the era, and we do know that it was performed on 1 January 1596 at Burley-on-the-Hill in Rutland, the seat of Sir John Harington (later Lord Harington of Exton).[5] That in itself suggests that it was worthy of performance at court. Similarly *Richard II* was probably the play that Sir Edward Hoby had staged at his house on the Strand for Sir Robert Cecil on 9 December 1595 (Chambers 1923: 3.194n), and if this was the play that the Chamberlain's Men were commissioned to perform on the eve of the Essex Rebellion in February 1601, it must have acquired some notoriety from that. Both plays, moreover, were among the most reprinted of Shakespeare's texts prior to 1623: *Titus* in 1594, 1600, and 1611; *Richard II* in 1597, 1598 (twice), and 1608 (in two states). If, as is likely, reprints often accompanied stage revivals, that suggests that both remained in the repertoire and would have been vying for the attention of the Master of the Revels. It surely tells us something that Henry Herbert chose *Richard II* at the Globe for his summer benefit in 1631, clearly expecting a good profit (Bawcutt 1996: 173).

Whatever else we make of the changes between the three different versions of *2 Henry IV*, it seems indisputable that Shakespeare continued to work on the text beyond the authorial manuscript which lay behind QA. It would seem to have been completed, and the play performed, by 1598 at the latest. Censorship may have played its part, but it was at best inconsistent: the new scene in QB discusses Richard's history and the rebellion current in the play at length, turning around QA's marked reticence on those issues. If, however, the scene had recently received the Master of the Revels' blessing for performance at court, it would very probably have been allowed into print.[6] Conversely, if the eight passages which appeared for

---

[5] Henslowe's *Diary* records five performances in 1594, the year of its first publication, but lists no more once the Chamberlain's Men, who had inherited it from earlier companies, ceased to play in his theatres (Foakes 2002: 21, 22). Jonson mocked those 'that will swear *Jeronimo* [*The Spanish Tragedy*] or *Andronicus* are the best plays yet' in the Induction to *Bartholomew Fair* (1614).

[6] As I argued in *Mastering the Revels* (1991: 53–4), a licence to perform a play in the public theatres meant that it was fit to perform before the Queen: that was the standard of acceptability. Until 1606 licensing for performance and licensing for the press were handled by separate authorities, the Master of the Revels and the Bishop of London's clerical censors respectively. Sir George Buc then started licensing for the press; from 1610 he performed both roles, though he charged separate fees for each. In practice, however, plays often ducked under the requirement for press censorship, like ballads and other ephemera, and were 'allowed' under the authority of the Master and Wardens of the Stationers' Company alone. That seems to have been what happened to both *Richard II* and *2 Henry IV*, since both are entered in the Stationers' Register but no licenser is mentioned (Arber 1875: 3.89; 3.170).

the first time in F existed when QB went to press, it is difficult to see how censorship would account for some of them (such as Lady Percy's lament for Hotspur) not being printed at that time. This leaves open the distinct possibility that some of those passages were composed later than the 1600 printing of QA and QB, conceivably even as late as the known court performance in 1612/13.

2 Henry IV thus stands alongside plays such as *Richard III*, *Hamlet*, *King Lear*, *Othello*, and *Troilus and Cressida* where we seem to have a perfectly satisfactory court-performance text in quarto (here QB, if not also QA) but the editors of the First Folio, even where they followed those quartos to some degree, incorporated what may well be later elaborations. Sometimes the changes they made amount to no more than representing theatrical practice. But at other times they seem to have had access to what we can only call second, or even third thoughts on Shakespeare's part. There was no pressure on Shakespeare to keep 'tinkering' in this way for public performances. But there was almost certainly pressure—when the plays appeared at court—to make them as impressive and memorable as might be.

b. Jacobean Shakespeare

All of the 'bad' quartos (and most of the 'good' ones) are Elizabethan documents, all products of the first half of Shakespeare's career. Is this just a matter of chance? To what extent do they offer evidence about the production of his later works? The key question is whether Shakespeare's writing practices changed when King James came to the throne. It is usual to assume that the Chamberlain's and King's Men were, in effect, a seamless entity—*The Shakespeare Company*, as Andrew Gurr dubs it (2004a). Their personnel remained largely the same, and the Globe continued to be their sole London house until they also were able to use the Blackfriars after 1608. Yet there is an awful lot that we just do not know about the Jacobean Shakespeare, not least because the printing of his new plays virtually dries up. We do, however, get first sight of a new phenomenon: two 'good' but *different* texts of the same play, in *Hamlet*, *Troilus and Cressida*, *Othello*, and *King Lear*.[7] And there are other signs that the company may have rethought their use of one of their principal assets, their 'ordinary poet', Shakespeare.

THE CHANGE OF REIGN

The Chamberlain's Men ceased to be on 19 May 1603 and were replaced by the King's Men. I put it this way, rather than say that the Chamberlain's Men 'became' the King's Men, because in some important respects that is not what happened. To most appearances it is true that relatively little changed, except that James I was now their immediate patron, and the sharers in the company would henceforth wear his splendid scarlet livery in their largely honorary positions as Grooms of the Chamber.[8] In due course the other major companies also came under royal patronage (see p. 34).[9] As I argued earlier in the book, this did not signify a policy shift: it acknowledged the reality of the leading companies implicitly tied to the court, in an era of multiple royal households. The fact that the King's Men received their royal patent only eight days after James had entered his new capital was perhaps a

---

[7] Several other Elizabethan plays appeared in the First Folio in versions somewhat different from their 'good' quartos, including *Love's Labour's Lost*, *A Midsummer Night's Dream*, *Richard III*, and *2 Henry IV*.

[8] They did, however, form part of the retinue that attended upon the Spanish Ambassador Extraordinary during the peace negotiations with Spain in August 1604. For once they were bit parts in the actual drama of court life, rather than its dramatic interpreters (Gurr 2004a: 51).

[9] In later years Prince Charles and Princess Elizabeth also patronized companies, as did Elizabeth's husband, the Elector Palatine. After 1606, when Paul's Boys went out of business, all London-based companies had explicit royal patronage.

marker—not least to the City of London—of how important theatre was going to be in the new reign.

A straw in that wind was the inclusion of a new name in the list of sharers. Laurence Fletcher was named first in the patent, followed by William Shakespeare and then Richard Burbage. Fletcher's acting company had found favour with King James in Edinburgh in the years before he acceded to the English throne. His connections with James in fact went back at least as far as 1594, when he was one of the 'Inglis comedianis' recorded in Edinburgh and by 1601 he was referred to as 'Laurence Fletcher, comedian to his Majesty' (Chambers 1923: 2.269).[10] Since in fact we hear no more about him, there has long been suspicion that Fletcher's inclusion in the King's Men's patent was little more than a token gesture to a royal favourite (e.g. Chambers 1923: 2.209). But from the company's point of view in 1603, it was surely to their advantage to have in their ranks someone who knew something of the Scottish royal family's interest in theatre, and perhaps of their particular tastes. Fletcher may well have anticipated the explosion of theatricals at the English Jacobean court, where James had the much greater revenues of England and a wider array of acting talent at his disposal. Leeds Barroll has offered a useful corrective to fanciful notions that James was an avid lover of theatre and indeed that he was always present when plays were presented at court (1991: 22–69). But he fully understood the role played by actors at the court of England (and Spain, France, and elsewhere) in reflecting the splendour and bounty of their monarchs. Their shows befitted the magnificence of kings.

Moreover, as Fletcher doubtless knew, whatever James's personal view of plays and players, his queen and elder son were avid fans. Sir Dudley Carleton caught the spirit of all this perfectly during their first English Revels season of 1603/4: 'The first holy days we had every night a public play in the great hall, at which the king was ever present, and liked or disliked as he saw cause; but it seems he takes no extraordinary pleasure in them. The Queen and Prince were more the players' friends, for on other nights they had them privately, and hath since taken them to their protection' (Carleton 1972: 53). Arbella Stuart reported on 18 December that 'It is said there shall be 30 plays' that Revels season, reflecting the general amazement at the number of plays being staged (Stuart 1994: 197). In the event there were only sixteen, plus the first of Queen Anna's masques, *The Vision of the Twelve Goddesses*.[11] Even so it was more than twice as many as Elizabeth ever saw staged in a season. The King's Men alone put on eight, in addition to the one they had put on for the court's visit to the Earl of Pembroke's Wilton.

Queen Anna's particular enthusiasm for theatricals is borne out in a letter from the second Jacobean Revels season. It is from Sir Walter Cope to Robert Cecil, who was Principal Secretary to James as he had been to Elizabeth:

---

[10] See also Dibdin 1888: 20; Bain 1898–1915: 2.676; Calderwood 1842–9: 5.765 on Fletcher's career in Scotland.

[11] Plays were staged on fifteen nights. The number sixteen includes two plays performed by the King's Men on 1 January and assumes that only one play was performed on 20 February, by a joint troupe of the Prince's Men and Paul's Boys, rather than one play each.

I have sent and been all this morning hunting for players, jugglers and such kind of creatures, but find them hard to find; wherefore, leaving notes for them to seek me, Burbage is come, and says there is no new play that the Queen hath not seen, but they have revived an old one called *Love's Labour Lost*, which for wit and mirth he says will please her exceedingly. And this is appointed to be played tomorrow night at my Lord of Southampton's, unless you send a writ to remove the *corpus cum causa* to your house in Strand. Burbage is my messenger ready attending your pleasure.   (Chambers 1923: 4.139)[12]

At least two features of this are remarkable. One is that a man as busy and important as Robert Cecil was employing one of his principal agents in pursuit of actors and personally determining what they should act and where. (There was, to be sure, a diplomatic dimension to this, in that the Queen's brother, the Duke of Holstein, was visiting and all due courtesies had to be observed.) The other is that, by this account, Queen Anna had—between 30 June 1603, when she reached Windsor from Scotland, and January 1605—exhausted the entire current repertory of the King's Men, which on the comparative basis of Henslowe's *Diary* we might put at thirty plays. How precisely she managed this is far from clear, since the number of recorded court performances by the King's Men would hardly amount to so many in that time, and she certainly did not visit the public theatres. We can only suppose that more plays were staged at private residences, such as that at the Earl of Southampton, than we have knowledge of; or that documentation from the Queen's household is lost. But however she managed it, it was a harbinger of what was to come. And in that context the company (quite possibly advised by Tilney) must have thought carefully about their strongest asset, Shakespeare.

SHAKESPEARE'S CONTRACT

What might these changes, including this enormously expanded royal consumption of drama, have meant for William Shakespeare? The short answer is that we do not know. But circumstantial evidence allows us to make some informed guesses. For one thing, Jonson's *Sejanus* (1603) is the last play in which we know that he performed. He is not listed in any of the three subsequent King's Men's plays to appear in the Jonson folio, *Volpone*, *The Alchemist*, and *Catiline*. This does not strictly prove anything, since the principles by which Jonson decided which actors to mention are elusive. Robert Armin—whom we think of as a mainstay of the company—is only listed in *The Alchemist*. Jonson probably only included those in major roles, and Armin may have spread his comic talent around several smaller

---

[12] The dating of this letter has to be circumstantial. It is endorsed '1604' in the Cecil archives and was addressed to Robert Cecil as Viscount Cranborne, the title he bore from 20 August 1604 to 4 May 1605, when he became Earl of Salisbury. A letter of 15 January 1605 from Dudley Carleton to John Chamberlain seems to refer to the same events: 'The last night's revels were kept at my Lord Cranborne's, where the Q[ueen] with the D[uke] of Holst[ein] and a great part of the court were feasted, and the like two nights before at my Lord of Southampton's' (*State Papers Domestic, Jac.*1, 12: 13).

ones. Shakespeare may similarly have taken smaller roles after *Sejanus*. So there is a good chance that the Jacobean Shakespeare no longer appeared onstage, in his own plays or anyone else's; but if he did, he probably only played smaller roles.

His situation as player/playwright/shareholder in the Chamberlain's Men had been unique among the leading companies of the 1590s. The Admiral's Men did not then employ an 'ordinary poet', but commissioned plays from a stable of playwrights, often in collaboration. This was also true, as far as we can determine, of Pembroke's, Derby's, and Worcester's Men. And this must have been how the Chamberlain's Men acquired *most* of their plays. A house playwright like Shakespeare can only ever have contributed a small proportion of new plays to the company's repertoire. Henslowe's *Diary* shows that, between 1594 and 1597, the Admiral's Men staged successively twenty-one, nineteen, and fourteen new plays a year, the latter figure becoming something like a settled norm. Shakespeare normally averaged two plays a year in this period. Assuming the Chamberlain's Men recruited new work at a similar rate, he could only have contributed at most one in seven of the new plays put on.

On the other hand, of the twenty-one new plays staged by the Admiral's Men in 1594/5, only eight were acted again in subsequent seasons. The real value to a company of a well-chosen 'ordinary poet' lay in his ability to create plays which would become a regular feature of the future repertoire, bankable certainties. By 1603 this must have been emphatically the case with Shakespeare. Throughout their existence, the King's Men never abandoned the practice of having a retained playwright, though they did adapt it. When they recruited Nathan Field around 1615, they briefly replicated Shakespeare's 1594 situation, since Field was a player/playwright/shareholder, though—as a leading actor—never apparently as prolific as an author.[13] But they also retained the exclusive services of John Fletcher, who collaborated with Shakespeare in his final writings (*c.* 1613), and thereafter wrote exclusively for them until his death in 1625. He, however, was never an actor or a sharer in the company. The financial side of this agreement must presumably have been mutually advantageous. Fletcher had already made his mark writing for the boy companies and in his extremely popular collaborations with Francis Beaumont, some of which the King's Men commissioned. So his long-term value to the company was well established before he entered an extended contractual arrangement with them. The same was true of Philip Massinger, Fletcher's eventual successor, who co-authored a number of plays with both him and Field. The same was, finally, also true of James Shirley after Massinger; he had a solid track record with Queen Henrietta's Men behind him.

So, to return to the question of Shakespeare's situation in 1603: it is entirely plausible that there might be mutual agreement that Shakespeare's time was better spent writing plays than performing in them, producing more of the plays which

---

[13] Field's presence was only brief because he died in 1619 or 1620. No solo play by Field written while he was with the King's Men has survived, though five plays that he co-authored with John Fletcher and/or Philip Massinger in that period form part of the Beaumont and Fletcher corpus: *The Honest Man's Fortune*, *The Queen of Corinth*, *The Jeweller of Amsterdam*, *The Fatal Dowry*, and *The Knight of Malta*.

would form the bedrock of their repertory for years to come. The issue might have been even more charged if the company felt the need of a strategy to address acquiring plays specifically to match the demand from the court, as distinct from what they regularly offered at the Globe.

Something which certainly changed is that plays written by him after the accession of King James—and not just 'bad' quartos—all but stopped being printed. In the period from 1603 to 1616 only five plays which had not previously been published reached the press: the 1603 and 1604/5 quartos of *Hamlet*, the 1608 quarto of *King Lear*, and the 1609 quartos of *Pericles* and *Troilus and Cressida*.[14] Of those, the 1603 version of *Hamlet*, at least, was in origin an Elizabethan play, entered in the Stationers' Register in 1602; in the same way, a version of *Troilus and Cressida* was entered in the Register on 7 February 1603. *Pericles* is, of course, a notoriously problematic text, probably only partly by Shakespeare and not reprinted in the 1623 folio—though whether because of the editors' scruples or because they could not secure the rights is unknown. A quarto of *Othello* belatedly appeared, in 1622, shortly before the folio. But even that may not be in origin a Jacobean text. The editors of the *Oxford Shakespeare* date the play between the summers of 1603 and 1604 (Wells and Taylor 1986: 819), but E. A. J. Honigmann, the Arden 3 editor, suggests '1602 as the probable year of the play's first performance' (1997: 350). In short, *King Lear* is the only indisputably Jacobean play entirely by Shakespeare to see print in his own lifetime, or indeed down to the publication of the First Folio.

One of the strongest chapters in Lukas Erne's *Shakespeare as Literary Dramatist* is 'The players' alleged opposition to print', where he shows that the Chamberlain's Men in fact allowed into print as many of Shakespeare's plays as it is reasonable to assume that they held the rights to (2003: 115–28). They possibly even *encouraged* the publication of the 'good' quartos up to and including the 1604/5 *Hamlet*. Erne does this to argue that Shakespeare always wrote with a readership in view, whether it be readers of printed texts or of specially commissioned scribal copies. That may or may not be the case.[15] But that so many of Shakespeare's plays for the Chamberlain's Men found their way into print must have been a collective company decision, not Shakespeare's own.

And for some reason the situation changed when the King's Men came into being, in ways that Erne does not convincingly explain. He is, firstly, in thrall to the contention that there was no great appetite for printed plays and so no great demand for them from printers. He cites Peter Blayney on this: 'Everything depends on the axiom that the demand for printed plays greatly exceeded the supply—which happens to be untrue' (1997: 384). Blayney was here denying the existence of a

---

[14] Of plays probably written after 1603, the following were not printed until the First Folio: *Measure for Measure*, *All's Well that Ends Well*, *Timon of Athens*, *Macbeth*, *Antony and Cleopatra*, *Coriolanus*, *The Winter's Tale*, *Cymbeline*, *The Tempest*, and *Henry VIII*. *The Two Noble Kinsmen* was not printed until 1634, and *Cardenio* was never printed and is lost. I discuss *Othello* in the text.

[15] Shakespeare *did* provide signed dedications to the Earl of Southampton for the printed texts of *Venus and Adonis* and *The Rape of Lucrece*. It may be significant that, save only in *The Faithful Shepherdess*—written before his contract with the King's Men—John Fletcher also did not acknowledge the publication of his plays.

supposedly heavy demand for Shakespeare's plays, which A. W. Pollard had argued inspired the publishers of the 'bad' quartos to piracy (1920).[16] If Blayney's contention were true, the paucity of Shakespeare texts in the Jacobean era would simply confirm his case. But his statistics have been convincingly challenged by Zachary Lesser and Alan Farmer, in demonstrating that the trade in playbooks was sound, and indeed often flourishing, throughout the early modern period, if subject to occasional fluctuations. Plays in fact got reprinted more often than other comparable kinds of publication, a real marker of value and demand (Lesser and Farmer 2005a and b). In the Jacobean phase of his life, Shakespeare's own *Richard III* (1603, 1605), *Titus Andronicus* (1611), *Romeo and Juliet* (1609), *Richard II* (1608, 1615), *1 Henry IV* (1604, 1608, 1613), and *Hamlet* Q2 (1611) were all reprinted—and this says nothing of the seven texts reissued by Jaggard and Pavier as part of the so-called 'False Folio' in 1619.[17] The argument that there was just no demand for Shakespeare's new works at this time surely will not wash.

But Erne adduces other, equally questionable, contentions:

> What the total picture thus suggests is, I believe, not Shakespeare and his fellows' indifference to the publication of Shakespeare's plays during the years of James's reign. Such an indifference would be difficult to account for after a policy of regular and systematic publication from 1595 to 1603. Rather, print publication seems to have been postponed, possibly in lieu of manuscript presentation copies for influential patrons. (2003: 114)

If so, it is unfortunate that neither such manuscripts nor evidence of their existence have survived. Subsequently Erne speculates that 'Shakespeare, in agreement with his fellow players, held back his Jacobean plays in the prospect of a more prestigious (manuscript or print) publication' (2013: 89).

If that really was the intention, it took twenty years to realize.

What Erne will not countenance is the possibility that the formation of what was legally and factually a new playing company may have changed their policy on the issue of publication. He asserts that 'to claim that the change of reign and patron had in and of themselves anything to do with what may have been a new attitude toward the publication of Shakespeare's plays seems far-fetched and is not supported by any firm evidence' (109). But this may underestimate the special deference due to royalty. The publishing situation for plays had been very different in the late 1580s, but it is worth noting that no play by the old Queen's Men went into print until the company itself lost its court privileges in 1594. After 1603 all the companies employing 'ordinary poets' were under direct royal patronage. Plays written by the retained playwrights of such companies were not merely commercial products but acts of service to the royal patron, all the more so if the authors were shareholder members who became Grooms of the Chamber of that patron. As such, although there were occasional exceptions (like *King Lear* and Heywood's

---

[16] Blayney is almost certainly right on other grounds (to do with the functioning of the Stationers' Company, which oversaw all printing) that there was no 'piracy' of Shakespeare's plays; but not on supply and demand grounds.

[17] See Introduction, p. 3 n. 8.

Rape of Lucrece), it may in normal circumstances have seemed demeaning to reduce them to public print. Jacobean and indeed Caroline practice may only have been a continuation of an established deference to direct royal patronage.

Thomas Heywood's testimony is particularly compelling in this context because, of all his early Jacobean contemporaries, Heywood is the one whose position most closely approximated to Shakespeare's; he was a shareholder, actor, and 'ordinary poet' of Queen Anna's Men.[18] From the preface to the 1608 quarto of *The Rape of Lucrece* we know that he was not supposed to publish the plays that he wrote for them, without company permission. He apologizes for the fact that the play was coming into print at all (he insists that he was not responsible), but confirms the 'consent' of his colleagues to the exception to the rule. And these company restrictions seem to be what he alludes to many years later, in the preface to *The English Traveller*, in explaining why some of his plays are not in print: 'Others of them are still retained in the hands of some actors who think it against their peculiar profit to have them come in print' (Heywood 1633: A3r). Erne seeks to cast doubt on these claims by looking at Heywood's shifting statements elsewhere about the printing of his plays over the years (2003: 123–6). But they are quite consistent with the one set of contractual restrictions on an 'ordinary poet' of which we have details, those entered into by Richard Brome with the Salisbury Court company in the 1630s.

Brome was their 'ordinary poet', though he was never a shareholder or actor. He had two contracts with them and defaulted on both, failing to produce the required number of plays (three a year). The earlier contract made no stipulations about publication. But the second one—for which he received a higher salary—stated that the author 'should not suffer any play made or to be made or composed by him' under the terms of this contract to be printed with his consent or knowledge 'without the license from the said company or the major part of them' (Haaker 1968: 298).

This is where G. E. Bentley's argument about the publication of playbooks comes into its own, despite Erne's attempts to suggest that Bentley was finding resistance to print where it does not in fact exist (see 2003: 117, 122, 126, 127). Bentley contends that the Jacobean and Caroline companies were usually most reluctant to allow into print the plays of their 'ordinary poets'; he shows convincingly that the plays which Heywood, Fletcher, Massinger, Shirley, and indeed Brome wrote while they were under such contracts did not normally come into print so long as the contracts lasted. If the contracts of the others resembled Brome's second contract, we would have to conclude not only that these authors would require specific company permission to publish a play—but also that such permission would not normally be granted (Bentley 1971: 266–85).

And this seems on the whole to have applied to Shakespeare in respect of plays he wrote for the King's Men, even though it had not applied to those for the Chamberlain's Men.

---

[18] On the scope of Heywood's career, see Richard Rowland, *Thomas Heywood's Theatre, 1599–1639* (2010).

A NEW CONTRACT

Not only were Shakespeare's plays rarely published; there were also fewer of them. Contrary to what we might have expected (especially if he gave up or reduced his acting), the rate of production of his new plays actually declined. Between 1594 and 1602 Shakespeare wrote between sixteen and nineteen plays, all apparently unaided; that is of the order of two plays a year.[19] Between 1603 and 1613 he *at most* wrote unaided: *All's Well that Ends Well, Othello, Measure for Measure, Lear, Macbeth, Antony and Cleopatra, Coriolanus, Cymbeline, The Winter's Tale,* and *The Tempest*. He also collaborated on *Timon of Athens, Pericles, Henry VIII, The Two Noble Kinsmen,* and (perhaps) the lost *Cardenio*.[20] Even so, that is only ten complete plays and five part-plays in eleven years, almost halving his earlier output of new work.[21]

Some of this is traditionally ascribed to a slowing down as Shakespeare approached retirement, which may be true but can hardly be the whole story; he was not yet forty when James came to the throne. The fact of collaboration is new and distinctive. Although Shakespeare may have collaborated with others before 1594, it is not something we associate with his mid-career, from his association with the Chamberlain's Men onwards.[22] Was this change in policy on the part of the King's Men (and contractual for Shakespeare) possibly associated with the higher demands for drama at the court? Were the decisions to collaborate with Middleton and Fletcher made, at least in part, because both had made their names in writing for the indoor houses of the boy players, the characteristics of which Shakespeare would need to master once the King's Men took over the Blackfriars theatre?[23] Or

---

[19] These would be, in approximate order, *A Midsummer Night's Dream, Richard II, The Merchant of Venice, Romeo and Juliet, King John, Love's Labour's Lost, 1 Henry IV, Much Ado About Nothing, 2 Henry IV, As You Like It, Henry V, Julius Caesar, Merry Wives of Windsor, Hamlet, Twelfth Night,* and *Troilus and Cressida* (16). To say that he wrote these plays unaided does not preclude the possibility that one or two, like *King John* and *Love's Labour's Lost*, may be earlier works which Shakespeare revised in this period; but he did not, so far as we know, collaborate with others at this time. Less certainly within the time frame are *The Comedy of Errors*, which some date very early but others locate in 1594, and *All's Well that Ends Well* and *Othello*, which some date before the change of reigns, some after.

[20] There is now a considerable body of work arguing for Shakespeare as a collaborator in the last years of his career. This includes Hope (1994); Vickers (2002), who considers all the extant plays I have mentioned; and Jackson (2003) on *Pericles*.

[21] I have included *All's Well* and *Othello* as post-1603, though not all would agree with this. If they were indeed earlier, the disproportion is even more marked. I accept the argument that *Henry VIII* was co-written with Fletcher, though this is perhaps the most contentious case in the late canon. The most detailed recent assessment of the case is Vickers 2002: 333–432.

[22] Such collaborations might have included work not only on plays that were later credited solely to Shakespeare, such as the *Henry VI* plays and *Titus Andronicus*, but also on plays that significant numbers of scholars have only recently been prepared to concede he might have had a hand in. These include *Arden of Feversham* and *Edward III*. On *1 Henry VI* see Vickers 2007; on *Titus* see Vickers 2002: 148–243; on *Arden* and *Edward III*, see Will Sharpe in Bate and Rasmussen 2013: 650–7, 663–70.

[23] John Jowett in the *Oxford Middleton* dates the Middleton collaboration to 1605–6 (Taylor and Lavagnino 2007: 356–8), which would put this collaboration early in Shakespeare's Jacobean phase, still indisputably at the height of his powers, around the time of *King Lear* and *Macbeth*. Middleton's early association with Shakespeare might thus have brought to the King's Men plays like *The Yorkshire Tragedy* and *The Revenger's Tragedy*, if they are indeed his. On the other hand, Anthony Dawson and Gretchen Minton, in their Arden 3 edition of *Timon*, date it *c.* 1607 and so later than some of those plays, which goes to show just how fragile such narratives are: Middleton was more established and had already written for the King's Men (2008: 12–18). Nothing associates Shakespeare with Fletcher before 1613, the probable date of both *Henry VIII* (which was playing when the first Globe burnt

was it simply that both had indeed made their marks and the company was sizing up potential successors for Shakespeare? We really do not know.

Shakespeare's collaboration with George Wilkins, putative author of the first two acts of *Pericles*, is even less easy to explain (see Wells and Taylor 1987: 130, 557–9; Vickers 2002: 142–4, 291–332). What makes him, on the face of it, such an unlikely collaborator is that his first line of work was as a tavern and brothel keeper; he was also a particularly unsavoury character, with a track record of violence towards women (Nicholl 2008: 201–6). Yet Wilkins had a brief but productive period writing plays, during which he sole-authored *The Miseries of Enforced Marriage* and co-wrote *The Travels of the Three English Brothers* (both successful enough to be published) before co-writing *Pericles* with Shakespeare, the first and last of these for the King's Men. Shakespeare in fact knew Wilkins before he wrote those plays. This emerges from the *Bellott v. Mountjoy* lawsuit of 1612, in which Shakespeare made a deposition about marriage negotiations made at the house where he was lodging in 1604 (Schoenbaum 1987: 261–4; Nicholl 2008: 4–5, 290–1). This opens up the distinct possibility that Shakespeare was the connection which drew Wilkins into writing for the King's Men, if he did not positively encourage him to try his hand.

Might it have become part of Shakespeare's duties to search out and encourage new writers, who must surely always have been in short supply? One wonders, for example, how Barnabe Barnes came to write for the King's Men. His only surviving play, *The Devil's Charter*, was performed at court in the same season as *King Lear*. Barnes at least had a track record as a poet and writer before turning to the theatre, though again he was a questionable character: in 1598 he had been prosecuted in Star Chamber for trying to poison someone.

If Shakespeare was actively recruiting other playwrights for the company, and collaborating with some of them, we may consider that—as the resident playwright—he very probably had a role to play in making texts other than his own fit for the court. This is not necessarily to say that he did any rewriting himself (though see p. 7), but that he may have had a supervisory function and been the chief intermediary with Tilney and latterly Buc. As ever, the lack of real evidence makes it impossible to say anything categorical about this. Our knowledge of the Chamberlain's/King's Men's plays *other than* those by Shakespeare is quite staggeringly thin. In the period from 1594 to 1615 we know with reasonable assurance of forty-two of them.[24] In the same period Shakespeare himself appar-

---

down that year) and *The Two Noble Kinsmen*. Their collaboration may have been brought about by the withdrawal that year of Beaumont from his famous partnership with Fletcher; marriage and then a serious stroke took Beaumont out of writing altogether.

[24] This is a list of all known plays in the repertory of Shakespeare's company, other than by Shakespeare himself, in approximate order of composition, with name of author where known or suspected, up to 1615. (* Indicates that the play is lost). *Ur-Hamlet* (Kyd?*), *Mucedorus* (anon), *A Warning for Fair Women* (Heywood?), *Every Man In His Humour* (Jonson), *Every Man Out of His Humour* (Jonson), *A Larum for London* (anon), *Cloth Breeches and Velvet Hose* (anon*), *The Freeman's Honour* (Wentworth Smith?*), *Satiromastix* (Dekker), *Thomas, Lord Cromwell* (anon), *Sejanus* (Jonson), *The Tragedy of Gowrie* (anon*), *The Spanish Maze* (anon*), *The Fair Maid of Bristow* (anon), *The London Prodigal* (anon, 1605), *The Merry Devil of Edmonton* (Dekker? 1608), *Jeronimo* (anon*), *The Malcontent* (Marston and Webster), *The Miseries of Enforced Marriage* (Wilkins), *Volpone* (Jonson), *A Yorkshire Tragedy* (Middleton), *The Revenger's Tragedy* (Middleton), *The Devil's Charter* (Barnes),

ently wrote or co-wrote approximately thirty-two plays, all but one or two of which (*Love's Labour's Won; Cardenio*) have survived. If the Chamberlain's/King's Men recruited new plays at about the same annual rate reflected in Henslowe's *Diary c.* 1596–7, about fourteen, there would have been a total of 308—which means that we know nothing at all about some 234 plays, or approximately three-quarters of their repertoire. Of the forty-two non-Shakespearean titles we have, eleven are anonymous and ten are lost; of the remainder, five are by Jonson and no fewer than twelve by Fletcher (with or without Beaumont and possibly others). That leaves just fourteen other plays whose authorship we know, suspect, or can guess at, spread between eleven authors: Thomas Kyd, Thomas Heywood, Wentworth Smith, Thomas Dekker, John Marston, John Webster, George Wilkins, Thomas Middleton, Barnabe Barnes, Richard Niccolls, and Cyril Tourneur. If the parallels with the Henslowe operation are anything to go by, there may have been dozens more across the whole period.

During this period there are some 155 instances when we know that Shakespeare's company played at court, but for which we do not have the titles of the play; 33 of these were in Elizabeth's reign, 122 in James's. As I showed earlier, the—admittedly totally inadequate—evidence we have suggests that they performed about one play by Shakespeare against one play by anyone else, though that proportion diminished as the Beaumont and Fletcher supply came on stream from *c.* 1609 (p. 36). That gives us our best guess of how many times each of Shakespeare's own plays was performed at court, and we can only wonder on how many of those occasions he and the Master of the Revels felt that amendments were called for. But this also means that there were some seventy to eighty plays (up to sixty of them Jacobean), titles and authors unknown, which found their way to court—some of which may have needed revising on their way there.

I stress my earlier point that I do not believe that *all* plays were adapted for court performance—at most only some of those chosen for particularly notable holiday dates. In the two seasons during Shakespeare's career for which we are fortunate enough to have both the dates of performance *and* a good many of the titles performed, the King's Men staged the following plays on key dates: *1604/5*: 1 November (All Saints), *Othello*; 26 December (St Stephen's Day), *Measure for Measure*; 28 December (Holy Innocents or Childmas), *Comedy of Errors*; 2 February (Candlemas), *Every Man In His Humour*; 10 and 12 February (Shrove Sunday and Shrove Tuesday), *The Merchant of Venice* (repeated); *1611/12*: 1 November (All Saints), *The Tempest*; 26 December (St Stephen's Day), *A King and No King*; 1 January (New Year's Day), *The Twins' Tragedy*; 23 February (Shrove Sunday), *The Nobleman*.[25] How many of these might have required some interven-

Philaster (Beaumont and Fletcher), *The Alchemist* (Jonson), *The Maid's Tragedy* (Beaumont and Fletcher), *A King and No King* (Beaumont and Fletcher), *The Woman's Prize* (Fletcher), *Bonduca* (Fletcher), *The Captain* (Fletcher), *Valentinian* (Fletcher), *The Second Maiden's Tragedy* (Middleton), *The Duchess of Malfi* (Webster), *The Twins' Tragedy* (Niccolls*), *A Bad Beginning Makes a Good Ending* (Ford?), *The Nobleman* (Tourneur*), *The Scornful Lady* (Beaumont and Fletcher), *Love's Pilgrimage* (Fletcher), *The Honest Man's Fortune* (Fletcher), *Monsieur Thomas* (Fletcher), *The Laws of Candy* (Fletcher?), *The Knot of Fools* (anon*).

[25] Although we know the titles of the twenty plays the King's Men performed in the hectic season of 1612/13, we do not know their dates.

tion from Shakespeare—or of all their equivalents in the years for which this information is missing?

Two texts from the period survive which have sometimes been thought to reflect such interventions; these may or may not be by Shakespeare. One is the 1610 edition of *Mucedorus*, the additions to which we have already observed (p. 113); the other is *The Second Maiden's Tragedy*, which survives in manuscript. Propelled in good part by a pioneering essay by MacDonald P. Jackson (1964), Jonathan Bate and Eric Rasmussen have recently claimed the additions to *Mucedorus* for Shakespeare in their RSC Shakespeare *William Shakespeare and Others: Collaborative Plays* (2013). In the past there has been considerable resistance to the idea that Shakespeare could have written these additions, partly because scholars hesitated to associate him with the play's 'artless' mongrel tragicomedy at all. But the play is inescapably associated with the King's Men at this time, its tragicomic mode (and the bear) might be thought to have interest for Shakespeare in the period of his late plays, and the additions are distinctively different from the original. Leo Kirschbaum aptly described their style as 'Jacobean in its conceited and sometimes cynical crabbedness', a mode of which the co-author of *Timon* was certainly capable (1955: 4). And Jackson's article makes a substantial argument for Shakespeare's authorship. It seems to me a plausible case (see Will Sharpe in Bate and Rasmussen 2013: 710–16). I quoted Tiffany Stern early in this study on the likelihood that the writing of prologues, epilogues, and other incidentals might fall, as regular company dramatist, as 'an aspect of his job as company wordsmith' (see p. 7). And this may well have extended to 'patching' plays like this, making small but telling embellishments when a court performance was felt to require it.

The Second Maiden's Tragedy is now widely accepted as Middleton's. It bears Sir George Buc's licence for performance (dated 31 October 1611) and was indeed named by him, since no title was given. The manuscript is marked for cuts—some, but far from all, by Buc himself—but it also has a number of slips pasted which either revise the original or are entirely new. These 'were written out by the original scribe on a single folio sheet, cut into fine pieces and fastened to the manuscript at places marked with a circle in the margin by the bookkeeper' (Briggs 2007: 619). It also has some apparently late stage directions and seems to have been used by the King's Men as a prompt copy. The amendments to the text can be very clearly seen in the late Julia Briggs's *Oxford Middleton* edition, where the play is renamed *The Lady's Tragedy* (Middleton 2007a: 833–906). Briggs seeks to demonstrate that both the original text and the most substantial changes were by Middleton and so represent early and late versions of his intentions.

Whoever was responsible for the changes, in general 'the purpose of the additional passages seems to have been to tighten up the plot', while the cumulative effect of the cuts was dramatically to speed up the play (619). Both the main manuscript and the additional slips are in the same hand, that of a professional scribe, so they are no guide to authorship. That the additional passages are by Shakespeare was forcefully argued by Eric Rasmussen (1989). But the growing conviction that the original play is by Middleton seems to have given wider acceptance to the thought that the later changes may well be too. And the play is not included in

Bate and Rasmussen's *William Shakespeare and Others* (2013: see Will Sharpe, 728–9). This again seems to me an appropriate conclusion. The kinds of revision visible here are in no way typical of what we have observed in revisions for the court. They seem rather to represent a professional trimming and tightening of the script for regular performance, Middleton's own finishing touches.

The Second Maiden's Tragedy does not, therefore, add to the case for Shakespeare as a 'patcher' of other people's plays for court; but *Mucedorus* 1610 does, and it would be surprising if it was the only example. However, the very limited survival of King's Men's plays from the period, other than by Fletcher and Jonson (none of which Shakespeare has ever been thought to have revised), makes it impossible to develop the case. We may simply say that it is not unlikely that, in addition to recruiting new playwrights for the company, and collaborating with some of them, the Jacobean Shakespeare was partly employed in revising the company's plays—both his own and those of others—for court performance.

One further factor needs to be weighed in the balance in relation to the slowing down of Shakespeare's writing in this period, and that is the prevalence of plague in London throughout it. There were major breaks in theatrical playing because of it in 1603/4, 1606/7, and 1608/10, but also frequent lesser stoppages. Leeds Barroll calculates that in the period 1603–13, mainly because of the plague (but also factoring in suspensions caused by Lent and political disturbances), some 71 of the 132 months saw no playing at all, while a further 17 months were disrupted (Barroll 1991: esp. 173). The players' options were then limited. In the winter months they might remain in the London region—but far enough removed from the city for safety from contagion—hoping for remission. This is what the King's Men did in the winter of the 1603/4 plague. When they were summoned to perform for the court at the Earl of Pembroke's Wilton, they were staying in Mortlake in Surrey, near Richmond Palace, possibly in a house owned by Augustine Phillips (see p. 236).

But in the summer they would most likely look for income by touring. As we noted they are reported as playing at Oxford in May and June of 1603 (p. 236); it was a favourite location for them. They were there again in October 1605, July 1606 (perhaps when they performed *Volpone*, as the dedication of its 1607 quarto tells us they did), September 1607, August in 1610 (when performances of *Othello* and *The Alchemist* were recorded), and before November of 1613. But this was only one venue of many, on what would have been carefully planned itineraries—their visits are also recorded at Leicester, Dover, Saffron Walden, Marlborough, Barnstaple, Dunwich, Ipswich, New Romney, Hythe, Shrewsbury, Stafford, Folkestone, and Norwich (Gurr 1996: 304–5, 390). Their royal livery ensured at the least a civil reception and a fee higher than that of rival troupes. This was the way of life all the players had known before 1594.

What effect did this have on Shakespeare's writing? In *Politics, Plague, and Shakespeare's Theater*, Leeds Barroll argues that it had a profound effect: 'Shakespeare did not wish to write plays throughout the periods when the playhouses were shut—when he could not see productions at the Globe' (1991: 19). I think this is misguided for a number of reasons, as well as being unprovable. Mainly, however, I see no reason to suppose that *public* performance was of such crowning importance to Shakespeare. Whenever he imagines performance in his own plays, it is either at the courts of Theseus or Claudius or at the house of a grandee, like the Lord in *The Taming of the Shrew*—the touring and patronage theatre of his own early days, not performing in the great commercial outdoor auditoria of the London suburbs.

And such performances were still available to him during even the worst of the plague, merely by waiting for the next Revels season. The plague barely affected court performances which, as we have noted, proliferated throughout the period at an exponential rate. After James's first winter, Whitehall was the primary site of the winter court and its plays. Its location in Westminster was still physically distinct from London—and apparently considered safe, even when the plague raged at the other end of the Strand. Barroll suggests that plays were not performed at court until they had been tried out on the public stage, but there is no way to prove that, and the royal subventions in 1603/4, 1608/9, and 1609/10 to allow the players to rehearse even when the commercial theatres were closed argue against it (Chambers 1923: 4.168–9, 175, 176). Rehearsing *new* plays was always a more urgent consideration than ones more familiarly embedded in the repertoire.

There are, moreover, two entries in Henslowe's *Diary* that we have not considered. One is for 9 August 1598: 'lent unto Anthony Munday...in earnest of a comedy for the court called [missing] the sum of 10s' (Foakes 2002: 96).[26] The other is for 5 November 1602, to 'John Day in earnest of a book called *Merry as May Be* for the court, 40s' (206). Final payment for this play, £6, was made to Day, Wentworth Smith, and Richard Hathaway on 17 November. These entries say nothing about mending, adding, or altering, and they are all we ever hear about *Merry as May Be*, which seems to be a new play in 1602. Of course there may be other circumstances, which Henslowe fails to record, but on the face of it these were occasions in which the Admiral's Men were prepared to commission a new play specifically 'for the court'. This could, of course, only have been done at Tilney's instigation or with his close attention, including rehearsals at his Clerkenwell quarters.

This possibility begs all kinds of questions about Shakespeare's writing for the court, especially in James's reign, when the demand for court plays became so acute.

* * *

We have to consider the possibility that, even if Shakespeare was distracted by the business of recruiting new dramatists for the company, and sometimes co-authoring plays with them, as well as revising a growing number of plays for court performance (both his own and those of others), the pace of his new writing during the period may well have been driven in good measure by the prospect that these plays were likely to receive their *first* performances at court. He certainly produced fewer

---

[26] The entry includes a memorandum: 'Mr Drayton hath given his word for the book to be done within one fortnight, witness Thomas Downton' [a sharer in the Admiral's Men]. Both items were subsequently crossed out.

plays in his Jacobean period, but the ones he did write were, on average, markedly on the long side. That, at least, is true of the versions which happen to have survived. If we had a wider array of texts, as we have for so many of the Elizabethan plays, the picture might be different. But we do not.

THE LENGTH OF SHAKESPEARE'S JACOBEAN PLAYS

All's Well, at 2,738 lines is the longest comedy (as distinct from romance) that Shakespeare ever wrote, while *Measure for Measure* is little shorter at 2,660.[27] *Othello* (if it did originate in the new reign) is 3,055 in quarto, 3,222 lines in the folio; the quarto *Lear* is 3,092; *Antony and Cleopatra*, *Coriolanus*, *Cymbeline*, and *The Winter's Tale* as they have survived are, respectively, 3,016, 3,279, 3,264, and 2,925 lines long—all significantly longer than the median 2,500 lines we associate with the Globe. That is eight of the ten sole-authored plays from the Jacobean period, *Macbeth* (2,084 lines) and *The Tempest* (2,015) being the only exceptions.

To confront those exceptions first. Both show distinct signs of having been adapted for performance at the Blackfriars; both have fully articulated five-act structures (unlike, say, *Antony and Cleopatra*), consonant with the need to refresh the candles. And both call for the use of descent machinery, which was certainly available at the Blackfriars but less certainly a feature of earlier playhouses used by Shakespeare's company. No Globe play written before 1609, by Shakespeare or anyone else, can be shown to have used such a facility. We might, for example, have expected its use for the vision of Diana in *Pericles*, but the stage direction barely calls for '*Diana*' (Iv; 5.1.242.0). We might also have expected it in Barnes' *The Devil's Charter*, which apparently used just about every other resource of the Globe, including the upper stage, discovery space, trap door, and pyrotechnics.

The earliest play which explicitly requires descent machinery is *Cymbeline* (1609–10): 'Jupiter descends in thunder and lightning, sitting upon an eagle' (5.4.92.0–1; TLN 3,127–8). But does that text represent the play as it was performed at the Globe? I suggest not. It is, firstly, immensely long. And secondly, it was one of the plays that Simon Forman records having seen, probably at the Globe, and he makes no mention of Jupiter throwing thunderbolts as he descended, which surely would have been the spectacular highlight of the play.[28] Thirdly, the play is strongly associated with the celebrations for the investiture of Prince Henry

[27] I accept the argument that *Measure for Measure* as we have it was revised by Middleton. The version in the *Oxford Middleton* gives the most fully developed explanation of how, where, and when Middleton may have adapted Shakespeare's original text (Middleton 2007a: 1542–85). The case for this adaptation was first advanced by Gary Taylor and John Jowett (1993) and the thinking of both authors has developed since then, as summarized in Taylor and Lavagnino 2007: 681–3. None of this in and of itself affects the argument that *as a fundamentally Shakespearean comedy* it is very long.

[28] The portions of Forman's *Diary* in which he records his play going are reproduced in Chambers 1930: 2.339–40; cited here from Rowse 1976. The authenticity of his 'Booke of Plaies' is not beyond dispute. It has, however, been accepted by many serious scholars: see Wilson and Hunt 1947; Pafford 1959. Sceptics, however, remain: see Duncan-Jones 2001: xii–xiii. The accounts Forman gives of three extant plays—*Cymbeline*, *Macbeth*, and *The Winter's Tale*—square broadly with the versions we have, but are not detailed enough to confirm that they were either identical or adapted.

as Prince of Wales in 1610, and as such must have been written with the court in mind (Cull 2014: 137–45). None of this is conclusive, but it may well point to *Cymbeline* as we have it being a text for court, where descent machinery was certainly available—it was evidently used in the court performance of *Old Fortunatus*.[29] It would be unwise to argue for descent machinery at the Globe on the evidence of *Cymbeline* alone.

The Tempest and *Macbeth* as we have them both call for descents, but are markedly short texts—*Macbeth* remarkably so for a tragedy. This is in line with the earlier texts of *The Malcontent* and is a marker of writing or adaptation for the Blackfriars theatre, where music before the performance and during the inter-acts filled out the show (see pp. 74, 118).[30] *The Tempest* strikingly calls for a wider range of musical effects than any other play in the Shakespeare canon. The descent machinery at the Blackfriars seems to have been quite sophisticated, allowing for the protracted spectacular descent of Juno in her car in Prospero's masque in *The Tempest* (4.1) and the complex aerial business with Hecate in 3.5 of *Macbeth*. Here again, *Macbeth* is one of the plays seen by Simon Forman in 1611—explicitly, in this report, at the Globe—and again there is no mention of a descent, though he does mention the 'women fairies or nymphs', as he understood the witches (Rowse 1976: 308). The issue of the Hecate scene requires some unpacking for those unacquainted with the suggestion that Middleton is responsible for that scene.[31] What is indisputable is that the song in the scene, 'Come away, come away', also appears in Middleton's *The Witch* (1609–15), where it involves the descent of a spirit-cat in a cloud, which latterly takes Hecate up into the heavens. The argument—which I accept—is that the whole sequence was inserted into an adaptation of *Macbeth*, probably c. 1615 and possibly effected by Middleton. *Macbeth* is usually thought to have been written in 1606, since it contains echoes of the Gunpowder Plot of the year before. But the text that has survived is about a decade later and was probably for the Blackfriars.

These two texts apart, Shakespeare's Jacobean output contains a striking preponderance of notably long texts, especially if we add to the list the other texts that started life as Elizabethan but were either significantly revised or first published in the Jacobean period—*Hamlet* (in its second quarto and folio forms; 3,668 and

---

[29] At the court of the Soldan, Fortunatus receives a magic hat, with which he flies away to Cyprus. The stage direction merely registers '*Exit*', but the Soldan's reaction makes clear that he flies off: 'Treason, Lords, treason, get me wings, I'll fly / After that damned traitor through the air...Like a magician breaks he through the clouds' (2.1.110–11; 116). It is questionable if the Admiral's Men could have staged this at the Rose but the Office of Works could certainly have set it up at a royal palace. It would be called on to manage increasingly sophisticated stage machinery for the Jacobean court masques.

[30] Performances in the Blackfriars, both by the boys and by the adult companies, took place in the afternoons, parallel to those in the public playhouses (note the special restraints on Paul's Boys: p. 72). Candles augmented natural light but were not expected to substitute for it—unlike night-time performances at court, the Inns of Court, and university colleges, which must have required considerably more candles (Graves 2009: 535–42). It follows that, if the consort of musicians performed for up to an hour before the play, and during the inter-acts, their plays—like *The Malcontent*—were likely to be shorter.

[31] See the edition of *Macbeth* in *The Oxford Middleton* (Middleton 2007a: 1165–99, esp. 1185–6).

3,537 lines), and *Troilus and Cressida* (quarto and folio forms; 3,291 and 3,323 lines). It is, of course, a central contention of this book that such extreme lengths—by the standards of the day—are most likely to reflect versions of the plays prepared for court. What is different here from the texts where at least one version was published between 1594 and 1603 is that we have no simple 'before' and 'after' comparison by which we can say (however cautiously) that at some point there was a shorter version of the play and at another point a longer one, and debate the relationship between the two. As it happens, there *are* variations in length between the different *Jacobean* versions of *Hamlet*, *Troilus*, and *Othello* (and indeed of *King Lear*) but these—though interesting and significant—are all, as I would put it, within the noise. That is, they are all of court performance length, were probably revised for different court performances, and would not have been presented at those lengths on the public stage.

We must presume that all of Shakespeare's Jacobean plays (with the possible exception of the apparently unfinished *Timon*) appeared on the public stage *in some form or other*. We have Simon Forman's testimony that *Macbeth*, *Cymbeline*, and *The Winter's Tale* did so in 1611, two of them expressly at the Globe (see n. 28). And *Henry VIII* was playing there when it burned down in 1613. What I want to register here are firstly my doubts as to whether many of them have survived in the form they were seen in there. For instance, a feature of *The Winter's Tale* that Forman did not record is the 'dance of twelve Satyrs' (4.4.342.2; TLN 2,164), which Tiffany Stern speculates is 'a reuse, with light rewriting, of the satyrs' dance in [Jonson's] *Masque of Oberon*' (2009a: 150). It was presumably quite spectacular but, like Hecate's descent in *Macbeth*, apparently did not register with the astrologer. Stern nominates other court masques which seem to have served second duty in Shakespeare's Jacobean plays:

> Paired dancers perform a 'Country pastime' morris around a maypole in Shakespeare and Fletcher's *The Two Noble Kinsmen*, a dance that appears to me...taken from the second antimasque in Francis Beaumont's *Masque of the Inner Temple and Gray's Inn*...[Campion's *Lord Hay's Masque*] may survive in *Pericles*, where the dance of the knights 'in your Armours' oddly recalls a courtier's dance of knights with helmets [but the] most intriguing example of the transferred masque...is the dance from Jonson's *Masque of Queens* that seems to have made its way into Shakespeare's *Macbeth* via Middleton's *The Witch*. (150–1)

Stern then asks whether each of these was a permanent addition to the text or only 'a temporary visitor' and particularly wonders whether they were specifically associated with court performances—which would explain why Forman did not see the satyrs in *The Winter's Tale*: 'The question can even be raised as to whether all masques in plays were actually the preserve of the court alone' (151, 153).[32]

This can only be pure speculation. I certainly suppose that all of these masque elements were added to the plays for performances at court. They would readily

---

[32] Forman's interests as a playgoer were not necessarily our own; his failures to record the descent of Hecate in *Macbeth* or the Satyrs in *The Winter's Tale* actually prove nothing. They are, at most, suggestive.

add length, variety, and spectacle—without adding to the labours of their 'ordinary poet'. It may also have been done, at least in some cases, without additional cost. Presumably when the King's Men performed the antimasque elements in these shows at court, such as the satyrs in *The Masque of Oberon*, those costumes were supplied by the court office responsible—no longer at this date the Revels Office, but probably the associated Office of the Wardrobe (see p. 54; Astington 1999: 29). It should not have been difficult for Tilney or Buc to negotiate their reuse for a different type of court performance. But would the King's Men have been able to use them in their own playhouses? Such questions justify Stern's scepticism about whether these 'borrowed' masque elements ever appeared at the Globe or the Blackfriars. *The Tempest*, with its home-scripted masque, may have been particularly distinctive in this regard.

We recall that the quarto of *King Lear* announces that it is *As it was played before the King's Majesty at Whitehall upon S. Stephen's Night in Christmas Holidays* and performed 'By His Majesty's servants playing usually at the Globe on the Bankside', broadly suggesting that other (public) performances would have been different. I strongly suspect that the other long texts I have listed, overwhelmingly versions printed in the First Folio, often for the first time, could have been printed with similar claims. Proving such claims is, of course, an entirely different matter. It is certainly possible to show—as Alvin Kernan has in *Shakespeare, the King's Playwright* (1995), and David Bergeron in *Shakespeare's Romances and the Royal Family* (1985), among many others—that most of these plays were written with an eye to the tastes, interests, or preoccupations of the Jacobean royal family. *Lear* alludes to King James's ambitions to make the union of English and Scottish crowns a deeper bonding at the level of their Parliaments. *Cymbeline*, another text drawing on 'the matter of Britain', probably alludes to the formal creation of Prince Henry as Prince of Wales in 1610. And so on. But it is one thing to demonstrate such thematic links and another to show that particular texts were written *for* court performance; it is particularly ironic that two of the plays most often thought to have special court associations, *Macbeth* and *The Tempest*, survive in texts which leave no trace of performance there (see pp. 281ff).[33] Paul Yachnin's argument for a Shakespeare generating *populuxe* entertainment—using the privileged patronage situation of the company to tantalize popular audiences with glimpses into the royal world—makes a different and entirely plausible case for what was going on here (Dawson and Yachnin 2001: esp. 38–68; Yachnin 2005). My own argument is that in fact *both* things were going on here: Shakespeare was both writing *for* the court and also (in different texts—of which *Macbeth* is perhaps

---

[33] The most sustained attempt to link *Macbeth* with performance before royalty is H. N. Paul's *The Royal Play of 'Macbeth'* (1950), which argues that it was specifically performed at Greenwich in the summer of 1606, when the King's Men put on two plays for the visit of Christian IV of Denmark. The fact that the text as we have it reflects a later revision, with material imported from Middleton's *The Witch*, somewhat undermines Paul's argument. Arthur Quiller-Couch and John Dover Wilson argued in their 1921 edition of *The Tempest* that the text of the play that we have represents a revision for performance during the 1613 wedding festivities for Princess Elizabeth. Frank Kermode cogently rebutted the argument for such a revision in his Arden 2 edition (1954: xxii–xxiv). It nevertheless keeps resurfacing.

the best surviving example) *about* the court, for his different audiences. My particular contention is that, in the great majority of cases, it is the versions *for* the court which have survived. But only the quarto text of *King Lear* is absolutely explicit about that.

What we cannot tell, in the absence of evidence, is whether Shakespeare continued what I have tried to demonstrate was his usual practice in the last years of Elizabeth's reign: firstly writing a version for the public stage, which he would then augment, enlarge, or otherwise amend for the court, at the behest of Edmund Tilney. Or whether, given the new demands imposed by the Jacobean court, the King's Men determined that it made more sense—at least in some instances—for him to compose his new plays explicitly with court performance as the first priority, as Henslowe's *Diary* gives us some small grounds for supposing Day and his colleagues may have done with *Merry As May Be*. The case for *King Lear*, for example, being *conceived* as a court play is very strong. If so, is it possible that in the new reign Shakespeare, at least sometimes, worked in the way we have identified Jonson doing: producing extra-long court texts at virtually the same time as he produced versions suitable for the Globe (see p. 92)? The latter might have been produced in the manner of the 1676 *Players' Hamlet*, in which some 900 lines of the 1604/5 quarto text were marked for omission in performance, or the 1700 edition of *1 Henry IV*, which was reduced to between 2,500 and 2,600 lines (Erne 2003: 169). Those reductions, though generated by the very different playing environment of Restoration theatre, are much more orderly than anything we see in the relationships between 'good' and 'bad' Elizabethan texts.

In allowing this possibility I may seem to be contradicting the main premises of my argument about the 'bad' quarto plays. But that is not the case. My key argument throughout has been that everything we know about Shakespeare's texts marks them as plays *for the theatre, for performance*. Whether that performance was at the Theatre, the Globe, the Blackfriars, or the court is immaterial, though it is perfectly clear that Shakespeare was adept at suiting his plays to whatever venue was required. In the Elizabethan years the expectation of three or four court performances a year—and no more than one or two of those needing distinctive enhancement or grace notes—made occasional adaptation of plays already proven in the public theatres a logical *modus operandi*. But the court became a much more demanding patron under James and his family, and with that the possibility that Shakespeare's writing practices changed accordingly can hardly be ignored. Perhaps somewhere in his calculations he also did envisage eventual publication. But he was too busy and too professional to devote time to producing drama that was never going to be performed.

We should end, as the history of the publication of new plays within Shakespeare's own lifetime ended, with the publication of a quarto of *Troilus and Cressida* in 1609. A play by that title was entered in the Stationers' Register in the last days of Elizabeth's reign (7 February 1603), to 'Master [James] Roberts, entered for his copy...to print when he hath got sufficient authority for it, the book of Troilus and Cressida as it is acted by my Lord Chamberlain's Men'. Roberts already had title to *Hamlet*, of which he was to print (but not publish) the 1604/5 version.

But he apparently never acquired the necessary authority for *Troilus and Cressida*, which was entered in proper order to Richard Bonion and Henry Walley on 28 January 1609, and they were responsible for the version printed that year by George Eld.

The book they produced is a 'good' quarto, apparently deriving from an authorial draft, 'The History of Troilus and Cressida', and very long (3,291 lines). It would differ in many particulars from the version that appeared in the First Folio, where it erratically appeared as the first tragedy ('The Tragedy of Troilus and Cressida'). But that too is a sound text, authorial in derivation, though possibly marked up for theatrical use, and even longer (3,323 lines). The most distinctive feature of the quarto, however, is that its front-matter changed during the print run.[34] In its first state it proclaims the play to be 'As it was acted by the King's Majesty's servants at the Globe'. In the second state the title becomes 'The Famous History of Troilus and Cressid. Excellently expressing the beginning of their loves, with the conceited wooing of Pandarus, Prince of Licia', and it omits all reference to performance. An Epistle was then inserted, which appears in no other version of the play, 'A never writer, to an ever reader. News'. This begins: 'Eternal reader, you have here a new play, never staled with the stage, never clapper-clawed with the palms of the vulgar, and yet passing full of the palm comical'.

Apparently Bonion and Walley were unclear about the kind of text they had acquired, or perhaps about how best to advertise it. In the first state they treat it like any regular play performed by the King's Men—perhaps as the play might have been when Roberts tried to secure it (even fodder for a 'bad' quarto). In the second state they wrap it up in allusive mystery, on which a good deal of editorial ink has since been spilled. Their 'eternal reader' is being granted access to a work like Shakespeare's others in this vein, 'showing such a dexterity and power of wit that the most displeased with plays are pleased with his comedies'. This is not fare for 'dull and heavy-witted groundlings'. Lukas Erne suggests that this 'address presents us with the kind of anti-theatrical rhetoric characteristic of the "high culture drama" *à la* Jonson *et al*' (2013: 125). I hope that my own readers will appreciate by now that Bonion and Walley's Epistle, decorously and allusively selling a text 'never staled with the stage, never clapper-clawed with the palms of the vulgar', was describing it to a knowing readership as one performed—as virtually everything by Shakespeare was—at court.

---

[34] Strikingly, the same thing happened with another text printed by Eld that year, Middleton's *A Trick to Catch the Old One*. The title page of the first issue merely presented it 'As it hath been lately acted by the Children of Paul's'; the second issue is much more effusive: 'As it hath been often in action, both at Paul's and the Blackfriars. Presented before his Majesty on New Year's night last. Composed by T.M'. Eld may have alerted Bonion and Walley to the option of more enticing front-matter, focusing (as I suggest) on a court performance.

Conclusions

My argument is at bottom a simple one: that the courts of both Elizabeth and James loomed much larger in Shakespeare's creative life than is usually appreciated; that many—perhaps most—of his plays have survived in versions adapted for court purposes, where length was no object (and indeed encouraged) and rhetorical virtuosity was appreciated. Within that overarching claim I have made some specific, localized ones: most particularly I have argued that the formerly despised shorter quartos of *2* and *3 Henry VI*, *Romeo and Juliet*, *Henry V*, *Hamlet*, and *The Merry Wives of Windsor* were not created by a process of cutting from pre-existing longer quarto or folio versions, but were poorly reported versions of the plays as they originally existed, before they were transformed into the canonical versions we know best today. I have also discussed the possibility that smaller-scale transformations account for changes and additional materials found in later texts of *Richard II*, *Titus Andronicus*, *2 Henry IV*, and even *A Midsummer Night's Dream*.

I have located these arguments in relation to the evidence in Philip Henslowe's *Diary*, by far the most detailed picture we have of theatrical activity in the whole era. Even though we have only a small window—late 1597 to early 1603—in which we can trace Henslowe paying Dekker, Chettle, and others to amend texts, this coincides almost exactly with the period in which Shakespeare's short quartos were printed and more substantial versions followed not very long after. (In instances where more substantial texts do not appear until the First Folio, I have to argue circumstantial cases about when the revisions took place.) It also coincides with the period when printers made considerable capital out of Shakespeare's plays being augmented, amended, and enlarged. In the quarto of *Love's Labour's Lost* they explicitly correlate this with performance before the Queen in the Revels season. The *only* reason Henslowe ever gives for paying people to amend texts is that it was 'for the court'.

I have looked in some detail at the surviving plays of the Lord Admiral's Men that we know from Henslowe were revised for the court, the clearest example being *Old Fortunatus*. I have also looked at a good range of other texts from the period where there is evidence of revision. In many of these instances there is considerable circumstantial evidence that the changes were made for court performance, though relatively few publishers (not even the publisher of *Old Fortunatus*) chose to advertise the fact on their title pages—an intriguing cultural marker in itself, though one that makes this study all the harder. One salutary outcome of reviewing the non-Shakespearean revisions is to be reminded of just how *unusual* it is that so many of Shakespeare's texts have survived in multiple versions. It is only one measure of his uniqueness, but I suggest it is a direct consequence of his being the foremost provider of theatrical entertainment for the court during his working lifetime.

Looking, in particular, at the editorial history of *Romeo and Juliet*, *Henry V*, *Hamlet*, and *The Merry Wives of Windsor* has been both instructive and depressing. Editing since the New Bibliography of the early twentieth century has usually presented itself as a quasi-science, applying a body of acquired knowledge to make sense of the mysteries that surround the sacred texts. But it is very clear that editors are in fact just like other forms of literary critics, very much in the thrall of the theoretical fashions of their day, which very quickly cohere into unquestioned orthodoxies. When, finally, those orthodoxies are challenged—and some of them have evaporated, virtually overnight—they are very rapidly replaced by new ones, or revived old ones, equally authoritative and monolithic. This has applied very strongly to the so-called 'bad' quartos, whose transformation from pirated travesties of Shakespeare's texts to valuable evidence of how his plays were 'normally' staged at the Globe and elsewhere is a wonder worthy of the ending of one of his late romances.

The once almost-universal conviction that the shorter texts were somehow generated from the longer ones, and then somehow garbled, seems to me to be based, above all, on bad reading. The shorter texts are not simply the longer ones stripped of unnecessary detail and poetic language. In each case there has been a transformation at the level of plot or dramatic action which can only be accounted for by a purposeful imaginative re-engagement. The idea that such a re-engagement went in the direction of stripping complexity, character, theatrical technique, and poetic intensity in such a way as to leave no traces of them (even allowing for the garbling involved in 'memorial reconstruction' or stenography) seems to me unthinkable. Q1 of *Henry V* is a conceptually different piece of theatre from the folio version, one that anticipates a different kind of audience, different forms of engagement and discrimination. The folio text of *Merry Wives* is similarly addressing a different audience from the quarto version—in this instance more clumsily, perhaps because it reflects a difficult or incomplete manuscript. And so on.

If a process of redaction *was* a regular feature of Elizabethan theatre, why did Henslowe apparently never pay anyone to do it? He paid for additions, not for excisions. Lukas Erne and others have suggested that a form of redaction was a recognized practice before the closing of the theatres, since Humphrey Moseley speaks of it in the first Beaumont and Fletcher folio in 1647. In the prefatory material he claims: 'When these comedies and tragedies were presented on the stage, the actors omitted some scenes and passages (with the author's consent) as occasion led them; and when private friends desired a copy, they then (and justly too) transcribed what they acted' ('To the Reader', A3r; Erne 2003: 204; Blayney 1997: 393–4). But where texts have survived that may have been trimmed in the way Moseley describes, they seem only to have lost some redundancy (on a par with what we see in *The Second Maiden's Tragedy*: pp. 277–8). The clearest instance is *The Woman's Prize*, of which a manuscript survives in addition to the Folio version.[1] The manuscript is missing two scenes in their entirety (2.1, 4.1), which do not appreciably advance the narrative, and some ten passages of up to fourteen lines each—but several of the latter may well have been cut by Henry Herbert in his recall of the play in 1633 (see pp. 154–5). Not much more than 200 cut lines can safely be ascribed to the kind of abridgement that Moseley speaks of, far less than anything we find in Shakespeare's 'bad' quartos. Most critically, the play has not been *revised*, as all Shakespeare's texts have (Erne 2003: 148–58).

So this would not account for what we still know as the 'bad' quartos. The idea that these might have been mined from longer versions is clearly linked to the new conviction that they are 'performance' texts—and who better than the actors to know what will work best onstage? But Janette Dillon (1994), Zachary Lesser and Peter Stallybrass (2008), and Paul Menzer (2008) have in different ways convincingly challenged notions that the shorter quartos are inherently more 'performance' texts than other playbooks of the era or that they were sold to the public as such. In each case, as I argue, there was some level of purposeful, quasi-authorial intervention— whichever way we imagine the revision being conducted. *Someone* decided whether the Dauphin would be at Agincourt or not. *Someone* decided whether Gertrude was secretly in league with Hamlet and Horatio. *Someone* decided whether Balthasar or Peter should accompany Romeo to Juliet's tomb. In each case plausibility argues that Shakespeare made those decisions as he 'augmented' his texts, just as it does that the version of *Merry Wives* in which Ford disguises himself as 'Brooke' *preceded* the one in which he is 'Broome'.

One immediate consequence follows, if my argument carries any weight at all. The habit of conflating Shakespeare's texts really does have to stop. It is ironic that no sooner did *The Division of the Kingdoms* demonstrate to us that it was wrong to conflate the two versions of *King Lear* than the *Oxford Shakespeare* argued that the Dauphin should not appear at Agincourt in what is otherwise the folio version of *Henry V*: this on the authority of the quarto version and its performance street credentials. Editions of *2 Henry VI* incorporate parts of *The First Part of the Contention*. Some *Hamlets* continue to appear longer than anything Shakespeare ever wrote, because they conflate Q2 and F. Editors of *Merry Wives* try to resolve the perplexities of F by relying too mechanically on the stage directions in Q1. And so on.

My analysis in all of these cases suggests that each version of a play came together as it did at a specific time, for a known theatre, audience, and projected playing time. When Shakespeare revised them (most probably for the court), sometimes on a grand scale, sometimes in smaller details, he had a tendency to do so as a 'tinkering' or 'fidgeting' reviser and most commonly in a spirit of copious expansion, such that the later version both linguistically and conceptually might be very far removed from the earlier one. Of course there are always going to be occasions when we can safely make better sense of one text by reference to another version, usually in respect of mistakes or confusions that may have occurred in the print shop. But such a process must be handled sparingly and conservatively, with the essential aim of retaining the integrity

---

[1] The manuscript is in the Folger Shakespeare Library (MS.J.b.3).

of the copy-text being edited—not aiming to reconstruct lost originals, or hypothetical conditions of performance, like calling spirits from the vasty deep.

For many, however, the most disturbing feature of my argument is bound to be the way it ties Shakespeare's creativity to the court, pulling it away from the supposed democratic melting pot of the Globe and other public theatres. Let me quote once more from Alfred Harbage on the audiences he supposedly wrote for there: 'But most important of all, Shakespeare's audience was socially, economically, educationally heterogeneous. It was motley, and for this we must be thankful. An audience so mixed compelled the most discerning of authors to address himself to men and not to their badges, to men's intelligence and not to its levels... where all classes are there is no class; there is that common humanity which subtends all. To the kind of audience for which he wrote, and to the fact that he did write for it, we owe Shakespeare's universality' (1941: 162). The more poetic he waxes ('where all classes are there is no class') the further he drifts into a pipe dream.

The 'universality' which Harbage claims for Shakespeare attaches itself to Q2 *Romeo and Juliet*, not Q1; to F *Henry V*, not to Q1. But Q1 in each case, though we must hope in much more reliable versions, is very probably closer to what the public audiences got, at least in the first instance. Davenant's *The Players' Hamlet perhaps* gives us the most reassuring picture of what they might have been offered somewhat later, once the practice of augmenting plays for the court was established: Q2 *Hamlet* but with 'such places as might be least prejudicial to the plot or sense... left out upon the stage'. Public audiences thus saw and heard the real thing, but in more measured doses than the privileged audiences at court would be graced with. If that goes against the modern, democratic grain, we must remember that public audiences only had *that* access because the court secured the Chamberlain's and King's Men the privilege of performing in London. And it did so for its own purposes.

Time and again the Privy Council spelled out to the London authorities that certain troupes should be allowed 'to exercise playing within the City... by reason that [they] are appointed to play this time of Christmas before her Majesty' (1578); 'without frequent exercise of such plays as are presented before her Majesty, her servants cannot conveniently satisfy her recreation' (1583); 'my now company of players have been accustomed for the better exercise of their quality, and for the service of her Majesty if need so require, to play this winter time within the City' (1594); 'licence hath been granted unto two companies of stage players retained to us... to use and practice stage plays, whereby they might be better enabled and prepared to show such plays as they shall be required at times meet and accustomed, to which end they have been chiefly licenced and tolerated as aforesaid' (1598) (Gurr 1996: 55; Chambers 1923: 4.296, 4.316, 325).

With that protection, the leading companies were able to earn a more than tolerable living, in return for which producing plays each winter, suitable in every way—including length—to entertain the court, was a small reciprocal gesture. Under the informed and watchful eye of Tilney and then Buc, those plays were 'rehearsed, perfected, and corrected', a process which invited Shakespeare to expand his imaginative engagement either with his own old plays or with new materials; to try the range of his poetic, rhetorical, and dramatic skills, without the restraints that hemmed in daily performance. As I observed earlier, Shakespeare lived out what Frank Whigham and Wayne Rebhorn call 'the core fantasy' of Puttenham's *Art of English Poesy*, in which the poet, by the use of all his rhetorical skills, may rise to the service of the monarch (Puttenham 2007: 1). The court is what made Shakespeare Shakespeare.

Bibliography

Note: *Editions of Shakespeare (but not other early authors) are sorted and referred to by editor. So too are collections of early materials, such as E. K. Chambers's 'The Elizabethan Stage', R. A. Foakes's edition of Henslowe's 'Diary', N. W. Bawcutt's edition of Sir Henry Herbert's papers, and Edward Arber's 'Transcripts of the Stationers's Company Register'. Collected letters, however, are sorted by their authors. Co-authored or co-edited items are listed after items by the first-named author or editor.*

EDITIONS OF SHAKESPEARE CITED

Bate, Jonathan (ed.) (1995), *Titus Andronicus*, Arden 3 (London: Routledge).
Bate, Jonathan and Eric Rasmussen (gen. eds) (2007), *The Royal Shakespeare Company's Complete Works of William Shakespeare* (Basingstoke: Palgrave Macmillan).
Bate, Jonathan and Eric Rasmussen (eds) (2013), *William Shakespeare and Others: Collaborative Plays*, The RSC Shakespeare (Basingstoke: Palgrave Macmillan).
Bevington, David (ed.) (2008), *The Complete Works of William Shakespeare*. 6th edn (New York: Pearson Longman).
Cox, John D. and Eric Rasmussen (eds) (2001), *King Henry VI, Part 3*, Arden 3 (London: Thomson Learning).
Craik, T. W. (ed.) (1995), *King Henry V*, Arden 3 (London: Routledge).
Crane, David (ed.) (2010), *The Merry Wives of Windsor*, New Cambridge Shakespeare (1997; Cambridge: Cambridge University Press).
Daniell, David (ed.) (1998), *Julius Caesar*, Arden 3 (London: Thomas Nelson).
Dawson, Anthony and Gretchen Minton (eds) (2008), *Timon of Athens*, Arden 3 (London: Ceneage Learning).
Edwards, Philip (ed.) (1984), *Hamlet, Prince of Denmark*, New Cambridge Shakespeare (Cambridge: Cambridge University Press).
Erne, Lukas (ed.) (2007), *The First Quarto of Romeo and Juliet*. The Early Quartos (Cambridge: Cambridge University Press).
Gibbons, Brian (ed.) (1980), *Romeo and Juliet*, Arden 2 (London: Methuen).
Gossett, Suzanne (ed.) (2004), *Pericles*, Arden 3 (London: Thomson Learning).
Green, William (ed.) (1965), *The Merry Wives of Windsor*, Signet Classic (New York and Toronto: New American Classics).
Greenblatt, Stephen (gen. ed.) (1997), *The Norton Shakespeare: Based on the Oxford Edition*, with Walter Cohen, Jean Howard and Katharine Eisaman Maus (New York: W. W. Norton).
Greg, W. W. (ed.) (1910), *The Merry Wives of Windsor, 1602*. Malone Society Reprints (Oxford: Oxford University Press).
Gurr, Andrew (ed.) (1992), *Henry V*, New Cambridge Shakespeare (Cambridge: Cambridge University Press).
Gurr, Andrew (ed.) (2000), *The First Quarto of King Henry V*. The Early Quartos (Cambridge: Cambridge University Press).
Halio, Jay L. (ed.) (2008), *Romeo and Juliet: Parallel Texts of Quarto 1 (1597) and Quarto 2 (1599)* (Newark: University of Delaware Press).
Hammond, Anthony (ed.) (1981), *Richard III*, Arden 2 (London: Methuen).

Hart, H. C. (ed.) (1904), *The Merry Wives of Windsor*, Arden 1 (London: Methuen).
Hattaway, Michael (ed.) (1991), *2 Henry VI*, New Cambridge Shakespeare (Cambridge: Cambridge University Press).
Hattaway, Michael (ed.) (1993), *3 Henry VI*, New Cambridge Shakespeare (Cambridge: Cambridge University Press).
Hibbard, G. R. (ed.) (1973), *The Merry Wives of Windsor*, New Penguin Shakespeare (Harmondsworth: Penguin Books).
Hibbard, G. R. (ed.) (1990), *Love's Labour's Lost*, The Oxford Shakespeare (Oxford: Clarendon Press).
Hinman, Charlton (ed.) (1996), *The First Folio of Shakespeare, Based on Folios in the Folger Shakespeare Collection*. 2nd edn, with an introduction by Peter W. M. Blayney (1968; New York: W.W. Norton & Co.).
Honigmann, E. A. J. (ed.) (1997), *Othello*, by William Shakespeare, Arden 3. (Walton on Thames: Thomas Nelson & Sons).
Hughes, Alan (ed.) (2006), *Titus Andronicus*, New Cambridge Shakespeare (1994; Cambridge: Cambridge University Press).
Humphreys, Arthur (ed.) (1960), *King Henry IV, Part 1*, Arden 2 (London: Methuen).
Humphreys, Arthur (1966), *King Henry IV, Part 2*, Arden 2 (London: Methuen).
Humphreys, Arthur (ed.) (1980), *Henry V*, New Penguin Shakespeare (Harmondsworth: Penguin).
Irace, Kathleen O. (1999), *The First Quarto of Hamlet*. First Quartos (Cambridge: Cambridge University Press).
Jenkins, Harold (ed.) (1982), *Hamlet*, Arden 2 (London: Methuen).
Johnson, Samuel (ed.) (1765), *The Plays of William Shakespeare*, 8 vols (London: J & R. Tonson).
Jowett, John (ed.) (2000), *Richard III*, Oxford Shakespeare (Oxford: Clarendon Press).
Kastan, David S. (ed.) (2002), *1 Henry IV*, Arden 3 (London: Thompson Learning).
Kermode, Frank (ed.) (1954), *The Tempest*, Arden 2 (London: Methuen).
Kliman, Bernice W. and Paul Bertram (eds) (2003), *The Three-Text 'Hamlet': Parallel Texts of the First and Second Quartos and First Folio*. 2nd edn (1991; New York: AMS Press).
Knowles, Ronald (ed.) (1999), *King Henry VI, Part 2*, Arden 3 (London: Thomson Learning).
Levenson, Jill (ed.) (2000), *Romeo and Juliet*, The Oxford Shakespeare (Oxford: Clarendon Press).
Lull, Janis (ed.) (1999), *Richard III*. New Cambridge Shakespeare (Cambridge: Cambridge University Press).
Malone, Edmond (ed.) (1790), *Plays and Poems of Shakespeare*, 11 vols (London).
Martin, Randall (ed.) (2001), *Henry VI Part Three*, The Oxford Shakespeare (Oxford: Clarendon Press).
Melchiori, Giorgi (ed.) (1989), *The Second Part of King Henry IV*, New Cambridge Shakespeare (Cambridge: Cambridge University Press).
Melchiori, Giorgi (ed.) (2000), *The Merry Wives of Windsor*, Arden 3 (Walton-on-Thames: Thomas Nelson & Sons).
Pope, Alexander (ed.) (1725), *The Works of Shakespeare*, 6 vols (London: Jacob Tonson).
Quiller-Couch, Sir Arthur and John Dover Wilson (eds) (1921), *The Tempest*, New Cambridge Shakespeare (Cambridge: Cambridge University Press).
Quiller-Couch, Sir Arthur and John Dover Wilson (eds) (1923), *Love's Labour's Lost*, New Cambridge Shakespeare (Cambridge: Cambridge University Press).
Rowe, Nicholas (ed.) (1709), *The Works of William Shakespear* (London: Jacob Tonson).

Steevens, George (ed.) (1766), *Twenty of the Plays of Shakespeare* (London: J. & R. Tonson).
Taylor, Gary (ed.) (1982), *Henry V*, The Oxford Shakespeare (Oxford: Clarendon Press).
Thompson, Ann and Neal Taylor (eds) (2006), *Hamlet*, Arden 3, 2 vols (London: Thomson Learning).
Walter, John H. (ed.) (1954), *Henry V*, Arden 2 (London: Methuen).
Warren, Roger (ed.) (2002), *2 Henry VI*, The Oxford Shakespeare (Oxford: Clarendon Press).
Weis, René (ed.) (1998), *Henry IV, Part 2*, The Oxford Shakespeare (Oxford: Clarendon Press).
Wells, Stanley and Gary Taylor (eds) (1986), *The Oxford Shakespeare: The Complete Works of William Shakespeare* (Oxford: Clarendon Press).
Wilson, J. Dover (ed.) (1947), *Henry V*, New Cambridge Shakespeare (Cambridge: Cambridge University Press).

EDITIONS OF OTHER EARLY MODERN AUTHORS

Barnes, Barnabe (1904), *The Devil's Charter*, ed. R. B. McKerrow (Louvain: A. Uystpruyst).
Barnes, Barnabe (1980), *The Devil's Charter by Barnabe Barnes. A Critical Edition*, ed. Jim C. Pogue (New York: Garland Publishing).
Beaumont, Francis and John Fletcher (2003), *Philaster*, ed. Andrew Gurr (1969; Manchester: Manchester University Press).
Bevington, David (gen. ed.) (2002), *English Renaissance Drama: A Norton Anthology*, with Lars Engle, Katharine Eisaman Maus and Eric Rasmussen (New York: W. W. Norton).
Blount, Thomas (1656), *Glossographia* (London).
Buck, Sir George (1982), *The history of King Richard the Third*, ed. A. N. Kincaid (1979; Stroud: Sutton Publishing).
Carleton, Dudley (1972), *Dudley Carleton to John Chamberlain, 1603–1624; Jacobean Letters*, ed. Maurice Lee (New Brunswick, NJ: Rutgers University Press).
Chamberlain, John (1939), *The Letters of John Chamberlain*, ed. Norman E. McClure, 2 vols (Philadelphia: American Philosophical Society).
Collins, A. (ed.) (1746), *Letters and Memorials of State. Written and Collected by Sir Henry Sydney, Sir Philip Sydney, Sir Robert Sydney &c.*, 2 vols (London).
Corbin, Peter and Douglas Sedge (eds) (1991), *The Oldcastle Controversy* (Manchester: Manchester University Press).
Dekker, Thomas (1953–61a), *Old Fortunatus*, in *The Dramatic Works of Thomas Dekker*, ed. Fredson Bowers, 4 vols (Cambridge: Cambridge University Press), 1: 105–206.
Dekker, Thomas (1953–61b), *Satiromastix*, in *The Dramatic Works of Thomas Dekker*, ed. Fredson Bowers, 4 vols (Cambridge: Cambridge University Press), 1: 299–395.
Dennis, John (1702), *The Comical Gallant: or the Amours of Sir John Falstaff* (London).
Drayton, Michael (1596), *Matilda the fair and chaste Daughter of the Lord Robert Fitzwater, the true Glory of the noble House of Sussex*, printed with *The Tragical Legend of Robert, Duke of Normandy* ([1594] London).
Elizabeth I, Queen (2000), *Elizabeth I: Collected Works*, ed. Leah S. Marcus, Janel M. Mueller and Mary Beth Rose (Chicago: University of Chicago Press).
Erasmus (1963), *On Copia of Words and Ideas*, trans. D. B. King and H. D. Rix (Milwaukee: Marquette University Press).
Fletcher, John (1951), *Bonduca*, ed. W. W. Greg. Malone Society Reprints (Oxford: Oxford University Press).
Henslowe's *Diary*: see Foakes 2002; Greg 1907.

Herbert, Sir Henry, papers: see Adams 1917; Bawcutt 1996.
Heywood, Thomas (1612), *An Apology for Actors* (London).
Heywood, Thomas (1633), *The English Traveller* (London).
Heywood, Thomas (1637), *Pleasant Dialogues and Dramas* (London).
Jonson, Ben (1971), *Every Man In His Humour: A Parallel-text edition of the 1601 Quarto and the 1616 Folio*, ed. J. W. Lever (Lincoln: University of Nebraska Press).
Jonson, Ben (2008), *Epicene*, ed. Richard Dutton (Manchester: Manchester University Press).
Jonson, Ben (2012a), *The Cambridge Edition of the Works of Ben Jonson*, gen. eds David Bevington, Ian Donaldson and Martin Butler, 7 vols (Cambridge: Cambridge University Press).
Jonson, Ben (2012b), *The Alchemist*, ed. Peter Holland and William Sherman; in Jonson 2012a: 2.541–710.
Jonson, Ben (2012c), *Bartholomew Fair*, ed. John Creaser; in Jonson 2012a: 3.351–68.
Jonson, Ben (2012d), *Cynthia's Revels* (Quarto Version), ed. Eric Rasmussen and Matthew Steggle, in Jonson 2012a: 1.429–547.
Jonson, Ben (2012e), *Cynthia's Revels* (Revised Scenes from the 1616 Folio), ed. Eric Rasmussen and Matthew Steggle; in Jonson 2012a: 5.1–100.
Jonson, Ben (2012f), 'The Entertainment at Britain's Burse', ed. James Knowles; in Jonson 2012a: 3.351–68.
Jonson, Ben (2012g), *Every Man In His Humour* (quarto text), ed. David Bevington; in Jonson 2012a: 1.111–227.
Jonson, Ben (2012h), *Every Man In His Humour* (folio text), ed. David Bevington; in Jonson 2012a: 4.617–728.
Jonson, Ben (2012i), *Every Man Out of His Humour*, ed. Randall Martin; in Jonson 2012a: 1.235–428.
Jonson, Ben (2012j), *Informations to William Drummond of Hawthornden*, ed. Ian Donaldson; in Jonson 2012a: 5.351–91.
Jonson, Ben (ed.) (2012k), *Volpone*, ed. Richard Dutton; in Jonson 2012a: 3.1–191.
Jupin, Arvin H (ed.) (1987), *A Contextual Study and Modern-Spelling Edition of 'Mucedorus'* (New York: Garland Publishing).
Kyd, Thomas (1986), *The Spanish Tragedy*, ed. Philip Edwards, The Revels Plays (1959; Manchester: Manchester University Press).
Kyd, Thomas (1989), *The Spanish Tragedy*, ed. J. R. Mulryne (1970; London: A. C. Black).
La Broderie, Antoine de (1750), *Ambassades de Monsieur de La Broderie en Angleterre, 1606–11*, 5 vols (Paris: Publiées par Paul Denis Burtin).
Lodge, Thomas (1596), *Wit's Misery* (London).
Marlowe, Christopher (1950), *Marlowe's 'Dr Faustus' 1604–1616: Parallel Texts*, ed. W. W. Greg (Oxford: Clarendon Press).
Marlowe, Christopher (1993), *Doctor Faustus, A- and B-Texts (1604, 1616)*, ed. David Bevington and Eric Rasmussen, The Revels Plays (Manchester: Manchester University Press).
Marlowe, Christopher (1995), *Dr Faustus and Other Plays*, ed. David Bevington and Eric Rasmussen, World's Classics (Oxford: Oxford University Press).
Marlowe, Christopher (1999), *Christopher Marlowe: The Complete Plays*, ed. Mark Thornton Burnett, Everyman (London: J. M. Dent).
Marlowe, Christopher (2005), *Dr Faustus*, ed. David Scott Kastan (New York: W. W. Norton).
Marlowe, Christopher (2007), *Christopher Marlowe's 'Dr Faustus'*, ed. Michael Keefer (1991; Peterborough, Ontario: Broadview Press).

Marston, John (1975), *The Malcontent*, ed. George Hunter. The Revels Plays (Manchester: Manchester University Press).
Middleton, Thomas (1999), *'Women Beware Women' and Other Plays*, ed. Richard Dutton. World's Classics (Oxford: Oxford University Press).
Middleton, Thomas (2007a), *Thomas Middleton: The Collected Works*, gen. eds Gary Taylor and John Lavagnino (Oxford: Clarendon Press).
Middleton, Thomas (2007b), *The Lady's Tragedy*, ed. Julia Briggs, in Middleton 2007a: 833–906.
Middleton, Thomas and William Rowley (2007c), *A Fair Quarrel*, ed. Suzanne Gossett, in Taylor and Lavagnino 2007: 1209–50.
Munday, Anthony (1965), *The Downfall of Robert Earl of Huntingdon 1601*, ed. John C. Meagher. Malone Society Reprint (Oxford: Oxford University Press).
Munday, Anthony and others (1961), *The Book of Sir Thomas More*, ed. W. W. Greg. Malone Society Reprint, updated by Harold Jenkins ([1911]; Oxford: Oxford University Press).
Munday, Anthony (1990), *Sir Thomas More*, ed. Vittorio Gabrieli and Giorgio Melchiori. The Revels Plays (Manchester: Manchester University Press).
Nashe, Thomas (1904–10), *The Works of Thomas Nashe*, ed. R. B. McKerrow, 5 vols (Oxford: Clarendon Press).
Nichols, John (ed.) (1828), *The Progresses, Processions, and Magnificent Festivities of King James the First*, 4 vols (London).
Puttenham, George (2007), *The Art of English Poesy: A Critical Edition*, ed. Frank Whigham and Wayne A. Rebhorn (Ithaca, NY: Cornell University Press).
Shirley, James (1640), *The Coronation* (London).
Stationers' Register, transcripts: see Arber 1875.
Stuart, Lady Arbella (1994), *The Letters of Lady Arbella Stuart*, ed. Sara Jayne Steen (Oxford: Oxford University Press).
Tilney, Edmund (1992), *The Flower of Friendship: A Renaissance Dialogue Contesting Marriage*, ed. Valerie Wayne (Ithaca, NY: Cornell University Press).
Webster, John (1995), *The Works of John Webster*, ed. David Gunby, David Carnegie, and Antony Hammond, 3 vols (Cambridge: Cambridge University Press).

OTHER WORKS CITED

Adams, Joseph Quincy (ed.) (1917), *The Dramatic Records of Sir Henry Herbert* (New Haven: Yale University Press).
Alexander, Peter (1924), '*3 Henry VI* and *Richard, Duke of York*', *Times Literary Supplement*, 13 November: 730.
Alexander, Peter (1929), *Shakespeare's Henry VI and Richard III* (Cambridge: Cambridge University Press).
Arber, Edward (ed.) (1875), *A Transcript of the Registers of the Company of Stationers of London, 1554–1640*, 5 vols (London: privately printed).
Astington, John (1999), *English Court Theatre* (Cambridge: Cambridge University Press).
Astington, John (2009), 'Court Theatre', in *The Oxford Handbook of Early Modern Theatre*, ed. Richard Dutton (Oxford: Oxford University Press), 307–22.
Bain, J. (ed.) (1898–1915), *Calendar of the State Papers relating to Scotland... 1547–1603*, 9 vols (London: HMSO).
Bains, Y. S. (1995), *Making Sense of the First Quartos of Shakespeare's 'Romeo and Juliet', 'Henry V', 'The Merry Wives of Windsor' and 'Hamlet'* (Rashtrapati Nivas: Indian Institute of Advanced Study).

Bald, R. C. (1942), *Evidence and Inference in Bibliography* (New York: Columbia University Press).

Baldwin, T. W. (1944), *William Shakespere's Small Latine and Lesse Greeke*, 2 vols (Urbana: University of Illinois Press).

Barroll, Leeds (1991), *Politics, Plague and Shakespeare's Theatre* (Ithaca, NY: Cornell University Press).

Bawcutt, N. W. (1996), *The Control and Censorship of Caroline Drama: The Records of Sir Henry Herbert, Master of the Revels 1623–73* (Oxford: Clarendon Press).

Beckerman, Bernard (1962), *Shakespeare at the Globe, 1599–1609* (New York: Macmillan).

Bednarz, James P. (2001), *Shakespeare and the Poets' War* (New York: Columbia University Press).

Bednarz, James P. (2006), 'When Did Shakespeare Write the Choruses of *Henry V?' Notes and Queries* 53: 486–9.

Bentley, G. E. (1971), *The Profession of Dramatist in Shakespeare's Time, 1590–1642* (Princeton: Princeton University Press).

Bentley, G. E. (1984), *The Profession of Player in Shakespeare's Time, 1590–1642* (Princeton: Princeton University Press).

Bergeron, David M. (1985), *Shakespeare's Romances and the Royal Family* (Lawrence: University of Kansas Press).

Berringer, Ralph W. (1943), 'Jonson's *Cynthia's Revels* and the War of the Theaters', *Philological Quarterly* 22: 1–22.

Berry, Herbert (1986), *The Boar's Head Playhouse* (Washington, DC: Folger Shakespeare Library).

Birch, T. (1754), *Memoirs of the Reign of Queen Elizabeth from the Year 1581 to Her Death*, 2 vols (London).

Blayney, Peter (1982), *The Texts of 'King Lear' and Their Origins. Volume 1, Nicholas Okes and the First Quarto* (Cambridge: Cambridge University Press).

Blayney, Peter (1987), 'Shakespeare's Fight with *What* Pirates?' Paper presented at the Folger Shakespeare Library, May 1987.

Blayney, Peter (1989), 'A Groatsworth of Evidence', Paper delivered at the SAA annual meeting, Austin, TX, April 1989.

Blayney, Peter (1991), *The First Folio of Shakespeare* (Washington, DC: Folger Books).

Blayney, Peter (1997), 'The Publication of Playbooks', in John D. Cox and David Scott Kastan (eds), *A New History of Early English Drama* (New York: Columbia University Press), 383–422.

Boas, F. S. (1914), *University Drama in the Tudor Age* (Oxford: Oxford University Press).

Bourus, Terri (2014), *Young Shakespeare's Young Hamlet: Print, Piracy, and Performance* (New York: Palgrave Macmillan).

Bowen, Catherine Drinker (1956), *The Lion and the Throne: The Life and Times of Sir Edward Coke (1552–1634)* (Boston: Little, Brown & Co.).

Bowers, Fredson (1955), *On Editing Shakespeare and the Elizabethan Dramatists* (Philadelphia: University of Pennsylvania Library).

Bradley, David (1992), *From Text to Performance in the Elizabethan Theatre* (Cambridge: Cambridge University Press).

Briggs, Julia (2007), 'Textual Introduction to *The Lady's Tragedy*' [*The Second Maiden's Tragedy*] in Taylor and Lavagnino 2007: 619–26.

Bruster, Douglas (2013), 'Shakespearean Spellings and Handwriting in the Additional Passages Printed in the 1602 Spanish Tragedy', *Notes and Queries* 60: 420–4.

Butler, Martin (1992), 'Ecclesiastical Censorship of Early Stuart Drama: The Case of Jonson's *The Magnetic Lady*', *Modern Philology* 89: 469–81.
Butler, Martin (1993), 'Jonson's Folio and the Politics of Patronage', *Criticism* 35: 377–90.
Butler, Martin (1995), 'Sir Francis Stewart: Jonson's Overlooked Patron', *The Ben Jonson Journal* 2: 101–27.
Calderwood, David (1842–49), *History of the Kirk of Scotland*, 8 vols (Edinburgh: for The Wodrow Society).
Carson, Neil (1988), *A Companion to Henslowe's 'Diary'* (Cambridge: Cambridge University Press).
Cerasano, Susan P. (1998), 'Edward Alleyn's "Retirement", 1597–1600', *Medieval and Renaissance Drama in England* 10: 98–112.
Chambers, Sir. E. K. (1923), *The Elizabethan Stage*, 4 vols (Oxford: Clarendon Press).
Chambers, Sir. E. K. (1930), *William Shakespeare: A Study of Facts and Problems*, 2 vols (Oxford: Clarendon Press).
Chambers, Sir. E. K. (1933), 'The Disintegration of Shakespeare', in *Aspects of Shakespeare* ([1924]; Oxford: Clarendon Press), 23–48.
Clare, Janet (1990), *'Art Made Tongue-Tied by Authority': Elizabethan and Jacobean Dramatic Censorship* (Manchester: Manchester University Press).
Clegg, Cyndia Susan (1997), ' "By the Choice and Inuitation of Al the Realm": *Richard II* and Elizabethan Press Censorship', *Shakespeare Quarterly* 48: 432–48.
Cohen, Walter (1985), *Drama of a Nation* (Ithaca, NY: Cornell University Press).
Craig, Hardin (1927), 'The Relation of the First Quarto Version to the First Folio Version of Shakespeare's *Henry V*', *Philological Quarterly* 6: 225–34.
Crofts, J. E. V. (1937), *Shakespeare and the Post Horses: A New Study of 'The Merry Wives of Windsor'* (Bristol: University of Bristol Press).
Cull, Marisa R. (2014), *Shakespeare's Princes of Wales* (Oxford: Oxford University Press).
Danby, John F. (1965), 'Beaumont and Fletcher: Jacobean Absolutists', in *Elizabethan and Jacobean Poets* (London: Faber & Faber), 152–83.
Davies, Sir John (1876), *The Complete Poems of Sir John Davies*, ed. A. Grosart, 2 vols (London: Chatto and Windus).
Dawson, Anthony and Paul Yachnin (2001), *The Culture of Playgoing in Shakespeare's England: A Collaborative Debate* (Cambridge: Cambridge University Press).
Dessen, Alan C. (2009), 'Stage Directions and the Theater Historian' in *The Oxford Handbook of Early Modern Theatre*, ed. Richard Dutton (Oxford: Oxford University Press), 513–27.
Dibdin, James C. (1888), *Annals of the Edinburgh Stage* (Edinburgh: R. Cameron).
Dillon, Janette (1994), 'Is there a Performance in this Text?' *Shakespeare Quarterly* 45: 74–81.
Doran, Madeleine (1928), *Henry VI, Parts II and III: Their Relation to* The Contention *and* The True Tragedy, *University of Iowa Studies* 4.
Doran, Madeleine (1931), *The Text of 'King Lear'* (Stanford: Stanford University Press).
Duncan-Jones, Katherine (2001), *Ungentle Shakespeare: Scenes From His Life* (London: Arden Shakespeare).
Dusinberre, Juliet (2003), 'Pancakes and a Date for *As You Like It*', *Shakespeare Quarterly* 54: 371–405.
Duthie, G. I. (1949), *Elizabethan Shorthand and the First Quarto of 'King Lear'* (Oxford: Blackwell).

Dutton, Richard (1974), 'The Significance of Jonson's Revision of *Every Man In His Humour*', *Modern Language Review* 69: 241–9.
Dutton, Richard (1991), *Mastering the Revels: The Regulation and Censorship of English Renaissance Drama* (Basingstoke: Macmillan; and Iowa City: University of Iowa Press).
Dutton, Richard (1993), 'Ben Jonson and the Master of the Revels', in *Theatre and Government under the Early Stuarts*, ed. J. R. Mulryne and Margaret Shewring (Cambridge: Cambridge University Press), 57–86.
Dutton, Richard (ed) (1999), *Thomas Middleton: 'Women Beware Women' and Other Plays* (Oxford: Oxford University Press).
Dutton, Richard (2000), *Licensing, Censorship and Authorship in Early Modern England: Buggeswords* (Basingstoke: Palgrave).
Dutton, Richard (2002), 'The Revels Office and the Boy Companies, 1600-1613: New Perspectives', *English Literary Renaissance* 32: 324–51.
Dutton, Richard (2005), '"Methinks the Truth Should Live from Age to Age": The Dating and Contexts of *Henry V*', in *The Uses of History in Early Modern England*, ed. Paulina Kewes. Special issue of *The Huntington Library Quarterly* 68.1–2: 173–204.
Dutton, Richard (2008), '"Not One Clear Item but an Indefinite Thing which is in Parts of Uncertain Authenticity"', *Shakespeare Studies* 26: 114–21.
Dutton, Richard (ed) (2009a), *The Oxford Handbook of Early Modern Theatre* (Oxford: Oxford University Press).
Dutton, Richard (2009b), 'The Court, the Master of the Revels, and the Players', in *The Oxford Handbook of Early Modern Theatre*, ed. Richard Dutton (Oxford: Oxford University Press), 362–79.
Dutton, Richard (2009c), '*The Famous Victories* and the 1600 Quarto of *Henry V*' in *Locating the Queen's Men, 1583–1603: Material Practices and Conditions of Playing*, ed. Helen Ostovich, Holger Schott Syme, and Andrew Griffin (Farnham: Ashgate), 135–44.
Dutton, Richard (2011), 'A Jacobean *Merry Wives*?' *Ben Jonson Journal* 18: 1–18.
Dutton, Richard (2014), '*Hamlet* and Succession', in *Doubtful and Dangerous: The Question of Succession in Late Elizabethan England*, ed. Susan Doran and Paulina Kewes (Manchester: Manchester University Press).
Dutton, Richard and Steven Galbraith (eds) (2015), Thomas Drue, *The Duchess of Suffolk* (Columbus: Ohio State University Press).
Eccles, Mark (1933a), 'Barnabe Barnes', in *Sir Thomas Lodge and Other Elizabethans*, ed. C. J. Sisson (Cambridge, MA: Harvard University Press), 166–241.
Eccles, Mark (1933b), 'Sir George Buc, Master of the Revels', in *Sir Thomas Lodge and Other Elizabethans*, ed. C. J. Sisson (Cambridge, MA: Harvard University Press), 409–506.
Edmond, Mary (1987), *Rare Sir William Davenant: Poet Laureate, Playwright, Civil War General, Restoration Theatre Manager* (Manchester: Manchester University Press).
Egan, Gabriel (2010), *The Struggle for Shakespeare's Text: Twentieth-Century Editorial Theory and Practice* (Cambridge: Cambridge University Press).
Egan, Gabriel (2011), 'Review of Stern, Tiffany. *Documents of Performance in Early Modern England*', *Early Modern Literary Studies* 15.3: 6.
Erne, Lukas (2003), *Shakespeare as Literary Dramatist* (Cambridge: Cambridge University Press).
Erne, Lukas (2013), *Shakespeare as Literary Dramatist*. 2nd edn (Cambridge: Cambridge University Press).
Farmer, Alan B. and Zachary Lesser (eds) (2007), *DEEP: Database of Early English Playbooks*. <http://deep.sas.upenn.edu>.

Feuillerat, Albert (ed.) (1908), *Documents Relating to the Office of the Revels in the Time of Queen Elizabeth* (Louvain: A. Uystpruyst).
Feuillerat, Albert (ed.) (1914), *Documents Relating to the Revels at Court in the Time of King Edward VI and Queen Mary* (Louvain: A. Uystpruyst).
Foakes, R. A. (ed.) (2002), *Henslowe's Diary*. 2nd edn (Cambridge: Cambridge University Press).
Freedman, Barbara (1994), 'Shakespearean Chronology, Ideological Complicity, and Floating Texts: Something is Rotten in Windsor', *Shakespeare Quarterly* 45: 190–210.
Freeman, Arthur and Paul Grinke (2002), 'Four New Shakespeare Quartos', *Times Literary Supplement*, 5 April: 17–18.
Gair, Reavley (1982), *The Children of Paul's: The Story of a Theatre Company, 1553–1608* (Cambridge: Cambridge University Press).
Gants, David L. (1999), 'The Printing, Proofing and Press-Correction of Ben Jonson's Folio *Workes*', in *Re-Presenting Ben Jonson: Text, History, Performance*, ed. Martin Butler (Basingstoke: Macmillan), 39–58.
Gopnik, Adam (2007), 'The Corrections: Abridgment, Enrichment, and the Nature of Art', *The New Yorker* 83, 22 October: 66–76.
Gossett, Suzanne (2007a), '*A Fair Quarrel*: Canon and Chronology', in Taylor and Lavagnino 2007: 398–400.
Gossett, Suzanne (2007b), 'The Texts: *A Fair Quarrel*', in Taylor and Lavagnino 2007: 633–40.
Graves, R. B. (1999), *Lighting the Shakespearean Stage, 1576–1642* (Carbondale and Edwardsville: Southern Illinois University Press).
Graves, R. B. (2009), 'Lighting', in *The Oxford Handbook of Early Modern Theatre*, ed. Richard Dutton (Oxford: Oxford University Press), 528–42.
Graves, T. S. (1913), *The Court and the London Theatres during the Reign of Elizabeth* (Menasha, WI: The Collegiate Press).
Green, William (1962), *Shakespeare's Merry Wives of Windsor* (Princeton: Princeton University Press).
Greenfield, Peter (2009), 'Touring', in *The Oxford Handbook of Early Modern Theatre*, ed. Richard Dutton (Oxford: Oxford University Press), 292–306.
Greg, W. W. (ed.) (1907), *Henslowe's Papers* (London: A. H. Bullen).
Greg, W. W. (ed.) (1904–8), *Henslowe's Diary*, 2 vols (London: A. H. Bullen).
Greg, W. W. (1928), 'Reply to Albright', *Review of English Studies* 4: 202–4.
Greg, W. W. (1939–59), *A Bibliography of the English Printed Drama to the Restoration*, 4 vols (London: Bibliographical Society).
Greg, W. W. (1954), *The Editorial Problem in Shakespeare*. 3rd edn ([1942]; Oxford: Clarendon Press).
Greg, W. W. (1955), *The Shakespeare First Folio* (Oxford: Clarendon Press).
Gurr, Andrew (1996), *The Shakespearian Playing Companies* (Oxford: Clarendon Press).
Gurr, Andrew (1999), 'Maximal and Minimal Texts: Shakespeare v. the Globe', *Shakespeare Survey* 52: 68–87.
Gurr, Andrew (2002), 'Privy Councillors as Theatre Patrons', in *Shakespeare and Theatrical Patronage in Early Modern England*, ed. Paul Whitfield White and Suzanne R. Westfall (Cambridge: Cambridge University Press), 221–45.
Gurr, Andrew (2004a), *The Shakespeare Company, 1594–1642* (Cambridge: Cambridge University Press).
Gurr, Andrew (2004b), *Playgoing in Shakespeare's London*, 3rd edn (1987; Cambridge: Cambridge University Press).

Haaker, Ann (1968), 'The Plague, the Theater, and the Poet', *Renaissance Drama*, ns 1: 283–306.
Hackel, Heidi Brayman (1999), '"Rowme" of its Own: Printed Drama in Early Libraries', in *A New History of Early English Drama*, ed. John D. Cox and David Scott Kastan (New York: Columbia University Press), 113–30.
Hackett, Helen (2012), '"As the Diall Hand Tells Ore": The Case for Dekker, not Shakespeare, as Author', *The Review of English Studies* 63: 34–57.
Halstead, W. L. (1939), 'A Note on Dekker's *Old Fortunatus*', *Modern Language Notes* 54: 351–2.
Harbage, Alfred (1941), *Shakespeare's Audience* (New York: Columbia University Press).
Hart, Alfred (1932), 'The Number of Lines in Shakespeare's Plays,' *Review of English Studies* 8: 19–28.
Hart, Alfred (1934), *Shakespeare and the Homilies* (Melbourne: Melbourne University Press).
Hart, Alfred (1942), *Stolne and Surreptitious Copies: A Comparative Study of Shakespeare's Bad Quartos* (Melbourne: Melbourne University Press).
Hart, Alfred (1944), 'Did Shakespeare Produce his own Plays?' *Modern Language Review* 36: 173–83.
Hattaway, Michael (2009), 'Dating *As You Like It* and the Problems of "As the *Dial Hand* Tells *O'er*"', *Shakespeare Quarterly* 60: 154–67.
Herz, Von E. (1903), 'Englische Schauspieler und englisches Schauspiel zur Zeit Shakespeares in Deutschland', *Theatergeschichtliche Forschungen* 18.
Hillebrand, Harold N. (1964), *The Child Actors* (1926; New York: Russell and Russell).
Hirrel, Michael J. (2010), 'Duration of Performances and the Length of Plays: How Shall We Beguile the Lazy Time?' *Shakespeare Quarterly* 61: 159–82.
Hirschfeld, Heather Anne (2004), *Joint Enterprises: Collaborative Drama and the Institutionalization of English Renaissance Theatre* (Boston: University of Massachusetts Press).
Hodgdon, Barbara (1986), 'Gaining a Father: The Role of Egeus in the Quarto and the Folio', *Review of English Studies* n.s. 37: 534–42.
Honigmann, E. A. J. (1965), *The Stability of Shakespeare's Text* (London: Edward Arnold).
Honigmann, E. A. J. (1996), *The Texts of 'Othello' and Shakespearean Revision* (London: Routledge).
Hope, Jonathan (1994), *The Authorship of Shakespeare's Plays: A Socio-Linguistic Study* (Cambridge: Cambridge University Press).
Hotson, Leslie (1931), *Shakespeare Versus Shallow* (London: Nonesuch Books).
Hotson, Leslie (1949), *Shakespeare's Sonnets Dated and Other Essays* (New York: Oxford University Press).
Hotson, Leslie (1952), *Shakespeare's Motley* (New York: Oxford University Press).
Howard-Hill, T. H. (1972), *Ralph Crane and Some Shakespeare First Folio Comedies* (Charlottesville, VA: Bibliographic Society of the University of Virginia).
Howard-Hill, T. H. (1988), 'Buc and the Censorship of *Sir John Van Olden Barnavelt* in 1619', *Review of English Studies* n.s. 39: 39–63.
Howard-Hill, T. H. (1992), 'Shakespeare's Earliest Editor, Ralph Crane', *Shakespeare Survey* 44: 113–29.
Hoy, Cyrus (1980), *Introductions, Notes, and Commentaries to Texts in 'The Dramatic Works of Thomas Dekker'*, ed. Fredson Bowers, 4 vols (Cambridge: Cambridge University Press).
Hume, M. A. S. (ed.) (1892–99), *Calendar of Letters and State Papers, relating to English Affairs, Principally in the Archives of Simancas*, 4 vols (London).

Hunt, Mary Leland (1911), *Thomas Dekker: A Study* (New York: Columbia University Press).
Hunter, George (1962), *John Lyly: The Humanist as Courtier* (London: Routledge).
Hyman, Stanley Edgar (1955), *The Armed Vision: A Study in the Methods of Modern Literary Criticism* (New York: Knopf).
Ingram, William (1978), *A London Life in the Brazen Age: Francis Langley, 1548–1602* (Cambridge, MA: Harvard University Press).
Ingram, William (1992), *The Business of Playing: The Beginnings of the Adult Professional Theater in Elizabethan London* (Ithaca, NY: Cornell University Press).
Ioppolo, Grace (1991), *Revising Shakespeare* (Cambridge, MA: Harvard University Press).
Irace, Kathleen O. (1994), *Reforming the 'Bad' Quartos: Performance and Provenance of Six Shakespearean First Editions* (Newark: University of Delaware Press, 1994).
Jackson, MacDonald P. (1964), 'Edward Archer's Ascription of *Mucedorus* to Shakespeare', *Journal of the Autralasian Universities Language and Literature Association* 22: 233–48.
Jackson, MacDonald P. (2003), *Defining Shakespeare: 'Pericles' As Test Case* (Oxford: Clarendon Press).
James, Mervyn (1986), *Society, Politics and Culture: Studies in Early Modern Culture* (Cambridge: Cambridge University Press).
Johnson, Gerald D. (1992), 'Thomas Pavier, Publisher, 1600–1625', *Library*, 6th series, 14: 12–50.
Johnson, W. (1987), 'An Enginer Hoist With His Own Petard', *International Journal of Mechanical Sciences* 29: 587–600.
Jones, John (1995), *Shakespeare at Work* (Oxford: Clarendon Press).
Jowett, John (1987), *2 Henry IV*, in Wells and Taylor 1987: 351–3.
Jowett, John and Gary Taylor (1987), 'The Three Texts of *2 Henry IV*', *Studies in Bibliography* 40: 31–50.
Kathman, David (2009), 'Inn-yard Playhouses', in *The Oxford Handbook of Early Modern Theatre*, ed. Richard Dutton (Oxford: Oxford University Press), 153–67.
Kay, W. David (1970–71), 'The Shaping of Ben Jonson's Career: A Reexamination of Facts and Problems', *Modern Philology* 67: 224–37.
Kay, W. David (1995), *Ben Jonson: a Literary Life* (Basingstoke: Macmillan).
Kernan, Alvin (1995), *Shakespeare, the King's Playwright: Theatre in the Stuart Court, 1603–1613* (New Haven and London: Yale University Press).
Kerrigan, John (1983), 'Revision, Adaptation, and the Fool in *King Lear*', in Taylor and Warren 1983: 195–239.
Kerrigan, John (2001), 'Shakespeare as Reviser', in *On Shakespeare and Early Modern Literature: Essays* (Oxford: Oxford University Press), 3–22.
Kincaid, Patrick (1999), 'A Critical Edition of William Percy's *The cuckqueans and cuckolds errants*', 2 vols (unpublished doctoral thesis, University of Birmingham).
Kirschbaum, L. (1945), 'An Hypothesis Concerning the Origin of the Bad Quartos', *PMLA* 60: 697–715.
Kirschbaum, L. (1955), 'The Texts of *Mucedorus*', *Modern Language Review* 50: 1–5.
Klein, David (1967), 'Time Allotted for an Elizabethan Performance', *Shakespeare Quarterly* 18: 434–8.
Knutson, Roslyn Landor (1985), 'Henslowe's Diary and the Economics of Play Revision for Revival', *Theatre Research International* 10: 1–18.
Knutson, Roslyn Landor (1991), *The Repertory of Shakespeare's Company, 1594–1613* (Fayetteville: Univ. of Arkansas Press).
Knutson, Roslyn Landor (2001), *Playing Companies and Commerce in Shakespeare's Time* (Cambridge: Cambridge University Press).

Knutson, Roslyn Landor (2010), 'What's So Special About 1594?' *Shakespeare Quarterly* 61: 449–67.
Kolbert, Elizabeth (2011), 'Sleeping with the Enemy', *The New Yorker* 87, 15 and 22 August: 64–75.
Lawrence, W. J. (1919), 'The abridged rural prompt-book theory': letter to the *Times Literary Supplement*, 21 August.
Lesser, Zachary (2015), *'Hamlet' After Q1: An Uncanny History of the Shakespearean Text* (Philadelphia: University of Pennsylvania Press).
Lesser, Zachary and Alan Farmer (2005a), 'The Popularity of Playbooks Revisited', *Shakespeare Quarterly* 56: 1–13.
Lesser, Zachary and Alan Farmer (2005b), 'Structures of Popularity in the Early Modern Book Trade', *Shakespeare Quarterly* 56: 206–13.
Lesser, Zachary and Peter Stallybrass (2008), 'The First Literary *Hamlet* and the Commonplacing of Professional Plays', *Shakespeare Quarterly* 59: 371–420.
Loewenstein, Joseph (1988), 'Plays Agonistic and Competitive: The Textual Approach to Elsinore', *Renaissance Drama* 19: 63–96.
Logan, Terence P., and Denzell S. Smith (eds) (1977), *The New Intellectuals: A Survey and Bibliography of Recent Studies in English Renaissance Drama* (Lincoln: University of Nebraska Press).
Long, John H. (1952), 'Another Masque for *The Merry Wives of Windsor*', *Shakespeare Quarterly* 3: 39–43.
Long, William B. (1985), ' "A Bed / for Woodstock": a Warning for the Unwary', *Medieval and Renaissance Drama in England* 2: 91–118.
Long, William B. (1997), 'Perspective on Provenance: The Contexts of Varying Speech-heads', in *Shakespeare's Speech-Headings: Speaking the Speech in Shakespeare's Plays*, ed. George W. Williams (Newark: University of Delaware Press), 21–44.
Long, William B. (1999), ' "Precious Few": English Manuscript Playbooks', in *A Companion to Shakespeare*, ed. David S. Kastan (Oxford: Blackwell), 414–33.
MacCaffrey, Wallace T. (1961), 'Place and Patronage in Elizabethan Politics', in S. T. Bindoff et al. (eds), *Elizabethan Government and Society* (London: Athlone Press), 97–126.
MacLean, Sally-Beth (2002), 'Tracking Leicester's Men: The Patronage of a Performance Troupe', in Paul Whitfield White and Suzanne R. Westfall (eds), *Shakespeare and Theatrical Patronage in Early Modern England* (Cambridge: Cambridge University Press), 246–71.
MacLean, Sally-Beth (2003), 'A Family Tradition: Dramatic Patronage by the Earls of Derby', in Richard Dutton, Alison Findlay, and Richard Wilson (eds), *Region, Religion and Patronage: Lancastrian Shakespeare* (Manchester: Manchester University Press), 205–26.
Maguire, Laurie E. (1996), *Shakespearean Suspect Texts: The 'Bad' Quartos and Their Contexts* (Cambridge: Cambridge University Press).
Maguire, Laurie E. and Thomas L. Berger (eds) (1998), *Textual Formations and Reformations* (Newark and London: Associated University Presses).
Manley, Lawrence, and Sally-Beth MacLean (2014), *Lord Strange's Men and Their Plays* (New Haven: Yale University Press).
Marcham, Frank (1925), *The King's Office of the Revels 1610–1622* (London: Frank Marcham).
Marcus, Leah (1988), *Puzzling Shakespeare: Local Reading and Its Discontents* (Berkeley: University of California Press).
Marcus, Leah (1991), 'Levelling Shakespeare: Local Customs and Local Texts', *Shakespeare Quarterly* 42: 168–78.

Marino, James J. (2011), *Owning William Shakespeare: The King's Men and Their Intellectual Property* (Philadelphia: University of Pennsylvania Press).

Martin, Randall (2002), 'Reconsidering the Texts of *The True Tragedy of Richard Duke of York* and *3 Henry VI*', *Review of English Studies* 53: 8–30.

Mason, John Monck (1785), *Comments on the Last Edition of Shakespeare's Plays* (London).

Mateer, David (2006), 'New Light on the Early History of the Theatre in Shoreditch', *English Literary Renaissance* 36: 335–75.

McKerrow, R. B. (1931), 'The Elizabethan Printer and Dramatic Manuscripts', *The Library* 12: 253–75.

McKerrow, R. B. (1935), 'A Suggestion Regarding Shakespeare's Manuscripts', *Review of English Studies* 11: 459–65.

McKerrow, R. B. (1939), *Prolegomena for the Oxford Shakespeare* (Oxford: Clarendon Press).

McLeod, Randall (Random Cloud, pseud.) (1982), 'The Marriage of Good and Bad Quartos', *Shakespeare Quarterly* 33: 421–31.

McManaway, James G. (1969), *Studies in Shakespeare, Bibliography, and the Theater* (New York: The Shakespeare Association of America).

McMillin, Scott (1987), *The Elizabethan Theatre and 'The Book of Sir Thomas More'* (Ithaca, NY: Cornell University Press).

McMillin, Scott (ed.) (1989), *Shakespeare and 'Sir Thomas More': Essays on the Play and Its Shakespearian Interest* (Cambridge: Cambridge University Press).

McMillin, Scott and Sally-Beth MacLean (1999), *The Queen's Men and their Plays* (Cambridge: Cambridge University Press).

McPherson, David (1976), 'The Origins of Overdo', *Modern Language Quarterly* 37: 221–33.

Melchiori, Giorgi (1992), '*Hamlet*: The Acting Version and the Wiser Sort', in Clayton 1992: 195–210.

Menzer, Paul (2006), 'The Tragedians of the City? Q1 *Hamlet* and the Settlements of the 1590s', *Shakespeare Quarterly* 57: 162–82.

Menzer, Paul (2008), *The 'Hamlets': Cues, Qs and Remembered Texts* (Newark: University of Delaware Press).

Mommsen, Tycho (1857), '*Hamlet*, 1603; and *Romeo and Juliet*, 1597', *The Athenaeum* 29.

Mullaney, Steven (1995), *The Place of the Stage: License, Play, and Power in Renaissance England* (Chicago: Chicago University Press).

Mullinger, James Bass (1873), *The University of Cambridge*, 2 vols (Cambridge: Cambridge University Press).

Murphy, Andrew (2003), *Shakespeare in Print: A History and Chronology of Shakespeare Publishing* (Cambridge: Cambridge University Press).

Murphy, Andrew (ed.) (2007), *A Concise Companion to Shakespeare and the Text* (Oxford and Malden, MA: Blackwell).

Nelson, Alan H. (ed.) (1989), *Records of Early English Drama: Cambridge* (Toronto: University of Toronto Press).

Nelson, Alan H. (1998), 'George Buc, William Shakespeare, and the Folger *George a Greene*', *Shakespeare Quarterly* 49: 74–83.

Nelson, Alan H. (1999), 'The Universities: Early Staging in Cambridge', in *A New History of Early English Drama*, ed. John D. Cox and David Scott Kastan (New York: Columbia University Press), 59–67.

Nicholl, Charles (2008), *Shakespeare the Lodger: His Life on Silver Street* (New York: Viking Penguin).

Nicholson, Brinsley (1881), 'The Relation of the Quarto to the Folio Version of *Henry V*', *Transactions of the New Shakespeare Society* 8: 77–102.
Orgel, Stephen (1988), 'The Authentic Shakespeare', *Representations* 2: 1–25; reprinted in *The Authentic Shakespeare* (New York, 2002).
Pafford, J. H. P. (1959), 'Simon Forman's Bocke of Plaies', *Review of English Studies*, n.s. 10: 289–91.
Palfrey, Simon and Tiffany Stern (2007), *Shakespeare in Parts* (Oxford: Oxford University Press).
Paul, H. N. (1950), *The Royal Play of 'Macbeth'* (New York: Macmillan).
Pitcher, Seymour (1961), *The Case for Shakespeare's Authorship of The Famous Victories* (New York: State University Press).
Pollard, A. W. (1909), *Shakespeare's Folios and Quartos: A Study in the Bibliography of Shakespeare's Plays 1594–1685* (London: Methuen).
Pollard, A. W. (1920), 'Variant Settings in *II Henry IV*', *Times Literary Supplement*, 21 October: 680.
Pollard, Alfred W. and J. Dover Wilson (1918–19), 'The "Stolne and Surreptitious" Shakespearian Texts', *The Times Literary Supplement*, 9 January 1918: 18; 16 January 1918: 30; 13 March 1919: 134; 7 August 1919: 420; 14 August 1919: 434.
Pyle, Fitzroy (1969), *'The Winter's Tale': A Commentary on the Structure* (New York: Barnes and Noble).
Rasmussen, Eric (1989), 'Shakespeare's Hand in *The Second Maiden's Tragedy*', *Shakespeare Quarterly* 40: 1–20.
Rasmussen, Eric (1993), *A Textual Companion to 'Dr Faustus'* (Manchester: Manchester University Press).
Riddell, James A. (1997), 'Jonson and Stansby and the Revisions of *Every Man In His Humour*', *Medieval and Renaissance Drama in England* 9: 81–91.
Riggs, David (1989), *Ben Jonson: A Life* (Cambridge, MA: Harvard University Press).
Rix, H. D. (1946), 'The Editions of Erasmus's *De Copia*', *Studies in Philology* 43: 595–618.
Roberts, Jeanne A. (1976), 'The *Merry Wives* Q and F: The Vagaries of Progress', *Shakespeare Studies* 8: 143–76.
Roberts, John (1729), *An Answer to Mr Pope's Preface to Shakespear* (London).
Rowland, Richard (2010), *Thomas Heywood's Theatre, 1599–1639* (Farnham: Ashgate Publishing).
Rowse, A. L. (1976), *The Casebooks of Simon Forman: Sex and Society in Shakespeare's Age* (London: Pan Books).
Rutter, Tom (2008), *Work and Play on the Shakespearean Stage* (Cambridge: Cambridge University Press).
Savage, J. E. (1949), 'The "Gaping Wounds" in the Text of *Philaster*', *Philological Quarterly* 28: 443–57.
Schlueter, June (2013), 'New Light on Dekker's *Fortunati*', *Medieval and Renaissance Drama in England* 26: 120–35.
Schoenbaum, S. (1987), *William Shakespeare: a Compact Documentary Life* (1977; Oxford: Oxford University Press).
Schoone-Jongen, Terence G. (2008), *Shakespeare's Companies* (Farnham: Ashgate).
Scott, Alison V. (2006), *Selfish Gifts: The Politics of Exchange and English Courtly Literature 1580–1628* (Madison: Fairleigh Dickinson University Press).
Scoufos, Alice-Lyle (1979), *Shakespeare's Typological Satires: A Study of the Falstaff-Oldcastle Problem* (Athens, OH: University of Ohio Press).
Shapiro, James (2005), *1599: A Year in the Life of William Shakespeare* (London: Faber and Faber).

Shapiro, Michael (1977), *Children of the Revels: The Boy Companies of Shakespeare's Time and Their Plays* (New York: Columbia University Press).
Shapiro, Michael (2006), 'The Westminster Scholars' *Sapientia Solomonis* as Royal Gift Offering', in Paul Menzer (ed.), *Inside Shakespeare: Essays on the Blackfriars Stage* (Selinsgrove: Susquehanna University Press), 118–22.
Sharpe, Kevin (1979), *Sir Robert Cotton, 1586–1631: History and Politics in Early Modern England* (Oxford: Oxford University Press).
Sisson, C. J. (1936), *Lost Plays of Shakespeare's Age* (Cambridge: Cambridge University Press).
Sisson, C. J. (1960), 'The Laws of Elizabethan Copyright: The Stationers' View', *The Library*, 5th ser., 15: 8–20.
Smith, Robert A. H. (1998), 'Thomas Creede, *Henry V* Q1, and *The Famous Victories of Henrie the Fifth*', *Review of English Studies* 49: 60–4.
Smith, Warren D. (1954), 'The *Henry V* Choruses in the First Folio', *Journal of English and Germanic Philology* 53: 38–57.
Somerset, Alan (2009), 'Not Just Sir Oliver Owlet: From Patrons to "Patronage" of Early Modern Theatre', in *The Oxford Handbook of Early Modern Theatre*, ed. Richard Dutton (Oxford: Oxford University Press), 343–61.
Spong, Andrew (1996), 'Bad Habits, "Bad" Quartos, and the Myth of Origin', *New Theatre Quarterly* 12: 65–70.
Steggle, Matthew (2004), 'Udall, Nicholas (1504–1556)', *Oxford Dictionary of National Biography* (Oxford: Oxford University Press); online edn, Oct 2006. [http://www.oxforddnb.com.proxy.lib.ohio-state.edu/view/article/27974, accessed 1 Oct 2008]
Stephenson, Joseph. F. (2006), 'On the Markings in the Manuscript of *Sir John Van Olden Barnavelt*', *Notes and Queries* 53: 522–4.
Stern, Tiffany (2000), *Rehearsal from Shakespeare to Sheridan* (Oxford: Clarendon Press).
Stern, Tiffany (2009a), *Documents of Performance in Early Modern England* (Cambridge: Cambridge University Press).
Stern, Tiffany (2009b), 'Actors' Parts', in *The Oxford Handbook of Early Modern Theatre*, ed. Richard Dutton (Oxford: Oxford University Press), 496–512.
Stern, Tiffany (2013), 'Sermons, Plays and Note-Takers: *Hamlet* Q1 as a "Noted" Text', *Shakespeare Survey* 66: 1–23.
Streitberger, W. R. (1978), 'On Edmond Tyllney's Biography', *Review of English Studies* n.s. 29: 11–35.
Streitberger, W. R. (1980), 'The Armada Victory Procession and Tudor Precedence', *Notes and Queries* 225: 310–12.
Streitberger, W. R. (ed.) (1986a), *Jacobean and Caroline Revels Accounts, 1603–1642*. Malone Society Collections XIII (Oxford: the University Press for the Malone Society).
Streitberger, W. R. (1986b), *Edmond Tyllney, Master of the Revels and Censor of Plays: A Descriptive Index to his Manual on Europe* (New York: AMS Press).
Streitberger, W. R. (2004), '"Last of the Poore Flocke of Hatfield": Sir Thomas Benger's Biography', *Review of English Studies* n.s. 55: 662–89.
Streitberger, W. R. (2007), 'The Earl of Sussex, the Revels Office, and London Commercial Theatre, 1572-1583', *Review of English Studies* n.s. 58: 34–63.
Streitberger, W. R. (2008), 'Chambers on the Revels Office and Elizabethan Theater History', *Shakespeare Quarterly* 59: 187–209.
Syme, Holger Schott (2010), 'The Meaning of Success: Stories of 1594 and its Aftermath', *Shakespeare Quarterly* 61: 490–525.

Syme, Holger Schott (2012), 'Fact and Factitiousness: Theatre History and Irresponsible Scholarship', <http://www.dispositio.net/archives/date/2014/1>.

Taylor, Gary (1979), *Modernizing Shakespeare's Spelling: With Three Studies of the Text of 'Henry V'* (Oxford: Clarendon Press).

Taylor, Gary (1985), 'The Fortunes of Oldcastle', *Shakespeare Survey* 38: 85–100.

Taylor, Gary (1987), 'William Shakespeare, Richard James and the House of Cobham', *Review of English Studies* 38: 334–54.

Taylor, Gary (2007), 'Introduction: The Middleton Canon', in Taylor and Lavagnino 2007: 331–4.

Taylor, Gary and John Jowett (1993), *Shakespeare Reshaped 1606–1623* (Oxford: Clarendon Press).

Taylor, Gary and John Lavagnino (gen. eds) (2007), *Thomas Middleton and Early Modern Textual Culture* (Oxford: Clarendon Press).

Taylor, Gary and Michael Warren (eds) (1983), *The Division of the Kingdoms: Shakespeare's Two Versions of 'King Lear'* (Oxford: Clarendon Press).

Thomas, Sidney (1984), 'Shakespeare's Supposed Revision of King Lear', *Shakespeare Quarterly* 35: 506–11.

Thornberry, Richard (1977), 'A Seventeenth-Century Revival of *Mucedorus* in London before 1610', *Shakespeare Quarterly* 28: 362–4.

Traversi, Derek (1957), *An Approach to Shakespeare*, 2nd rev. edn ([1938]; London and Glasgow: Sands and Co.).

Tricomi, Albert H. (1971–2), 'The Revised *Bussy D'Ambois* and *The Revenge of Bussy D'Ambois*: Joint Performance in Thematic Counterpoint', *English Language Notes* 9: 253–62.

Tricomi, Albert H. (1973), 'The Revised Version of *Bussy D'Ambois*: A Shift in Point of View', *Studies in Philology* 70: 288–305.

Trousdale, Marion (1982), *Shakespeare and the Rhetoricians* (Chapel Hill: University of North Carolina Press).

Turner, Robert K. (1957), 'The Relationship of *The Maid's Tragedy* Q1 and Q2', *PBSA* 51: 322–7.

Urkowitz, Steven (1987), *Shakespeare's Revision of 'King Lear'* (Princeton, NJ: Princeton University Press).

Urkowitz, Steven (1988), ' "If I Mistake in those Foundations which I Build Upon": Peter Alexander's Textual Analysis of *Henry VI Parts 2 and 3*', *English Literary Renaissance* 8: 230–56.

Urkowitz, Steven (2012), 'Did Shakespeare's Company Cut Long Plays Down to Two Hours' Playing Time?' *Shakespeare Bulletin* 30: 239–62.

Van Es, Bart (2013), *Shakespeare's Company* (Oxford: Oxford University Press).

Vickers, Brian (2002), *Shakespeare, Co-Author* (Oxford: Oxford University Press).

Vickers, Brian (2006), 'By Other Hands', *Times Literary Supplement* [London, England] 11 Aug: 10+. *Times Literary Supplement Historical Archive*. Web. 21 July 2015.

Vickers, Brian (2007), 'Incomplete Shakespeare: Or, Denying Coauthorship in *Henry the Sixth, Part 1*', *Shakespeare Quarterly* 58: 311–52.

Vickers, Brian (2012), 'Identifying Shakespeare's Additions to *The Spanish Tragedy* (1602): A New(er) Approach', *Shakespeare* 8: 13–43.

Walsh, Brian (2009), *Shakespeare, the Queen's Men, and the Elizabethan Performance of History* (Cambridge: Cambridge University Press).

Warren, Michael (1978), 'Quarto and Folio of *King Lear* and the Interpretation of Albany and Edgar', in *Shakespeare: Pattern of Excelling Nature*, ed. David Bevington and Jay H. Halio (Newark, DE: University of Delaware Press), 95–107.

Wells, Stanley and Gary Taylor (1987), *William Shakespeare: A Textual Companion* (Oxford: Oxford University Press).

Werstine, Paul (1990), 'Narratives About Printed Shakespeare Texts: "Foul Papers" and "Bad" Quartos', *Shakespeare Quarterly* 41: 65–86.

Werstine, Paul (1998), 'Touring and the Construction of Textual Criticism', in Maguire and Berger: 45–66.

Werstine, Paul (1999), 'A Century of "Bad" Shakespeare Quartos', *Shakespeare Quarterly* 50: 310–33.

Werstine, Paul (2009), 'The Continuing Importance of New Bibliographical Method', *Shakespeare Survey* 62: 30–45.

Werstine, Paul (2012), *Early Modern Playhouse Manuscripts and the Editing of Shakespeare* (Cambridge: Cambridge University Press).

Westfall, Suzanne R. (1990), *Patrons and Performance: Early Tudor Household Revels* (Oxford: Clarendon Press).

White, Paul Whitfield (2002), 'Shakespeare and the Cobhams', in *Shakespeare and Theatrical Patronage in Early Modern England*, ed. Paul Whitfield White and Suzanne R. Westfall (Cambridge: Cambridge University Press), 64–89.

Wickham, Glynne (1959–81), *Early English Stages 1300–1660*, 3 vols (London: Routledge & Kegan Paul).

Wickham, Glynne, Herbert Berry and William Ingram (eds) (2000), *English Professional Theatre, 1530–1660* (Cambridge: Cambridge University Press).

Wiles, David (1987), *Shakespeare's Clown: Actor and Text in the Elizabethan Playhouse* (Cambridge: Cambridge University Press).

Wilson, J. Dover and R. W. Hunt (1947), 'The Authenticity of Simon Forman's Bocke of Plaies', *Review of English Studies* 23: 193–200.

Winwood, Sir Ralph (1725), *Memorials of Affairs of State in the Reigns of Queen Elizabeth and King James*, ed. E. Sawyer, 3 vols (London).

Woudhuysen, H. R. (2004), 'Ferrers, George (*c.* 1510–1579)', *Oxford Dictionary of National Biography* (Oxford: Oxford University Press). [http://www.oxforddnb.com.proxy.lib.ohio-state.edu/view/article/9360, accessed 1 Oct 2008]

Yachnin, Paul (2005), ' "The Perfection of Ten": Populuxe Art and Artisanal Value in *Troilus and Cressida*', *Shakespeare Quarterly* 56: 306–27.

Index of Offices and Organizations, Events and Editions, Things and Theories

Note that adult playing companies are listed by the title [e.g. Leicester, Worcester, Queen Anna] or the principal offices [e.g. Admiral, Lord Chamberlain, King] of their patron.

Academic theatricals, length of 85–6
   Responses to: Elizabeth 85, James 85–6, Charles 86
Act for the Punishment of Vagabonds 15, 16
Admiral's Men (patron Lord Admiral Howard) 8, 16, 25, 28 & n. 13, 29–30 & n. 15, 31–3, 34 & n. 18, 35, 46, 53 n. 15, 54, 58, 80, 89, 90, 93, 99–100, 102, 105, 116 & n. 32, 156, 164 n. 85, 166, 167, 168, 209, 252 n. 41, 270, 281 n. 29, 286
   At court 48, 49, 50, 55, 69, 82, 103 & n. 10, 104, 107, 108, 111, 279 & n. 26
'Allowed book': *see* Licensing of plays by Master of the Revels
Amplificatio (rhetorical theory) 189–99
Apology for Actors, An (Thomas Heywood) 6, 46, 57, 231

'Bad' quartos: *see* Editing (of Shakespeare): Theories
Blackfriars boys (Children of the Queen's Revels, Children of the Blackfriars: *see* 231 n. 18) 90, 91, 92, 93 & n. 30, 113, 118 n. 36, 160, 231 & nn. 18 and 20, 232, 236, 281 n. 30
Blackfriars liberty 19, 21, 39, 62, 73, 88, 93
Blackfriars playhouse (built 1596) 1, 21 n. 10, 37, 59, 61, 72, 73, 74, 87 n. 22, 90, 92, 93, 113, 118, 161, 231–2, 242, 260, 267, 274, 280, 281 & n. 30, 283, 284, 285
Blackfriars Theatre, Staunton, Virginia 77, 79
Boar's Head 33, 69, 71 n. 4
Boy companies: *see* Blackfriars boys, Chapel Boys/Children of the Chapel Royal, Children of the Queen's Revels (Queen Anna's), Children of Westminster, Children of the Whitefriars, Children of Windsor Chapel

Chamberlain's Men (patron Thomas Radclyffe, Earl of Sussex, Lord Chamberlain 1572–83) 44, 47
Chamberlain's Men (patrons Henry and George Carey, Lords Hunsdon, 1594–1603) 7, 8, 14, 21, 25, 27, 28, 29, 30 & n. 15, 33, 34 & n. 18, 58, 62, 76, 80, 81 & n. 16, 90,
91, 93, 110 nn. 22 and 23, 116, 142, 156, 166–7, 167–8, 169, 188 n. 25, 190, 209, 213, 214, 232, 247, 251, 253, 265 & n. 5, 267, 270, 271, 273, 274, 275–6, 284, 289
   At court 28 & n. 13, 30, 33, 34–5, 36, 46, 49, 69, 109, 209–10
Chandos's Men (patron Grey Bridges, Lord) 16
Children of the Chapel Royal (Children of the Queen's Chapel, the Chapel Boys 20, 21, 34 & n. 18, 40, 41, 42, 47 & n. 6, 49, 90, 91 n. 27, 92–3, 118, 231 & n. 18, 232
Children of the Queen's Revels (Queen Anna's) 34, 118 n. 36, 231 n. 18; *see also* Blackfriars boys
Children of Westminster 40 & n. 3, 41, 49
Children of the Whitefriars 19, 40 n. 26, 93
Children of Windsor Chapel 40, 41, 44, 45, 49
Christmas Revels 38–66
Clerk and Clerk Controller of the Revels 3, 9, 41, 42, 44, 51
Clerkenwell 20, 44, 54, 157, 279
Clinton's Men (patron Lord Admiral Clinton) 41, 45
Costs of courtly theatricals 19ff, **22**, 39, 41–7, **53**, 57; cutting down costs of 22ff
Court dramatist 1–2, 7, 290
Court-identified companies/privileged playing companies 20, 25, 27 n. 12, 31–3, 34 n. 18, 63, 69, 70, 76, 111, 160, 167, 283
   See also Children of the Queen's Chapel, Chamberlain's Men (Sussex's and Hunsdons'), Admiral's Men, Warwick's Men, Leicester's Men, Essex's Men, Paul's Boys, Derby's Men, Worcester's Men, Blackfriars boys
Court performances of note in Shakespeare's time
   See (Jonson) *Bartholomew Fair* 87–9, *Cynthia's Revels* 91–2, *Every Man Out of his Humour* 91 & n. 27; (Shakespeare) *A Midsummer Night's Dream* 59ff, *Love's Labour's Lost* 109–10, *King Lear* 64–5, *Othello* 65, *Pericles* 83–4; (Barnes) *The Devil's Charter* 64–5; (Munday) *Downfall of Robert, Earl of Huntingdon* 103ff; (Dekker) *Phaeton* 103 & n. 10, *Old Fortunatus* 107ff

Court performances of note in Shakespeare's time (*cont.*)
  At the court of Charles I (Shakespeare) *The Taming of the Shrew* 65, 153–4; (Fletcher) *The Woman's Prize* (*The Tamer Tamed*) 65, 153–4; (Heywood) *The Fair Maid of the West* (two parts) 65
  As described by foreign ambassadors 82, 83
  Length of court performances (plays and masques) 83–4
  Parallel staging of plays in courtiers' houses 84–5
  Prologues and choruses for court performance 80, 87, 101 & nn. 7 and 8, 102
Curtain playhouse, The 1, 19 n. 6, 21, 26, 30, 33, 69, 71, 72, 186, 187–8 & n. 25

Derby's Men (patron William Stanley, sixth Earl of) 29 & n. 14, 31, 34 & n. 18, 93 n. 30, 160, 166, 200, 209 & n. 47, 270; *see also* Strange's Men
Duopoly theory 29, 30, 34–5 & n. 18

Editing (of Shakespeare): Theories
  'foul papers' 5, 98 & n. 3, 120, 122, 123 n. 43, 125, 129, 137, 138, 142, **143–6**, 147, 150, 168, 174, 201, 202, 203, 211, 224, 225–6, 247, 249, 258
  'bad' quartos 5, 9, 67, 92, 97 n. 2, 98 & n. 3, 109, 112, 117, 119, 122, 129, 134, **139–42 & n. 62**, 143, 145–9, 150, 168–70, 178, 179, 204, 208, 211, 212, 233, 243, 244, 245, 267, 271, 272, 284, 285, 287, 288
  continuous copy 112 n. 27, 123, **151–2**, **159**, 163, 168, 212, 227
  shorthand 5, 138, **140–1**, 146, 169, 213, 228–9
  abridgement for touring 142
  memorial (re)construction **141–3**, **147–8**
Editors and editions of Shakespeare's plays
  John Heminge and Henry Condell vii, 2, 138, 188 & n. 26, 189, 257, 261 n. 1;
  Samuel Johnson 97 & n. 2, 139, 201;
  Edmund Malone 139, 201, 202;
  Alexander Pope vii, 97 & n. 1, 98, 246–7;
  Nicholas Rowe 166, 246, 249; George Steevens 97 & n. 2; (twentieth century onwards) Sir Jonathan Bate 3 n. 2, 7, 99 n. 5, 116, 149, 259–60, 274 n. 22, 277–8; John D. Cox 9, 149, 202, 208; David Crane 98 & n. 3, 249, 254, 257; Anthony Dawson and Gretchen Minton 274 n. 23; Brian Gibbons 129, 142, 211–12, 214 n. 7; Suzanne Gossett, 3 n. 2, 58, 114–15; W. W. Greg 6, 32, 62, 117, 129, 132, 138, 141–2, 143, 144 & n. 65, 145 & n. 68, 146, 151, 157, 168, 174, 211, 226, 245, 247, 253; Andrew Gurr 9, 80, 119, 150, 174 & n. 3, 177 n. 9, 178–9, 212; Anthony Hammond 130, 237; Michael Hattaway 101 nn. 7 and 8, 131 n. 56, 201–2; G. R. Hibbard 129, 248; E. A. J. Honigmann 146, 271; Harold Jenkins 139, 142, 150, 226–8, 229, 232; John Jowett 130, 146, 263 n. 3, 274 n. 23, 280 n. 27; David Scott Kastan 117 n. 33, 127 n. 49, 135, 252; Ronald Knowles 9, 201 n. 37, 202, 204–6; Jill Levenson 150, 212, 214 n. 6, 222 n. 11; Janis Lull 130; Randall Martin x, 89, 139, 178 n. 11, 201 n. 37, 202–4, 209; Giorgio Melchiori 9, 98, 229, 245 & n. 31, 246 n. 32, 248–9; William Montgomery 131 n. 56, 146, 202; Eric Rasmussen 3 n. 2, 7, 9, 99 n. 5, 116, 149, 201 n. 37; Gary Taylor: see *Oxford Shakespeare* and 174 nn. 2 and 3, 177 n. 9, 180–1, 249–50, 252, 265 n. 3; Ann Thompson 150, 229 n. 15; Roger Warren 176 n. 7, 201, 204, 207 & n. 44, 208; Stanley Wells: see *Oxford Shakespeare*
  Arden Shakespeare 6, 9, 98, 150, 202, 211, 226, 229 n. 15, 245, 248, 259, 271, 274 n. 23, 283 n. 33; *Oxford Shakespeare* (Stanley Wells and Gary Taylor, with John Jowett and William Montgomery) 3 n. 3, 6–7, 60 & n. 21, 102, 111 n. 26, **146–7 & n. 69**, 149, 151, 159, 173 n. 1, 202, 248, 271, 288; *New Cambridge Shakespeare* (Sir Arthur Quiller-Couch and John Dover Wilson) 129, 151, 283 n. 33; (current series) 97, 150, 201, 230 n. 16, 260; *Shakespearean Originals* (Graham Holderness and Bryan Loughrey) 150; *Complete Works of William Shakespeare* (2008) (David Bevington) 9, 60 n. 21, 173, 220, 223 n. 12, 232, 243, 255 n. 44, 256 n. 49; *Folger Shakespeare Editions* (Barbara Mowat and Paul Werstine) 150; *William Shakespeare and Others: Collaborative Plays* (Sir Jonathan Bate and Eric Rasmussen) 3 n. 2, 7, 99 n. 5, 116, 149, 274 n. 22, 277–8
Essex's Men (patron Walter Devereux, second Earl of) 20–1
Essex Rebellion: *see* Essex, Robert Devereux, third Earl of

Fortune playhouse, The 19 n. 6, 25, 33, 87, 116, 159, 160

Gift-exchange economy and theatricals 14ff, 26, 33, 40, 41, 48, 49
Globe playhouse, The ix, 1, 10, 14, 18, 19 n. 6, 33, 61, 64, 70, 72 & n. 5, 79, 80, 87, 89, 106, 110, 113, 118, 119, 130, 148, 177, 178, 186, 187 & n. 25, 190, 230, 260, 261, 271, 278, **280–1**, **282**, **283**, 284–9

Index of Offices and Organizations

Gray's Inn 28 n. 13, 40, 48, 83, 84, 282
Grooms of the Chamber 23, 114, 267, 272
Gunpowder Plot (1605), The 65, 281

Henslowe's *Diary*: entries under Henslowe, Philip
Hertford's Men (patron Edward Seymour, Earl of) 34
Hope playhouse, The 19 n. 6, 72, 88, 165 n. 86
Howard's Men: *see* Admiral's Men
Hunsdon's Men: *see* Chamberlain's Men

Inner Temple 41, 59, 84, 282
Inns of Court 16, 38, 48, 52, 191 n. 29, 281 n. 30
See also Gray's Inn, Inner Temple, Middle Temple

King's Men ix, 2, 4 n. 8, 7, 13, 16, **34**, 35–6 & nn. 24 and 25, 50, 52–3, 58, 60 n. 22, 61, 62, 65 & n. 23, 72 & n. 5, 80, 83, 84 n. 18, 87 n. 22, 88, 90 n. 25, 93 & n. 28, 95, 113, 114, 118 & n. 36, 119, 122, 123 & n. 43, 136, 143–4, 153, 154–5, 158 & n. 80, 162, 163–4, 188 n. 26, 231 n. 20, 235, 236, 237 & nn. 23 and 24, 241, 244, 252 n. 41, 253, 258 n. 50, 261, **267–9**, 270 & n. 13, 271 & n. 15, 273–4 & n. 23, 275, 276 & n. 25, 277–8, 283 & n. 33, 284, 285, 289

Lady Elizabeth's Men (patron Princess Elizabeth Stuart) 52–3, 59 n. 17, 88, 93 & n. 28, 158 & n. 80, 159–60 & n. 81
Leicester's Men (patron Robert Dudley, Earl of) 15–17, 18, 21 & n. 8, 22, 24, 29, 45, 47, 49, 70
Length of plays in performance
 Academic theatricals 84–5
 At court (revels): times of night 82–4; masques 84–5
 At public playhouses, start and end times: before 1594 69; after 1594 70ff; at Blackfriars 281 n. 30; at Paul's playhouse 72–3; 'two-hours traffic' theory 68ff; negotiations between Privy Council and City authorities 69ff
 Line-delivery (speed) 77ff; American Shakespeare Center 79, Royal Shakespeare Company 77
 Line-lengths as measure of performance time 5 n. 10, 75–7, 89, 108, 118, 280; Shakespeare line lengths before and after 1596 81; Jonson's exceptional line lengths 89ff
 Timing of action within plays (*The Tempest*, *The Alchemist*) 74–5
Licensing of plays by Master of the Revels 'Allowed book' 63, 75, 76, 152–3, 155, 158 & n. 80, 160–2, 168, 243

Payment/fees: for revisions 154ff; for sections of plays 155ff
Performances without a license, consequences of 153
Lord Admiral's Men: *see* Admiral's Men
Lord Mayors of London 14, 20, 21, 26, 69, 70–1
 Privy Council Letter to Lord Mayor (1578), court-identified companies 20
 Lord Hunsdon Letter to Lord Mayor (1594) 70
Lord of Misrule 39; *see also* George Ferrers

Masques: Elizabethan 39, 41–2, 44–5, 47, 48, 49; Jacobean 39, 40, 50, 51 & n. 11, 52, 54, 65, 89, 90, 91, 94, 95–6, 256–7, 268, 281 & n. 29, 282–3
Master of the Revels: evidence of activity from attendance fees at court 20, 24, 25, 47–8, 51, 53, 55, 82, 168
 As director and creative consultant for the Revels season 39, 43, 46
 loses responsibilities for court masques 52
 Changes to role with Tilney 52ff
 Involved in revision of plays for court 44, 45, 47, 48, 51 & n. 12, 53ff
 See also Licensing of plays by Masters of the Revels; performing rights from Master of the Revels' licence; Thomas Cawarden, Thomas Blagrave, Sir Thomas Benger, Edmund Tilney, Sir John Astley, Sir Henry Herbert
Merchant Taylors' Boys 41, 44, 49
Middle Temple 49

New Bibliographers: *see* R. B. McKerrow, W. W. Greg, A. W. Pollard
Newington Butts playhouse 19 & n. 6, 21, 28, 233

Oldcastle/Falstaff 165–6, 246, 249ff
Order of the Garter **245–58**
Oxford Shakespeare, The: see Editors and editions of Shakespeare's plays
Oxford's Men (patron, Edward de Vere, seventeenth Earl of) 19, 24, 34

Palsgrave's Men (patron Frederick V, Elector Palatine, husband of Princess Elizabeth) 93, 160, 267 n. 9
Patronage culture 19, 23, 26, 40 & n. 4, 55, 64, 89, 90, 92, 96
Patronage of playing companies 1, 8, 13–15 & n. 1, 16, 19–20, 21, 23, 24, 29 & n. 14, 30 & n. 15, 32 n. 16, 34, 39, 40 n. 2, 46, 47 n. 7, 49, 52, 54, 55, 104, 109 & nn. 20 and 21, 114, 118 n. 36, 165 n. 86, 247, 267 & n. 9, 272–3, 279, 283, 284; *see also* individual companies

Paul's Boys 20, 21, 34, 40, 41, 47, 48, 49, 70, 91, 110 n. 22, 157, 231, 232, 267 n. 9, 268 n. 11, 281, 285 n. 34
Pembroke's Men (patron Henry Herbert, second Earl of) 29 & n. 14, 31, 34 & n. 18, 93 n. 30, 160, 166, 200, 209 & n. 47, 270
Performing rights from Master of the Revels' licence 75
Petition of Blackfriars residents (1619) 73
Plague years 17; *1592–4* 5, 13, 29, 30 n. 15, 58, 69; *1603–4* 5, 13, 38, 90 n. 26, 235–6, 278; *1608–10* 5, 13, 279
Playbook printing and rights attached 57–8, 140, 146, 210, 272, 273; *see also* Stationers' Company
Plays with single-sequence additions: see *A Fair Quarrel*, *Titus Andronicus*, *Richard II*, *2 Henry IV*
Prince Charles's Men (patron Prince Charles, Duke of York; subsequently Charles I) 52, 53, 93 & n. 28, 114, 267 n. 9
Prince Henry's Men (patron Henry, Prince of Wales) 34, 52, 53, 83
Privy Council 14, 19, 20, 21, 23–4, 26, 27, 29–32 & n. 16, 33, 34, 39, 69, 166, 235, 240 n. 26, 247, 254, 289
Prompt copy of plays 142–3, 144, 145 n. 67, 146–7, 150–1, 153, 162, 164, 211, 277

Queen Anna's Men (patron Anna of Denmark) 34, 36 & n. 25, 52, 53, 93, 273
Queen's Men (patron Queen Elizabeth I) viii, 16, **23–4**, 26, 27 n. 12, 28, 29, 48, 49, 83, 125 n. 48, 132, 148, 166, 174, 175 n. 5, 177, 272

Red Bull playhouse, The 71 & n. 4, 158
Rehearsal 6, 20, 26, 39, 44, 45–6, 48, 51, 53–4, 70, 108, 153, 155, 158, 159, 164, 167, 279, 289
Revels calendar, special days: All Hallows Night, St. Stephen's Day, Twelfth Night, Shrove Sunday, Shrove Tuesday, New Year's Day, Candlemas 24, 34 n. 18, 39, 42 & n. 5, 45, **48–50**, 52, 65, **82**, 83, 88, 95; as noted on title pages 50
Rich's Men (patron Robert Rich, second Lord) 41
Rose playhouse, The 19 & n. 6, 25, 29, 30–3, 69, 72, 106, 108, 115, 116, 281 n. 29

Shoreditch 18, 19 n. 6, 30, 69, 70, 72, 73 n. 6
Sir Percival Hart's Sons 40
Sir Robert Lane's Men 41, 43

Stationers' Company 3 n. 8, 36, 139, 140, 166, 178 n. 10, 200, 233, 265 n. 6, 271, 272 n. 16, 284
Strange's Men (patron Ferdinando Stanley, Lord; later fifth Earl of Derby)
Sussex's Men (patron Thomas Radclyffe, Earl of; Lord Chamberlain 1572–83): *see* Chamberlain's Men (Radclyffe)
Swan playhouse, The 19 n. 6, 30, 31, 33, 54, 69

Theatre, The 1, 18, 19 & n. 6, 21, 25, 26, 29, 30, 33, 61, 69, 72, 130, 148, 188 n. 25, 233, 284; *see also* James Burbage, John Brayne
Theories of play-revision:
Shakespearean versus non-Shakespearean drama 99, 102; *see also* Roslyn Landor Knutson
Styles of revision, tinkerers and interpolators, *see* John Kerrigan
See notable examples: *A Midsummer Night's Dream*, *The Woman's Prize*, *Phaeton*, *Robin Hood*, *Love's Labour's Lost*, *Mucedorus*, *A Fair Quarrel*, *The Spanish Tragedy*, *Doctor Faustus*, *The Malcontent*, *Philaster*, *The Maid's Tragedy*; especially *Old Fortunatus*
Title page information about revision
'Augmented' 126, 128–31; see also *Romeo and Juliet*, *Love's Labour's Lost*, *Richard III*, *The Malcontent*, *The Devil's Charter*, *The Maid's Tragedy*
'Enlarged' 126, 131–2; see also *The Spanish Tragedy*, *Hamlet*, *The First Part of the Contention*, *The True Tragedy*, *The Maid's Tragedy*
'Amended' 126, 132; see also *The Spanish Tragedy*, *Soliman and Perseda*, *Philaster*, *Bussy D'Ambois*, *Romeo and Juliet*
'With Additions' 127, 133; see also *The Spanish Tragedy*, *The Malcontent*, *Richard II*, *Mucedorus*, *A Fair Quarrel*, *Doctor Faustus*
'Corrected' 127–8, 133–5; see also *The Spanish Tragedy*, *Love's Labour's Lost*, *Romeo and Juliet*, *Soliman and Perseda*, *The Devil's Charter*, *The Whole Contention*, *Philaster*, *Bussy D'Ambois*, *Locrine*, *1 Henry IV*, *Parasitaster, or The Fawn*, *Jack Drum's Entertainment*, *The Faithful Shepherdess*, *Merry Wives*, *Love's Mistress*

Warwick's Men (patron Ambrose Dudley, Earl of) 19, 20, 21, 29, 41, 47 & n. 6
Worcester's Men (patron Edward Somerset, Earl of Worcester) 34, 54, 100, 270

Index of Plays and Other Dramatic Texts

Aeneas and Dido (Anonymous) 83
Ajax Flagellifer (Sophocles) 85, 86
Alchemist, The (Jonson) 36, **74–5**, 90, 93 & n. 29, 94 & n. 32, 96, 112, 269, 276 n. 24, 278
All is True / Henry VIII (Shakespeare and Fletcher) 3, 57, 68, 77, 79, 271 n. 14, 274 & nn. 21 and 23, 282
All's Well That Ends Well (Shakespeare) 3, 271 n. 14, 274 & nn. 19 and 21, 280
Alphonsus, King of Aragon (Greene) 58
Antony and Cleopatra (Shakespeare) 3, 78, 81, 101, 177, 233, 240, 274 n. 19
Arraignment of Paris, The (Peele) 58
As You Like It (Shakespeare) 3, 77, 101, 177, 233, 240, 274 n. 19
Aulularia (Plautus) 85

Bad Beginning Makes a Good Ending, A (Ford (?) 36, 276 n. 24
Bartholomew Fair (Jonson) 36 n. 23, 50, 64, 84, 90, 92, 95, 265 n. 5
  Length and playing time, professional theatre and court versions 78, **87–9**
Baxter's Tragedy (Anonymous) 156
Beauty and Desire (Anonymous) 41
Believe as Ye List (Massinger) 122 n. 42, 152
Black Dog, The (Anonymous) 101
Bonduca (Fletcher) 143–4 & n. 63, 276 n. 24
Bussy D'Ambois (Chapman) 66, 112, 127–8, 132–3, 137, 159
Byron plays (Chapman) 23, 240 n. 26

Campaspe (Lyly) 50, 109 n. 19, 187
Cardenio (Shakespeare and Fletcher) 3 n. 2, 36 & nn. 23 and 25, 237 n. 23, 271 n. 14, 274, 276
Cardinal, The (Anonymous) 156
Cardinal Wolsey (Chettle) 101 & n. 6, 102, 155–7 & n. 78
Catiline His Conspiracy (Jonson) 87, 90, 94, 96, 112, 187 n. 23, 269
Changeling, The (Middleton and Rowley) 115
1 Civil Wars of France (Drayton and Dekker) 164
Cloridon and Radiamanta (Anonymous) 43
Comedies, Histories and Tragedies of Mr. William Shakespeare (First Folio, Shakespeare) vii & n. 1, 2 & nn. 2 and 3, 4 & n. 9, 5, 9, 10 & n. 14, 81, 97 n. 2, 98, 106 n. 14, 111, 125, 134, 138–9, 141, 144, 147, 158 & n. 36, 159, 185, 188 & n. 26, 200 & n. 36, 203, 211 n. 1, 223–4 & n. 12, 226, 233, 245, 259, 260, 261 & n. 1, 263, 266, 267, 271 & n. 14, 283, 285, 286

Comedy of Errors, The (Shakespeare) 3, 28 n. 13, 35, 74 n. 8, 77, 81, 224, 236
Comical Gallant, The: or the Amours of Sir John Falstaff (Dennis) 246
Contention Between Liberality and Prodigality, The (Anonymous) 35 n. 20, 125
Coriolanus (Shakespeare) 3, 78, 271, 274, 280
Coronation, The (Shirley) 235
Cutting Dick (Heywood) 101
Cymbeline (Shakespeare) 3, 77, 78, 261 n. 1, 271 n. 14, 274, 280 & n. 28, 281–3
Cynthia's Revels (Jonson) **90–2**, 94, 95, 99 n. 4, 110 & n. 22, 112

Death of Robert, Earl of Huntington, The (aka *Robin Hood*; Munday) 102
Devil's Charter, The (Barnes) 36, 50, 58, **64–5**, 89, 90 n. 26, 126–8, 130, 133, 136, 137, 275 & n. 24, 280
Dido (Anonymous) 85
Doctor Faustus (Marlowe) 2, 8, 9, 65, 99–100, 101–2, 115, **116–17 & n. 33**, 124, 127, 130, 133, 135, 137, 204
Downfall of Robert, Earl of Huntington, The (aka *Robin Hood*; Munday) **102–4 & n. 11**, 106
Duchess of Malfi, The (Webster) 89, 130, 137, 276 n. 24

Eastward Ho! (Chapman, Jonson and Marston) 93 n. 30, 161, 231
Emperor Otho, The (Herbert) 59
Endymion (Lyly) 50
English Traveller, The (Heywood) 273
Epicene (Jonson) 90 & n. 26, 93, 94, 96 n. 34
Estrild (Charles Tilney?) 58
Every Man In His Humour (Jonson) 36, 50, 90, **94–5**, 110 n. 22, 112, 236, 275 n. 24, 276
Every Man Out of His Humour (Jonson) 35 n. 19, 36, **89–91 & n. 27**, 92, 95, 110 n. 22, 177 n. 10, 187 n. 23, 236, 275 n. 24
Ezechias (Udall) 85

Fair Maid of Bristow, The (Anonymous) 36, 125, 237 n. 24, 275 n. 24
Fair Maid of the West (Heywood) **65–6** & n. 24
Fair Quarrel, A (Middleton and Rowley) 112, **114–15**, 133, 137, 159, 259, 260
Faithful Shepherdess, The (Beaumont and Fletcher) 128, 133, 271 n. 15

Famous Victories of Henry V, The (Anonymous) viii, 8, 140, 148, 166, 174, **175–8**, 180–2, 184–6, 198, 199, 201, 206, 208, 250
First Part of the Contention of the Two Famous Houses of York and Lancaster, The (Shakespeare) 3, 4, 9, 81, 169, **200–10**, 288
Fleire, The (Sharpham) 62
Fortunatus (Dekker): see *Old Fortunatus*
Friar Bacon & Friar Bungay (Greene) 101

Galathea (Lyly) 48, 50
Game at Chess, A (Middleton) 115, 122 n. 42, 163, 258 n. 50, 261 n. 1
George a Greene, the Pinner of Wakefield (Greene) 58
Gorboduc (Norton and Sackville) 41, 232, 238, 241, 258

Hamlet (Shakespeare) 3, 5, 9, 10 n. 14, 45, 67, 76, 77 & n. 12, 78, 80, 81, 84, 93, 97 n. 2, 98, 110 & n. 23, 111, 112 & n. 27, 116, 123, 126, 130 n. 53, 131, 134 n. 58, 136, 137, 139, 141, 144, 149 & n. 72, 150, 151, 159, 163, 164 & n. 84, 166–7, 169, 177, 179, 197, 211, **226–44**, 266, 267, 271, 272, 274 n. 19, 275, 281, 282, 284, 286, 287–9
1 Henry IV (Shakespeare) 3 & n. 7, 36 n. 25, 77, 81, 110 & n. 24, **127 & n. 49**, 128, 130, 133, 134 n. 58, 135, 136, 174, 196, 210, 237, 248, 250–2, 264, 272, 274 n. 19, 284
2 Henry IV (Shakespeare) 3, 4, 36 & n. 25, 78, 81, 101, 109, 110, 116, 174, 175, 185, 189 n. 27, 197, 209, 210, 247, 248, 250, 251, 252 n. 40, 259, **263–6**, 267 n. 7, 274 n. 19, 286
Henry V (Shakespeare) 3, 4, 5, 8, 9, 35, 67, 76, 78, 80, 81, 93, 97, 98, 109, 110, 116, 123, 139, 140, 147, 169, 170, 171, **173–99**, 201–4 & n. 38, 208, 210, 212, 216, 225, 229, 236, 247, 248, 251, 252 n. 39, 257, 264, 274 n. 19, 286, 287–9
1 Henry VI (Shakespeare) 3, 28, 81, 184–6, 209 n. 47, 249, 253, 274 n. 22
2 Henry VI (originally *The First Part of the Contention of the Two Famous Houses of York and Lancaster*) (Shakespeare) 3, 5, 9, 78, 81, 93, 123, 131 n. 56, 134, 139, 151 n. 74, 166, 176 n. 7, 184, **200–10**, 286, 288
3 Henry VI (originally *The True Tragedy of Richard Duke of York, and the death of good King Henry VI*) (Shakespeare) 5, 9, 27, 78, 81, 93, 98, 123, 131, 139, 151 n. 74, 166, 178 n. 11, **200–10**, 286

Henry VIII (All is True) (Shakespeare and Fletcher): see *All Is True*
Hieronimo (Kyd): see *The Spanish Tragedy*
Honour of Young Ladies, The (Brome) 161
Hot Anger Soon Cold (Jonson) 93

If It Be Not Good, the Devil is In It (Dekker) 68
If You Know Not Me, You Know Nobody (Heywood) 125 & n. 47, 141
Ignoramus (Ruggles) **85–6**
Isle of Dogs, The (Thomas Nashe and Ben Jonson) 31, 32, 35 n. 18, 93 n. 30, 160
Isle of Gulls, The (Day) 231

Jack Drum's Entertainment (Marston) 128, 133, 134
Jephthah Judge of Israel 156, 164 & n. 85
Jew of Malta, The (Marlowe) 100, 165
Julius Caesar (Shakespeare) 3, 36, 70, 81, 177, 187 n. 25, 233, 239, 274 n. 19

King and No King, A (Beaumont and Fletcher) 36, 276 & n. 24
King John (Shakespeare) 3 & n. 4, 77, 81, 97, 151 n. 74, 163, 164, 166, 274 n. 19
King Lear (Shakespeare) 3, 36, 50, 64, 78, 80, 87, 89, 90 n. 26, 93, 110, 145, 148, 149, 163, 169, 237, 239, 242, 266, 267, 275, 282, 288
  The History of King Lear 3, 36, 50, 64, 78, 80, 87, 89, 90 n. 26, 110, 111–12, 141, 187, 237, 266, 271, 272, 274 n. 23, 275, 283–4
  The Tragedy of King Lear 111–12, 237, 266
Knot of Fools (Anonymous) 36, 276 n. 24

Lady Barbara (Anonymous) 43
Locrine (Charles Tilney? Peele?) 3 n. 2, 7, 58, 127, 133, 135
Love Parts Friendship (Chettle and Smith) 156
Love's Labour's Lost (Shakespeare) 3, 35, 77, 81, **109–10**, 126–7, 128–9, 133, 134 & n. 58, 135–7, 168, 187, 198, 200 n. 35, 214, 236, 267 n. 7, 274 n. 19, 286
Love's Labour's Won (Shakespeare) 276
Love's Mistress (Heywood) 128

Macbeth (Shakespeare) 1, 3, 37, 74 n. 8, 77, 239, 271 n. 14, 274 & n. 23, 280 & n. 28, **281–2 & nn. 31** and **32**, 283 & n. 33
Machiavelli and the Devil (Daborne) 157
Magnetic Lady, The (Jonson) 155 n. 77, 161–2, 187 n. 23
Maid's Tragedy, The (Beaumont and Fletcher) 36, **123–4**, 125, 126, 131–2, 136, 137, 169, 276 n. 24
Malcontent, The (Marston) 80, **118**, 126, 127, 130, 133, 136, 137, 275 n. 24, 281 & n. 30

Index of Plays and Other Dramatic Texts 315

Marriage of Thames and Rhine (Beaumont) 84
Martyred Soldier, The (Shirley) 59 n. 17, **159–60**
Masque of Blackness, The (Jonson) 65, 90, 95
Masque of Goddesses [and] Huntresses (Anonymous) 39
Masque of Hercules (Anonymous) 39
Masque of Oberon (Jonson) 282, 283
Masque of Queens (Jonson) 96, 282
Masque of the Inner Temple and Gray's Inn (Beaumont) 282
Masque of Turkish Magistrates (Anonymous) 39
Masque of Venetian Senators (Anonymous) 39
Match Me in London (Dekker) 161 & n. 81
Measure for Measure (Shakespeare) 3, 35, 77, 236, 261 n. 14, 274, 276, 280 & n. 27
Merchant of Venice, The (Shakespeare) 3, 4, 36, 37, 81, 109, 236, 274 n. 19, 276
Merry as May Be (Day and colleagues) 279, 284
Merry Devil of Edmonton, The (Anonymous) 36, 65 n. 23, 275
Merry Wives of Windsor (Shakespeare) ix, 3 & n. 3, 5, 9, 35, 63, 77, 81, 93, 97–8 & nn. 1 and 3, 110 & n. 23, 123, 124, 128, 133, 136, 137, 139, 141, 165–6, 169, 187–211, 224, 236, **245–58**, 261 n. 1, 274 n. 19, 286, 287, 288
Midas (Lyly) 35 n. 20, 50, 109 n. 19
Midsummer Night's Dream, A (Shakespeare) 3, 4 n. 8, 10, 35, 59, 77, 81, 109, 111 n. 24, 153, 237 & n. 24, 267 n. 7, 274 n. 19, 286
  evidence of revision from Q1 to F **59–63**
Miseries of Enforced Marriage, The (Wilkins) 275 & n. 24
Misfortunes of Arthur (Hughes) 48
Mucedorus (Anonymous) 3 n. 2, 36, 37, 50, 106, 112, **113–14**, 115, 127, 128, 133, 137, 154, 231 n. 20, 253, 259, 275 n. 24, **277**, 278
Much Ado About Nothing (Shakespeare) 3, 36, 77, 81, 110 & n. 24, 220, 240, 274 n. 19
Murderous Michael (Anonymous) 49
Mutius Scaevola (Ireland) 49

Narcissus (Anonymous) 42
Nobleman, The (Tourneur) 36, 276 & n. 24

Old Fortunatus (Dekker) 35, 67, 87, 88, 101, 102, **106–8** & n. 17, 124, 136, 164, 167, 168, 177 n. 10, 187 & n. 24, 188, 204, 253, 281 & n. 29, 286
Old Joiner of Aldgate, The (Chapman) 157
Oldcastle (Dekker): see *1 Sir John Oldcastle*
Othello (Shakespeare) 3, 35, 36, 65, 78, 87, 93, 112, 134 n. 58, 149, 169, 236, 237, 258, 260, 266, 267, 271 & n. 14, 274 & nn. 19 and 21, 276, 278, 280, 282

Page of Plymouth (Jonson) 93
Panecia (Anonymous) 45
Parasitaster, or The Fawne (Marston) 127, 133
Patient Grissell (Chettle and Dekker) 58
Peaceable King or the Lord Mendall (Anonymous) 158
Peddler's Masque, The 45
Pericles (Shakespeare and Wilkins) 2 & n. 2, 3, 58, 77, **85**, 139 & n. 60, 187, 271, 274 & n. 20, 275, 280, 282
Perseus and Andromeda (Anonymous) 49
Phaeton (Dekker) 8, 88, 101, 103 & n. 10, 107, 108, 136
Philaster, Or Love Lies A-Bleeding (Beaumont and Fletcher) 36, **118–23**
Philotas (Daniel) 160, 231, 240 n. 26
Phoenix, The (Middleton) 125
Players' Hamlet, The (Davenant) 242, 243, 244, 284, 289
Poetaster (Jonson) 90, 91 n. 27, 232
Pompey (Anonymous) 49
Pontius Pilate (Anonymous) 101
Predor and Lucia (Anonymous) 49
Pretestus (Anonymous) 45
Prince of Pallaphilos, The 41
Proud Woman, The (Chettle) 101

Quintus Fabius (Anonymous) 49

Ralph Roister-Doister (Udall) 40
Rape of Lucrece, The (Heywood) 36, 125 n. 46, 141, 273
Respublica (Udall) 40
Revenge of Bussy D'Ambois, The (Chapman) 66, 132
Revenger's Tragedy, The (Middleton?) 65, 274 n. 23, 275 n. 24
Richard II (Shakespeare) 3, 4, 77, 81, 109, 110 n. 24, 116, 127, 133, 136, 184, 200 n. 35, 210, 259, **261–3**, 264, 265 & n. 6, 272, 274 n. 19, 286
Richard III (Shakespeare) 3, 4, 78, 81, 109, 110, 126, 128, 130, 133, 134 n. 58, 135, 136, 137 n. 59, 145, 184, 185, 200 n. 35, 210, 237, 266, 267 n. 7, 272
Richard Crookback (Jonson) 93
Rival Friends, The (Hausted) 86
Robert II of Scotland (The Scots Tragedy) (Jonson) 93
Robin Hood (Chettle) 100–9
Romeo and Juliet (Shakespeare) 3, 5, 9, 67, 68, 76, 77 n. 12, 81, 93, 97, 98, 109, 110 & n. 23, 123, 126–9, 132, 133, 134–7, 139, **150**, 169, **170–1**, 179, 207, **211–25**, 237, 257, 261 n. 1, 272, 274 n. 19, 286, 287, 289

Sappho and Phao (Lyly) 50, 187
Satiromastix (Dekker) **90–1**, 110 n. 22, 232, 275 n. 24

316 Index of Plays and Other Dramatic Texts

Scottish History of James the Fourth, The (Greene) 59
Second Maiden's Tragedy, The (Middleton) 153, 276 n. 24, **277–8**, 287
Sejanus (Jonson) 90 & n. 26, 93 & n. 30, 94, 187 n. 23, 269, 270, 275 n. 24
Shoemaker's Holiday, The (Dekker) 35, 50, 108 n. 18, 187
Silver Age, The (Heywood) 36
Sir Clyomon and Clamydes (Peele) 58
1 Sir John Oldcastle, The (Munday, Drayton, and others) 4 n. 8, 102, 135, 252 n. 41
Sir John van Olden Barnavelt (Fletcher and Massinger) 152, 162
Sir Thomas More, The Book of (Munday and Chettle) 3 n. 2, 151, 152, 162
Soliman and Perseda (Anonymous) 126–7, 132, 133
Spanish Maze, The (Anonymous) 36, 236, 275 n. 24
Spanish Tragedy, The (aka *Hieronimo*; Kyd) 2, 3 n. 2, 8, 67, 93, 99 & nn. 4 and 5, 100, 102, 112, **115–16** & n. 32, 117 n. 34, 118 n. 35, **126–8**, 131, 132, 133, 134, 136, 137, 228, 259, 260, 265 n. 5
Spanish Viceroy, The (Massinger) 153, 161, 188
Staple of News, The (Jonson) 90
Stepmother's Tragedy, The (Chettle) 157–8

Tale of a Tub, A (Jonson) 90
Tamer Tamed, The (Fletcher): see *The Woman's Prize*
Taming of a Shrew, The (Anonymous) 3 n. 4, 139 n. 61, 163
Taming of the Shrew, The (Shakespeare) 3 & n. 4, 65, 77, 81, 151 n. 74, 154, 166, 209, 279
Tasso's Melancholy (Dekker) 101–2, 136
Tempest, The (Shakespeare) 3, 36, 37, 57, 74–5, 77, 87 n. 22, 242, 261 n. 1, 271 n. 14, 274, 276, **281**, 283 & n. 33
Tethys' Festival (Daniel) 84
3 Thomas Strowde, The (Haughton and Day) 155–7
Three Plays in One (Anonymous) 49
Timoclia at the Siege of Thebes (Anonymous) 44–5, 49
Timon of Athens (Shakespeare) 3, 77, 271 n. 14, 274 & n. 23, 277, 282
Titus and Gisippus (Anonymous) 49

Titus Andronicus (Shakespeare) 3 & n. 7, 4, 29, 77, 81, 106, 109, 200 n. 35, **259–61**, 264, 265, 272, 274 n. 22, 286
Tobias Comedy (Chettle) 156
Tragedy of Tancred and Gismund, The (Wilmot and others) 59
Travels of the Three English Brothers, The (Wilkins) 275
Trick to Catch the Old One, A (Middleton) 50, 285 n. 34
Troilus and Cressida (Shakespeare) 3, 4, 78, 89, 149, 266, 267, 271, 274 n. 19, 282, **284–5**
Troublesome Reign of King John, The (Anonymous) 3 n. 4
True Tragedy of Richard, Duke of York, The (Shakespeare) 3 & n. 5, 9, 81, 109, 126, 131 & n. 54, 139, 169, 178 n. 11, **200–11**
Truth, Faithfulness, and Mercy (Anonymous) 49
Twelfth Night (Shakespeare) 3, 121, 223, 274 n. 19
Twins' Tragedy, The (Nicholls?) 36, 276 & n. 24
Two Angry Women of Abingdon, The (Porter) 158
Two Gentlemen of Verona, The (Shakespeare) 3, 77, 81, 261 n. 1
Two Noble Kinsmen, The (Shakespeare and Fletcher) 3 n. 2, 36 n. 23, 68, 271 n. 14, 274, 275 n. 23, 282

Unfortunate Lovers, The (Davenant) 68

Vertumnus (Gwynn) 86
Vision of the Twelve Goddesses, The (Daniel) 268
Volpone (Jonson) 65 n. 23, 90 & n. 26, 94, 96, 112, 269, 275 n. 24, 278

White Devil, The (Webster) 71
Whole History of Fortunatus, The (Dekker) 101, 106, 107
Winter's Tale, The (Shakespeare) 3, 36, 77, 113, 158 & n. 80, 160, 242, 261 n. 1, 271 n. 14, 274, 280 & n. 28, 282 & n. 32
Wise Man of West Chester, The (Anonymous) 106, 165
Witch, The (Middleton) 282, 283 n. 33
Woman is a Weathercock, A (Field) 125
Woman's Prize, The (aka *The Tamer Tamed*; Fletcher) 65, **153–5** & n. 77, 158, 160, 161, 162, 276 n. 24, 288

Index of Persons

Note: works of non-dramatic literature are listed under authors.

Adams, Joseph Quincy 33 n. 17, 237 n. 24, 243 n. 28
Alexander, Peter 142, 201, 207 & n. 43
Alleyn, Edward (actor) 29, 79, 100, 116, 137, 165
Anna (Anne) of Denmark, Queen of England 34, 50, 65, 83, 118, 231, 254, 258, 268, 269 & n. 12
Armin, Robert (actor) 79, 113, 118, 252, 269
Aspley, William (publisher) 118
Astington, John 7, 35, 54, 83 n. 17, 84 n. 19, 109, 283
Astley, Sir John (Master of the Revels 1622–23) 59 n. 17, 90, **160**

Bacon, Sir Francis 84
Bacon, Sir Nicholas (Lord Keeper of the Seal) 193
Baldwin, T. W. 193
Barnes, Barnabe (dramatist) 36, 50, 58, 64–5, 126, 128, 130, 136, 275 n. 24, 276, 280
Baroll, Leeds 268, 278–9
Bate, Sir Jonathan: *see* Editors and editions of Shakespeare's plays
Bawcutt, n.W. 27, 55, 65, 81, 119, 122 n. 42, 132, 137 n. 59, 152–5 & n. 77, 159, 160 n. 81, 161–2, 265
Beaumont, Francis (dramatist) 36, 68, 84, 118, 119, 122, 123 n. 43, 126–8, 144, 235 n. 21, 270 & n. 13, 275 n. 23, 276 & n. 24, 282, 287
Beckerman, Bernard 13–14, 16
Beeston, Christopher 159
Beeston, William 68, 153
Belleforest, François de (*Histoires Tragique*) 233, 243
Benger, Sir Thomas (Master of the Revels 1560–77) 19, 23, 24, **41–4**, 48, 52, 53, 57, 59 n. 17
Bentley, G. E. 7, 65–6, 72, 99, 102, 273
Bergeron, David M. 1, 283
Betterton, Thomas (actor) 242
Bevington, David 95, 99, 117 & n. 33; *see also* Editors and editions of Shakespeare's plays
Birch, Thomas 83
Bird, William (alias Bourne; actor) 8, 31, 99, 100, **101–2**, 103 & n. 10, 117
Blagrave, Thomas (Clerk and acting Master of the Revels) 44–6, 49, 52

Blayney, Peter 10, 140, 146, 166, 271–2 & n. 16, 287
Blount, Charles, Lord Mountjoy 182
Blount, Thomas 38
Bonion, Richard (publisher) 285
Bowers, Fredson 145 & n. 67
Brayne, John 18 & n. 5, 20 n. 7
Briggs, Julia 277
Brome, Richard (dramatist) 161, 273
Brooke, Arthur (*The Tragicall Historye of Romeus and Juliet*) 222
Brooke, Henry (eleventh Lord Cobham) **250ff**, 288
Brooke, William (tenth Lord Cobham; Lord Chamberlain 1596) 247
Bruster, Douglas 116
Buc, Sir George (Master of the Revels 1610–22) viii, 23, 25, 27, 33, 48, 51, 52 n. 13, 56, 59 n. 17, 63, 85, 88, 90, 92, 118 n. 36, 119 n. 37, 122, 152, 158, 162, 168, 174 & n. 4, 265 n. 6, 275, 277, 283, 289; relationship to Shakespeare 57, 58–9; writings and publications (*Daphnis Polystephanos*, *The Art of Revels*, 'The Third University of England', *The History of King Richard III*, *The Baron*) 46, 56–7; interest in theatre / playbook annotations / identifier of anonymous plays **57–9**
Buchanan, George 238
Burbage, James (builder of The Theatre and the Blackfriars playhouse) 18 & n. 5, 19, 20 n. 7, 21 n. 10, 28, 29, 118
Burbage, Richard 28, 29, 65, 79, 84 n. 18, 116 & n. 32, 118, 197, 225, 263, 264, 269
Burby, Cuthbert (publisher) 129
Burghley, William Cecil, first Lord (Lord Treasurer 1572–97) 20, 44, 53, 56, 62, 93 & n. 32
Butts, Henry 86

Camden, William 95
Carey, George (second Lord Hunsdon; Lord Chamberlain 1597–1603) 32 n. 16, 109 n. 21, 247, 250, 251 & n. 37, 252, 254 n. 43
Carey, Henry (first Lord Hunsdon; Lord Chamberlain 1585–96) 28, 29, 32 n. 16, 62, 70–1, 79, 109 n. 21
Carleton, Sir Dudley (English ambassador) 83 n. 17, 237 n. 24, 268, 269 n. 12

Index of Persons

Carow, John (property-maker) 42
Carson, Neil 164
Castiglione, Baldassare (*The Book of the Courtier*) 56, 192
Cawarden, Sir Thomas (Master of the Revels 1544–59) 39, 41, 53
Cecil, Sir Robert (Principal Secretary of State under both Elizabeth I and James I) 56, 84, 209 n. 46, 235, 250, 251 n. 37, 265, 268–9 & n. 12
Chamberlain, John (letter-writer) 84, 85, 269 n. 12
Chambers, E. K. 35 n. 21, 53, 84, 91, 92, 95, 119 n. 37, 151 & n. 74, 247
  The Elizabethan Stage 9, 14, 17, 28, 32, 36 n. 24, 50, 51 n. 11, 52, 59, 71, 72 n. 5, 82, 83, 84, 85, 116 n. 32, 119 n. 37, 188, 236, 237 n. 24, 247, 265, 268–9, 279, 289
Chapman, George (dramatist) 54, 56, 93 n. 30, 112, 127–8, 132, 157 & n. 79, 161, 231, 240 n. 26
Charles I, King of England 39, 52, 53, 64, 82, 86, 114, 115 & n. 31, 122 & n. 42, 154, 262 n. 9; *see also* Prince Charles
Chettle, Henry (dramatist) 33, 54, 58, 93, 101–3 & n. 12, 104–7, 157–8, 217, 286
Christian IV, King of Denmark and Norway 234, 253, 283 n. 33
Clegg, Cyndia Susan 262
Cobham family: *see* Henry Brooke, William Brooke
Condell, Henry (actor) vii, 2, 138, 188 & n. 26, 189, 257, 261 n. 1
Cope, Sir Walter 268
Cotton, Sir Robert 56
Cox, John D.: *see* Editors and editions of Shakespeare's plays
Craig, Hardin 127
Crane, David: *see* Editors and editions of Shakespeare's plays
Crane, Ralph (scrivener) 162, 163, 245, 256, 257, 258 n. 50, 261 n. 2
Creede, Thomas (printer) 129–30, 140

Daborne, Robert (dramatist) 157, 162
Daniel, Samuel (dramatist) 231, 240 n. 26; and licensing of plays 118 n. 36, 160
Davenant, Sir William (dramatist) 68, 153, 242–3 & nn. 28 and 30, 244, 289
Davies, Sir John 73
Dawes, Robert (actor) 72
Day, John (dramatist) 155, 279
Dekker, Thomas (dramatist) 8, 33, 35, 50, 54, 58, 68, 80, 87, 88, 90–2, 93, 101–2, **106–8**, 124, 136, 167, 168 & n. 87, 177 n. 10, 187–8, 232, 276, 286
Dennis, John (dramatist) 246

Dessen, Alan C. 260
Dillon, Janet 143, 150, 243, 288
Donne, John 38
Doran, Madeleine 145, 201
Downton, Thomas (actor) 31, 101 n. 7, 107, 108, 279 n. 26
Drayton, Michael (dramatist) 105, 279 n. 26
Duthie, G. I. 5, 141
Dutton, Lawrence (actor) 24, 45

Edward VI, King of England 39
Elizabeth I, Queen of England viii, 1, 8, 10, 13, 14, 16, 25, 27, 28, 34ff, 41, 43, 48, 56, 58, 59 n. 17, 62, 82–3, 85, 90 n. 26, 91 & n. 27, 93, 97, 106, 187, 188, 192, 209 & n. 46, 232–5, 246, 248, 253, 254, 258, 262, 268, 276, 284, 286
Elyot, Sir Thomas (*The Book Named The Governor*) 192
Erasmus, Desiderius (*De verborum ac rerum Copia*) 193, 194; (*The Education of a Christian Prince*) 238
Erne, Lukas ix, 5 & n. 10, 7, 67, 68, 76–8 & n. 10, 79–80, 87–9, 96, 128 n. 51, 129 n. 52, 131, 145 & n. 68, 170–1, 179–80, **189–94**, 212, 213, 216, 229, 243, 271–3, 285, 287
Essex, Robert Devereux, third Earl of 232ff

Farmer, Alan x, 125 n. 45, 272
Farrant, Richard 21, 41, 44, 45
Ferrers, George (courtier, Lord of Misrule) 39
Feuillerat, Albert 27
Field, Nathan (actor, dramatist) 88 & n. 24, 93 & n. 28, 125, 270 & n. 13
Fletcher, John (dramatist) 2 n. 2, 36 & n. 23, 65, 68, 80, 87 n. 23, 113, 118–22, 123 n. 43, 126–8, 143–4, 153–4, 162, 235 n. 21, 270 & n. 13, 271 n. 15, 273, 274 & nn. 21 and 23, 275 n. 23, 276, 278, 282, 287
Fletcher, Laurence (actor) 237, 268 & n. 10
Foakes, R. A. 9, 25, 32, 156; *see also* Philip Henslowe
Ford, John (dramatist) 36, 276 n. 24
Ford John (film director) 248
Forman, Simon (astrologer, play-goer) 280 & n. 28, 281–2
Foxe, John (*Book of Martyrs*) 250

Garrick, David (actor) 243
Gibbons, Brian: *see* Editors and editions of Shakespeare's plays
Gopnik, Adam 226
Gossett, Suzanne: *see* Editors and editions of Shakespeare's plays
Grammaticus, Saxo (*Historiae Danicae*) 233
Green, William 247–9, 253, 258

Index of Persons

Greene, Robert (dramatist) 28, 35 n. 20, 55, 58, 59, 125 n. 48, 200;
Menaphon 233
Greenfield, Peter x, 16, 27 n. 12, 252 n. 39
Greg, W. W.: *see* Editors and editions of Shakespeare's plays
Gurr, Andrew 5, 7, 19, 20, 23, 24, 26, 29, 31, 64, 67, 68 & n. 2, 75–6, 77–80, 86, 119, 145, 150, 152, 164, 166, 174, 175 n. 6, 178–9, 212, 236, 267, 278, 289; *see also* Editors and editions of Shakespeare's plays

Halio, Jay L. 214 n. 5, 216–17
Hall, Edward (*Chronicle: The Union of the Noble and Illustre Families of Lancaster and York*) 203
Halstead, W. L. 67–8, 108 & n. 17
Hammond, Anthony: *see* Editors and editions of Shakespeare's plays
Harbage, Alfred (*Shakespeare's Audience*) 2, 289
Harington, Sir John 265
Hart, Alfred 5 n. 10, 67, 68, 75, 76–7 & n. 12, 78, 79, 80, 82, 89, 108, 114, 171 n. 1, 208
Harvey, Gabriel 191–2 & n. 30
Hattaway, Michael: *see* Editors and editions of Shakespeare's plays
Heminge, John vii, 2, 38 n. 4, 138, 158, 188 & n. 26, 189, 236, 257, 269 n. 1
Henrietta Maria, Queen of England 81, 86, 137 n. 59, 154 & n. 76, 161
Henry VIII, King of England 103–4, 106, 234
Henry, Prince of Wales 52–3, 64, 84, 115 n. 31, 122 & n. 41, 240, 253, 280–1, 283
Henslowe, Philip ix, 6, 8, 9, 25, 27, 28, 29, 31, 32, 33, 53 n. 15, 54, 55, 67, 82, 89, **99–109**, 111, 113, 115, 116 n. 32, 117, 133, 136, 137, 144, 150, 153, **155–8**, 159, 164 & n. 85, 165 n. 86, 167–8, 204, 209 n. 47, 233, 265 n. 5, 269, 270, 276, 279, 284, 286–7; *see also* R. A. Foakes
Herbert, Sir Henry (Master of the Revels 1623–42) 27, 59 & n. 17, 64, 65, 66, 122 n. 42, 137 n. 59, 150, 152, 153–5 & n. 77, 158, 159–60, 161–2, 265, 288
Herbert, Sir Philip 84
Heywood, Thomas (dramatist) 6, 36 & n. 25, 46, 53, 57, 65–6 & n. 24, 80, 101, 108, 125 & nn. 46 and 47, 128, 141, 168, 231, 272–3, 275 n. 24, 276; *An Apology for Actors* 6, 46, 57, 108, 168, 289
Hibbard, G. R.: *see* Editors and editions of Shakespeare's plays
Hirrel, Michael J. 67, 69, 71 n. 4, 73–5
Holderness, Graham: *see* Editors and editions of Shakespeare's plays
Holinshed, Raphael (*Chronicles of England, Scotland, and Ireland*) 174, 176–7, 182–6, 198, 203, 209
Holland, Peter 74
Honigmann, E. A. J.: *see* Editors and editions of Shakespeare's plays
Howard: Charles, Lord Howard of Effingham, later Earl of Nottingham (Lord Chamberlain 1583–5, Lord Admiral 1585–1619) 19–20 & n. 7, 23, 24, 26, 29, 32 n. 16, 44, 55, 56

Ioppolo, Grace 99, 102, 129, 130, 136, 148–9, 185, 198, 212 n. 3

Jackson, MacDonald P. 277
Jaggard, William 3 n. 8, 131, 272
James I, King of England viii, ix, 1, 13–14, 25, 37, 38, 39–40, 48, 50, 51 & n. 11, 52, 56, 62, 64, 65, 82, 85–6, 88–9, 91 n. 27, 94, 113, 122 & n. 42, 167, 188, 209, 232, 234, 235–6 & n. 22, 237 & n. 24, 238, 240, 241, 252, 253–4, 255, 262, 267–8, 272–3, 274, 276, 279, 283–4, 286
Jeffes, Humphrey (actor) 209
Jenkins, Harold: *see* Editors and editions of Shakespeare's plays
Johnson, Samuel: *see* Editors and editions of Shakespeare's plays
Jones, John 149 & n. 72
Jonson, Ben (dramatist) viii, 2, 8, 31, 35 n. 19, 36 & n. 23, 50, 54, 56, 59 n. 17, 64, 68, 74–5, 77, 78, 80, 93 n. 30, 94 nn. 31 and 32, 99, 100, 101–2, 110 n. 22, 112, 116 n. 32, 137, 155 n. 77, 160, 161–2, 177 n. 10, 187 n. 23, 231, 232, 260, 265 n. 5, 269, 275 n. 24, 276, 278, 284, 285; length of plays 79, **87–96**; court performances **88–96 & nn. 26** and **27**; masques 90, 95, 96, 258, 282
Jowett, John: *see* Editors and editions of Shakespeare's plays
Juby, Edward (actor) 58

Kastan, David Scott: *see* Editors and editions of Shakespeare's plays
Kathman, David 17–18, 69
Kemp, William 28, 79, 113, 170, 252 n. 39; role in *Romeo and Juliet* 213–14, 215, **219–25**
Kernan, Alvin 1, 49, 85–6, 283
Kerrigan, John **111–12**, 117, 123, 132, 179, 204, 207, 237, 242, 260
Kirschbaum, Leo 120, 277
Klein, David 67–8, 87
Knell, William (actor) 24, 55
Knight, Edward (bookkeeper for the King's Men) 144 & n. 65, 154–5

Knowles, Ronald: *see* Editors and editions of Shakespeare's plays
Knutson, Roslyn Landor ix, 7, 29, **100–2**, 113, 114, 116, 122, 165, 166, 226, **230–2**, 235
Kolbert, Elizabeth 226
Kyd, Thomas (dramatist) 2, 8, 55, 67, 99, 126–7, 132, 133, 134, 136, 259, 276

La Broderie, Antoine de (French ambassador) 83
La Trémoille (French ambassador) 83
Laud, William (Archbishop of Canterbury) 86, 155 n. 77, 161
Lawrence, W. L. 142
Leicester, Robert Dudley, Earl of 15 & n. 1, 16, 20, 21 & nn. 8 and 9, 23, 41, 83
Lesser, Zachary x, 97 n. 2, 125 n. 45, 228, 243 & n. 30, 272, 288
Levenson, Jill: *see* Editors and editions of Shakespeare's plays
Long, John H. 257
Long, William B. x, 7 & n. 12, 59 n. 19, 146
Loughrey, Bryan: *see* Editors and editions of Shakespeare's plays
Lull, Janis: *see* Editors and editions of Shakespeare's plays
Lyly, John (dramatist) 27, 35 n. 20, 40, 48, 50, 55–6, 66, 90, 91, 109 n. 19, 125 n. 48, 187

McKerrow, R. B. 6, 130 n. 53, 144, 146, 226
MacLean, Sally-Beth 7, 15 n. 1, 23, 24, 26, 27 n. 12, 30 n. 15
McMillin, Scott 7, 23, 24, 26, 27 n. 12, 148 & n. 71, 155, 169
Maguire, Laurie 6, 141, 142
Malone, Edmund: *see* Editors and editions of Shakespeare's plays
Marcus, Leah 64, 256 n. 47
Marino, James ix, 3 n. 4, 4 n. 8, 5, 6, 7, 112 n. 27, 137, 151–2, **163–8**, 200, 233, 252
Marlowe, Christopher (dramatist) 2, 8, 28, 55, 99, 117 & n. 33, 127, 166
Marston, John (dramatist) 54, 93 n. 30, 118, 126–8, 133–4, 136, 231, 275 n. 24, 276
Martin, Randall: *see* Editors and editions of Shakespeare's plays
Mary I, Queen of England 39–40, 41, 142
Mary, Queen of Scots 58
Mason, John Monck 235 & n. 21
Massai, Sonia 7 & n. 13
Massinger, Philip (dramatist) 7, 122 n. 42, 152–3, 162, 270 & n. 13, 273
Maus, Katharine Eisaman 49
Meagher, John 103 n. 11, 105–6
Melchiori, Giorgio: *see* Editors and editions of Shakespeare's plays
Menzer, Paul 5, 7, 18, 69, 112 n. 27, **151–9**, 161–3, 165, 168, 228, 230, 243, 288

Meres, Francis (*Palladis Tamia*) 248
Middleton, Thomas (dramatist) viii, 50, 68, 101, 112, 114–15, 122 n. 42, 125, 127, 163, 258 n. 50, 274 & n. 23, 275 n. 24, 276, 277–8, 280 n. 27, 281 & n. 31, 282–3, 285 n. 34
Millington, Thomas (publisher) 139–40, 200
Montgomery, William: *see* Editors and editions of Shakespeare's plays
Mulcaster, Richard 41, 44
Mullaney, Steven 18
Mulryne, J. R. 67–8
Munday, Anthony (dramatist) 102–6 & nn. 11 and 14, 151, 279

Nashe, Thomas (dramatist) 28, 31, 55, 93 n. 30, 160, 233
Nelson, Alan 58–9, 85, 174 n. 4, 190 n. 39
Nichol, Charles 47, 58, 275
Nicholls, Richard 33
Nicholson, Brinsley 174

Orgel, Steven 67–8, 74, 75, 78–80

Pavier, Thomas 3 n. 8, 131, 272
Peele, George (dramatist) 55, 58, 127, 200
Pembroke, William Herbert, third Earl of 84 n. 18, 90, 94 & n. 32, 96, 188 n. 26, 236, 254; Jonson and patronage of 90, 94 & n. 32
Percy, William (dramatist) 68, 72–3
Philip II, King of Spain 82, 234
Phillips, Augustine (actor) 278
Platter, Thomas (Swiss visitor) 70–3, 187 n. 25
Playstowe, William 156
Pollard, A. W. 2, 5, 80, 129, 139–40, 141, 142, 146, 150, 151, 178, 245
Pope, Alexander: *see* Editors and editions of Shakespeare's plays
Porter, Henry (dramatist) 158
Prince Charles (later Charles I) 52, 53, 64, 114, 122, 267 n. 9
Princess Elizabeth (later Queen of Bohemia) 36 n. 25, 37, 53, 57, 84, 85, 237 n. 23, 267 n. 9, 283 n. 33
Puttenham, George (*The Art of English Poesy*) 192–4, 196, 290

Quiller-Couch, Sir Arthur 129, 283 n. 33

Ralegh, Sir Walter 84, 252, 253 n. 42
Rasmussen, Eric 92, 117 & n. 33; *see also* Editors and editions of Shakespeare's plays
Rebhorn, Wayne 192 n. 31, 193, 290
Riggs, David 91
Roberts, James (printer) 284–5
Roberts, John 97
Rowe, Nicholas: *see* Editors and editions of Shakespeare's plays

Index of Persons

Rowley, Samuel (dramatist) 8, 99, 100, 101, 102, 117
Rowley, William (dramatist) 112, 114–15, 127
Rutter, Tom x, 104 & n. 13

Sackville, Sir Richard 82
Sackville, Thomas (dramatist; later Earl of Dorset and Lord Treasurer) 254
Savage, Jerome (actor) 19
Scaliger, Julius Caesar 57
Schlueter, June 107–8 & n. 16
Schoone-Jongen, Terence 28
Seymour, Edward (Earl of Hertford) 233
Shakespeare, William
  Career before 1594 28; with Lord Chamberlain's Men 28–37; with the King's Men 267–85; contracts 7, 269ff, 274ff
  Dealings with Masters of the Revels 30, 54ff, 58–9, 62–3; plays at court 35ff, 276ff; length of plays 81, 173, 211, 245, 280ff and *passim*; publication of plays 3–5, 271ff; *Venus and Adonis*, *The Rape of Lucrece* 4, 271 n. 15
Shapiro, James 77
Sharpe, Will 274 n. 22, 277, 278
Sherman, William 74
Shirley, Henry (dramatist) 159
Shirley, James (dramatist) 235 & n. 21, 270, 273
Sidney, Sir Philip 161
Sidney, Sir Robert 84, 94 n. 32, 252
Silva, Don Diego Guzman De (Spanish ambassador) 82–3
Sims, Valentine (printer) 118
Sinklo or Sincler, John (actor) 209
Sisson, C. J. 140, 157
Smith, Warren D. 188
Smith, Wentworth (dramatist) 275, 276, 279
Spenser, Gabriel (actor) 209
Stansby, William (printer and publisher) 95
Steevens, George: *see* Editors and editions of Shakespeare's plays
Stephenson, F. J. 162–3
Stern, Tiffany 5, 7, 45, 94, 101 n. 8, 108, 123 n. 44, 141, 151–2, **159–63**, 168, 169, 179, 187, 213, 228–9 & n. 14, 243, 277, 282–3
Stow, John (*Annals of England*) 23–4, 56
Streitberger, W. R. 7, 22, 23–4, 25, 35 n. 21, 40 & n. 2, 41, 43–4, 51–2, 56
Stuart, Lady Arbella (cousin of James I) 90 n. 26, 120 n. 38, 234, 252, 268

Taylor, Gary 111, 119 n. 37, 145, 148 & n. 70, 274 n. 23, 280 n. 27; *see also* Editors and editions of Shakespeare's plays
Thompson, Ann: *see* Editors and editions of Shakespeare's plays
Tilney, Edmund (Master of the Revels 1579–1610) vii, 8, 13
  appointment and expectations 19–30, 31–45
  patent (1579) and special commission (1581) 22
  evolving role 46–50, 51–4
  literary and scholarly qualifications (*The Flower of Friendship*, 'Topographical descriptions, regiments, and policies') 55–6
Topcliffe, Richard (pursuivant and torturer) 31
Tourneur, Cyril (dramatist) 36, 276 & n. 24
Trousdale, Marion 194
Tudor, Margaret (sister of Henry VII, wife of James IV of Scotland) 234

Udall, Nicholas (dramatist) 40, 85
Urkowitz, Steven 67, 75, 77–80 & n. 15, 163, 201

Walley, Henry (publisher) 285 & n. 34
Walsh, Brian 107
Warren, Michael 111 & n. 25, 145, 148
Warren, Roger: *see* Editors and editions of Shakespeare's plays
Webster, John (dramatist) 71, 80, 89, 118, 126–7, 130, 136–7, 275 n. 24, 276 n. 24
Wells, Stanley: *see* Editors and editions of Shakespeare's plays
Werstine, Paul x, 59 n. 19, 142–4 & nn. 63 and 64, 146, 150, 202
Westcott, Sebastian 41
Whigham, Frank 192 n. 31, 193, 290
Whitgift, John (Archbishop of Canterbury) 26
Whyte, Rowland (letter-writer) 84
Wiles, David 220ff
Wilkins, George (dramatist, tavern keeper) 2 n. 2, 58, 275 & n. 24, 276
Wilson, John Dover 129, 142, 151, 212, 283 n. 33
Wilson, Robert (actor, dramatist) 23, 24
Winwood, Sir Ralph 84

Yachnin, Paul 283

Printed and bound by CPI Group (UK) Ltd, Croydon, CR0 4YY